Lecture Notes in Computer Science   9296

Commenced Publication in 1973
Founding and Former Series Editors:
Gerhard Goos, Juris Hartmanis, and Jan van Leeuwen

More information about this series at http://www.springer.com/series/7409

Julio Abascal · Simone Barbosa
Mirko Fetter · Tom Gross
Philippe Palanque · Marco Winckler (Eds.)

Human-Computer Interaction – INTERACT 2015

15th IFIP TC 13 International Conference
Bamberg, Germany, September 14–18, 2015
Proceedings, Part I

 Springer

Editors
Julio Abascal
Universidad del País Vasco/Euskal Herriko
  Unibertsitatea
Donostia-San Sebastián
Spain

Simone Barbosa
PUC-Rio
Rio de Janeiro
Brazil

Mirko Fetter
University of Bamberg
Bamberg
Germany

Tom Gross
University of Bamberg
Bamberg
Germany

Philippe Palanque
University Paul Sabatier
Toulouse
France

Marco Winckler
University Paul Sabatier
Toulouse
France

ISSN 0302-9743   ISSN 1611-3349   (electronic)
Lecture Notes in Computer Science
ISBN 978-3-319-22700-9   ISBN 978-3-319-22701-6   (eBook)
DOI 10.1007/978-3-319-22701-6

Library of Congress Control Number: 2015946321

LNCS Sublibrary: SL3 – Information Systems and Applications, incl. Internet/Web, and HCI

Springer International Publishing AG Switzerland is part of Springer Science+Business Media
(www.springer.com)

Foreword

The 15th IFIP TC.13 International Conference on Human–Computer Interaction, INTERACT 2015, was held during September 14–18, 2015, in Bamberg, Germany, organized by the University of Bamberg. The city of Bamberg is proud of its more than 1,000-year-old center. It has more than 2,400 historically listed buildings and became a UNESCO World Cultural Heritage Site in 1993. With 70,000 inhabitants, Bamberg is a small town in the heart of Europe.

The theme of the 2015 edition was "Connection, tradition, innovation." In its relatively short history, the human–computer interaction (HCI) area has experienced impressive development. Theories, methodologies, procedures, guidelines, and tools have been progressively proposed, discussed, tested, and frequently adopted by academia and industry. The protagonists of this development created in a short period of time a scientific and technological tradition able to produce high-quality interaction systems. However, the evolution of the computers and networks pose new challenges to all stakeholders. Innovation, based on tradition, is the only way to face these challenges, even if innovation often requires breaking the tradition. In order to make this process possible, INTERACT 2015 provides diverse and abundant connection opportunities. A multidisciplinary approach is characteristic of the HCI field. INTERACT 2015 aimed to connect all the matters able to contribute to the quality of the future interactions among people and computers.

The series of INTERACT international conferences (started in 1984) is supported by Technical Committee 13 on Human–Computer Interaction of the International Federation for Information Processing (IFIP). This committee aims at developing the science and technology of the interaction between humans and computing devices.

IFIP was created in 1960 under the auspices of UNESCO with the aim of balancing worldwide the development of computer technology and Science. Technical Committee 13 is fully conscious of the social importance of information and communication technologies for our world, today and in the future. Therefore, INTERACT 2015 made efforts to attract and host people from all over the world, and to pay attention to the constraints imposed on HCI by differences in culture, language, technological availability, physical, as well as sensory and cognitive differences, among other dimensions of interest.

INTERACT 2015 gathered a stimulating collection of research papers and reports of development and practice that acknowledge the diverse disciplines, abilities, cultures, and societies, and that address all the aspects of HCI, including technical, human, social, and esthetic.

Like its predecessors, INTERACT 2015 aimed to be an exciting forum for communication with people of similar interests, to foster collaboration and learning. Being by nature a multidisciplinary field, HCI requires interaction and discussion among diverse people with different interests and backgrounds. INTERACT 2015 was directed both to the academic and industrial world, always highlighting the latest developments in the discipline of HCI and its current applications. Experienced HCI researchers and professionals, as well as newcomers to the HCI field, interested in the design or evaluation of interactive software, development of new technologies for interaction, and research on general theories of HCI met in Bamberg.

We thank all the authors who chose INTERACT 2015 as the venue to publish their research. This was again an outstanding year for the conference in terms of submissions in all the technical categories.

We received 651 submissions. Of these, the following were accepted: 93 full research papers; 74 short research papers; eight demos; 30 interactive posters; four organizational overviews; three panels; six tutorials; 11 workshops; and 13 doctoral consortium papers.

The acceptance rate for the full papers was 29.6 % and 26.8 % for short papers.

In order to select the highest-quality contributions, an elaborate review system was organized including shepherding of 38 full research papers that went through a second and sometimes a third round of review. That process was primarily handled by the 32 meta-reviewers who willingly assisted and ensured the selection of high-quality full research papers to be presented at INTERACT 2015.

The final decision on acceptance or rejection of papers was taken in a plenary Program Committee meeting held in Tampere (Finland) in February 2015, aimed to discuss a consistent set of criteria to deal with inevitable differences among the large number of reviewers who were recruited and supported by the meta-reviewers. The technical program chairs and the track chairs, the general chairs, and the members of IFIP Technical Committee 13 participated in the meeting.

Special thanks must go to the track chairs and all the reviewers, who put in an enormous amount of work to ensure that quality criteria were maintained throughout the selection process. We also want to acknowledge the excellent work of the co-chairs of the different sections of the conference and the meta-reviewers of the full research paper track.

We also thank the members of the Organizing Committee, especially Mirko Fetter, local organization chair, who provided us with all the necessary resources to facilitate our work. Finally, we wish to express a special thank you to the proceedings publication chair, Marco Winckler, who did extraordinary work to put this volume together.

September 2015

Tom Gross
Julio Abascal
Simone Barbosa
Philippe Palanque

IFIP TC13

Established in 1989, the International Federation for Information Processing Technical Committee on Human–Computer Interaction (IFIP TC13) is an international committee of 37 national societies and nine working groups, representing specialists in human factors, ergonomics, cognitive science, computer science, design, and related disciplines. INTERACT is its flagship conference, staged biennially in different countries in the world. From 2017 the conference series will become an annual conference.

IFIP TC13 aims to develop the science and technology of human–computer interaction (HCI) by: encouraging empirical research, promoting the use of knowledge and methods from the human sciences in design and evaluation of computer systems; promoting better understanding of the relation between formal design methods and system usability and acceptability; developing guidelines, models, and methods by which designers may provide better human-oriented computer systems; and, cooperating with other groups, inside and outside IFIP, to promote user orientation and humanization in system design. Thus, TC13 seeks to improve interactions between people and computers, encourage the growth of HCI research and disseminate these benefits worldwide.

The main orientation is toward users, especially non-computer professional users, and how to improve human–computer relations. Areas of study include: the problems people have with computers; the impact on people in individual and organizational contexts; the determinants of utility, usability, and acceptability; the appropriate allocation of tasks between computers and users; modeling the user to aid better system design; and harmonizing the computer to user characteristics and needs.

While the scope is thus set wide, with a tendency toward general principles rather than particular systems, it is recognized that progress will only be achieved through both general studies to advance theoretical understanding and specific studies on practical issues (e.g., interface design standards, software system consistency, documentation, appropriateness of alternative communication media, human factors guidelines for dialogue design, the problems of integrating multimedia systems to match system needs and organizational practices, etc.).

In 1999, TC13 initiated a special IFIP Award, the Brian Shackel Award, for the most outstanding contribution in the form of a refereed paper submitted to and delivered at each INTERACT. The award draws attention to the need for a comprehensive human-centered approach in the design and use of information technology in which the human and social implications have been taken into account. 2007 IFIP TC 13 also launched an accessibility award to recognize an outstanding contribution with international impact in the field of accessibility for disabled users in HCI. In 2013, IFIP TC 13 launched the Interaction Design for International Development (IDID) Award, which recognizes the most outstanding contribution to the application of interactive systems for social and economic development of people in developing countries. Since the process to decide the award takes place after papers are submitted for publication, the awards are not identified in the proceedings.

IFIP TC 13 also recognizes pioneers in the area of HCI. An IFIP TC 13 pioneer is one who, through active participation in IFIP Technical Committees or related IFIP groups, has made outstanding contributions to the educational, theoretical, technical, commercial, or professional aspects of analysis, design, construction, evaluation, and use of interactive systems. IFIP TC 13 pioneers are appointed annually and awards are handed over at the INTERACT conference.

IFIP TC13 stimulates working events and activities through its working groups (WGs). WGs consist of HCI experts from many countries, who seek to expand knowledge and find solutions to HCI issues and concerns within their domains, as outlined here.

WG13.1 (Education in HCI and HCI Curricula) aims to improve HCI education at all levels of higher education, coordinate and unite efforts to develop HCI curricula and promote HCI teaching.

WG13.2 (Methodology for User-Centered System Design) aims to foster research, dissemination of information and good practice in the methodical application of HCI to software engineering.

WG13.3 (HCI and Disability) aims to make HCI designers aware of the needs of people with disabilities and encourage development of information systems and tools permitting adaptation of interfaces to specific users.

WG13.4 (also WG2.7; User Interface Engineering) investigates the nature, concepts, and construction of user interfaces for software systems, using a framework for reasoning about interactive systems and an engineering model for developing user interfaces.

WG 13.5 (Resilience, Reliability, Safety, and Human Error in System Development) seeks a framework for studying human factors relating to systems failure, develops leading-edge techniques in hazard analysis and safety engineering of computer-based systems, and guides international accreditation activities for safety-critical systems.

WG13.6 (Human–Work Interaction Design) aims at establishing relationships between extensive empirical work-domain studies and HCI design. It will promote the use of knowledge, concepts, methods, and techniques that enable user studies to procure a better apprehension of the complex interplay between individual, social, and organizational contexts and thereby a better understanding of how and why people work in the ways that they do.

WG13.7 (Human–Computer Interaction and Visualization) aims to establish a study and research program that will combine both scientific work and practical applications in the fields of HCI and visualization. It will integrate several additional aspects of further research areas, such as scientific visualization, data mining, information design, computer graphics, cognition sciences, perception theory, or psychology, into this approach.

WG13.8 (Interaction Design and International Development) are currently working to reformulate their aims and scope.

WG13.9 (Interaction Design and Children) aims to support practitioners, regulators, and researchers to develop the study of interaction design and children across international contexts.

New Working Groups are formed as areas of significance to HCI arise. Further information is available on the IFIP TC13 website: http://ifip-tc13.org/

IFIP TC13 Members

Officers

Chair
Jan Gulliksen, Sweden

Vice-chair
Philippe Palanque, France

Vice-Chair for WG and SIG
Simone D.J. Barbosa, Brazil

Treasurer
Anirudha Joshi, India

Secretary
Marco Winckler, France

Webmaster
Helen Petrie, UK

Country Representatives

Australia
Henry B.L. Duh
Australian Computer Society

Austria
Geraldine Fitzpatrick
Austrian Computer Society

Belgium
Monique Noirhomme-Fraiture
Fédération des Associations
  Informatiques de Belgique

Brazil
Raquel Oliveira Prates
Brazilian Computer Society (SBC)

Bulgaria
Kamelia Stefanova
Bulgarian Academy of Sciences

Canada
Heather O'Brien
Canadian Information Processing Society

Chile
Jaime Sánchez
Chilean Society of Computer Science

Croatia
Andrina Granic
Croatian Information Technology
  Association (CITA)

Cyprus
Panayiotis Zaphiris
Cyprus Computer Society

Czech Republic
Zdeněk Míkovec
Czech Society for Cybernetics &
  Informatics

Denmark
Torkil Clemmensen
Danish Federation for Information
  Processing

Finland
Kari-Jouko Räihä
Finnish Information Processing
  Association

France
Philippe Palanque
Société des Electriciens et des
  Electroniciens (SEE)

Germany
Tom Gross
Gesellschaft fur Informatik

Hungary
Cecilia Sik Lanyi
John V. Neumann Computer
  Society

Iceland
Marta Kristin Larusdottir
The Icelandic Society for Information
  Processing (ISIP)

India
Anirudha Joshi
Computer Society of India

Ireland
Liam J. Bannon
Irish Computer Society

Italy
Fabio Paternò
Italian Computer Society

Japan
Yoshifumi Kitamura
Information Processing Society of Japan

Korea
Gerry Kim
KIISE

Malaysia
Chui Yin Wong
Malaysian National Computer
  Confederation

The Netherlands
Vanessa Evers
Nederlands Genootschap voor
  Informatica

New Zealand
Mark Apperley
New Zealand Computer Society

Nigeria
Chris C. Nwannenna
Nigeria Computer Society

Norway
Dag Svanes
Norwegian Computer Society

Poland
Marcin Sikorski
Poland Academy of Sciences

Portugal
Pedro Campos
Associação Portuguesa para o Desen-
  volvimento da Sociedade da Infor-
  mação (APDSI)

Slovakia
Vanda Benešová
The Slovak Society for Computer
  Science

South Africa
Janet L. Wesson
The Computer Society of South Africa

Spain
Julio Abascal
Asociación de Técnicos de Informática
  (ATI)

Sweden
Jan Gulliksen
Swedish Computer Society

Switzerland
Solange Ghernaouti
Swiss Federation for Information
Processing

Tunisia
Mona Laroussi
Ecole Supérieure des Communications
  De Tunis (SUP'COM)

UK
Andy Dearden
British Computer Society (BCS)

USA
Gerrit van der Veer
Association for Computing Machinery
  (ACM)

Expert Members

Nikos Avouris (Greece)
Simone D.J. Barbosa (Brazil)
Peter Forbrig (Germany)
Joaquim Jorge (Portugal)
Paula Kotzé (South Africa)
Masaaki Kurosu (Japan)

Gitte Lindgaard (Australia)
Zhengjie Liu (China)
Fernando Loizides (Cyprus)
Dan Orwa (Kenya)
Frank Vetere (Australia)

Working Group Chairs

WG13.1 (Education in HCI and HCI Curricula)
Konrad Baumann, Austria

WG13.2 (Methodologies for User-Centered System Design)
Marco Winckler, France

WG13.3 (HCI and Disability)
Helen Petrie, UK

WG13.4 (also 2.7) (User Interface Engineering)
Jürgen Ziegler, Germany

WG13.5 (Resilience, Reliability, Safety and Human Error in System Development)
Chris Johnson, UK

WG13.6 (Human–Work Interaction Design)
Pedro Campos, Portugal

WG13.7 (HCI and Visualization)
Achim Ebert, Germany

WG 13.8 (Interaction Design and International Development)
José Adbelnour Nocera, UK

WG 13.9 (Interaction Design and Children)
Janet Read, UK

Conference Organizing Committee

General Conference Co-chairs
Tom Gross, Germany
Julio Abascal, Spain

Tutorials Co-chairs
Christoph Beckmann, Germany
Regina Bernhaupt, France

Full Papers Chairs
Simone D.J. Barbosa, Brazil
Philippe Palanque, France

Workshops Co-chairs
Christoph Beckmann, Germany
Víctor López-Jaquero, Spain

Short Papers Co-chairs
Fabio Paternò, Italy
Kari-Jouko Räihä, Finland

Doctoral Consortium Co-chairs
Geraldine Fitzpatrick, Austria
Panayiotis Zaphiris, Cyprus

Posters and Demos Co-chairs
Stephen Brewster, UK
David McGookin, UK

Proceedings Chair
Marco Winckler, France

Madness Co-chairs
Artur Lugmayr, Finland
Björn Stockleben, Germany
Tim Merritt, Denmark

Organization Overviews Co-chairs
Melanie Fitzgerald, USA
Kori Inkpen, USA

Panels Co-chairs
Anirudha N. Joshi, India
Gitte Lindgaard, Australia

Local Organization Co-chairs
Mirko Fetter, Germany
Claudia Tischler, Germany

Open Space Co-chairs
Christoph Beckmann, Germany
Achim Ebert, Germany

Student Volunteers Co-chairs
Robert Beaton, USA
Sascha Herr, Germany

Program Committee

Meta-reviewers
Birgit Bomsdorf, Germany
Gaëlle Calvary, France
José Campos, Portugal
Pedro Campos, Portugal
Luca Chittaro, Italy

Torkil Clemmensen, Denmark
Paul Curzon, UK
Achim Ebert, Germany
Peter Forbrig, Germany
Michael Harrison, UK

Anirudha Joshi, India
Denis Lalanne, Switzerland
Effie Law, UK
Célia Martinie, France
Laurence Nigay, France
Monique Noirhomme, Belgium
Fabio Paternò, Italy
Helen Petrie, UK
Antonio Piccinno, Italy
Aaron Quigley, UK
Kari-Jouko Räihä, Finland
Virpi Roto, Finland

Luciana Salgado Cardoso de Castro,
  Brazil
Paula Alexandra Silva, Ireland
Frank Steinicke, Germany
Simone Stumpf, UK
Allistair Sutcliffe, UK
Jean Vanderdonckt, Belgium
Gerhard Weber, Germany
Astrid Weiss, Austria
Marco Winckler, France
Panayiotis Zaphiris, Cyprus

Reviewers

José Abdelnour-Nocera, UK
Al Mahmud Abdullah, Australia
Silvia Abrahão, Spain
Funmi Adebesin, South Africa
Ana Paula Afonso, Portugal
David Ahlström, Austria
Pierre Akiki, Lebanon
Deepak Akkil, Finland
Hannu Alen, Finland
Jan Alexandersson, Germany
José Carlos Bacelar Almeida, Portugal
Florian Alt, Germany
Julian Alvarez, France
Junia Coutinho Anacleto, Brazil
Leonardo Angelini, Switzerland
Craig Anslow, New Zealand
Mark Apperley, New Zealand
Nathalie Aquino, Paraguay
Liliana Ardissono, Italy
Carmelo Ardito, Italy
Oscar Javier Ariza Núñez, Germany
Myriam Arrue, Spain
Ilhan Aslan, Austria
Simon Attfield, UK
Nikolaos Avouris, Greece
Chris Baber, UK
Myroslav Bachynskyi, Germany
Jonathan Back, UK
Gilles Bailly, France
Liam Bannon, Ireland

Emilia Barakova, The Netherlands
Javier Barcenila, France
Louise Barkhuus, USA
Barbara Rita Barricelli, Italy
Valentina Bartalesi, Italy
Mohammed Basheri, Saudi Arabia
Christoph Beckmann, Germany
Yacine Bellik, France
Vanda Benešová, Slovak Republic
Kawtar Benghazi, Spain
David Benyon, UK
François Bérard, France
Regina Bernhaupt, Austria
Karsten Berns, Germany
Nadia Berthouze, UK
Raymond Bertram, Finland
Mark Billinghurst, New Zealand
Dorrit Billman, USA
Silvia Amelia Bim, Brazil
Fernando Birra, Portugal
Renaud Blanch, France
Ann Blandford, UK
Mads Boedker, Denmark
Davide Bolchini, USA
Birgit Bomsdorf, Germany
Rodrigo Bonacin, Brazil
Paolo Gaspare Bottoni, Italy
Fatma Bouali, France
Chris Bowers, UK
Giorgio Brajnik, Italy

Manuel Fonseca, Portugal
Peter Forbrig, Germany
Marcus Foth, Australia
Andre Freire, Brazil
Carla D.S. Freitas, Brazil
Jonas Fritsch, Denmark
Luca Frosini, Italy
Dominic Furniss, UK
Nestor Garay-Vitoria, Spain
Jérémie Garcia, France
Roberto García, Spain
Jose Luis Garrido, Spain
Franca Garzotto, Italy
Isabela Gasparini, Brazil
Miguel Gea, Spain
Patrick Gebhard, Germany
Cristina Gena, Italy
Giuseppe Ghiani, Italy
Patrick Girard, France
Kentaro Go, Japan
Daniel Gonçalves, Portugal
Rúben Gouveia, Portugal
Nicholas Graham, Canada
Andrina Granic, Croatia
Toni Granollers, Spain
Saul Greenberg, Canada
John Grundy, Australia
Nuno Guimaraes, Portugal
Jan Gulliksen, Sweden
Rebecca Gulotta, USA
Mieke Haesen, Belgium
Hans Hagen, Germany
Jonna Häkkilä, Finland
Jukka Häkkinen, Finland
Jaakko Hakulinen, Finland
Lynne Hall, UK
Arnaud Hamon, France
Chris Harrison, USA
Daniel Harrison, UK
Michael Harrison, UK
Ruediger Heimgaertner, Germany
Tomi Heimonen, Finland
Matthias Heintz, UK
Ingi Helgason, UK
Susan Catherine Herring, USA
Wilko Heuten, Germany

Martin Hitz, Austria
Thuong Hoang, Australia
Rüdiger Hoffmann, Germany
Jennifer Horkoff, UK
Heiko Hornung, Brazil
Ko-Hsun Huang, Taiwan,
 Republic of China
Alina Huldtgren, The Netherlands
Ebba Thora Hvannberg, Iceland
Aulikki Hyrskykari, Finland
Ioanna Iacovides, UK
Netta Iivari, Finland
Mirja Ilves, Finland
Yavuz İnal, Turkey
Poika Isokoski, Finland
Minna Isomursu, Finland
Howell Istance, Finland
Ido A. Iurgel, Germany
Mikkel R. Jakobsen, Denmark
Francis Jambon, France
Jacek Jankowski, Poland
Maddy Janse, The Netherlands
Nuno Jardim Nunes, Portugal
Caroline Jay, UK
Kasper Løvborg Jensen, Denmark
Mikael Johnson, Finland
Matt Jones, UK
Joaquim Jorge, Portugal
Rui Jose, Portugal
Anirudha Joshi, India
Christophe Jouffrais, France
Anne Joutsenvirta, Finland
Marko Jurmu, Finland
Eija Kaasinen, Finland
Jari Kangas, Finland
Anne Marie Kanstrup, Denmark
Victor Kaptelinin, Sweden
Evangelos Karapanos, Portugal
Kristiina Karvonen, Finland
Dinesh Katre, India
Manolya Kavakli, Australia
Patrick Gage Kelley, USA
Ryan Kelly, UK
Rabia Khan, UK
Hideki Koike, Japan
Christophe Kolski, France

Hannu Korhonen, Finland
Nataliya Kosmyna, France
Paula Kotze, South Africa
Christian Kray, Germany
Per Ola Kristensson, UK
Sari Kujala, Finland
Todd Kulesza, USA
Denis Lalanne, Switzerland
David Lamas, Estonia
Michael Lankes, Austria
Rosa Lanzilotti, Italy
Przemyslaw Lasota, USA
Yann Laurillau, France
Effie Law, UK
Shaimaa Lazem, UK
Xavier Le Pallec, France
Eric Lecolinet, France
Jong-Seok Lee, South Korea
Asko Lehmuskallio, Finland
Antti Leino, Finland
Juha Leino, Finland
Tuomas Leisti, Finland
Jair Leite, Brazil
Alexander Lenz, UK
Barbara Leporini, Italy
Sophie Lepreux, France
Karen Y. Li, UK
Edirlei Lima, Brazil
James Lin, USA
Mats Lind, Sweden
Agnes Lisowska Masson, Switzerland
Zhengjie Liu, China
Sara Ljungblad, Sweden
Corrado lo Storto, Italy
Steffen Lohmann, Germany
Fernando Loizides, Cyprus
Víctor López-Jaquero, Spain
Fabien Lotte, France
Maria Dolores Lozano, Spain
Yichen Lu, Finland
Paul Lubos, Germany
Stephanie Ludi, USA
Bernd Ludwig, Germany
Andreas Luedtke, Germany
Christopher Lueg, Australia
Jo Lumsden, UK
Christof Lutteroth, New Zealand

Kris Luyten, Belgium
Anderson Maciel, Brazil
I. Scott MacKenzie, Canada
Allan MacLean, UK
Christian Maertin, Germany
Charlotte Magnusson, Sweden
Ana Gabriela Maguitman, Argentina
Päivi Majaranta, Finland
Marco Manca, Italy
Nicolai Marquardt, UK
Célia Martinie, France
Paolo Masci, UK
Masood Masoodian, New Zealand
Maristella Matera, Italy
Denys J.C. Matthies, Germany
Peter W. McOwan, UK
Gerrit Meixner, Germany
Guy Melançon, France
Amaia Mendez Zorrilla, Spain
Maria Menendez Blanco, Italy
Zdenek Mikovec, Czech Republic
Jan-Torsten Milde, Germany
Nicole Mirnig, Austria
Giulio Mori, Italy
Roxana Morosanu, UK
Christiane Moser, Austria
Marcelle Mota, Brazil
Omar Mubin, Australia
Chrystie Myketiak, UK
Miguel Nacenta, UK
Lennart Nacke, Canada
Mathieu Nancel, Canada
Bonnie Nardi, USA
David Navarre, France
Ather Nawaz, Norway
Luciana Nedel, Brazil
Alexandra Nemery, France
Vania Neris, Brazil
Daniel Nesbitt, UK
Lene Nielsen, Denmark
Anton Nijholt, The Netherlands
Laurence Nigay, France
Manuel Noguera, Spain
Monique Noirhomme, Belgium
Julianne Nyhan, UK
Clemens Nylandsted Klokmose,
    Denmark

Harri Siirtola, Finland
Paula A. Silva, Ireland
Bruno S. Silva, Brazil
Carlos CL Silva, Portugal
João Carlos Silva, Portugal
Jose Luis Silva, Portugal
Paula Alexandra Silva, Ireland
Milene Silveira, Brazil
Carla Simone, Italy
Shamus Smith, Australia
Andreas Sonderegger, Switzerland
Keyur Sorathia, India
Fabio Sorrentino, Italy
Hamit Soyel, UK
Oleg Spakov, Finland
Lucio Davide Spano, Italy
Mark Vincent Springett, UK
Jan Stage, Denmark
Christian Stary, Austria
Katarzyna Stawarz, UK
Frank Steinicke, Germany
Gerald Stollnberger, Austria
Markus Stolze, Switzerland
Simone Stumpf, UK
Noi Sukaviriya, USA
Allistar Sutcliffe, UK
David Mark Swallow, UK
Tapio Takala, Finland
Chee-wee Tan, Denmark
Franck Tarpin-Bernard, France
Carlos Teixeira, Portugal
Luis Teixeira, Portugal
Daniel Tetteroo, The Netherlands
Jakob Tholander, Sweden
Nigel Thomas, UK
Liisa Tiittula, Finland
Nava Tintarev, UK
Martin Tomitsch, Australia
Ilaria Torre, Italy
Marilyn Tremaine, USA
Daniela Trevisan, Brazil
Sanjay Tripathi, India
Janice Tsai, USA
Manfred Tscheligi, Austria
Huawei Tu, UK
Outi Tuisku, Finland
Phil Turner, UK

Susan Ellen Turner, UK
Markku Turunen, Finland
Blase Ur, USA
Heli Väätäjä, Finland
Stefano Valtolina, Italy
Judy van Biljon, South Africa
Jos P. van Leeuwen, The Netherlands
Paul van Schaik, UK
Jeroen Vanattenhoven, Belgium
Jean Vanderdonckt, Belgium
Jari Varsaluoma, Finland
Radu-Daniel Vatavu, Romania
Angel Velazquez-Iturbide, Spain
Hanna Venesvirta, Finland
Jayant Venkatanathan, India
Gilles Venturini, France
Arnold Vermeeren, The Netherlands
Karel Vermeulen, UK
Frédéric Vernier, France
Markel Vigo, UK
Nadine Vigouroux, France
Chris Vincent, UK
Giuliana Vitiello, Italy
Arnd Vitzthum, Germany
Dhaval Vyas, Australia
Mike Wald, UK
Jim Wallace, Canada
Tanja Carita Walsh, Finland
Robert Walter, Germany
Leon Watts, UK
Gerhard Weber, Germany
Rina Wehbe, Canada
Astrid Weiss, Austria
Janet Louise Wesson, South Africa
Graham Wilson, UK
Stephanie Wilson, UK
Marco Winckler, France
Theophilus Winschiers, Namibia
Chui Yin Wong, Malaysia
Wolfgang Wörndl, Germany
Volker Wulf, Germany
Yeliz Yesilada, Turkey
Salu Ylirisku, Finland
Nur Haryani Zakaria, Malaysia
Massimo Zancanaro, Italy
Panayiotis Zaphiris, Cyprus
Jürgen Ziegler, Germany

Sponsors and Supporters

Sponsors

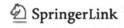

Supporters

Contents – Part I

Brain-Computer Interaction

Cognitive Factors

Contents – Part II

Evaluation Methods/Usability Evaluation

Eye Tracking

Gesture Interaction

HCI and Security

HCI for Developing Regions and Social Development

HCI for Education

Contents – Part III

Human-Robot Interaction

Interactive Tabletops

Mobile and Ubiquitous Interaction

Participatory Design

Pointing and Gesture Interaction

Social Interaction

Contents – Part IV

Visualization

Visualization 3D

Visualization in Virtual Spaces

Wearable Computing

Demonstrations

Organizational Overview

Panels

Tutorials

Workshops

Assisted Interaction Data Analysis
of Web-Based User Studies

Xabier Valencia, J. Eduardo Pérez, Unai Muñoz,
Myriam Arrue$^{(\boxtimes)}$, and Julio Abascal

EGOKITUZ: Laboratory of HCI for Special Needs,
University of the Basque Country (UPV/EHU), Informatika Fakultatea,
20018 Donostia, Spain
{xabier.valencia, juaneduardo.perez, unai.munoz,
myriam.arrue, julio.abascal}@ehu.eus

Abstract. User behaviour analysis requires defining experimental sessions with numerous participants. In this context, the specification of experiments is a demanding task, as several issues have to be considered such as the type of experiment, the type and number of tasks, the definition of questionnaires and the user interaction data to be gathered. The analysis of collected data is also complex and often requires repeatedly examining recorded interaction videos. In order to deal with these tasks, we present a platform called RemoTest which assists researchers to specify and conduct experimental sessions as well as to gather and analyse the interaction data. This platform has been applied to define different formal user studies on the web and has assisted researchers in detecting the main interaction characteristics of different user profiles and settings.

Keywords: Web accessibility · User testing · User behaviour · Accessibility in use

1 Introduction

User behaviour when interacting with the Web has been extensively studied in the last decade. This significant research area requires the conducting of experimental sessions with large and diverse groups of users. Experimental sessions have to be carefully planned in order to obtain meaningful results because a minor fault in the design could lead to an erroneous interpretation of results. Researchers need to clearly define the objectives of the experiment, the type of experiment, the stimuli to be presented to participants, the tasks to be performed and the procedure of the experimental sessions. In addition, sometimes specific questionnaires are required in order to explicitly obtain certain data from the participants. The experiment design process is demanding and involves knowledge from different areas such as human factors, hypertext, web technology, etc.

The designed experiments are intended to gather significant interaction data. This data could be gathered through combining different methods such as the traditional ones of recording sessions with video cameras or using specific software components to conveniently collect and store it.

© IFIP International Federation for Information Processing 2015
J. Abascal et al. (Eds.): INTERACT 2015, Part I, LNCS 9296, pp. 1–19, 2015.
DOI: 10.1007/978-3-319-22701-6_1

Interaction data analysis is a tedious task especially when only traditional recording methods have been used. Researchers are required to view the recorded videos repeatedly and annotate every meaningful interaction event and data. Among others, cursor movement events are of vital importance when studying the accessibility-in-use of websites or web navigation strategies. For instance, actions such as pointing to a target (buttons, scroll bars, check boxes and radio buttons, etc.), clicking on a target or providing accurate text entry could be very difficult for people with motor impairments due to their lack of dexterity [23]. Examining the cursor movements on recorded images is a hard task that can be alleviated through the application of software components. These components should be efficient in appropriately storing, presenting and preparing all this interaction data for analysis.

In addition, involving an appropriate number of participants for a specific experiment is also challenging. Frequently, this is due to the location and the rigorous timing of sessions. Nowadays, there is an increasing interest in using software tools for conducting experiments remotely. That means that participants are observed while they perform the tasks in their habitual daily environment. This particularly facilitates the conduction of experiments with disabled people, as their environment is already adapted to their needs. Moreover, this type of experiments gathers real interaction data without any obtrusive observation mechanism [2]. It also makes it possible to involve a larger number of participants, as they do not have to physically get to a specific location.

This paper presents a platform called RemoTest that can be applied in remote and in situ experimental sessions. Its objective is to assist researchers when designing experiments, conducting experimental sessions and analysing data gathered in the sessions. A case study based on a real in situ exploratory study with 16 participants (11 people with physical impairments and 5 able-bodied participants) is described in Sect. 4. The objective of this experiment was to analyse the differing interaction characteristics of users with physical impairments and able-bodied users. The interaction of the 11 participants with physical impairments was manually analysed based on the video recordings and results are presented and discussed in [20]. The RemoTest platform was also applied to analyse the data of all the participants so the results of manual and automated analysis are contrasted in this paper as a proof-of-concept of the proposed platform.

2   Related Work

In the last few years, the use of tools for remotely conducting user tests has come to the attention of researchers. These tools can be classified depending upon their architecture: server-side tools, proxy tools and client-side tools. Each one has its drawbacks and advantages. Server-side tools are the most unobtrusive. Participants are not required to install or configure anything on their systems. Among the HTTP requests from the servers, user interaction data could be also gathered by modifying the web pages with code to track the interaction data (for instance, JavaScript). One drawback is that the conducted tests could be only based on websites located on the servers researchers have access to. Contrarily, proxy tools require participants to configure their web browser in order to access to the proxy. This type of tool enables more information to be gathered than via the server logs as well as permitting the tests to be conducted on any website but however, it is not possible to capture all the participants actions, such as the events on the browser. Finally, client-side tools are the most obtrusive ones since they require the installation of some add-on applications to the participant's system. Nevertheless, they are the best option for researchers because they capture all the user interaction data needed in a user behaviour study, such as cursor movements, scroll events, clicking actions, browser events (backward/forward button, print/save page, add bookmark), etc. without modifying the original web pages.

There are some commercial tools such as Google Analytics [11], Loop11 [15] and Morae [17]. Google Analytics is a server-side tool. Its objective is to obtain general connection data about the users of a specific web site but not to conduct formal experiments. It records information such as the network provider or the browser used by users accessing to a specific web site enriched with Google Analytics. Loop11 is a proxy tool developed for conducting user tests. It includes features that facilitate the definition of web tasks or questionnaires. Regarding the data analysis, it provides click stream reports to visualize the paths that the user followed, click heat maps and the option of visualizing the data in real time. There is a version of Loop11 using AccessWorks devoted to performing user tests with disabled people. Nevertheless this tool does not capture browser events. These events can be used as user disorientation indicators (for example, several clicks on the browser backward button in a task may sometimes imply user orientation problems). Morae is a client-side tool which stores user interaction data when interacting with either standalone applications or web sites. In addition, it provides tools to enable the observation and annotation while the user is performing the test. The tool is quite complex to configure due to the amount of available options provided. Sometimes, programmer skills are required in order to gather some interaction events.

There are many examples of tools developed in academic contexts. Webquilt [12] is a proxy-based tool that stores only information obtained from HTTP requests. NIST WebMetricsSuite [5, 22] is a server-side tool that provides methods to assess the usability of web pages by analysing the path followed by the user. These tools only gather events related to clicks. Therefore, no user interaction data is gathered. Other tools such as WET [8] or USAPROXY [3] are more comprehensive as they also enable the detection of problematic web elements by gathering user interaction data such as mouse movements and keyboard events by injecting Javascript code to the original web pages. Nevertheless, these tools do not assist in formal experiment definition, as they do not include features for task definition or the elaboration of questionnaires. WebRemUSINE tool [18] provides researchers with features for defining formal experiments. It is a client-side tool that uses both technologies Java Applets and JavaScript code to capture the interaction events. The tool is based on ConcurTaskTrees (CTT) task model annotation [19] for defining experiments. It detects usability problems analyzing the differences between the path followed by users to perform the defined tasks and the specified task model in CTT. It requires high knowledge levels and expertise to define the task models, making this tool only usable by expert researchers. In addition, this tool does not provide features for defining questionnaires to fill in by participants during the experimental sessions.

On the contrary, Curious Browser [5] presents questionnaires to the user after every new visited page, with the aim of rating its interest. Nevertheless the tool does not provide methods to define formal experiments like defining tasks, pre/post task questionnaires and so on. Uzilla [7] is another comprehensive tool for defining formal experiments. It also provides features for defining questionnaires to be filled in by participants during the session. However, there is not much information about the suitability of the created questionnaires for people with disabilities.

Some other approaches can be found relating to the study of users' interaction performance in the wild. Gajos et al. [9] developed a system devoted to minimize the gap between the results of pointing performance in a laboratory and those in the wild. The tool distinguishes between deliberate and distracted mouse pointer movements. Another similar tool was proposed by Hurst et al. [14]. This tool classifies users' characteristics based on their input events. Both tools provide valuable information about user behaviour or characteristics but do not allow performing formal experiments.

Power et al. list a number of requirements that a remote user tool should meet to be able to conduct experimental sessions with users with disabilities [21]. Some of them are related to participants and other to researchers. The requirements related to participants include the following: provide features to record demographic data (P1), specify the technology used (OS, browser, assistive technology) (P2), select the trials (P3). The ones related to researchers are the following: provide features to test customized and "real" websites (R1), define tasks for a set of users (R2), specify a set of questions to the user, before and/or after the task has been completed (R3), provide instructions and training documents for each trial (R4). Table 1 shows the requirements fulfilled by the academic context tools presented in this section.

Table 1. Classification of user testing tools according to the requirements proposed by Power et al. and their location.

Name	Location	P1	P2	P3	R1	R2	R3	R4
NISTWebMetrics Suite	Sever	No	No	No	Partial	No	No	No
WET	Server	No	No	Yes	Partial	No	No	No
WEBQUILT	Proxy	No	No	No	Yes	No	No	No
Curious Browser	Client	No	No	No	Yes	No	Partial	No
UsaProxy	Proxy	No	No	No	Yes	No	No	No
WebRemUSINE	Server	No	No	Yes	Yes	Yes	No	No
Uzilla	Client	Yes	Yes	Yes	Yes	Yes	Yes	Yes
Gajos et al.	Client	No	No	No	Yes	No	No	No
Hurst et al.	Client	No	No	No	Yes	No	No	No

The Remotest platform is a client-side tool that provides all the necessary features for defining formal experiments and fulfils the requirements proposed by Power and colleagues. In addition, the questionnaires created by the tool have proven to be accessible to people with disabilities in several evaluations.

3 The Remotest Platform

The RemoTest platform provides the necessary functionalities to assist researchers to define experiments, manage experimental remote/in situ sessions and analyse the gathered interaction data. This platform admits a wide range of experiments. The objective can be, for instance, to study user behaviour when performing a task in different websites, to analyse and compare navigational strategies of different types of participants when interacting with the same website, to evaluate the accessibility-in-use of several websites, to gather significant information through surveys, to measure user satisfaction when using a certain web service and to analyse user performance improvement when interacting with adapted versions of original web pages and so on.

The architecture of the platform has been designed taking all these different types of experiments into consideration. In this case, we opted for a hybrid architecture model that includes some functions in a client-side module and the other ones in some server-side modules. The platform is split into four modules: Experimenter Module (EXm), Participant Module (PAm), Coordinator Module (COm) and Results Viewer Module (RVm).

3.1 Experimenter Module

This module provides a set of functionalities for defining all the components of the experiments. It is a server-side module which can be accessed by experimenters from any computer with an Internet connection. All the definition process is performed by the use of a web application and has been divided into five main steps:

Step 1: Specifying the type of experiment. This first step is intended to specify the type of the experiment (survey or navigation tasks on the web) and general characteristics of the experiment such as the stimuli to be presented in experimental sessions, number of questionnaires (demographic data questionnaire, satisfaction questionnaire, etc.)

Step 2: Determining the tasks and stimuli of the experimental sessions. Depending on the type of experiment specified in Step 1 the platform would ask to provide information about the tasks to be performed by participants and the stimuli to present. Two main types of tasks can be defined: "Fill in Questionnaire" and "Web Navigation". There is no limit to the number of tasks per experiment

For each task some details have to be provided. For instance, for the "Fill in Questionnaire" task the questions, the type of questions (open-ended or closed) and possible options for answers (likert scales, ranges) have to be defined. There is some other information regarding title, id, etc., that has to be completed in order to ensure the accessibility of the created questionnaire. The "Web Navigation" task also requires some data. Currently, there are two types of tasks in this category: "searching target" tasks and "free navigation" tasks. The former one refers to tasks where participants are required to find a specific target (such as a specific button, link, form, etc.) whereas the latter one entails navigation without any concrete objective. Both require certain information from the experimenter, for instance, the starting URI, time limit for the task, etc. Searching target tasks also require the specific target URI to be provided. In addition, a title and a description can be added to each task so that, in the experimental sessions, an accessible task explanation web page is presented to participants before starting the task and an alert after performing the task.

Once all the tasks are defined, the dependencies between them have to be explicitly stated. This module provides features to define if any task should be presented just before or after another one. For example, in an experiment to measure satisfaction of users when interacting with a certain website, a "Fill in Questionnaire" task about satisfaction has to be presented just after a "Web Navigation" task.

Step 3:   Defining the procedure of the experimental sessions. In this step, the number of groups of participants, the tasks presented to each group and the task sequence for each group has to be defined. Experimenters are asked to provide the number of groups in the sample. Specifying a unique group leads to a within-subject experiment. Therefore, each participant will perform all the defined tasks. The task sequence should be counterbalanced between participants and the experimenter is required to define one method (manual, latin square, rotation or random). In between-groups experiments, the tasks to perform by each group are manually selected by the experimenter. The task sequence for each group can be defined manually or automatically (using random method). In all cases, the EXm considers the dependencies between tasks and any other detected inconsistencies are notified to the experimenter

Step 4:   Specifying interaction data to be gathered. The experimenter selects the interaction data to be gathered in the experimental sessions. This data will be automatically gathered by the PAm during the experimental sessions. Currently, the interaction data gathered by the platform are the following:

- Browser related events. Active tab, opening tab, closing tab, changing tab, backward button, forward button, vertical/horizontal scroll movements, screen resolution, window size, mouse context menu, favourites management...
- Cursor/Mouse related events. Clicking left button, clicking right button, using mouse wheel, size of clicked elements, hover events, size of hovered elements, tracking cursor movements.
- Keyboard related events. Key down, key up, key pressed.

Step 5:   Selecting the sample of participants. The RemoTest platform provides functionalities to maintain information about participants in a database through the module EXm. This tool includes options such as manual selection of participants in each group, randomly creating groups from the selected participants or establishing some kind of criteria to select the sample, (such as gender, age, assistive technology used, etc.), applying filtering criteria to the query

The information about the experiments is stored in an XML-based language specifically developed for this platform, the Experiment Specification Language.

3.2 Coordinator Module

The Coordinator Module is a server-side type module which has been developed as a Web Service. The objectives of this module are the following:

- Storing and managing the experiments defined by different experimenters applying features of EXm.
- Creating stimuli to present during the experimental sessions (questionnaires, task description web page, task completion alert, etc.).
- Defining the personalized experimental sessions specifications.
- Collecting and storing interaction data obtained in experimental sessions.
- Maintaining information about experimenters, experiments, participants in databases.

This module creates all the necessary stimuli for the experiments (surveys, questionnaires, task description web pages, alerts, etc.) according to the definition provided by means of the Experiment Specification Language. In addition, it prepares the participant groups and performs the counterbalancing methods, when necessary, in order to create personalized experimental sessions for each participant or group of participants. This leads to the obtaining of specific personalized experimental session specifications for each participant defined in an XML-based language developed for this purpose, the Experimental Session Controlling Language. The interaction data created in the sessions are managed and stored in a MongoDB database.

3.3 Participant Module

The participant module is a client-side type module. Therefore participants have to install this module in their computers. It is currently an add-on for Firefox browser but it can be easily migrated to other platforms, since this module is mostly based on JavaScript and XML. It processes the Experimental Session Controller Language for correctly conducting participants' experimental sessions. In addition, it gathers all the interaction data, as well as the HTTPRequest information during the whole session and asynchronously sends to COm by using AJAX technology.

3.4 Results Viewer Module

The RVm is a server-side type module which deals with the presentation of the interaction data gathered in experimental sessions. For this purpose, RVm implements functions for collecting the data from COm, structuring it in understandable blocks of events and presenting them to the experimenter as a web application. Some statistics by pages, tasks or users can be visualized:

- Rapidity measures: Time on page, cursor average speed, cursor acceleration.
- Accuracy measures: Trajectory distance (cursor travel distance), curvature index (CI) relation between optimal path and path followed, distances to the centre of the target and to the last click and ratio of start-end position amplitude to start-target centre amplitude [1].

Figure 1 shows the information presented regarding the performance of a participant in a visited web page.

Rapidity Measures	
Time on page:	00:00:16 (hh:mm:ss)
Average-speed:	91,92 Pixels/seconds
Number of ZA:	56
Number of acceleration to deceleration phases:	27
Number of deceleration to a acceleration phases:	22
Accuracy Measures	
Trajectory distance:	1470,78 Pixels
Curvature Index:	1,21
Distance between start to end point:	1213,66 Pixels
Distance between start point to target center:	1180,15 Pixels
Ratio of start-end position amplitude to start-target center amplitude:	1,03

Fig. 1. General information about the performance of a participant in a visited web page.

This module includes a tool for comparing the performance of each participant in all the visited pages. Figure 2 show the charts generated for comparing the trajectory distance of a participant in the visited pages.

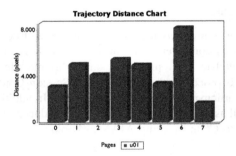

Fig. 2. Comparing chart about the trajectory distance parameter of a participant

The general information shown by the RemoTest platform assist researchers to obtain detailed information about the performance of each participant during the experimental session. In addition, this module also provides several graphs for each visited page. One is the "Distance to target chart", where the distance to the target at every moment can be seen. With this chart researchers can easily identify users' problems when aiming at the target, see Fig. 3 Left. As can be seen, once cursor is in the target nearby the user requires several attempts to place the cursor on it.

Furthermore, associated with this first chart the tool also provides another graph that shows the distance to the target but starting from users' intention time to click the

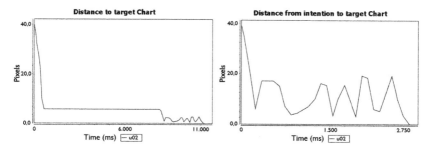

Fig. 3. "Distance to target" (Left) and "Distance from intention to target" (Right) charts

target, see Fig. 3 Right. The intention time to click is automatically calculated by the algorithm described in the Sect. 3.4.1.

In addition, graphs of cursor's movement speed and acceleration charts can be found. Through these graphs researchers can appreciate for instance, the different cursor movements taking into account the input device used by the user.

Figure 4 shows one participant (who moves the cursor by pressing the numerical keypad with a head pointer) creates similar speed and acceleration peaks followed by short pauses, the time it takes the user to change direction to press another key with the head pointer.

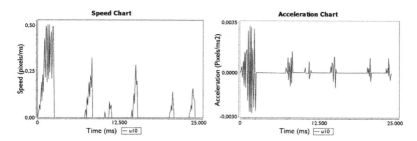

Fig. 4. Speed chart (left) and acceleration chart (right) of a participant (U10 in the case study)

Another important feature is the ability of the tool to make comparisons. In first place, researchers can view a comparison between different statistics about all visited pages in a task of a selected user. In the same way, the application also allows to compare these statistics to all participants for a given task. So, RVm is able to display automatically generated bar charts comparing the average or median, of the trajectory distances, curvature index, times to point and click or cursor speeds.

This straightforward visualization may assist experimenters in discovering relevant bits of users' interactions, and in case of also having complementary video recordings, fast locating the corresponding moments and save huge amount of time viewing and analysing video images.

In order to extract aimed movements from all the cursor's kinematic data recorded by the RemoTest platform and study pointing trajectory-related measures, we have processed the data as follows.

3.4.1 Delimiting Pointing Trajectories

A pointing trajectory starts when a user resolves to move the cursor to reach an objective. Controlled laboratory experiments can specify restricted interactions to make the beginning of cursor movement explicit [9]. In contrast to those studies, more naturalistic settings with untagged web interactions do not permit the register of any explicit trace of the cognitive process behind the users' intention. In those cases, as in ours, heuristics are needed to estimate the beginning of the aimed movements [4, 10].

Among the other possible aimed movements within web GUIs (e.g., hovering over an element to see its tooltip), we have decided to focus on pointing trajectories that end with a navigational click and a posterior page load event. In our case we have considered the following bases for delimiting pointing trajectories.

Beginning of movement. A pointing to navigational click trajectory may correspond to the complete cursor movement recorded along a page, however behaviours such as moving the cursor while reading the content of the page provoke the need to analyse all the cursor trajectory throughout every page.

We have considered the first cursor move event recorded within every page as the beginning of movement candidates for pointing to navigational click trajectories. Each time a page scroll interaction occurs, actual cursor trajectory (if it exists) is rejected as a page candidate for pointing to navigational click trajectory, restarting a new pointing trajectory when the next cursor move event is triggered.

Additionally, pauses take place along cursor trajectories are useful to segment pointing trajectories. Aimed movements consist of several sub-movements separated by pauses [16], so trying to delimit a pointing trajectory as a cursor movement without pauses is not feasible.

Calculating Valid User Pauses. A pause during an aimed movement may correspond to a sub-movement transition, or in case of being long enough (movement stop) to cursor trajectory segmentation (Fig. 5).

Unlike other studies where a unique value for all users serves to distinguish between valid pauses during cursor aimed movements and movement stops [4, 10], we have followed an individual approach for this purpose. As we have observed from the interaction of the physically impaired participants of our study, valid pauses during aimed movements vary among users depending on the computer pointing device used and their ability with it (Fig. 5). For instance, a numeric keypad user needs more time to change cursor trajectory (notable pauses between strokes) than a joystick user. We believe that calculating a movement stop threshold for every user will improve the quality of the segmentation and therefore the pointing trajectory-related measures.

To calculate each user movement stop threshold, we have taken into account all the intervals in which the cursor velocity falls to zero within each every page, registering these time durations by user. From this data, we have calculated the median value of all

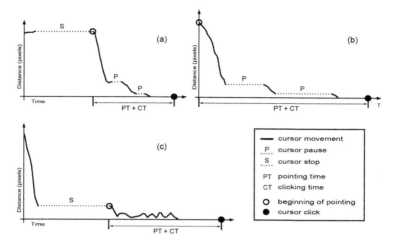

Fig. 5. Beginning of pointing trajectories estimations for 3 physically impaired participants using different computer pointing devices: (a) joystick, (b) numeric keypad with a head pointer and (c) oversized trackball.

collected observations by user, and so discarded stops duration that were two quartile deviations or more away from the participant's median. We have used the median and quartile deviation values to reduce the importance of outliers within each distribution. Through an extensive observation of our data we have concluded that values obtained this way were reasonable.

End of movement. As mentioned above, we only focus on pointing trajectories that end with a navigational click and a posterior page load event. Thus we have discarded all pages from our data logs without pointing to navigational click trajectories, for instance using keyboard shortcuts or browsing history navigation without moving the cursor.

4   Case Study

This section is devoted to describing the benefits of using the RemoTest platform to define experiments, conducting experimental sessions and collecting and analyzing interaction data. This case study is based on a specific experiment carried out by the authors with 16 participants, 11 people with upper-body physical impairments (U01–U11) and 5 able-bodied people (U12–U16). The objective of the experiment was to analyse the different navigation strategies used by the participants. Web expertise varied among participants as well as the assistive technology and input devices used for accessing the Web. Table 2 shows information about the participants.

The experimental sessions were carried out locally in different settings (experimenters moved to the specific location and assisted participants during all the session) and used different computers: 7 experimental sessions were conducted at the Elkartu

Table 2. Information about the participants

User	Expertise	Input devices	Setting
U01	Medium	Reconfigured mouse and keyboard	Elkartu
U02	High	Oversized trackball and keyboard	Lab
U03	High	Joystick and keyboard with cover	Home
U04	Medium	Joystick and keyboard	Elkartu
U05	Medium	Joystick and on screen keyboard	Elkartu
U06	Low	Joystick and keyboard with handstick	Elkartu
U07	Low	Reconfigured touchpad and keyboard	Elkartu
U08	High	Numeric keypad and keyboard	Home
U09	High	Numeric keypad and keyboard	Home
U10	High	Head pointer and reconfigured keyboard	Elkartu
U11	Medium	Head pointer and reconfigured keyboard	Elkartu
U12	High	Standard mouse and keyboard	Lab
U13	High	Standard mouse and keyboard	Lab
U14	High	Standard mouse and keyboard	Lab
U15	High	Standard mouse and keyboard	Lab
U16	High	Standard mouse and keyboard	Lab

premises (a local association of people with physical disabilities), 6 participants carried out the experimental session in a laboratory of the Computer Science School at the University of the Basque Country and the remaining experimental sessions (3 of 16) were conducted at the participant's home. The platform used was similar in all cases: Windows operating system (Windows 7 except of U02 who used Windows XP) and Mozilla Firefox browser.

Participants were asked to install the PAm module on the local computer (their usual computer in some cases). To this end, the PAm Firefox add-on was placed on an URL and a web page with clear instructions of how to install it was created. This task was useful for detecting some minor issues in the instructions that needed to be fixed. Even though it was not the object of the study, this preliminary installation task was also useful in order to test the adequacy of using a client-side tool for conducting experimental sessions. Despite only one participant (U02) having previous experience in installing this type of software, all participants were able to install the PAm module including the ones with low-level expertise in using the computer (U06, U07).

4.1 Experiment Definition

The experiment consisted of three tasks: filling in a questionnaire about demographic data (Task 1), free navigation task with 5 min duration (Task 2) and searching for a target task with a maximum duration of 10 min (Task 3).

Web navigation tasks (Task 2 and Task 3) were performed on the Discapnet website [www.discapnet.com] which is specialized in providing information to people with disabilities. The order of these tasks was predefined since the free navigation task was intended to familiarize the users with the website.

RemoTest platform was used for defining the experimental sessions. The definition process was as follows:

Step 1:   Specifying the type of experiment. This experiment was a web navigation experiment

Step 2:   Determining the tasks and stimuli of the experimental sessions

- Task 1: The EXm module guided the researcher in the process of defining the questions and possible options for responses.
- Task 2: This task was a "Web Navigation" type task with free navigation category. The EXm module asked for information regarding this task such as: duration, task description text, URL of the website, task completion text, etc.
- Task 3: This task was "Web Navigation" type task and search target category. The EXm module asked for similar information as in Task 2 and, in addition, the specific target has to be defined. In this case the target is a specific URL in Discapnet.

Step 3:   Defining the procedure of the experimental sessions. In this experiment all participants had to do the same tasks and the order was the same in all cases. This information was inserted in the RemoTest platform

Step 4:   Specifying interaction data to be gathered. The EXm module presents all the interaction data PAm module is prepared to be gathered so the experimenter could select the most interesting in each case

Step 5:   Selecting the sample of participants. The RemoTest platform provides functions to select the participants of an experiment

The experiment definition process leads to obtain an XML file containing the experiment definition based on the Experiment Specification Language.

4.2 Creating the Experimental Sessions

The COm module automatically created the necessary stimuli for the experiment based on its definition. In this particular case study, the stimuli to create were the following: the demographic data questionnaire, the free navigation task description web page, the free navigation task completion web page, the target searching task description web page and the target searching task completion web page.

In addition, the information included in the experiment definition XML file is applied to create the personalized experimental sessions. In this specific case study, all the experimental sessions will be similar.

4.3 Conducting the Experiment

The PAm module installed on the client-side guided participants throughout the experimental session based on the XML file in Experimental Session Controlling Language. It managed the duration of tasks, the sequence, the presentation of stimuli, the gathering of data provided by each participant in questionnaires and the interaction data. All the information gathered by this module (that explicitly provided by the participant by answering questionnaires, and the interaction data implicitly obtained by the platform) were sent to the COm module in an asynchronous manner without interrupting the participant session. The experimental session completion web page was shown when all tasks were completed.

4.4 Interaction Data Analysis

The analysis presented in this section is focused on the cursor movement characterization features included in the RVm module and described in Sect. 3.4. These features were applied to the interaction data gathered in Task 3 (Searching a target task) allowing the researchers to identify navigation patterns and profiles between the participants. In this case, a total number of 323 web pages were visited by participants in this task. Note that U11 had to be excluded from the analysis due to fact that she decided to leave the experimental session before finishing the tasks. Applying the pre-processing algorithm defined in Sect. 3.4.1, the data of 133 web pages were selected to perform the cursor movement characterization analysis (23 web pages were excluded because of their lack of cursor movements as they were the result of repeatedly pushing the browser back button, 167 web pages were removed due to some detected problems in the PAm module when gathering interaction data when the cursor was out of the web browser window, a new web page was loaded, cursor position errors with *iframe* components in the page). Table 3 shows the total number of the visited pages by each participant and the total number of pages to be considered for the cursor movement characterization.

The information in Table 3 allows researchers to select the participants for further analysis. For instance, some of the participants (U04, U05, U06, U07 and U13) have fewer than 5 pages for analysing. Some parameters (curvature index, pointing time, clicking time) may not be accurate enough due to this lack of data. At this point, it is possible to select the participants to be excluded for the cursor movement characterization process. In this case, we excluded those with fewer than 5 pages to be analysed.

Some parameters were calculated based on the interaction data obtained in Task 3 for the rest of participants. Median values of cursor speed were automatically calculated for each participant. Figure 6 shows the resulting values. There is a considerable difference in speed parameter between participants. Able-bodied participants using standard mouse and keyboard (U12,U14,U15,U16), obtained the highest values.

The curvature index parameter allows problematic cursor movement patterns to be detected. It measures the relation between the optimal path and the followed path. The calculated values are shown in Fig. 7. U02 has the highest value meaning that there is a lack of precision in cursor movements. Actually, he was a trackball user with low

Table 3. Information about the total number of visited pages (VP) in Task 3 and the analysed pages (AP) for cursor movement characterization.

User	Visited pages	Analysed pages
U01	8	5
U02	32	10
U03	33	12
U04	14	1
U05	5	3
U06	5	2
U07	6	2
U08	31	15
User	**Visited pages**	**Analysed pages**
U09	15	7
U10	13	6
U12	26	10
U13	9	4
U14	40	24
U15	50	15
U16	36	17

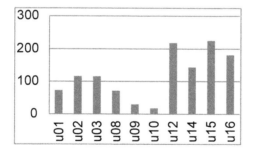

Fig. 6. Comparing chart about the speed parameter automatically obtained for each participant.

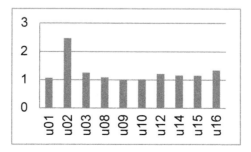

Fig. 7. Comparing chart about the curvature index automatically obtained for each participant

upper-body movement precision. Users using numeric keypad (U08,U09,U10) are the ones with the best values (1.09, 1.01 and 1.02 respectively). Actually, the use of keypad for moving the cursor produces linear and more precise movements.

Other significant measures for characterizing cursor movements are the time required for pointing a target and the time required for clicking on a target. Both measures are considered for detecting problematic situations in cursor movements. For instance, a high value of time for clicking on a target may indicate that the user has problems trying to perform the click action due to the size of the target and lack of precision or some distracting content around the target. The algorithm presented in Sect. 3.4.1 is applied for calculating both measures for each participant. Figure 8 shows the means of these measures for each participant automatically obtained by the RemoTest platform. It can be observed that participant U02 has the highest mean value for clicking on targets (3059 ms) whereas U14 is the one with lowest mean value (536 ms). U02 is one of the participants with physical disabilities using a trackball and U14 is an able-bodied participant. Able-bodied participants (U12,U14,U15,U16) obtained the better values for both measures (mean value for clicking is 855.32 ms and mean value for pointing is 1931.41 ms) than participants with physical impairments (mean value for clicking is 1872.53 ms and mean value for pointing is 4351.27 ms).

Recordings of participants with physical disabilities were manually analyzed and the time required for pointing to a target measure was annotated for each visited web page. The mean of automatically obtained values was compared with the mean of those obtained manually. These values can be found in Table 4. It can be observed that the values obtained automatically were generally lower than those manually gathered from the video analysis. Kendall's Concordance Tests was performed to analyse the agreement between rankings provided by both measures. The value obtained by the

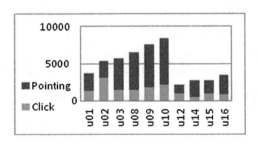

Fig. 8. Comparing chart about the time for pointing a target and time for clicking on a target for each participant in the experiment

Table 4. Mean values of the time required for pointing to a target automatically obtained by RemoTest platform (APM) and manually obtained based on video analysis (MPM).

	U01	U02	U03	U08	U09	U10
APM (ms)	2318	2314.6	4289.5	5107.6	5728.7	6349.2
MPM (ms)	6440	5080	3240	7190	8570	20480

concordance coefficient was 0.73 (p = 0.055) meaning that there is some correlation between both rankings.

5 Discussion

The results automatically obtained by the RemoTest platform proved to be useful for characterizing the cursor movements and detecting different profiles between partici-pants in a formal experiment. In fact, the observation of values obtained in curvature index, cursor speed and the time to clicking on a target assists researchers in detecting problematic situations in experimental sessions due to lack of precision, inappropriate target dimension, features of assistive technology used by participants, etc. It would be possible to detect some problematic situations, even if the experiment were carried out in remote settings. For instance, behaviour of participant U01 who uses a standard mouse differs in speed values for other participants using the same input device. It may be concluded that this participant requires some assistance by means of web interface adaptation mechanisms in order to improve his performance.

Observing the results in Fig. 9 it can be appreciated that participants U08, U09 and U10 obtained considerably higher values for their typical pauses between cursor sub-movements. These values may indicate some difficulties for starting the cursor movements as well as participants' fatigue during experimental sessions. In this case study, U10 is the one with the highest value (955.5 ms). This participant used a head pointer that may cause fatigue and sometimes disorientation as the cursor is out of sight when pressing the key during the cursor movements.

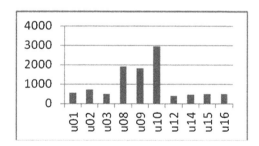

Fig. 9. Median values by user for motionless intervals along cursor trajectories

The algorithm for automatically calculating the required time for pointing to a target proved to be useful for ranking purposes. The values obtained are not accurate comparing with the values obtained manually. However, this could be due to lack of data used for automated analysis after the pre-processing. The current version of RemoTest platform will be more accurate in this sense as some of the errors when gathering coordinates of the cursor position have been fixed.

6 Conclusions

The RemoTest platform was conceived with a clear objective of assisting experimenters when dealing with the tedious task of carrying out remote/in situ experiments with web systems. The functionalities included in the platform support experimenters throughout the entire process: designing the experiment, conducting experimental sessions, gathering interaction data and analyzing results.

The experiment definition features consider the specification of different kind of studies. For instance, user behaviour studies on concrete web tasks, comparative studies on navigational strategies when using different types of assistive technology, accessibility-in-use evaluations, web surveys for collecting specific information, user satisfaction measuring, user performance improvement analysis when applying adaptation techniques and so on.

Moreover, the RemoTest platform includes features for assisting with the analysis of interaction data recorded during experiments. A straightforward visualization of each participant interaction data in an understandable mode helps experimenters discovering valuable issues occurred during experiments at a glance, and saving huge amount of time when analysing complementary video recordings if available. Additionally, the tool also performs heuristic estimations in order to obtain pointing trajectory-related measures that enable further understandings within participants' behaviours. Future work will be focused on testing new performance measures to enrich users' characterization, searching for additional parameters that lead to better aimed movements estimations, and studying the application of the RemoTest tool for analysing interaction data of other groups of impaired users.

Acknowledgements. The authors gratefully acknowledge the support of the Spanish Ministry of Science and Innovation through Project ModelAccess (TIN2010-15549). The EGOKITUZ Research Laboratory is supported by the Department of Education, Universities and Research of the Basque Government (Grant# IT-395-10) and the University of the Basque Country (Grant# UFI11/45).

References

1. Almanji, A., Davies, T.C., Stott, N.: Using cursor measures to investigate the effects of impairment severity on cursor control for youths with cerebral palsy. Int. J. Hum. Comput. Stud. **72**(3), 349–357 (2014)
2. Apaolaza, A., Harper, S., Jay, C.: Understanding users in the wild. In: 10th International Cross-Disciplinary Conference on Web Accessibility (W4A 2013), Article 13, p. 4. ACM, New York (2013)
3. Atterer, R., Wnuk, M., Schmidt, A.: Knowing the user's every move: user activity tracking for website usability evaluation and implicit interaction. In: 15th International Conference on World Wide Web, pp. 203–212. ACM, New York (2006)
4. Chapuis, O., Blanch, R., Beaudouin-Lafon, M.: Fitts' law in the wild: a field study of aimed movements. Technical report 1480, LRI, University Paris-Sud, France, p. 11 (2007)

5. Claypool, M., Le, P., Wased, M, Brown, D.: Implicit interest indicators. In: 6th International Conference on Intelligent User Interfaces (IUI 2001), pp. 33–40. ACM, New York (2001)
6. Cugini, J., Scholtz, J.: VISVIP: 3D visualization of paths through web sites. In: 10th International Workshop on Database and Expert Systems Applications, pp. 259–263, IEEE (1999)
7. Edmonds, A.: Uzilla : a new tool for web usability testing. Behav. Res. Meth. Instrum. Comput. **35**(2), 194–201 (2003)
8. Etgen, M., Cantor, J.: What does getting WET (Web Event-logging Tool) mean for web usability? In: 5th Conference on Human Factors and the Web (1999)
9. Gajos, K.Z., Weld, D.S., Wobbrock, J.O.: Automatically generating personalized user interfaces with Supple. Artif. Intell. **174**, 910–950 (2010)
10. Gajos, K., Reinecke, K., Herrmann, C.: Accurate measurements of pointing performance from in situ observations. In: Proceedings of the SIGCHI Conference on Human Factors in Computing Systems (CHI 2012), pp. 3157–3166. ACM, New York (2012)
11. Google Analytics 2014. http://www.google.es/analytics
12. Hong, J., Heer, J., Waterson, S., Landay, J.A.: WebQuilt: a proxy-based approach to remote web usability testing. ACM Trans. Inf. Syst. **19**(3), 263–285 (2001)
13. HttpFox 2014. https://addons.mozilla.org/es/firefox/addon/httpfox/
14. Hurst, A., Hudson, S.E., Mankoff, J., Trewin, S.: Distinguishing users by pointing performance in laboratory and real-world tasks. ACM Trans. Access. Comput. **5**(2), 27 (2013)
15. Loop11 2014. http://www.loop11.com
16. Meyer, D., Smith, J., Kornblum, S., Abrams, R., Wright, C.: Optimality in human motor performance: ideal control of rapid aimed movements. Psychol. Rev. **95**, 340–370 (1988)
17. Morae 2014. http://www.techsmith.com/morae.html
18. Paganelli, L., Paternò, F.: Intelligent analysis of user interactions with web applications. In: 7th International Conference on Intelligent User Interfaces (IUI 2002), pp. 111–118.3. ACM, New York (2002)
19. Paternò, F., Mancini, C., Meniconi, S.: ConcurTaskTrees: a diagrammatic notation for specifying task models. In: Howard, S., Hammond, J., Lindgaard, G. (eds.) IFIP TC13 Interantional Conference on Human-Computer Interaction, pp. 362–369. Chapman and Hall Ltd., London, UK (1997)
20. Pérez, J.E., Arrue, M., Valencia, X., Moreno, L.: Exploratory study of web navigation strategies for users with physical disabilities. In: Proceedings of the 11th Web for All Conference, Article 20, p. 4. ACM, New York (2014)
21. Power, C., Petrie, H., Mitchell, R.: A framework for remote user evaluation of accessibility and usability of websites. In: Stephanidis, C. (ed.) Universal Access in HCI, Part I, HCII 2009. LNCS, vol. 5614, pp. 594–601. Springer, Heidelberg (2009)
22. Scholtz, J., Laskowski, S., Downey, L.: Developing usability tools and techniques for designing and testing web sites. In: 4th Conference on Human Factors and the Web (1998)
23. Trewin, S.: Physical impairment. In: Harper, S., Yesilada, Y. (eds.) Web Accessibility - A Foundation for Research, pp. 37–46. Springer, London (2008)

Technology Acceptance Evaluation by Deaf Students Considering the Inclusive Education Context

Soraia Silva Prietch$^{(\boxtimes)}$ and Lucia Vilela Leite Filgueiras

Escola Politénica, Universidade de São Paulo, Av. Prof. Luciano Gualberto,
Trav. 3, N. 158, São Paulo, Sao Paulo 05508-970, Brazil
soraia.roo@gmail.com, lfilguei@usp.br

Abstract. As a consequence of the National Policy on Special Education on the Perspective of Inclusive Education in Brazil, established in 2007, mainstream schools have begun receiving a greater number of Deaf or Hard of Hearing (D/HH) students that previously attended specialized schools. However, data point to the declining number of D/HH students enrolled from primary school to secondary school; i.e., there are reasons to believe that educational barriers are imposed on the means these students have of conquering a complete education. In this context, the goal of this work is to propose a technology acceptance model that takes into account constructs that involve aspects of the inclusive education context, as well as performing a pilot test on the interaction of 16 D/HH users with a mobile application, called SESSAI, to evaluate the model. SESSAI consists of a technology-mediated form of communication, which allows hearing persons and D/HH individuals to interact through an automatic recognition system. Among the constructs of the model, one of them refers to the potential educational barriers experienced by D/HH students in inclusive classrooms. With regard to research methodology, the study was developed in cycles of literature review and conduction of tests. The proposed model has shown positive results in capturing factors that influence technology acceptance given the domain specific context, since they incorporate aspects of pragmatic quality and hedonic quality (emotional user experience), and also considers issues related to perceived usefulness in minimizing potential educational barriers, future expectations, and facilitating conditions. We conclude that the model encompasses both users' personal motivation and context of use aspects, and it can be used for the purpose for which it was proposed. Further investigations need to be conducted in order to adjust the model questionnaire and to recruit a broader number of participants.

Keywords: Assistive technology · Technology-mediated communication · Country specific developments · Human-computer interaction · Media in education

1 Introduction

According to 2010 Brazilian census [13], the country's population reached 190.755.799 inhabitants; among which, approximately, 46 million declared themselves to have some kind of disability. Within this number, among people who are Deaf or

© IFIP International Federation for Information Processing 2015
J. Abascal et al. (Eds.): INTERACT 2015, Part I, LNCS 9296, pp. 20–37, 2015.
DOI: 10.1007/978-3-319-22701-6_2

Hard of Hearing (D/HH), over 300 thousand people informed census takers that do not hear any sound; almost two million people stated that they hear with great difficulty; and, over seven million people declared that they have some difficulty in hearing. Also, it was observed that people who are D/HH with an age between 0 and 50 account for 1.191.682 inhabitants, indicating an expressive number of potential students, from day care center assistance to adult education.

During the past decade, a growth in the number of students with disabilities enrolled in inclusive schools and a decrease in the number enrolled in special schools has been observed through the Brazilian education census [13]. Another observed statistic was the decrease in the number of students who are D/HH concluding primary and reaching secondary schools. In order to not segregate the expressive number of people with disabilities in Brazilian special schools, in 2007, the National Policy for Special Education under the perspective of Inclusive Education was enacted, intending to provide accessibility in inclusive environments in attendance of the different stages and types of education. Thus, every student attends regular classes together in inclusive schools, in which some schools offer specialized educational services in a special education resource room during hours opposite those of regular classes.

In both cases (regular classrooms and special education resource rooms), we believe that technology can help minimize educational barriers that prevent students who are D/HH from completing regular educational stages. However, technology-based products by themselves can not improve complex scenarios such as inclusive schools. For that matter, it is important to study the aspects that influence the acceptance or rejection of technology, considering the specific characteristics of the application.

By specific characteristics we mean the target users, context of use, type of technology and tasks to be accomplished by users. In this sense, it is not enough to simply decide to develop a new technology and, later, verify if users are adopting it, but evaluate its acceptance during the prototyping stage. So, there is a difference between the adoption and acceptance of a technology. Davis [8] informs that technology adoption is a goal for designers/developers/owners, and technology acceptance is related to design and selection processes that constitute stages previous to that of adoption; therefore, acceptance evaluation may prevent expenses with coding and launch in the case of rejection of the early concept.

People who are D/HH may use one or more modes of communication, switching between written language, oral language and lip reading and sign language, among other possibilities. This characteristic of target users shows how diverse this group can be. Language preference or use depends on many factors, well described by [6], including educational background, family support, amongst others.

Given the problematic presented, the goal is to propose a technology acceptance model that takes into account representative constructs of an inclusive education context, and to conduct a pilot test with D/HH students using a technology-based product to evaluate the proposed model. Throughout this work, we were concerned with answering two questions: What constructs are important during acceptance evaluations considering technology use by D/HH students in inclusive classrooms? Is the proposed model able to cover constructs that can identify the acceptance of technology in inclusive educational environments by D/HH students?

To answer these research questions, this paper is organized as follows: in Sect. 2, related literature reviews are presented; Sect. 3 reports the pilot test and findings of research; in Sect. 4, results and research questions are discussed; and, Sect. 5 presents conclusions.

2 Literature Review

The proposition of technology solutions, which may minimize potential barriers in inclusive educational environments for D/HH students, permeates questions regarding acceptance. According to [8], technology acceptance models are a means to explain reasons why people decide to use or not use a particular technology.

The literature review was conducted in two forms: exploratory and systematic reviews. Exploratory reviews were carried out to find which consolidated acceptance models have been used by researchers, what aspects of user experience are present in acceptance models, and to become familiar with existing AT models. Also, one systematic review was conducted; in this case, we intended to find related works that report research conducted regarding technology acceptance evaluations of technology-based interaction with people who are deaf.

2.1 Exploratory Literature Reviews

We carried out three stages of exploratory review, which included: (i) the study of consolidated technology acceptance models; (ii) evidence of user experience aspects in technology acceptance models; and (iii) the analysis of AT evaluation models.

As a starting point, three consolidated models caught our attention for their popularity in academic research. The first two are acceptance models and the third is an adoption model: Technology Acceptance Model (TAM) [8]; Unified Theory of Acceptance and Use of Technology (UTAUT) [32]; and Innovation-Decision Process (IDP) [28]. Davis [8] proposed TAM with the goal of explaining technology acceptance behavior by new users in an organizational context. With this purpose in mind, [8] investigated which, and how, variables and constructs influence the behavior of using technology, and in what manner could user motivation be measured. As a result, [8] postulated that user motivation involves three main constructs: *Perceived usefulness* (PEU) and *Perceived ease of use* (EOU) representing cognitive responses, and *Attitude toward Technology* (ATT) representing affective responses. Design features of technology are considered as external variables that influence PEU and EOU. Also, in TAM [8]: EOU influences PEU; PEU and EOU influence ATT; PEU and ATT influence directly *Behavioral intention* to use (BI); and, BI influences *Actual system use*. *Behavioral intention* is not a construct in the model, but a desired outcome.

It is worth mentioning that, in TAM, PEU has a stronger influence than EOU on BI, because this construct directly influences ATT and BI, reinforcing its importance. In this regard, [8] informs that users are willing to accept a technology that is difficult to use if it provides task accomplishment, rather than accept an easy-to-use system that does not allow users to reach their goals.

The second model, UTAUT [32], is the result of the unification of eight technology acceptance models, including TAM; and, it is interested in explaining user behavior towards technology acceptance and use in organizational contexts. This model is composed of four constructs and four moderating variables. *Performance expectancy* (PE), *Effort expectancy* (EE) and *Social influence* (SI) are constructs that influence *Behavioral intention* (BI), while *Facilitating conditions* (FC) is a construct that directly influences on *Use behavior*. [32] equate PE to *Perceived usefulness* (TAM) and EE to *Perceived ease of use* (TAM), since they have similar definitions. As moderating variables, the authors verified that there are four factors that influence relations between constructs, differently from each other: Gender influences the relation of PE, EE, SI with BI; Age influences the relation of PE, EE, SI with BI, and FC with *Use behavior*; Experience influences the relation of EE, SI with BI, and FC with *Use behavior*; and Voluntariness of use influences only the relation of SI with BI.

The third model, concerned with technology adoption and known as IDP [28], was defined as a model of five stages which an individual or a group must go through in order to decide whether to adopt or reject a technology. These five stages are: (i) Knowledge; (ii) Persuasion; (iii) Decision; (iv) Implementation; and, (v) Confirmation. To measure confirmation of adoption, [28] informs that five variables can determine the rate of adoption of innovations: the perceived attributes of innovations; type of innovation-decision; communication channels; nature of the social system; and, extent of change agents' promotion efforts. The resulting rates indicate adoption classification as innovators, early adopters, early majority, late majority, and laggards.

Over the years, evolutionary technology acceptance models have been proposed, for example: TAM2 [8, 31] and UTAUT2 [33]. These new models are variants of original models, which include new constructs and moderating variables. It is worth noting that in UTAUT2, the authors added *Hedonic motivation* as a construct that directly influences *Behavioral intention*, which "is defined as the fun or pleasure derived from using a technology" [33] (p. 161).

With respect to evidence of user experience aspects in technology acceptance models, [15] demonstrates concern not only with the quality of the technology itself but also with the quality of using the technology as perceived by its users; where quality in use comprises aspects beyond usefulness and usability. The quality in use may be measured by user experience evaluations, in which everything that involves the human-computer interaction must be considered. [12] report that "UX is a consequence of a user's internal state (predispositions, expectations, needs, motivation, mood, etc.), the characteristics of the designed system (e.g. complexity, purpose, usability, functionality, etc.) and the context (or the environment) within which the interaction occurs (e.g. organizational/social setting, meaningfulness of the activity, voluntariness of use, etc.)" (p. 95).

In this sense, [10] presents two dimensions of how users perceive interactive technologies: pragmatic and hedonic quality. According to the author, pragmatic quality is related to manipulation, involving "relevant functionality (i.e., utility) and ways to access this functionality (i.e., usability)" [10] (p. 34), and "supports the achievement of 'do-goals'" [11] (p. 12). On the other hand, hedonic quality refers to stimulation, identification and evocation, involving personal preferences, past experiences and well-being; supporting the achievement of 'be-goals' [11] (p. 12). [10] states that "typical hedonic attributes of software products are 'outstanding', 'impressive', 'exciting' and 'interesting'" (p. 35), so in this paper we use the term 'hedonic quality attributes' as synonyms for emotional outcomes (forms of describing felt emotions during human-computer interactions) in evaluations.

Referring to emotional outcomes, [22] describes that in emotional design three dimensions have to be taken into account: visceral, behavioral and reflective. The visceral dimension is concerned with appearance, aesthetics; the behavioral dimension is related to pleasure and effectiveness of use; and the reflective dimension considers the rationalization and intellectualization of a product. From this, in evaluations, we can assume the visceral and reflective dimensions [22] are responsible for triggering emotions associated to hedonic quality [10]; and, that the behavioral dimension is associated to pragmatic quality. In this context, [24] mention that "UX is surely about how the user feels and how the interaction with the product makes them feel, not only their evaluation of the product or service" (p. 3848) and, fundamentally, this is the reason why we consider important the presence of hedonic qualities in technology acceptance models.

2.2   Systematic Literature Review

Here, we intended to find related works on technology acceptance evaluations involving people who are deaf (target users), in order to know what types of technology were considered and to verify what types of constructs were used.

The systematic review protocol was defined so that works should be found in the English language only and be published from 2003 to 2013, using three repositories ACM DL, IEEEXplore DL and SpringerLink. Eighteen keywords were used in the search: ("Technology Acceptance Model" *XOR* UTAUT) *AND* (deaf *XOR* "hearing impaired"); ("Technology Acceptance Model" *XOR* UTAUT) *AND* ("Assistive technology" *XOR* Chat) *AND* (deaf *XOR* "hearing impaired"); ("Technology Acceptance Model" *XOR* UTAUT) AND ("Automatic speech recognition" *XOR* "Speech-to-text") *AND* (deaf); as well as (Acceptance) *AND* (ASR *XOR* "Speech-to-text") *AND* (deaf). The exclusion criteria for paper selection were: repeated items, table of contents, item with several abstracts, not available for download, medical emphasis, and keywords within papers that were found only in references or were merely mentioned in the text. From this search, 175 items were found and, after applying exclusion criteria, it resulted in 07 included papers. Therefore, from this review, seven papers were selected [3, 5, 16, 18, 23, 26, 27].

On the subject of types of technology considered by researchers, [3] proposed a mobile application that translates a given English written phrase to Signwriting and vice versa, as an alternative to exchanging SMS between people who are D/HH and hearing individuals; [5] conceived a speech rehabilitation system for D/HH children between 1 and 4 years old that use cochlear implants; [16] proposed a prototype of Sign Language Interpreter Module (SLI Module) to improve Web accessibility for deaf users, providing alternative information formats, which was evaluated by thirty one D/HH students with ages between 15 and 21; [18] evaluated mixed reality, using animated avatars, within an assistive learning system with hearing and deaf students;

[23] proposed a Semantic and Syntactic Transcription Analysing Tool (SSTAT) to improve the quality of transcriptions delivered by automatic speech recognition systems, and evaluated it with deaf and hearing students; [26] investigated acceptance of the Dictation function of Nuance's Sample Voice Recognition App among eleven D/HH students with age average of 28; and, [27] chose Digital TV as the technology which was subsequently evaluated by people who are deaf and hearing individuals.

With respect to the constructs used by these researchers, [5] conducted acceptance evaluation with TAM but did not use other constructs; [26] used TAM in their investigation, including other factors that were relevant for technology use in educational environments, such as: hedonic quality attributes (emotional user experience), usability, future expectations of educational improvement, social influence, empowerment of technology, educational barriers; [27] proposed ADOPT-DTV model, adapted from UTAUT, and included three constructs - self-sufficiency, anxiety, attitudes - regarding the use of technologies and intention of adoption (will adopt, undecided, won't adopt).

References [3, 16, 18, 23] proposed a new technology and conducted technology acceptance evaluations; however, these authors did not use or propose structured models [3]. Evaluated preference between SMS and translation, acceptance, system functionalities, ease of use, and consistency between desktop and mobile systems; [16] evaluated usability (including satisfaction, ease of use and comprehension), sign language interpreter (including lip reading and hands-movements), subtitles (including size and readability), and video playback controls (including size of buttons and usefulness); [18] evaluated percentage of acceptance, effectiveness, absent-mindedness, and quality of animated avatars; and, [23] evaluated the following aspects: (i) perception of transcription quality (accuracy); (ii) perceived acceptance of transcripts (between having transcription or not); (iii) usefulness (referring to the quality of transcripts); and, (iv) perceived usability (also referring to the quality of transcripts).

3   Model Proposition: TAM4 IE

The proposed model, which is the aim of this paper in particular, was named as TAM4 IE (Technology Acceptance Model for Inclusive Education), which came as a result of theoretical and empirical research conducted in previous studies [25, 26].

It was noticed that the specific application in hands was not fully covered by consolidated technology acceptance models. When we say specific application, we mean the coverage of context of use, characteristics of target users (people who are deaf), type of technology, tasks to be accomplished and facilitating conditions for users. Many authors, inspired by consolidated models, proposed different research models in order to reach their goals, such as, [9, 27, 34], because they felt that the existing models did not meet their needs. Constructs and hypotheses of the proposed model are illustrated in Fig. 1.

Important aspects were mapped into constructs in this new technology acceptance model for use in inclusive education, which were five: *Subjective perception*; *Perceived usability*; *Perceived usefulness*; *Future expectations*; and *Facilitating conditions*. This new model was called Technology Acceptance Model for Inclusive Education

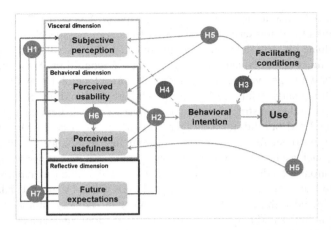

Fig. 1. Constructs and hypotheses of the proposed model (Own source)

(TAM4 IE). Being TAM4 IE a new model, it was necessary to formulate research hypotheses about the relationship between the proposed constructs. Thus, seven hypotheses were elaborated, which are listed below:

- H1: *Subjective perception* has a significant influence on *Perceived usability* and on *Perceived usefulness*;
- H2: *Perceived usability*, *Perceived usefulness* and *Future expectations* have a significant influence on *Behavioral intention*;
- H3: *Facilitating conditions* do NOT have a significant influence on *Behavioral intention*;
- H4: *Subjective perception* do NOT have a significant influence on *Behavioral intention*;
- H5: *Facilitating conditions* have a significant influence on *Perceived usefulness*, *Perceived usability* and *Subjective perception*;
- H6: *Perceived usability* has a significant influence on *Perceived usefulness*;
- H7: *Future expectations* have a significant influence on *Perceived usefulness*, *Perceived usability* and *Subjective perception*.

Subjective Perception (SP) construct was shaped by literature on user experience aspects in technology acceptance models [10, 11, 12, 22], on works that proposed technology acceptance models while taking hedonic quality into account [1, 9, 33, 34], and on those papers that were essential to create Emotion-LIBRAS.[1] Emotion-LIBRAS is an emotional user experience evaluation instrument for use by deaf participants, which was proposed and tested in previous work [25] and is shown in Fig. 2.

Subjective perception is about emotions felt by users during interaction with technology. Such emotions are associated to the visceral dimension [22], being used as

---

[1] The word LIBRAS stands for Brazilian Sign Language as an acronyms for its Portuguese meaning, and it is the official language of deaf individuals in Brazil.

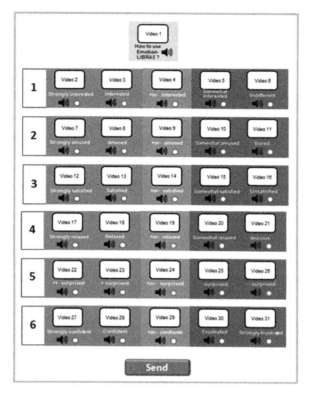

Fig. 2. Emotion-LIBRAS 2.4 (Own source) (The instrument is composed of three parts: (i) An initial video explaining how to use Emotion-LIBRAS, (ii) Six rows of responses (interested/indifferent, amused/bored, satisfied/unsatisfied, relaxed/anxious, positively surprised/not surprised, and confident/frustrated), with 05 mutually exclusive alternatives each. The alternatives are organized as a differential semantic 5-point scale, going from strong and positive intensity of emotion, in green; passing through neutral emotion, in grey; to strong and negative intensity of emotion, in red. All alternative responses have three different ways of displaying the same information: in sign language video, in written language and in audio; and (iii) a send button).

triggers to understand two other constructs: *Perceived usability* and *Perceived usefulness*. In this way, the *Subjective perception* construct is defined as *"the result of measuring hedonic quality attributes triggered during human-computer interaction"*. The instrument of measurement of hedonic quality attributes of TAM4 IE is Emotion-LIBRAS, since target users are represented by D/HH students.

According to [10, 11], both pragmatic and hedonic qualities must be evaluated in order to fully include user experience aspects. Thus, in TAM4 IE we included all of those aspects, represented by usefulness, usability and hedonic attributes. During a previous test with TAM [26], it was verified that *Perceived usefulness* and *Perceived ease of use* were not capable of representing the totality of this complexity. To complement that, Emotion-LIBRAS was also used to understand if hedonic quality attributes could influence these two constructs of TAM and, as result, in the new model (Fig. 1), *Subjective perception* is placed as a construct that may influence *Perceived usefulness* and *Perceived usability*.

In TAM4 IE, the construct called *Perceived ease of use* in TAM is encompassed by *Perceived usability*, considered a broader construct, which is kept close to the *Perceived usefulness* construct to represent pragmatic quality attributes in the model. Together, *Perceived usability* and *Perceived usefulness* compose the behavioral dimension [22]. Also, we believe that these two constructs influence the Behavioral intention to use technology. However, in TAM4 IE, differently from TAM, both constructs have the same weight in the scale.

[8, 10, 11, 21, 22] were the references that inspired the inclusion of **Perceived usability** (PUB) as a construct in the new model. Thereby, this construct was defined as *"the result of the perception of usability inherent in the technology"*, which intends to ensure that interaction with technology is not hindered due to diversion of attention of the user's goal caused by difficulties in interaction. This means that usability problems may negatively mask the potential perceived usefulness of technology.

To measure *Perceived usability*, the following attributes were considered while elaborating the questionnaire used in the test: learnability [15, 21], memorability [21], accessibility [15], and aesthetics [15]. Satisfaction also was an investigated attribute but was allocated to the *Subjective perception* construct. As a consequence, in the TAM4 IE structure, *Perceived usability* was positioned in a border zone (Fig. 1), aggregating characteristics from visceral and behavioral dimensions [22].

Perceived Usefulness (PUF) was conceived based on previous works [25], and it was defined as *"the degree to which an individual believes that the use of a technology can minimize educational barriers faced by him/her"*. To measure *Perceived usefulness*, attributes related to educational barriers faced by D/HH students are investigated. The educational barriers included in the questionnaire of the pilot test were the following: (1) Difficulty to follow simultaneous activities during classes; (2) Embarrassment to ask questions in sign language; (3) Difficulty to take notes during classes; (4) Lack of possibility to revise class content; and, (5) Lack of sufficient number of interpreters or unprepared interpreter.

The **Future Expectations** (FE) construct was included in TAM4 IE considering three constructs of UTAUT [32]: Effort expectancy, Performance expectancy and Social influence; the value empowerment of technology, and, conceptual aspects of the Decision stage in IDP [28]. This construct has a direct relation to Behavioral intention, in the sense that the intention to use technology is molded by users' expectations. In this sense, if expectations are high, intention of use is highly favorable; otherwise, if expectations are low, intention of use is unfavorable, with expectations being directly proportional to intention of use.

Also, [28] mentions that during decision-making about technology adoption, users reflect upon the consequences that a technology might bring to their lives and weigh the advantages and disadvantages of these situations. Therefore, the *Future expectations* construct allows users to ponder their values and imagine future experiences of technology use.

Because of this perspective, the *Future expectations* construct was placed in the reflective dimension [22] in the TAM4 IE structure (Fig. 1), and it was defined as *"the result of user's reflection with respect to potential future benefits reached by the use of technology"*. Future benefits need to be defined by researchers taking into account their application, since objectives, context of use and the nature of technology may be different from case to case. In TAM4 IE, we are interested in minimizing educational barriers faced by D/HH students in inclusive educational environments; therefore, future benefits are those with the potential to improve some aspects that hinder these students from completing educational stages.

The concept of the *Future expectations* construct is aligned with the *benefits* mentioned by [2], which was defined as "perceived advantages of using computers in the class" (p. 94) [20]. Included *expected consequences of use* in their research model, defined as "the better the task-technology fit the more positive the anticipated consequences of use of a system" (p. 499). Also, [7] proposed *learning expectancy* as a construct in his research model, which was defined as "the expectations for learning performance" (p. 1502).

The **Facilitating Conditions** (FC) construct originally was included from the UTAUT model [32], which was defined as *"the degree to which an individual believes that an organizational and technical infrastructure exists to support use of the system"* (p. 453). Also, in UTAUT, this construct directly influences Use behavior. This relation was kept in TAM4 IE.

The definition of *Facilitating conditions* used in UTAUT is organization-oriented, and we are interested in inclusive education; however, a global concept of this construct is desired in TAM4 IE because it includes aspects of assistive technology evaluation models. These aspects are concerned with external factors (neither user nor technology) that may facilitate or hinder technology use in specific contexts, such as: national policies; school infrastructure (e.g., Internet connection); school management (e.g., internal policies of technology use); device cost; technical support (technology and special education professionals); privacy policies; and, training for teachers; among others.

It is worth noting that, besides the inclusion of new constructs, none of constructs from previous models were left out of the new model, they were just adapted with other names or its definition were aggregated to compose a new construct.

After defining constructs, the questionnaire of the pilot test was elaborated in a 5-point Likert scale format (1-Strongly agree; 2-Agree; 3-Neither agree nor disagree; 4-Disagree; 5-Strongly disagree) with one group of questioning for five constructs and for Behavioral intention. For questioning participants regarding *Subjective perception* the Emotion-LIBRAS instrument (Fig. 2) was used. In Table 1, these constructs, their related questions and their references are presented (some questions are equal to those presented in the original reference and others were adapted from references). Also, the type of technology to be evaluated, using the model, was taken into account to elaborate the questions. For this matter, SESSAI, a mobile application for the Android platform was developed, which consists of an instant messaging system for groups with an automatic speech recognition system.

4 Pilot Test with TAM4IE

After the elaboration of the TAM4IE proposal, a pilot test was carried out in a semi-controlled environment of a special school for deaf students. This school offers both fulltime education regular primary education and an integral youth and adult education program in primary education, with 130 D/HH students, in total, amongst the student population. Conducting the test in the school was considered positive due to the fact that students, and their parents, felt comfortable knowing the place and the school staff; on the other hand, a negative point was the lack of control over infrastructure such as Internet connection, cameras and research staff positioning. In order to carry out the test, a mobile application for the Android platform was developed. This application was called SESSAI (acronym in Brazilian Portuguese for Support to Deaf Students in Inclusive Classrooms).

Table 1. Constructs, questions and references

Constructs	Questions	References
PUB1	It is easy to learn how to use	[19, 26]
PUB2	It is easy to remember how to use again later	
PUB3	It promotes accessibility for D/HH students	
PUB4	Aesthetics of user interface is beautiful and attractive	
PUF1	In an inclusive school, while teacher speaks, it is useful to have SESSAI for note taking	[21, 29, 33]
PUF2	SESSAI is useful for review content after class	
PUF3	In an inclusive school, if there is no interpreter or the interpreter is not prepared, SESSAI is useful to follow classes	
PUF4	In an inclusive school, if many individuals (teacher and classmates) are speaking simultaneously, SESSAI is useful by delivering transcription that can be read	
PUF5	In an inclusive school, if someone is embarrassed to make a comment or a question in LIBRAS during classes, SESSAI is useful for sending and receiving comments or questions in written language	
FE1	In the future, SESSAI can help to raise my chances to improve my grades in school evaluations	[2, 6, 21, 25]
FE2	In the future, if only I use SESSAI in class, I will feel important	
FE3	In the future, if only I use SESSAI in class, I will feel impotant	[27]
FE4	In the future, I want SESSAI installed in my cell phone	[33]
FC1	I have the knowledge necessary to use SESSAI	[4]
FC2	I find important to have someone available to help me when I have difficulties in using SESSAI	[32]
BI1	I have intention to use SESSAI in the classroom	[31]
BI2	I would rather have this transcript than not have any transcripts at all	[28]
BI3	I would use even if I would have to pay	[24]

The sample used in the investigation was defined by convenience, because there were a small amount of D/HH participants interested in contributing to the research. The research script consisted of the sequence: profile questionnaire application, followed by interaction of participant with SESSAI and, lastly, acceptance evaluation questionnaire application. In total, 16 D/HH students participated in seven interviews (individual, in pairs or in trio), and each interview took in average 53 min.

During interactions with SESSAI, simple questions were asked the participants, such as: what is your favorite color?; what soccer team do you support?; when is your birthday?; what is your name?. We chose simple questions because in a previous test with TAM [26] we had selected phrases that contained some metaphors, which led to difficulties in participants understanding the question.

With respect to participants' profiles, among the 16 D/HH students, there were 04 women and 12 men; the minimum age was 13 and the maximum 42, with an average age of 21.37 years. Concerning participants' educational level, since the special school offers regular primary education and a program for primary education for youth and adult education, all participants were enrolled at the primary stage of education; however, in Brazil, primary school is divided into two categories: level 1, between 1st and 5th cycles; and level 2, between 6th and 9th years. Among the 16 students, 12 were in level 2, and 04 in level 1, with 03 of level 1 primary education students participating in the youth and adult education program.

With regard to preferences in modes of communication, among those who answered: 14 participants chose sign language as their favorite mode of communication; as their second favorite, 07 chose written language, and 07 oral language/lip reading; 10 participants did not chose Signwriting as a possible mode of communication used by them; and, 01 student marked written language as first mode of communication. Responses for self-reporting on participants' level of written language proficiency showed that 11 classified themselves as regular, 03 as high, and 02 as low. With respect to ownership and experience with technology, 09 participants informed that they did not have their own cell phone; 06 students of the 07 that did report having a cell phone also reported accessing the Internet using their device, and frequently using Whatsapp.

To perform the pilot test, we formed a team with one researcher, two research assistants and one interpreter (sign/oral language), and we were equipped with two smartphones (Samsung GalaxyNote GT-N7000 and Galaxy Ace GT-S5830B), one notebook, one filming camera, printed materials (terms of consent and questionnaires) and pens. The two smartphones were used in order to simulate interaction with multiple persons, using the SESSAI app, where one smartphone was used by the researcher who asked simple questions by speaking, while the other smartphone was used by participants to read transcriptions produced by the app and answer them by typing.

Those simple questions were previously trained using SESSAI, in order to ensure 100 % correctness of automatic recognition, due to the fact that we wanted to produce an interaction free of risk of influence on acceptance results, as a way of simulating a situation that would leave D/HH students comfortable to interact with technology without having the fear of misunderstanding what was asked.

The technology acceptance evaluation questionnaire included 18 questions plus the 06 questions on Emotion-LIBRAS instrument, as can be seen in Table 1 and Fig. 2.

To investigate the hypotheses of this study, the Spearman correlation coefficient was calculated between the variables of interest, since all quantitative variables are ordinal. In this case, a significance level (p-value) for the obtained coefficient was observed. Thus, to reject the null hypothesis means that the correlation is statistically significant. All tests of hypotheses developed assumed a significance level of 5 %, i.e., the null hypothesis was rejected when p-value was less than or equal to 0.05.

It is important to mention that during the interviews two students did not answer 08 questions and one student did not answer 07 questions; these students, all over 30 years old, participated together as a group during interviews and had difficulties in communication, since they had been learning sign language for a short time and were studying in level 1 of primary school. As a result, for some tests of the hypotheses, we consider only 13 answers (Number of participants = N).

- H1: *Subjective perception* has a significant influence on *Perceived usefulness* and on *Perceived usability* (N = 16). Tests results between *Subjective perception* (answers from Emotion-LIBRAS) and *Perceived usefulness* show that: (i) the higher participants rate SESSAI as useful in a situation of embarrassment to make a comment or a question in LIBRAS during classes, the higher the interest (p-value = 0.0048) and more relaxed (p-value = 0.0399) in using SESSAI in class and the lower the feeling of frustration (p-value = 0.0305); and, (ii) the higher participants state SESSAI is useful in a situation of many individuals (teacher and classmates) speaking simultaneously, the less participants are amused (p-value = 0.0411). With respect to the relationship between *Subjective perception* and *Perceived usability*: (i) the better participants declare the interface aesthetics, the stronger participants state their satisfaction (p-value = 0.0411) with SESSAI; and, (ii) the easier participants find it to remember how to use the app again later, the less frustrated they feel (p-value = 0.0011).
- H2: *Perceived usability*, *Perceived usefulness* and *Future expectations* have a significant influence on *Behavioral intention* (N = 13). Between *Perceived usability* and *Behavioral intention* one statistically significant positive correlation was found: the higher participants rated finding SESSAI easy to remember how to use, the higher they state they would rather have this transcript than not have any transcripts at all (p-value = 0.0135). Regarding *Perceived usefulness* and *Behavioral intention* there were more statistically significant positive correlations than negative ones: (i) the higher participants state it is useful to use SESSAI to take notes (transcript) while the teacher speaks during class, the higher they state they would rather have this transcript than not have any transcripts at all (p-value = 0.0002); (ii) the higher participants find SESSAI useful for review content after class, the higher they state the intention to use SESSAI in the classroom (p-value = 0.0004) and that they would even pay to use the app (p-value = 0.0413); and, (iii) the higher participants find SESSAI useful in situation of embarrassment to make comments or pose questions in LIBRAS during classes, the less they state their intention to use SESSAI in the classroom (p-value = 0.0055). With respect to the relationship between *Future expectations* and *Behavioral intention*, no statistically significant correlations were observed.

- H3: *Facilitating conditions* do NOT have a significant influence on *Behavioral intention* (N = 13). Regarding to the relationship between *Facilitating conditions* and *Behavioral intention*, no statistically significant correlations were observed.
- H4: *Subjective perception* do NOT have a significant influence on *Behavioral intention* (N = 13). One statistically significant positive correlation was found between intention of using SESSAI in the classroom and the emotion of being positively surprised (p-value = 0.0365); which consists of a denial of this hypothesis.
- H5: *Facilitating conditions* have a significant influence on *Perceived usefulness*, *Perceived usability* and *Subjective perception* (N = 13). With respect to the relationship between *Perceived usefulness* and *Facilitating conditions*, no statistically significant correlations were observed. As a result from tests conducted between *Perceived usability* and *Facilitating conditions*, it was verified that the higher participants rate as important having someone available to help them when they have difficulties in using SESSAI, the easier they find to remember how to use SESSAI again. Regarding to the relationship between *Subjective perception* and *Facilitating conditions*, the higher participants find it important to have someone available to help them when they have difficulties in using SESSAI, the higher they rate feeling frustrated (p-value = 0.0199).
- H6: *Perceived usability* has a significant influence on *Perceived usefulness*. From this hypothesis test, we observed that the higher participants find SESSAI useful to follow classes when there is no interpreter present or the interpreter is present but not prepared, the higher they believe SESSAI can promote accessibility for D/HH students (p-value = 0.049, N = 16).
- H7: *Future expectations* have a significant influence on *Perceived usefulness*, *Perceived usability* and *Subjective perception*. Only statistically significant correlations were identified between *Future expectations* and *Perceived usefulness*, in which: (i) the higher participants find SESSAI useful to follow classes when there is no interpreter present or the interpreter present is not prepared, and they perceive it is useful when there are many individuals speaking simultaneously, with SESSAI in class, they would feel more important if they were the only one in class using SESSAI (respectively, p-value = 0.0085 and p-value = 0.0278, N = 16); and, (ii) the higher participants rate SESSAI as useful in situation of embarrassment to make a comment or ask a question in LIBRAS during classes, the higher they believe SESSAI can help raise the chances of improving their grades in school evaluations in the future (p-value = 0.0449, N = 13).

4.1   Discussion of the Findings

As a result from the tests of hypotheses, we had a full confirmation of H1, since the attributes of the hedonic quality (*Subjective perception*) influence the perception of usability and usefulness of technology for minimizing the educational barriers of deaf students in inclusive classrooms. Also, we had a partial confirmation of H2 because a significant correlation was found between *Perceived usability* and *Perceived usefulness* with *Behavioral intention*; although, *Future expectations* did not show influence on *Behavioral intention*.

With respect to H3, we observed a full confirmation, that *Facilitating conditions* do not have a significant correlation with *Behavioral intention*. This result confirms the statement is consistent with UTAUT [32], where *Facilitating conditions* influence directly actual usage (adoption of technology). The result from H4 was a denial, since we verified the *Subjective perception* influence on *Behavioral intention*. This evidence shows that subjective perception not only influences *Perceived usability* and *Perceived usefulness*, but *Behavioral intention* directly; as a consequence, this construct represents a significant weight in technology acceptance.

Testing H5, we found that *Subjective perception* and *Perceived usability* can be influenced by *Facilitating conditions*, because if the environment provides support for the use of technology it can be interesting and pleasant, and also might become easier and more intuitive to use. On the other hand, *Facilitating conditions* did not show influence on *Perceived usefulness* on minimizing educational barriers for deaf students in inclusive settings. With respect to H6 results, we identify that accessibility (*Perceived usability*) is an important issue for participants, since the mobile app evaluated was stated as useful when it is not possible to communicate using sign language through a professional interpreter in the classroom (*Perceived usefulness*).

Finally, the testing of hypothesis H7 showed that, although *Future expectations* have no influence on *Subjective perception* or on *Perceived usability*, this construct has influence on *Perceived usefulness*. These constructs make sense together since the usefulness of the mobile app, in this case, is motivated by an interest in minimizing educational barriers and finding answers to questions associated with future expectations that include desired situations for overcoming some of the negative outcomes of those barriers. The final structure of the model is presented in Fig. 3.

Regarding the research questions of this work, which investigated: *"What constructs are important during acceptance evaluations considering technology use by D/HH students in inclusive classrooms?"*; and, *"Is the proposed model able to cover constructs that can identify the acceptance of technology in inclusive educational environments by D/HH students?"*.

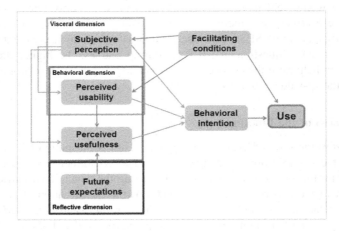

Fig. 3. Final structure of the model TAM4 IE (Own source)

We begin with a review of the relevant literature, where it was possible to verify the existence of consolidated models of technology acceptance and adoption, new models or adapted models from consolidated ones that incorporate hedonic quality attributes as constructs, and research on technology acceptance with D/HH users. This theoretical foundation showed that given differences in the type of application, in the context of use and in target users, it is necessary to reflect upon model characteristics in order to understand if a model's composition can capture the essence of aspects that influence decision-making towards technology acceptance.

Previous work [26] was a great motivator in composing a new model with constructs that could represent more truthfully the context of use and target users of technology, and also that could incorporate aspects of user experience.

It was observed from the results of the test with TAM4 IE showed more significant and positive correlations than negative ones. However, in this study, we included a small number of participants in order to be able to assert a concrete answer. These findings can be seen as a shed of light over a path that can be followed as evidence. The literature review also confirms some of the findings, showing concrete results of the relationship between constructs used in TAM4 IE, such as *Facilitating conditions* with *User behavior* [32], *Perceived usefulness* with *Behavioral intention* [8] and *Subjective perception* with *Perceived usefulness* [1, 34].

Future expectations did not show an influence on *Behavioral intention* in the test. This result is consistent with findings of [7, 20], in which *Learning expectancy* did not present significant influence on *Behavioral intention* to use technology. However, we consider that this construct could be kept in order to compare initial expectations of the students (raised from acceptance evaluation) with results of learning assessments to verify if expectations become reality.

5 Conclusions

We believe the goal of this research was met, since we proposed a technology acceptance model that takes into account representative constructs of inclusive education aspects, and conducted a test with D/HH students using a technology-based product (SESSAI app) to evaluate the proposed model.

As a result, in the pilot test, we found acceptance of SESSAI by participants, who were mostly positively surprised and stated that this technology would be useful to them in an inclusive education context. Also, it was evidenced that the proposed model was able to capture every aspect concerning technology acceptance in an inclusive education setting as can be seen in the final structure of TAM4 IE.

Along the way, we identified other gaps not explored that can be suggested as future work. Regarding Emotion-LIBRAS, we suggest as future work modifying the focus of evaluation; rather than discovering individual emotions, investigate emotions considering the collective, highlighting social relations. Computational systems have enabled the narrowing of human relationships through digital media, social networks, collaborative systems, and virtual learning environments, amongst others. Therefore, evaluation results of emotions with D/HH users may be different than those found for individual identification. Moreover, it is important to highlight that questions of the acceptance evaluation questionnaire (Table 1) can be modified according to technology, users and their specific educational barriers. The model can not be attached to technology or type of user, and because of that its questionnaire must be adapted.

Further investigations using TAM4 IE also deserve attention, especially as regards: (i) to investigate if the emotions 'Interested' and 'Positively surprised' are only identified when technology is new to participants; (ii) to evaluate technology acceptance in a natural environment, comparing results with research conducted in a controlled environment; and, (iii) to investigate other stakeholders in an inclusive educational environment, such as: hearing students, teachers, interpreters, managers, and parents of D/HH students. Also, other aspects from the educational environment can be included as questions in constructs already proposed in the new model, such as teaching-learning strategies, school projects, and the interface between school and universities.

References

1. Abad, M., Díaz, I., Vigo, M.: Acceptance of mobile technology in hedonic scenarios. In: Proceedings of the 24th BCS Interaction Specialist Group Conference (2010)
2. Agyei, D.D., Voogt, J.M.: Exploring the potential of the will, skill, tool model in Ghana: predicting prospective and practicing teachers' use of technology. Comput. Educ. **56**, 91–100 (2011)
3. Ahmed, A.S., Seong, D.S.K.: Signwriting on mobile phones for the deaf. Mobility, Bangkok, 25–27 Oct 2006
4. Ajzen, I.: The theory of planned behavior. Organ. Behav. Hum. Decis. Process. **50**(2), 179–211 (1991)
5. Bozelle, C., Betrancourt, M., Deriaz, M., Pelizzone, M.: Evaluation of technology acceptance of a computer rehabilitation tool. In: IDC 2008, 11–13 June 2008, Chicago, IL, USA (2008)
6. Cavender, A., Ladner, R.E.: Hearing impairments. In: Harper, S., Yesilada, Y. (eds.) Web Accessibility. Springer, London (2008)
7. Chen, J.-L.: The effects of education compatibility and technological expectancy on e-learning acceptance. Comput. Educ. **57**(2011), 1501–1511 (2011)
8. Davis, F.D.: A technology acceptance model for empirically testing new end-user information systems: theory and results. Doctoral dissertation, MIT Sloan School of Management, Cambridge (1986)
9. Fuchsberger, V., Moser, C., Tscheligi, M.: Values in action (ViA) – combining usability, user experience and user acceptance. CHI, Austin, USA (2012)
10. Hassenzahl, M.: The thing and I: understanding the relationship between users and product. In: Blythe, M.A., Overbeeke, K., Monk, A.F., Wright, P.C. (eds.) Funology: From Usability to Enjoyment, pp. 31–42. Kluwer, The Netherlands (2003)
11. Hassenzahl, M.: The interplay of beauty, goodness, and usability in interactive products. Hum. Comput. Interact. **19**, 319–349 (2004)
12. Hassenzahl, M., Tractinsky, N.: User experience – a research agenda. Behav. Inf. Technol. **25**(2), 91–97 (2006)
13. IBGE. www.ibge.gov.br (2015). Accessed 13 Jan 2015
14. INEP. portal.inep.gov.br/ (2015). Accessed 13 Jan 2015
15. ISO/IEC 25010: systems and software engineering — systems and software quality requirements and evaluation (SQuaRE) — system and software quality models (2011)

16. Kosec, P., Debevc, M., Holzinger, A.: Sign language interpreter module: accessible video retrieval with subtitles. In: Miesenberger, K., Klaus, J., Zagler, W., Karshmer, A. (eds.) ICCHP 2010, Part II. LNCS, vol. 6180, pp. 221–228. Springer, Heidelberg (2010)
17. Kuo, T.C.T., Shadiev, R., Hwang, W.-Y., Chen, N.-S.: Effects of applying STR for group learning activities on learning performance in a synchronous cyber classroom. Comput. Educ. **58**, 600–608 (2012)
18. Luo, X., Han, M., Liu, T., Chen, W., Bai, F.: Assistive learning for hearing impaired college students using mixed reality: a pilot study. In: International Conference on Virtual Reality and Visualization (2012)
19. Matthews, T.L., Carter, S.A., Pai, C., Fong, J., Mankoff, J.: Scribe4Me: evaluating a mobile sound transcription tool for the deaf. Technical report No. UCB/EECS-2006-49. http://www.eecs.berkeley.edu/Pubs/TechRpts/ (2006). Accessed 13 Jan 2015
20. Mcgill, T.J., Klobas, J.E.: A task-technology fit view of learning management system impact. Comput. Educ. **52**, 496–508 (2009)
21. Nielsen, J.: Usability Engineering. Morgan Kaufmann, San Francisco (1993)
22. Norman, D.A.: Emotional Design: Why We Love (or Hate) Everyday Things. Perseus Books Group, NewYork (2004)
23. Papadopoulos, M., Pearson, E.: Improving the accessibility of the traditional lecture: an automated tool for supporting transcription. In: Proceedings of the BCS HCI, People and Computers XXVI, Birmingham, UK (2012)
24. Petrie, H., Harrison, C.: Measuring users' emotional reactions to websites. In: CHI, Spotlight on Works in Progress, USA, 4–9 Apr 2009
25. Prietch, S.S., Filgueiras, L.V.L.: Developing emotion-libras 2.0 - an instrument to measure the emotional quality of deaf persons while using technology. In: Blashki, K., Isaías, P. (eds.) Emerging Research and Trends in Interactivity and the Human-Computer Interface. IGI Global Publishers, Hershey (2013)
26. Prietch, S.S., de Souza, N.S., Filgueiras, L.V.L.: A speech-to-text system's acceptance evaluation: would deaf individuals adopt this technology in their lives? In: Stephanidis, C., Antona, M. (eds.) UAHCI 2014, Part I. LNCS, vol. 8513, pp. 440–449. Springer, Heidelberg (2014)
27. Quico, C., Damásio, M.J., Henriques, S.: Digital TV adopters and non-adopters in the context of the analogue terrestrial TV switchover in Portugal. In: EuroITV 2012, Germany (2012)
28. Rogers, E.M.: Diffusion of Innovations. The Free Press, New York (1995)
29. Taylor, S., Todd, P.A.: Assessing IT usage: the role of prior experience. MIS Q. **19**(2), 561–570 (1995)
30. Taylor, S., Todd, P.A.: Understanding information technology usage: a test of competing models. Inf. Syst. Res. **6**(4), 144–176 (1995)
31. Venkatesh, V.: Determinants of perceived ease of use: integrating control, intrinsic motivation, and emotion into the technology acceptance model. Inf. Syst. Res. Informs **11**(4), 342–365 (2000)
32. Venkatesh, V., Morris, M., Davis, G., Davis, F.: User acceptance of information technology: toward a unified view. MIS Q. **27**(3), 425–478 (2003)
33. Venkatesh, V., Thong, J., Xu, X.: Consumer acceptance and use of information technology: extending the unified theory of acceptance and use of technology. MIS Q. **36**(1), 157–178 (2012)
34. Zhang, P., Li, N.: The importance of affective quality. Commun. ACM. **48**(9), 105–108 (2005)

Understanding Touch and Motion Gestures
for Blind People on Mobile Devices

Marco Romano$^{(\boxtimes)}$, Andrea Bellucci, and Ignacio Aedo

Universidad Carlos III de Madrid, Leganés, Madrid, Spain
{mromano,abellucc}@inf.uc3m.es, aedo@ia.uc3m.es

Abstract. Considering users preferences and behaviour is a necessity to develop accessible interaction for blind people. Mainstream mobile devices are widely used by people with disabilities but, despite the growing interest of the research community around accessibility issues of touch interfaces, there is still much to understand about how best to design the interaction of blind people with mobile technologies. To this end, we conducted a preliminary elicitation study (8 participants) to understand how blind people perform touch and motion gestures for common tasks on a mobile phone. We found that blind people do not use motion gestures. We provide a discussion of our results according to the type of gestures performed.

Keywords: User-defined · Gestures · Blind · Accessibility · Touch screens

1 Introduction

Mainstream mobile devices, like smartphones, are widely used by blind people [7]: they offer opportunities to increase their level of independence by making it possible to keep in touch with family and caregivers [18], orientate themselves in the street [3] and have portable access to assistive technologies like screen-readers [11]. Apart from screen-reading software that are now included in major mobile platforms, the interaction with mobile devices presents important accessibility barriers, since touch-enabled displays are designed for sighted interactions —users need to locate objects on the screen— and do not provide tactile feedback, conversely from hardware buttons.

Likewise previous research [6, 8], we are interested in understanding how to improve the accessibility of modern mobile interaction. Off-the-shelf mobile phones allow to interact both by touch and motion gestures to perform specific computing tasks: our goal is to explore the design space and provide insights to understand how best to design gestural interaction with mobile devices for a blind person.

Here we present results of a preliminary elicitation study [19] in which 8 blind users are asked to provide touch or motion gestures for common tasks on a mobile device. Our insights provide "prima facie" implications for the design of accessible mobile gestures sets. Compared with the study of Kane et al. [8], in which researchers used a 10.1-inches tablet pc to elicit touch gestures from 10 blind people, our results suggest that users have different gestures preferences for a mobile form factor. Moreover, we found that blind people are not particularly keen to motion gestures.

© IFIP International Federation for Information Processing 2015
J. Abascal et al. (Eds.): INTERACT 2015, Part I, LNCS 9296, pp. 38–46, 2015.
DOI: 10.1007/978-3-319-22701-6_3

2 Background

Our research is informed by previous work on touch and motion gestures, accessible mobile touch interface for blinds and user-defined gestures for surface computing.

Touch and Motion Gestures. *Touch gestures* (or surface gestures) are hand movements performed on a two-dimensional surface, like the touch-screen of a mobile phone [13]. Over the last two decades, surface gestures have been studied under different perspectives, from enabling hardware [15], to software frameworks and architectures [4], to design principles and taxonomies for touch interaction and evaluations of gestures vocabularies [13]. Modern mobile devices allow users to perform also *motion gestures* that are gestures performed in three dimensions by translating and rotating the device thanks to embedded sensors [17]. One of the first examples of a motion gesture was provided by Rekimoto [16], who exploited tilting data to interact with virtual objects. Recently, motion gestures have been explored for a variety of input tasks, such as text entry [5] and maps navigation [2]. *One of the limitations of gestural interaction is the fact that, without any user participation, the gestures set is defined by designers. Although such gestures can be legitimate to test technical aspects of gesture systems —since they are easy to recognize— they do not consider users preferences and performances.*

User-Defined Gestures for Surface Computing. Previous research exhibits that users preference patterns match better with gestures created by groups of potential users rather than expert designers [10]. To this end, researchers have begun to focus on participatory design techniques [19] to elicit touch gestures from users, aiming at generating better interactions that are directly informed by users behaviour. In their influential study, Wobbrock et al. [20] created a *user-defined* touch gestures set for surfaces by showing the outcome of an action to participants and asking them to provide a gesture that would produce that action. In the recent past a plethora of other studies have exploited the same method to elicit user preferences for a variety of conditions, e.g.: motion gestures for mobile devices [15], touch gestures for coupling mobile devices with interactive surfaces and multi display environments [9] or for discerning cultural differences and similarities in touch behaviours [12]. Significant to our research is the work of Kane et al. [8]: they applied the method of Wobbrock et al. with the goal of devising what kind of gestures are the most intuitive and easy to perform for blind people. In their study they asked participants to provide touch gestures for standard tasks on a touch-enabled 10.1–inches tablet. Insights from the study provide implications for the design of accessible touch interfaces for blind user, such as avoiding symbols used in print writing, use physical edges and corners as landmarks and reduce the need of spatial accuracy.

Our study follows the method proposed by Wobbrock et al. *[20] and differs from the study of Kane* et al. *[8] in the following aspects: (1) we explore gesture preferences for a different form factor —a 3.5-inches smartphone— since the size of a device can be an important factor for the definition of a gestures set, and (2) we include motion gestures, which are a relevant input modality supported by modern smartphones that, nonetheless, is underutilized [16]. Moreover, there is a lack of knowledge if or not motion gestures can be a valid input method for blind users.*

Mobile Touch Interfaces for Blind People. The widespread diffusion of mobile devices requires to assess accessibility issues of touch interfaces in order to provide efficient interaction techniques for *visual impaired users* [1]. Speech, audio and haptic has been widely used as output channels. For instance, screen-readers have been developed for different platforms, such as VoiceOver[1] for Apple OS or Eyes-Free Shell[2] for Android. The Talking Tactile Tablet [10] uses a special hardware with an overlay that enables tactile feedback. With respect to the input, various touch techniques have been explored for eyes-free interactions. Slide Rule [6], for example, offers adapted gestural interaction for navigating lists of items. Lastly, the role of touch location has been studied in order to provide different triggers for gestures that depend on the screen region [17].

Research on touch interaction techniques for blind people shows that we have not yet developed a clear understanding of users preferences, which can be achieved by involving the end users in the design process [19]. The results are promising, since it has been shown that blind people have significant spatial and tactile abilities and therefore are capable of using touch- and motion-based interfaces [8].

3   User Study

We are interested in understanding what kind of gestures blind users consider intuitive for mobile devices and whether or not motion gestures can be a valid input modality together with touch gestures. We conducted a preliminary study with a group of 8 blind people in which participants were asked to perform touch or motion gestures for common tasks on a mobile phone.

We recruited 8 users, 4 male and 4 female with average age 61.1 (SD = 11.29). Participants were selected considering their level of blindness and their familiarity with touch technologies. Participants have congenital blindness (2 of 8) or are early blind (6 of 8), a condition that requires the use of a screen reader to access digital information. As one of the participants stated *"blind people are not an homogeneous population"* and there are differences, for instance, with respect to spatial perception between early and late blind [14]. Since it would not have been possible, at this stage, to isolate this condition, we recruited the subjects in order to have a sample as uniform as possible. The participants belong to a Spanish organization for blind people (ONCE). The organization provides general IT education and technological support to their members. In particular, it offers a course that focuses on interaction with iPhone, in which attendees learn how to interact with the VoiceOver interface. All of our participants attended the course and are familiar with IT technologies. They use a desktop pc daily for working purposes and use touch-screen devices mainly as personal assistants both when they are at home (e.g. reading emails) or outside (e.g. getting the current location and routes). Moreover, all participants consider themselves as technologically proactive and eager to improve the access of their peers to mobile technologies. We conducted the

---

[1] https://www.apple.com/es/accessibility/ios/voiceover/.

[2] https://code.google.com/p/eyes-free/.

study in a laboratory setting: we chose the ONCE central office to make participants comfortable, since the location was well known by all.

The study was conducted on a 3.5 inches iPhone 4s running iOS 7.1.2. We developed an HTML5 and Javascript application that captures multi-touch and motion gestures. As in [8], we used an operating system-agnostic application aiming to provide a neutral setup for the experiment. The ubiquity of HTML allows to repeat the experiment with heterogeneous hardware without implementing an ad hoc version of the application. The application stores gestures data in a XML-formatted file and provides the researchers with a visualization tool for the later analysis. Figure 1(a) shows a participant performing a touch gesture (on the left) and the resulting data captured by the application (on the right). All the sessions were video-recorded with a stationary camera pointing to the device to capture the interactions and protect subjects' privacy. No other objects were present and the users sat to side of a table during the whole session. Just a ONCE helper was present in case of necessity.

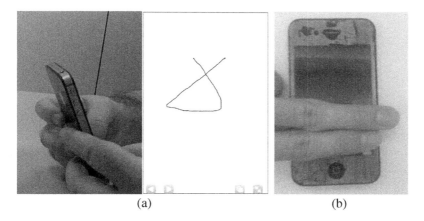

(a)   (b)

Fig. 1. (a) Example of a touch gesture and its visualization. (b) A no traditional gesture.

Previous to the experiment, we interviewed one of the ONCE IT specialists in order to fine-tune the setup. From the interview, we decided to give participants 10 min to get familiar with the device, since the IT specialist reported that "*it is paramount for visually impaired users to understand the dimensions of the screen in order to create a mental map of the device they are going to use*". We also estimated each session to last less than 40 min, which is the time limit the specialist suggested to avoid excessively stressing the users. Each session began with an interview on the kind of disability, technological skills, and the participant experience with mobile technologies. Participants were then introduced to the tasks. They had to invent two gestures (a preferred one and a second choice), motion or touch, which can be used to trigger a specific command. We used the command list from Kane et al. [8], which we reviewed and modified in collaboration with ONCE IT specialist in order to match the context of mobile devices and to assure that all the participants could know and understand it.

Selected commands were: *Context menu, Help, Undo, Switch application, Next, Previous, Ok, Reject, Move object, Open, Close, Copy, Cut, Paste, Quit, Select, Change input field, Answer up, Hang up*. Participants were asked to think aloud while performing the gestures and motivate their preferences. Before performing a gesture for a command, the experimenter read the name of the command and a description of the expected outcome.

Results. The 8 participants were asked to perform 2 gestures for 19 commands for a total of 304 samples. Some of them were not able to provide two different gestures for the same command, therefore we have 152 gestures as first choice plus 126 for the second choice (total of 278). Only 12 of the 278 (4,32 %) were motion gestures while multi-finger were 43 (15,46 %). Figure 2 illustrates the gesture rationale for each category. We classified motion and touch gestures using the nature dimension of the taxonomy from Wobbrock et al. [20], in the same way Kane et al. [8] did for touch gestures and Ruiz et al. [17] for motion gestures.

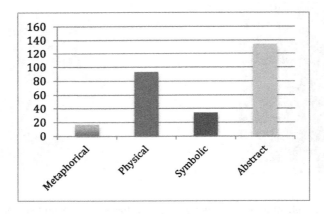

Fig. 2. Gestures rationale according to the nature dimension.

The nature dimension groups together *symbolic, metaphorical, physical and abstract gestures*. Gestures are defined as metaphorical when they represent the metaphor to act on an object different from a mobile phone (e.g., emulating an eraser on the touch-screen to remove an object). They are physical when they act directly on an object (e.g., drag and drop), symbolic when gestures indicate a symbol (e.g., typographic symbols like '?'). Finally gestures are abstract when their mapping is arbitrary (e.g., double tap). We grouped our samples taking into account users explanations and direct observations. The *abstract* gestures are the largest category, with 134 samples (48.02 %), followed by *physical* gestures (93 samples), *symbolic* (34) and *metaphorical* (17). The *abstract* category presents the highest prevalence of multi-finger gestures (24 gestures, 15 physical and 4 metaphor). Multi-finger gestures have been employed 18 times as first choice, 25 as second. Finally, 37 % of the provided gestures stem from previous experiences with desktop and touch interfaces as explicitly commented by the testers.

4 Discussion

When compared with the study of Kane et al. [8], in which metaphorical and abstract gestures were dominant for a tablet form factor, our results show that physical and abstract are prevailing for a mobile device. Those results suggest that the physicality of the device, which determine the way users interact with it (e.g., making gestures with the same hand that is holding the device), the tasks selected for the mobile context (e.g., answering the phone) and the user background (e.g., technological knowledge) influence the kind of gestures made by blind users. In particular, the physical nature of the gestures is prevalent for the following commands: *previous* (60 %), *next* (47 %), *move object* (67 %), *cut* (36 %), *reject* (47 %). Some users commented to be inspired by the interaction mechanisms of real world that make them to feel the interaction as more "natural". In general abstract is the main gesture category and get the best percentages in commands such as *ok* (75 %), *copy* (64 %) and *select* (77 %). Many of the abstract gestures stem from participants experience with the other user interfaces. For example, regarding the *ok* command, 7 users performed a tap or a double tap because it is what they normally do in their mobile or desktop devices. Moreover most of the elicited gestures (203) are one-finger and multi-finger variations of tap or flick (an unidirectional movement of the finger). This is probably due to the fact that the VoiceOver interface, which participants have learnt to operate in the IT courses, uses mostly tap and flick gestures. Flicks vary on the number of fingers, from one to four. Taps vary on the number of fingers, one or two, and repetitions. In VoiceOver multi-finger gestures are mainly used for system control or are personalized gestures. This suggests the reason why testers demonstrated to be familiar with multi-finger gestures but to prefer mainly one-finger strokes.

Our study shows that blind people tent to use gestures that are different from common touch interfaces for sighted users but that are familiar to them. For instance, the 2-finger double-tap gesture is used frequently in the VoiceOver interface: its uses include answering and ending phone calls, starting and stopping music and video playback, etc. A preliminary advice for the designers of mobile accessible interaction is to consider the technological literacy of the users and exploit their familiarity with touch gestures.

Another outcome of the study is related to the reduced use of motion gestures. Causes are due to users lack of familiarity with motion gestures and because they were afraid to hit some objects moving the device. Conversely from other studies that focus on sighted users [17] and show that motion gestures are a significant for mobile devices, we found that motion gestures do not seem to be suitable for blind people: there is no general agreement in using a common gesture for a given command.

Together with touch gestures that can be easily recognized, participants provided other kinds of no traditional hand postures, consisting in covering portions of the screen, that are not detected by current mobile phones hardware and software. Such gestures were performed by three different users for four different commands. For instance, covering the bottom part of the screen was used to confirm a choice, as it recalls the paper's position in which we usually sign an agreement, as depicted in Fig. 1(b). Another participant used the palm to cover the whole screen with the intent to trigger the quit command.

A considerable number of gestures was performed in specific screen locations that participants associated to a semantic interpretation. Performing gestures in the left side was interpreted as "go back" or "recover from an action". For instance gestures on the left side were associated to commands like undo, previous, reject, close, quit and hang up. On the other hand, the right side was associated to opposite actions, such as next, accept, open, answer a call.

With respect to spatial awareness, Kane et al. [8] suggest to favor edges and corners of the screen because they can be used as physical landmarks that help blind people to locate spots in the surface. Our study reveals that this behavior largely depends on the experience of the users with mobile technology. We observed that users with less experience start by searching for the edges of the touch-screen and, when they are ready, they perform the gesture nearby it. Users with more years of experience with touch-screens generally start their gestures from the center of the device.

5 Conclusions and Future Work

We presented a preliminary elicitation study to understand preferences of blind people with respect to touch and motion gestures on mobile devices. First insights from our study can be summarized as follows: (1) our results highlight that gestures are influenced by the form factor and the users background, (2) the gesture rationale is prevalently abstract and physical, (3) users tend to assign a behavior to screen locations, (4) users prefer touch gestures rather than motion gestures. Our work provides new insights on how blind people use mobile technologies. However, given the open-ended nature of the study, further research is needed. Since the lack of prior knowledge and experience affects the users' preferences, we consider that an in-depth study could reveal new interesting insights. We plan to modify the experiment requiring users to provide and then evaluate both a touch and a motion gesture for each command. This is to confirm whether motion gestures can be an effective input modality. The final aim is to reach an agreement on the mapping between gestures and commands and thus to define a robust and accessible gestures set for mobile phones.

Acknowledgement. This work is supported by the project CREAx grant funded by the Spanish Ministry of Economy and Competitivity (TIN2014-56534-R). We also thank the collaboration and the support of the ONCE organization of Madrid.

References

1. Abascal, J., Civit, A.: Mobile communication for people with disabilities and older people: new opportunities for autonomous life. In: Proceedings of ERCIM Workshop 2000, pp. 255–268 (2000)
2. Bellucci, A., Malizia, A., Diaz, P., Aedo, I.: Don't touch me: multi-user annotations on a map in large display environments. In: Proceedings of AVI 2010, pp. 391–392, ACM (2010)
3. Di Chiara, G., Paolino, L., Romano, M., Sebillo, M., Tortora, G., Vitiello, G., Ginige, A.: The framy user interface for visually-impaired users. In: 2011 Sixth International Conference on Digital Information Management (ICDIM), vol., no., pp. 36–41, 26–28 Sept 2011
4. Echtler, F., Klinker, G.: A multitouch software architecture. In: Proceedings of NordiCHI 2008, p. 463, ACM Press (2008)
5. Jones, E., Alexander, J., Andreou, A.: GesText: accelerometer-based gestural text-entry systems. In: Proceedings of CHI 2010, pp. 2173–2182 (2010)
6. Kane, S., Bigham, J., Wobbrock, J.: Slide rule: making mobile touch screens accessible to blind people using multi-touch interaction techniques. In: Proceedings of SIGACCESS 2008, pp. 73–80, ACM Press (2008)
7. Kane, S.K., Jayant, C., Wobbrock, J.O., Ladner, R.E.: Freedom to roam: a study of mobile device adoption and accessibility for people with visual and motor disabilities. In: Proceedings of SIGACCESS 2009, pp. 115–122, ACM Press (2009)
8. Kane, S., Wobbrock, J., Ladner, R.: Usable gestures for blind people: understanding preference and performance. In: Proceedings of CHI 2011, pp. 413–422, ACM Press (2011)
9. Kristensson, P.O., Clawson, J., Dunlop, M., et al.: Designing and evaluating text entry methods. In: CHI EA 2012, p. 2747, ACM Press (2012)
10. Landau, S., Wells, L.: Merging tactile sensory input and audio data by means of the talking tactile tablet. In: Proceedings of EuroHaptics 2003, vol. 60, pp. 291–297 (2003)
11. Manduchi, R., Coughlan, J.M.: Portable and mobile systems in assistive technology. In: Miesenberger, K., Klaus, J., Zagler, W.L., Karshmer, A.I. (eds.) ICCHP 2008. LNCS, vol. 5105, pp. 1078–1080. Springer, Heidelberg (2008)
12. Mauney, D., Howarth, J., Wirtanen, A., Capra, M.: Cultural similarities and differences in user-defined gestures for touchscreen user interfaces. In: CHI EA 2011, pp. 4015–4020, ACM Press (2010)
13. Morris, M., Wobbrock, J., Wilson, A.: Understanding users' preferences for surface gestures. In: Proceedings of GI 2010, Canadian Information Processing Society, pp. 261–268 (2010)
14. Postma, A., Zuidhoek, S., Noordzij, M.L., Kappers, A.M.: Differences between early-blind, late-blind, and blindfolded-sighted people in haptic spatial-configuration learning and resulting memory traces. Perception 36(8), 1253–1265 (2007)
15. Rekimoto, J.: Smartskin: an infrastructure for freehand manipulation on interactive surfaces. In: Proceedings of CHI 2002, pp. 113–120, ACM Press (2002)
16. Rekimoto, J.: Tilting operations for small screen interfaces. In: Proceedings of UIST 2016, pp. 2–3, ACM Press (1996)
17. Ruiz, J., Li, Y., Lank, E.: User-defined motion gestures for mobile interaction. In: Proceedings of CHI 2011, pp. 197–206, ACM Press (2011)
18. Sánchez, J., Aguayo, F.: Mobile messenger for the blind. In: Stephanidis, C., Pieper, M. (eds.) ERCIM Ws UI4ALL 2006. LNCS, vol. 4397, pp. 369–385. Springer, Heidelberg (2007)

19. Schuler, D., Namioka, A.: Participatory design: Principles and Practices. L. Erlbaum Assoc. Inc., Hillsdale (1993)
20. Wobbrock, J., Morris, M., Wilson, A.: User-defined gestures for surface computing. In: Proceedings of CHI 2009, pp. 1083–1092, ACM Press (2009)

Virtual Buttons for Eyes-Free Interaction:
A Study

Jens Bauer[(✉)] and Achim Ebert

Computer Graphics and HCI Group, TU Kaiserslautern, Kaiserslautern, Germany
{j_bauer, ebert}@cs.uni-kl.de

Abstract. The touch screen of mobile devices, such as smart phones and tablets, is their primary input mechanism. While designed to be used in conjunction with its output capabilities, eyes-free interaction is also possible and useful on touch screens. One of the several possible techniques for eyes-free interaction is the virtual button method, where the screen is divided into a regular grid of buttons that can be pressed even without looking at the screen.

This paper contains an exploratory study about influence factors on this interaction method. Results indicate, that not only the size of the buttons matter, but also the device orientation and user dependent factors, such as the age or general experience with touch screens. By involving small children in the evaluation we can see the validity of this approach even for the youngest users.

Keywords: Eyes-free · Evaluation · Virtual buttons · Mobile devices

1 Introduction

In most cases, interaction with mobile phones and tablets is done via the touch screen of those devices. Users will naturally look at the screen while using it. However, there are some cases, where looking at the screen might not be possible or viable, e.g. while driving or when interacting with another system via the mobile device. This is called eyes-free interaction. A comprehensive list of such cases is presented by Yi et al. [7]. Consumer-level devices do not provide haptic feedback on their screens, thus making this style of interaction difficult. One possibility of dealing with this is to divide the screen into a grid of virtual buttons. Other common approaches are described in the Related Work section later. There are studies showing the impact of different grid sizes on the accuracy (i.e., the hit-miss-ration of the user) for this kind of interaction. The paper from Wang et al. [6] is a prime example of this. More are covered later in the Related Work. No research has yet been done on the impact of different devices and their sizes on the accuracy and the duration of actually interacting, since the device size impacts those values inversely.

In this paper, we describe an exploratory study of eyes-free virtual button presses. Unlike previous studies, we look for the impact of not only the number of virtual buttons on the touch screen, but also the size of the device itself, attributes of the user, etc. To get further insight into the general usability of this method our participants are not only adults, but also small children. Children are getting their own mobile phones

© IFIP International Federation for Information Processing 2015
J. Abascal et al. (Eds.): INTERACT 2015, Part I, LNCS 9296, pp. 47–54, 2015.
DOI: 10.1007/978-3-319-22701-6_4

(with touch screens) in early age, thus it is important to know, if methods working well for adults are actually viable for them.

In the next section we will give a brief overview of related literature. Then we will present the design of our evaluation and the process, followed by the actual evaluation of the results. We finish with the conclusions of the results.

2 Related Work

Yi et al. [7] presented a classification of motives for eyes-free interaction and identified several actual reasons. The four main categories are *Environmental, Social, Device Features* and *Personal*. The number and variety of reasons shows that eyes-free interaction is an important topic.

Alternatives for eyes-free interaction to the virtual button approach include Bezel Swipe [5] and Touch Gestures [2]. Bezel Swipe requires the user to touch one of the sides of the screen and swipe inwards. The tactile feedback with this technique makes it viable for eyes-free interaction. Touch gestures, which do not require any special position on the screen, such as a simple pinch gesture are also easy to use eyes-free.

Azenkot and Zhai [1] evaluated the effect of using a finger, a thumb or two thumbs on text input on touch capable smart phones.

An evaluation about virtual buttons on smart phones was done by Wang et al. [6]. They found that grid sizes of bigger than 3×3 are not feasible to use for almost any user. Their evaluation was only done with one touch screen capable phone and only using one handed-interaction.

A huge evaluation done by Henze et al. [3] focuses on the impact of several hardware design factors, such as device size, screen resolution, target sizes and position. They gathered data through a game distributed in an official app store. However their study was by design not abled to measure those effects on eyes-free interaction.

3 Evaluation

3.1 Design

The main goal of the study was to find out how different factors impact on the eyes-free usability of virtual buttons. Those factors are the size of the virtual buttons, as given by the touch screen size and the layout of the button grid. According to the results of Wang et al. [6], button grids with more than 3 buttons in any direction were excluded, as were trivial layouts with only one or two buttons in total. The remaining grid layouts were: 1×3, 2×3, 3×3, 3×2 and 3×1. To gain insight about the effect of device size, we also used three different devices, an iPad 2 (241.2 mm $\times$ 185.7 mm, 9.7 in. display), iPad Mini (200 mm $\times$ 134.7 mm, 7.9 in. display) and an iPhone 4S (115.2 mm $\times$ 58.6 mm, 3.5 in. display). We chose to use only this device family to minimise hardware influences on the tests. For example the resolution of touch input (*not* screen pixels) is similar on all devices. This assures the App to behave the same on all devices, too. Since the device orientation might impact user performance as well, all tests were to be done in both landscape and portrait orientation. As shown by Azenkot and Zhai [1], usage of thumb vs. finger can have an impact, too, and according to Karlson et al. [4] this is the primary way of mobile touch interaction. Therefore each user was asked to complete all tests a second time using only one thumb in portrait orientation and two thumbs in landscape. In the other test runs, user had the freedom of choice of how to interact with the device, the only constraint being, the device has to be held with at least one hand and may not be put down on a table or anywhere else. Because of the physical size of the devices, this was only done for the phone. For additional data, users were asked for their experience with touch devices (self perceived), age and gender.

The evaluation design is straightforward. Every user is presented a grid of virtual buttons, displayed not on the mobile device, but on a separate computer screen, as we focus on eyes-free interaction. The mobile device screen stays completely blank, so if a user accidentally looks at the mobile device, they get no additional insight, and thus no advantage over other participants not looking at the device.

Depending on the complexity of the grid, 20, 30, or 40 touches were needed per grid layout and device orientation (more complex layouts needing more touches). Considering that every participant was asked to perform the test with three different devices and one device having an additional test run under special conditions described later, every user had to perform a total of 1520 touches. We used three different mobile device sizes, large tablet, small tablet and mobile phone to measure the impact of the device/screen size on the test.

To have a wider age range in the evaluation, we decided to not only have adult participants. To see how age actually affects the results of our study, we created another design, targeted at small children. This will help to understand if virtual buttons is a concept simple enough for even children to understand. We can also get an insight on the effect the grid layout and device size has on their performance, given their smaller hand sizes.

To get results across all possible grid setups, we reduced the number of touches needed per grid layout to ten. Also to help the children understand the task they were supposed to accomplish, their test started with a short example of the test with the grid visible on both the mobile device and the computer screen. These touches were, of course, not counted in the evaluation. The Thumb-Only run on the mobile phone was also not done by the children, since their hands were not big enough to accomplish it. To not negatively influence the study due to the children getting bored by the tasks, they had the option of stopping the test after each device. Thus, less data is available from the children's test, but still enough for an evaluation.

For the evaluation we developed a simple mobile application connected to a desktop application. The desktop application will display the current grid of virtual buttons and highlight the button the user is supposed to be pressing. To avoid confusion, the system guarantees that no button will be highlighted twice in a row, giving reliable feedback to the participants. The system automatically randomizes the test order (order of device, grid layout and button to press) to avoid learning effects affecting the results. The grid was displayed on a standard LCD computer display with 21 in. of size, connected to a desktop PC. A dedicated WiFi connected the PC and the mobile device.

Each touch was recorded individually. Accuracy and duration was measured by aggregating the gathered data. Accuracy is simply the ration of hitting the correct button and the total number of button requests. Duration is the total time between a button prompt being displayed and it being pressed, summed up for each test run.

For the test involving adults, we had 44 participants (30 of them male, 14 female) in the age range of 21 to 62 years. All test candidates were asked to rate their own experience with touch screen interaction (on a Likert-scale of 1–5) and to state if they own a touch device themselves (which the majority of 34 users did). The average experience level was 3.57, unsurprisingly due to the high number of touch device owners in the test. As a side note, the high number of touch device owners shows the ubiquity of these devices and does not affect the viability of the test as we still have 10 participants not owning such a device.

The 29 children (18 male, 11 female) were between 4 and 6 years old. They were not asked to rate their experience, as children of that age are unreliable of their self-assessment. But they were asked, if anybody in their family owns a touch device that they are allowed to use on a regular basis. 18 of the 29 children confirmed that, while 9 had no prior access to touch devices (2 children opted to not to answer that question).

3.2   Results

To get basic results from the study, we tested for influence of four basic factors on the accuracy. The factors are the device orientation (Landscape/Portrait), a combined factor of the device used and if the user was asked to use only their thumb, if the user actually owns a touch device, and the self-rated experience value.

The mean values are given in Table 1 below. As supposed from the related work, the accuracy results are above 90 % for adults. Children's accuracy is significantly lower at values between 70 % and up to more than 90 %. This shows, that children are actually able to understand the concept of virtual buttons, even for eyes-free interaction. But due to the lower hit-ratio, care must be taken to allow undo-operations or similar mechanisms when designing applications for children.

Portrait orientation supports higher accuracy for both adults and children. It also influences the duration, with adults being faster in portrait orientation. Interestingly children were faster using the (less accurate) landscape orientation. More evaluation is needed in order to gain insight into this.

As expected, bigger devices allow for higher accuracy. It also seems, that the bigger device size does not cause the duration to go up (due to longer ways to move fingers), but instead seem to lower the duration. This is probably caused by users being more confident in hitting the desired area.

Using the thumbs only for interaction with the phone seems to actually increase accuracy and interaction speed. Since the alternative involves moving the whole hand to reposition the finger, this is not surprising.

Experience levels do also influence both accuracy and duration, mostly in the expected way. There is a outlier in the data, as the low experience level of 2 performed faster than levels 1, 3 and 4. The cause of this is unclear at this point.

Gender does not seem to influence accuracy at all for the adults. Though male candidates performed the requested tasks quicker than females. The cause of this needs more evaluation. Even more interesting is the fact, that with children this is actually reversed. Girls were more accurate hitting the virtual buttons and even performed fasters.

Table 1. Base results. Values are divided into children and adult values. Duration is average duration per touch in seconds.

Classification	Accuracy		Duration	
	Adults	Children	Adults	Children
Orientation				
Portrait	0.9638	0.8222	0.7840	3.008
Landscape	0.9538	0.7928	0.8534	2.972
Device				
iPad 2	0.9736	0.8571	0.7689	1.629
iPad Mini	0.9687	0.8115	0.7736	1.434
iPhone 4S	0.9300	0.7566	0.8863	5.887
iPhone 4S (Thumb)	0.9500	N/A	0.8440	N/A
Owns Touch Device				
No	0.9515	0.8595	0.9207	6.175
Yes	0.9631	0.7756	0.7947	1.579
Experience Level				
1	0.9203	N/A	0.9637	N/A
2	0.9391	N/A	0.7848	N/A
3	0.9717	N/A	0.8681	N/A
4	0.9798	N/A	0.8277	N/A
5	0.9695	N/A	0.7405	N/A
Gender				
Male	0.9557	0.7637	0.7640	3.967
Female	0.9597	0.8948	0.9341	1.648

Looking at the actual target button sizes, as defined by touch screen size and the grid layout yields the results seen in Tables 2 and 3. For Table 2 the results were grouped by the minimal dimension of the button. For example, a button size of 10×15 mm would then have a minimal dimension of 10 mm. In Table 3 the whole square size is used to group the results. Roughly the results reinforce the hypothesis, that bigger target sizes will lead to better accuracy and execution speed. Not all bigger sizes perform better than smaller sizes. More research is needed here to find the cause of this. Generally the standard deviation (and therefore variance) of accuracy and duration decreases with increasing button size (in both tables). This might be a sign of users being more confident with bigger sizes or simply more users can reliably use the virtual buttons as their size increases. There also seems to be a point till where user performance increases faster with increasing size. Unfortunately our data is not abled to support such a hypothesis statistically, so this is also a point needing further research.

Table 2. Accuracy and duration by minimal dimension of target button (i.e., a button size of 10 × 15 mm has a minimal dimension of 10 mm). Columns contain mean values and standard deviation. Size is given in milimeters and duration in seconds.

Min.	Accuracy		Duration	
Size	Adults	Children	Adults	Children
19.5	0.9349 ± 0.1103	0.7448 ± 0.2805	0.9191 ± 1.2987	5.647 ± 16.3594
29.3	0.9569 ± 0.1009	0.8139 ± 0.2489	0.8223 ± 0.6596	6.238 ± 23.7814
38.4	0.9464 ± 0.1071	0.7595 ± 0.2443	0.7452 ± 0.2164	5.681 ± 17.0854
44.9	0.9645 ± 0.0907	0.8050 ± 0.2595	0.7843 ± 0.1672	1.524 ± 0.6258
61.9	0.9683 ± 0.0679	0.8464 ± 0.1685	0.7896 ± 0.2002	1.660 ± 0.6454
66.7	0.9665 ± 0.0749	0.7970 ± 0.2514	0.7764 ± 0.2366	1.344 ± 0.6166
67.4	0.9790 ± 0.1026	0.8735 ± 0.2013	0.7333 ± 0.1874	1.385 ± 0.6058
80.4	0.9692 ± 0.0666	0.8711 ± 0.1413	0.7591 ± 0.1591	1.678 ± 0.7999
92.9	0.9938 ± 0.0166	0.8965 ± 0.1803	0.7190 ± 0.1111	1.503 ± 0.5611

Table 3. Accuracy and duration by size of the button. Columns contain mean values and standard deviation. Size is given in square millimeters and duration in seconds.

Sq.	Accuracy		Duration	
Size	Adults	Children	Adults	Children
750	0.9223 ± 0.1048	0.7192 ± 0.3213	0.9038 ± 0.2660	5.8143 ± 17.620
1125	0.9397 ± 0.1203	0.7679 ± 0.2690	0.8764 ± 0.9219	6.4241 ± 24.571
1688	0.9777 ± 0.0805	0.8415 ± 0.2279	0.8240 ± 0.9643	5.6302 ± 16.959
2250	0.9538 ± 0.0918	0.7573 ± 0.2474	0.8348 ± 1.5992	5.5466 ± 16.877
2993	0.9611 ± 0.0781	0.7941 ± 0.2644	0.8260 ± 0.1703	1.6114 ± 0.5039
4490	0.9645 ± 0.0992	0.8012 ± 0.2779	0.7965 ± 0.2172	1.4944 ± 0.6702
4977	0.9625 ± 0.0836	0.8297 ± 0.1682	0.8210 ± 0.1668	1.7047 ± 0.4986
6735	0.9790 ± 0.1026	0.8735 ± 0.2013	0.7333 ± 0.1874	1.3853 ± 0.6058
7465	0.9700 ± 0.0625	0.8734 ± 0.1535	0.7905 ± 0.1977	1.8205 ± 0.8531
8980	0.9710 ± 0.0569	0.8058 ± 0.2277	0.7063 ± 0.1505	1.3203 ± 0.6133
11198	0.9938 ± 0.0166	0.8965 ± 0.1803	0.7190 ± 0.1111	1.5032 ± 0.5611
14930	0.9718 ± 0.0583	0.8527 ± 0.1573	0.7108 ± 0.1632	1.4917 ± 0.6016

We did a Pearson's test of correlation between the accuracy, user's age, the virtual button size, the minimal length or width of a button (called MinSize for the remainder of this paper) and the duration of a test. We got a significant correlation between accuracy and age, button size and MinSize for both test groups. The same goes for duration, respectively. Since Pearson's test of correlation is well known to be impacted by outliers, we confirmed our results with an additional Spearman-correlation test. All correlations were confirmed, except for the correlation of duration and MinSize in the children group, so correlation here is improbable.

Analyses of Variance (i.e. ANOVE) was then done to test the influence of the virtual button position on the accuracy. Separate ANOVAs were performed for each combination of device and grid layout. One of the interesting findings here is the fact, that for all devices the middle button in the 1×3 (one single row of 3 buttons) layout was significantly (on a 5 % level) harder to hit, while this does not hold true for the 3×1 layout. Here no significant differences could be found. Other layouts with statistically significant inaccurate buttons are 2×3, 3×2 and 3×3.

For the 3×3 layout, the buttons in the middle column had least accuracy, with the top and bottom button in this column having even lesser accuracy than the middle one. This holds true on all devices. For this layout the middle device size has the highest accuracy for all individual buttons. In the 3×2 and 2×3 layouts, also the middle buttons had lower accuracy than the other buttons, again on all devices. This is probably due to the fact that buttons near a corner are easier to find without looking on the device.

4 Conclusion

Our evaluation shows, that there are several influence factors confirmed for eyes-free virtual button interaction on smart phones and tablets. The device size is important as one might assume as is the actual size of the target. As the improvement of accuracy when using the iPad over the iPad Mini is not significant, this hints, that there is a point, where enlarging the mobile device does not yield better results for accuracy. Since grid sizes bigger than 3×3 virtual buttons are strongly discouraged by Yi et al. [7], this is understandable.

For the design of virtual buttons we can conclude, that it is important to use the minimal possible amount of buttons and to move secondary functionality into other interaction mechanisms, like gestures or an on-screen menu. Especially since application designers cannot influence the factors of age and touch screen experience of their potential users, they are well-advised to keep the user interface as simple as possible. Especially when developing for platforms that target several different device sizes (such as Android or iOS), the designers have to keep in mind, that they might not know the actual device size their application is used and thus not the actual target sizes of virtual buttons they use.

When using only three different buttons, it is advised to arrange them in column order, as there is no button with lower accuracy in that layout as found out above. In general the 3×1 and 2×2 layouts are most suited for eyes-free interaction. If more functions are needed, applications designers should take care to identify critical functionality, that causes most problems if invoked by mistake. Important functions should be assigned to a button in a corner of the device, unimportant ones can be connected with the middle buttons. The centre button in the 3×3 layout has a special role, as it has higher accuracy than the buttons to its sides, but less than the corner buttons.

We can also conclude, that virtual buttons is a concept, that is simple enough for even some small children to understand and use properly. As the number of children owning their own touch device is steadily increasing, this is an important point for application design. While the actual accuracy numbers are fairly low for the children test group, one has to keep in mind that eyes-free interaction is not easy for children at all. As future work the results mentioned in this paper need thorough evaluation to statistically prove their validity. Especially looking for a perfect size and the influence of grid layout and device size is very interesting for further evaluation. Still the results presented can be used as a hint for designing apps using the virtual button approach.

References

1. Azenkot, S., Zhai, S.: Touch behavior with different postures on soft smartphone keyboards. In: Proceedings of the 14th International Conference on Human-Computer Interaction with Mobile Devices and Services, pp. 251–260. ACM (2012)
2. Bragdon, A., Nelson, E., Li, Y., Hinckley, K.: Experimental analysis of touch-screen gesture designs in mobile environments. In: Proceedings of the SIGCHI Conference on Human Factors in Computing Systems, pp. 403–412. ACM (2011)
3. Henze, N., Rukzio, E., Boll, S.: 100,000,000 taps: analysis and improvement of touch performance in the large. In: Proceedings of the 13th International Conference on Human Computer Interaction with Mobile Devices and Services, pp. 133–142. ACM (2011)
4. Karlson, A., Bederson, B., Contreras-Vidal, J.: Understanding single-handed mobile device interaction. In: Handbook of Research on User Interface Design and Evaluation for Mobile Technology, pp. 86–101 (2006)
5. Roth, V., Turner, T.: Bezel swipe: conflict-free scrolling and multiple selection on mobile touch screen devices. In: Proceedings of the SIGCHI Conference on Human Factors in Computing Systems, pp. 1523–1526. ACM (2009)
6. Wang, Y., Yu, C., Liu, J., Shi, Y.: Understanding performance of eyes-free, absolute position control on touchable mobile phones. In: Proceedings of the 15th International Conference on Human-Computer Interaction with Mobile Devices and Services, MobileHCI 2013, pp. 79–88. ACM, New York, NY, USA (2013)
7. Yi, B., Cao, X., Fjeld, M., Zhao, S.: Exploring user motivations for eyes-free interaction on mobile devices. In: Proceedings of the SIGCHI Conference on Human Factors in Computing Systems, CHI 2012, pp. 2789–2792. ACM, New York, NY, USA (2012)

Comparing Concurrent and Retrospective Verbal Protocols for Blind and Sighted Users

Andreas Savva$^{(\boxtimes)}$, Helen Petrie, and Christopher Power

Human Computer Interaction Research Group, Department of Computer Science,
University of York, York YO10 5GH, UK
{asl517,helen.petrie,christopher.power}@york.ac.uk

Abstract. Verbal protocols are widely used in user studies for evaluating websites. This study investigated the effectiveness and efficiency of concurrent and retrospective verbal protocols (CVP and RVP) for both blind and sighted participants, as well as participant workload and attitudes towards these methods. Eight blind and eight sighted participants undertook both protocols in a website evaluation. RVP was more effective as measured by problems encountered for both groups, although it was no more efficient than CVP. The severity of problems identified by both protocols was equivalent. As measured on the NASA TLX, participants found RVP found more demanding than CVP. Sighted participants found rating problems during CVP more disruptive than blind participants. These results show that RVP is a more useful protocol for practitioners and researchers even though it takes more time and is more demanding for participants. It is equally applicable for both blind and sighted participants.

Keywords: User evaluation · Think aloud protocol · Concurrent verbal protocol · Retrospective verbal protocol · Web accessibility · Web usability · Blind users

1 Introduction

In user-based studies to evaluate websites, participants typically "think aloud" while undertaking tasks to identify problems. The thinking aloud may be performed concurrently with conducting the task, known as a concurrent verbal protocol (CVP), or retrospectively while reviewing recordings of their performance on a task, known as a retrospective verbal protocol (RVP). A number of studies have compared these two types of verbal protocol with sighted participants, in terms of the information gathered [3, 17] and the number of problems revealed [25, 26]. However, a comparison of these protocols when used with blind participants has not yet been performed, in spite of the fact that there are a number of studies which have used verbal protocols with blind participants [8, 12, 19, 20, 22]. CVP may add additional effort particularly for blind participants, as the mental effort of using the web for blind users with screen readers is typically greater than understanding the web visually. This is because blind users need to recall all the keyboard commands that they use to interact with the web, whereas sighted users can rely on recognition of icons and menu items if need be.

© IFIP International Federation for Information Processing 2015
J. Abascal et al. (Eds.): INTERACT 2015, Part I, LNCS 9296, pp. 55–71, 2015.
DOI: 10.1007/978-3-319-22701-6_5

However, few studies have compared the two verbal protocols in terms of the workload they place on participants. In addition, there are no studies comparing the two protocols with blind participants in terms of information gathered, problems revealed and the workload of the protocol. As blind participants are the most common disabled user group to participate in evaluations of websites for their accessibility, research is needed to establish which protocol is better to use.

We conducted a study with blind and sighted participants, performing both CVP and RVP, to compare the two protocols in terms of effectiveness, efficiency and the effect the protocols have on the two participant groups.

2 Related Work

In user-based studies of websites, a number of users who represent the target audience perform a number of tasks on the target websites. The most basic user evaluation has users performing a task in order to measure the users' performance on it. In addition, users can perform tasks while performing a verbal protocol, which can offer insight into the users' thought processes, the problems they encountered and their problem solving strategies [15]. The verbal protocol derives from the work of Ericsson and Simon, and was originally used as a research method in cognitive psychology [7]. It was introduced into the usability field by Lewis [13]. The underlying concept of this approach is the passive role of the evaluator, as there is no interaction between the evaluator and the participants while they perform the verbal protocol, except to remind them to think out loud if they become silent. Even the verbal protocol is based on this approach, some practitioners and researchers do not maintain the passive role of the evaluator [1, 16, 23].

Boren and Ramey [1] observed the verbal protocol methods used in two companies. Their results demonstrated that evaluators did not instruct participants comparably, as there were variations in instructions on how to think out loud. Moreover, most of the practitioners started immediately with the tasks, without giving participants any practice in the verbal protocol technique. Also, Boren and Ramey found inconsistencies among the prompts that evaluators used to remind participants when they fell silent for a period of time. Finally, most evaluators intervened in ways that did not reflect the approach of Ericsson and Simon. Based on these observations, Boren and Ramey [1] proposed a new approach, based on speech communication theory, in which evaluators have a more active role in comparison to the Ericsson and Simon approach.

Several studies have investigated if the change in approach affects participants' performance [9, 18]. In 2004, Krahmer and Ummelen [9] conducted a study with 10 participants, who performed a verbal protocol using either the original Ericson and Simon approach or the more active Boren and Ramey approach. They found that the approach did not affect the number of problems detected, however there was difference in participants' performance. Participants using the Boren and Ramey approach were more successful in completing tasks. Olmsted-Hawala et al. [18] compared the two approaches in a study with 80 participants. They found no differences in participants' performance between the two approaches.

As mentioned above, the verbal protocol may be performed concurrently or ret-rospectively. In CVP participants think out loud while doing the task, whereas in RVP participants perform the task first in silence and then think out loud while watching a video of themselves doing the task [6, 15, 21]. In the case of blind participants, they listen to the audio of themselves using the screen reader, which is the equivalent cue for them.

Several studies have been conducted to compare the differences found in the information gathered between the two methods [3, 10, 17]. Bowers and Snyder [3] conducted a study comparing the two protocols in a multiple window task. Their results revealed that during CVP more procedural information was collected, whereas during RVP more design changes and explanations were collected. Ohnemus and Biers [17] found that in RVP participants produced more statements which were useful for designers than in CVP. Kuuesela and Paul [10] compared the two protocols in terms of effectiveness for revealing human cognitive processes. Their results showed that CVP provides more insight into decision making processes, whereas RVP provides more statements about the participants' final choice.

Studies have also been conducted to compare the effects of the two protocols on participants' performance. A number of studies found that there is no difference between the two protocols in terms of task performance [17, 25, 26]. However, there are also several studies that showed that verbalization could have an impact on par-ticipants performance: either improved [30] or worsened it [29].

Uncovering user problems is one of the most important features in conducting user-based evaluations. A number of studies compared the number of problems revealed between the two protocols and most of them have demonstrated that the two protocols revealed a comparable set of problems [25–28]. However, these studies have some limitations, as only one website was used in each one of the studies. More extended research needs to be conducted to compare the two protocols in terms of the number of user problems revealed.

Some user-based evaluation studies are undertaken with disabled people to identify accessibility problems. The most frequent disabled groups involved are blind users. Studies that have included blind participants have almost exclusively had them perform CVP [8, 12, 19, 20, 22]. While it seems the standard protocol to use, it is a method that adds additional workload to the users in vocalizing their thoughts about their actions and the problems they encounter while trying to undertake a task. For blind users in particular, it is likely that the workload of the task is already high when they are working with a screen reader due to the need to remember several different modes, shortcut keys and settings. As their workload is likely to be higher than that of sighted participants, it is possible that RVP is more appropriate for blind participants and that this protocol will yield better results. No research could be found with comparing the verbal methods with any disabled user group.

Chandrashekar et al. [4] conducted a user-based evaluation study with six visually impaired participants, evaluating a website using CVP. They noted that blind partici-pants did not respond when they were prompted using defined time intervals. More-over, they stated that it is not feasible to have blind participants think aloud concurrently, as they use the screen reader to read the text on the page. Some partic-ipants were not willing to stop the screen reader in order to think out loud, as it interrupted the flow of the task. Also, they noted that the participants did not offer many comments, even though the researcher prompted them. Our experience of conducting many evaluations with blind participants is that they are quite happy to mute the screen reader when they are think out loud; even if they fail to remember to do this, it is usually possible to understand both what the participant is saying and the screen reader output. However, it may well be the case that this interrupts the flow of the task more than it would for sighted participants.

Even though some variations of verbal protocols for blind participants have been proposed [2, 24], they have not being used by other researchers. Further research needs to be conducted to compare the two verbal protocols, with both blind and sighted participants.

In this paper, a user-based study with blind and sighted participants comparing the two protocols, CVP and RVP, is presented. This study addressed a number of research questions, which can be grouped into three areas:

Effectiveness of CVP versus RVP:

- Does one protocol identify more distinct problems than the other?
- Do blind and sighted participants identify the same number of problems with each protocol?
- Does one protocol identify more severe problems than the other?
- Do the two protocols identify the same problems?

Efficiency of CVP versus RVP:

- Does one protocol identify problems more rapidly?

Effect of CVP and RVP on blind and sighted participants:

- Does one protocol demand greater workload for participants, either blind or sighted?
- Does one protocol make participants more self-conscious than the other?
- Do participants prefer one method in comparison to the other?

3   Method

3.1   Design

This study was a task-based user evaluation with blind and sighted participants using two different verbal protocols, CVP and RVP. A mixed design was used with user group as the between-participant independent variable with two levels (blind or sighted participants) and the within-participant independent variable with two levels (CVP and RVP).

Participants evaluated two websites with each protocol. In addition to talking the researcher through about what they were thinking, each time a participant encountered a problem, they were asked to rate its severity on a scale from 1 (cosmetic) to 4 (catastrophic). Problems were considered everything that participant felt that was a problem, whether it was caused by the website, the browser or the screen reader. After each session, participants were asked to complete the NASA TLX, a subjective workload questionnaire [14], as well as a questionnaire about their experience with the methods they had used.

3.2 Participants

Sixteen participants took part in the study, eight blind screen reader users and eight sighted users. Six of the blind participants were men and two were women. Ages ranged from 23 to 64 years (median = 43 years). Three of the participants were congenitally blind while the remaining five lost their sight between the ages of 26 and 49.

Sighted participants were selected to achieve as close a matched sample as possible with the blind participants on gender, age, operating system used, web experience and web expertise. Thus, six of the sighted participants were men and two were women. Ages ranged from 22 to 55 years (median = 40 years).

Participants rated their experience and expertise on the web using a five-point Likert items (1 = Very low to 5 = Very Good). The average rating for web experience for blind participants was 4, whereas for sighted participants was 4.5. On web expertise, the average rating of blind participants was 3.8, for sighted participants it was 3.6.

All blind participants used screen readers to access computers and the web for home and work. Five used JAWS (running on the Windows OS) and three used VoiceOver (running on Mac OSX). The JAWS version varied from JAWS 12.0 to JAWS 15.0 (the latter being the latest version of JAWS when the study was conducted). Participants who used VoiceOver used the latest version on the Mac OS Mavericks operating system (the latest version of Mac OS when the study was conducted). Blind participants were asked to rate their experience and expertise of using screen readers on a five-point Likert item (1 = "Very Low" to 5 = "Very Good"). The average rating for experience and expertise using screen readers was 4 and 3.9, respectively.

Six participants used Mac OSX (three blind and three sighted) and 10 participants used Windows (five blind and five sighted). The majority of the blind participants who used Windows mentioned Internet Explorer as their primary browser and all of the participants who used Mac OSX reported using Safari as their primary browser. Of the sighted participants, the ones who used Windows mentioned Chrome as their primary browser and one of them mentioned Internet Explorer. Of the ones using Mac OSX, one of them mentioned Chrome, whereas the other two mentioned Safari as their primary browser.

3.3 Equipment and Materials

For participants who use the Windows OS, the study was conducted using a desktop computer running Windows 8 with speakers, keyboard and a 2-button mouse with scroll wheel. For participants who use the Mac OSX, the study was conducted using a MacBook Pro laptop running the Mavericks Operating System, with speakers, and 2-button mouse with scroll wheel. In addition, blind participants used the version of

JAWS they were most familiar with or used the VoiceOver version that comes with Mavericks OS.

The sessions were recorded using Morae 3.1 on Windows or ScreenFlow 4.0.3 on Mac OSX. These recordings included audio, for analyzing the verbal protocols, screen activity for understanding the users' actions, and participants' facial expressions.

After each session participants completed the NASA TLX, a subjective workload questionnaire [14]. NASA TLX measures the overall effort or workload of the task, but also six different measurements of mental demand, physical demand, temporal demand, effort, frustration and performance of the participant.

At the end of the CVP session participants completed a questionnaire about the method using 5-point Likert items:

- Protocol interrupt (Q1): To what extent did thinking aloud during the task interrupt the flow of the task?
- Rating interrupt (Q2): To what extent did having to rate the problems for severity during the task interrupt the flow of the task?
- Protocol concentration (Q3): To what extent did thinking aloud during the task affect your concentration during the task?
- Rating concentration (Q4): To what extent did having to rate the problems for severity during the task affect your concentration during the task?
- Protocol real life (Q5): To what extent do you feel that thinking aloud during the task changed the way you did the tasks in comparison on how you might do it in real life?
- Protocol tiring (Q6): How tiring was it to do think aloud during the task?

Participants answered Q1 – Q5 using a scale: 1 = "Not at all" to 5 = "Very much", and Q6 using a scale: 1 = "Not at all tiring" to 5 = "Very tiring".

At the end of both verbal protocols participants were asked to complete the following question:

- To what extent did thinking aloud during the task/replay of the task made you self-conscious about what you were doing?

Participants answered this question using a scale: 1 = "Not at all" to 5 = "Very much".

Finally at the end of the session, participants were asked to select which one of the two verbal protocols they preferred conducting and to explain why they chose that preference.

3.4   Websites and Tasks

Four websites from different domains were used: a government website (www.gov.uk), a real estate website (www.rightmove.co.uk), an ecommerce website (www.boots.com) and a news website (www.channel4.com).

The tasks used were:

- Gov.uk: Find how much it is going to cost to arrange a meeting to apply for a National Insurance number from your mobile phone number.

- Rightmove: Find a house to rent with a minimum of two bedrooms and a rent of no more than £1200 per month, near to a secondary school (a postcode was provided).
- Boots: Find the cheapest, five-star rated car seat for a two-year old child who weights 24 kg.
- Channel4: Find which movie will be on Film4 at 9 pm the day after tomorrow.

The tasks that were used investigate different design aspects of the websites, such as information architecture, navigation, content, headings, links, images, forms and tables. Tasks were undertaken by the first author using JAWS 15.0 and VoiceOver, to check that it was possible for screen reader users to be able to complete the tasks.

3.5 Procedure

The study took place in the Interaction Laboratory at the Department of Computer Science of the University of York and at the National Council For the Blind of Ireland (NCBI) in Dublin. Participants were first briefed about the study and were asked to sign an informed consent form. In order to avoid any conflicts between the technology and participants' preferences, participants were asked which browser they would like to use. Blind participants were also asked which screen reader they preferred and which version. They were also given the option to adjust the computer display, sound and related software to their preferences in order to match to their usual setup.

The researcher gave a demonstration on how to perform the verbal protocol the participant was about to conduct. Participants tried the protocol out using a practice website not analysed in the study.

When participants were comfortable doing the appropriate verbal protocol, they were asked to perform each task. Depending on which protocol participants were using, they performed CVP or RVP. The verbal protocol approach that was used was based on the Boren and Ramey [1] approach. During the CVP condition they thought out loud as they performed the tasks. When participants were quiet for an extended period of time, they were prompted with "What are you thinking about?" to remind them to vocalize their thoughts. No predetermined time intervals were used to remind blind participants, as there were occasions when blind participants were silent for a long time because they were clearly listening to the text from the website using the screen reader. Thus, the use of reminding prompts relied on researcher's discretion. When participants encountered a problem, however minor, the researcher asked them to describe the problem and rate its severity using a four-point scale. The rating scale is based on Nielsen's severity ratings for usability [15]. However the description of the problem was adapted to a user-centred description, as follows:

- Cosmetic problem (1): This problem on the website is making it slightly difficult to complete my task
- Minor problem (2): This problem on the website is making it difficult to complete my task
- Major problem (3): This problem on the website is making it very difficult to complete my task
- Catastrophic problem (4): This problem on the website makes my task impossible to complete

During the RVP condition participants performed the task in silence, then they reviewed the task as the video (or for the blind participants, the audio) of the task was played back. Participants controlled the video/audio using the spacebar button of the computer to pause and resume the flow, in order to think out loud. Similar prompting and problem severity rating procedures were used in the RVP conditions as in the CVP.

This procedure was repeated for each website. After doing two websites with one protocol participants were asked to complete the NASA TLX and the questionnaire about the method they used. The procedure was then repeated for the second verbal protocol.

After completing both protocols, participants were asked to choose which one of the two protocols they preferred and to explain why, as well as to complete a demographic questionnaire. Finally, participants were debriefed about the study and the researcher answered their questions.

3.6 Data Analysis

The video recordings of each participant were reviewed, in order to code the problems and perform a problem matching technique. In the first phase of analysis, the problems identified by the users were structured using a variation of the model of Lavery et al. [11], in which the problems are analysed in relation to four components: cause, breakdown, outcome and design change. For this study, the design change component was not used. The second phase of analysis involved identifying distinct problems. Problem instances checked if there were distinct problems, that is a problem that may have been encountered by more than one participant or by the same participant on more than one occasion on the same website in the same context.

In order to check the validity of the analysis, inter-coder reliability was performed by another researcher of the Human Computer Interaction Research Group on a sample of the data. This yielded an agreement of more than 90 % on both phases of the analysis.

For this analysis we concentrate only on the number of problems and their severity rating, not the different causes or different types of the problems.

4 Results

A total of 260 instances of problems yielded 136 distinct problems were identified, across both protocols and both user groups. The average number of instances of problems was 8.13 per participant per website.

To investigate whether one protocol identified more problem instances than the other and whether blind or sighted participants identified more problem instances, a 2-way mixed ANOVA was conducted on the number of problem instances identified in each protocol condition and by blind and sighted participants. The analysis revealed a significant main effect for protocol ($F = 6.93$, $df = 1,14$, $p < 0.05$). The mean number of problem instances identified using CVP was 6.56 ($SD = 2.39$), whereas in RVP it was 9.69 ($SD = 4.27$). There was no significant main effect for user group ($F = 3.06$, df = 1,14, n.s.). Thus, there was no difference between blind and sighted participants in the number of problem instances identified. Finally, there was no interaction between protocol and user group (F = 0.00, df = 1,14, n.s.).

To investigate the severity of problem instances identified in the two protocols and by blind and sighted participants, a 2-way mixed ANOVA was conducted on the severity ratings of the problem instances. There was no main effect for protocol (F = 0.62, df = 1,14, n.s.) or user group (F = 0.00, df = 1,14, n.s.) and no interaction between protocol and user group (F = 0.09, df = 1,14, n.s.).

To investigate whether the two protocols identified the same distinct problems and what percentage of problems was identified by each protocol, the distribution of distinct problems identified by each method and by both methods was calculated for blind and sighted participants separately. Figure 1 shows that for all participants 27 % of the distinct problems were found by both CVP and RVP, with a slightly lower figure for sighted participants (23 %) than for blind participants (31 %). In total, RVP identified around 76 % of the distinct problems, whereas CVP only identified 51 % of the distinct problems.

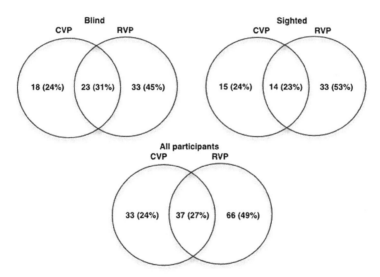

Fig. 1. Numbers and percentages of distinct problems identified for each protocol for the two user groups and for all participants across the four websites

The severity ratings of the problems identified by one protocol only and by both protocols were also investigated. The mean severity ratings are shown in Fig. 2, note that the mean severity ratings for all participants are the means for each user group weighted by the number of problems found by each user group. To investigate whether the problems by blind and sighted participants were rated more severely by one of the two protocols, the severity ratings of the problems that were found by both protocols were analysed. For blind participants, 23 problems were found by both protocols. The mean severity of these problems when found using CVP was 2.43 (SD = 0.98), whereas when found using RVP it was 2.12 (SD = 0.65). A paired sample t-test showed that there was no significance difference between these ratings from the two protocols (t = 1.81, df = 22, n.s.). For sighted participants, 14 distinct problems were found by both protocols. The mean severity of these problems when found using CVP was 2.33 (SD = 0.93), whereas when found using RVP it was 2.40 (SD = 0.55). Again, a paired sample t-test showed that there was no significance difference between the ratings from the two protocols (t = -0.23, df = 13, n.s).

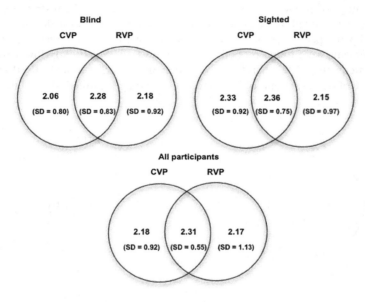

Fig. 2. Severity ratings of distinct problems identified for each protocol for the two user groups and for all participants across the four websites

To investigate the efficiency of the two protocols an analysis of the number of distinct problems identified per hour of evaluation time was conducted. A 2-way mixed ANOVA revealed that there was no main effect for protocol (F = 1.62, df = 1,14, n.s.). However, there was a main effect for user group (F = 30.17, df = 1,14, p < 0.001). The average number of distinct problems identified per hour for blind participants was 9.59 (SD = 4.36), whereas for sighted participants the average was 28.47 (SD = 9.96). Finally, there was no interaction between protocol and user group (F = 0.66, df = 1,14, n.s.).

To investigate the workload of undertaking the protocols for blind and sighted participants, an analysis of the NASA TLX scores was conducted. Table 1 shows the mean scores for each of the NASA TLX subscales and the overall mean score. A 3-way ANOVA (protocol x user group x NASA TLX subscale) revealed a significant main effect for protocol (F = 4.63, df = 1,14, p < 0.05). The overall mean NASA TLX score for CVP was 22.17 (SD = 13.76), whereas for RVP it was 22.77 (SD = 15.74). There was no significant main effect for the NASA TLX subscale ($F = 3.20$, df = 1,14, n.s.) and user group ($F = 2.28$, df = 1,14, n.s.). Finally, there were no significant interactions between protocol, user group and NASA TLX subscales. To investigate whether there were any significant differences on any of the individual NASA TLX subscales between CVP and RVP, post hoc paired t-tests were conducted between each of the six pairs, but this failed to show any significance differences.

Table 1. Means on NASA TLX subscales for CVP and RVP

NASA TLX sub-scale	CVP Mean/SD	RVP Mean/SD
Mental Demand	40.50 (SD = 18.18)	40.44 (SD = 15.08)
Physical Demand	2.38 (SD = 5.44)	5.25 (SD = 10.68)
Temporal Demand	16.50 (SD = 12.25)	18.25 (SD = 20.13)
Performance	15.50 (SD = 8.83)	19.31 (SD = 16.12)
Effort	33.94 (SD = 18.29)	45.00 (SD = 20.43)
Frustration	24.19 (SD = 26.63)	38.38 (SD = 33.21)
Mean:	22.17 (SD = 13.76)	27.77 (SD = 15.74)

To investigate participants' attitudes towards the two protocols, an analysis of the ratings on the six questions answered after completing CVP was conducted. A 2-way ANOVA revealed that there was no main effect for question ($F = 1.38$, df = 1,14, n.s.). There was a trend towards a significant difference for user group ($F = 3.19$, df = 1,14, $p = 0.09$). The average rating for questions asked about CVP from blind participants was 1.92 (SD = 0.96), whereas for sighted participants it was 2.46 (SD = 0.94), meaning sighted participants found CVP more disruptive than sighted participants. Finally, there was no interaction between questions and user group ($F = 0.97$, df = 1,14, n.s.).

Looking more specifically at the differences between the two user groups on the six questions (see the means in Tables 2 and 3), sighted participants found rating the severity of problems interrupted the flow of the task more than blind participants (Sighted mean: 3.0; Blind mean: 1.50) and also that it interrupted their concentration more (Sighted mean: 3.0; Blind mean: 2.00).

One-sample t-tests were conducted for each of the six questions for blind and sighted participants separately to investigate whether participants ratings were significantly above the "not at all" point and significant different from the midpoint of the scale ("moderately"). The one-sample t-tests that were compared with value 1 were one tailed, whereas the other one-sample t-tests were two tailed.

Table 2 shows the results of the one-sample t-tests for blind participants. It shows that blind participants found thinking out loud interrupted the flow of the task (Q1) and their concentration (Q3) significantly more than "not at all", but significantly less than "moderately". They found that rating problems for their severity interrupted their concentration significantly more than "not at all" but significantly less than "moderately" (Q4). Blind participants also found that performing the CVP was significantly different than the way they might do the tasks in real life (Q5). Further, they found that performing the CVP was significantly more tiring (Q6) than not performing it at all.

Table 2. One-sample t-tests for blind participants' questions about CVP

Question	Mean/SD	Test value = 1 df = 7 in all cases	Test value = 3 df = 7 in all cases
Protocol interrupt (Q1)	2.13 (SD = 0.64)	t = 4.97 p < 0.001	t = -3.86 p < 0.01
Rating interrupt (Q2)	1.50 (SD = 0.76)	t = 1.87 n.s.	t = -5.61 p < 0.01
Protocol concentration (Q3)	2.00 (SD = 1.07)	t = 2.65 p < 0.05	t = -2.65 p < 0.05
Rating concentration (Q4)	2.00 (SD = 0.93)	t = 3.06 p < 0.01	t = -3.06 p < 0.05
Protocol real life (Q5)	2.13 (SD = 1.64)	t = 1.94 p < 0.05	t = -1.51 n.s.
Protocol tiring (Q6)	1.75 (SD = 0.71)	t = 3.00 p < 0.01	t = -5.00 p < 0.01

Table 3 shows the results from the same one-sample t-tests for the sighted participants. It shows that sighted participants found that thinking aloud (Q1, Q3) and rating the problems for their severity (Q2, Q4) significantly interrupted the flow of the task and their concentration more than "not at all". They also found that performing CVP changed the way they perform the tasks compared with real life (Q5) and that it was significantly more tiring (Q6) than not performing it at all. In comparison to the moderate midpoint, the results showed that sighted participants found that thinking aloud interrupted the flow of the task (Q1) and their concentration (Q3), although the interruption was significantly less than the midpoint of the scale. Also they found performing CVP to be significantly less tiring (Q6) than the midpoint of the scale.

Table 3. One-sample t-tests for sighted participants' questions about CVP

Question	Mean/SD	Test value = 1 df = 7 in all cases	Test value = 3 df = 7 in all cases
Protocol interrupt (Q1)	2.25 (SD = 0.89)	t = 3.99 p < 0.01	t = -2.39 p < 0.05
Rating interrupt (Q2)	3.00 (SD = 0.93)	t = 6.11 p < 0.001	t = 0.00 n.s.
Protocol concentration (Q3)	2.25 (SD = 0.89)	t = 3.99 p < 0.01	t = -2.39 p < 0.05
Rating concentration (Q4)	3.00 (SD = 0.93)	t = 6.11 p < 0.001	t = 0.00 n.s.
Protocol real life (Q5)	2.50 (SD = 1.31)	t = 3.24 p < 0.01	t = -1.08 n.s.
Protocol tiring (Q6)	1.75 (SD = 0.71)	t = 3.00 p < 0.01	t = -5.00 p < 0.01

Participants were asked to rate how much thinking aloud during the tasks (for CVP) or during the replay of the task (during RVP) made them self-conscious about what they were doing (on a scale from 1 = "Not at all" to 5 = "Very much"). A 2-way ANOVA revealed that there was no main effect for the protocol (F = 0.13, df = 1,14, n.s.) or for the user group (F = 0.09, df = 1,14, n.s.) and no interaction between protocol and user group (F = 2.02, df = 1,14, n.s.).

One-sample t-tests were also conducted for the self-conscious question comparing the participants' ratings for each protocol with a value of 1, (not making them self-conscious at all) and the midpoint value of 3 (making them moderately self-conscious). Table 4 shows the results from these one-sample t-tests. Blind participants found both protocols made them significantly more self-conscious about what they were doing than not doing them at all. However, when the results were compared with the midpoint value of 3, blind participants found that doing CVP made them significantly less self-conscious than the midpoint of the scale. Sighted participants found only that doing CVP made them significantly more self-conscious about what they were doing than not doing nothing at all.

Table 4. One sample t-test on ratings of self-consciousness of the two protocols, for blind and sighted participants

User group/ protocol	Mean/SD	Test value = 1 df = 7 in all cases	Test value = 3 df = 7 in all cases
Blind/CVP	1.87 (SD = 0.83)	t = 2.96, p < 0.05	t = -3.81, p < 0.01
Blind/RVP	2.25 (SD = 1.04)	t = 3.42, p < 0.05	t = -2.05, n.s.
Sighted/CVP	2.50 (SD = 1.07)	t = 3.97, p < 0.05	t = -1.32, n.s.
Sighted/RVP	1.88 (SD = 1.36)	t = 1.83, n.s.	t = -2.35, n.s.

Finally participants selected which of the two protocols they preferred undertaking. Five out of eight sighted participants preferred CVP and three preferred RVP, whereas of the eight blind participants four preferred CVP and four preferred RVP. A chi-square test showed that there was no difference between user groups in preference for the protocols and no difference overall in preference for one protocol over the other ($X^2 = 0.25$, df = 1, n.s.).

5 Discussion

This study investigated the use of two verbal protocols for conducting evaluations in terms of effectiveness, efficiency and the effects they had on blind and sighted participants.

In terms of effectiveness, the results indicate that RVP is more effective than CVP. RVP identified more distinct problems than CVP for both blind and sighted participants. In addition, there was no difference in the severity ratings of the distinct problems identified between the two protocols. Comparing the two protocols in terms of whether they identify the same problems, we found that only 27 % of the distinct problems were identified by both protocols. Van den Haak et al. [25–28] also compared overlap between the two protocols in their studies. The overlap in most of the studies

[25–27] was similar with the overlap reported in the study here, except for one study [28]. Unfortunately, van den Haak et al. did not specifically report the overlap between CVP and RVP, as they included other protocols in their studies. However, found that the overlap between protocols which included CVP and RVP ranged from 25 % to 39 %. In addition, in this study RVP revealed 76 % of the total number of distinct problems, whereas CVP revealed only 51 % of the total number of distinct problems, with very similar figures for both blind and sighted participants. Finally, there was no difference between the severity ratings of the distinct problems found by both protocols from either user group and the severity of the problems that RVP failed to uncover was relatively low.

Although CVP is the more commonly used protocol [8, 12, 19, 20, 22], in this study CVP only identified approximately half of the distinct problems, whereas RVP identified three quarters. This contradicts the results of previous studies conducted by van den Haak et al. [25–28], that compared the two verbal protocols with sighted participants and found that they were comparable in terms of effectiveness. One possible explanation as to why the results are different lies in what van den Haak et al. identify as a user problem. In their studies, van den Haak et al. relied on a combination of user identified problems (i.e. problems that users verbalized themselves as problems) and problems identified by experts from reviewing the videos after the evaluation with the participants. In this study we were more conservative in our definition of user problems, in that we only considered those that were verbalized by participants.

In terms of efficiency, there was no difference between the two protocols. However, there was a significant difference in efficiency between the two user groups. Sighted participants identified nearly three times the number of distinct problems per hour compared with blind participants. This is not surprising as blind users interact with websites differently from sighted users and typically take longer to complete tasks. In this study, the blind participants typically took three times as long to complete tasks as the sighted participants, results very much in line with results from the Disability Rights Commission investigation of web accessibility [5], and also in line with the difference in efficiency with sighted participants.

In terms of the effects of the protocols on participants, the NASA TLX showed that RVP demanded more workload than CVP for both blind and sighted participants. However were a number of differences between blind and sighted participants on their perceptions of the two protocols, with sighted participants finding the rating of the severity of problems more disruptive than blind participants. However, comparing the ratings of the blind and sighted participants separately against "not at all" disruptive and "moderately" disruptive points revealed that both groups did find that CVP interrupted the flow of the task and concentration somewhat.

Comments from blind participants on this disruption included:

"when I think aloud I may miss what JAWS is talking to me and I may forget what I was doing and where I was"

"when I was trying to find things I had to think aloud and interrupted my concentration … it is difficult and sometimes frustrating"

"I was not listening 100 % on JAWS … there is a lot of processing information I had to use a lot of senses"

"I was not listening 100 % on JAWS ... there is a lot of processing information I had to use a lot of senses"

These comments highlight how blind participants found thinking aloud interrupted their concentration and may cause them miss output from the screen reader. It was difficult for them to think aloud while they were trying to process the output of the screen reader and perform the task at the same time.

Comments from sighted participants on the disruption included:

"... trying to think aloud did interrupt the flow of the task"
"...by verbalizing my thoughts through process I assumed I was missing something"

These comments highlight how sighted participants found that thinking aloud interrupted the flow of the task and their concentration.

The two protocols are comparable in terms of how self-conscious the participants were about what they were doing. There was no difference between user groups in preference for the protocols. Participants were also asked to explain their choice. Comments from participants who preferred RVP included:

"I found [RVP] more easy to follow during the replay of the task"
"it was easier to do the tasks [in RVP] in silence you were able to concentrate more on what you were doing ... RVP was easier because it was easier to listen to VoiceOver"
"thinking aloud during the task was hard ... forgetting what I was doing ... it was a distraction ... RVP was easier but demanded more time"

Comments from participants who preferred CVP included:

"It was my normal way ... I talk to the screen regularly"
"because it's quicker"
"it's in real time ... beneficial at the time"

The comments show that some participants found it easier to perform RVP, as it did not interrupt them, especially blind participants who had to process the output of the screen reader in addition to performing the protocol. However, other participants preferred CVP because it was quicker compared to RVP.

6   Conclusions

This study compared two verbal protocols, CVP and RVP, with blind and sighted participants. The two protocols were compared in terms of effectiveness, efficiency and the effect they have on participants. The study provides insight in terms of which verbal protocol is appropriate for use in studies with both blind and sighted participants.

The key results are that RVP outperforms CVP in terms of effectiveness but is no more efficient than CVP. RVP identifies more distinct problems and problem instances than CVP for both blind and sighted participants. Also, both of the protocols are comparable in terms of identifying more severe problems. Further, the study demonstrated that there was quite a low overlap in the problems between the two protocols identified for both blind and sighted participants. In addition, RVP identified three-quarters of the total number of distinct problems, whereas CVP only identified half of the distinct problems. In terms of efficiency, the protocols are comparable.

Even though RVP created a significantly higher workload for participants and CVP was perceived as being somewhat disruptive of the flow of the task, there was no clear preference amongst participants for one protocol over the other, so these did not strongly differentiate between the protocols.

Our future research will examine whether there is difference into the type of problems that the two protocols reveal. Also, an investigation whether there is difference into the problems that the two user groups reveal will be conducted.

Acknowledgements. We thank the National Council for the Blind of Ireland for their assistance in running this study, and all the participants for their time. Andreas Savva thanks the Engineering and Physical Science Research Council of the UK and the Cyprus State Scholarship Foundation for his PhD funding.

Research Data Access. Researchers wishing to access the data used in this study should visit the following URL for more information:

http://www.cs.york.ac.uk/hci/as1517/

References

1. Boren, T., Ramey, J.: Thinking aloud: reconciling theory and practice. IEEE Trans. Prof. Commun. **43**, 261–278 (2000)
2. Borsci, S., Federici, S.: The partial concurrent thinking aloud: a new usability evaluation technique for blind users. Assistive technology from adapted equipment to inclusive environments—AAATE, vol. 25, pp. 421–425 (2009)
3. Bowers, V.A., Snyder, H.L.: Concurrent versus retrospective verbal protocol verbal for comparing window usability. In: Human Factors and Ergonomics Society Annual Meeting, pp. 1270–1274 (1990)
4. Chandrashekar, S., Stockman, T., Fels, D., Benedyk, R.: Using think aloud protocol with blind users: a case for inclusive usability evaluation methods. In: 8th international ACM SIGACCESS Conference on Computers and Accessibility, pp. 251–252. ACM, New York (2006)
5. Disability Rights Commission.: The Web: Access and inclusion for disabled people. The Stationery Office, London (2004)
6. Dumas, J.F., Redish, J.C.: A practical Guide to Usability Testing. Greenwood Publishing Group Inc., Westpost, CT, USA (1993)
7. Ericsson, K.A., Simon, H.A.: Protocol Analysis. MIT-press, Cambridge (1984)
8. Harrison, C., Petrie, H.: Severity of usability and accessibility problems in eCommerce and eGovernment websites. In: BryanKinns, N., Blandfor, A., Curzon, P., Nigay, L. (Eds.), People and Computers XX - Engage. pp. 255–262, Godalming: Springer-Verlag London Ltd (2007)
9. Krahmer, E., Ummelen, N.: Thinking about thinking aloud: a comparison of two verbal protocols for usability testing. IEEE Trans. Prof. Commun. **47**, 105–117 (2004)
10. Kuusela, H., Paul, P.: A comparison of concurrent and retrospective verbal protocol analysis. Am. J. Psychol. **113**(3), 387–404 (2000)

11. Lavery, D., Cockton, G., Atkinson, M.P.: Comparison of evaluation methods using structured usability problem reports. Behav. Inf. Technol. **16**, 246–266 (1997)
12. Lazar, J., Olalere, A., Wentz, B.: Investigating the accessibility and usability of job application web sites for blind users. J. Usability Stud. **7**, 68–87 (2012)
13. Lewis: Using the Thinking Aloud Method in Cognitive Interface Design, Technical report. IBM Research Center (1982)
14. NASA TLX: Task Load Index, http://humansystems.arc.nasa.gov/groups/tlx/
15. Nielsen, J.: Usability Engineering. Elsevier (1994)
16. Nørgaard, M., Hornbæk, K.: What do usability evaluators do in practice?: an explorative study of think-aloud testing. In: 6th Design Interactive systems conference, pp. 209–218, ACM, New York (2006)
17. Ohnemus, K.R., Biers, D.W.: Retrospective versus concurrent thinking-out-loud in usability testing. In: Human Factors and Ergonomics Society Annual Meeting, pp. 1127–1131 (1993)
18. Olmsted-Hawala, E.L., Murphy, E.D., Hawala, S., Ashenfelter, K.T.: Think-aloud protocols: a comparison of three think-aloud protocols for use in testing data-dissemination web sites for usability. In: SIGCHI Conference on Human Factors in Computing Systems, pp. 2381–2390. ACM, New York (2010)
19. Petrie, H., Kheir, O.: The relationship between accessibility and usability of websites. In: SIGHI conference on Human Factors in Computing Systems, pp. 397–406. ACM, New York (2007)
20. Power, C., Freire, A., Petrie, H., Swallow, D.: Guidelines are only half the story: accessibility problems encountered by blind users on the web. In: SIGHI Conference on Human Factors in Computing Systems, pp. 433–442, ACM, New York (2012)
21. Rogers, Y., Sharp, H., Preece, J.: Interaction Design: Beyond Human-Computer Interaction. John Wiley & Sons, Hoboken (2011)
22. Rømen, D., Svanæs, D.: Validating WCAG versions 1.0 and 2.0 through usability testing with disabled users. Univ. Access Inf. Soc. **11**, 375–385 (2012)
23. Shi, Q: A field study of the relationship and communication between Chinese evaluators and users in thinking aloud usability tests. In: 5th Nordic conference on Human-Computer Interaction: Building Bridges, pp. 344–352. ACM, New York (2008)
24. Strain, P., Shaikh, A.D., Boardman, R.: Thinking but not seeing: think-aloud for non-sighted users. In: CHI 2007 Extended Abstracts on Human Factors in Computing Systems, pp. 1851–1856. ACM, New York (2007)
25. van den Haak, M.J., De Jong, M.D., Schellens, P.J.: Employing think-aloud protocols and constructive interaction to test the usability of online library catalogues: a methodological comparison. Gov. Inf. Q. **16**, 1153–1170 (2004)
26. van den Haak, M.J., De Jong, M.D., Schellens, P.J.: Evaluating municipal websites: A methodological comparison of three think-aloud variants. Gov. Inf. Q. **26**, 193–202 (2009)
27. van den Haak, M.J., De Jong, M.D., Schellens, P.J.: Evaluation of an informational web site: three variants of the think-aloud method compared. Tech. Commun. **54**, 58–71 (2007)
28. van den Haak, M.J., De Jong, M.D., Schellens, P.J.: Retrospective vs concurrent think-aloud protocols: testing the usability of an online library catalogue. Behav. Inf. Technol. **22**, 339–351 (2003)
29. van den Haak, M.J., De Jong, M.D.: Exploring two methods of usability testing: concurrent versus retrospective think-aloud protocols. In: IEEE International Professional Communication Conference. pp. 285–287 (2003)
30. Wright, R.B., Converse, S.A.: Method bias and concurrent verbal protocol in software usability testing. In: Human Factors and Ergonomics Society Annual Meeting, pp. 1220–1224 (1992)

Exploring Map Orientation with Interactive Audio-Tactile Maps

Alistair D.N. Edwards$^{(\boxtimes)}$, Nazatul Naquiah Abd Hamid,
and Helen Petrie

Department of Computer Science, University of York, York YO10 5GH, UK
{alistair.edwards,nhah501,helen.petrie}@york.ac.uk

Abstract. Multi-modal interactive maps can provide a useful aid to navigation for blind people. We have been experimenting with such maps that present information in a tactile and auditory (speech) form, but with the novel feature that the map's orientation is tracked. This means that the map can be explored in a more ego-centric manner, as favoured by blind people. Results are encouraging, in that scores in an orientation task are better with the use of map rotation.

Keywords: Multi-modal maps · Blind people · Tactile · Speech · Rotation

1 Introduction

When travelling to an unfamiliar location people may prepare in a number of ways. Sighted people will often rely on their vision – supported by visual cues such as signs to navigate on arrival. They may also prepare in advance by consulting a map (increasingly this may be on-line). Maps designed for sighted users are overloaded with information, combining a range of visual encodings: geometrical, symbolic, textual, colour etc. The important point is that users can cope with this complexity because of the power of the visual channel. They can – literally – focus on the information that is relevant to their current task and ignore that which is not relevant.

Blind people can also benefit from the use of (non-visual) maps. Indeed, they may have more of a need to do so, since it is not possible for them to use vision to navigate in situ. In creating maps for blind users one encounters what is known as the 'bandwidth problem', which is to say that the non-visual senses simply do not have the same capacity to carry so much information that can be filtered as necessary. In this situation it is common to use as many of the non-visual senses together in the form of multimodal interaction, with the objective that the whole may be greater than the sum of the parts. Thus there has been developed the concept of the multimodal map (e.g. [1, 6, 10]). This paper presents the results of experiments with multimodal maps that combine haptic interaction with auditory output, but introducing the novel aspect of using the map's orientation as an additional interactive element.

The primary objective of the research is to find out whether blind people can be better prepared to navigate in unfamiliar environments, given this form of multimodal map. A secondary aspiration is to find out more about the kinds of internal representations such people use.

© IFIP International Federation for Information Processing 2015
J. Abascal et al. (Eds.): INTERACT 2015, Part I, LNCS 9296, pp. 72–79, 2015.
DOI: 10.1007/978-3-319-22701-6_6

2 Background

As argued above, maps can be very powerful tools. One role for (non-visual) maps is for planning. That is to say that before arriving at a new location the person may prepare, becoming familiar with the area by exploring a map of it. Increasingly it is the case that when in the location other technology (usually GPS-based) will be used to assist guidance, but there is still a role for the map to be used as a means of learning about the layout of the place in planning a visit.

It is relatively easy to manufacture tactile maps, using technology such as swell-paper [13], although designing such maps to be usable is quite difficult, given the limitations of the haptic senses. One approach to overcoming some of the limitations of tactile maps is to make them interactive and to provide other non-visual cues. Thus, a tactile map can be mounted on a touch-sensitive pad. This can track the location of the user's finger as well as haptic gestures that they may make, such as pressing on the map. Then appropriate auditory feedback can be provided, such as speech or non-speech sounds.

Previous audio-tactile maps systems (for example [1, 6, 10]) used tactile maps as an overlay where the systems were designed and used by the user to learn maps in a static orientation. A possible limitation of any conventional tactile map – that we have set out to explore – has to do with the style of interaction. As illustrated in Fig. 1, the user may be tracing a path in a forwards direction (Fig. 1.1 and 1.2). When they reach a corner where the path turns to the left (1.3) they keep the map in the same orientation and move their finger sideways (1.4).

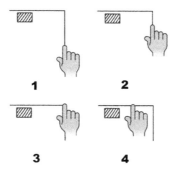

Fig. 1. The conventional, 'allocentric' approach to tactile map reading.

Of course, this does not correspond to the way that they would behave in the real world. There, on reaching such a corner, a person would turn to the left and continue walking forwards. This is the basis of our experiments. By being able to detect the orientation of the map, it is possible (as illustrated in Fig. 2) that when the map-user reaches the corner (2.3) they can then rotate the map and continue to trace in a forwards direction (2.4).

It seems likely that such a map will generate a more useful representation in the user's mind. For instance, the building represented by the grey rectangle in Figs. 1 and 2 will be to the left of the finger following the turn (2.4) – and will be to the user's left if they walk that way in the real world. However, there is evidence that this kind of approach is particularly appropriate for blind people because they tend to use an ego-centric spatial frame of reference as opposed to the external, allocentric one which sighted people tend to use [11].

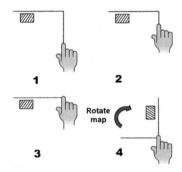

Fig. 2. Tracing a tactile map with rotation, a more 'ego-centric' approach.

The long-term aim of this work is to develop and test a fully-functional multimodal map system, incorporating tactile interaction with speech and non-speech audio output. However, the main focus of the experiments reported herein is the specific facility of map rotation. This builds on previous work on the role of map orientation for both sighted and blind people, as explained in the following section.

3   Experimental Precursors

Levine et al. [4] have carried out experiments on simple map use by sighted people. Rossano and Warren [7] extended this work to blind people. In their experiments blind people were presented with tactile maps and then asked to perform an orientation task in the real world. For instance, they might explore the map in Fig. 3 and then be given an instruction such as, 'Imagine that you are standing on point B of the path that I just showed you, with point A directly in front of you—indicate the direction you need to go to get to point C.'

The maps were presented to the participants in one of three orientations:

- *aligned* (i.e. for the example, in which the participant is to imagine being at point B facing A, the map would be in that orientation, as it is in Fig. 3).
- *contra-aligned* (that is Fig. 3 rotated through 180°)
- *mis-aligned* (aligned at 45°, 90° or 135°)

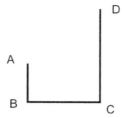

Fig. 3. A simple map, as used in this and other experiments

Rossano and Warren [7] found that blind participants were much more accurate in the aligned condition, achieving a correctness score of 85 %.

Giudice et al. [3] also carried out work based on these experiments. They found evidence to support a hypothesis that spatial images are stored in an amodal representation, in both sighted and blind people. Of interest in the context of this work, though, was the fact that their experiments included elements of rotation. However it is not possible to make any direct comparison between their results and ours. Pielot et al. [14] have also conducted experiments on auditory tangible maps with rotation. In their case they spatialized the audio feedback to match the orientation of a tangible avatar. In the experiments reported herein we did not spatialize the sounds, though we plan to do so in future developments.

4   Experimental Outline

Our experiment had a number of objectives:

1. Are blind participants more accurate in pointing to a landmark when they have used a rotatable audio-tactile map in comparison to a static audio-tactile map?
2. Does their performance on this task correlate with their sense of direction?
3. What is their subjective preference for the Static and Rotation conditions?

Further data was collected which might shed some light on the results. For instance, is it possible to identify why people are particularly good or bad at the task and can we find something about the cognitive representations that people use in the task? This paper reports on the investigation of objective 1. Further data was collected addressing 2 and 3 which will be reported in future publications.

5   Method

The method was based on that of Rossano and Warren. Tactile maps were produced, based on the guidelines in [4]. Alphabetical labels were provided through synthetic speech. That is to say, that if the participant pressed on the point B (Fig. 3), then they would hear the label 'B'. There were two conditions in the experiment: *Static*, in which it was not possible to rotate the map, and *Rotation*, in which it was possible to rotate it.

All participants experienced both conditions but the order of presentation was counter-balanced (i.e. 50% of the participants undertook the static condition followed by the rotation condition, and vice-versa).

Note that in the rotation condition participants were not obliged to use rotation. Whether they did or not was noted and their results analyzed accordingly. One suggestion was that in the rotation condition, most participants would rotate the map, corresponding to the aligned condition in Rosanno and Warren's experiments, so that we might expect similar results between the aligned and mis-aligned conditions.

5.1   Materials

Our experiments were based on a device that we have dubbed the *T4* (Fig. 4). This consists of a T3, Talking Tactile Tablet[1] mounted on a turntable. The T3 has a 38 cm × 30.5 cm surface on which a tactile overlay can be placed. It can detect a single point of pressure on the surface that it communicates to a computer via a (wireless) USB port. The turntable detects the angle or orientation.

Fig. 4. A participant exploring a map on the T4

5.2   Procedure

Each participant was briefed and gave consent for the experiment. They then verbally completed a pre-test questionnaire. The questionnaire was constructed in different sections to obtain information on their mobility experience, experience in using tactile maps, experience in using audio-tactile maps and demographics.

They were then introduced to the T4. They sat by the device and were able to explore a practice map. Then they were given the experimental map in one of four orientations. Then they were given the task (e.g. 'Imagine that you are standing on point B of the path, with point A directly in front of you. What is the direction to point C?') In the rotation condition they were then allowed to rotate the map as they wished.

When they felt they were ready they stood up and, guided by a handrail, walked to the centre of the room. They were given a beanbag in their hand, asked to point in the

---

[1] http://touchgraphics.com/.

required direction and to drop the beanbag to mark the direction. The position of the beanbag was recorded by an overhead camera.

Each participant would complete the test under the current condition (Static or Rotation) for the same map presented in each of five orientations. They would then complete them in the other orientation.

On completions of the tests, the participant was given a post-test interview to ascertain their preferences. Twelve blind or visually impaired people undertook the experiment. They were volunteers but received an Amazon voucher for £25 in compensation for their time.

6   Results

The distribution of the pointing accuracy measures was inspected for all conditions. The distribution was approximately normal with a mean accuracy error of 12.5° and a standard deviation of 40.6°. However, there were three outliers in which the pointing accuracy error was close to 180°, which suggested that the participants were making reflection errors, confusing a point in front of them with a point behind. The three instances were from three different participants, two in the Static condition and one in the Rotation condition, so there was no particular pattern to these errors. Including these measures in the analyses would have skewed the results substantially, so they were removed from the dataset. In order to use the rest of the data from the three participants, these measures were replaced by the mean pointing accuracy for either the Static or Rotation condition, depending on which the error occurred. This resulted in an overall distribution of pointing accuracy measures with a mean of 9.2° and a standard deviation of 32.2°.

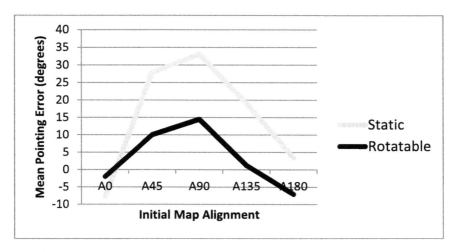

Fig. 5. Mean errors in the pointing task in the Static versus Rotation conditions.

In the Rotation condition participants were not required to rotate the map. In practice 3 participants did not always use rotation when they might have, in a total of 11 instances. In that case their data was treated with the Static data.

To investigate whether the use of a static or rotatable map affected the accuracy of pointing, a two way repeated measures analysis of variance was conducted, with Static vs Rotation as one independent variable and Initial Map Alignment as the other independent variable. There was a trend towards a significant effect for Static vs Rotatable ($F = 3.32$, df = 1,10, $p = 0.09$) and a significant effect for Initial Map Alignment ($F = 3.35$, df = 4,40, $p < 0.05$). There was no significant interaction between the two variables. Figure 5 shows that there was a substantially larger error in pointing accuracy with the Static Map condition for all alignments, apart from at Zero Alignment. There was also an increase in error for both Static and Rotation conditions as the alignment increased to 90°, which then decreased as the alignment increased further to 180°.

7   Discussion

Participants in the Rotation condition are more accurate in the pointing task than in the Static condition. However, the difference fails to reach significance at the 0.05 level. It is planned to continue the experiments with a larger numbers of participants to see whether a significant result will be achieved.

This experiment was based on those reported in [7]. Rossano and Warren did not allow rotation as such, but it was assumed that when in our experiments participants rotated the map into alignment, their results would be similar to those in Rossano and Warren's aligned condition. However, it is difficult to make any comparison because of the way Rossano and Warren treated their data. They classified responses as either correct or not, depending on whether the response was within ±30° of the target. A superficial examination does appear to show differences: participants in our experiment scored more highly in all conditions. This warrants further investigation.

8   Further Work

We also collected further data in this experiment, relating to participants' sense of direction, their ability to recreate the maps they used in tactile form and their subjective preferences. These have yet to be analyzed. Specifically, where participants have made errors, it may be possible to use their map reconstructions to identify the nature of the error, and thereby to see whether it is possible to promote less error-prone cognitive maps. Furthermore, more-reliable results will be obtained if we can run more participants.

It has also been mentioned that this is also only a small part of the development of the T4. In the long run we plan to develop it into a multimodal tool. We plan to experiment with the use of auditory environmental cues to help users in navigation tasks. Given that the results in these simple experiments on rotation are encouraging, we would experiment with spatialized sounds that are linked to the map orientation.

It is envisaged that a map of this form would be used in preparation for visiting a new, unfamiliar location. Clearly experiments to see whether the learning from such a map transfers to the real world would be called for.

9 Conclusions

We have experimented with a multimodal, non-visual map which has the novel facility that it can be rotated to match orientation in the real world. Our results (while not achieving statistical significance) suggest that errors in an orientation/pointing task are less when map rotation is used than in a static condition. This gives encouragement to further develop the system.

References

1. Brock, A., et al.: Usage of multimodal maps for blind people: why and how. In: ACM International Conference on Interactive Tabletops and Surfaces (2010)
2. Hamid, N.N.A., Edwards, A.D.N.: Facilitating route learning using interactive audio-tactile maps for blind and visually impaired people. In: Extended Abstracts CHI 2013, pp. 37–42. ACM Press (2013)
3. Giudice, N., Betty, M.R., Loomis, J.M.: Functional equivalence of spatial images from touch and vision: evidence from spatial updating in blind and sighted individuals. J. Exp. Psychol. Learn. Mem. Cogn. 37(3), 621–634 (2011)
4. Levine, M., Jankovic, I.N., et al.: Principles of spatial problem solving. J Environ. Psychol. Gen. 111, 157–175 (1982)
5. MacEachren, A.M.: Learning spatial information from maps: can orientation-specificity be overcome? Prof. Geogr. 44(4), 431–443 (1992)
6. Paladugu, D.A., Wang, Z., Li, B.: On presenting audio-tactile maps to visually impaired users for getting directions. In: Extended Abstracts CHI 2010, pp. 3955–3960. ACM (2010)
7. Rossano, M.J., Warren, D.H.: The importance of alignment in blind subjects' use of tactual maps. Perception 18(6), 805–816 (1989)
8. Rossano, M.J., Warren, D.H.: Misaligned maps lead to predictable errors. Perception 18, 215–229 (1989)
9. Shepard, R.N., Hurwitz, S.: Upward direction, mental rotation, and discrimination of left and right turns in maps. Cognition 18, 161–193 (1984)
10. Wang, W., Li, B., Hedgpeth, T., Haven, T. Instant tactile-audio map: enabling access to digital maps for people with visual impairment. In: ACM SIG ASSETS (2009)
11. Millar, S.: Understanding and Representing Space: Theory and Evidence from Studies with Blind and Sighted Children. Oxford University Press, New York (1994)
12. Halko, M.A., Connors, E.C., Sánchez, J., Merabet, L.B.: Real world navigation independence in the early blind correlates with differential brain activity associated with virtual navigation. Hum. Brain Mapp. 35, 2768–2778 (2014). doi:10.1002/hbm.2236
13. Eriksson, Y., Strucel, M.: A Guide to the Production of Tactile Graphics on Swellpaper. The Swedish Library of Talking Books and Braille, Stockholm (1995)
14. Pielot, M., Henze, N., Heuten, W., Boll, S.: Tangible user interface for the exploration of auditory city maps. In: O, I., Brewster, S. (eds.) HAID 2007. LNCS, vol. 4813, pp. 86–97. Springer, Heidelberg (2007)

Inclusive Production of Tactile Graphics

Jens Bornschein$^{(\boxtimes)}$, Denise Prescher, and Gerhard Weber

Technische Universität Dresden, Institut für Angewandte Informatik,
Nöthnitzer Straße 46, 01187 Dresden, Germany
{jens.bornschein,denise.prescher,
gerhard.weber}@tu-dresden.de

Abstract. In this article a collaborative workstation for creating audio-tactile graphics is presented. The system is based on a common open source office suite and supports a transcriber for tactile graphics with several tools. In addition the system allows a blind reviewer to get involved at every stage of the creation process. This is achieved through a refreshable two-dimensional tactile display. The blind participant can independently manipulate graphical objects and make annotations in parallel. As a result, a tandem team of a sighted graphic creator and a blind partner may create a tactile graphic with better quality.

Keywords: Tactile graphics · Blind users · Collaboration · Pin-matrix device

1 Introduction

While the visual world gets more connected and data gets more complex, visual presentation is an effective means to convey information. Problems arise if participants cannot access the presented information, in particular blind people. Non-visual access to graphics is often provided by a verbal description, which is not always a satisfying solution. To create an alternative textual description can be challenging for some graphics, for example maps, complex diagrams or images containing some kind of graphical notation. In addition, verbal descriptions can be incomplete or can contain wrong interpretations. This can change the meaning of an image or can lead to mis-understanding its intention. For this reason, a combination of a description and a transcribed tactile representation should be provided for important graphical data as it improves comprehension by blind people [1]. For some photographs or art it is hard to create even a suitable tactile counterpart, access to them remains to be limited.

Creating tactile graphics is also not an easy task, especially if the creator has only little experience. In a survey in German speaking countries, we found that only 5 % of the 78 blind and visually impaired participants generally prefer image descriptions over tactile graphics [2]. Conversely, most blind people wish to get more tactile graphics as they not only allow for an independent exploration, but also for a better spatial com-prehension of the content. However, a basic requirement for an effective reading is a sufficient quality of tactile graphics. In most institutions it is common to check some of their produced materials by visually impaired colleagues to ensure a good quality [2]. In the conventional production process it is necessary to produce a digitally mastered tactile graphic for every change again to show it to a blind reader. In contrast, we use a

© IFIP International Federation for Information Processing 2015
J. Abascal et al. (Eds.): INTERACT 2015, Part I, LNCS 9296, pp. 80–88, 2015.
DOI: 10.1007/978-3-319-22701-6_7

refreshable tactile pin-matrix device to include a blind user in early stages of the production process within a collaborative workstation.

2 Tactile Graphics

Tactile graphics allow readers to feel presented structures, graphic elements or Braille text, through their tactile perception. Several different production methods exist. They all differentiate in their ability of presenting tactile structures. Differing features are, for example, possible resolution, the ability of allowing different raise levels, stability, speed and costs for reproducibility. While microcapsule paper and matrix embossers can produce tactile graphics from digital data without big additional effort, reliefs and other production methods need some manual post-processing or long production times. In this paper we focus on digital production methods, such as normal printing and embossing. Tactile embossers allow resolutions form 10 dpi for Braille embossers up to 20 dpi with different height levels for matrix embossers. Microcapsule paper is able to present detailed tactile structures printed with a normal printer on a special paper that rises on dark areas while heated under a special lamp.

Instead of conventional static production media refreshable two-dimensional tactile displays can be used to interactively present tactile graphical and textual information. For instance, the BrailleDis 7200 [3] allows to show content on a 120×60 pins large display area as binary tactile image with a resolution of about 10 dpi. Because of its zooming and panning possibilities, theoretically, each type of graphic can be shown on the pin device. However, there are some limitations. For instance, it is hard to handle graphics that use colors or different height levels. Very fine-grained structures, rounded objects and non-orthogonal lines can also lead to problems in their recognizability on such low-resolution devices. Reducing the complexity is a main requirement for tactile graphics; therefore these kinds of structures should be avoided in any case.

2.1 Tools for Preparing Tactile Graphics

The creation of a tactile graphic is not the challenging part of a transcription process. Almost every source image can be directly transformed into a grayscale or binary image which can then be produced as tactile version, for example, on microcapsule paper or with a matrix-embosser. The main problem is the readability and recognition of objects. Structures and shapes often get lost due to the low resolution. Therefore, a transcriber needs to prepare the image with respect to simplification and readability.

Several drawing tools exist to support transcribers. They contain functions for filling objects with different tactile patterns or allow redrawing image parts in a way that they fit into the embossing matrix of the related embosser. Some of them also apply graphic filters for grayscale or binary transformation as well as for finding and high-lighting the outlines of objects (e.g. PictureBraille[1]). Creating Braille labels is another task for transcribers. The TGA system [4], for example, supports the translation of text

---

[1] http://www.pentronics.com.au/index_files/PictureBraille.htm.

in images by semi automatic OCR-mechanisms. However, it seems that mostly standard office or image processing software is used [2].

In contrast, suppliers for tactile graphic production hardware often deliver their own production software. For example, the audio-tactile graphic exploration system IVEO[2] comes with a touch-sensitive image frame and its own tactile graphic production software for creating scalable vector graphic (SVG) images with the feature to add a two-level description to graphic elements. Technically, SVG is utilized for annotating a title and description of tactile objects.

2.2   Tactile Graphics by Blind People

Drawing graphics without vision is difficult. Blind pupils learn to create drawings by different techniques. Most of them are based on handicraft techniques or combine tactile primitives to more complex structures [2]. Creating freehand drawings can be done by scratching tactile perceptible structures into special foils or wood plates. These are all analog methods and, therefore, hard to reproduce. The digital creation of a drawing by a blind user is more complex and with limited tactile feedback. Often Braille characters form drawings or command languages define graphical structures. All analog techniques have the disadvantage that an error correction is almost impossible for the creator. For the digital methods this is also very exhausting because it needs a lot of mental imagination.

2.3   Quality of Tactile Graphics

The dissemination of tactile graphics among blind people lacks behind their importance. Due to lack of training many blind users have difficulties in recognizing complex tactile graphics [5]. Reasons may be, for instance, the overloading of a graphic with too much information, the reduced distinctiveness among different objects as well as the limited preservation of orientation [2]. To minimize such problems some kind of quality management for tactile graphics is important.

There are several guidelines (see [6]), which should improve the quality of tactile materials. However, such guidelines are often complex and general, which complicates their practical application - especially for non-expert sighted persons who commonly produce tactile graphics [2]. We propose the inclusion of blind users into the creation process. Therefore, we have developed a collaborative workstation as described in the following section.

The main purpose of our system is to allow a simplified inclusion of blind users in the production process as well as to support inexperienced sighted users. Besides, the system can also be used for sketching difficult concepts with and for a blind user, for instance in learning or working scenarios. First user observations in a collaborative

[2] http://www.viewplus.com/products/software/hands-on-learning/.

graphic production scenario have shown that it is not effective to let the blind user follow the creation of a graphic from the beginning. It is more effective to include the blind user after a first draft of the graphic is produced. The blind reviewer can than check the graphic and make some annotations and changes if necessary. The sighted user can also ask for specific problems which can lead to further discussions and improvements of the resulting tactile graphic.

3 Collaborative Workstation for Tactile Graphics

Compared to cooperation, where each individual works separately on his own part, collaboration requires direct interaction and discussions among the participants [7]. For an efficient collaboration between a sighted and a blind user, the visual and the non-visual workspace have to remain consistent and have to be synchronized in a multimodal sense. The Tangram collaborative workstation not only has to allow for the creation and modification of tactile and visualized graphics by both users. It also has to support the communication between the partners by focusing on objects of interest jointly. Beyond basic graphics operations, the workstation also has to include functions for annotation and quality management. In the following, the general architecture of the Tangram workstation as well as the mechanisms for supporting the collaborative production of tactile graphics by sighted and blind users are presented.

3.1 Architecture of the Tangram Workstation

The Tangram workstation consists of two parallel I/O workspaces connected to one computer (see Fig. 1). The sighted user uses mouse and standard keyboard as input and a monitor screen for the visual output. The blind user on the other hand uses the dynamic pin device BrailleDis 7200 for tactile output and its 28 buttons as well as its touch-sensitive display area as input device for keying in commands, Braille text and gestural input [3]. In addition, auditory feedback is given, consisting of sound and text-to-speech output. With the exception of non-visual drawing, all basic tasks for

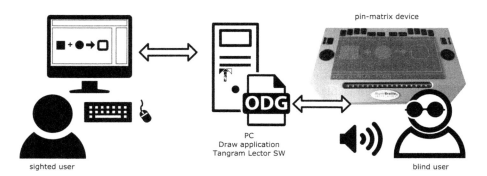

Fig. 1. Schematic representation of the Tangram workstation

transcription can be mapped to interactive operations at which the two partners do not hinder each other while working on the same document independently and in parallel.

As basic drawing system the open source office suites OpenOffice[3] and LibreOffice[4] can be used. These programs are free to use, even in a commercial context, and produce vector graphics which can be exported to several different document formats. Multiple tools have been added to implement the working process for creating audio-tactile graphics.

For the blind user a special screen reader has been implemented that allows access to the accessible interface of the office suite as well as to the document object structure [8]. This enables the blind user to manipulate the graphical and textual document elements. The presentation of the graphical content is realized by rendering a tactile screenshot of the working area window on the pin device. Thereto, a configurable filter is applied to the screenshot, converting lighter points to lowered pins and darker points to raised ones. The user can freely explore the tactile screenshot by zooming and panning operations. Additional information is added to the screenshot image, such as a dotted frame resembling the size and position of the sheet to draw on within the working area. The blind user can retrieve further information on document objects by pointing at them while pressing a button.

The blind users' input and output system is realized with our open-source framework BrailleIO [9]. This framework allows for a fast and easy implementation of a basic windowing system for two-dimensional tactile pin devices. Furthermore, the framework also allows the Tangram workstation software to be applied to other pin device types besides the BrailleDis 7200.

3.2   Supporting the Sighted User

Especially for sighted producers with little experiences, the provision of a specialized toolbar by the graphic editing software itself can reduce some of the deficits when designing tactile graphics on a visual screen. This can include the specification of predefined sets of filling patterns, line styles or elementary graphical primitives, such as arrows or tactile symbols. Moreover, an easier access to important properties of graphical objects, such as position, size and textual information (title and description), can also be helpful for enhancing the productivity of a sighted user. The implemented toolbar supports the following tasks (compare Fig. 2):

- position properties: edit x and y position of the selected object.
- size properties: specify width and height of the selected object.
- keep ratio toggle: enable and disable preservation ratio of width and height.
- unit selection: select measuring unit for presentation of position and size.
- line styles: select a tactile perceivable line style (solid, dotted and dashed) for the selected object.

---

[3] www.openoffice.org.

[4] www.libreoffice.org.

position   size   unit   line styles   pattern styles

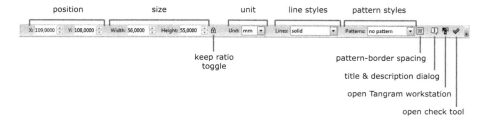

keep ratio
toggle

pattern-border spacing

title & description dialog

open Tangram workstation

open check tool

Fig. 2. Toolbar for supporting the sighted user in producing tactile graphics

- pattern styles: select a texture for filling the selected graphical object. We have tested the suitability and discriminability of the provided patterns for utilization with different tactile graphics technologies (microcapsule paper, matrix embossed printing and pin-matrix device) in an unpublished study with 12 blind users.
- pattern-border spacing: add or remove white space between the filling pattern and the border of the selected object to increase distinctiveness and outline perception.
- title and description dialog: open or hide a docking window for annotating title and description of graphical objects.
- open Tangram workstation: start the Tangram workstation for the blind reviewer. Besides, document properties are adapted, such as standard colors and font style.
- open check tool: open a dialog for reviewing tactile graphics based on our authoring guidelines.

3.3   Supporting the Blind User

The blind user manipulates graphic objects independently on the pin-matrix device by a rotating menu with five different editing modes. Input is realized by the buttons of the right cursor key pad of BrailleDis 7200 (see Fig. 3). If an element of the graphic is selected, the user can start it's editing by pressing the center key. Initially, the move mode is activated. By pressing one of the four direction buttons the element is moved into the chosen direction. The current editing mode can be changed by pressing the center key iteratively. In this way an element can be moved, scaled, rotated, and its texture and line style can be changed. The assignment of functions to the cursor key pad buttons is dependent on the current mode (see Fig. 3). Therefore, the user doesn't have to remember many button combinations. Furthermore, one hand may remain on the cursor key pad while the other hand can monitor the changes on the element in real time. Bi-manual operation has been found to be effective for most interaction tasks [10]. One drawback is the reduced efficiency due to the modal menu. Nevertheless, an informal discussion with four blind users showed that this is acceptable if there are not too many modes.

Besides the editing of the appearance of graphic objects, the blind user also can annotate the tactile graphic, for instance, by adding a title and description for each element. Thereto, he can open a dialog in the detail region of the pin-matrix device, where reading and editing of Braille content is performed. Either a text field for the title or for the description is shown. The user can switch between these two by using the up or down button of the right cursor key pad. For writing, the Braille input keys on the BrailleDis are used. Finally, the data have to be saved by calling the save menu, which is realized by pushing the center button of the right cursor key pad. Using the left or right button the user can choose between the following menu options: save, not save or cancel. All options are presented in Braille, where the current selected option is underlined and also is spoken out.

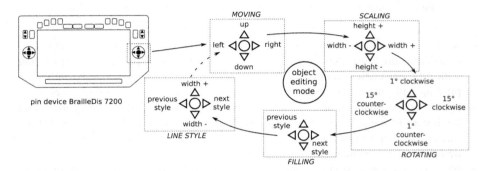

Fig. 3. Usage of the cursor keys within the five editing modes in the non-visual user interface

3.4   Collaboration

The blind user can edit the graphic elements independently from the sighted user, as mentioned above. Therefore, it is necessary to have two separate foci: the standard GUI focus, which will be called mouse focus in the following, and the pin device focus which refers to the DOM objects of the drawing document. The latter will be called Braille focus. To enable an effective collaboration, the two users have to be aware of these focus concepts.

Allowing the blind user to follow his sighted partner's activities, the selected GUI element can be highlighted on the pin device, and a follow mouse focus mode can be activated. In this mode, the element which is currently selected by the sighted user, is not only spoken by audio output, but also is signaled by a blinking pin frame and is shown in the center of the pin device. If the sighted user selects another element, the tactile output is refreshed automatically. In this way the blind user can easily track the mouse focus. If he wants to edit the element which has the mouse focus, he can set the Braille focus to that element and quit the follow mouse focus mode with a single button command. By this means, the sighted is able to show the blind user an element and ask him to do some improvements, for example.

On the other side, the blind user can also highlight the Braille focus for his sighted partner on the GUI to indicate the element he is currently editing. Therefore, a blinking overlay window is shown for some seconds above the corresponding element.

4 Conclusion and Outlook

A collaborative workstation for producing tactile graphics was implemented. This allows blind users to actively take part in the transcription process for tactile graphics from early stages. As they are the target user group of the materials created, this should increase the quality of the resulting images. First prototyping tests with four blind users showed that the editing functionalities on the pin device were rated as useful and intuitive. Nevertheless, a high learning curve was mentioned. The focus concepts were rated as understandable, but the effective usage in collaboration with a sighted partner needs a lot of training, practice and coordination.

As the next step a real scenario user study with pairs of blind and sighted subjects reworking a previously transcribed tactile graphic will be conducted. Thereby, we will be able to assess usability and accessibility of the Tangram workstation's approach to collaboration. It already became clear that blind reviewers would like to do some changes in existing tactile graphics. In our studies, we want to find out if materials produced by professionals will be improved by a blind user, too.

Acknowledgements. We thank our blind participants for the rich discussion about the concepts of our tactile user interface. The Tangram project is sponsored by the Federal Ministry of Labour and Social Affairs (BMAS) under the grant number R/FO125423.

References

1. Edman, P.K.: Tactile Graphics. AFB Press, New York (1992)
2. Prescher, D., Bornschein, J., Weber, G.: Production of accessible tactile graphics. In: Miesenberger, K., Fels, D., Archambault, D., Peňáz, P., Zagler, W. (eds.) ICCHP 2014, Part II. LNCS, vol. 8548, pp. 26–33. Springer, Heidelberg (2014)
3. Prescher, D.: Redesigning input controls of a touch-sensitive pin-matrix device. In: Zeng, L., Weber, G. (eds.) Proceedings of the International Workshop on Tactile/Haptic User Interfaces for Tabletops and Tablets (2014)
4. Jayant, C., Renzelmann, M., Wen, D., Krisnandi, S., Ladner, R., Comden, D.: Automated tactile graphics translation: in the field. In: Proceedings of the 9th International ACM SIGACCESS Conference on Computers and Accessibility, pp. 75–82. ACM (2007)
5. Bentzen, B.L.: Tangible graphic displays in the education of the blind persons. In: Schiff, W., Foulke, E. (eds.) Tactual Perception: A Sourcebook. Cambridge University Press, Cambridge (1982)
6. Braille Authority of North America and Canadian Braille Authority: Guidelines and standards for tactile graphics (2010). http://www.brailleauthority.org/tg/web-manual/index.html
7. Kozar, O.: Towards better group work: seeing the difference between cooperation and collaboration. Eng. Teach. Forum **48**(2), 16–23 (2010)
8. Bornschein, J., Prescher, D.: Collaborative tactile graphic workstation for touch-sensitive pin-matrix devices. In: Zeng, L., Weber, G. (eds.) Proceedings of the International Workshop on Tactile/Haptic User Interfaces for Tabletops and Tablets (2014)

9. Bornschein, J.: BrailleIO - a tactile display abstraction framework. In: Zeng, L., Weber, G. (eds.) Proceedings of the International Workshop on Tactile/Haptic User Interfaces for Tabletops and Tablets (2014)
10. Morash, V.S., Pensky, A.E.C., Tseng, S.T., Miele, J.A.: Effects of using multiple hands and fingers on haptic performance in individuals who are blind. Perception **43**(6), 569–588 (2014)

Navigation Problems in Blind-to-Blind Pedestrians Tele-assistance Navigation

Jan Balata$^{(\boxtimes)}$, Zdenek Mikovec, and Ivo Maly

Faculty of Electrical Engineering, Department of Computer Graphics and
Interaction, Czech Technical University in Prague, Prague, Czech Republic
{balatjan, xmikovec, malyil}@fel.cvut.cz

Abstract. We raise a question whether it is possible to build a large-scale navigation system for blind pedestrians where a blind person navigates another blind person remotely by mobile phone. We have conducted an experiment, in which we observed blind people navigating each other in a city center in 19 sessions. We focused on problems in the navigator's attempts to direct the traveler to the destination. We observed 96 problems in total, classified them on the basis of the type of navigator or traveler activity and according to the location in which the problem occurred. Most of the problems occurred during the activities performed by the navigator. We extracted a set of guidelines based on analysis of navigation problems and successful navigation strategies. We have partially mapped the problem of tele-assistance navigation to POMDP based dialogue system.

Keywords: Visually impaired · Navigation · Tele-assistance · User study

1 Introduction

The ability to explore the neighborhood independently and to travel to a desired destination is required for satisfactory level of quality of life and of self-confidence. According to Golledge [11], visual impairment primarily restricts a person's mobility. Golledge et al. [13] show that restrictions on the mobility of visually impaired people significantly reduce their travel-related activities. Although visually impaired people undergo special training to learn specific navigation and orientation techniques and strategies, it has been observed that 30 % of them never leave their homes alone [7, 34]. Moreover, only a fraction of blind people travel independently to unknown places [12]. Interestingly, the percentage of visually impaired people who never travel alone has remained constant over decades, despite the fact that more and more assistive aids have become available. This leaves a space for research in the area of blind user navigation.

The level of mobility is influenced by the efficiency of the wayfinding process, which consists of two parts: immediate environment sensing (avoiding obstacles and hazards), and navigation to remote destinations [17]. Both parts of the wayfinding process can be supported by navigation aids that will assist the visually impaired. The basic criteria for evaluating navigation aids were defined by Armstrong [1] as safety, efficiency, and stress level.

© IFIP International Federation for Information Processing 2015
J. Abascal et al. (Eds.): INTERACT 2015, Part I, LNCS 9296, pp. 89–109, 2015.
DOI: 10.1007/978-3-319-22701-6_8

One already existing solution is a navigation aid based on a tele-assistance center with professional navigators (see Subsect. 2.2). The main problem of this solution is its scalability, as the gathering of a suitable set of landmarks for particular area often requires the physical presence of the professional navigator on the spot. According to a study by Balata et al. [3], visually impaired people memorize relatively long routes at a very high level of detail. It was also shown that 67 % of visually impaired people have experience with sharing their route with friends/family via email, phone, or messaging [2], and that they prefer navigation provided by a blind person to that of the sighted public (also supported by [4, 16]). This opens the possibility to base a tele-assistance navigation service on visually impaired volunteers, and to build up an efficient large-scale system where one visually impaired person navigates another. In this situation, the blind navigator (*navigator*) forms a natural source of suitable landmarks with their descriptions and with routing strategies optimized for blind travelers (*traveler*).

According to the functional model of a general navigation system for the blind [18], the *navigator* in such tele-assistance navigation service fully covers components providing a description of the environment (typically some kind of geographic information system), route planning, auditory display and speech input. The only component that cannot be covered independently by the *navigator* is the component responsible for determining the *traveler's* position and orientation. Here, collaboration with the *traveler* is needed. The *traveler* serves as a sensor gathering necessary data for the *navigator*, and/or can determine the position and orientation on her/his own.

A key feature of such tele-assistance navigation service is its non-stop availability. Here an automated dialogue-based navigation can be employed. There are several approaches to dialogue management: finite state machine, information state, grammar-based, plan-based and data-driven approach. Our case is highly complex and thus a data-driven approach like POMDP based dialogue managers is a suitable solution [30].

Based on [17, 18], we identified the following five activities (three for *navigator* and two for *traveler*) that we wanted to observe in our experiment: The *navigator* describes the environment, plans the route (gives navigation instructions), and determines the blind *traveler's* position [18]. The *traveler* travels to a remote destination (executes navigation instructions), and senses the environment (identifies landmarks) [17].

Our main goal is to investigate the process of tele-assistance-based navigation by blind people, with special reference to navigation problems that occur during these activities. Based on an analysis of the navigation problems we will develop recommendations for improving the training procedures in order to increase the efficiency of wayfinding in situations where tele-assistance takes place. Further, we will map the problem of tele-assistance-based navigation to POMDP based dialogue system in order to replace *navigator* with the computer system in the future.

2   Related Work

2.1   Pedestrian Navigation

For successful navigation and orientation in a space, we need to build up spatial knowledge about the given environment. According to Siegel and White [29], there are three levels of spatial knowledge: landmark knowledge, route knowledge, and over-view knowledge. Route knowledge can be further subdivided into two levels [12]:

- a procedural level, based on fixed reaction patterns that follows after exposure to a part of the route. These reactions can be automated, and do not require conscious effort. This leads to lower requirements on attention and on working memory.
- a declarative level, based on knowledge of particular landmarks on the route and abstract rules on how to navigate between these landmarks. This level of knowledge requires greater attention and more working memory.

Overview knowledge concerns relations between objects. These relations are repre-sented for example by angles or distances between two objects, which are not neces-sarily related to the route itself.

It has been shown that landmarks (representing landmark knowledge) are by far the most frequently-used category of navigation cues for pedestrians [19] (unlike junctions, distance, road type and street names or numbers). A study conducted by Ross et al. [27] states that the inclusion of landmarks within the pedestrian navigation instructions increased user confidence, and reduced or eliminated navigation errors. Rehrl et al. [26] showed that voice-only guidance in an unfamiliar environment is feasible, and that participants clearly preferred landmark-enhanced instructions.

The fact that humans rely primarily on landmarks to navigate from point A to B is reflected in many experimental designs of navigation systems, e.g. the system of Millonig and Schechtner [22]. The system designed by Hile et al. [14] presents a set of heuristics for selecting appropriate landmarks along the navigation path.

In our experiment, where the *navigator* instructs the *traveler* remotely without being physically present on the route and without any visual feedback, a declarative level of route knowledge is needed. The *navigators* were therefore thoroughly trained in compliance with official training methodology in the region where the tests were conducted [36]. The *navigators* were also introduced to objects that were not located on the test route. Finally, they checked a tactile map of the route and its environment to gain overview knowledge. In the training procedures for our experiment, we paid special attention to introducing all important landmarks and describing them to the *navigators* in order to support the creation of landmark knowledge (see Apparatus, Sect. 3).

2.2   Orientation and Navigation of the Blind

In large spaces where body movement is necessary, visually impaired pedestrians use different cognitive strategies from those used by sighted pedestrians for navigation and orientation, based on egocentric frames [20, 21]. Typically, they have to memorize a large amount of information [32] in the form of sequential representation [20] based on routes. Route knowledge has to be acquired on a declarative level [12]. Fortunately, it seems that visually impaired people acquire superior serial memory skills. A study by Raz et al. [25] discovered that congenitally blind people are better than sighted people in both item memory and serial memory, and that their serial memory skills are out-standing, especially for long sequences. In a study by Bradley and Dunlop [4], it was revealed that in a situation of pre-recorded verbal navigation, the blind navigator navigated the blind traveler significantly faster than a sighted navigator.

There are numerous navigation aids for visually impaired pedestrians. Some use special sensors to identify objects on the route, e.g. cameras [6], or an RFID based electronic cane [10]. Others are based on a concept described in [23], and rely on some kind of positioning system (e.g. GPS) in combination with the GIS system to identify objects and navigate the pedestrian, e.g. Ariadne GPS, BlindSquare. There have also been attempts to develop special interaction techniques for presenting navigation instructions, e.g. an auditory display [17] or a tactile compass [24].

The navigation aids based on major GIS systems (Google Maps, Apple Maps, OSM Maps, Nokia HERE Maps) suffer from an inappropriate description of the environment for visually impaired pedestrians. The available description may be imprecise (e.g. missing sidewalks or missing handrails), or may be ambiguous (e.g. an inadequate description of pedestrian crossing, meaning that it cannot be localized and identified without visual feedback) or it may ignore specific navigation cues (e.g. the surface structure of the sidewalk, acoustic landmarks such as the specific sound of a passage, the traffic noise of a busy street, or other sensory landmarks, such as the smell of a bakery). In addition, routing algorithms can encounter problems with non-trivial adjustments to the preferences and abilities of visually impaired people, e.g. their inability to cross open spaces (e.g. large squares).

Both inappropriate descriptions and unsuitable routing algorithms can be avoided by introducing navigation systems based on tele-assistance with a trained human agent. Various approaches have been proposed on the basis of various ways to identify the position and the environment of the pedestrian, like transmission of chest mounted camera view to the navigator [6], a verbal description from the pedestrian optionally combined with GPS location and GIS [8, 31], or purely based on a verbal description and knowledge of the environment [33]. Namely Navigational Centre for the Blind [8], operating since 2007, proved to be helpful tele-assistance navigation service widely used (6650 cases in years 2008–2013 [9]) by community of visually impaired people.

In our experiment navigation was performed in a way similar to that used in [4, 33].

3   Experiment

In our experiment we observed the process of navigation by a *navigator* navigating *traveler* by means of tele-assistance. The goal is to identify navigation problems in the following activities:

1. *Navigator* describing the environment,
2. *Navigator* giving navigation instructions,
3. *Navigator* determining *traveler's* position,
4. *Traveler* executing navigation instructions,
5. *Traveler* identifying landmarks.

The experiment consisted of 19 sessions. There were two participants per session, one in the *traveler* role and the other in the *navigator* role. Each session lasted 100 min.

Participants. 25 visually impaired participants (12 females, 13 males) were recruited via three methods: an e-mail leaflet sent to a group of Czech Blind United [8] clients, direct recruiting of our long term collaborators, and snowball technique. The participants in the experiment were aged from 25 years to 66 years (*mean* = 43.44, *SD* = 13.27). Fourteen participants had Category 4 vision impairment (light perception); 11 participants had Category 5 vision impairment (no light perception) [35]; 12 participants were congenitally blind, 13 participants were late blind. All of the participants were native Czech speakers. None of the participants in the *traveler* role knew the route before the experiment, though the character of environment was familiar to them. During recruitment, the participants were asked whether they are willing to participate in both roles, as the *traveler* in the first session, and then as the *navigator* in the following session. Table 1 contains details about the participants. Table 2 contains details about the sessions and about the roles that the participants took (the session IDs do not necessarily correspond to their real order). We tried to balance onset of impairment, category of impairment and gender of the participants in the sessions as much as possible. All of the participants (except P23) were active and regularly traveled alone. Several researchers have noted that it is quite difficult to acquire blind pedestrians as a target user group for a usability study [4, 6]. However, we had established a relationship with blind communities during our previous studies, and this made it comparatively easy to recruit a considerable number of blind participants for our experiment.

Apparatus. *Training methodology.* The goal of the training was to learn the *navigators* the route for regular independent walking, i.e. to form a declarative level of the route knowledge. We arranged several meetings with the chief methodologist from the Czech Blind United [8]. One of the chief methodologist's fields of expertise is in the training visually impaired people in spatial orientation and in preparing itineraries for their regular routes (i.e. routes to work, to a shop, to a public transport station/stop, etc.) in accordance with their navigation strategies. In order to conform with the official training methodology [36] used by the chief methodologist, we proceeded as follows: (1) We selected the route, identified important landmarks, and consulted possible dangers on the route together with the chief methodologist. (2) Together, we prepared a tactile map of the route and printed it on a paper using foil fuser technology. (3) The experimenter observed the chief methodologist training the *navigator* in the first pilot session. (4) The experimenter trained the *navigator* according to the observed methodology under the supervision of the chief methodologist in the second pilot session. (5) The trained experimenter trained the *navigators* in all subsequent sessions of the experiment.

Description of the route. For our experiment, we selected a city center outdoor environment. Environments for this type of experiment are usually real environments [4, 26] rather than artificial (lab) environments, though exceptions are possible [28]. The location of the route was in a quiet area in the city center of Prague, Czech Republic (see Figs. 1 and 2). It was 256 m in total length (from S via D1–D5 to B11) and navigation via phone took place on the 105 m long final part of this route (from D1 to B11). In the initial part (from S to D1) of the route the *traveler* walked alone. This was done to allow the *traveler* to get oriented and to get familiar with the surrounding

Table 1. List of participants, including onset of the impairment (congenital – C, late – L), category of visual impairment [35], gender (male – M, female – F), and age.

Part. No.	P1	P2	P3	P4	P5	P6	P7	P8	P9	P10	P11	P12	P13	P14	P15	P16	P17	P18	P19	P20	P21	P22	P23	P24	P25
Onset	C	L	C	C	C	L	C	C	C	C	L	L	L	C	C	L	L	L	L	L	C	L	C	L	L
Category	5	5	4	5	5	4	5	4	5	4	4	5	4	4	5	4	5	4	4	5	5	4	5	5	5
Gender	F	M	F	F	M	M	M	F	M	F	M	M	M	F	M	F	M	F	M	F	F	F	F	M	M
Age	38	60	37	42	29	61	43	27	32	29	36	37	50	38	43	38	60	50	62	66	25	65	29	31	58

environment of D1. Along the route there were 5 decision points (D1–D5) to which the *navigator* tries to navigate the *traveler*, number of surface changes (SFx), acoustic landmarks (Ax), vertical traffic signs and columns (Cx), and doors (Bx) (see Fig. 2).

Fig. 1. Panorama from the beginning of the route containing decision points D1 and D2 (top), and from the end of the route containing decision points D3, D4, and D5 (bottom).

Equipment. Our equipment and the data we collected is based on field laboratory design presented in Hoegh et al. [15]. The *traveler* was equipped with a Nokia 6120 mobile phone with a lanyard which hung from his/her neck. In this way, the phone was protected from being dropped unintentionally, and the *traveler* was able to release it and have an empty hand when needed, and s/he could also find it again quickly. The mobile phone was set to Czech language, and it was equipped with the MobileSpeak text-to-speech (TTS) screen reader application by CodeFactory. The *navigator* was located in the usability lab dedicated to executing user tests equipped with a laptop and the Skype application with Skype Out capabilities for connection with the mobile phone network. The laptop speakers and the internal microphone were used as input and output devices. Communication between the *traveler* and the *navigator* was recorded using MP3 Skype Recorder v3.1 (left/right channel separated for *traveler*/ *navigator* communication).

In each session, we also recorded two video streams of the *traveler's* activities. The first camera (GoPro Hero 3) recorded 1st person view and was installed on a shoulder strap of the backpack that was carried by the *traveler* during the session, while the second camera (Panasonic SDR-S150) recorded a 3rd person view by the experimenter shadowing the *traveler*.

Procedure. Before the session started, both participants were briefed, and the purpose of the experiment was explained to them separately.

The experiment session consisted of two phases. In the first phase, the *navigator* was taught the route by the experimenter. In the second phase, the *navigator* navigated the *traveler* along the route. Both of the participants were asked to proceed as quickly and accurately as possible. The *traveler* was asked either to hold the phone in a hand or to leave it on the lanyard, according to his/her own preference.

The first phase of the experiment involved training the *navigator*. The training consisted of three walkthroughs. The first two walkthroughs of the route were done with the experimenter, and the third was done alone, with the experimenter in the vicinity. During the first two walkthroughs, the experimenter described the landmarks (see Fig. 2) along the route and offered as many details as possible. During the third walkthrough, the *navigator* walked alone and asked the experimenter about the landmarks in cases when s/he was uncertain, so that s/he could remember better, but mostly to verify that s/he had learned the route sufficiently. After the walkthroughs, the *navigator* was accompanied into our usability lab and was presented with a tactile map of the overview of the route and the destination details. From this point, the *navigator* waited in the usability lab with the experimenter for a call from the *traveler*.

The second phase of the experiment consisted of a walkthrough of a part of the route by the *traveler*, and of navigation of the *traveler* by the *navigator*. This phase consisted of three parts. In the first part, the *traveler* was accompanied to the starting point of the route[S] and was given the task. The task was given as follows: *"You have a meeting at Hostel Emma[B11] (see Fig. 2) on Na Zderaze Street. Now you are on the corner[S] of Dittrichova Street and Resslova Street. Continue approximately 80 meters slightly downhill along Dittrichova Street to the first crossroad. The building will be on your right hand side, and on the left there will be cars parked on the sidewalk. Then turn right and continue approximately 80 meters uphill along Zahoranskeho Street to the crossroad[D1] with Na Zderaze Street. To reach the destination, you will have to call the navigator who knows the location very well. At the crossroad, you will be assisted with dialing the phone. Proceed as if you were alone, but we will be watching for your safety from a distance."* Then the *traveler* started out. The second part consisted of assisting the *traveler* with making the phone call from the corner[D1] where the navigation with *navigator* starts. The phone call was initiated by the experimenter in the lab, who relayed the call to the *navigator*. Then the *traveler* accepted the phone call and started a dialog with the *navigator*. The third part consisted of navigating the *traveler* by the *navigator* via a phone call. The *navigator* described the environment, gave navigation instructions, and determined the *traveler's* position. The *traveler* executed the navigation instructions, and identified the landmarks. The experimenter observed the whole session from nearby to ensure the safety of the *traveler*. If the *traveler* got lost beyond the possibility of finding the destination, and/or was in distress, the experimenter terminated the session. Otherwise, the *traveler* was not interrupted by the experimenter. After reaching the destination, the *traveler* was accompanied into the usability lab, where both participants were debriefed and received their payment.

Measures. During the sessions we measured the time to reach the destination in successful sessions and the number of navigation problems in all sessions. For the activities *Navigator* describing the environment and *Navigator* giving navigation instructions we define the navigation problem as deviation from the training navigators went through (see paragraph Apparatus – Training methodology). A navigation problem in the activity *Navigator* determining *traveler's* position is defined as

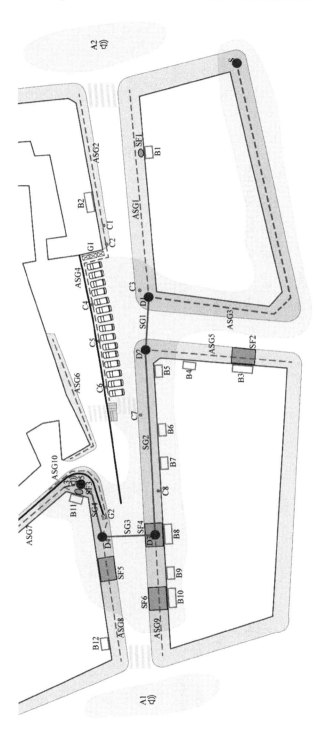

Fig. 2. Schematic illustration of the route and its adjacent area. The rightmost red dot depicts the starting point of the route[S], red dots depict decision points[Dx], blue lines depict segments[SGx] of the route (bold solid – route segments traveled with the *navigator*, bold dashed – adjacent segment[ASG3] walked without the *navigator* from the starting point, dashed – adjacent segments[ASGx]), orange boxes depict buildings[Bx], dark grey boxes and ovals depict surface landmarks[SFx] such as a rubber mat[SF1,SF3] or differences in material, e.g. cobblestone[SF2,SF4,SF6] and a broken sidewalk.[SF5] speaker icons depict acoustic landmarks[Ax], such as busy streets[A1,A2] or echoes[A3], crossed circles depict vertical traffic signs and columns[Cx], crossed squares depict waste containers of various sizes[Gx]. The green area contains landmarks taught to the *navigator* in the training phase of the experiment. Bold black lines depict stone walls. Gray areas depict sidewalks (Color figure online).

Table 2. List of sessions, including participants' role in the experiment, duration of navigation (minutes), success of session, and the number of navigation problems.

Session	S_1	S_2	S_3	S_4	S_5	S_6	S_7	S_8	S_9	S_{10}	S_{11}	S_{12}	S_{13}	S_{14}	S_{15}	S_{16}	S_{17}	S_{18}	S_{19}
Traveler	Pl	P3	P5	P6	P4	P8	P10	Pll	P13	P14	P16	P17	P18	P19	P22	P21	P23	P24	P25
Navigator	P2	P4	P6	P3	P7	P9	Pll	P12	P12	P15	P17	P18	P14	P20	P19	P22	P2	P23	P24
Duration	11:23	5:17	7:06	-	-	-	-	4:20	4:15	8:41	-	9:32	6:01	8:51	4:32	-	-	-	4:52
Success	Yes	Yes	Yes	No	No	No	-	Yes	Yes	Yes	No	Yes	Yes	Yes	Yes	No	No	No	Yes
Problems	1	1	4	8	11	7	4	0	1	3	11	4	4	7	3	4	3	12	8

concurrent occurrence of two events: the *traveler's* physical position differs from the *navigator's* imagination of the *traveler's* physical position, and the *navigator* is not determining the *traveler's* physical position. Problems in the *traveler's* activities (i.e. *Traveler* executing navigation instructions, *Traveler* identifying landmarks) are defined as fail to execute the navigation instruction and fail to identify the landmark.

Collected Data. Nineteen Skype call audio files were recorded. Nineteen video files were recorded from a 3rd person view observing the *traveler*, and eighteen video files were recorded using a GoPro camera on the *traveler's* shoulder from the 1st person view (one file was not recorded, due to a hardware malfunction). These files were then merged and aligned by time into a single multimedia file for each session.

In order to analyze the data, we developed an application that allows time-stamped annotation of the *traveler's* physical position and the *navigator's* imagination of the *traveler's* physical position in the map. After annotation, the multimedia file from the session and both annotated positions in the map could be browsed side-by-side.

4 Results and Discussion

Eleven sessions finished with successful arrival at the destination after between 4 min 15 s and 11 min 23 s (*mean* = 6 min. 48 s., *SD* = 2 min. 28 s.). One session was inconclusive due to intervention of the experimenter. Seven sessions failed. In this section, we describe the navigation problems observed during navigation of the *traveler* by the *navigator*. Initially, we focus on general results, and then we describe selected navigation problems in various types of situations.

We analyzed the navigation problems in all the sessions, and classified them into the corresponding activities performed by *navigators* and *travelers*, and into different types of situations. Out of the total of 96 problems, 71 were problems identified on the route, and 25 were problems identified off the route. Sixty problems were identified in the failed sessions, and 36 problems were identified in the successful sessions (see Table 2). Most of the navigation problems on the route (44 of 71) occurred in two activities: *Navigator* describing the environment, and *Navigator* giving navigation instructions (see Table 3). It was shown that the *navigator's* problems on the route were greater than the *traveler's* (53 vs. 18), but off the route there the difference was smaller (15 vs. 10).

A majority of the navigation problems that occurred in the activity *Navigator* describing the environment on the route were related to column^{C8} (8 out of 23) and decision point [D3] (7 of 23). *Navigators* did not mention column^{C8}, door^{B8}, and cobblestones^{SF4} while *traveler* was approaching decision point [D3].

Along with the navigation problems in various types of situations (i.e. reorientation at a corner, crossing from corner to corner, traveling along a building, reorientation at a building, crossing from building to building, finding a landmark), we observed four other phenomena that affected successful navigation. They were: similarities in the environment; temporary changes of environment; landmark confusions; recovery from going astray.

Table 3. Occurrence of navigation problems in the activities performed by *navigators* and *travelers* in different situations on and off the route.

Situation (Landmark)	*Navigator* describing the environment	*Navigator* giving navigation instructions	*Navigator* determining *traveler's* position	*Traveler* executing navigation instructions	*Traveler* identifying landmarks
On the route					
Reorientation at a corner (D1, D2)	2	10	0	0	2
Crossing from corner to corner (SG1)	0	1	0	2	0
Traveling along a building (SG2, SG4)	4	4	2	3	1
Reorientation at a building (D3, D4)	0	3	1	0	0
Crossing from building to building (SG3)	0	1	0	1	0
Finding a landmark (B8, C8, SF3, SF4)	17	2	6	5	4
Total on the route	23	21	9	11	7
Off the route					
Traveling along building (ASGx)	4	1	10	4	5
Finding landmark (B1)	0	0	0	1	0
Total off the route	4	1	10	5	5
All navigation problems	27	22	19	16	12

4.1   Reorientation at a Corner

There were 14 navigation problems in reorientation at a corner. For example, the *navigator* did not instruct the *traveler* to turn left [D1, $S_{6,18}$]. The *navigator* did not relate the position of the *traveler* to the building [D1, S_{16}]. The *navigator* was unable to give the *traveler* unambiguous instructions on how to stand at the corner: *"Turn so you have the corner at your back."* [D1, S_{13}]. The *navigator* could not determine the *traveler's* position on the corner, i.e. which side s/he was on [D2, S_{12}]. The *navigator* wrongly instructed the *traveler* and confused *"turn left"* with *"have the building on your left"* [D2, S_{11}]. It seems that this situation was one of the most difficult for the participants.

However, several successful navigation strategies were used to reorient at the corner. For example, the *navigator* instructed the *traveler* to turn his/her back towards the building before s/he turned the corner [D1, S_{15}]. The *navigator* instructed the *traveler* to check if s/he could hear a busy street from the right [D1, S_4]. The *navigator* described the surrounding streets and gave their names at [D1, S_8]. The *navigator* checked on which side the *traveler* had a building and what the slope of the sidewalk was [D2, S_6]. The *navigator* asked the *traveler* on which side the downhill sidewalk was [D2, S_{12}].

4.2   Crossing from Corner to Corner

We found 3 navigation problems when the street was crossed from corner to corner [D1, D2]. For example, the *traveler* did not execute the instruction to come back slightly from the corner[D1] to the street, so s/he arrived at the opposite corner[D2], while the *navigator* expected him/her on the left from the opposite corner [S_{11}]. The *traveler* did not walk straight while crossing the street and missed the opposite corner [S_{17}].

However, several successful navigation strategies were used to cross the street from corner to corner. For example, the *navigator* instructed the *traveler* to return back to the street and cross, in order not to miss the corner on the other side [$S_{10,17}$]. The *navigator* instructed the *traveler* to walk around the cars from the left side in order not to miss the corner [S_{12}]. The *navigator* instructed the *traveler* to cross the street to the opposite sidewalk. In this way, the *navigator* used *traveler's* previously traveled route and the fact, that the street had sidewalk on both sides, for giving the instruction [S_8].

4.3   Traveling Along a Building

In the situation when traveling along a building, we observed 14 navigation problems. For example, the *traveler* did not describe the slope of the sidewalk precisely when the *navigator* was trying to determine his/her position [SG2, S_{16}]. The *traveler* did not execute the instruction to walk along the building [SG2, S_7]. The *navigator* did not know about two restaurants[B6,B7] that the *traveler* asked about [SG2, S_7]. The *navigator* did not instruct the *traveler* to walk along the building in order to find the rubber mat[SF3] [SG4, $S_{3,4,5,15,19}$].

However, several successful navigation strategies were also used for traveling along building. For example, the *navigator* described the sidewalk made of small paving blocks [SG2, $S_{3,14}$]. The *navigator* checked that the building was on the left-hand side of the *traveler* [SG2, $S_{7,8}$]. The *navigator* checked the sound from the busy street[A1] in front of the *traveler* [SG2, S_{14}]. The *navigator* described the restaurants[B6,B7] on the left-hand side [SG2, $S_{3,8}$].

4.4   Reorientation at a Building

We found 4 navigation problems during reorientation at a building. For example, the *navigator* did not determine the position of the *traveler* when s/he reached the doors[B8] and instructed him/her to turn right instead of instructing him/her to turn about face when s/he was facing the door[B8] [D3, S_3]. The *navigator* did not determine the *traveler's* orientation when s/he reached the other side of the street [D4, S_3].

However, several successful navigation strategies were also used for reorientation at the building. For example the *navigator* checked that the building was on the left-hand side of the *traveler* after s/he had crossed the street [D4, $S_{3,8,9}$]. The *navigator* instructed the *traveler* to have the doors[B8] behind his/her back [D3, S_4].

4.5   Crossing from Building to Building

Two navigation problems were observed during crossing the street from one building to another building [D3, D4]. For example, the *navigator* instructed the *traveler* to turn right if s/he found cars parked along the sidewalk, instead of bypassing them [S_3]. The *traveler* did not execute the instruction to cross the street to the building, and stopped at the edge of the sidewalk [S_{15}].

However, several successful navigation strategies were also used for crossing from building to building. For example the *navigator* instructed the *traveler* to walk around the parked cars from the left [S_1].

4.6   Finding a Landmark

In the situation of finding a landmark, we observed 34 navigation problems. For example, the *navigator* did not describe the column[C8] [$S_{2,4,12,13,14}$]. Similarly, the *traveler* did not identify the same column[C8] even if s/he struck it [S_{14}]. The *navigator* did not describe the wooden doors[B8] with metal fittings and a handle at head level [$S_{10,11,14}$]. The *traveler* failed to check the material of the doors[B8] and the handle [$S_{15,18}$]. The *traveler* did not execute the instruction to stop at the cobblestones[SF4] although s/he did find them [S_{19}]. Alternatively, the *traveler* did not identify the cobblestones[SF4] at all [$S_{10,12}$].

However, several successful navigation strategies were also used for finding a landmark. For example, the *navigator* described the cobblestones[SF4] [$S_{5,13}$]. The *navigator* described the wooden door[B8] with metal fittings and a handle at head level [$S_{1,4,12}$]. The *navigator* described exact position of the column[C8] – 15 cm from the building on the left side [$S_{5,7,8,9,18}$]. The *navigator* described the distance to the column[C8] from the corner [D2, $S_{8,9,19}$]. The *navigator* described the acoustics[A3] at the corner [D5, $S_{12,13,18,19}$]. The *navigator* described a rubber mat[SF3] on the sidewalk [SG4, $S_{12,14,18}$].

4.7   Similarities in the Environment

If the *traveler* was inattentive to the details of landmarks, two parts of the route can seem to be very similar. The similar parts can be characterized by the same sequences of similar landmarks (e.g., route part R consists of landmarks A, B, C and route part R' consists of landmarks A', B', C', where A is similar to A', B to B', and C to C').

There was similarity between one sidewalk[ASG8] from restaurant[B12] to place with broken sidewalk[SF5] and another sidewalk[SG2] from shop[B5] to the cobblestones[SF4] [S_5] (see Fig. 3(a)). The *navigator* thought that the *traveler* had crossed the street and returned back (from SG4 back to the other side of the road to SG2 and farther away to D2), as they could not find the destination[B11]. This was because of incorrect instructions from the *navigator* – s/he did not stress that the *traveler* should go along the building to find the rubber mat[SF3] at the destination[B11] [SG4]. The *navigator* checked the acoustic landmark[A2] and the *traveler* acknowledged that there was indeed a busy road[A1] behind his/her back; however, it was the other one[A2]. They did not check the material of sidewalks: on one[SG2] there are small paving blocks, whereas on the other one[ASG8] there is asphalt.

There was similarity between one sidewalk[ASG5] from corner[D2] to cobblestones[SF2] and another sidewalk[SG2] from corner[D2] to cobblestones[SF4] [S_{11}] (see Fig. 3(b)). The *navigator* confused the navigation instruction (left vs. right), and the *traveler* continued to the left[ASG5] instead of to the right[SG2] [D2]. The *navigator* did not check whether the *traveler* had buildings on his/her left side, and did not check which side the landmarks reported by the *traveler* were on. Both sidewalks[ASG5,SG2] are downhill, but the first[ASG5] is much steeper. The *navigator* checked for the slope and the *traveler* acknowledged that it was downhill but not how steep it was. Navigation continued until the *traveler* reached cobblestones[SF2]. The material of the doors[B3] did not match the right one[B8], however the *navigator* instructed the *traveler* to continue further downhill[ASG5].

There was similarity between one sequence of sidewalks[ASG4,ASG2,ASG1] from column[C4] near stone wall[ASG4] to doors[B1] with rubber mat[SF1] and another sequence of sidewalks[SG2,SG3,SG4] from corner[D2] to doors[B11] with rubber mat[SF3] [S$_{18}$] (see Fig. 3(c)). The *navigator* forgot to turn the *traveler* to the left to cross the street[SG1] and the *traveler* ended up by stone wall[ASG4]. The *traveler* continued along the wall[ASG4] and reported cars along the buildings. The *navigator* acknowledged, but did not check how far from the building the cars were. The *traveler* reported wooden doors[B2] but the *navigator* did not check for cobblestones[SF4], which are missing there[B2]. After crossing the street from the doors[B2], the *traveler* did not find the corner on the right side and decided to walk to the left in the opposite direction[ASG1], but the *navigator* did not make any comment. The *traveler* reported that s/he was at the destination at doors[B1] with rubber mat[SF1].

4.8   Landmark Confusion

Travelers often had to make a further examination of a landmark that they had discovered, in order not to confuse it with another object. The *traveler* confused a railing with a temporary traffic sign placed next to a column[C3] [S$_1$]. The *traveler* confused a garbage container[G1] with a trash can[G2] [S$_5$]. The *traveler* confused cars with garbage containers[G1] [S$_{18}$]. The traveler confused a passage with a van parked along the sidewalk [D3, S$_{19}$]. *Travelers* confused a building with a stone wall[ASG4] [S$_{6,16,18}$].

4.9   Temporary Changes of Environment

An urban environment has a rhythm of its own. Streets that are busy during the day are silent at night, and the shops are closed. Some shops open at 9:00 am, while some restaurants and coffee bars do not open until 11 o'clock. There is also a weekly rhythm of dustmen and periodic street cleaning. All of these changes have an impact on the environment and affect some of the landmarks. In our case, there was increased traffic in an otherwise quiet street near [D1, S$_{14}$], a temporary traffic sign next to column[C3] [S$_1$], a dustbin put outside a door[B8] for the garbage collectors [S$_7$], a van parked on the sidewalk [D3, S$_{19}$], or a missing advertising stand, which led to session failure [D2, S$_{16}$].

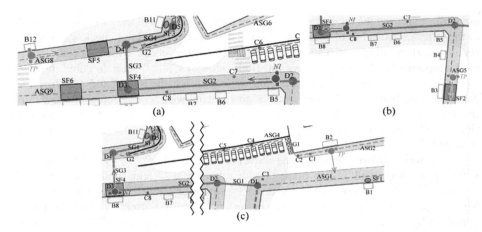

Fig. 3. Similarities in sessions S_5 (a), S_{11} (b), and S_{18} (c). The green figure represents the *traveler's* physical position and direction (TP). The red figure represents the *navigator's* imagination of the *traveler's* physical position and direction (NI) (Color figure online).

4.10   Recovery from Going Astray

During the sessions, we observed *traveler* going astray. In a moment when the *navigator* or the *traveler* realized that the *traveler* is out of the route they started to recover from this situation and get back on the right route. The recovery process can be divided into three subsequent steps: (1) realize that the *traveler* went astray, (2) determine the *traveler's* real position, (3) take the *traveler* back on the route.

The *traveler* walked relatively long time without mentioning that s/he went astray. This especially happened when the *navigator* did not determine the *traveler's* physical position on regular basis and when the *traveler* failed to identify the landmarks. For example, at second cobblestones[SF6], the *traveler* realized that s/he probably did not identify the first ones[SF4] as the door[B10] material did not match the *navigator's* description [S_4]. However, neither the *traveler* nor the *navigator* realized that the *traveler* went astray, but they were convinced that they reached the destination[B11], even though they were at different doors[B1] [ASG1, S_{18}].

In order to take the *traveler* back on the route the *navigator* had to determine the *traveler's* position and direction. For example, when the *navigator* realized the *traveler* went astray, s/he asked direction of busy street[A2]. When the *traveler* confirmed the *navigator* determined his/her position at stone wall[ASG4] near 3rd column[C4] [S_6]. However, neither the *navigator* did not determine the *traveler's* position until experimenter terminated the session [$S_{4,5}$].

The last step is the attempt to take the *traveler* back on the route. This was typically done by backtracking to last known point on the route. For example, the *navigator* successfully instructed the *traveler* to cross the street from stone wall[ASG4] near 3rd column[C4] [S_6]. The *navigator* successfully instructed the *traveler* to return back from end of the street[ASG9] back to first cobblestones[SF4] [S_{12}]. However, the *traveler* was not able to cross the street from stone wall^{ASG4} and the session was terminated on his/her request [S$_{17}$].

After successful recovery they tried to identify the error either in giving the navigation instruction by the *navigator* or in executing the navigation instruction by the *traveler*. The most common error was not identifying a cobblestones^{SF4} by the *traveler*. The common solution was returning back and trying to identify the landmark [S$_{4,12,14}$].

Table 4. Guidelines extracted from observed navigation problems and successful navigation strategies, their application, and some of the examples from the experiment.

	Activity	Guideline	Example (situation)
G1	*Navigator* describing the environment	*Navigator* should describe the environment in detail, with focus on tactile properties (materials, changes of materials, slopes) and auditory properties (traffic sounds, echoes).	✓ The *navigator* described the sidewalk made of small paving blocks (4.3). ✓ The *navigator* described the surrounding streets and gave their names (4.1). ✗ The *navigator* did not describe the wooden doors (4.6).
G2	*Navigator* giving navigation instructions	*Navigator* should relate the orientation of *traveler* to the environment, to *traveler*'s previous route, and/or to auditory landmarks; *navigator* should describe landmarks along the route, mention on which hand side is the leading line (building, edge of sidewalk), and mention auditory properties.	✓ The *navigator* instructed the *traveler* to have the doors behind his/her back (4.4). ✓ The *navigator* instructed the *traveler* to walk around the parked cars from the left (4.5). ✗ The *navigator* did not relate the position of the *traveler* to the building (4.1).
G3	*Navigator* determining *traveler*'s position	*Navigator* should regularly check *traveler*'s position e.g. ask about execution of instruction and discovered landmarks.	✓ The *navigator* checked that the building was on the left-hand side of the *traveler* (4.3). ✓ The *navigator* checked the sound from the busy street in front of the *traveler* (4.3). ✓ The *navigator* checked on which side the *traveler* had a building and what the slope of the sidewalk was (4.1).
G4	*Traveler* executing navigation instructions	*Traveler* should listen to whole navigation instruction before execution, restate instruction, acknowledge both understanding and execution of the instruction.	✗ The *traveler* did not execute the instruction to come back slightly from the corner to the street (4.2). ✗ The *traveler* did not execute the instruction to cross the street to the building, and stopped at the edge of the sidewalk (4.5). ✗ The *traveler* did not execute the instruction to walk along the building (4.3).
G5	*Traveler* identifying landmarks	*Traveler* should describe the environment in detail, with focus on tactile and auditory properties.	✗ The *traveler* failed to check the material of the doors (4.6). ✗ The *traveler* did not describe the slope of the sidewalk precisely when the *navigator* was trying to determine his/her position (4.3). ✗ The *traveler* did not execute the instruction to stop at the cobblestones although s/he did find them (4.6).

4.11   Guidelines

We extracted the following five guidelines based on an analysis of 96 navigation problems and successful navigation strategies collected during the experiment (see Table 4).

4.12   POMDP Based Dialogue System

The findings obtained in the study can be used for POMDP based dialogue system definition [5, 37]. In our case, the system is represented by the *navigator* and the environment is represented by the *traveler*.

A POMDP is defined by sextuplet $<S, A, Z, T, O, R>$, where S is a set of states (*Traveler's* states), A is a set of the system's actions (*Navigator's* actions), Z is a set of observations the system can experience (a set of *Navigator's* observations), T is a transition model, O is an observation model, and R is a reward model.

The state set $S = <I_t \times P_t \times D_t>$ is composed of three features: *traveler's* action (I_t), which corresponds to *Traveler* executing navigation instruction activity, *traveler's* 2D coordinate position (P_t), and *traveler's* direction (D_t) as an absolute angle. In the future the state set can be extended with features such as *traveler's* type of disability or his/her experience. The action set $A = <I \times L>$ is composed of two features: action (I), and landmarks (L). The actions are passed to *traveler* during the *Navigator* giving navigation instruction activity. The observation set $Z = <OI_t \times OL_t \times OD_t>$ is composed of three features: *traveler's* observed action (OI_t), *traveler's* observed landmarks (OL_t), which corresponds to the *Traveler* identifying landmarks activity, and *traveler's* observed direction (OD_t) as a relative angle. The observation set is acquired during the *Navigator* determining *Traveler's* position activity. To parameterize the transition model $T(s', s, a) = p(s'|s, a)$ we can use the *Traveler* executing navigation instruction activity. In the future the transition model can be used for personalization based on types of disability or experience (from the state set) such as adjustment of segment length, or usage of specific landmarks. The observation model $O(s', a, z) = p(z|s', a)$ is represented by GIS-like data structure with probable *traveler's* states. Findings from Sects. 4.7–4.9 can be used for parameterization. In the future the observation model can be used for probability distribution visualization of *traveler's* position. In the future the reward model $R(s, a): S \times A \rightarrow R$ can be parameterized by stress function i.e. whether to re-plan or back-track when the *traveler* went astray and his/her stress level became high (see Sect. 4.10).

5   Conclusion

We have gathered a set of problems that occur during the process of blind-to-blind navigation by means of tele-assistance. These problems have been classified into activities performed by the *navigator* and by the *traveler* and have been assigned to categories of situations where these problems occurred. We have also described in detail behavior of *navigators* and *travelers* in special situations (i.e. similar parts of the route, temporary changes in the environment, landmark confusion, and recovery from going astray). It seems that substantial number of problems are related to activity *Navigator* giving navigation instructions. These findings can serve as a basis to improve the training for visually impaired people to make the wayfinding process more efficient in situations when tele-assistance takes place. Furthermore, our results are suitable for parameterization of POMDP based dialogue systems, which can form a step towards replacement of human *navigator* by a computer system.

Future research should focus on experiments in different environments (e.g. city park, indoors) and on development of efficient training methods for blind-to-blind pedestrian tele-assistance-based navigation.

Acknowledgments. This research has been supported by the project Design of special user interfaces funded by grant no. SGS13/213/OHK3/3T/13 (FIS 161 – 832130C000).

References

1. Armstrong, J.: Evaluation of man-machine systems in the mobility of the visually handicapped. In: Picket, R.M., Triggs, T.J. (eds.) Human Factors in Health Care, pp. 331–343. Lexington Books, Lexington (1975)
2. Balata, J., Mikovec, Z., Slavik, P.: Mutual communication in navigation of visually impaired. CogInfoCom **445**, 08854-4141 (2012)
3. Balata, J., Franc, J., Mikovec, Z., Slavik, P.: Collaborative navigation of visually impaired. J. Multimodal User Interfaces **8**(2), 175–185 (2014)
4. Bradley, N.A., Dunlop, M.D.: An experimental investigation into wayfinding directions for visually impaired people. Pers. Ubiquit. Comput. **9**(6), 395–403 (2005)
5. Bui, T.H., Poel, M., Nijholt, A., Zwiers, J.: A tractable hybrid DDN–POMDP approach to affective dialogue modeling for probabilistic frame-based dialogue systems. Nat. Lang. Eng. **15**(2), 273–307 (2009)
6. Bujacz, M., Baranski, P., Moranski, M., Strumillo, P., Materka, A.: Remote guidance for the blind – a proposed tele-assistance system and navigation trials. In: HSI 2008, pp. 888–892. IEEE (2008)
7. Clark-Carter, D., Heyes, A., Howarth, C.: The efficiency and walking speed of visually impaired people. Ergonomics **29**(6), 779–789 (1986)
8. Czech Blind United. http://www.sons.cz/. Accessed Sept 2014
9. Czech Blind United: Annual Report (2013) (in Czech). http://www.sons.cz/docs/Vyrocni_zprava_SONS_2013.pdf. Accessed Sept 2014
10. Faria, J., Lopes, S., Fernandes, H., Martins, P., Barroso, J.: Electronic white cane for blind people navigation assistance. In: WAC 2010, pp. 1–7. IEEE (2010)
11. Golledge, R.G.: Geography and the disabled: a survey with special reference to vision impaired and blind populations. Trans. Inst. Br. Geogr. **18**, 63–85 (1993)
12. Golledge, R.G.: Human wayfinding and cognitive maps. In: Golledge, R.G. (ed.) Wayfinding Behavior: Cognitive Mapping and Other Spatial Processes, pp. 5–45. Johns Hopkins Press, Baltimore (1999)
13. Golledge, R.G., Klatzky, R.L., Loomis, J.M.: Cognitive mapping and wayfinding by adults without vision. In: Portugali, J. (ed.) The construction of cognitive maps, pp. 215–246. Springer, Dordrecht (1996)

14. Hile, H., Grzeszczuk, R., Liu, A., Vedantham, R., Košecka, J., Borriello, G.: Landmark-based pedestrian navigation with enhanced spatial reasoning. In: Tokuda, H., Beigl, M., Friday, A., Brush, A., Tobe, Y. (eds.) Pervasive 2009. LNCS, vol. 5538, pp. 59–76. Springer, Heidelberg (2009)
15. Høegh, R.T., Kjeldskov, J., Skov, M.B., Stage, J.: A field laboratory for evaluating in situ. In: Lumsden, J. (ed.) Handbook of Research on User Interface Design and Evaluation for Mobile Technology, pp. 982–996. IGI Global, Hershey (2008)
16. Kulyukin, V.A., Nicholson, J., Ross, D.A., Marston, J.R., Gaunet, F.: The blind leading the blind: toward collaborative online route information management by individuals with visual impairments. In: AAAI Spring Symposium: Social Information Processing, pp. 54–59 (2008)
17. Loomis, J.M., Golledge, R.G., Klatzky, L.: Navigation system for the blind: Auditory display modes and guidance. Presence-Teleop. Virt. 7(2), 193–203 (1998)
18. Loomis, J.M., Golledge, R.G., Klatzky, R.L., Speigle, J.M., Tietz, J.: Personal guidance system for the visually impaired. In: Assets 1994, pp. 85–91. ACM (1994)
19. May, A.J., Ross, T., Bayer, S.H., Tarkiainen, M.J.: Pedestrian navigation aids: information requirements and design implications. Pers. Ubiquit. Comput. 7(6), 331–338 (2003)
20. Millar, S.: Understanding and Representing Space: Theory and Evidence from Studies with Blind and Sighted Children. Oxford University/Clarendon Press, Oxford (1994)
21. Millar, S.: Space and sense. Psychology Press, New York (2008)
22. Millonig, A., Schechtner, K.: Developing landmark-based pedestrian-navigation systems. ITSC 2007 8(1), 43–49 (2007)
23. Petrie, H., Johnson, V., Strothotte, T., Michel, R., Raab, A., Reichert, L.: User-centred design in the development of a navigational aid for blind travellers. In: Howard, S., Hammond, J., Lindgaard, G. (eds.) Human-Computer Interaction – INTERACT 1997. LNCS (IFIP), pp. 220–227. Springer, New York (1997)
24. Pielot, M., Poppinga, B., Heuten, W., Boll, S.: A tactile compass for eyes-free pedestrian navigation. In: Campos, P., Graham, N., Jorge, J., Nunes, N., Palanque, P., Winckler, M. (eds.) INTERACT 2011, Part II. LNCS, vol. 6947, pp. 640–656. Springer, Heidelberg (2011)
25. Raz, N., Striem, E., Pundak, G., Orlov, T., Zohary, E.: Superior serial memory inthe blind: a case of cognitive compensatory adjustment. Curr. Biol. 17(13), 1129–1133 (2007)
26. Rehrl, K., Häusler, E., Leitinger, S.: Comparing the effectiveness of gps-enhanced voice guidance for pedestrians with metric- and landmark-based instruction sets. In: Fabrikant, S. I., Reichenbacher, T., van Kreveld, M., Schlieder, C. (eds.) GIScience 2010. LNCS, vol. 6292, pp. 189–203. Springer, Heidelberg (2010)
27. Ross, T., May, A., Thompson, S.: The use of landmarks in pedestrian navigation instructions and the effects of context. In: Brewster, S., Dunlop, M.D. (eds.) Mobile HCI 2004. LNCS, vol. 3160, pp. 300–304. Springer, Heidelberg (2004)
28. Schinazi, V.R.: Spatial representation and low vision: two studies on the content, accuracy and utility of mental representations. In: International Congress Series, vol. 1282, pp. 1063–1067. Elsevier (2005)
29. Siegel, A.W., White, S.H.: The development of spatial representations of large-scale environments. Adv. Child Dev. Behav. 10, 9 (1975)
30. Skantze, G.: Error Handling in Spoken Dialogue Systems – Managing Uncertainty, Grounding and Miscommunication (2007)
31. Talkenberg, H.: Electronic guide dog a technical approach on in-town navigation. In: Rank Prize Funds Symposium on Technology to Assist the Blind and Visually Impaired, Gramere, Cumbria, England (1996)

32. Thinus-Blanc, C., Gaunet, F.: Representation of space in blind persons: vision as a spatial sense? Psychol. Bull. **121**(1), 20 (1997)
33. Vystrcil, J., Maly, I., Balata, J., Mikovec, Z.: Navigation dialog of blind people: recovery from getting lost. In: EACL 2014, p. 58 (2014)
34. White, R.W., Grant, P.: Designing a visible city for visually impaired users. In: Proceedings of the 2009 International Conference on Inclusive Design (2009)
35. WHO: ICD update and revision platform: change the definition of blindness (2009). http://www.who.int/blindness/Change%20the%20Definition%20of%20Blindness.pdf
36. Wiener, W.R., Welsh, R.L., Blasch, B.B.: Foundations of Orientation and Mobility, vol. 1. American Foundation for the Blind, New York (2010)
37. Young, S., Gasic, M., Thomson, B., Williams, J.D.: Pomdp-based statistical spoken dialog systems: a review. Proc. IEEE **101**(5), 1160–1179 (2013)

Prototyping TV and Tablet Facebook Interfaces for Older Adults

José Coelho$^{(\boxtimes)}$, Fábio Rito, Nuno Luz, and Carlos Duarte

LaSIGE, University of Lisbon, Lisbon, Portugal
{jcoelho,faarito,nmluz}@lasige.di.fc.ul.pt,
caduarte@fc.ul.pt

Abstract. With the daily problem of social isolation comes an aggravation of older adults' general health. Social Network Services like Facebook have the potential to ameliorate the social connectivity of this segment of the population. However, they are still not fully adopted by them, whether because of age-related limitations or the lack of appropriate technological skills. In this paper we argue that the development of SNSs based on technology already used by older adults, like Television, or technology which has proven to be more accessible to them, like Tablets, can improve the ability of older adults to use these systems. We report findings from a study composed of semi-structured interviews and focus groups which aimed at the development of two Facebook-based prototypes for TV and Tablet. Results show good receptiveness from older adults to perform social tasks on TV and Tablet-based applications, for interacting using alternative modalities like speech, or back-of-device tapping, and for the use of adaptation mechanisms. Informed by the study results the main contributions are the two prototypes, and a collection of recommendations regarding the design of TV and tablet based interfaces for this population.

Keywords: Facebook · Older adults · Social isolation · Tablet · Television · Semi-structured interviews · Focus groups · Participatory design · Prototyping

1 Introduction

Older adults face daily a serious problem called loneliness. They spend a lot of time alone in their homes which contributes to increase social isolation [10]. The resulting decrease of social skills can lead to illness or other problems which can increase their mortality risk [2]. Technology can have an important role to improve social abilities in seniors [2]. However, they are quite resistant to adopt new technologies, which hinders the introduction of solutions benefiting social life. Additionally, age-related impairments limit the way these users interact with technology [23]. Online social network services (SNS) have the potential to ameliorate the social life of older adults, allowing users to create and share media content among each other. The main reason for seniors to adopt SNSs is the ability to improve online and offline relationships between them and family and close friends. Facebook, as the most popular SNS [1], constitutes the ideal vehicle for this use. However, a considerable number of older adults still do not adopt or

© IFIP International Federation for Information Processing 2015
J. Abascal et al. (Eds.): INTERACT 2015, Part I, LNCS 9296, pp. 110–128, 2015.
DOI: 10.1007/978-3-319-22701-6_9

make a limited use of this SNS. Main limitations are design complexity [9, 15, 20], privacy issues [9, 15, 16, 24] and preconceptions about its use [9, 15, 20] and the inability to use and learn technology used for SNS access [23].

To improve the ability of older adults to access SNSs we argue that its development should be based on technology already used by older adults (like Television) and technology which has proven to be more accessible to them (like Tablets). Television (TV) is the most used technology by older adults [3]. By exploring this close relationship, TV can be used to introduce social applications to older adults. Tablets support direct object manipulation, which has proven to be useful for older adults, because they allow the user to focus only on the screen without requiring attention to the input hardware [28]. Additionally, by being lightweight, small-scaled, and providing internet access everywhere, tablets could help captivate older users [13, 23]. Furthermore, to deal with seniors' disabilities and differences when interacting with technology, we advocate that these social applications should resort to multimodal and adaptive interfaces. Taking the Tablet and TV roles into consideration, as well as the role of multimodality and adaptation, we performed a user study composed by semi-structured interviews and focus group sessions. Main goals were to collect user requirements for a more inclusive design regarding the senior population and to gather information required for the design of two Facebook based prototypes: one TV-based and one Tablet-based. We also wanted to understand preferred alternatives to interact with TV and tablet applications and to evaluate how this population perceives personalization and adaptation concepts.

This paper main contributions are a study which provides relevant indications about how TV and Tablet devices can be used to simplify SNS access among older adults; and two Facebook-based high-fidelity prototypes which aim to ease this access. Concerning the study, results show older adults like to interact with TV and would like to perform social tasks through TV-based applications. When considering Tablet devices, results also indicate that older users would like to interact using several modalities like speech, and back-of-device tapping. The first because it simplifies the interaction without requiring too much effort, while the latter could be especially useful for interacting with the device without hiding information on the screen. Concerning the prototypes, a collection of recommendations is provided regarding the design of TV and tablet based interfaces for this population.

We start by presenting related work on the use of SNS by older adults, and what advantages Tablet and TV can bring to the elderly. We also summarize past research on what multimodal and adaptive interfaces can bring to the older population. Next, we describe the methodology we followed for our study, and follow that with a detailed analysis of the results and respective recommendations for the development of the two prototypes and describe them in detail. We end the paper with the main conclusions.

2   Related Work

2.1   Older Adults and Social Network Services

Technology could be an important collaborator to scale down loneliness and consequently to mitigate social isolation. SNS are the most important technology to confront this problem [2, 20]. There are two distinct types of SNSs that could make older adults more active in social aspects. The first ones are SNSs uniquely designed for older adults however these tend to expire shortly after being launched [15]. The second type are typical SNSs which could be used by older adults if they are designed having this population in consideration like Facebook. Research showed that the first approach excluded older adults' family and close friends which were the main reason for them to adopt SNS in the first place [15, 16]. Therefore, recently several authors developed solutions based on existing SNSs which can be adapted to the older segment of the population: Tlatoque [9] was an aSNS (ambient SNS), that collected Facebook content and presented it to older adults. It gave support for interacting with SNS using different technologies: a digital frame and a multi-touch PC. Results showed an increase in online and offline relationships between older adults and family; Gomes G. et al. [16] developed a tablet Facebook interface that allowed older adults to see, create and share content with close relatives. They compared it with the Facebook native application for tablets, and showed that older adult's acceptance increased because of the focus on family and close friends. Users also esteemed that content could be filtered by family, close friends and personal content. Privacy and usability issues were also identified as problematic; Norval et al. [24] also explored how SNSs could be accessible for older adults. They presented a comparison between a Facebook application with less functionalities and a SNS designed based on gathered requirements. Their results indicated that the second approach allowed applications to achieve a higher usability level. Users could also perform tasks with less effort and in a shorter time which could lead to an increase of users in SNSs that follow these recommendations. Our prototypes take advantage of the requirements found in these studies that could lead seniors to adopt and use SNSs. Additionally, we will include a new concept of TV shared content that will allow users to share what they are seeing on TV. None of the aforementioned studies attempted to evaluate this context of interaction.

2.2   Television, Multimodality and Older Adults

Older adults are often in front of TV and this can lead them to adopt new technologies based on this device [3, 20]. However, it is crucial to recognize that when interacting with SmartTVs they face problems raised by age-related disabilities [21], Electronic Program Guides (EPGs) [11], or insufficient number of accessible user interfaces [8]. In recent years, several researchers have turned their attention to the potential of TV-based applications: Karahasanovic et al. [19] showed that TV with additional features could be a valid solution for older adults to create and share contents "because it takes less time to turn it on and it should be much simpler to work on"; Gaver et al. developed Photostroller [14], an application based on a device that simulated a TV and offered a slideshow of photos retrieved from Flickr. Their findings demonstrated that the use of a remote controller (RC) to interact with the system caused a greater acceptance and that the use of the system increased the number of offline interactions; GUIDE [7] developed a framework to create TV based applications. They showed that multimodality and adaptation could make them more accessible to older adults with disabilities by providing different ways of interaction that fit their characteristics. Their findings also suggested that although RC should be the default way to interact with TV, voice and gestures were seen as better ways to do it; Bobeth J. et al. [3] compared four different techniques for gesture interaction in TV applications. They demonstrated that not only gestures are an accessible modality for older adults to interact with TV applications, but also that older adults prefer an indirect pointing approach to direct pointing, directional gestures or to TV parallel circular movements; finally, the same authors [4], compared the usage of tablet, gestures and RC by older adults in a TV context. They used two applications to show that the use of a tablet to interact with TV applications was appreciated by both older adults and younger people. Gestures were also enjoyed but for very limited interaction, while the RC was appreciated for linear tasks. From all this past research, it is evident the fulcral value of multimodality when concerning more accessible TV-based applications. The You, me & TV TV-based prototype proposed in this paper builds from this necessity and focuses its design on providing alternative ways of interacting with the TV: RC interaction, speech and gestures.

2.3 Tablet Devices, Multimodality and Older Adults

Older adults have difficulties using particular devices. They do not have too much strength for holding heavy devices as laptops and the usual computer graphical user interface can also be complicated for them. This is mainly because these interfaces require splitting users' attention between input hardware and the screen content [6]. The use of Tablet devices, by being "eyes-free, button-free, and silent" has been seen as a way to facilitate interaction and increase older adults' accessibility [28]. Other work also showed that Tablet devices offer flexibility which makes adaptation to older adults' characteristics, preferences and heterogeneity easier [11]. Because of these characteristics, the use of Tablet devices as a new bridge between older adults and their social communities has been very successful in recent years. Several projects were based on supporting the exchange of lightweight information, and took advantage of Tablet device features like Internet connectivity, in built-camera and virtual keyboard for capturing, sending and receiving messages and photos for and from older adults' relatives. Examples are applications like PersonCard [21], Wayve [22] and Enmesh [29] or systems like Building Bridges [13]. Other example of the potential of Tablet devices for accessing features typically present in a SNS was Cornejo et al. aSNS [9], which was built on top of Facebook and was also based on a multi-touch screen resembling a tablet. This last example, not only was an incentive for online social relationships but also led to an increase of in-person encounters. Additionally, the majority of these projects was also based on the use of several modalities for facilitating interaction with the Tablet. PersonCard and Wayve made use of SMS features, a virtual keyboard and the possibility of performing handwritten messages; Building Bridges focused on adding a Tablet touch, look and feel interface to phone functionalities which made use of speech; even Cornejo's SNS was based on a PC resembling a Tablet and made use of touch interaction, gesture interaction and ambient aware interaction. Like past research focused on TV-based applications for older adults, work performed on Tablets also supports itself on the value of multimodal interaction. Therefore, the Tablet-based prototype proposed in this paper is built with support for a large set of interaction possibilities: touch, gestures, speech, tilting and back-touch interaction. While the first three were already heavily used on past research, the latest two have not been tested on seniors before.

2.4   Adaptation and Older Adults

In a similar fashion to multimodal interfaces, adaptation and personalization mechanisms can be used to help older adults interact. From the end of the 20th century, several projects focused on the adaptation and personalization of user interfaces having older adults in mind. This was done either by adapting dynamic characteristics [27], by changing layout and font size [12], or by offering multimodal interaction along with the transformation of applications appearance and presentations style to fit user's characteristics [8]. Moreover, and since about 2009, researchers have been verifying that personalization and adaptation are even more highly appreciated by older adults when considering SNS profile presentation [20] and SNS features [5, 22]. Additionally, other studies focused on the differences concerning awareness and communication needs [19], and regarding distinct chunks of information [17] among older adults. In common, both these studies evidenced the need for these differences to be considered when designing a service usable by older adults, and again, the importance of adaptation mechanisms for this end. Both You, me & TV and YouTablet prototypes will build from this evidence on the necessity of turning to adaptation features when designing SNS applications more accessible to older adults. Therefore the study reported in this paper will also be concerned with understanding the perception of older adults regarding adaptation mechanisms and chances for personalization.

3   Methodology

The main goal behind this work is designing two Facebook based prototypes that allow to close the gap between SNSs and older adults. To promote their adoption prototypes will be based on two elderly friendly technologies - Tablet and TV. Both prototypes should be based on design recommendations for seniors collected through previous studies and, given the novel platforms, a further study of our own. This study will heavily involve end-user representatives following a participatory design methodology. This paper covers work developed on the first two phases, the population characterization and the participatory design phases. The last phase involving longitudinal evaluation is under way but will not be focused on this paper.

3.1   Population Characterization

To understand which requirements exist for older adults to make use of SNS technology it is paramount to characterize them concerning their technological expertise and age related limitations. We also attend to their opinions on the use of different technologies to access SNS. Consequently, we defined a set of research questions. The first will be concerned about what distinguishes older adults who use Facebook from older adults who do not and what are the main reasons for non-adoption or limited use (RQ1). Other research questions will be concerned with TV and Tablet as vehicles for older adults to adopt SNSs like Facebook. Are the elderly receptive to use social applications on TV (RQ2) or Tablet devices (RQ3)? We are also concerned with what modalities older adults prefer for interacting with TV (RQ4) and tablets (RQ5). Finally, the last research questions will be concerned with the concepts of adaptation and personalization. Which of these concepts is preferred by seniors (RQ6)? What issues should be taken into account in the implementation of each of these concepts (RQ7)? In order to answer the research questions we decided to conduct semi-structured interviews which allowed us to learn more about the population that we are studying. This method allow us to collect more data than simple questionnaires, because when necessary, reasons for a particular response can be asked by the interview conductor.

3.2 Participatory Design

Once the research questions are answered, it is crucial to gather design recommendations. Those allow us to develop Facebook based prototypes and should be clustered into two distinct groups. A group for the recommendations that improve the development of TV interfaces and other group for the development of tablet prototypes. For that end we decided to carry out focus groups in order to bring older adults to participate in the design process of these prototypes. These focus groups also allow to validate the findings of the interviews before turning them into recommendations to follow for the design of the interfaces. For this validation we developed low fidelity prototypes. The modularity of these prototypes allowed seniors to build together the system's information architecture. Building was achieved by combining elements of the interface represented in pieces of paper over a previously constructed layout (Fig. 1).

Fig. 1. Low-fidelity prototype of TV interface.

3.3 Validation

Both prototypes should be validated through tests with older users. The main goal of these tests is to validate if both approaches taken have a social impact in older adults life. Thus, we planned longitudinal tests at older adults' homes to realize their initiative for using the system in real contexts. To measure social isolation we will consider the basis of Cornwell et al. study [10] and their measures of social disconnectedness and perceived isolation. These tests are under way and will run for two to three months.

4 User Study

4.1 Semi-Structured Interviews

Participants. A total of 31 participants (11 male, 20 female) participated in the semi structured interviews. These had a duration of approximately one hour each. All participants were volunteers and more than 60 years of age. Age was not asked directly, participants indicated which of the age ranges they were. There were 6 different categories (Between 60 and 64 (19.35 %), Between 65 and 70 (23.6 %), Between 71 and 75 (35.5 %), Between 76 and 80 (19.4 %) and More than 80 (3.2 %)). About 93 % of the participants indicated having visual impairments, 36 % have hearing disabilities and about 33 % complained that they forget events that happened some time ago. In a Likert scale of 1 (nothing satisfied) to 5 (very satisfied) participants averaged 3.55 (SD = 1.31, MED = 4.00, mode = 5) in terms of social satisfaction. Concerning the use of technology, participants reported difficulties, with only 23 % stating to be comfortable using some technology and about 52 % having some to a lot of difficulties interacting with technology. Anonymity was kept at all times, with each user being identified exclusively by an id number. All data was saved in a secure repository.

Procedure. We first inquired older adults about five main fields. First, profiling questions concerning gender, age, education and household composition, self-characterization in terms of general and emotional health, social feelings and age-related impairments were asked. Second, they were inquired about their interest concerning distinct types of technology and about PC, TV and Tablet devices in terms of how easy they are to use in general and in specific tasks. Third, questions related with TV were asked focusing on viewing frequency, TV features, TV-related tasks, and TV content. Older adults were also asked to classify both traditional and alternative ways of interacting with TV. Fifth, participants classified in terms of easiness, satisfaction and effort the different ways of interacting with a Tablet device and ranked their interests in performing typical technological tasks using speech, gesture, or Tablet-base modalities like frame-based interaction, back-touch and tilting. Finally, participants answered to questions related with adaptation and personalization of user interfaces. On a last note, although specific questionnaires for accessing technological expertise and other skills' characterizing instruments already exist we decided against using such instruments due to 1) the increase it would represent in what contributes already for a long interview; 2) most of them being based on self-reported data nonetheless.

4.2   Focus Groups

Participants. A total of 17 participants (3 male and 14 female) participated in the focus groups. The first two focus groups focused on the TV-based prototype, and were composed by two groups of 6 participants. The third focus group focused on the Tablet-based prototype and was attended by 5 participants. Each focus group had a duration of about one hour. All participants were volunteers and more than 60 years of age. From the first two sessions, only one stating to have difficulties interacting with the TV in his daily life. No one saw TV as very easy to interact with. Only 4 in 12 used a PC, with only two considering it easy to use, while two used and considered easy to use the Tablet, and 2 from the 3 who used Facebook considered it easy to use. Thus few participants made use of technologies other than the TV which made them ideal to generate discussion around this platform. On the last focus group, no one had or made use of a Tablet, all classified TV as being easy to use. Three made use of a PC but only one classified it as easy to use, and 3 made use of Facebook, with 2 classifying it as easy to use. This shows this group was more technologically proficient than the other two, however no one had experience with the device on which the discussion was focused.

Procedure. Focus groups were performed at two distinct senior universities and allowed us to define how would the information architecture be organized on both the TV-based (the first two focus groups) and the Tablet-based (the third focus group) Facebook prototypes. Participants were asked to have an active role in changing each detail of the user interface by moving, placing and ordering the distinct components on the cardboard (which simulated the screen). We started by explaining the system and what we wanted to achieve with the discussions. We also asked them to complete a brief questionnaire concerning what technology they use and are familiar with. This served as a basis for characterizing each group. In the first two focus groups, the discussion began around functionalities they see as more important, and how they would like to see the menu and contact information presented. How to group information and contacts and how to filter media content were discussed next. Finally, some discussion was generated around the concepts of personalization and adaptation. In the last focus group, discussion begun with similar topics, the feed functionality, the menu composition and group visualization. More discussion focused around how to perform different tasks in several distinct modalities like speech, back-touch, tilting and touch. Finally, a concept called "digital frame", in which users can watch a slideshow of their contact photos and status updates, was also appreciated by the participants.

5   User Study Findings

Results from the structured interviews are presented below. Special consideration is given towards answering each research question identified in the methodology.

5.1   What Distinguishes Older Adults Who Use Facebook from Those Who Do not (RQ1)?

From the thirty elderly individuals interviewed, about half uses Facebook (48.4 %). This serves as an appropriate basis for a comparison between the two populations. We first observed that there are no major differences between them in terms of age-related limitations. Next, we found differences related to the age range of users and non-users. An association shows that the younger elderly population is the one that uses Facebook more (graphic A on Fig. 2). This association is particularly visible from 60 to 71 years of age, as percentage of Facebook users' drops. Further, there is also an association between the use of Facebook and the way participants appreciate using a computer (graphic B on Fig. 2), meaning that non users like PC less than Facebook users. In the same way, non-users also like TV more than Facebook users (graphic C on Fig. 2), and they would enjoy less accessing it on a TV context than Facebook users (graphic D on Fig. 2) (answers on both, were obtained through Likert scale from 1 (do not like it at all) to 5 (like it very much)). This can be partially explained if we consider that during the interviews it was observed a tendency of non-users to reject all alternatives for accessing Facebook. The main reasons for this population group to not use this SNS are related with privacy issues ("I think that Facebook is not safe. How do I know if talking to a person on Facebook, that person is the only one that sees what I write"). Another reason appointed is related to negative feelings about what people do in the SNS ("I do not like Facebook, because people expose their lives there"). These results showed that younger elderly use Facebook more. Users of this SNS prefer using the computer more than non-users, and vice versa concerning use of TV. We also found that the reason for non-users of Facebook to reject all alternatives for accessing this SNS, are related with privacy issues and negative feelings about the way that people expose their lives. These findings support previous findings [9, 15, 24] regarding the use of Facebook by this population.

5.2   Are the Elderly Receptive to Use Social Applications on TV (RQ2)?

The findings about the usage of Facebook, related with the usage of computer and the feelings towards TV already reported when answering RQ1, (chart B and C on Fig. 2 respectively) also allow us to discuss that TV could be a way for non-Facebook users to adopt SNS. By not using a computer, they currently cannot make use of Facebook, but their general appreciation towards TV could make this context ideal for the use of SNS. However, when considering their perceived interest in doing so, they rejected it (chart D on Fig. 2). Still, as we have seen when answering RQ1, this rejection could be strongly associated with bad feelings about the word "Facebook". In this sense, SmartTV technology could be one way for older adults to access SNS like Facebook. However, this technology has not yet reached the older population: 94 % have never used SmartTVs and 71 % do not know what that concept is. Still, when we explained what it is about, they were very enthusiastic. Some of them even said they would buy a SmartTV if they had the chance. From the several tasks they would like to perform using one, tasks related with SNS such as viewing photos and videos of family and close friends, creating events with these groups and sending messages were highlighted. Furthermore, they were also interested in talking to family and friends through video conference, as this would allow them to see people on a larger screen. One participant even said "So I could talk and see my granddaughter on TV when she went to Covilhã". These results are an important outcome of this study as they clearly show that seniors want to perform social tasks through TV. Older adults enjoyed the idea of recording and sharing TV content with family and friends if those contents are related with news, documentaries and debates (Fig. 3 (left)). In fact, some of them already do this without this technology: "I'm watching TV and call friends to tell them to switch to what I am seeing". This led to including TV content sharing functionality within the TV based SNS prototype. This also provides excellent feedback to answer this research question, because through a TV-based SNS, older adults have the opportunity to directly share TV contents with their family and close friends. Finally, some older adults proposed a new functionality. They have plenty of printed photos they would like to share with their family and friends through TV. Thus, we have included in the TV-based prototype the possibility to digitize their digital photos and share them through their online network. These results clearly show older adults' interest towards using a TV-based SNS application. Older adults want to make social tasks on TV, such as, talk with their family, sharing TV content and printed photos with their family and close friends.

5.3   Are the Elderly Receptive to Use Social Applications on Tablet Devices (RQ3)?

The majority (77 %) of the participants interviewed said they had never used a tablet but would appreciate the opportunity to do it. In a Likert scale of 1 (I do not like to use

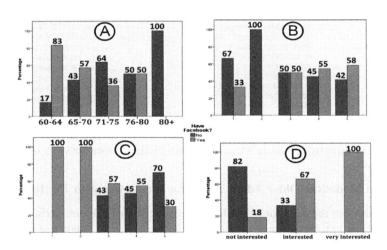

Fig. 2. Differences between users of Facebook and non-users of this SNS: (A) Age distribution; (B) Like using computer; (C) Feelings about TV; (D) Interest accessing SNS in TV.

a Tablet at all) to 5 (I really like to use a Tablet) they averaged 3.29 (SD = 1.54, MED = 4.00, mode = 5). In the same way, the ones who use a Tablet, are very satisfied with the way it works (M = 4.14, SD = 0.69, MED = 4.00, mode = 4). When questioned about the reasons for using it, they appointed portability associated with talking with family and friends and playing games with their grandchildren. The last two are tasks supported by Facebook. Results from the structured questions regarding easiness of tasks indirectly show that they use it primarily to access the Internet, view and write emails and view photos and videos of family and close friends (Fig. 3 (right)). This last functionality is again the main reason appointed by older adults to make use of a SNS like Facebook. However, these results also show that about 71 % of them do not use it to access Facebook. Similar to what happened before regarding the possible use of SNS on TV, this could also have been influenced by the negative feelings towards the word "Facebook". Additionally, negative feelings were also felt concerning privacy issues when using Facebook on a tablet device because of the device specific properties ("I think Facebook in the tablet device is less secure" or "I do not know who sees what I put on Facebook through the tablet device"). Inspired by previous work which made use of Tablet devices as a digital photo frame [9] or as a device for sending and receiving photos from family members [21] we inquired participants about the idea of having it as a photo frame that displays content shared by their family on Facebook. In a Likert scale from 1 (not interesting at all) to 5 (very interesting), they generally enjoyed it, averaging 3.65 (SD = 1.52, MED = 4.00, mode = 5). Although results do not clearly show older adults interest in accessing Facebook through a Tablet-based application, the tasks they perform or would like to perform through this device, along with the preconceived negative feelings about Facebook, could indicate the opposite.

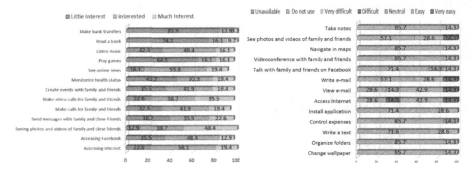

Fig. 3.   Interests on sharing TV content (left). Preferred tablet activities (right).

5.4   What Modalities Older Adults Prefer for Interacting with TV (RQ4)?

When asked about the need for help when interacting with TV-based SNS, older adults showed interest in a broad range of alternatives. The preferred manner of assistance is voice feedback (81 %), followed by help through a virtual character (avatar) (71 %) and textual help (55 %). The preference for voice support was justified as being the one more close to the traditional ways of communication they use daily. Some seniors also underlined that having an application talking to them could make them feel less alone. Several structured questions showed the preferences concerning seniors' interaction with a TV-based SNS. Figure 4 (left) shows older adults prefer both the traditional way (RC) and speech for this interaction but are also open to interact through gestures. Based on these results, we decided to include these two modalities in the TV-based prototype. Finally, in respect to new ways of interaction with the TV, it is important to highlight that seniors found interest to have a tablet as a device for help in two distinct situations (answers were obtained through Likert scale from 1 (totally disagree) to 5 (totally agree)): when they cannot see specific TV-content they would like to have a tablet displaying it at a larger size (M = 3.81,MED = 4, mode = 5); and for showing content related with what they are watching, meaning providing additional information about TV-content. (M = 4.00, MED = 4, mode = 4). These results show that older adults are strongly interested in having alternative ways of interacting with a TV-based SNS, such as voice and gestures, at the same time as they preserve the traditional interaction (RC) and are helped by contextual information in both audio, visual forms.

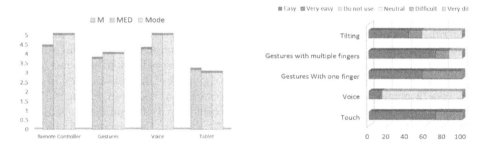

Fig. 4. Older adults preferred modalities for interact with TV (left chart) and tablet (right chart).

5.5   What Modalities Older Adults Prefer for Interacting with Tablets (RQ5)?

Similar to what happens on a TV context, when asked about the need for help interacting with Tablet-based SNS, older adults showed interest in a broad range of alternatives. Ratios and reasons for preferring speech are the same as for TV interaction, and ratios for avatar and text are also similar. With regard to what modalities older adults prefer to interact with SNS for tablet devices (Fig. 4 (right)), seniors appointed first the simplicity of traditional touch interaction as well as gesture interaction using both one or multiple fingers. However, the study obtained some interesting findings that open the possibility to interact in new ways which satisfy the needs of the elderly. About 50 % see tilt interaction as easy or very easy. When asked for further explanation about this, participants told they were used to this way of interaction from when they play games on the tablet device. As a result, we considered providing navigation on the tablet prototype menu by tilting the device. Additionally, voice interaction on the

Tablet is almost unknown to older adults. However, when asked about the possibility of using it, they foresee advantages on tasks such as: browsing photos and videos (75 %), adjust the tablet volume (78 %), play the media content (74 %), and perform speech-to-text tasks like writing emails (68 %) and notes (71 %). As a result, we will provide speech navigation for every interaction on the Tablet device. Moreover, seniors found interesting to interact with the tablet using touches on the back of the device. They recognized it could constitute an advantage when they need the screen to be completely visible (like playing/pausing a video (47 %)) and for basic tasks such as media content navigation (52 %). As a result, we considered exploring this interaction for tasks such as seeing extra information about a post. These results show that older adults are strongly interested in having alternative ways of interacting with a Tablet-based SNS, such as, voice, tilting and back-of-device touch. Additionally, they preserve the traditional interaction (touch and gestures) and are helped by contextual information in both audio, visual forms.

5.6 Concerning the Concepts of Adaptation and Personalization, Which Is Preferred by Seniors (RQ6)?

Concepts of personalization and adaptation were explained to older adults before asking them about any preference. After acknowledging the concepts, they were asked about the possibility of changing content size, and increase/decrease audio volume within the application, both by doing it manually (personalization) or being done automatically (adaptation). Results show a strong interest in both features in both concepts (averaging from 4.10 to 4.35 for personalization, and from 4.29 to 4.32 for adaptation). Results obtained through a Likert scale from 1 (I think that is bad) to 5 (I think that is good) averaged 4.39 (SD = 0.72, MED = 5.00, mode = 5) for personalization and 4.32 (SD = 1.013, MED = 5.00, mode = 5) for adaptation. We also verified that there is not a clear preference for either one. As a result, we decided to implement personalization features related with increasing and decreasing interface elements and audio volumes, on both prototypes. These results indicate that seniors have a strong interest in adaptation and personalization concepts, showing preference for neither.

5.7 What Issues Should Be Taken into Account in the Implementation of Adaptation and Personalization Concepts (RQ7)?

We also observed older adults opinions about other conditions related with the concepts of adaptation and personalization. In general, they found interesting to have a technology tailored to their needs (M = 3.52, SD = 1.48, MED = 4.00, mode = 5) and would not mind if both adaptation (87 %) and personalization (83 %) would make their interfaces different from others. However, almost every participant (90 %) argue for the necessity of having control over what interface features could be adapted. Finally, when asked if they would mind if the technology collected data about the way they interact with it for adaptation purposes, participants showed tolerance (M = 3.90, SD = 1.30, MED = 4.00, mode = 4). Those with less tolerance justified it with concerns of privacy ("I do not know what "they" are going to do with my data"). These results indicate that older adults do not mind if adaptation and personalization make user interfaces different from others, although it is imperative that they retain control over what can be changed. Additionally, they do not mind if data about the way they interact with the systems is gathered for adaptation or personalization purposes.

6 Developing TV and Tablet Interfaces

In this section, we present both prototypes taking into account all the recommendations and results from the structured interviews highlighted in the previous section. Additionally, for a better understanding of what was validated or discussed on the focus groups, we will make a reference to that process every time we present a new feature.

6.1 You, Me and TV Prototype

You, me & TV prototype provides three different modalities (RC, voice and gestures) which were indicated during interviews with older adults. RC interaction is done with directional arrows and the OK button as previous research confirms that this is the best approach for older adults [7]. Additionally, remaining keys can be used to perform social tasks, such as making a post with a press of a button. Another modality implemented is speech recognition. This modality has two distinct approaches. The first is based on voice commands that perform a particular action depending on the current application context task. The second is based on speech-to-text. Both approaches were implemented using the Kinect microphone. The last modality is gesture recognition that allow users to perform gestures to control the application. We follow the mouse cursor metaphor approach, as Bobeth et al. [3] had confirmed through studies with senior users that this would be the best approach. We decided to validate two different ways to implement confirmation of actions with gestures. In the first option confirming is done through the hand closing. In the second option, conforming is done by leaving the "mouse cursor" three seconds over the object that user wants to select. Both approaches are being validated during the longitudinal tests.

The prototype (Fig. 5) focuses on three main functionalities: content publishing, content visualization and group management. Content publishing functionality addresses the types of media content that is possible to share through TV technology. As it was possible to understand from interviews and focus groups, older adults enjoyed further to share photos and TV content with family and close friends. These two types of content lead seniors to mention two different usage contexts. The possibility to share printed photos that older users have in their albums; and the possibility to share what seniors are seeing on TV at a specific time. Both actions end with the posting of a publication on Facebook. Content visualization allows older users to see photos, videos and text content of their family and close friends. The prototype has two main areas, in one it is possible to see family members and in other to see friends, as requested in the focus groups. If a user wants to see information about a specific member he should select it and the prototype presents an area with all the information. The information is divided in photos, videos, publications and general profile and interests. This division was also informed by older adults in the focus groups. Finally, the third main functionality allows users to manage sub groups inside family and close friends' screens. This was a surprising feature raised by older adults as they wanted to create sub groups inside family and friends. They gave us some examples like "I had gymnastics friends and coffee friends and I want to distinguish these two groups". We also perceived that if a friend belongs to two groups then it should appear in both groups.

Fig. 5. TV-based prototype You, Me & TV

6.2 YouTablet Prototype

The YouTablet prototype (Fig. 5 (right)) offers five modalities of interaction: touch, gesture, speech, tilting and back-of-device touch. As requested on the focus groups, touch interaction will be based on providing touch buttons for every possible action. Additionally, gestures will be supported as intuitive options to accomplish the same actions. Speech interaction, like on the You, Me & TV prototype, will be based on both voice commands and speech-to-text functionalities using the Android speech recognition module. Tilting will be offered as an exploratory interaction, based on a "press to tilt" concept where the user has to press a button on the interface and at the same time tilt the device. This concept was inspired by both the "squeeze and tilt" concept [18], and Rekimoto concept for tilting operations on small screen devices [25]. Tilting will be offered for menu navigation and scrolling tasks, as suggested by older adults opinions on both the interviews and the focus groups - they perceived it as very useful and easy to do, however they expressed the need for help on the first interaction, especially regarding what button to press to begin the interaction -. Finally, and also as a result of the structured interviews, YouTablet will support back-of-device interaction inspired by Robinson et al. [26] for tasks related with getting extra information from interface items. For implementing this feature we followed an approach based on a state machine algorithm (Fig. 6).

Regarding functionalities, YouTablet focuses on content publishing, content visualization, group visualization and digital photo frame. Content publishing is based

Fig. 6. Tablet-based Facebook prototype (right).

on providing the traditional posting options already available in Facebook; YouTablet approach on content visualization is based on presenting posts one by one. Each post's content is fitted to the screen in order to focus older adults' attention. This concept was validated on the focus groups, being approved by all participants. Navigation through posts is based on a next and previous approach, and supported by four distinct modalities of interaction: gestures, voice commands, buttons by touch and tilting. In the focus groups, swipe was seen as the main modality to achieve this navigation. It was also referred the need for providing help throughout the application regarding which voice commands could be used. Button navigation also seemed intuitive, although some participants expressed the desire for having buttons on each side of the content, even at the expense of having to grab the tablet only with one hand. As a result, the location of the buttons could be considered as a personalization option. Still, regarding content visualization, flipping the post to see its comments and likes was implemented as it provides more space to organize the graphic elements on interface and allow for a larger font. Back-of-device touch will be offered to achieve this, as focus groups participants perceived it as a very natural action. Additionally, this can also be achieved by using buttons labelled "See comments" and "See likes". Regarding group visualization, YouTablet will offer the possibility of filtering posts by groups and navigating through its members. Additionally, options for managing groups suggested in the You, Me & TV prototype were also validated by the participants. Digital photo frame is a slide show mode, which presents the Family group members photos like a digital frame. It has an automatic activation and deactivation. When the tablet is not being used, it starts the slide show until the user grabs the tablet again. This functionality was first perceived as a good idea on the interviews and further validated on the focus groups. The latter participants requested an option to directly access the content being shown, and an option for also visualizing events. Finally, concerning the top action bar and the existence of symbols as shortcuts for features, participants pointed out the need for additional help in understanding its purposes or the addition of text labels (Fig. 7).

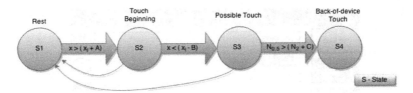

Fig. 7. The back-of-device touch state machine: from a rest position (S1), the algorithm measures the device spatial variation on the 3 axis. When a positive peek A first happens, the machine transits to S2. Then, when a peek B happens in the opposite direction, the machine reaches S3. Finally, if the device's microphone detects a sound variation of at least C it reaches S4. Reaching S4 means the machine recognized a touch. In S2 and S3, if the transition condition is not met in a set amount of time, the machine goes back to S1

7   Conclusion

Social isolation seriously damages the health of older adults leading to a progressive increase in the risk of mortality. Facebook has the potential to increase the number of social interactions of older people with relatives and friends by getting them to feel less isolated. We conducted a study consisting of 30 semi-structured interviews and 3 focus groups. In the interviews we sought to differentiate older adults who use Facebook from the ones who do not, and to perceive the opportunities for using multimodal adaptive TV and tablet devices as ways for non-users of SNS to gain access to them. Focus groups allowed to involve older people in the design of Facebook prototypes for TV and tablet. The results showed that the elderly are receptive to using SNSs on TV and Tablet and that these applications must meet a number of recommendations: they should provide different modalities like RC, voice and gestures for TV, and touch, gestures and voice for Tablet; exploratory modalities like tilting and back-of-device touch can also be used for menu navigation and showing contextual information on Tablet; older adults highlighted the importance of always getting contextual help through several outputs and appreciate the concepts of adaptation and personalization. Finally, the study also suggested new features such as sharing of printed photos through the TV-based prototype and a digital photo frame through a Tablet-based interface which presents the family members photos in a slide show mode like a digital frame. Both prototypes and design decisions are being further validated through a longitudinal study.

Acknowledgments. We would like to thank to Universidade Sénior de Massamá e Monte Abraão and all the participants for making this study possible. This work was partially supported by Fundação para a Ciência e Tecnologia (FCT) through Multiannual Funding to the LaSIGE research unit and the Individual Doctoral Grant SFRH/BD/81115/2011.

References

1. Top 15 Most Popular Social Networking Sites — January 2015 (2015). http://www.ebizmba.com/articles/social-networking-websites

2. Alaoui, M., Lewkowicz, M.: A LivingLab approach to involve elderly in the design of smart TV applications offering communication services. In: Ozok, A., Zaphiris, P. (eds.) OCSC 2013. LNCS, vol. 8029, pp. 325–334. Springer, Heidelberg (2013)
3. Bobeth, J., Schmehl, S., Kruijff, E., Deutsch, S., Tscheligi, M.: Evaluating performance and acceptance of older adults using freehand gestures for TV menu control. In: EuroiTV 2012, pp. 35–44. ACM, New York, NY, USA (2012)
4. Bobeth, J., Schrammel, J., Deutsch, S., Klein, M., Drobics, M., Hochleitner, C., Tscheligi, M.: Tablet, gestures, remote control?: influence of age on performance and user experience with iTV applications. In: TVX 2014, pp. 139–146 (2014)
5. Burke, M., Kraut, R., Marlow, C.: Social capital on facebook: differentiating uses and users. In: CHI 2011, pp. 571–580 (2011)
6. Chen, Y.: Usability analysis on online social networks for the elderly. Technical report, Helsinki University of Technology (2009)
7. Coelho, J., Biswas, P., Duarte, C., Guerreiro, T., Langdon, P., Feiteira, P., Costa, D., Costa, D., Neves, B., Alves, F.: Involving all stakeholders in the development of TV applications for elderly. Int. J. Adv. Intell. Syst. 5(3–4), 427–440 (2012)
8. Coelho, J., Duarte, C., Biswas, P., Langdon, P.: Developing accessible TV applications. In: ASSETS 2011, pp. 131–138. ACM (2011)
9. Cornejo, R., Tentori, M., Favela, J.: Enriching in-person encounters through social media: a study on family connectedness for the elderly. Int. J. Hum.-Comput. Stud. 71(9), 889–899 (2013)
10. Cornwell, E.Y., Waite, L.J.: Measuring social isolation among older adults using multiple indicators from the NSHAP study. J. Gerontol. 64B(suppl 1), i38–i46 (2009)
11. Findlater, L., Wobbrock, J.: Personalized input: improving ten-finger touchscreen typing through automatic adaptation. In: Proceedings of CHI 2012. pp. 815–824. ACM (2012)
12. Gajos, K.Z., Wobbrock, J.O., Weld, D.S.: Automatically generating user interfaces adapted to users' motor and vision capabilities. In: UIST 2007, pp. 231–240 (2007)
13. Garattini, C., Wherton, J., Prendergast, D.: Linking the lonely: an exploration of a communication technology designed to support social interaction among older adults. Univers. Access Inf. Soc. 11(2), 211–222 (2012)
14. Gaver,W., Boucher, A., Bowers, J., Blythe, M., Jarvis, N., Cameron, D., Kerridge, T., Wilkie, A., Phillips, R., Wright, P.: The photostroller: Supporting diverse care home residents in engaging with the world. In: CHI 2011, pp. 1757–1766. ACM (2011)
15. Gibson, L., Moncur, W., Forbes, P., Arnott, J., Martin, C., Bhachu, A.S.: Designing social networking sites for older adults. pp. 186–194. British Computer Society (BCS), UK (2010)
16. Gomes, G., Duarte, C., Coelho, J., Matos, E.: Designing a facebook interface for senior users, Sci. World J., Article ID 741567, p. 8 (2014)
17. Grosinger, J., Vetere, F., Fitzpatrick, G.: Agile life: addressing knowledge and social motivations for active aging. In: OzCHI 2012, pp. 162–165 (2012)
18. Harrison, B.L., Fishkin, K.P., Gujar, A., Mochon, C., Want, R.: Squeeze me, hold me, tilt me! an exploration of manipulative user interfaces. In: CHI 1998 pp. 17–24 (1998)
19. Judge, T.K., Neustaedter, C., Harrison, S., Blose, A.: Family portals: Connecting families through a multifamily media space. In: CHI 2011 pp. 1205–1214 (2011)
20. Karahasanovi, A., Brandtzg, P.B., Heim, J., Lders, M., Vermeir, L., Pierson, J., Lievens, B., Vanattenhoven, J., Jans, G.: Co-creation and user-generated contentelderly peoples user requirements. Comput. Hum. Behav. 25(3), 655–678 (2009)
21. Lindley, S.E., Harper, R., Sellen, A.: Desiring to be in touch in a changing communications landscape: attitudes of older adults. In: Proceedings of CHI 2009, pp. 1693–1702 (2009)
22. Lindley, S.E.: Shades of lightweight: supporting cross-generational communication through home messaging. Univers. Access Inf. Soc. 11(1), 31–43 (2012)

23. McLaughlin, A.C., Rogers, W.A., Fisk, A.D.: Using direct and indirect input devices: attention demands and age-related differences. ACM Trans. Comput.-Hum. Interact. **16**(1), 2:1–2:15 (2009)
24. Norval, C., Arnott, J.L., Hanson, V.L.: What's on your mind?: Investigating recommendations for inclusive social networking and older adults. In: CHI 2014, pp. 3923–3932. ACM, NY (2014)
25. Rekimoto, J.: Tilting operations for small screen interfaces. In: UIST 1996, pp. 167–168 (1996)
26. Robinson, S., Rajput, N., Jones, M., Jain, A., Sahay, S., Nanavati, A.: Tapback: Towards richer mobile interfaces in impoverished contexts. In: CHI 2011, pp. 2733–2736 (2011)
27. Stephanidis, C., Paramythis, A., Sfyrakis, M., Stergiou, A., Maou, N., Leventis, A., Paparoulis, G., Karagiannidis, C.: Adaptable and adaptive user interfaces for disabled users in the avanti project. In: IS&N 1998, pp. 153–166 (1998)
28. Stobel, C., Blessing, L.: Mobile device interaction gestures for older users. In: NordiCHI 2010, pp. 793–796 (2010)
29. Waycott, J., Vetere, F., Pedell, S., Kulik, L., Ozanne, E., Gruner, A., Downs, J.: Older adults as digital content producers. In: Proceedings of CHI 2013, pp. 39–48. ACM (2013)

Socially Networked or Isolated? Differentiating Older Adults and the Role of Tablets and Television

José Coelho$^{(\boxtimes)}$ and Carlos Duarte

LaSIGE, University of Lisbon, Lisbon, Portugal
{jcoelho,cad}@di.fc.ul.pt

Abstract. Population is aging. With it comes social isolation which leads to drastic health degrading situations. Facebook has the potential to assist older adults in maintaining relationships. Still problems like unclear purposes, design complexity and privacy issues have contributed to a lower uptake. We conducted a study to understand how to draw Facebook closer to older adults, investigate the main difficulties and motivations towards its use and adoption, and inquire about the possibilities of using Tablet and Television as alternatives to the traditional PC for accessing this kind of services. Findings show correlations between self-belief in technical skills, motor limitations, and tablet use and the use of Facebook. It also shows that the complexity of Facebook's user interface limits its use by the older adults that use it and works as a barrier for its adoption by the seniors who still don't. We also identified distinct groups and distinct feelings about the use of Television as a vehicle for social interaction. We derived a set of recommendations to consider when designing solutions for tackling social isolation.

Keywords: Facebook · Older adults · Social isolation · Tablet · Television · Questionnaire

1 Introduction

Population all over the world is aging [9]. As people get old, several physical and social problems arise. One of the most concerning issues is social isolation, which typically "kicks in" at retirement age, and leads to drastic health degrading situations [15]. Satisfying social needs through participation in social networks is the only way to fight isolation. These serve a great number of functions, providing social and emotional support, information resources and ties to other people [28]. Social Network Services (SNS) are an on-line equivalent to off-line Social Networks. In the words of Burke, "SNS are designed to connect people with friends, family and other strong ties, as well as to efficiently keep in touch with a larger set of acquaintances and new ties, without having to share the same space" [2]. A growing body of evidence suggests there are many social and cognitive benefits for older adults that make use of these technologies to create content and actively participate in reciprocal information sharing with family and friends [17, 19]. However, although SNSs have the potential to assist older adults in maintaining relationships, uptake by this segment of the population is still low. Much of

© IFIP International Federation for Information Processing 2015
J. Abascal et al. (Eds.): INTERACT 2015, Part I, LNCS 9296, pp. 129–146, 2015.
DOI: 10.1007/978-3-319-22701-6_10

the literature overlaps, with several emerging themes such as preconceptions about SNSs [13, 18], design complexity [13, 23], loss of a deeper way of communication [2, 14], and above all privacy [13, 14, 18, 23], being suggested as the main causes for the low participation. Additionally, even SNS developed specifically for older adults have not achieved popularity [4, 29], mainly because younger counterparts - the main reason for the use of SNSs in the first place [4] - are not interested in using these tailored solutions. Additionally, while traditional technology like the PC could compensate some of the age-related changes in older adults' physical, social and cognitive resources, enhancing their quality of life, they in many cases get disinterested and frustrated by too complex technology [21, 26].

Hence, the challenges are not only resolving interface problems related with well-known (and used by everyone) SNS like Facebook, but mostly providing technology that encourages older people to actively engage in technology-mediated communication and to use Facebook [7, 17]. New technologies like Tablet devices or older technology like Television (TV) can be ideal solutions for these goals: TV as a technology present "in every home" could help reduce the gap between old and new technology [17, 24], while Tablet devices built on top of mobile device advantages like simplicity and touch interaction, could help captivate older users [16, 27].

In this paper we begin with a review of the relevant literature that examined older adults' experiences and attitudes towards SNS. We also focus on how both Tablet and Television have been known to play a role in the interaction with this population. We then try to answer the main goal of this research which consists of how to draw older adults closer to Facebook, especially those who still do not make use of it. We designed and applied a questionnaire to be able to infer the current state of use of the most worldwide used SNS by older adults, the main difficulties and motivations towards its use and adoption, and the possibilities of using Tablet and Television as alternatives for accessing this kind of services. As contributions, we present the main findings and provide a discussion regarding not only the role these platforms can play in decreasing social isolation, but also the way older adults' confidence in their own abilities is fundamental in adopting and using new technology and for the purposes of social engagement.

2   Related Work

2.1   Older Adults and Social Network Services

Since 2005 it has been shown that the most obvious motive for older adults to join a SNS like Facebook is the need for integration and social interaction [1, 22]. Because older adults are typically more isolated than younger segments of the population, identifying with others and gaining a sense of belonging is essential for them; as well as finding a basis for social interaction by connecting with family, friends and society, and gaining insight into the circumstances of others. These findings have been supported by both earlier and more recent research: the preference to communicate with relatives involving social activities [25]; the enrollment in offline and online social networks as a way of dealing with the inevitable mental and physical deterioration after retirement [26];

the importance of staying connected with geographically remote grandchildren as a major motivation for the use of technology like SNS [18]; the confirmation that greater SNS use is associated with increased social capital and reduced loneliness [3]; and the association between the use of SNSs and health benefits, like a decrease of loneliness, an increase in social well-being, longevity and both mental and physical health [13].

However, in spite of the mentioned advantages, older adults are still keeping distance from these type of services as they largely overlook their needs in several distinct domains: the difficulty in grasping the purpose of SNSs and the impact of adverse media stories [13], the problems with privacy controls [13, 14, 17, 18, 23], the need for varying degrees of reciprocity and ways of expressing deeper communication [13, 14], the need for better designed grouping functionalities [13], the necessity of focusing interaction around strong-tie relationships (like family members and close friends) [2, 14, 23], interface aspects related with complexity and technical terms and symbols [23] and the need for supporting adaptation or alternative ways of interaction [2, 17].

2.2 Tablet Devices and Older Adults

The use of Tablet devices by being "eyes-free, button-free, and silent" was first seen as a way to facilitate interaction, and increase accessibility for older adults. Especially if the interaction is designed to match patterns and symbols they are familiar with, and their execution is tolerant to motor impairments an older user might display [16, 27]. They also constitute an ideal platform for older adults when dealing with numeric entry tasks, not forcing users to divide their attention between the input device and screen content [5], and they offer high flexibility making it possible to adapt to distinct users' needs and preferences like the ones present in the old aged population [10].

Hence, the design of new ways of interaction based on Tablet devices, can result in valuable contributions for the older segment of the population. More specifically, when working as a bridge for the adoption of Internet-based services like social applications and services capable of tackling social isolation. Examples of these were: Lindley et al. PersonCard concept [19] which allowed for lightweight information to be sent and displayed within an older adult's home using a photo frame enhanced with touch-screen functionalities (much like a Tablet device); Lindley et al. situated messaging device called Wayve [20] which was based on the same principles and made use of a device even similar to a Tablet; the Building Bridges project [11], a 12-inch touch screen device in a custom-made stand (the same principles as a Tablet) and a built-in phone handset, which was built with the goal of providing opportunistic social interaction among old adults who did not know each other before and which resulted in a very simplified use and in new social interactions (even outside the system); the Emnesh [29] which took advantage of the Internet connectivity and iPad features like an in-built camera and a virtual keyboard, for both capturing, exchanging and controlling photographs and messages around the screen and enabled older users to build rapport and find common interests; and Cornejo et al. ambient SNS called Tlatoque [7] based on a multi-touch screen resembling a tablet, which communicated to Facebook to expose photographs in the user's home enabling a more natural interaction with the social information and contributing to enriching in-person encounters.

2.3   Television and Older Adults

Recently, digital TV as a media consumption platform has increasingly turned from a simple receiver and presenter of broadcast signals, to an interactive and personalized media terminal, with access to Internet-based services. TV panels currently on the market offer embedded digital processing platforms (connected TV), which have the potential to turn the TV into an application platform and service terminal. At the same time, it is recognized that older adults still face problems when using this kind of TV-based services mainly because of functional limitations related with age-impairments [19], with typical barriers raised by digital menus and Electronic Program Guides (EPGs) [8], and mainly because of the lack of provision of accessible user interfaces [6].

Still, the development of connected TV and its relation with common Information and Communication Technologies (ICT) applications like social media applications could make a big difference for older adults' living quality and help fight issues related with social isolation. Example of this can be found in work from Karahasanovic et al. who investigated user requirements related to consumption and co-creation of content in new media. They showed that a TV with additional functionality might offer a solution for older adults who are afraid of computers, because it takes less time to turn on and is much simpler to work on [17]. Additional examples can also be found in Meeteetse, a social well-being system based on place attachment which established a connection between homes and a local community and made use of several TV screens [1]; and the Photostroller, a device designed for use by residents of a care home for older people, which showed a continuous slide-show of photographs and made use of a sort-of old Television screen which could move around the house [12].

2.4   Discussion

There is a vast amount of related work concerning Facebook and older adults, and more specifically concerning the issues which make this service less easy to use for this segment of the population. However, limited research has focused in what distinguishes older adults who make use of Facebook from older adults who have not yet adopted it. The understanding of these differences can provide valuable knowledge concerning the motivations to use this SNS. At the same time the understanding of issues which negatively influence both, could help identify more broad design problems which do not consider third-age problems. In this paper we build from previous research and try to understand what those differences are with the goal of finding ways to bring Facebook closer to the older population.

Moreover, the understanding of the benefits that the interaction with Tablet devices can bring to the older population, and the way it has been used for keeping older adults in contact with their family, are good indicators that it can also be useful as a bridge for accessing Facebook. However, no previous work has focused on the validation of that possibility. Additionally, and concerning TV, the expansion of SmartTVs and the opportunities they can provide in terms of getting Internet services - like Facebook - closer to older adults have also not yet been explored in detail. Taking into consideration the way older adults use TV almost every day, the possibility of using Facebook to keep in contact with family and close friends on a daily basis, represents a valuable opportunity that should be explored. Taking into consideration previous indicators, in this paper we also focus on how older adults would perceive the possibility of using these two alternative ways of interaction for keeping in touch and accessing typical content and features like the ones present in Facebook.

3 Methodology

The main goal behind this work is to find ways on how to draw Facebook closer to the older segment of the population so they can take advantage of its features as a means of fighting social isolation. To be able to do that, we must first understand the relationship between older adults and SNSs, and the technology that might support SNS dissemination. Consequently, the main research question (RQ1) underlying this research will be concerned with what distinguishes Facebook users and non-users (across the older population). We want to check if older adults not using Facebook have the desire to use it, and try to understand the main reasons behind its non-adoption or limited use. We also want to understand the differences between these older adults and the ones which use Facebook, considering their education, gender, age-range, age-related limitations and the way they believe in themselves concerning the use of technology. We want to understand if these factors can influence the adoption and use of a SNS like Facebook. Additionally, we want to consider two more research questions: (RQ2) could TV or (RQ3) Tablet devices be good alternatives for older adults to access Facebook or Facebook related features. To answer these questions we need to characterize both platforms in terms of their current use, and understand if SNSs are one of the reasons for their use, and, if not, if interacting with Facebook could be something that older adults consider when thinking about this platforms.

We considered collecting richer data from interviews or focus groups, or pooling a larger number of sources with user surveys. Even though richer data would be helpful for more in-depth characterization of some of the topics to be addressed, we opted to conduct a larger user survey and leave other instruments to later in the project's lifecycle. For the user survey, we prepared a questionnaire, which we made available online to an international audience, with three translations: English, Portuguese and Spanish. It was announced in several mailing lists, with focus on healthcare and research. The online survey was available for a period of four months. Additionally, the questionnaire was administered in person at three senior institutions (two senior universities and one retirement home).

3.1 Participants

141 participants (64 male, 77 female) answered the questionnaire. 129 questionnaires were answered online, while 12 were answered by administering it in person. All participants were volunteers and more than 55 years old. We did not restrict participants to more than 60 or 65 years of age, as we also wanted to reflect the importance of

individuals which will be considered older adults in the next five years. Age was not asked directly, participants selected the appropriate age range from 6 different categories which spanned from "less than 60" to "more than 80". Table 1 shows how participants spanned over those categories. Anonymity was kept at all times, with each user being identified exclusively by an id number. All data was saved in a secure repository.

Table 1. Participants' age range distribution.

Age categories	Frequency	Percentage
Less than 60	46	32.6
Between 60 and 64	29	20.6
Between 65 and 70	33	23.4
Between 71 and 75	14	9.9
Between 76 and 80	7	5.0
More than 80	12	8.5
Total	141	100.0

3.2   Questionnaire

First, profiling questions concerning age, gender, education, household composition, the way participants see themselves concerning the use of technology, and regarding difficulties and impairments, were asked. Second, participants were asked about Facebook awareness, how frequently they make use of it, or how much times they have tried it. These questions were followed by Likert scale questions where participants had to classify their agreement (on a scale from 1 (strongly disagree) to 5 (strongly agree)) with possible reasons why they use or why they would like to use Facebook. Sentences were related with getting information about what's going on in the world, family and friends, making new friendships, privacy issues, usability and satisfaction.

Questions related with both Television and Tablet were asked next. For the first platform no questions related with awareness or frequency of use were asked, as it was assumed that every user had a television (one user in fact questioned this option, and noticed she neither had nor wanted to have one). Likert scale questions (with the same scale as above) were asked regarding reasons why participants use Television and how easy it is for them to interact with this traditional technology, followed by matters related with their familiarity with smart-TVs or access to Internet through Television, and concerning their willingness to use this platform as a way of accessing Facebook or related social activities and content.

For the Tablet questions, a similar approach to the one followed regarding Facebook was adopted. Some questions related with Tablet awareness and use, and about frequency of use were first asked and used to filter the remainder of the questionnaire. Then, participants answered to a series of Likert scale questions where they were asked to classify their agreement with the reasons why they use or why they would like to use Tablet devices. Finally, multiple choice questions were asked where participants would choose activities and applications they typically perform in Tablet devices.

On a last note, although specific questionnaires for accessing technological expertise and other skills' characterizing instruments already exist we decided against using such instruments due to (1) the increase it would represent in what constitutes already a long questionnaire; (2) most of them being based on self-reported data nonetheless.

4 Findings

4.1 Technologic Expertise and Age Related Limitations

Concerning the use of technology, we inquired users about their self-characterization regarding technical expertise and the technologies widely available in the market. More than half of the participants (58 %) considered themselves as being capable of using typically available technology and only about one fourth considered to have some difficulties interacting with technology.

Concerning the matter of age-related limitations each participant answered from their own perspective selecting the type and severity of impairments they feel to have. About one third considered not having any impairment, while 45 % considered to have only one type, with about 10 % having two types, 9 % having three different types of impairments and a total of 5 participants (3.5 %) having the whole range of hearing, vision, motor and cognitive impairments. Additionally, in terms of severity of the limitations, 53 % of the participants considered to have only minor impairments, leaving only about 14 % considering to have more severe limitations. Lastly, and concerning the type of impairments, the most frequent ones were related with vision, with more than half (51 %) of participants considering to have this kind of difficulties. Additionally, 20 % considered to have hearing difficulties, about 15 % considered to have motor limitations and 15 % considered to have cognitive difficulties as a result of the ageing process.

4.2 Facebook

Regarding Facebook, almost everyone (97 %) is aware of what it is, and about 67 % makes use of it with about 40 % doing it every day (which represents 62 % of the ones which use Facebook). Additionally, only one fifth of the participants never experienced it. Still in terms of Facebook usage, 50 % of in-person respondents were users, while this number grew to 69 % for online respondents. While expectably bigger, it did not cause any significant differences in the findings.

When questioned about the reasons behind the use of this SNS (Table 2), participants gave the most relevance to keeping in contact with family and close friends. This is in-line with related work which focused on the importance of family in the use of Facebook [2, 14, 18, 25]. Additionally, they also give an almost equivalent relevance to keeping in contact with friends. This result contrasts previous findings, where older adults did not attribute this degree of importance to all friends. Moreover, they are more or less neutral regarding the use of Facebook as a means for accessing information about what is going on in the world, and tend to reject the use of Facebook as a platform for making new friends. This confirms findings from previous studies on the main reasons for older adults to use this type of platform [3, 13, 18, 23].

Table 2. Willingness to use Facebook.

I use Facebook to...	Know what's going on in the world	Know about my relatives and close friends	Know what's going with all my friends	Make new friendships
Mean	2.68	3.56	3.26	1.63
Median	3.00	4.00	3.00	1.00
Mode	1	4	4	1

When posing the same questions to participants who do not use Facebook all possible reasons for using the platform in the future were rejected (averages between 1.96 and 1.82 and modes of 1). This shows that the majority of older adults who do not make use of Facebook do not see any advantage on doing so, which in turn can indicate that the majority of non-users, even if they had heard about Facebook, lack real knowledge about what it can offer. This is also supported by the fact that from the 30 % of participants which are non-users of Facebook, only one third had actually experimented the SNS. Therefore, until older adults become acquainted with the possibilities of Facebook they will most probably reject its utility.

When confronting Facebook users with the problems which contribute the most for its limited use, participants appointed privacy issues (Mean = 3.18, Median = 3.00 and Mode = 5) as the major factor. At the same time, they also rejected not liking Facebook (Mean = 2.23, Median = 2.00 and Mode = 1) or not knowing how to use it (Mean = 1.69, Median = 1.00 and Mode = 1) as reasons for not taking full advantage of it.

In the same way, when asking non-users of Facebook about the same reasons, privacy was even more strongly appointed as the main barrier for making use of it (Mean = 3.73, Median = 4.00 and Mode = 5). However, in the case of these participants, the pre-conceived idea of not liking Facebook is also appointed as having a direct influence in not adopting it as a social tool (Mean = 3.39, Median = 3.00 and Mode = 3). All these results are also in-line with previous related work on these matters, as privacy issues related both with the way privacy settings are designed and the controversial stories about invasion of privacy are known to influence Facebook use and adoption.

Differences Between Facebook Users and Non-users. The understanding of the differences between Facebook users and non-users when considering older adults was one of the major goals of this study. From the findings regarding Facebook use we got some insights regarding the way older adults see this tool and regarding the general problems that lead to its limited use or adoption. However, more insights are needed regarding what makes an older adult, a Facebook user. One of those insights takes into consideration the possible influence of older adults' self-belief in their capabilities on the use of Facebook. We tested for a possible correlation between the way participants classify themselves in terms of technical expertise and the use of the SNS (Table 3).

Performing a Pearson's correlation test we found a negative correlation ($r = -0.243$, $p = 0.004$) between both variables. This means that there is a relation between the way participants believe in their capabilities and the use of Facebook.

Table 3. Facebook use vs. Technical expertise

Technical expertise classification	Facebook non-user	Facebook user
I use any typical technology available nowadays	4	30
I'm comfortable working with some technology	19	30
I have minor issues dealing with technology	6	13
I have some difficulties with technology	14	20
I have a lot of difficulties with technology	4	1
Total	47	94

Because self-belief could be influenced by the limitations that each person has, and because some influences between limitations and the use of Facebook can be expected, we also checked for possible correlations on this. However, no correlation was found regarding the number of limitations a participant reported and the use of technology. No correlations were also found regarding the severity of each ones' limitations and they tend to use Facebook less. This relation between motor limitations and Facebook use can have several interpretations, especially concerning the technology older adults make use to access the SNS.

Taking into consideration the possible influence of education, or the possibility that older adults with more or less studies have distinct probabilities of using Facebook, we also performed a Pearson's correlation test on these variables. However not only no statistical significance was found, but the biggest percentage of Facebook users (78 %) were older adults with the 12th grade (middle of the education scale), while about 65 % of participants with the 9th grade, a graduate degree and a Masters/PhD were Facebook users. Therefore, education seems not to have a relevant role on influencing the use of Facebook.

Considering that past studies showed differences between distinct genders regarding the use of SNS, supporting that female were more predisposed than male for the use of this kind of services, we also checked for possible differences in this study. However, not only we did not find significant differences favoring the female gender but in fact we observed a slight difference favoring man (69 % uses Facebook against 65 % of woman). Still this difference is also non-significant.

Lastly, we also inquired about the possible influence of living alone or accompanied, or how the number of people with who the user lives with influences the use of Facebook (Table 4). Based on the results obtained by cross checking both variables we performed a Pearson's correlation test and found a significant correlation ($r = 0.233$, $p = 0.006$). This shows that the more people a user lives with, higher the probability of using Facebook.

Distinct Groups. During the analysis we found some distinct groups of users which can provide additional findings regarding the differences between users and non-users.

Table 4. Facebook use vs. Number of people the participant lives with.

	Facebook non-user	Facebook user
Alone	14	18
One other	22	35
2 to 3 other	10	25
4 to 5 other	1	13
More than 5	0	3
Total	47	94

First, following previous findings concerning older adults who live alone, we checked for differences between the ones who live alone and do not use Facebook (group 1) and the ones who, in the same conditions use the SNS (group 2): the first difference concerns the use of Tablets with only 15 % of the participants in group 1 using one, while 56 % of the participants in the second group use one; secondly, about 28 % of participants in the first group consider themselves capable of using any typical technology without difficulties, while this percentage raises to 60 % in group 2; thirdly, and concerning age, all participants in the first group are older than 71 years of age, with about 43 % being older than 80. This value decreases significantly in the second group, with only one fourth (26 %) being older than 71 and 2.6 % having more than 80 years of age. These numbers suggest the use of Tablet devices, the way participants consider themselves capable of using technology and age, as factors which can influence the use of Facebook, especially when living alone. If the first factor is for the first time suggested by these findings, the second factor is a confirmation of previous findings of this paper, and the third one shows that, if we consider isolation as a sum of living alone and also not connecting to others using Facebook, the most isolated users are also the most aged ones.

Additionally, when comparing these differences with the differences found between older adults who live accompanied and make use of Facebook and the ones that in the same conditions do not, we find that the use of Tablet is not influenced by being alone or accompanied, while the other two factors are more critical the less company the older adult has. Therefore, the oldest older adults are also the ones who believe less in their capabilities concerning technology and that leads them to not make use of Facebook.

Finally, we checked for differences concerning the reasons appointed for not using Facebook and the way they vary with older adults' self-belief in their technical capabilities. Relevant results were found for two of these reasons: the first regarding "I do not use Facebook because of privacy issues" where the value remained constant regardless of the technical expertise of the participants, which suggests that privacy issues are not related with technical skills and are a transversal problem to the whole older adult population; and secondly the concordance with the sentence "I do not make use of Facebook because I don't know how to use it" increased as older adults consider themselves less technologically skilled. This suggests that Facebook does not look simple enough to be used by anyone, and that the way it is designed leaves less-skilled or less-brave users out, or simply frightens these older adults.

4.3 Television

Concerning the use of television, and when asked about the main reasons that characterize its mainstream use by the older population (Fig. 1), almost everyone agreed on
it being easy to use (mean of 4.56), and on the importance of watching their favorite
programs and shows (4.14) and getting information about what is going on in the world
(4.12). This shows the importance of using TV both as a means of accessing new
information and as a vehicle of entertainment. These uses are not well aligned with
Facebook's main purposes, which focus on communication with family and friends. In
fact, when asked about the possibility of using Television for distinct purposes of the
ones they are used to, only about 26 % of the participants showed interest in using it for
accessing the Internet or to get information about family and close friends, and a fewer
percentage (about 16 %) implicitly showed interest in accessing Facebook. Additionally, and concerning the latter, about 57 % were against it.

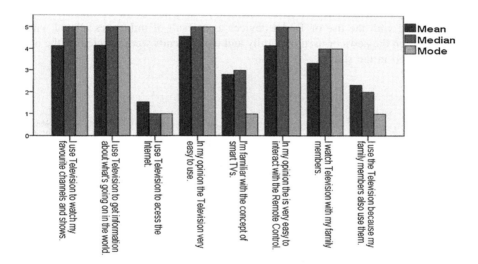

Fig. 1. Reasons behind the use of television (Color figure online).

Although these preliminary findings could be interpreted as an indication that TV
may not be an appropriate alternative for reducing the gap between Facebook and older
adults, additional findings can somehow rebut this. For example, we have to take into
consideration that participants are not familiarized either with the concept of
smart-TVs, or accessing the Internet through TV and, as we have seen earlier, it is
common that by not having experienced new ways of using the television they refuse
using it for anything else than what they are already used to. Additionally, there are
also differences regarding the acceptance of these new ways of using TV when comparing Facebook users and non-adopters, with the mode increasing by one value. This
also supports the previous argument, showing that the most knowledge older adults
have about technology the most receptive they will be about adopting it, or at least,
experimenting it.

4.4 Tablet

About 87 % of the participants are aware of what is a Tablet, however only 37 % makes use of one, and a similar percentage (35 %) never tried one. Of the ones who use a Tablet about 67 % uses it every day (which represents one fourth of all participants).

When talking about the reasons behind the use of tablet devices (Fig. 2) the possibility of using it anywhere and the simplicity behind its use were the ones which collected more concordance from the participants. Additionally, also relevant was the fact that the use of certain applications was the third most supported reason (only 25 % of participants disagreed with it) for using a Tablet. Moreover, we looked specifically at the applications users reported to use and verified a close relation with SNSs and Facebook: about 67 % said to use the Tablet to access SNSs, and about three fourths (73 %) said to use Facebook. This is a first indication that suggests a relation between the use of Tablets and access to Facebook. Still, regarding reasons for using the Tablet, sentences related with communication with family and friends tended to be classified as neutral, and participants were also divided concerning the price of the device. All factors related with the use of Tablet devices as a result of influences related with it being talked on the news or used by family and close friends were rejected by the older adults involved in the study.

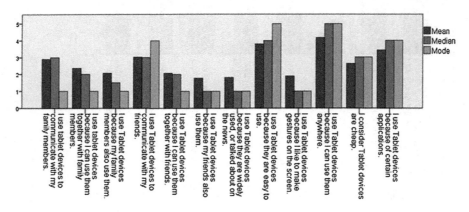

Fig. 2. Reasons behind the use of tablet (Color figure online).

When asking participants who do not make use of Tablets if the same statements would be reasons for wanting to use the device, the same order of preference between statements was verified, however with much lower concordance values. As a result only the possibility of making use of the tablet anywhere was supported by the majority (mean of 3.46 and mode of 5), with easiness of use, and the ability of using certain applications having means a little lower than neutral (2.90 and 2.80 respectively), and with communication with family and friends a bit lower (2.65 and 2.49). Additionally, and just like the ones who already make use of tablets, also the non-users rejected the sentences related with the influence of family and friends on the willingness to use the device.

Taking into consideration participants that make use of Facebook and participants who do not, we found differences regarding the way the first ones see tablet more like a communication device for connecting with family (mean of 3.06 and median of 3 while non-users tend to reject the statement with a mean of 2.33 and a median of 2) and friends (mean of 3.27 and median of 3 while non-users tend to reject the statement with a mean of 2.17 and a median of 2). This could mean that participants that are already familiar with SNS interactions and capabilities see the Tablet as a viable way of mediating those kind of interactions while participants who are not familiar with online social interactions like the ones available through Facebook, do not see that potential in the tablet. This is also in line with other previous findings concerning the use of Television for accessing SNSs or for means of keeping in touch, and the way older adults reject using technology for purposes they are not familiar with.

Considering the previous indications related with the use of Tablet devices for accessing Facebook and having in mind a possible influence of the use of the device and the adoption of the technology, we performed a cross-check analysis between Tablet use and Facebook use. In this analysis although we observed no relation between using a Tablet and being aware of what Facebook is (100 % of users which make use of a Tablet are aware of what Facebook is, while in the case of non-users this percentage is around 95 %) we found that 85 % of Tablet users make use of Facebook, while only 56 % of participants who do not use a Tablet use this SNS. In this case, a Pearson's correlation test found a positive correlation between the use of Tablet devices and Facebook ($r = 0.291$, $p < 0.001$). This suggests that by using Tablet devices participants are closer to using Facebook.

Lastly, and considering the previous findings which showed the existence of a correlation between the severity of motor limitations and the use of Facebook, we also expected to find differences regarding the use of Tablet devices as motor limitations increase in severity. However, in this case, and although differences exist with percentages of tablet users decreasing with the increase in severity, a Pearson correlation test showed no statistical significance.

5   Discussion

The major point of discussion of this paper concerns the understanding of what makes an older adult a Facebook user and the differences when compared with non-users (RQ1). Building from this, it is important to discuss solutions to approximate Facebook to older adults who do not make use of it, so they can take advantage of its features as a means of fighting social isolation.

The first relevant finding showed the **importance of older adults' self-belief, or how by considering themselves capable of interacting with technology or being confident in their technical skills, older adults are more likely to use Facebook**. In this context, and knowing that less skilled users see Facebook as a more complex service (or interface) than users who believe in their technical capabilities, the effort should be on simplifying the user interface or the way older adults have access to it. This is even further supported by the fact that, not only non-adopters, but also Facebook users consider, for example, privacy settings as the major factor for its limited use, which shows that the way the interface is designed is not even tailored for them. Additionally, it is also necessary to promote this simplicity so that older adults can give the SNS a second chance. Secondly, limitations have shown no influence in the use of Facebook with the exception for the way motor limitations evolve. **Older adults with tremors, trouble moving arms, difficulties grasping a mouse, or positioning and controlling a cursor, tend to use Facebook (or the technology which permits accessing Facebook) less than users with just a small portion of these problems, and much less than users with none.** One possible reason for this, and also slightly indicated by the results, is that older adults with these issues cannot make use of Tablet devices in the same way as older adults with no motor limitations, and consequently they also have less opportunities to use Facebook. Other reason is related with the use of the more traditional ways of accessing Facebook through a computer, where limitations on the use of a mouse results in inability to use the whole service. Concerning these limitations, solutions should focus on making alternative modalities of interaction available, particularly voice, other type of gestures, or a combination of both. Or in providing adaptation mechanisms capable of attenuating the differences. Moreover, the smaller the number of people there is in a household the least probable is for an older adult to use Facebook, i.e., **the more isolated (at least physically) older adults are, the less they use Facebook.** Therefore the way the SNS is currently designed does not seem to target socially isolated users, but the maintenance of existing and technological savvy social ties. As it is, the use of Facebook approximates more to a tool for expressing existing social connections - as valid as a phone call, exchanging messages or even being face to face, than a tool for regaining contact with family members and friends.

Taking all these findings into consideration, the main differences between older adults who use Facebook and older adults who do not make use of Facebook, are mainly related with the number of people they live with, the severity of motor limitations they have and the way they believe in themselves concerning the use of technology.

Additionally, answers to the second (RQ2) and third (RQ3) research questions were also obtained with this questionnaire.

In what concerns TV (RQ2) the fact that it is used by older adults for opposite purposes of Facebook, that is, mainly for entertainment, might discourage its role in targeting social isolation. This might be aggravated by older adults' tendency for, not only rejecting the use of technology they do not know for purposes they know well (like the use of Facebook for keeping in contact with family and friends), but also rejecting the use of technology they know well for purposes they are not familiar with (like the use of Television as a bridge for that Facebook access). However, **for older adults aged more than 80 years old who live alone and are generally not familiar with Facebook in its traditional form, integrating Facebook features in a simplified form on the TV might help**. Additionally, while solutions are not experienced by older adults we cannot know for sure, and with the rise of smart TVs it might be only a matter of time until Facebook reaches the big screen. When this happens, older adults should be considered the main use case for this transition.

Findings showed **benefits on using a Tablet device especially in terms of adoption (high perceptions regarding ease of use) and long-term use**

(higher numbers of Facebook users among Tablet users in single person households, those that are, potentially, more isolated). Therefore, Tablet might in fact facilitate the access to a tool like Facebook, by either being more simple to interact than the original computer or because the mobile interface is more simple than the desktop one, or even by other factors such as the possibility of using it anywhere. Additionally, the use of Tablet devices for activities related with connecting with family and friends also seems even more relevant when older adults already have an idea of what is Facebook. This makes Tablets a good vehicle and a good entrance point for respectively experienced users and non-adopters, of Facebook.

Finally, no relevant differences were found between online respondents and in-person respondents, with exception for a higher percentage of Facebook users on the first group than in the second. Still, and as a major limitation, the results of this study can more confidently be applied for more technology-experienced than less technology-experienced older adults.

5.1   Tackling Isolation Through Design

From the findings obtained through this study we also compiled a list of design directions that should be considered when designing not only for inclusion but more importantly when targeting social isolation, which is critically present in the older segment of the population.

Focus on Functionalities for Keeping in Contact. Issues related with social isolation should be the main target of a SNS like Facebook when considering older adults, especially by providing opportunities and functionalities to keep in contact with family and friends. This is not only supported by previous related work but also appointed in this study as the main reason for using Facebook. Additionally, and contrary to what has been defended in the past, these functionalities should focus not only on family and close friends, but also on other friends specially for the purpose of providing users with more interaction possibilities with already existing contacts and for making possible the revival of old connections.

Simplify Facebook's Interface. Facebook's user interface does not look easy to older adults who "defy" technology fears and make use of it, or to older adults who consider not having the necessary amount of skills to experiment it. Explanations for this can be related with the way the user interface looks non-intuitive, with the way privacy settings are designed, with it having too many features which older adults do not grasp the concept, or with the fact that it is offered to the older segment of the population without considering their different needs and limitations. Facebook's user interface is not an interface that fits all, because it introduces new concepts in a non-intuitive manner which requires learning. This study supports previous findings on this with participants appointing the complexity of Facebook user interface as a reason for not using the application, and supports previous indications that to be used by the majority of the older population, Facebook should be redesigned having simplicity in mind, as this is the only way of supporting learning through experimentation. Reducing the number of functionalities to only the more relevant ones, pushing the most used functionalities to a simpler and more prominent menu (or to more central areas), increasing the size of menus, and showing less information on each screen, are all examples (showed in previous research) of what could make Facebook simpler.

Tackle Privacy Issues. We have seen once more in this paper that both Facebook users and older adults who still not make use of the tool, have, in privacy issues, the main cause for a limited use of the SNS. Additionally, we have several indications from these findings that these privacy issues are independent of their self-belief in technology. This means that privacy settings are not simple enough for the ones who already use Facebook and frighten the ones who still do not. One possible solution would be to redesign privacy settings to be less open as a default, keeping any post private or open only to a restricted set of contacts (family members or contacts approved manually by the user) as well as making possible for the user to gradually expand these settings (and including more contacts).

Use Adaptation Mechanisms. This study shows that age-related impairments related with motor limitations are not the only factors which lead to differences in the use of Facebook. The differences concerning preferences and habits of the older population - e.g. the self-belief in their technology skills - also play a differentiation role as valid as any other. To get around these differences, both Facebook and the devices through which Facebook is accessed, should offer mechanisms which tailor both presentation and interaction to each user characteristics. And although older adults are the ones in more need of these type of mechanisms, they should support the use of the SNS by both skilled and less-skilled, younger and older, confident and less-confident, and traditional and less-traditional users. Examples of these adaptations (and valid ways of compensating for both limitations and preferences) are features like reducing the sensibility of touch operations for scrolling up and down and zooming in and out, increasing the size of selectable items, or increasing the space between interface items. Additionally, the provision of several modalities of interaction like supporting speech-based interactions instead of touch-based ones, or supporting audio and haptic feedback (or even both at the same time) could also play a decisive role on the adoption of SNSs by older adults.

Use Technologies Closer to the User. Tablet and TV are seen by older adults in a distinct manner. Depending on how isolated and aged the individual is, and how easily he/she deals with technology, one or other have a potential to bridge the gap to Facebook use. Still, the technology should embrace the older adult and not the other way around. Tablet should be the main vehicle for targeting Facebook adoption by the generality of older adults, while TV should work as a secondary vehicle and target adoption by the oldest (and more isolated) older adults. While in the first case (Tablet) the use is already associated with Facebook, in the second case (TV) the solution might be introducing Facebook features without giving the idea that users are using a new service, but rather that they are only expanding the use of a technology they are already familiar with.

6 Conclusion

Facebook has the opportunity of tackling older adults' social isolation. However several difficulties related with the way the service is designed have been presented in recent years which show that this opportunity is not being explored. In this study we inquired older adults about habits and concerns related with the most used SNS, and understood differences between users and non-users of the service. We also explored older adults' receptiveness to the possibility of using alternative technology like Tablets and TV, to facilitate Facebook adoption. Findings showed how believing in their own technical skills, and having different degrees of motor limitations can make a difference, showed differences between older old adults and younger old adults in terms of social context, and evidenced how users which make use of a Tablet are more probable to also make use of Facebook. They also show a strong necessity for simplifying the design of the SNS. Based on the findings we derived a set of recommendations which should be considered when designing solutions to tackle social isolation.

Acknowledgments. We thank all participants who voluntarily participated in our study. This work was partially supported by Fundação para a Ciência e Tecnologia (FCT) through Multi-annual Funding to the LaSIGE research unit and the Individual Doctoral Grant SFRH/BD/81115/2011.

References

1. Brunette, K., Eisenstadt, M., Pukinskis, E., Ryan, W.: Meeteetse: social well-being through place attachment. In: Proceedings of CHI 2005, pp. 2065–2069. ACM (2005)
2. Burke, M., Kraut, R., Marlow, C.: Social capital on facebook: differentiating uses and users. In: Proceedings of CHI 2011, pp. 571–580. ACM (2011)
3. Burke, M., Marlow, C., Lento, T.: Social network activity and social well-being. In: Proceedings of CHI 2010, pp. 1909–1912. ACM (2010)
4. Chen, Y.: Usability analysis on online social networks for the elderly. Technical report, Helsinki University of Technology (2009)
5. Chung, M.K., Kim, D., Na, S., Lee, D.: Usability evaluation of numeric entry tasks on keypad type and age. Int. J. Ind. Ergon. **40**(1), 97–105 (2010)
6. Coelho, J., Duarte, C., Biswas, P., Langdon, P.: Developing accessible TV applications. In: Proceedings of ASSETS 2011, pp. 131–138. ACM (2011)
7. Cornejo, R., Tentori, M., Favela, J.: Enriching in-person encounters through social media: a study on family connectedness for the elderly. Int. J. Hum.-Comput. Stud. **71**(9), 889–899 (2013)
8. Epelde, G., Valencia, X., Carrasco, E., Posada, J., Abascal, J., Diaz-Orueta, U., Zinnikus, I., Husodo-Schulz, C.: Providing universally accessible interactive services through TV sets: implementation and validation with elderly users. Multimedia Tools and Applications pp. 1–32 (2011)
9. Eurostat European Commission: Population structure and ageing (2012)
10. Findlater, L., Wobbrock, J.: Personalized input: improving ten-finger touchscreen typing through automatic adaptation. In: Proceedings of CHI 2012, pp. 815–824. ACM (2012)

11. Garattini, C., Wherton, J., Prendergast, D.: Linking the lonely: an exploration of a communication technology designed to support social interaction among older adults. Univers. Access Inf. Soc. **11**(2), 211–222 (2012)
12. Gaver, W., Boucher, A., Bowers, J., Blythe, M., Jarvis, N., Cameron, D., Kerridge, T., Wilkie, A., Phillips, R., Wright, P.: The photostroller: supporting diverse care home residents in engaging with the world. In: Proceedings of CHI 2011, pp. 1757–1766. ACM (2011)
13. Gibson, L., Moncur, W., Forbes, P., Arnott, J., Martin, C., Bhachu, A.S.: Designing social networking sites for older adults. In: Proceedings of BCS 2010, pp. 186–194 (2010)
14. Hope, A., Schwaba, T., Piper, A.M.: Understanding digital and material social communications for older adults. In: Proceedings of CHI 2014, pp. 3903–3912. ACM (2014)
15. Joinson, A.N.: Looking at, looking up or keeping up with people? motives and use of facebook. In: Proceedings of CHI 2008, pp. 1027–1036. ACM (2008)
16. Kallio, S., Korpipää, P., Linjama, J., Kela, J.: Turn-based gesture interaction in mobile devices. In: Hailes, S., Sicari, S., Roussos, G. (eds.) S-CUBE 2009. LNICST, vol. 24, pp. 11–19. Springer, Heidelberg (2010)
17. Karahasanovic, A., Brandtzaeg, P.B., Heim, J., Luders, M., Vermeir, L., Pierson, J., Lievens, B., Vanattenhoven, J., Jans, G.: Co-creation and user-generated content-elderly people's user requirements. Comput. Hum. Behav. **25**(3), 655–678 (2009)
18. Lehtinen, V., Näsänen, J., Sarvas, R.: "A little silly and empty-headed": older adults' understandings of social networking sites. In: Proceedings of BCS 2009, pp. 45–54. British Computer Society
19. Lindley, S.E., Harper, R., Sellen, A.: Desiring to be in touch in a changing communications landscape: attitudes of older adults. In: Proceedings of CHI 2009, pp. 1693–1702. ACM (2009)
20. Lindley, S.E.: Shades of lightweight: supporting cross-generational communication through home messaging. Univers. Access Inf. Soc. **11**(1), 31–43 (2012)
21. McLaughlin, A.C., Rogers, W.A., Fisk, A.D.: Using direct and indirect input devices: attention demands and age-related differences. ACM Trans. Comput.-Hum. Interact. **16**(1), 1–15 (2009)
22. Morris, M.: Social networks as health feedback displays. Internet Computing, IEEE **9**(5), 29–37 (2005)
23. Norval, C., Arnott, J.L., Hanson, V.L.: What's on your mind? investigating recommendations for inclusive social networking and older adults. In: Proceedings of CHI 2014, pp. 3923–3932. ACM
24. Plaza, I., Martin, L., Martin, S., Medrano, C.: Mobile applications in an aging society: status and trends. J. Syst. Softw. **84**(11), 1977–1988 (2011)
25. Santana, P.C., Rodríguez, M.D., González, V.M., Castro, L.A., Andrade, A.G.: Supporting emotional ties among Mexican elders and their families living abroad. In: Proceedings of CHI 2005, pp. 2099–2103. ACM (2005)
26. Sayago, S., Santos, P., Gonzalez, M., Arenas, M., López, L.: Meeting educational needs of the elderly in ICT: two exploratory case studies. Crossroads 14(2) (2007)
27. Stobel, C., Blessing, L.: Mobile device interaction gestures for older users. In: Proceedings of NordiCHI 2010, pp. 793–796. ACM (2010)
28. Sundar, S.S., Oeldorf-Hirsch, A., Nussbaum, J., Behr, R.: Retirees on Facebook: can online social networking enhance their health and wellness? In: Proceedings of CHI 2011, pp. 2287–2292. ACM (2011)
29. Waycott, J., Vetere, F., Pedell, S., Kulik, L., Ozanne, E., Gruner, A., Downs, J.: Older adults as digital content producers. In: Proceedings of CHI 2013, pp. 39–48. ACM (2013)

Using Photo Diaries to Elicit User Requirements from Older Adults: A Case Study on Mobility Barriers

David Swallow$^{(\boxtimes)}$, Helen Petrie, Christopher Power,
and Alistair D.N. Edwards

Human Computer Interaction Research Group, Department of Computer Science,
University of York, York YO10 5GH, UK
{david.swallow,helen.petrie,christopher.power,
alistair.edwards}@york.ac.uk

Abstract. Older adults encounter numerous barriers to mobility, many of which are in the built environment. Technological solutions may enable them to mitigate these barriers and promote physical activity. To design appropriate technological solutions, it is crucial to understand the specific barriers to mobility older adults face from their perspectives. Photo diary studies allow older adults to autonomously document their experiences to support generation of user needs and requirements. We investigate the methodological appropriateness of photo diaries for exploring experiences of older adults and eliciting their requirements for new technologies. A photo diary study was conducted with 26 older adults, who were given disposable cameras to document things that affect their mobility. As well as presenting a selection of the mobility barriers identified in this study, the paper outlines a number of methodological issues relating to the use of photo diaries for eliciting the needs and requirements of older adults.

Keywords: Photo diaries · User study · Participatory design · Older adults · Mobility barriers · Built environment

1 Introduction

Older adults encounter many barriers to mobility as a consequence of major changes in their lives. For instance, losing a partner or becoming a carer for someone, losing a driving licence due to illness or disability, and changing circumstances, such as retiring or moving house, can have a huge impact on the physical activity of older adults in the built environment.

Many mobility barriers that older adults encounter are in the built environment. This term refers to aspects of the physical environment that are constructed by human activity [9]. It includes the physical infrastructure of roads, pavements, cycle paths, railways, and bridges; transportation systems, such as bus and rail networks; the design of urban areas and the physical elements within them; and the distribution of activities (e.g. residential, commercial, industrial etc.) across these areas [5].

Technology can be used to support the mobility of older adults in the built environment. For example, walking aids, such as canes, crutches, and walkers assist people

© IFIP International Federation for Information Processing 2015
J. Abascal et al. (Eds.): INTERACT 2015, Part I, LNCS 9296, pp. 147–164, 2015.
DOI: 10.1007/978-3-319-22701-6_11

with walking impairments. People with visual impairments commonly use canes as mobility aids. Wheelchairs and mobility scooters support people with more severe physical impairments. These mobility aids represent low-technology mechanical solutions for supporting mobility in older adults. Opportunities exist however, for high-technology solutions that enable older adults to mitigate the barriers they encounter and promote physical activity.

To design technology for supporting mobility in older adults, we must first understand how they experience and interact with the built environment. Many studies have investigated the impact of different characteristics of the built environment upon mobility in older adults (for reviews, see [8, 14]). Studies of this nature tend to assess the built environment either by objective measures of demographic and socio-economic characteristics (e.g. population density, land use diversity, street connectivity, or walkability indexes) or by subjective perceptions of local area characteristics (e.g. perceived neighbourhood security or the quality of neighbourhood facilities).

Whilst both objective and subjective measures show positive associations with mobility in older adults [1, 14], they each have potential drawbacks. Objective measures may be too general to identify specific mobility barriers, whereas subjective measures rely upon participants' perceptions of problems, as opposed to the actual presence of mobility barriers [8]. Further, neither approach is particularly suitable for eliciting the needs and requirements of older adults for high-technology solutions. A more appropriate method may be to have older adults identify specific mobility barriers in the built environment themselves.

Diary studies are a commonly adopted technique in the field of Human Computer Interaction for actively involving potential users in the requirements elicitation process [7]. These typically require participants to autonomously document their experiences through a series of diary entries that may later be used to prompt discussion with the users. Photographs, audio recordings and other media can be incorporated into diary entries both to enrich the data and ease the burden on participants to capture and later recall their contents. Indeed, a study investigating the use of different media in diary studies [2] demonstrated that photo diaries are the easiest for participants to capture and recognise at a later date.

Despite the apparent benefits of photo diaries, few studies could be found that utilise the method to examine the experiences of older adults. This paper explores the methodological appropriateness of photo diaries for examining the experiences of older adults and eliciting requirements for high-technology solutions. It investigates whether the application of photo diary studies can contribute to a greater understanding of the barriers that older adults encounter in the built environment and possible technological solutions to these barriers.

2   Related Literature

Many studies have considered the impact of characteristics of the built environment upon the mobility of older adults. Yen, Michael and Perdue [14] conducted a systematic review of 33 such studies conducted in the USA, Europe and Australia published between 1997 and 2007, concluding that the neighbourhood environment has a large impact on older adults' health and functioning. Rosso, Auchincloss and Michael [8] conducted a similar systematic review of 17 studies conducted predominantly in the USA and published between 1990 and 2010, also identifying an association between characteristics of the built environment and mobility in older adults.

Yen et al. [14] included studies measuring both objective and subjective characteristics of neighbourhoods. Objective measures include demographic and socioeconomic composition, land use diversity, street connectivity, and 'walkability' indexes, derived from census and other administrative data. Subjective measures include perceptions of local area characteristics, such as perceived neighbourhood security or the quality of neighbourhood facilities, derived from survey data. Rosso et al. [8] only included studies measuring objective measures of the built environment.

Both objective and subjective measures of the built environment are positively associated with mobility in older adults [1], albeit potentially in different ways, as subjective measures show stronger associations with physical activity than objective measures [14]. Nevertheless, both approaches have potential methodological drawbacks. Objective measures may be the most common approach and the easiest for policymakers to tackle (e.g. installing cycle paths and walkways to promote a more active lifestyle [10]). However, they may be too broad to identify specific barriers to mobility in older adults and too impersonal to elicit the specific concerns of participants. Subjective measures, on the other hand, may be driven by psychological affect (the tendency to report consistently positively or negatively) [1], eliciting unfounded concerns that may be difficult to address. Indeed, Rosso et al. [8] excluded studies that used subjective measures because they rely upon participants' perceptions of problems as opposed to the actual presence of barriers.

A more appropriate method combining the subjective perceptions of older adults with the objective identification of mobility barriers is to have older adults identify specific mobility barriers in the built environment themselves. Diary studies are a commonly adopted technique in the field of Human Computer Interaction for actively involving potential users in the requirements elicitation process (for a summary, see [7]). These typically require participants to autonomously document their experiences through a series of diary entries that can later be used to prompt discussion. Photographs, audio recordings and other media can be incorporated into diary entries both to enrich the data and ease the burden on participants to capture and later recall their contents. A study by Carter and Mankoff [2] investigating the use of different media in diary studies demonstrated that photo diaries are the easiest for participants to capture and recognise at a later date. Though Carter and Mankoff do not specify the ages of participants, they do not appear to include older adults. Given the apparent benefits of photo diaries, it is surprising that we could find few studies that utilise the method for examining the experiences of older adults and eliciting their needs and requirements for technological solutions to mobility problems.

Ståhl, Carlsson, Hovbrandt and Iwarsson [12] identified environmental barriers and risk factors by accompanying older adult participants on walks along predetermined neighbourhood routes. This was triangulated with questionnaire data and focus group discussions, which identified and prioritised several measures aimed at increasing accessibility and safety for pedestrians in the built environment. These measures included: the separation of pedestrians and cyclists; lower speed limits; and better maintenance of pavement surfaces. Whilst this study was successful in engaging older adults in the generation of needs and requirements, the methodology, by the authors' own admission, was demanding and complex to coordinate. Furthermore, the presence of a researcher during the observed neighbourhood walks as well as the use of predetermined routes may have compromised the spontaneity of participants' observations.

Schmehl, Deutsch, Schrammel, Paletta, Tscheligi [11] identified mobility barriers in the use of public transport using a modified cultural probe methodology. Unlike Gaver's original methodology [3], which is designed to elicit a holistic contextual experience, Schmehl et al. deployed directed cultural probes that were restricted to a specific issue. People with visual, cognitive or language-related disabilities, including older adults, were asked to document as many mobility barriers as possible during a two-week period using written diaries, cameras, voice recorders and checklists. Though the authors consider their approach to be an expedient modification of cultural probes, the number of diary entries generated by participants and the derived number of mobility barriers was disappointingly small.

A related technique, called *photovoice*, in which participants use cameras to record and reflect on their daily lives, has found several applications, including the identification of environmental barriers to and facilitators of walking in older adults [6]. While *photovoice* incorporates aspects of photo diary studies, its intended purpose is to engage communities, policymakers and stakeholders through focus groups and group discussions [13]. We found no studies that use photo diaries for the explicit purpose of eliciting the needs and requirements of older adults for technological solutions.

In this paper, we present a photo diary study of older adults on both barriers and aids to mobility they encounter in the built environment. We seek to answer the following questions:

1. What mobility barriers and aids do older adults encounter in the built environment?
2. Are photo diary studies an appropriate methodology for eliciting older adults' needs and requirements for new technologies?

3 Method

3.1 Design

Older adult participants were provided with disposable cameras. They were asked to take the cameras with them on any journeys they made outside of their homes during approximately two weeks and use them to take photos of things that affect their travels, both in positive and negative ways. This was followed by an interview in the participant's home during which they were asked to describe what they had taken in their photos and how it affected their mobility.

Participants were recruited from three locations in the UK: Hexham, a small town in Northumberland (population: 11,446); Leeds, a large city in West Yorkshire (757,700); and York, a small city in North Yorkshire (153,717). These locations were chosen as diverse examples of built environments, whose design, topography and infrastructure present a range of mobility barriers.

3.2   Participants

Twenty-six participants, all from the UK, took part in the study. Their demographics are summarised in Table 1. They were an invited subset of those taking part in the Co-Motion project[1], which is investigating the links between mobility and well-being in older adults. Participants were recruited on the basis that they were sufficiently mobile and willing to document their journeys. They received a £20 gift voucher in compensation for their time and effort.

Table 1. Demographic characteristics of participants.

Total	Gender		Age			Location		
	Male	Female	55–64	65–74	75–84	Hexham	Leeds	York
26	9	17	11	8	7	8	8	10

3.3   Equipment and Materials

Participants were provided with a Kodak Fun Flash disposable camera with 39 exposures. Three participants opted to use their own camera or mobile phone camera. One participant opted to use the disposable camera but supplement it with photos taken with their own camera. Participants using a disposable camera were provided with a freepost envelope in which to return the camera to the research team for processing. Participants using their own camera were asked to email their photos to the research team.

Participants were provided with a detailed information sheet about the photo diary study, as well as a short reminder sheet describing the key objectives of the study. At the start of the follow-up interview, participants were asked to complete an informed consent form.

3.4   Procedure

Participants were invited to take part in the photo diary study based on their involvement in the Co-Motion project. Those who agreed were provided with the equipment and materials described above. Participants were asked to take the camera with them on any journeys they made during approximately two weeks and use it to take photos of things that affected their travels – both in positive and negative ways. Though the disposable cameras contained 39 exposures, participants were assured that they did not have to use them all and could take as many or as few photos as they felt necessary. Participants who wanted to take more than 39 exposures were encouraged to use their own camera or mobile phone camera. Once participants had taken the photos, they were asked to send the cameras back to the research team.

Approximately one week into the exercise, a member of the research team contacted each participant by phone to check how they were doing with the study and to

---

[1] http://www.york.ac.uk/chp/expertise/co-motion/.

answer any questions. This contact point was also used as an opportunity to arrange follow-up interviews to discuss the participants' photos.

The follow-up interviews took place in participants' homes. Participants were asked how they found the photo diary study and whether they had encountered any problems, either in finding things to photograph or in using the disposable camera. The interviewer then went through the participants' photos and asked them to describe what they had taken and how it affected their mobility. Participants were assured of the confidentiality of the data they provided and that any identifiable aspects of the photos (e.g. faces, number plates etc.) would be obscured. The participants' consent for publication of the anonymised photos was obtained. Participants were also given the opportunity to exclude any of the photos from use in the investigation if they wished. With the participant's permission, audio of their voice was recorded for later analysis. The interviews lasted approximately 50 min.

3.5   Data Analysis

The audio recordings of each participant were fully transcribed prior to analysis. The photos were anonymised to ensure participants and anyone else appearing in the photos could not be identified. The transcriptions, with the accompanying photos, were then reviewed for all utterances that could be interpreted as representing either a barrier or aid to mobility.

This process built up a large collection of mobility barriers and aids. These were classified, using an emergent grounded theory approach [4]. The initial classification grouped the mobility barriers and aids according to different aspects of the built environment (e.g. pavements, roads, public transport etc.). Further analysis identified several distinct themes incorporating mobility barriers and aids from across all aspects of the built environment.

During the initial coding stage, the primary coder coded all 653 photos (and accompanying interview snippets) generated by all participants in the study. Two secondary coders coded approximately 10 % of the photos (and accompanying interview snippets) to establish inter-coder reliability.

4   Results

4.1   Productivity of the Photo Diary Study Method

Participants generated a total of 653 photos (mean number of photos per participant = 25; min = 9; max = 44). The photos were accompanied by a total of 21 h of interview data (approximately 50 min per participant). A total of 1,384 instances of mobility barriers and aids were identified across all study locations (Hexham, Leeds, and York). This includes 816 instances of mobility barriers and 568 instances of mobility aids. Many of the photos incorporated multiple barriers and/or aids to mobility.

Many participants identified similar barriers and aids to mobility. Taking this into account, a total of 354 unique barriers and aids to mobility were identified across all study locations. This includes 187 unique mobility barriers and 167 unique mobility aids.

4.2   Thematic Analysis of Barriers and Aids to Mobility

The grounded theory analysis identified six distinct themes incorporating mobility barriers and aids from across all aspects of the built environment.

Stability and Consistency of the Built Environment. A number of participants were unsteady on their feet or concerned for others with such mobility problems. Consequently, many barriers and aids to mobility were related to physical aspects of the built environment and the objects within it. Figure 1A is an example of a participant's photo from this category.

Fig. 1. Examples of participants' photos of barriers and aids to mobility: A: Broken pavement. B: Electronic display board. C: Busy road.

Participants identified many mobility barriers relating to the poor condition of pavement and road surfaces. These included tripping hazards caused by protruding gratings and drains, broken or uneven paving slabs, and exposed tree roots. Several participants attributed these mobility barriers to poor workmanship and a lack of local authority funding. One participant said, about the local council: "They just never seem to get round to doing anything. And in these days of health and safety, they seem to get so uptight about health and safety and then these things can lie around like that. Potential hazards."

Environments that are stable, consistent and free of physical hazards promote mobility in older adults. Participants identified many mobility aids relating to pavements and road surfaces that are in good condition. Smooth, wide pavements that are open and free of clutter were identified as being particularly important. Several participants described how they were used to identifying aspects of the built environment that help and hinder mobility. One participant said: "When I'm pushing the wheelchair, I'm spending the time looking on the ground. People say hello and then I look up and see them. I'm always looking for hazards."

Although technology is unable to directly address many physical mobility barriers, it may allow older adults to circumvent them. Navigation apps, such as Google Maps[2], already supplement driving directions with traffic information, weather reports and business data. An extension of this could supplement walking directions with data on mobility barriers, allowing older adults to plan routes that will avoid them.

Clarity and Visibility of the Built Environment. Participants identified many barriers and aids to mobility related to the clarity and visibility of aspects of the built environment. This not only included the physical infrastructure, such as roads, pavements and street furniture, but also information sources, such as bus or train timetables and street signs. Figure 1B is an example of a participant's photo from this category.

Poor clarity of pavements and roads were the cause of numerous mobility barriers, particular in areas shared by different users (motorists, pedestrians, cyclists etc.), where there may be little distinction between the two. This was a particular concern where pavements are divided into separate lanes for cyclists and pedestrians and unclear signage can lead to confusion. One participant said, about shared pathways: "Cyclists don't always realise that pedestrians may be coming off the pathway to cross the road. So they're cycling along at a mad speed, they don't ring the bell, and the pedestrian, who is probably slightly hard of hearing anyway, turns to cross and is at risk of being knocked down."

Environments that are easy to perceive and understand promote mobility in older adults. Clear and accurate information sources, such as bus and train timetables that are easy to read and include route maps, precise times, and other useful information, were identified as important aids to mobility. Electronic display boards for buses and trains were considered particularly useful. They not only provide reassurance that a bus or train is coming but also avoid lengthy waits at bus stops or train platforms. One participant said, about electronic display boards: "You have the backup of when the next bus is due, which means if you get there too early and it says 15 min to go, you can always nip into the shop or something rather than stand there in the cold."

Technology such as electronic display boards evidently goes some way to improving information delivery within the built environment. Although travel information is increasingly available via mobile apps, it is often limited to a particular location, company, or mode of transport. Greater unity and integration of travel information will make it easier for older adults both to plan journeys before leaving the home and access up-to-date travel information on the move.

Safety and Security of the Built Environment. Participants identified many barriers and aids to mobility related to the safety and security of the built environment. These impact upon both the physical safety of older adults as well as their emotional security and well-being. Figure 1C is an example of a participant's photo from this category.

Participants identified many mobility barriers relating to busy roads that are difficult and dangerous for motorists and pedestrians to navigate. One participant said: "It is a problem for pedestrians to know precisely 'can I cross here or not safely?' So, some

---

[2] http://www.google.com/mobile/maps/.

will think 'ah yeah, I can put a foot out into the road and get across' but there's no legal obligation on cars to stop."

Several mobility barriers were related to perceived threats to safety in the built environment, such as vandalism, the absence of street lighting, and a perceived lack of concern about such matters from the police and local authorities. One participant said, about an arson attempt in their local area: "If you report that to the police, they won't even bother coming out. But if it was cleaned more regularly, would vandals still do it? Would they think that someone was keeping an eye on it and think, 'Well, we won't bother'?" Whilst such problems may not represent direct barriers to mobility, they can result in older adults being reluctant to leave their homes.

Environmental features that promote safety, such as pedestrianised streets and shared spaces, traffic light-controlled pedestrian crossings or footbridges, and traffic-calming measures, such as speed bumps and speed restrictions, were identified as important mobility aids. One participant said: "The pedestrianised area is flat and easily accessible and less of a danger for people who are either elderly or frail. And for children to be able to run around a little bit as well. A pedestrianised precinct in certain areas is really positive for everybody of all ages."

Technology has an important role in promoting safety and security for older adults in the built environment. The mere presence of a mobile phone often provides passive reassurance to older adults and builds confidence in leaving the home. Mobile phones also provide a convenient means of reporting crime or alerting emergency services.

Beauty and Upkeep of the Built Environment. Participants identified many barriers and aids to mobility related to the aesthetics of the built environment. These referred to both the inherent physical appearance of the built environment as well as the upkeep and maintenance of objects within it. Figure 2D is an example of a participant's photo from this category.

Fig. 2. Examples of participants' photos of barriers and aids to mobility: D: Mobility scooter in crowded area. E: Handy bench. F: Local bus service.

The poor appearance of pavements, roads and street furniture, properties that are standing empty, litter and animal mess, the absence of trees, flowerbeds or hanging baskets, as well as the dull appearance of urban areas were the cause of several mobility barriers. One participant remarked: "What a dull and dismal place to live! Why don't we have a tree? … We get coachloads of tourists! Okay, it's not helped by the fact it's raining but why not some imagination?"

Similarly, the upkeep and maintenance of objects in the built environment, such as overgrown trees and bushes and the debris they produce, blocked drains, and water-logged pavements, was the cause of many mobility barriers. Participants attributed many mobility barriers to a lack of local authority funding, support and attention. One participant said: "I don't think it's cuts, I think it's full stop. Cuts mean you cut down a bit but maintenance just seems to have stopped and it's going to cost a fortune isn't it?"

Environments that are well maintained and attractive promote mobility in older adults. The presence of trees, gardens and flowerbeds were identified as important aids to mobility. Whilst the appearance of the built environment may not directly impact upon mobility, it evidently influences the well-being of older adults and their desire to be mobile.

Though technology may be unable to increase local authority budgets, it may assist in prioritising and allocating resources. For example, older adults could use cameras in mobile phones and tablets to capture mobility barriers in situ and report them to local authorities, alerting them to aspects of the built environment that need attention.

Propriety and Thoughtfulness in the Built Environment. Participants identified many barriers and aids to mobility relating to the behaviour of individuals and consideration for certain groups of people, such as older adults or mobility scooter and wheelchair users. Courtesy and respect for each other promotes mobility in older adults. Figure 2E is an example of a participant's photo from this category.

Aspects of the built environment shared by different groups of people, such as pavements, roads, and public transport, inspired several barriers and aids to mobility. Many related to the use, and misuse, of pavements, such as cars parking on or over-hanging pavements or pavement obstructions (including bin bags and refuse bins, roadworks, A-boards[3], and restaurant chairs and tables). One participant said: "The A-boards were there and I was in the wheelchair, and I couldn't get round. It was just dreadful. And when people put chairs and tables outside. It's alright if there's plenty of pavement, but when there isn't…".

Participants identified many mobility aids relating to the provision of facilities for people with mobility problems. These include benches and places to sit, disabled parking spaces and wide parking bays for easy access, dedicated assistance on trains and planes, and considerate use of pavements and public areas. One participant said: "Putting a seat on stone paving in the middle of a grassy area for the elderly to rest. I thought that was good, the way it wasn't just put down but on a nice firm footing because it can be very muddy. So that's a positive. I thought that seat was good. Nice, well-planned, well thought out."

In spite of many displays of carelessness in the built environment, there are many examples of thoughtfulness and consideration for older adults, be it wheelchair-accessible routes or convenient benches. Technology could be used to pool awareness

---

[3] A-boards are a type of advertising placed on pavements outside shops, cafes or other businesses. They comprise two boards displaying text or images hinged to form an 'A' shape.

of mobility aids among older adults and promote positive aspects of the built environment.

Freedom and Flexibility Within the Built Environment. Participants identified many barriers and aids to mobility relating to individual freedom and flexibility within the built environment. This freedom and flexibility may be a consequence of personal finance or health, or it may be due to public transport systems and provisions for older adults. Figure 2F is an example of a participant's photo from this category.

Irregular public transport and the absence of connecting routes between certain locations were identified as mobility barriers. One participant said: "Where I used to live before it was one bus but now I have to get two buses there and it's quite a journey. It takes about an hour and coming back in the dark." This was considered to be a particular problem at night, when irregular or absent bus services may discourage older adults from venturing out. One participant said: "The #7 bus, which is very frequent in the day stops completely. So if I go out at night, unless I want to walk, I have to get a taxi, which costs a lot. My difficulty is if something has finished, a concert maybe, there's nowhere to wait in the warm."

Having a driving licence and access to a car was identified as an important aid to mobility, offering freedom and independence in older age. One participant said: "I took a picture of my car because I love it so much. I didn't start driving until quite late on in my 50s. I don't know what I'd do if I couldn't drive. It represents enormous freedom." However, the cost of running a car as well as the cost of parking was identified as a major mobility barrier. One participant said: "Parking charges … are as expensive as London. And the council are deliberately trying to get people to use the Park and Ride[4]. They want to kick people out of the city centre. I just think they've got a really anti-car attitude within the town."

Similarly, the cost of taxis and train tickets were identified as barriers to mobility but transport schemes such as the Senior Railcard and the free older person's bus pass[5] were highly praised by many participants. One participant said: "The best thing is the free bus. There's no doubt about it. I mean, in theory, I can go to London… if I wanted to travel on 30–40 buses and take 4 days! That's the beauty of it. That's the best thing."

Technology has a vital role in enabling freedom and flexibility within the built environment. Whether this involves clarifying and tailoring travel information, identifying accessible routes between locations, highlighting potential hazards or promoting positive experiences, there is huge potential for high-technology solutions to support the mobility of older adults.

Design Solutions. A potential high-technology solution that draws together each of these themes is a mobile navigation app that allows older adults to plan walking routes in their local area. The app could identify routes that not only direct users away from known mobility barriers (e.g. roadworks, uneven surfaces, or steep steps) but also

---

[4] Park and Ride is a scheme to reduce car traffic in city centres. Free car parks are provided on the city outskirts, from where occupants can take a dedicated bus into the centre.

[5] People of pensionable age and disabled people in England are entitled to free off-peak travel on all local bus services anywhere in England.

direct users towards known mobility aids (e.g. pedestrianised areas, good transport links, or simply nice places that encourage mobility). The data for such an app could be generated by users themselves and used to not only refine potential walking routes but also inform local authorities of neighbourhood mobility barriers.

Such an app could also be used to identify pedestrian desire lines. These are paths that pedestrians take informally, rather than using pavements or set routes. The app could (literally) crowd-source movement patterns in busy urban areas to identify routes taken by different user groups. The app could then use this data to create 'digital desire lines' informing users of the safest and most efficient route to take.

4.3   Methodological Reflections on the Photo Diary Method

In addition to identifying the barriers and aids to mobility that older adults encounter in the built environment and suggesting potential high-technology solutions, we also reflected on different methodological aspects of the photo diary method.

Familiarity with Camera Technology. The use of disposable cameras in this study was reasonably successful. Although participants were permitted to use their own camera or mobile phone camera, the majority of them used the disposable camera provided.

In addition to the reduced cost and lower risk of using disposable cameras, we anticipated that older adults would be more comfortable using this type of camera. Surprisingly, several participants said that they were more familiar with digital cameras and that it took them a while to reacquaint themselves with what they considered "primitive" or "prehistoric" technology. Not being able to immediately view photos resulted in many participants being uncertain about whether the camera had worked properly. Only one participant said they enjoyed using a disposable camera, remarking: "It was quite nice having what I would call an 'old-fashioned' type of camera. It wasn't digital. I didn't have to understand, I just had to point and press and wind on. I enjoyed that."

Four participants used their own camera or mobile phone camera to take photos. This proved to be a more efficient process, reducing the cost of processing, producing better quality photos, and allowing participants to use a camera that they are familiar with. Though only a small number of participants in this study were willing to use their own camera or mobile phone camera, we anticipate that older adults' increasing familiarity with digital technology will reduce the need for future studies of this nature to provide disposable cameras.

Feelings of Self-consciousness. Taking photos of mobility barriers in public places made many participants feel slightly uncomfortable. Eight participants commented that they had felt awkward or self-conscious. For some participants, this was due to the unusual nature of the exercise. One said: "Yes [there are difficulties], if you start taking photographs of inanimate objects. There was a sign where there was a road closed, and I was stood taking a photograph of that. That felt a bit odd." Another participant said: "There's a little snickleway[6]. As I approached it, there were two men and a woman

---

[6] 'Snickleway' is a Yorkshire dialect word for a small alleyway.

who were taking pictures of the snickleway, so I had to wait for them to finish. And I felt a bit weird. They're taking a picture, they're probably tourists, and I'm taking a picture and I live here! It just felt a bit peculiar."

Other participants were more concerned about what other people might think. One said: "I find it quite difficult going around taking pictures because some people look very suspiciously at you if you stop and take pictures outside their shop. They want to know what it's all about and what you're doing, which is understandable." Another said: "[I was] fine, once I stopped feeling a little bit conscious that people would think I was spying on them. When you're doing it in your local area, you know other people in the houses, you're thinking they're going to wonder what on earth I am doing here!"

In spite of these concerns, three participants commented that once they informed observers about what they were doing, the observers became very interested. One participant said: "When I was taking the [photos] of the cars parked on the road, I had to wait several times for pedestrians to walk past. And they said: 'What are you doing taking pictures of the cars parked on the pavement?' And they all agreed that it was a nightmare." Another said: "I had one of the security men coming over and stood at the side of me and looking to see what I was doing. But he was really interested when I started telling him what it was about."

Remembering to Take Photos and Recall Them Later. Diary studies place a considerable burden on participants to conscientiously document their experiences. Photo diaries may ease this burden by simplifying the process of creating diary entries. However, participants must still remember to take the camera with them and use it once they are out and about. Several participants in this study commented that they had struggled with this. One said: "With the photos, I sort of had to think. I had to remember to take the camera and then think to actually take anything. Sometimes I'd seen something I wanted to take and I'd forgotten the camera." Another said: "I've got out of the habit of looking at things with a view to photographing them. Time was, I wouldn't move without my camera. So, it was quite hard to think about what I was looking at and to see if there was a study for photographing."

Diary studies also require participants to recognise and discuss their diary entries during follow-up interviews. Photo diary studies have been shown to have advantages over other diary methods in this regard [2]. Despite an interval of approximately one to two weeks between the study period and follow-up interviews in the current study, several participants had forgotten what they had taken or why they had taken it. This resulted in some photos being unnecessarily discarded.

Flexibility of Study Duration. We recruited participants over a period of approximately 12 months. This meant that they completed the photo diary exercise at different times of the year. Though this did not cause any major problems, several participants who we recruited in the winter months commented that bad weather during the study period prevented them from going out and taking as many photos as they would have liked. Conversely, a number of participants who we recruited in the summer months expressed disappointment at being unable to take photos of weather-related mobility barriers, such as snow and icy surfaces.

The photo diary exercise required a reasonable degree of commitment and dedication from participants. Some participants felt the study period (approximately two weeks) was too short and they had run out of time. Others felt the study period was unnecessarily long. Their attitude appeared to depend on how they had approached the exercise. Some participants completed all diary entries in a single journey and found the study period too long. Others completed diary entries on different journeys throughout the study period and found the study period too short. Though the latter approach is what we originally encouraged participants to take, it did not seem to make any difference to the quality or variety of photos they produced.

Spontaneity of Photo Diary Entries. Participants differed according to the spontaneity of their photo diary entries. The majority of participants completed diary entries whenever they noticed barriers or aids to mobility. However, some participants planned their diary entries beforehand. For example, one participant commented that they had completed the exercise "straight away, the first day I got it, I went out and managed to take quite a lot of photos. I knew the kind of things that I wanted to take." Another described how they "made a list of 18 [mobility barriers/aids]. I lay there and thought, 'right, this is what you're aiming for' and that's what I did, basically." Another participant said: "Once I started doing it, then ideas kept coming to us. As I drove round, there's some stuff I saw at random, and other stuff that I thought I would go and have a look at anyway."

Several participants found it difficult to capture certain barriers and aids to mobility in situ. For example, one participant mentioned they were unable to take a photo of them struggling to get onto a train with a heavy suitcase because they would have needed an extra hand. Some participants addressed this problem by taking photos to represent problems (e.g. a suitcase) rather than the actual situation in which they occurred. One participant said: "When you're travelling along you've already gone past something and you think 'I wish I'd taken that'. And it's too late then. So it's quite hard actually to find things to actually take photos of."

Attitudes Towards the Diary Study Method. Many participants commented that they had enjoyed taking part in the photo diary study. One said: "It was a really nice project to do. It was like being back at school. I got really enthusiastic about it." Several participants commented how the photo diary study had made them more aware of barriers and aids to mobility in the built environment. One participant said: "I found it quite interesting thinking of the things that are good and then also the sort of hiccups that might cause chaos." Though we gave participants a £20 gift voucher for completing the photo diary study, several commented that they enjoyed merely being involved in the project and were not expecting a monetary incentive.

Some participants struggled with the photo diary exercise. Despite giving them an information sheet, a reminder sheet, and verbal instructions, several participants were still uncertain about what to take photos of. One participant said: "I had no problems taking the photographs, except I was a bit uncertain of what things would be best to take. Certain things that I thought in retrospect would have been better to take didn't get taken. Some things I took might have been better not taken."

Though we instructed participants to take as many or as few photos as they felt appropriate, the number of available exposures in the disposable camera (39) was too many for several participants, who felt pressured to use them all. One said: "With there being 30-odd photos, I found it difficult. I felt that I wasn't doing enough and I didn't want to repeat things." Another participant said: "[I found it] quite hard really. Because I don't get out, well, I do I get out a lot but it's all in this area and I tend to repeat the same journeys. So I had to actually look for things." Another participant said: "It's not easy. The biggest hazard is uneven pavements. But there's only so many uneven pavements you can take."

5 Discussion

The results indicate that photo diaries are an appropriate methodology both for identifying barriers and aids to mobility in the built environment and eliciting needs and requirements from older adults for high-technology solutions. Participants generated a substantial number of photos identifying numerous barriers and aids to mobility.

A grounded theory analysis of the data identified six distinct themes incorporating mobility barriers and aids from across all aspects of the built environment. These themes provide a basis for generating requirements for high-technology solutions that will enable older adults to mitigate mobility barriers and promote physical activity.

Many of the barriers and aids to mobility identified in the current study are similar to those identified in previous studies. Ståhl et al. [12], identified barriers relating to uneven pavement surfaces, busy roads, difficult road crossings, and the inappropriate behaviour of cyclists – all of which participants identified in the current study. Though Schmehl et al. [11] focused specifically on public transport, several of the mobility barriers they identified, such as inaccessible steps and exposed bus shelters, were also identified by participants in the current study. The focus groups and public discussions conducted by Lockett et al. [6] also elicited similar mobility barriers and aids to the current study, such as the difficulty of having insufficient time to cross busy roads or the benefit of pavements that have been cleared of snow and ice.

The similarity of the barriers and aids to mobility identified in these studies is perhaps unsurprising, given the similarity of the participants and study locations. However, in comparison to focus groups, cultural probes and accompanied walks, the photo diary method used in the current study offers a much simpler and less time-consuming approach, both for participants and researchers. Photo diaries elicit a combination of the subjective perceptions of older adults and the objective identification of mobility barriers, avoiding many of the pitfalls of studies that rely exclusively on objective or subjective measures of the built environment (e.g. [8, 14]). The autonomous nature of photo diaries also omits the need for researchers to be present, as in Ståhl et al. [12], allowing for greater spontaneity and ecological validity of the data. Furthermore, depending on the purpose of the investigation, the data from photo diaries could easily be shared with policymakers and stakeholders, as in Lockett et al. [6], to stimulate broader discussions.

There were some limitations to the photo diary methodology used in this study. For example, the use of a camera possibly biased participants towards taking journeys on foot and identifying barriers and aids to mobility from that perspective. This was not always the case, as participants took a number of photos on public transport, on bikes, and in cars, but the vast majority of photos were taken from the pedestrian perspective. Similarly, the instructions we gave to participants possibly biased them towards taking photos of very 'concrete' physical barriers and aids to mobility in the built environment. Again, this was not always the case, as participants took photos of people, places, and artifacts such as bus passes or mobile phones, but the vast majority of photos taken were of physical barriers or aids to mobility. While there is great potential to address such barriers via appropriate policy interventions [8], the scope for addressing physical barriers through high-technology solutions is more limited. In light of this, it may be necessary to refine the photo diary methodology to encourage older adult participants to consider a broader range of barriers and aids to mobility.

Participants in this study were an invited subset of those taking part in the Co-Motion project and were recruited on the basis that they were sufficiently mobile and willing to document their journeys. This meant that Co-Motion participants who were less mobile, and perhaps faced the biggest mobility barriers, were typically not invited to take part in the photo diary study. Future studies should aim to recruit a broad selection of participants who vary in mobility. Some of the more able-bodied participants in the photo diary study felt it was intended more for people with severe mobility problems. As a result, they tended to take photos of things that might help or hinder people with mobility problems (but did not actually affect them personally). There is a danger with this approach that the study only captures perceived, rather than actual, barriers and aids to mobility. Future studies should perhaps place greater emphasis on issues that directly affect participants.

Carter and Mankoff [2] demonstrated that photo diaries are the easiest method for participants, both for generating diary entries and later recognising their contents. However, some of the older adult participants in this study experienced difficulties both in remembering to use the camera and recalling what they had taken during the follow-up interview. In some photo diary studies, researchers prompt participants to complete diary entries at particular times of day [7]. Such an approach would not have been appropriate in the current study, given the emphasis on capturing mobility barriers and aids whenever and wherever they occur. The follow-up phone call made to participants in the middle of the study period did however prove useful for providing additional guidance and encouragement. Ensuring a minimal amount of time between the study period and follow-up interview also ensures that participants recall as much information as possible. Some participants in this study kept notes of what they had taken, which they used as prompts during the follow-up interview. Though this would add to participants' workload, it may be a sensible recommendation for any future studies.

Participants in this study differed according to how they completed their diary entries. Some planned their entries before embarking on a journey; others captured diary entries more spontaneously. Similarly, some participants completed all diary entries in a single journey; others completed them on different journeys throughout the study period. Though we encouraged participants to make spontaneous entries diary entries throughout the duration of the study period, it did not seem to make any difference to the quality or variety of photos they produced. However, for participants who planned their photos beforehand, it is, again, possible that they were capturing perceived, rather than actual, barriers and aids to mobility. For instance, one participant said: "The only thing I couldn't find when I wanted one was an overhanging tree. That was something I couldn't get. All the ones along here that had been annoying me for weeks have all been cut back." Future studies should perhaps place greater emphasis on issues that actually, rather than potentially, affect participants.

Many of these methodological drawbacks could easily be addressed in future studies. The feelings of awkwardness or self-consciousness that many participants experienced when taking photos of mobility barriers in public places may be more difficult to address. Future studies should perhaps encourage participants to discuss what they are doing with interested observers, as this appeared to satisfy their curiosity in this study. Ultimately, many participants in this study enjoyed the photo diary exercise and felt it had raised their awareness of barriers and aids to mobility. With some methodological adjustments, photo diary studies can be considered an appropriate methodology for eliciting older adults' needs and requirements for new technologies.

6 Conclusions

In this paper, we have presented a photo diary study conducted with 26 older adults in the UK who were given disposable cameras to document things that affect their mobility. We have presented a selection of the mobility barriers and aids identified in this study, grouped according to six distinct themes reflecting older adults' experiences from across all aspects of the built environment. We have also outlined several methodological issues relating to the use of photo diaries for eliciting needs and requirements from older adults.

The photo diary method is not without its limitations. We have outlined several issues relating to the use of disposable cameras with older adults; older adults' self-consciousness when photographing their neighbourhoods; older adults' difficulties in remembering to create photo diary entries; and older adults' differing interpretations of the study protocol.

However, this study has shown that photo diaries are an efficient, flexible, and productive method both for identifying barriers and aids to mobility in the built environment and eliciting needs and requirements from older adults for new technologies.

Research Data Availability. Researchers wishing access to the data used in this study should visit the following URL for more information: http://www.cs.york.ac.uk/hci/comotion.

Acknowledgments. This research was conducted as part of the Co-Motion project [EP/K03748X/1], a Design for Well-Being: Ageing and Mobility in the Built Environment Initiative funded by the Engineering and Physical Sciences Research Council, the Economic and Social Research Council, and the Arts & Humanities Research Council. We are grateful to the project partners for their hard work and support. We also thank all the participants in the study for their time and effort.

References

1. Bowling, A., Stafford, M.: How do objective and subjective assessments of neighbourhood influence social and physical functioning in older age? Findings from a British survey of ageing. Soc. Sci. Med. **64**(12), 2533–2549 (2007)
2. Carter, S., Mankoff, J.: When participants do the capturing: the role of media in diary studies. In: 23rd SIGCHI Conference on Human Factors in Computing Systems, pp. 899–908. ACM, New York (2005)
3. Gaver, B., Dunne, T., Pacenti, E.: Design: cultural probes. Interactions **6**(1), 21–29 (1999)
4. Glaser, B., Strauss, A.: The Discovery of Grounded Theory. Weidenfield & Nicholson, London (1967)
5. Handy, S.L., Boarnet, M.G., Ewing, R., Killingsworth, R.E.: How the built environment affects physical activity: views from urban planning. Am. J. Prev. Med. **23**(2), 64–73 (2002)
6. Lockett, D., Willis, A., Edwards, N.: Through seniors' eyes: an exploratory qualitative study to identify environmental barriers to and facilitators of walking. Can. J. Nurs. Res. **37**(3), 48–65 (2005)
7. Palen, L., Salzman, M.: Voice-mail diary studies for naturalistic data capture under mobile conditions. In: Conference on Computer Supported Cooperative Work, CSCW 2002, pp. 87–95. ACM, New York (2002)
8. Rosso, A.L., Auchincloss, A.H., Michael, Y.L.: The urban built environment and mobility in older adults: a comprehensive review. J. Aging Res. **2011**, 1–10 (2011)
9. Saelens, B.E., Handy, S.L.: Built environment correlates of walking: a review. Med. Sci. Sports Exerc. **40**(7 Suppl), S550–S566 (2008)
10. Sallis, J., Bauman, A., Pratt, M.: Environmental and policy interventions to promote physical activity. Am. J. Prev. Med. **15**(4), 379–397 (1998)
11. Schmehl, S., Deutsch, S., Schrammel, J., Paletta, L., Tscheligi, M.: Directed cultural probes: detecting barriers in the usage of public transportation. In: Campos, P., Graham, N., Jorge, J., Nunes, N., Palanque, P., Winckler, M. (eds.) INTERACT 2011, Part I. LNCS, vol. 6946, pp. 404–411. Springer, Heidelberg (2011)
12. Ståhl, A., Carlsson, G., Hovbrandt, P., Iwarsson, S.: "Let's go for a walk!": identification and prioritisation of accessibility and safety measures involving elderly people in a residential area. Eur. J. Ageing **5**(3), 265–273 (2008)
13. Wang, C., Burris, M.A.: Photovoice: concept, methodology, and use for participatory needs assessment. Health Educ. Behav. **24**(3), 369–387 (1997)
14. Yen, I.H., Michael, Y.L., Perdue, L.: Neighborhood environment in studies of health of older adults: a systematic review. Am. J. Prev. Med. **37**(5), 455–463 (2009)

Design Criteria for Stimulating Emotions
in Web Applications

Giulio Mori[✉], Fabio Paternò, and Ferdinando Furci

ISTI – CNR, Via Moruzzi, 1, 57126 Pisa, Italy
{giulio.mori,fabio.paterno,ferdinando.furci}
@isti.cnr.it

Abstract. This work aims to identify the main aspects of Web design responsible for eliciting specific emotions. For this purpose, we performed a user study with 40 participants testing a Web application designed by applying a set of criteria for stimulating various emotions. In particular, we considered six emotions (hate, anxiety, boredom, fun, serenity, love), and for each of them a specific set of design criteria was exploited. The purpose of the study was to reach a better understanding regarding what design techniques are most important to stimulate each emotion. We report on the results obtained and discuss their implications. Such results can inform the development of guidelines for Web applications able to stimulate users' emotions.

Keywords: Web guidelines · Emotions · Affective interfaces · Adaptable interfaces

1 Introduction

Emotions have acquired increasing importance in HCI [1–3]. However, little work has addressed how to take them into account when designing Web applications, which are the most widely used ones. Therefore, Web developers and designers have difficulties in identifying the most relevant design criteria (such as choice of user interface widgets, navigation and interaction style, suitable colours, etc.) that can stimulate specific emotional states. Understanding the effects of certain design criteria is not only important for the awareness of Web designers, but also useful for many Web application domains such as educational environments, telemedicine, online psychological platforms, games, home automation applications, or tools oriented to help people with disabilities or the elderly.

The literature contains various contributions investigating the effects of aesthetics in Web sites [4–6], what influences users' preferences [7], or analysis of the emotional appeal of hedonic elements in Web sites (such as colour, images, shapes and photographs) [8], but none of these studies provides indications about the effectiveness in stimulating specific emotions of the various aspects of Web design. One study [3] aims to understand the relations between the design factors and emotional dimensions of many evocative homepages. In particular the study identified 13 emotional dimensions (each one based on some adjective provided by the users), and some main design factors (shape, texture and colour for the background; title, menu and main images for

© IFIP International Federation for Information Processing 2015
J. Abascal et al. (Eds.): INTERACT 2015, Part I, LNCS 9296, pp. 165–182, 2015.
DOI: 10.1007/978-3-319-22701-6_12

the elements). Unfortunately, even if the study aimed to associate the emotional dimensions with the proposed design factors, as the authors indicate, their study cannot determine which design factors are closely related to which feelings. In addition, the study analyses just only some design factors for the home pages. An approach [2] comparing two different Web sites (differing in content as well as in graphic design, colour schemes, and balance between text versus illustrations) has been proposed to identify the relations between the design elements of Web pages, perceived usability, and emotional responses, but it does not suggest any concrete indication of Web design aspects for stimulating specific emotions. A series of studies [9–11] show that first impressions of a Web site can affect the appealing judgment before users can consciously notice any details, but they do not go deeper to identify the most important aspects for each specific affective state. Unfortunately, the effects of Web design features on the emotional state is not yet a known field. In fact, Internet is still full of Web sites (implemented also by professional designers) with banners, popups, media or layout and colour complexity, that often elicit unsuitable emotional reactions from visitors [1, 2]. Different interfaces with poor usability can stimulate different negative emotional reactions, just as different usable interfaces can elicit different positive emotional states [12]. This denotes that there is a need to understand more the emotional impact of the various Web design criteria.

In this paper we aim to investigate the effectiveness of some Web design criteria to stimulate a certain emotional state in the user. In order to understand if some aspects of Web design can be more relevant than others to stimulate an emotional reaction, we have designed and implemented a Web application able to adapt the design depending on the chosen emotion (hate, anxiety, boredom, fun, serenity, love). Moreover, we have conducted a user test with 40 users to evaluate the emotional impact of the proposed Web designs and to collect indications about the design criteria perceived by the user as more relevant than others to elicit the selected emotional state.

Previous work [12] investigated the impact of some Web design criteria to elicit specific emotions independently of the contents and the application domain. For this purpose, a survey and one user test were carried out. The survey involved 57 users and aimed to understand the most recurring emotions during Web interaction and the relative Web features. Each users was asked to propose a certain number (maximum 8) of typical emotions during Web interaction, and then to associate each proposed emotion with specific choices for the main Web design aspects (such as colours, page structures and contents distribution, type of media, navigation & interaction elements, etc.). When the users proposed negative emotions, they also had to suggest a positive counterpart, and finally order them (on the basis of their perception) from the most negative to the most positive. After having filtered (discarding synonyms, emotions with low number of preferences, and emotions having similar Web design characteristics associated), the 219 negative and 219 positive collected emotions became six: *hate, anxiety, boredom, fun, serenity* and *love*. Hate and love indicate the sense of disliking/liking typical of social environments, anxiety and serenity denote the emotions during critical/safe operations (e.g. buying using the credit card), while boredom and fun express how the contents are presented to attract the user. These six emotions are probably not exhaustive for the Web, but rather than a further general emotion classification (many are present in literature [13–15]), we need a basic set of emotions that can be considered typical of Web applications. The six-emotion universal cultural classification proposed by Ekman [13] has not been considered typical for the Web interaction by the users that we recruited. The results of that user study emphasized that different Web designs can stimulate different emotional states on the users. Bad or good usability, although an important factor that can elicit a negative or positive emotional state, is not sufficient to elicit specific emotional reaction. In fact, different unusable/usable interfaces elicited different negative/positive emotions from the users. Positive emotions were perceived important to improve the user experience (at different levels), but also negative emotions were perceived useful in some cases depending on their applications (e.g. educational or learning tools where it is necessary to increase the awareness of children about the difference between good and bad behaviours). Designers need to be aware of the emotional effects of the Web design aspects.

Unfortunately, such previous study [12] did not clarify if some aspects of Web design can be more important than others to stimulate a certain emotional state, so in this work we seek to address this issue. For this purpose, we have designed and implemented a Web application able to adapt its design to the emotional state selected by the user and performed a user test to check the validity of the design criteria applied. Section 2 describes the Web application adapting the design to six emotions, and the applied design criteria for each, while Sect. 3 reports the user test results and discusses them. Finally, we draw some conclusions and discuss ideas for future work.

2 The Design of a Web Application Adapting to Elicit Emotions

We designed and implemented a Web application, *Emotional Music System*, where the user can select an emotion and search for one musical author or a band. After the emotion has been selected, the associated Web design criteria (aiming to elicit that emotion) are applied by the system replacing the initial neutral interface (without any particular Web design criteria). Music streams can be exploited through the Spotify (http://www.spotify.com) widgets present in the interface. In particular, we designed two versions implemented through two CSS (*Cascading Style Sheets*) for each emotion: (a) **the first version**: applied design criteria similar to those in the previous user test [12], though improved based on the collected results, (b) **the second option**: similar to the first version but with different small aspects that resulted controversial regarding their emotional effectiveness in the previous user test (such as colours and visual characteristics, blurred or clear text and dimension of images & videos).

The design criteria applied consider the main Web design aspects: colours and visual characteristics, page structures & content distribution, presence and type of multimedia elements, type of navigation and interaction elements, elements for text insertion. In the following we detail how their applications varied depending on the emotion to elicit.

Web Interface to Elicit Hate. The widgets are disposed in a confused layout, adding further obstacles during the user interaction (such as some advertisement pop-ups). In addition, the TAB key has been designed to have an unpredictable behaviour (i.e. for each click of the TAB key the focus goes randomly to one element of the interface), instead of sequential. The contents are distributed in just one long page with totally black background, blurred white text and big blurry black & white images. We used textual elements for navigation and interaction. Figure 1 shows the first design of a zoomed extract of the form from the whole long Web page showing the confusing positioning of the form elements and the blurry black & white text and images/videos. Figure 1 also shows a pop-up introducing further difficulties during the user interaction (appearing randomly when the user clicked on some fields) and forcing the user to intervene actively.

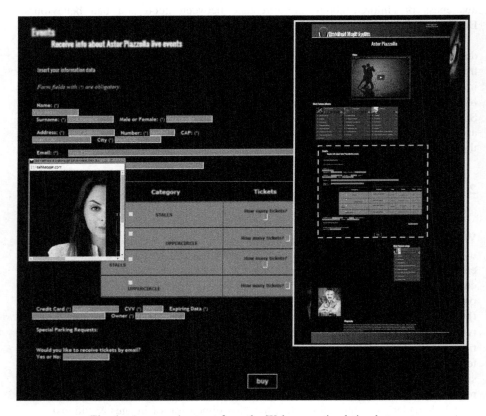

Fig. 1. A zoomed extract from the Web page stimulating hate

In the *second option design* we removed the visual decorations in the background, and reduced also the dimension of images and videos.

Web Interface to Elicit Anxiety. The elements of the Web interface include intermittent light effects, distortion and jerky transformations. The Web pages have been enriched with intermitting de-saturated icons, and the content has been distributed over three pages: the *author* page contains the biography, the audio player, the video, the albums section; the *events* page contains the form to buy the virtual tickets; and the *albums* page presents three Spotify players of three famous albums. The page background is totally black with light effects, blurred text in combination with blurred and small de-saturated images. We have used standard navigation and interaction elements with dynamic effects (distortion and shrinkage). Standard textboxes were used to insert data in the form (such as personal data, number of tickets) and one text area was used to insert special requests. Figure 2 shows an extract of the form of the *event page* and a complete view of the *author* page with light effects, distortion and jerky transformations of the elements. With the goal of creating stress and anxiety, in the *events* Web page, the form tilts when the mouse hovers over that area. In addition, we have added a countdown clock showing the remaining time to complete the data insertion. The clock was simply an element to add pressure to the user.

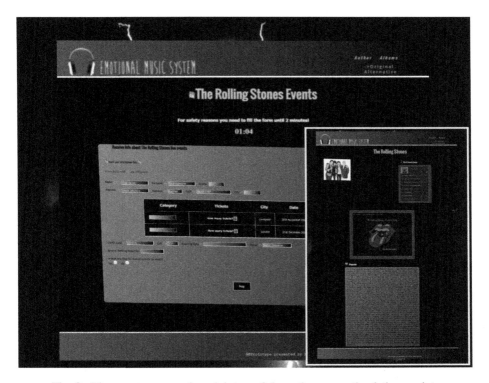

Fig. 2. The events page and a miniature of the author page stimulating anxiety

In the *second option design* we just changed the black background colour and the grey colour of the section area to navy blue. We have also removed the visual decorations in the background.

Web Interface to Elicit Boredom. The contents of the interface have been distributed in one long page. We have not included images and videos. The background of the page shows rain drops, while the colour of the area containing the contents is totally grey with blurred text. Accepting the suggestions of the users in the survey, with respect to the other interfaces, we have added more text in the biography and some extra required fields in the form. We have used static elements for navigation and interaction. Standard textboxes have been used to insert data (such as personal data, number of tickets, or special requests). Figure 3 shows an extract of the Web page to elicit boredom.

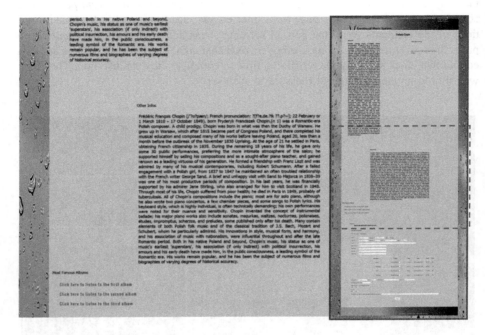

Fig. 3. A zoomed extract from the Web page stimulating boredom

In the *second option design* we have substituted the grey colour with silver, and changed the rain background with a foggy one. Considering that in the previous user test, many users said that the blurred text (instead of clear) was probably not so determinant in making the interaction boring (many users considered the blurred text as a nuisance), we have applied clear text.

Web Interface to Elicit Fun. The Web interface presents unpredictable animations and dynamic effects of the elements, with the goal of surprising positively and entertaining the user. The users had suggested that dynamic effects of the areas or elements should not be excessive in number (avoiding them when useless), and they should facilitate the user interaction. Thus, we applied the dynamic effects only to the navigation elements and the biography area (zooming at the passage of the mouse over). The contents have been distributed in three pages: the *author* page containing the biography, the audio player, the video, the albums section; the *events* page, containing the form to buy the virtual tickets, and the *albums* page containing three Spotify players of three famous albums. We have enriched the pages with graphical decorations and icons emphasizing each section of each page. The background of the page shows spring flowers, while the areas present a gradient of yellow (remembering the light and sun) and the text is colourful (maintaining a readable contrast between the clear text and the background). We have used dynamic elements of navigation (rotating and enlarging at the passage of the mouse over). In addition, we have used dynamic elements of interaction in general (the survey reported dynamic effects as an important key factor independently of the type of interaction elements used). Standard textboxes have been used to insert data (such as user personal data, number of tickets, or special requests).

Figure 4 shows the author page with graphical decorations and the rotation of the *events* link in the navigation bar, in combination with the enlargement of the biography section when the mouse is over that area. In the *events* page containing the form to buy tickets, the fields change their colours to facilitate the interaction when the user clicks on them.

Fig. 4. The author Web page stimulating fun and a zoomed extract of the navigation elements.

In the *second option design* we have substituted the flowers background with a rainbow background. We have changed yellow and green with orange and fuchsia and the graphical decoration of the frame has been reduced, substituting each border of the interface, with just only some flowers (fuchsia instead of green) in the corners.

Web Interface to Elicit Serenity. We have designed this Web interface with the goal of minimizing the user effort during the interaction and maintaining the simplicity of the interface in order to allow users to interact easily.

The contents have been distributed in three pages accessible through TABs: the *author* page containing the biography, the audio player, the video, the albums section; the *events* page, containing the form to buy the virtual tickets; and the *albums* page, containing three Spotify players of three famous albums. The elements of the pages are completely static avoiding that dynamic effects could distract the user. The page background shows an open space panorama, while the colours of the area and text are soft aqua and green. Standard textboxes have been used to insert data (such as personal data, number of tickets), and one text area has been used to insert special requests. Figure 5 shows the *author* page where TAB elements in the top-left area of the interface facilitate the navigation. In the *events* page containing the form to buy tickets, we have reduced the required fields to simplify the user effort. Besides, the credit card field has been split into 4 groups (each 4 digits long) in order to facilitate the reading and the insertion. When the user fills in a group of 4 credit card digits, the system moves the cursor automatically to the next group (corresponding to the next 4 digits). We have added a famous logo for secure transaction, so that the user could feel her/himself safe.

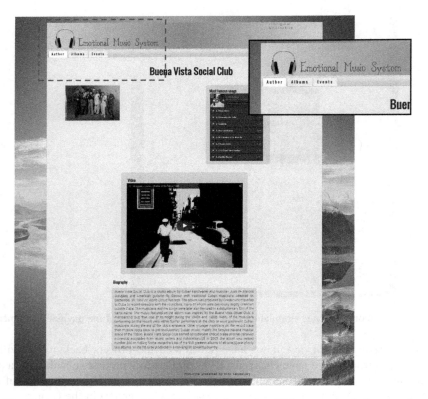

Fig. 5. A zoomed extract of the TABs, and the author Web page stimulating serenity

In the *second option design* we have substituted the open space mountain panorama background with a sea view, and blue and teal are the new colours applied.

Web Interface to Elicit Love. We have designed this Web interface with the goal of attracting the user to frequently interact and use the interface, through the aesthetic in combination with good usability. The contents have been distributed in one long page. Details have been enriched graphically in order to be more appealing, together with graphical icons emphasizing each section of the page. The background of the page shows indefinite and abstract textures, while the gradient of colours of the area containing the contents are red and pink. Considering the critics of users about the too shocking colours previously tested, we have taken into consideration soft colours. We have applied white text maintaining a readable contrast between the clear text and the red background. We have used smooth dynamic hover effects and graphical for the navigation and interaction elements. We have applied standard textboxes to insert data (such as personal data, number of tickets), and one text area to insert special requests. As the interface should elicit serenity, the form aims to simplify the interaction. In particular, the credit card field has been split into 4 groups, each 4 digit long, to facilitate the reading and insertion and required fields for the user's data have been reduced. Figure 6 shows the Web page to elicit love, in which graphics has been enhanced with graphical enrichments and textures.

Fig. 6. The Web page stimulating love

In the *second option design,* we have taken into account the received critics about the used colours (red and pink), we have decided to test different warm colours (orange and yellow), substituting also the abstract textures of the background. We have also reduced the dimension of the images and videos.

3   The User Test

The purpose of the user test was to understand whether some aspects of Web design can be more important than others to elicit a specific emotion. We recruited 40 users who had not participated to any our previous user test, and were divided into two groups of 20 users each: (a) the group A tested only the *first design* for the six emotions, (b) the group B tested only the *second option design.* For each emotion, we asked each user to select the main three aspects of Web design that they considered important to elicit that emotional state.

3.1   Description of the Tasks and the Questionnaire

We performed a between-subjects test in order to avoid that using both versions the order could influence the emotional perception. For each emotion, each user had to choose one different author or band and perform three tasks: (1) find the birth date of the author or in case of a band, the date of constitution, (2) select the second song from the third album in the *Most Famous Albums* section, (3) fill in a form to buy some virtual tickets (using the assigned imaginary user profile). The three tasks had respectively the objectives to try out: (1) text reading, (2) navigation, and (3) interaction with the interface elements and their disposition on the layout.

Users had to fill in an online questionnaire. The questionnaire was composed of four parts, asking the users: (PART A) some personal information, (PART B) a judgment about the emotional effectiveness of the analysed interface, (PART C) to choose the main three aspects of Web design from a proposed list for the current emotion, (PART D) some suggestions and comments. PART A had to be filled in before starting the user test, and PART D had to be filled in at the end, while PART B and PART C had to be filled in after having performed the three tasks for each interface aiming at eliciting one of the six emotions.

Each user of both groups (A and B) evaluated the emotional effectiveness of the six designs in random order. The users gave their ratings in a scale from 1 to 5 (where the value 1 indicated that the page was very ineffective to elicit the proposed emotion, while value 5 indicated that the page was very effective, and the value 3 represented the neutrality). Besides, each user had to choose the main three aspects of Web design from a proposed list. The list was composed by every Web design feature applied to each one of the six analysed interfaces. The users did not know the Web design features applied to the current evaluated interface, and the execution of the three tasks had the goal to help them to understand concretely if certain Web design characteristics could be really important to stimulate the specific emotion. In details, the list of all Web design characteristics was structured by couples of opposite features or groups of choices and they have been provided to the users together with their meanings as following: **(a) confused layout/ordered layout** (indicates if the elements of the interface are misaligned horizontally and/or vertically or well aligned; see Fig. 1), **(b) non-semantic/semantic effects** (indicates if the functionalities triggered by the widgets of the interface can accomplish or not their purpose), **(c) stressing/reassuring elements** (indicates if the interface allows the user to perceive some risk factors, such as the sense of losing data and money, providing limited time to complete a task, etc. or on the contrary, if the interface supports the user with continuous feedbacks, famous logos, no deadlines, etc.), **(d) excessive/moderate information** (indicates if the interface contains too much text and requires too much data to insert, or if the amount of text and data is a proper trade-off), **(e) difficult/easy interaction** (indicates if the interface requires excessive mouse movements to navigate, contains selection widgets with too many choices, elements in difficult position to be reached, obstacles such as popup or windows, etc., or on the contrary, if the position of the elements minimize the effort and movements, contains interactive elements for selection with few choices, no pop-up and no open windows appear, etc.), **(f) ugly/appealing aesthetic and graphics** (it is a subjective aspect depending on visual complexity and colourfulness [16]), **(g) different/used colours** (indicates if different colours (from the applied) are considered better for the emotional effect, or if the chosen colours are appropriate, **(h) blurred/clear text & images/videos** (indicates if the blurred text or multimedia can produce appropriate emotional effect comparing with clear text and multimedia), **(i) medium-small/medium-big images/videos** (indicates which dimension of the images/videos can affect the emotional state), **(j) black & white, de-saturated, coloured images/videos** (indicates which type of the images/videos can affect the emotional state), **(k) absence/presence of images/videos** (indicates if the multimedia elements should be present or not), **(l) one page or many pages** (indicates the number of pages for distributing the contents and the elements), **(m) different/used interaction and navigation elements** (indicates if the different elements for interacting or navigate (from the applied) are considered emotionally effective, or if the applied elements are appropriate), **(o) text edit or text area** (indicates which way for inserting text is more appropriate for the emotional effect).

3.2   Results

The test was carried out by 40 users (average completion time per user was about 45 min). For sake of simplicity and lack of space, below we report only the first five more important Web aspects perceived by the two groups for each emotion (avoiding minor aspects with few preferences) so they can be easily comparable.

The participants in group A were 11 females and 9 males, with an average age of 26, 95 years (ranging from 22 to 51). Five users had a five-year degree, 1 user had a four-year degree, 11 users had a bachelor's degree, while 3 users had an high school diploma. Users were used to surf the Internet (16 users were connected to the Web every day, and 4 users navigated three times per week). The sample considered both experienced and inexperienced users in Web development (at different levels, 8 users had implemented some Web interfaces, while 12 users had little or no knowledge on Web programming).

The participants in group B were 14 females and 6 males, with an average age of 24, 6 years (ranging from 19 to 34). Four users had a five-year degree, 12 users had a bachelor's degree, while 4 users had an high school diploma. Users were used to surf the Internet (15 users were connected to the Web every day, 4 users navigated three times per week, and 1 user used the Web one time every fifteen days). The sample considered both experienced and inexperienced users in Web development (at different levels, 8 users had implemented some Web interfaces, while 12 users had little or no knowledge on Web programming).

Hate. The average effectiveness has been evaluated 4.75 by group A with a standard deviation 0.71. The average judgment of group B about the effectiveness of this second option Web design to stimulate hate became 4.65 with a standard deviation 0.67. The ranking of the users' preferences regarding the main factors of the two Web design responsible to elicit hate are reported in Table 1.

Table 1. Ranking of main Web aspects for the two designs eliciting hate.

Main first design aspects	N°	Main second option design aspects	N°
Confused layout	12	Confused Layout	11
Difficult interaction & navigation	10	Blurred text & images/video	11
Non-semantic effects	10	Difficult interaction and navigation	9
Stress factors	8	Non-semantic effects	8
Blurred text & images/videos	7	Stress factors	6

Anxiety. The average effectiveness has been evaluated 4.25 by group A with a standard deviation 1.06. The average judgment of group B about the effectiveness of this second option Web design to stimulate anxiety became 4.3 with a standard deviation 0.73. The ranking of the users' preferences regarding the main factors of the two Web design responsible to elicit anxiety are reported in Table 2.

Table 2. Ranking of main Web aspects for the two designs eliciting anxiety.

Main first design aspects	N°	Main second option design aspects	N°
Stress factors	14	Stress factors	17
Blurred text & images/videos	12	Blurred text & images/video	9
Dynamic effects	10	Dynamic effects	9
Confused layout	6	Difficult interaction & navigation	9
Difficult interaction & navigation	4	Confused layout	6

Boredom. Actually, the average effectiveness has been evaluated 3.65 by group A with a standard deviation 1.18. The average judgment of group B about the effectiveness of this second option Web design to stimulate boredom became 3.5 with a standard deviation 1.19. The ranking of the users' preferences regarding the main factors of the two Web design responsible to elicit boredom are reported in Table 3.

Table 3. Ranking of main Web aspects for the two designs eliciting boredom.

Main first design aspects	N°	Main second option design aspects	N°
Excessive info	14	Excessive Info	10
No effects (static)	11	No Effects (Static)	10
Absence of images/videos	9	Absence of images/videos	10
Difficult interaction & navigation	4	Used colours	5
Used colours, Unpleasant graphic	3	Unpleasant graphic	4

Fun. Currently, the average effectiveness has been evaluated by group A 3.33 with a standard deviation 1.08. The average judgment of group B about the effectiveness of this second option Web design to stimulate fun surprisingly improved, now becoming 3.75 with a standard deviation 0.91. The ranking of the users' preferences regarding the main factors of the two Web design responsible to elicit fun are reported in Table 4.

Table 4. Ranking of main Web aspects for the two designs eliciting fun.

Main first design aspects	N°	Main second option design aspects	N°
Appealing graphics & aesthetics	11	Dynamic effects	12
Dynamic effects	10	Appealing graphics & aesthetics	10
Colour images/videos	9	Colour images/videos	8
Ordered layout	6	Semantic effects	8
Easy interaction & navigation	6	Ordered layout	7

Serenity. The average effectiveness has been evaluated by group A 4.2 with a standard deviation 0.61. The average judgment of group B about the effectiveness of this second option Web design to stimulate serenity was 4.0 with a standard deviation 0.72. The ranking of the users' preferences regarding the main factors of the two Web design responsible to elicit serenity are reported in Table 5.

Table 5. Ranking of main Web aspects for the two designs eliciting serenity.

Main first design aspects	N°	Main second option design aspects	N°
Ordered layout	14	Ordered layout	11
Reassuring elements	12	Easy interaction and navigation	10
Easy interaction & navigation	9	Reassuring elements	9
Appealing graphics & aesthetics	6	Semantic effects	7
Semantic effects, Used colours	5	Used colours	6

Love. The users judged the average effectiveness of the interface stimulating love by group A 4.15 with a standard deviation 0.67. The average judgment of group B about the effectiveness of this second option Web design to stimulate love became 3.85 with a standard deviation 1.03. The ranking of the users' preferences regarding the main factors of the two Web design responsible to elicit love are reported in Table 6.

Table 6. Ranking of main Web aspects for the two designs eliciting love.

Main first design aspects	N°	Main second option design aspects	N°
Appealing graphics & aesthetics	13	Appealing graphics & aesthetics	11
Used colours	11	Clear text & images/videos	9
Reassuring elements	7	Reassuring elements	8
Easy interaction & navigation	6	Used colours	6
Semantic effects	5	Easy interaction & navigation	5

3.3   Discussion

Comparing the results of group A and B composed of different users interacting with slightly different designs, we can notice similar indications. In particular, comparing the average judgment for each emotion and the first three main aspects eliciting a specific emotions for group A and B (even if some times in slightly different order) we can find interesting consistent results.

Hate. The average judgments about the emotional design impact in the two groups are high effective and similar: 4.75 for group A and 4.65 for group B. This it is a clue that the applied characteristics are effective to stimulate hate. In particular, **confused layout, difficult interaction and navigation** are the common main aspects of Web design considered in group A and group B. However, the five common aspects in the first five positions (even if in different order) denote that the **difficulty or obstacles during the interaction are clearly considered predominant to stimulate the emotion hate**. These factors seem to be fundamental for the user to hate the Web interface and leaving it. Dimensions of images and videos do not seem to be relevant.

Anxiety. The average judgments about the emotional impact of the designs in the two groups are still high effective and similar: 4.25 for group A and 4.3 for group B. This it is a clue that the applied characteristics are effective to stimulate anxiety. In particular, **stress factors, blurred text and images/videos**, and **dynamic effects** are the common main aspects of Web design considered in group A and B. The two groups show five common aspects (even if with slight different number of the user's preferences). Looking at the gap of number of user's preferences, **the stress factors** and **dynamic transformation of the elements are the predominant keys to stimulate anxiety**. The presence of some aspects hindering the interaction, typical of hate, such as blurred text & images or difficult interaction and navigation, in close positions in the scale indicate that there is not a clear distinction between these two emotions.

Boredom. The average judgments about the emotional impact of the designs in the two groups are similar and a little bit over the neutrality: 3.65 for group A and 3.5 for group B. The judgments have decreased comparing to the previous user test, where the average judgment was 4.16 with a standard deviation 0.88. The reason of this lower evaluation is justified by the fact that the first assigned task was not particularly appropriate. In fact, we asked the birth date of the author or the date of constitution of the band, but this information was at very beginning of the text, saving the user to read it entirely. The fact that the user is forced to manage too much information as input (i.e. filling a form) or as output (i.e. reading text) is a clue of becoming bored. Long text seems to be more relevant than blurred or clear text. This is shown also by the fact that the **excessive information,** together with the **absence of dynamic effect** and **absence of images or videos** (in the first three positions) are considered important in both groups A and B. These three aspects indicate that **the presence of too much information without a way of distraction, such as image or videos or dynamic effects, are considered causes of boring**. Considering that there is an important gap in terms of number of preferences after these aspects, this denotes that the other characteristics are considered secondary.

Fun. The average evaluation of the emotional impact of the designs in the two groups are a little bit different: 3.33 for group A and 3.75 (quite high) for group B. The average judgment of the design in group A (where we applied just only useful animations to facilitate the interaction) is similar to the previous user test (average 3.32 with a standard deviation 1.21). On the contrary, the average judgment for group B (where we maintained the same dynamic effects of group A, but we reduced also the graphics decorations) is improved. This denotes that useful dynamic effects for the interaction and proper graphic and aesthetics have considerable importance to stimulate fun, so finding a suitable compromise can be important. **Appealing graphics and aesthetics, dynamic effects** and **colour images & videos** are considered the main aspects for both group A and B to elicit fun. Looking at the other aspects in different order in Table 4, we notice characteristics (such as ordered layout, easy interaction & navigation and semantic effects) facilitating the interaction. Obviously, an interface difficult to use cannot stimulate fun, but the results denote that a usable interface is not sufficient, an some extra factors such as unexpected reactions are important. From our research **this emotion is the more critical and difficult comparing with the others because it requires a suitable mix and compromise of different factors**, such as unusual graphics, dynamic effects or animation, and appealing colours.

Serenity. The average evaluation of the emotional impact of the designs in the two groups are high and similar: 4.2 for group A and 4.0 for group B. The high and rather homogeneous judgment indicates that the applied characteristics are effective to stimulate serenity. In particular, **ordered layout, reassuring elements** and **easy interaction and navigation** are common characteristics to the group A and group B, as an indication of important aspects to stimulate serenity. Looking at the results, **the stimulation of serenity requires minimization of the user's effort and his/her reassurance** (with known logos or elements reducing the fear and risk of losing something).

Love. The average judgments of the emotional impact of the designs in the two groups are rather over the neutrality: 4.15 for group A and 3.85 for group B. They are both better than the previous user test where the average judgment was 3.64 with a standard deviation 1.06. The differences of the two groups can indicate that colours have also a certain influence. The **appealing graphics and aesthetics** and **the reassuring elements** are considered important factors to stimulate love, involving the user to use the interface again many times. Looking at the other common aspects in Table 6 of groups A and B, easy interaction and navigation denote that **a good usability is an important factor to stimulate love, but they should be mixed properly with an appealing graphics/aesthetic, and reassuring elements**. Dimensions of images and videos do not seem to be relevant.

There are many studies about the effects of the colours and emotions [16–19]. However, after this analysis, the fact that the two user groups did not consider the colours as a principal factor of Web design for stimulating a specific emotion, but they rather indicated interaction factors as more important, is not trivial at all. In fact, excluding love emotion where colours seem to have a certain influence, they are not perceived from the users as an important factor of Web design to stimulate a particular emotion (at least for the six emotions we have analysed). We cannot say in this phase that colours have not at all an emotional impact on the user, but colours do not seem to be perceived fundamental as other characteristics of Web design. The interactive Web features perceived by the users as fundamental to elicit each emotional state are intuitive and this is a positive aspect, even if a deeper statistical analysis with larger samples is necessary. In addition, the closer emotions present common design aspects, but with different percentage of perceived importance. This indicates that the emotions are complex and there is not a well definite distinction between similar (but not equal) emotional states.

4   Conclusions and Future Work

The goal of this work has been to understand whether some particular factors of Web design are responsible to stimulate a specific emotional state on the users. The collected results are consistent and encouraging, and provide useful indications about the main aspects of Web design, even if further investigation is necessary. The fact that colours are not perceived as a main aspect to elicit emotions is not trivial, and we plan to perform different user tests with wider samples of users for further statistical verifications. We are also considering for the future implementation of the next user tests, to exploit various physiological sensors in order to monitor the emotional changes according to the Web design changes during the interactions. In addition, we are thinking to introduce the support of an eye-tracker to investigate the emotional effects of the elements disposed in different positions, and a neuro-headset measuring the EEG signal to detect when users are focused and concentrated. We plan to involve professional Web designers to learn more about the potential impact of the identified criteria.

The final goal of this research aims to formalize a set of guidelines to design Web applications able to elicit a particular emotional state of the user during the interaction. As a further step, we plan to investigate the design of Web applications capable to monitor and take into account the current emotional state of the user, adapting the Web design to stimulate more positive emotions, for a better user experience.

References

1. Hassenzahl, M.: The thing and i: understanding the relationship between user and product. In: Blythe, M., Overbeeke, K., Monk, A., Wright, P. (eds.) Funology. Human Computer Interaction Series, vol. 3, pp. 31–42. Springer, Dordrecht (2005)
2. Karlsson, M.: Expressions, emotions, and web site design. CoDesign 3(1), 75–89 (2007)
3. Kim, J., Lee, J., Choi, D.: Designing emotionally evocative homepages: an empirical study of the quantitative relations between design factors and emotional dimensions. Int. J. Hum Comput. Stud. 56(6), 899–940 (2003)
4. Hartmann, J., Sutcliffe, A., De Angeli, A.: Investigating attractiveness in web user interfaces. In: Proceedings of the CHI 2007. ACM Press (2007)
5. Lindgaard, G., Dudek, C., Sen, D., Sumegi, L., Noonan, P.: An exploration of relations between visual appeal, trustworthiness and perceived usability of homepages. ACM Trans. Comput.-Hum. Interact. 18, 1 (2011)
6. Zheng, X., Chakraborty, I., Lin, J., Rauschenberger, R.: Correlating low-level image statistics with users' rapid aesthetic and affective judgments of web pages. In: Proceedings of the CHI (2009)
7. De Angeli, A., Sutcliffe, A., Hartmann, J.: Interaction, usability and aesthetics: what influences users' preferences? In: Proceedings of the DIS 2006, pp. 271–280, ACM Press (2006)
8. Cyr, D.: Emotion and web site design. In: Soegaard, M., Dam, R.F. (eds.) The Encyclopedia of Human Computer Interaction, 2nd edn., (Chapter 40), Interaction Design Foundation. http://www.interaction-design.org/encyclopedia/emotion_and_website_design.html
9. Lindgaard, G., Fernandes, G., Dudek, C., Brown, J.: Attention web designers: you have 50 milliseconds to make a good first impression! Behav. Inf. Technol. 25(2), 115–126 (2006)
10. Tractinsky, N., Cokhavi, A., Kirschenbaum, M., Sharfi, T.: Evaluating the consistency of immediate aesthetic perceptions of web pages. Int. J. Hum.-Comput. Stud. 64, 1071–1083 (2006)
11. Tuch, A.N., Presslaber, E., Stoecklin, M., Opwis, K., Bargas-Avila, J.: The Role of visual complexity and prototypicality regarding first impression of web sites: working towards understanding aesthetic judgments. Int. J. Hum. Comput. Stud. 70(11), 794–811 (2012)
12. Mori, G., Paternó, F., Furci, F.: Design criteria for web applications adapted to emotions. In: Casteleyn, S., Rossi, G., Winckler, M. (eds.) ICWE 2014. LNCS, vol. 8541, pp. 400–409. Springer, Heidelberg (2014)
13. Ekman, P., Friesen, W.V.: Constants across cultures in the face and emotions. J. Pers. Soc. Psychol. 17(2), 124–129 (1971)
14. Bànziger, T., Tran, V., Scherer, K.R.: The Geneva emotion wheel. J. Soc. Sci. Inf. 44(4), 23–34 (2005)
15. Cowie R., Douglas-Cowie E., Savvidou S, McMahon E.: 'FEELTRACE': an instrument for recording perceived emotion in real time. In: Proceedings of the ISCA workshop on Speech and Emotion pp. 19–24 (2000)

16. Reinecke K., Yeh T., Miratrix L., Mardiko R., Zhao Y., Liu J., Gajos K. Z.: Predicting users' first impressions of web site aesthetics with a quantification of perceived visual complexity and colorfulness. In: Proceedings of the CHI 2013, pp. 2049–2058 (2013)
17. Cyr, D., Head, M., Larios, H.: Colour appeal in website design within and across cultures: a multi-method evaluation. Int. J. Hum.-Comput. Stud. **68**(1–2), 1–21 (2010)
18. Bonnardel, N., Piolat, A., Le Bigot, L.: The impact of colour on website appeal and users' cognitive processes. Disp. J. **32**(2), 69–80 (2011)
19. Ou, L.C., Luo, M.R., Woodcock, A., Wright, A.: A study of colour emotion and colour preference. Part I: colour emotions for single colours. Color Res. Appl. **29**(3), 232–240 (2004)

Emotion Detection in Non-native English Speakers' Text-Only Messages by Native and Non-native Speakers

Ari Hautasaari$^{(\boxtimes)}$ and Naomi Yamashita

NTT Communication Science Laboratories, Kyoto, Japan
ari.hautasaari@lab.ntt.co.jp, naomiy@acm.org

Abstract. When people from different language backgrounds communicate, they need to adopt a common shared language, such as English, to set up the conversation. In conversations conducted over text-only computer-mediated communication (CMC) mediums, mutual exchange of socio-emotional information is limited to the use of words, symbols and emoticons. Previous research suggests that when message receivers share the same native language with the authors, they are more accurate at detecting the emotional valence of messages based on these cues compared to non-native speaking receivers. But is this still true when the messages are written by non-native speakers? Moreover, what message properties influence the accuracy of emotional valence detection? In this paper, we report on an experiment where native English speakers and Japanese non-native English speakers rate the emotional valence of text-only messages written by Japanese non-native English speaking authors. We analyze how three message properties, grammatical correctness, fluency of language and use of symbols and emoticons, influence emotional valence detection for native and non-native speakers. Based on our results, we propose theoretical and practical implications for supporting multilingual socio-emotional communication in text-only CMC.

Keywords: Computer-mediated communication · Text-only message · Non-native speaker · Emotion detection

1 Introduction

In face-to-face meetings, or during conversations on the phone, people are in general able to judge their conversational partners' emotional states based only on their facial expressions or the tone of their voice [1, 2]. However, geographical distribution, social dynamics and diverse language backgrounds of interlocutors often lead them to rely on text-only computer-mediated communication (CMC) mediums, such as email or instant messaging, to set up the conversation [3–6]. These lean communication mediums lack the vocal and non-verbal cues available in richer mediums, such as video conferencing [7], making it more difficult for message receivers to determine the author's emotional states and tone [8–11].

Exchange of socio-emotional information in current text-only CMC mediums is limited to the use of words, symbols and emoticons as emotional cues [8, 11], which

© IFIP International Federation for Information Processing 2015
J. Abascal et al. (Eds.): INTERACT 2015, Part I, LNCS 9296, pp. 183–200, 2015.
DOI: 10.1007/978-3-319-22701-6_13

inhibits the mutual exchange of emotional and interpersonal information between interlocutors [12]. Moreover, text-only CMC is often characterized as fragmented, agrammatical and incoherent [13], which may further impede detection of emotional information in the messages. In an effort to overcome these challenges and accurately convey their intended emotional tone, message authors often employ symbols and emoticons as emotional cues to enhance the verbal emotional content [14–16]. However, misunderstandings regarding the emotional tone of a message can sometimes occur even between conversational partners who share the same native language [17]. This problem is more salient when the message receivers are non-native speakers of the author's native language [18]. That is, non-native speaking receivers are less accurate than native speaking receivers at detecting the emotional valence of native speaking authors' messages. But, is this still true when the message author is a non-native speaker?

One pivotal aspect in multilingual communication over text-only CMC mediums is that non-native authors are generally less competent than native authors in using their second language. They rarely reach a native-level of grammatical correctness or the fluency of language when authoring messages [19]. They also often lack in experience using their non-native language outside a classroom [20, 21], which may in turn limit their competence in using symbols and emoticons to enhance the verbal content of their second language messages [22, 23]. Yet, previous research offers little indication how these limitations affect the exchange of socio-emotional information between non-native authors, and native and non-native receivers in text-only CMC.

In this paper, we will firstly explore how different message properties may affect socio-emotional communication in text-only CMC between native and non-native speakers. We focus on grammatical correctness, fluency of language, and the use of symbols and emoticons in relation to the verbal content of text-only messages authored by non-native speakers of English. Secondly, we aim to answer whether non-native speakers are still less accurate than native English speakers at detecting the emotional valence of messages when they share similar first and second language background with the authors. Answering these questions provides both theoretical and practical implications for supporting multilingual socio-emotional communication over text-only CMC mediums.

2 Related Work

2.1 Emotion Detection in Text-Only CMC

According to Social Presence theory, problems in detecting emotions in text-only CMC stem from the lack of non-verbal and vocal cues, which are available in richer mediums such as in video conferencing [7, 9]. Lack of these cues inhibits the mutual exchange of socio-emotional and interpersonal information between conversational partners [9]. However, according to Social Information Processing theory, emotional information is still available in text-only CMC environments, but it takes longer for interlocutors to detect this information [10].

The Social Information Processing view of emotion detection has been largely supported by recent literature on human-computer interaction and interpersonal communication in text-only CMC. Previous research suggests that interlocutors are able to distinguish between message author's positive and negative emotions in a text chat based only on the limited emotional cues [8, 14]. The emotional information for detecting some complex emotions, such as joy and anger, is also available in longer texts, such as online blogs [17, 24].

Exchange of emotional information in text-only CMC is in general limited to the use of words, symbols and emoticons used as emotional cues [14–16]. Besides explicit statements referring to the author's emotional state, such as "I am happy", the verbal and structural characteristics of a message may give receivers clues about the author's intended emotional tone. For example, authors expressing negative emotions use fewer words, more affective words and words conveying negative feelings and negations [8, 14]. Higher level of socio-emotional transmissions is also associated with conversational partners' tendency to use more emoticons and symbolic marks in their messages [25]. Emoticons indicate pauses in the emotional expression, such as laughter, that would occur in spoken dialogue in richer mediums or face-to-face settings [26]. Including emoticons in text-only messages strengthens the intensity of the verbal message, especially when the message is intended to carry a negative emotional tone [16, 27].

However, previous works focus largely on emotion and emotional valence detection based on the available cues by interlocutors who share the same native language, usually English. Indeed, misunderstandings about the emotional tone of text-only messages occur even between conversational partners who share the same native language [17, 25]. Yet, multinational organizations and intercultural working groups deal with communication problems caused by language diversity on a daily basis (e.g., [28]). In these multilingual environments, misunderstandings between native and non-native speaking conversational participants regarding the emotional tone of text-only messages, such as in email exchange, may be more salient.

2.2 Exchange of Socio-emotional Information Between Native and Non-native Speakers

To date, scarce research has focused on multilingual socio-emotional communication, particularly in text-only CMC, where conversational partners from different language backgrounds have to adopt a common shared language to set up a conversation, usually English. In these communicative situations, message receivers who do not share the same native language with the message author may experience much greater difficulties in detecting the author's intended emotional tone. Besides empirical and anecdotal evidence suggesting that non-native English speakers have only limited exposure to their second language outside a classroom [20, 21], communicative norms and display rules may be very different for native and non-native speakers [29, 30]. Absence of shared norms and display rules regarding emotional expression may cause receivers to misperceive the author's emotional tone in text-only CMC [31].

Besides different norms and rules regarding emotional expression, native and non-native speakers may experience the emotionality of words and phrases differently. In general, people experience the greatest emotional weight of emotionally arousing phrases in their native language [32]. Further, the social context of second language acquisition may mediate the emotionality of a language, where emotionality decreases the later the language is acquired [33, 34]. More detailed inquiries on the perceptions that interlocutors have regarding emotion and emotion-laden words in their native and non-native languages were reported by Russell [35], Romney et al. [36] and Moore et al. [37]. While they argued for the support of a shared model of semantic structure of emotion terms, they also highlighted discrepancies in how native and non-native speakers perceive the same emotion words in their shared language. In addition to emotion words and phrases, conversational participants make use of symbols and emoticons as emotional cues in text-only CMC [14–16]. However, previous research has found discrepancies in how interlocutors from different language and cultural backgrounds perceive these emotional cues [38]. Further, the adoption rate of different types of emoticons can vary greatly between languages and language groups, such as between Asia and North America [22, 23, 38], and non-native speakers may not be familiar with the emoticons commonly used in the shared language adopted with a native speaking conversational partner [23]. Altogether, these previous studies suggest that non-native conversational participants perceive the emotional nuances in words, symbols and emoticons differently from native speakers in text-only CMC, which may inhibit the mutual exchange of socio-emotional information.

Results reported in Hautasaari et al. [18] corroborate the findings in previous literature. Their results suggested that while non-native speakers are as accurate as native speakers at detecting the relevant emotional cues in messages written by native speaking authors, they are unable to reach similar accuracy when detecting the intended emotional valence of a message based on these cues. However, previous research gives little indication on whether this holds true when the message authors share similar first and second language background with the non-native speaking receivers. These discrepancies between native and non-native speaking conversational partners may, firstly, affect how accurately emotional valence is detected by receivers, and secondly, influence what emotional cues native and non-native authors choose to adopt to convey their emotional tone. Moreover, previous research has not addressed how different message properties, such as grammatical correctness of messages, affect the accuracy of emotional valence detection in text-only CMC between native and non-native speakers.

2.3 Grammatical Correctness and Fluency of Language in Text-Only CMC

In the previous section, we discussed how native and non-native speakers differ in their perception on the emotional nuances carried in words [32, 35–37], symbols and emoticons [22, 33, 38]. However, text-only CMC is also characterized as fragmented, agrammatical and often incoherent due to limitations imposed by the available mediums [13], which may inhibit the mutual exchange of socio-emotional information between interlocutors. This may be particularly problematic in text-only conversations between native and non-native speakers.

While previous research suggests that non-native English speakers consider achieving grammatical correctness in vocal and text-only CMC conversations a high priority [39, 40], non-native speakers rarely reach a native-level of grammatical correctness or fluency of language when authoring messages [19]. Further, even if native and near-native (i.e., non-native speakers with very high language proficiency) speakers of a language appear equivalent in terms of language proficiency, they can still have markedly divergent perceptions on grammatical aspects of their shared language [41]. Non-native speakers may also end up with very different set of grammatical rules than native speakers, partly due to the second language education system [42].

Besides grammatical correctness, text-only messages are characterized by the fluency of language. Fluency refers to the clarity, consistency and naturalness of utterances or messages in relation to meaning and context. For non-native speakers', fluency in their second language generally increases as they progress as second language learners, and if they are able to use the non-native language in communicative contexts [43]. However, non-native speakers often lack this experience [20, 21], which may also further limit their competence in using symbols and emoticons to enhance the verbal content of their messages in text-only CMC [22, 23].

But, how do these properties of text-only messages influence the exchange of socio-emotional information between native and non-native conversational participants? That is, is emotional information more readily available in grammatically correct messages? How does the fluency of language used (i.e., the choice of words to express emotional tone) influence the detection of this information? Furthermore, how does the use of symbols and emoticons to enhance the verbal emotional content affect the transfer of emotional information? And lastly, considering the effects of these properties, how accurately native and non-native speaking receivers are able to detect the emotional valence of non-native speaking authors' text-only messages?

3   Current Study

In the current study, we explore how grammatical correctness, fluency of language, and use of symbols and emoticons affect emotional valence detection in text-only CMC between native and Japanese non-native speakers of English. Secondly, we compare native and non-native speakers' accuracy of detecting the emotional valence of non-native English speaking authors' messages. As a dataset for the analysis, we extracted 99 English public Facebook status updates from Japanese non-native English speakers. We use quantitative and qualitative data analysis to examine the following research questions.

3.1   Research Questions

Grammatical correctness of text-only messages may improve the comprehensibility of the verbal content. However, previous works imply that native and non-native speakers may possess different sets of grammatical rules for their shared language [41]. Furthermore, message authors who are non-native speakers rarely reach a level of grammatical correctness comparable to native speaking authors [19]. But, previous works have yet to answer how grammatical correctness of messages influences the exchange of socio-emotional information between non-native authors, and native and non-native receivers. Thus, we ask the following research question:

RQ1: Does the increase in grammatical correctness of non-native speakers' text-only messages increase the accuracy of emotional valence detection for native and non-native receivers?

Fluency refers to the clarity, consistency and naturalness of language used in a message. As non-native speakers advance as second language learners they are in general more fluent at expressing themselves [43]. Further, non-native speakers report being most fluent in their second language in text-only CMC mediums [6]. But, how does the fluency of language affect the exchange of socio-emotional information between non-native authors, and native and non-native receivers? We ask the following research question:

RQ2: Does the increase in fluency of language in non-native speakers' text-only messages increase the accuracy of emotional valence detection for native and non-native receivers?

Symbols and emoticons enhance the emotionality of the verbal content of a message [16, 27]. However, depending on their first language background, non-native speaking conversational participants may have different perceptions on the emotional nuances carried in these cues [22, 23, 38], and they may lack the experience in using them in text-only CMC [20–23]. How appropriately the symbols and emoticons are linked to the verbal socio-emotional information may affect emotional valence detection accuracy for native and non-native receivers [18]. Thus, we ask the following research question:

RQ3: How does the appropriateness of symbols and emoticons used to enhance the verbal content non-native speakers' text-only messages affect the accuracy of emotional valence detection for native and non-native receivers?

Native English speakers are able to detect the emotional valence of text-only messages written by other native English speakers more accurately than non-native speakers [18]. However, non-native receivers who share the same first and second language background with non-native authors may be more familiar with the emotional cues used by the authors [22, 23, 32, 35–38], and the norms and display rules to express emotions in their shared non-native language [29, 30]. Thus, we ask the following research question:

RQ4: Are non-native speakers more or less accurate than native speakers at detecting the emotional valence in text-only messages written by non-native authors with similar first and second language background?

4   Method

4.1   Overview

To answer our research questions, we tested whether language background (native vs. non-native), and level (low vs. medium vs. high) of grammatical correctness, fluency of language, and appropriateness of symbols and emoticons in relation to verbal content of a message influenced participants' emotional valence detection in messages authored by Japanese non-native English speakers. In this experiment, native and Japanese non-native English speaking participants rated the emotional valence in a set of text-only messages (public Facebook status updates) written by Japanese non-native English speakers. Each message in the dataset was categorized for the level of grammatical correctness, fluency of language, and appropriateness of symbols and emoticons by native English speaking annotators.

4.2   Authors

The non-native message authors (N = 5) were all Japanese native speakers and spoke English as a non-native language. Their average TOEIC[1] score (M = 888.75, SD = 107.81) and self-evaluated English language proficiency (M = 4.80, SD = 1.10: 1 = not fluent at all, 7 = very fluent) indicated that they speak English as a second language, but not fluently. Two of the non-native authors had resided in an English-speaking country, but lived in Japan at the time of the study. The rest of the authors had resided outside Japan for at least a year, where they primarily communicate in English. All authors had posted at least 20 public Facebook status updates in English.

The authors were contacted via email including an explanation of the study and a request to participate as message contributors. They were then asked to rate the emotional valence of their own English language messages on a 7-point Likert scale (1 = very negative, 4 = neutral, 7 = very positive). By doing this, we got a gold standard (i.e., author rating) for comparing the accuracy of emotional valence detection between native and non-native speaking participants.

4.3   Dataset

We extracted 99 messages (per author: M = 19.8, SD = 2.17) from Facebook with each author's consent, which formed the initial message pool for our experiment materials. All messages were public status updates written by Japanese non-native English-speaking authors. None of the messages included any other additional content besides English text (e.g., photos, hyperlinks). We fully anonymized all messages by excluding any names and affiliations.

Message Categorization. We hired three native English speakers to categorize the initial message pool for analysis. The three annotators were presented with the set of messages (N = 99) from Japanese non-native English speaking authors in a randomized order. The annotators were then asked to read and rate each message on three 7-point scales (1 – Not accurate/fluent/appropriate at all, 7 – Very accurate/fluent/appropriate):

---

[1] Test of English for International Communication.

Grammatical Correctness (Accuracy): How correct the grammar and vocabulary in the message is?

Fluency of Language (Fluency): How clear, concise and natural the language used in the message is?

Appropriateness of Symbols and Emoticons: How appropriately symbols (e.g., exclamation marks) and emoticons are used in the message in relation to the verbal content?

We averaged the ratings from the three annotators to categorize each message on these three scales. We then divided the messages to ordinal categories (low vs. medium vs. high) based on the average rating scores for grammatical correctness, fluency of language, and appropriateness of symbols and emoticons used in the message, and randomized the order to form the final dataset presented to the participants.

4.4 Participants

We hired 20 native English speakers and 20 non-native English speakers for this study. All native speaking participants had received their primary education (from the age of 6 to 18, elementary school to high school) in English speaking countries, and reported English as their only native language. All native speakers had lived in Japan for over two years at the time of the study (M = 9.98, SD = 6.65).

The non-native speaking participants in this study were all Japanese native speakers. They all had spent less than two years in English speaking countries. We required a minimum score of 750 in the TOEIC[1] English proficiency test for all non-native participants (M = 854.75, SD = 66.69). Their TOEIC[1] score and self-evaluated English language proficiency (M = 3.92, SD = 1.07; 1 = not fluent at all, 7 = very fluent) indicated that they speak English as their second language at similar level of fluency as the non-native English speaking message authors.

4.5 Procedures

We presented the native and non-native speaking participants a set of text-only messages on a laptop computer, and asked them to read and rate the emotional valence of each message on a 7-point Likert scale (1 = very negative, 4 = neutral, 7 = very positive). The participants were not informed of the authors' language background. Depending on the participant's speed, the experiment took 2–2.5 h including 15 min reserved for instructions for both native and non-native speaking participants. The task instructions for non-native speaking participants were given in Japanese. In order to reduce fatigue during the experiment, each participant was asked to take a 10–15 min break once they had rated half of the messages.

4.6 Measures

Participants' emotional valence detection in the message: native and non-native speaking participants rated their evaluation of the emotional valence of each message on a 7-point Likert scale (1 = very negative, 4 = neutral, 7 = very positive). The rating score reflects the participants' emotional valence detection in the message. The inter-rater reliability was lower among native (Krippendorff's α = .58) than non-native speakers (Krippendorff's α = .66), which indicated that native speakers had a more diverse perception than non-native speakers regarding the emotional valence in the non-native authors' messages.

5   Results

In the next sections, we explore how increase in grammatical correctness, fluency of language, and appropriateness of symbols and emoticons in relation to verbal content correspond to emotional valence detection accuracy for native and non-native speakers. We calculated the participants' emotional valence detection accuracy as a correlation (Spearman's correlation coefficient) with author ratings. We then compared the average correlations of native and non-native speakers.

5.1   Grammatical Correctness of Non-native Speaking Authors' Messages

To answer our *RQ1*, we conducted a 3 (grammatical correctness: low vs. medium vs. high) × (language background: native vs. non-native) mixed ANOVA analysis on native and non-native speakers emotional valence detection accuracy in non-native speaking authors' messages (Fig. 1). The average grammatical correctness was 4.06 (SD = 0.87) on a 7-point scale (1 – Not accurate (grammatically correct) at all, 7 – Very accurate (grammatically correct)).

There was a significant main effect of grammatical correctness on emotional valence detection accuracy ($F[2, 37] = 44..22$, $p < .001$), but no significant main effect for language background ($F[1, 38] = 0.01$, $p = n.s.$). The interaction effect between grammatical correctness and language background was also not significant ($F[2, 37] = 0.68$, $p = n.s.$). Bonferroni corrected post hoc tests showed that emotional valence

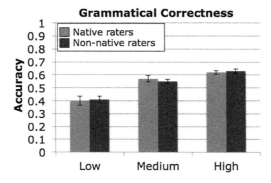

Fig. 1. Accuracy of emotional valence detection for native and non-native speakers in three levels of grammatical correctness of non-native authors' messages (N = 99). Error bars represent standard error of the mean.

detection accuracy differed significantly between all three levels of grammatical correctness (p < .016). These indicated that increase in grammatical correctness in non-native speaking authors' messages corresponded to increase in emotional valence detection accuracy for both native and non-native speaking raters (*RQ1*).

5.2   Fluency of Language in Non-native Speaking Authors' Messages

To answer our *RQ2*, we conducted a 3 (fluency: low vs. medium vs. high) × (language background: native vs. non-native) mixed ANOVA analysis on native and non-native speakers emotional valence detection accuracy in non-native speaking authors' messages (Fig. 2). The average fluency was 4.49 (SD = 0.68) on a 7-point scale (1 – Not fluent at all, 7 – Very fluent).

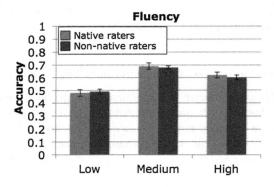

Fig. 2. Accuracy of emotional valence detection for native and non-native speakers in three levels of fluency in non-native authors' messages (N = 99). Error bars represent standard error of the mean.

There was a significant main effect of fluency on the emotional valence detection accuracy (F[2, 37] = 58.75, p < .001), but no significant main effect for language background (F[1, 38] = 0.27, p = *n.s.*). The interaction effect between fluency and language background was also not significant (F[2, 37] = 0.16, p = *n.s.*). Bonferroni corrected post hoc tests showed that emotional valence detection accuracy differed between all three levels of language fluency (p < .016), but decreased between medium-high levels. These indicated that increase in language fluency in non-native authors' messages did not correspond to increase in emotional valence detection accuracy for native or non-native speaking raters (*RQ2*).

5.3   Appropriateness of Symbols and Emoticons in Non-native Speaking Authors' Messages

To answer our *RQ3*, we conducted a 3 (appropriateness of symbols and emoticons: low vs. medium vs. high) × (language background: native vs. non-native) mixed ANOVA analysis on native and non-native speakers emotional valence detection accuracy in non-native speaking authors' messages (Fig. 3). The average appropriateness of symbols and emoticons was 4.61 (SD = 0.70) on a 7-point scale (1 – Not appropriate at all, 7 – Very appropriate).

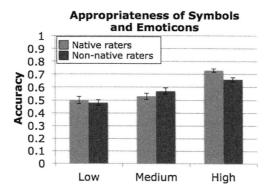

Fig. 3. Accuracy of emotional valence detection for native and non-native speakers in three levels of appropriateness of symbols and emoticons in non-native authors' messages (N = 99). Error bars represent standard error of the mean.

There was a significant main effect of appropriateness of symbols and emoticons on the emotional valence detection accuracy (F[2, 37] = 58.75, p < .001), but no significant main effect for language background (F[1, 38] = 0.91, p = *n.s.*). However, the interaction effect between appropriateness of symbols and emoticons and language background was significant (F[2, 37] = 3.49, p < .05). Bonferroni corrected post hoc tests showed that emotional valence detection accuracy differed between all three levels of appropriateness of symbols and emoticons (p < .016). Furthermore, planned pairwise comparisons showed that while native and non-native speakers' emotional valence detection accuracy did not differ significantly at low (F[1, 38] = 0.39, p = *n.s.*) and medium (F[1, 38] = 1.18, p = *n.s.*) levels of appropriateness of symbols and emoticons, native speakers (M = 0.73, SD = 0.06) were significantly more accurate than non-native speakers (M = 0.66, SD = 0.07) at high level of appropriateness (F[1, 38] = 10.70, p < .01).

These indicated that increase in appropriateness of symbols and emoticons used in relation to the verbal content in non-native authors' messages corresponded to the increase in emotional valence detection accuracy for both native and non-native speaking raters. However, native speakers' accuracy surpassed that of non-native speakers when the appropriateness of symbols and emoticons increased (*RQ3*). These results also answered our *RQ4*. There was no significant difference between native and non-native speakers in their emotional valence detection accuracy in non-native authors' messages.

6 Discussion

The goal of this study was to increase our understanding on the factors that influence the success of socio-emotional communication between native and non-native speakers in text-only CMC, such as via email or instant messaging. Taken together, our results demonstrate how grammatical correctness, fluency of language, and appropriateness of symbols and emoticons in relation to verbal emotional content affect emotional valence detection accuracy in non-native English speaking authors' messages.

Grammatical correctness of messages in text-only CMC, such as in the context of our dataset, is generally low [13]. While non-native authors tend to strive for writing grammatically correct messages [39], they rarely reach the level of native speaking authors [19]. Our results suggest that lower grammatical correctness in non-native authors' messages may have detrimental effects on the exchange of socio-emotional information between the author and receivers, regardless whether a receiver is a native or non-native speaker of the shared language (Example 1). That is, both native and non-native speakers were less accurate at detecting the emotional valence of non-native authors' messages as the grammatical correctness deteriorated (Fig. 1).

Example 1. Non-native author's message with low level of grammatical correctness.

Non-native author's message	Evaluation of the emotional valence
Even after i speak perfect japanese i was mistaken as a foreigner lololol wtf going on?? Lol at tea place :)	Author: Positive
	Native raters: Neutral
	Non-native raters: Neutral

The second message property we examined was the fluency of language used in the text-only messages, which refers to the clarity, consistency and naturalness of the language. While the fluency of language in non-native authors' messages is often lower than that of native authors [19], our results implied that increase in the level of fluency does not correspond to higher accuracy of emotional valence detection (Fig. 2). One possible explanation for this is that messages with higher fluency of language may lack some syntactic or orthographic emotional cues, such as abbreviations and use of capital letters as emphasis, which could carry information about the emotional tone (Example 2). However, fluency in second language generally increases as the non-native speakers become more experienced in communicating with it [43], but our results do not address how their messages might change over time. This question should be answered in future work.

Example 2. Non-native author's message with low level of fluency.

Non-native author's message	Evaluation of the emotional valence
BUUUUUUUSSSSSSSSSSYYYYYYYYYY but fiiiiiiiinally weeeeeekend!!!	Author: Positive
	Native raters: Positive
	Non-native raters: Positive

Our third message property of interest considered how appropriately symbols and emoticons are used in relation to the verbal content of the message. Our findings indicated that increase in the appropriateness of symbols and emoticons corresponded to increase in emotional valence detection accuracy for both native and non-native speakers. For one, appropriate use refers to enhancing text-only messages with emoticons in the same valence as the verbal emotional content of the message (Example 3).

Example 3. Non-native author's message with high appropriateness of symbols and emoticons.

Non-native author's message	Evaluation of the emotional valence
WHAT! "Your timeline foes live on April 28"? No,no,I'd rather use the current/previous version of Facebook!! I feel like I'm forced to use it. :(	Author: Slightly Negative
	Native raters: Negative
	Non-native raters: Slightly Negative

Furthermore, employing the use of emoticons in the same valence as the verbal emotional content in the message may increase receivers' emotional valence detection accuracy even in lower levels of grammatical correctness (Example 4).

Example 4. Non-native author's message with high appropriateness of symbols and emoticons and medium level of grammatical correctness.

Non-native author's message	Evaluation of the emotional valence
I never say it doesn't suit me, I make it suitable for me :)) That's my spirit :P	Author: Very Positive
	Native raters: Positive
	Non-native raters: Positive

However, inappropriate use of symbols and emoticons in a message can make it increasingly difficult for receivers to detect the emotional valence, particularly in messages with low grammatical correctness (Example 5). That is, if the valence of the emoticons used as emotional cues does not appropriately reflect the verbal emotional content.

Example 5. Non-native author's message with low appropriateness of symbols and emoticons and low grammatical correctness.

Non-native author's message	Evaluation of the emotional valence
Insects r coming after me. Animals and kids r staring at me and i play with them :)) And weirdos r … Well above all i have been horrified by harmful insects which r coming after me and also mosquitos lol any solution even I was safe but soooo scary to have experience some big bees r back of ur neck inside of ur hair lol Still haven't being bite except for mosquitos type though… Kowaiiii lol	Author: Very Positive
	Native raters: Slightly Negative
	Non-native raters: Slightly Negative

Furthermore, even if text-only messages have high grammatical correctness, omitting emoticons as emotional cues may lead the message receivers to misperceive the non-native author's intended emotional valence (Example 6).

Example 6. Non-native author's message with low appropriateness of symbols and emoticons and high grammatical correctness.

Non-native author's message	Evaluation of the emotional valence
Tomorrow, I will take a flight to Japan. Hot, Hot... melting Tokyo & Kyoto.	Author: Slightly Positive
	Native raters: Slightly Negative
	Non-native raters: Slightly Negative

Our results also revealed that when non-native authors employed symbols and emoticons as emotional cues more appropriately, the native speaking raters surpassed non-native raters in their emotional valence detection accuracy (Fig. 3). One possible explanation for this is that in these messages, the use of Western symbols and emoticons by the Japanese non-native authors was closer to how native English speaking authors would use them as emotional cues. Previous works suggest that non-native receivers may have trouble identifying the connection between the verbal emotional content and symbols and emoticons in native English speaking authors messages [15]. Hence, it is possible that non-native receivers have trouble detecting the emotional information in messages from non-native authors who have more experience communicating in English [20, 21], and are more accustomed to using Western symbols and emoticons [22, 23].

Finally, how does a shared first and second language background affect the exchange of socio-emotional information in text-only CMC? Hautasaari et al. [18] found implications that native English speaking receivers are more accurate than non-native receivers at detecting the emotional valence of text-only messages written by native English speaking authors. Our results suggest that when the non-native receivers share the same first and second language background with the authors, they are as accurate as native receivers at detecting the emotional valence. In part, this discrepancy may be explained by shared understanding on nuances in emotional cues [22, 23, 32, 35–38], and the norms and display rules to express emotions in the authors' and receivers' shared non-native language [29, 30]. However, it is important to note that combined these two results do not answer whether non-native speakers write more emotionally arousing messages, or whether it is in general easier for receivers to detect the socio-emotional information in non-native authors' messages. Answering these questions requires future research.

6.1 Design Implications

A large number of text-only CMC mediums are already fitted with automatic spell checkers, and our results suggest that increase in grammatical correctness of non-native authors' messages increases the accuracy of emotional valence detection. However, there is a need for a balanced approach that would potentially help non-native authors to produce messages with similar levels of grammatically correctness as native authors [19], while not forcing or suggesting them to omit any syntactic or orthographic emotional cues. For example, a system that would detect grammatical errors and inform the non-native authors about the potentially low emotional expressivity of their message might improve the quality of socio-emotional communication with native/non-native receivers in text-only CMC.

In previous work by Hautasaari et al. [18], the authors suggested a system for translating the emotional nuances in symbols and emoticons in native authors' messages for non-native receivers. Our results indicate that the connection between symbols and emoticons to the verbal content of a message is crucial in socio-emotional communication between non-native authors and native/non-native receivers. However, non-native authors may not be familiar with the nuances carried in these emotional cues in their second language [22, 23, 38]. For example, Asian non-native speakers of English may often be unaware of the emotional nuances carried in Western emoticons, and fail to connect them appropriately in relation to the verbal emotional content of their message. A system that would (1) detect the presence/absence of emotion and emotion-laden words in a text-only message, and (2) suggest including/removing symbols and emoticons in the same/opposite valence could help non-native speakers to author more emotionally coherent messages.

6.2 Limitations and Future Directions

Mining a larger set of English messages written by a large number of non-native speakers from different first language backgrounds (e.g., Twitter) could provide a more generalizable sample of non-native speakers' socio-emotional messages. In future studies, we are interested in exploring how our results may apply to various conversational contexts, such as multilingual group communication via email, or when the author and receiver are familiar with each other.

7 Conclusion

We examined how grammatical correctness, fluency of language, and appropriateness of symbols and emoticons influence the exchange of socio-emotional information in text-only CMC between non-native English speaking authors, and native and non-native English speaking receivers. Our results suggested that increase in grammatical correctness of text-only messages corresponds to increase in accuracy of emotional valence detection in the message for both native and non-native receivers. However, increase in fluency of language used in the message did not correspond to increase in the accuracy of emotional valence detection. A likely explanation is that messages with higher fluency lack syntactic or orthographic emotional cues, such as abbreviations and use of capital letters as emphasis. Increase in the appropriateness of how symbols and emoticons are used in relation to the verbal content of a message corresponded to increase in emotional valence detection accuracy. However, the accuracy of native speaking receivers' emotional valence detection surpasses that of non-native receivers as the non-native authors' use of symbols and emoticons as emotional cues borders that of native speaking authors.

Lastly, we found that while non-native English speakers are less accurate at detecting the emotional valence in native authors' messages, they are as accurate as native speakers when message authors are other non-native speakers with similar first and second language background. These findings have implications for our theoretical understanding of socio-emotional communication between native and non-native speakers in text-only CMC, and practical implications for communication tools to support multilingual socio-emotional communication.

Acknowledgements. We would like to extend our gratitude to the message authors who agreed to let us use their public Facebook status updates as part of our dataset. We would also like to thank the anonymous reviewers for their insightful comments and suggestions for improving this paper.

References

1. Buchanan, T.W., Lutz, K., Mirzazade, S., Specht, K., Shah, N.J., Zilles, K., Jäncke, L.: Recognition of emotional prosody and verbal components of spoken language: an fMRI study. Cogn. Brain. Res. **9**(3), 227–238 (2000)
2. Ekman, P.: Emotion in the Human Face, 2nd edn. Cambridge University Press, New York (1982)
3. Harzing, A.-W., Köster, K., Magner, U.: Babel in business: the language barrier and its solutions in the HQ-subsidiary relationship. J. World Bus. **46**(3), 279–287 (2011)
4. Mok, D., Carrasco, J.A., Wellman, B.: Does distance still matter in the age of the internet? Urban Stud. **46**(13), 2747–2783 (2009)
5. Olson, G.M., Olson, J.S.: Distance matters. Hum. Comput. Interact. **15**(2), 139–178 (2000)
6. Setlock, L.D., Fussell, S.R.: What's it worth to you? the costs and affordances of CMC tools to Asian and American users. In: Proceedings of 2010 ACM Conference on Computer Supported Cooperative Work, pp. 341–349. ACM (2010)
7. Dennis, A.R., Kinney, S.T.: Testing media richness theory in the new media: the effects of cues, feedback, and task equivocality. Inf. Syst. Res. **9**(3), 256–274 (1998)
8. Hancock, J.T., Gee, K., Ciaccio, K., Lin, J.M-H.: I'm sad you're sad: emotional contagion in CMC. In: Proceedings of the 2008 ACM Conference on Computer Supported Cooperative Work, pp. 295–298. ACM, New York (2008)
9. Short, J., Williams, E., Christie, B.: The Social Psychology of Telecommunications. Wiley, New York (1976)
10. Walther, J.B.: Interpersonal effects in computer-mediated interaction: a relational perspective. Commun. Res. **19**, 52–90 (1992)
11. Walther, J.B., Loh, T., Granka, L.: Let me count the ways: the interchange of verbal and nonverbal cues in computer-mediated and face-to-face affinity. J. Lang. Soc. Psychol. **24**(1), 36–65 (2005)
12. Murphy, K.L., Collins, M.P.: Development of communication conventions in instructional electronic chats. J. Distance Educ. **12**(1–2), 177–200 (1997)

13. Herring, S.: Interactional coherence in CMC. J. Comput. Mediated Commun. **4**(4) (1999)
14. Hancock, J.T., Landrigan, C., Silver, C.: Expressing emotion in text-only communication. In: Proceedings of 2007 ACM Conference on Human Factors in Computing Systems, pp. 929–923. ACM (2007)
15. Aman, S., Szpakowicz, S.: Identifying expressions of emotion in text. In: Matoušek, V., Mautner, P. (eds.) TSD 2007. LNCS (LNAI), vol. 4629, pp. 196–205. Springer, Heidelberg (2007)
16. Walther, J.B., D'Addario, K.P.: The impacts of emoticons on message interpretation in computer-mediated communication. Soc. Sci. Comput. Rev. **19**, 324–347 (2001)
17. Gill, A.J., Gergle, D., French, R.M., Oberlander, J.: Emotion rating from short blog texts. In: Proceedings of 2008 ACM Conference on Human Factors in Computing Systems, pp. 1121–1124. ACM (2008)
18. Hautasaari, A., Yamashita, N., Gao, G.: "Maybe it was a joke": emotion detection in text-only communication by non-native english speakers. In: Proceedings of 2014 ACM Conference on Human Factors in Computing Systems, pp. 3715–3724. ACM (2014)
19. Medgyes, P.: Native or non-native: who's worth more? ELT J. **46**(4), 340–349 (1992)
20. Benson, M.J.: Attitudes and motivation towards english: a survey of Japanese freshmen. RELC J. **22**(1), 34–48 (1991)
21. Hyland, F.: Learning autonomously: contextualising out-of-class english language learning. Lang. Awareness **13**(3), 180–202 (2004)
22. Nishimura, Y.: Linguistic innovations and interactional features of casual online communication in Japanese. J. Comput. Mediated Commun. **9**(1) (2006)
23. Park, J., Barash, V., Fink, C., Cha, M.: Emoticon style: interpreting differences in emoticons across cultures. In: Proceedings of the 7th International AAAI Conference on Weblogs and Social Media (ICWSM 2013), pp. 466–475. AAAI Press (2013)
24. Gill, A.J., French, R.M., Gergle, D., Oberlander, J.: The language of emotion in short blog texts. In: Proceedings of 2008 ACM Conference on Computer Supported Cooperative Work, pp. 299–302. ACM (2008)
25. Kato, S., Kato. Y., Akahori, K.: Study on emotional transmissions in communication using a bulletin board system. In: Proceedings of World Conference on E-Learning in Corporate, Government, Healthcare, and Higher Education (ELEARN) 2006, pp. 2576–2584. AACE, Chesapeake (2006)
26. Provine, R.R., Spencer, R.J., Mandell, D.L.: Emotional expression online: emoticons punctuate website text messages. J. Lang. Soc. Psychol. **26**(3), 299–307 (2007)
27. Derks, D., Bos, A.E.R., von Grumbkow, J.: Emoticons and online message interpretation. Soc. Sci. Comput. Rev. **26**(3), 379–388 (2008)
28. Harzing, A.-W., Köster, K., Magner, U.: Babel in business: the language barrier and its solutions in the HQ-subsidiary relationship. J. World Bus. **46**(3), 279–287 (2011)
29. Meierkord, C.: Interpreting successful Lingua franca interaction: an analysis of non-native-/non-native small talk conversations in English. Linguistik Online **5**(1) (2000)
30. Seidlhofer, B.: closing a conceptual gap: the case for a description of English as a Lingua Franca. Int. J. Appl. Linguist. **11**(2), 133–158 (2001)
31. Byron, K.: Carrying too heavy a load? the communication and miscommunication of emotion by email. Acad. Manag. Rev. **33**(2), 309–327 (2008)
32. Dewaele, J.-M.: The emotional weight of I love you in multilinguals' languages. J. Pragmat. **40**(10), 1753–1780 (2008)
33. Harris, C.L., Gleason, J.B., Aycicegi, A.: When is a first language more emotional? psychophysiological evidence from bilingual speakers. In: Pavlenko, A. (ed.) Bilingual Minds: Emotional Experience, Expression, and Representation, pp. 257–283. Multilingual Matters, Clevedon (2006)

34. Schumann, J.: The Neurobiology of Affect in Language. Blackwell, Malden (1997)
35. Russell, J.A.: Pancultural aspects of the human conceptual organization of emotions. J. Pers. Soc. Psychol. **45**(6), 1281–1288 (1983)
36. Romney, A.K., Moore, C.C., Rusch, C.D.: Cultural universals: measuring the semantic structure of emotion terms in English and Japanese. Proc. Natl. Acad. Sci. **94**(10), 5489–5494 (1997)
37. Moore, C.C., Romney, A.K., Hsia, T.-L., Rusch, G.D.: The universality of the semantic structure of emotion terms: methods for the study of inter- and intra-cultural variability. Am. Anthropol. **101**(3), 529–546 (1999)
38. Kayan, S., Fussell, S.R., Setlock, L.D.: Cultural differences in the use of instant messaging in Asia and North America. In: Proceedings of the 2006 ACM Conference on Computer Supported Cooperative Work, pp. 525–528. ACM (2006)
39. Lee, C.K.M.: Text-making practices beyond the classroom context: private instant messaging in Hong Kong. Comput. Compos. **24**, 285–301 (2007)
40. Zakura, N.: Focus on the form versus focus on the message in Lingua Franca conversations. Eesti Rakenduslilingvistika Uhingu Astaraamat **8**, 275–287 (2012)
41. Coppieters, R.: Competence differences between native and near-native speakers. Language **63**(3) (1987)
42. Dabrowska, E.: Different speakers, different grammars individual differences in native language attainment. Linguist. Approach Biling **2**, 219–253 (2012)
43. Housen, A., Kuiken, F.: Complexity, accuracy and fluency in second language acquisition. Appl. Linguist. **30**(4), 461–473 (2009)

Making Decisions About Digital Legacy with Google's Inactive Account Manager

Raquel O. Prates[1,2(✉)], Mary Beth Rosson[2], and Clarisse S. de Souza[3]

[1] Department of Computer Science, Federal University of Minas Gerais,
Belo Horizonte, Brazil
rprates@dcc.ufmg.br
[2] College of Information Science and Technology,
Pennsylvania State University, State College, PA, USA
mrosson@ist.psu.edu
[3] Department of Informatics, Pontifical Catholic University of Rio de Janeiro,
Rio de Janeiro, Brazil
clarisse@inf.puc-rio.br

Abstract. As information systems become more integrated into everyday use, people generate and store significant data through their lifetimes. Only recently have researchers and companies started to pay attention to digital legacy issues. Google has been one of the first companies to support users in planning the future of their digital assets through Google Inactive Account Manager (IAM). In this work, we present a systematic analysis of IAM and discuss how it structures users' digital legacy decision space and deals with challenges regarding future impact of these decisions.

Keywords: Digital legacy · Anticipation · Configuration settings · Future impact

1 Introduction

Digital technologies are embedded in many aspects of people's daily lives, in their work, entertainment and civic behavior. One result is that people generate and store significant data through their lifetimes [9]. Recently designers have begun to consider issues related to digital legacy [6, 7, 9]. These range from supporting the bereaved [8]; allowing users to plan what is to be done with their own digital legacy [5]; how to curate the digital legacy of a loved one [1, 9]; or even allowing users to create messages to be delivered after their death (e.g. DeadSocial - http://www.deadsocial.org).

One way that people can state their wishes regarding their physical legacy is to draw up a will. Similarly, systems are emerging in the virtual world that let users plan for what happens after their death by creating digital materials, messages or instructions to be sent to loved ones. Some systems use the metaphor of a safe where users can store digital copies of documents, online authentication credentials, and a list of beneficiaries who will have access to them in case of their deaths (e.g. SecureSafe - http://www.securesafe.com/en/product-blog/data-inheritance/). However, such provisions are still relatively rare. In April 2013, Google took a step in this direction with Inactive

© IFIP International Federation for Information Processing 2015
J. Abascal et al. (Eds.): INTERACT 2015, Part I, LNCS 9296, pp. 201–209, 2015.
DOI: 10.1007/978-3-319-22701-6_14

Account Manager (IAM), a tool that allows users to specify plans for online data associated with a subset of Google products.[1]

To activate IAM, the user specifies parameters to indicate a set of trusted individuals (or beneficiaries), these people's contact information, and relevant digital assets. This process might seem simple, but beyond the emotional cost of planning for one's own death, users must also anticipate the future system states that are desired and map these to software configurations; this anticipation includes data accesses and interactions that will be enabled or disabled by these states. Prates et al. [10] discuss the challenges of anticipating what interactions may occur over time from configuration decisions. For digital legacy, having a clear understanding of the impact of these decisions is especially relevant, because users will not be there to repair poor decisions.

In this paper, we present a systematic analysis of Google IAM. Our goal is twofold: discuss the digital legacy management interface; and show how to use Configurable Interaction Anticipation Challenges (CIAC) [10] to analyze support for user configuration over time. Google IAM presents only a few legacy configuration decisions at this point, but our analysis helps to articulate the system design space related to digital legacy management, as well as the more general challenge of supporting configuration processes that impact interaction over time.

2 Methodology

We analyzed Google IAM using the Semiotic Inspection Method (SIM) [3]. SIM is a method of Semiotic Engineering, a semiotic theory of HCI that views human-computer interaction as a special case of computer-mediated human communication involving a system's designers and users [2]. Through the interface, designers communicate to users their vision of who the system is intended to serve, what problems it can solve or experiences it can offer, and how users can interact with the system. In the case of collaborative systems, the designers' message includes the roles that members of a group can take, the relationships among roles and members, and the languages and protocols through which users can communicate. Users progressively unfold and grasp the designers' intended message as they interact with the system and with each other through the system, over time.

SIM can be used to evaluate how well a system conveys to users the designers' communicative intent and the system's underlying principles – the system's communicability [3]. SIM inspects communication looking at how the message is constructed, structured, expressed and delivered (the sender's side).

SIM analyzes communicability in five steps.[2] The first three steps deconstruct the designers' interactive message to users into three segmented views of communication; the final two steps reconstruct the designers' message with the result of the segmented analysis. Reconstruction involves contrasting the three views from previous steps, which allows the evaluator to spot possible inconsistency among messages and assess

---

[1] http://googlepublicpolicy.blogspot.com/2013/04/plan-your-digital-afterlife-with.html.

[2] Due to space limitation SIM is not detailed, for a complete description on SIM please see [3].

the designers' decisions about which kinds of signs convey what kinds of messages. In the final step the evaluator integrates all results, assessing the quality of the designers' communication from a message emission perspective.

In our analysis, we focused on how the designers of Google IAM communicate to users about *future impacts* of their digital legacy specifications. To guide the analysis we used CIAC, a set of concerns raised in an earlier conceptual discussion of issues in communicating how configurable interactions might evolve over time, particularly when the configurations include relationships with other users (see Table 1; the challenges are introduced and discussed in [10]).

Table 1. Configurable interaction anticipation challenges

Challenge	Brief description
Anticipation support	Can users anticipate and understand the possible impacts of the decisions being taken now and the potential future interaction scenarios that may result from it?
Representation	Can users represent future possible scenarios? Can they ask what-if questions? Does the representation make use of the system's interface language or propose a different representation?
Cost x benefits	What are the costs and benefits of representing future scenarios? If they cannot be represented, what are the costs and benefits of not being able to do so?
Conflict negotiation and mitigation	If users' decisions are able to impact other users, which conflicts (if any) can they generate? How can users negotiate or mitigate potential conflicts?
Definition of default values	Are there default values suggested regarding users' configuration of future scenarios?

The analysis of Google IAM was performed in March 2015 by an expert in Semiotic Engineering and HCI who has extensive experience in applying SIM. The inspection scenario described a Google user who had just learned about IAM and wanted to explore it to make decisions about her digital legacy assets.

3   Results

We present the results of our analysis in two sub-sections. First we explain the design space defined by IAM (part of the designers' communication message to users). Second we consider how IAM does or does not address the CIAC (Table 1) over time.

3.1   User's Decision Space in Google IAM

The Google IAM does not mention *"death"* or *"legacy"* in its interface or help; it refers to accounts becoming *"inactive"* for *"any reason"* (perhaps because discourse about death is taboo [8]). Nonetheless, in Google's Public Policy Blog, Google's product manager announced the IAM as a means to *"plan you digital afterlife"* (See footnote 1).

Activating the IAM involves four steps: (1) *Alert Me*: users submit contact information so they can be alerted if their account is about to become inactive; (2) *Timeout period*: users decide after what period of time without activity their account should be considered inactive; (3) *Notify contacts or share data*: users nominate people as trusted contacts to be informed and/or have access to (part of) their data once their account becomes inactive; (4) *Optionally delete account*: users decide whether or not their account should be deleted when it becomes inactive.

The *Alert Me* step is mandatory. The user's gmail account is used for this notification. Users must also provide a cell phone number and may add other email accounts. Once the cell phone number is provided, a verification code is sent to the phone and must be typed into the system. *Alert Me* intends to guarantee that an account will not become inactive without its user's knowledge.

In the *Timeout period* step, users may define what amount of time without use is sufficient to deem their account as inactive. Options vary from 3 to 18 months (in intervals of 3 months). In the *Notification* step, users can name trusted contacts. For each one the user must provide an email address and decide if the contact should have access to parts of their data or just be notified. The user must also write a message for each contact; this message will be sent to that person by Google once the account is deemed inactive. If the user decides to give data access to a trusted contact, s/he must choose which applications' data should be available and provide a cell phone number. The user is informed that to protect their data from unauthorized access, each trusted contact will receive a verification code over their phone, and that this will be needed in order to access the data. Finally users may write a message that will be sent automatically to anyone who sends them a message after their account becomes inactive.

Lastly, IAM users must decide whether they wish to have their data deleted (after requested actions have been completed). Once all five configuration steps are complete, the user must explicitly enable IAM (clicking on an *Enable* button). After IAM is enabled users can choose to receive a reminder about it being enabled every 3 months. They may go back at any time and change their settings or disable the IAM.

3.2 Addressing Configurable Interaction Anticipation Challenges

Next we present our analysis of how Google IAM addresses the challenges raised regarding groupware configuration impacts over time.

Anticipation Support. Users name trusted contacts, write a message to be sent to each, and decide which data can be accessed. The information about how the settings will impact future actions is explained to users through text. The IAM help page[3] presents answers to four questions, two of which are meant to help users anticipate the future impact of their decisions, (*What will trusted contacts receive?; What happens when your account gets deleted?*).

---

[3] https://support.google.com/accounts/answer/3036546?hl=en.

Configuration prompts and help pages explain that trusted contacts will only be notified once the account is considered inactive. The help page explains that Google will add text informing the contact that the user had instructed Google to send the message if the account became inactive (this information is not mentioned on the configuration page). If users decide to share data with a contact, then the configuration page informs that Google will add instructions on how to access data to users' message. The help page illustrates what the footer to be added to users' message **might** look like. Using the word "might" is a signal that the footer text may change between the time the user does the configuration and when the message is sent. Although an example is provided, configuration pages do not refer to it or to the help page in which it is available.

Google recognizes that when a trusted contact receives a (future) message on behalf of the user, s/he may have doubts about it – thus the help system includes one page about the IAM that is aimed at Trusted Contacts.[4] This page gives an overall view of the IAM, explains the need for the verification code that will be sent by phone to the trusted contact, and notes situations that might make the data inaccessible even to trusted contacts. Interestingly, the email given as an example does not mention the verification code, nor does it mention the help page that explains its role.

Regarding the effects of choosing to delete their account data, users are informed in the configuration page that their data will only be deleted after their requested actions have been completed. In the help page there is a (very) brief explanation about what it means to have one's data deleted.

Representation. In the configuration page IAM uses the same interface elements used in other Google products (dropdown lists, switch buttons, etc.). Nonetheless, there are new terms specific to IAM such as *"trusted contact"* or *"timeout period"* that are introduced in the configuration interface; for these, IAM offers a contiguous explanation in the interface. The representation of future impacts is accomplished with natural language at the configuration and help pages. In some cases, the information is spread across two pages, and users would need to read both to get a full understanding. Because there are only a few decisions and the explanations are not long, one could argue that reading it would be feasible. However, Google refers to the help page only once in the configuration dialog (within the *Delete account* step). Thus, the user must take initiative to look for relevant information. IAM does not provide users with means to preview (or experiment with) impacts that will result from their configuration, such as the final form of a notification message to be sent to a trusted contact, which will combine a user-generated message with Google's explanations.

Costs x Benefits. Planning the future of one's data once you are no longer able to manage it is the primary benefit from a digital legacy system [5]. With respect to cost, IAM setup is easy, requiring only four sets of decisions. Also, users need not make all decisions at once and can easily return to change their settings. In relation to the configuration, the existing costs are associated to anticipation, since it is only supported through explicative text spread through more than one page. Also, not all possible future scenarios are addressed in the explanation.

---

[4] https://support.google.com/accounts/answer/3036514?hl=en.

One reason an account may become inactive is due to its owner's death, which leads to the consideration of a possible emotional cost [6]. The emotional cost may be experienced particularly in writing messages to loved ones to be delivered after one's death (the message to trusted contacts is not optional). Also, there may be an emotional cost to contacts who receive an unexpected message and gain access to users' digital assets after their deaths (up to 18 months later), or even worse are informed that the user wanted them to have access to their data, but discover they are unable to do so (e.g. the cell phone number registered in the IAM settings is no longer active).

Conflict Negotiation and Mitigation. The access to a deceased person's assets in the physical world can be the source of a number of conflicts. The virtual world per se may solve some of the conflict sources (e.g. each beneficiary may have a copy of the assets, as opposed to dividing it among themselves [9]). The potential conflicts that could arise in the virtual world, are addressed by Google IAM by avoiding them in the users decision space or leaving them outside the scope of the system.

Being named as a beneficiary of another person's digital legacy may create discomfort if the person does not wish to be responsible for the curation of this legacy [1]. In IAM a nomination does not generate conflict within the system, because trusted contacts are not informed through the system at the time of their nomination, nor are they presented with the opportunity to decline it. Once the trusted contact is informed of the user's wishes, the user (probably) is no longer available for negotiation.

In IAM, users can only decide to *grant access* to their digital assets, which means that Google will allow the contact to download a copy of the data. Trusted contacts are not faced with decisions on what to do with the data (at least not within Google). Moreover, they are not informed if there are any other trusted contacts and who they are. If any conflicts take place regarding how trusted contacts choose to use the users' data, it takes place outside the system, and Google bears no responsibility over it.

The only potential conflict that may take place is between the trusted contact and Google. For example, a trusted contact might receive the message that grants him/her access to a user's data, but not have access any longer to the cell number registered in IAM; this would prevent access to the data. In this case, Google's position is supported by IAM rules which inform users of the need of a valid cell number for trusted contacts and how it will be used.

Definition of Default Values. IAM is associated with a person's Google account. To activate IAM, users must adjust their account settings (it is off by default). Of the four decisions available to users in IAM, only two have default values – *Timeout period* (default: 3 months) and *Delete account* (default: No). In the *Alert Me* step the user's gmail is used as the primary email for notification (it cannot be removed). All the other fields within IAM settings have to be provided by the user.

4   Google IAM's Communicability

Although Google IAM does not directly refer to death, we can see the IAM as a metaphor to drawing up a will; Google plays the role of a lawyer who executes the user's wishes according to the "law" (Google's terms and conditions, IAM rules).

IAM allows users to configure actions to be taken in a future time, when they likely will not be available to take actions regarding their data. The CIAC analysis of IAM indicates that Google supports users' anticipation of impacts their decisions will have in future scenarios by describing them in natural language. Even though the design space presented to users is small in IAM, some aspects about these future scenarios are not explained to users and are not easily explored. For instance, it is not clear why there is a time limit for trusted contacts to download the data even when users have chosen not to delete it. Also, during the configuration process there is no representation of all trusted contacts named thus far along with kinds of access that have been specified, or even whether Google knows about data that has not yet been addressed. Although users can gather this information from the interface, it might be costly (checking as many as 10 contacts and verifying who has access to as many as 10 classes of data). Also, users might have questions about future scenarios, such as *What is the data that would be available regarding a specific product? In which format would it be available? Which tools should contacts use to access the information?*

Previous literature has shown that allowing users to visualize the future states resulting from their decisions and exploring them (e.g., in a simulated environment) would improve their understanding of the decisions [10]. Building such supports would increase the cost of providing users with services like IAM. Nonetheless, if the design space for user decisions increase (for instance, allowing trusted contacts to make decisions in the user's name, or defining access to data not by the product it is associated to, but rather by use of finer criteria, such as the tags used to organize it) these tools may not only be desirable, but necessary for decision-making.

Dealing with digital legacy may involve deep emotions for all involved – users who must think about their own deaths and wishes, the bereaved who later receive instructions written by someone they cared about. IAM minimizes dealing with any emotional aspects by omitting references to death, framing it in a broader context. Even simple strategies such as allowing users to preview a message to a trusted contact could help them to gain a better idea of how to frame the request.

IAM avoids most foreseeable potential conflicts that may emerge in digital legacy; currently the decisions about data are based on the user's settings, Google's terms and conditions of use, and IAM rules. However the CIAC identified a potential conflict occurring when a trusted contact is asked to curate a digital asset but no longer has access to the data as intended (e.g., a new phone number). The decision to add a security layer for authorizing data access could have an undesirable effect, wherein the users' digital legacy cannot reach intended beneficiaries. One way to mitigate this would be to allow users to associate a "default" cell phone number to trusted contacts who have Google accounts, thus relying on the trusted others to maintain their own account information. Considering that active users probably maintain that information updated (since it might be needed to regain access to their account in some situations) it would probably decrease the chance of the information becoming outdated. The same strategy could be used in the *Alert Me* step regarding the user's own cell phone.

Finally, legal aspects regarding digital legacy are an open issue under discussion in many countries [4]. As countries regulate how data owned by deceased persons should be treated, companies responsible for such data will need to respect such regulations.

Still open is which country's law would prevail – the country of the company, the country in which the data is physically stored, in or the user's country [4].

5   Final Remarks and Next Steps

In this paper we present the results of a systematic analysis of the Google IAM. Our goal in doing so was twofold – contribute to research related to digital legacy, as well as that of configuration processes that impact interaction over time. Our findings discuss how IAM supports users planning for how to deal with their digital assets, describing the users' decision space, as well as how IAM deals with some of the issues raised in recent literature on digital legacy. The findings can be useful to researchers working on proposing requirements for such systems, and professionals involved in (re)designing digital legacy planning systems.

The research regarding anticipating impacts of configuration settings in collaborative systems over time covers a broader scope of domains. Nonetheless, digital legacy planning is an excellent domain for consideration, because all impacts will take place in a future in which users will not be around to check if their configuration decisions achieved their intended effects. By using the interaction anticipation challenges proposed in [10] we have generated a specific account of how these challenges can be useful to the designing or evaluating digital legacy systems. Also, the analysis illustrates how to use CIAC in combination with SIM.

In our work, by using SIM we analyzed designers' decisions; an interesting future work would be to contrast this analysis with one taking to a user's perspective. Future directions for digital legacy could involve analyzing other systems that help users to plan for their digital assets, and compare this to the decision space offered by Google. Moreover, it would be interesting to compare what we learned by analyzing IAM with the help of CIAC and SIM, with what can be gleaned from other analytical tools.

Acknowledgments. Raquel Prates thanks CNPq (grant #248441/2013-2) and the College of IST at Penn State; Clarisse de Souza thanks CNPq (grant #307043/2013-4) and FAPERJ (grant #E-26/102.770/2012) for partially funding their research.

References

1. Brubaker, J., Dombrowski, L., Gilbert, A., Kusumakaulika, N., Hayes, G.: Stewarding a legacy: responsibilities and relationships in the management of post-mortem data. In: Proceedings of CHI 2014, pp. 4157–4166. ACM (2014)
2. de Souza, C.: The Semiotic Engineering of Human-Computer Interaction. MIT press, Massachusetts (2005)
3. de Souza, C., Leitão, C.: Semiotic engineering methods for scientific research in HCI. Synth. Lect. Hum. Centered Inf. 2(1), 1–122 (2009)
4. Edwards, L., Harbinja, E.: "What happens to my facebook profile when i die?": legal issues around transmission of digital assets on death. In: Maciel, C., Pereira, V.C. (eds.) Digital Legacy and Interaction, pp. 115–144. Springer International Publishing, Switzerland (2013)

5. Gulotta, R., Odom, W., Faste, H., Forlizzi, J.: Legacy in the age of the internet: reflections on how interactive systems shape how we are remembered. In: Proceedings of DIS 2014, pp. 975–984. ACM (2014)
6. Maciel, C., Pereira, V.: Digital Legacy and Interaction. Springer, Heidelberg (2013)
7. Massimi, M., Odom, W., Banks, R., Kirk, D.: Matters of life and death: locating the end of life in lifespan-oriented HCI research. In: Proceedings of CHI 2011, pp. 987–996. ACM (2011)
8. Massimi, M., Baecker, R.: Dealing with death in design: developing systems for the bereaved. In: Proceedings of CHI 2011, pp. 1001–1010. ACM (2011)
9. Odom, W., Banks, R., Kirk, D.: Reciprocity, deep storage, and letting go: opportunities for designing interactions with inherited digital materials. Interactions **17**(5), 31–34 (2010)
10. Prates, R.O., Rosson, M.B., de Souza, C.S.: Interaction anticipation: communicating impacts of groupware configuration settings to users. In: Proceedings of IS-EUD 2015, p. 6 (2015)

Shedding Lights on Human Values:
An Approach to Engage Families
with Energy Conservation

Janine Huizenga[1,4], Lara S.G. Piccolo[2(✉)], Meia Wippoo[1],
Christoph Meili[3], and Andrew Bullen[4]

[1] WAAG Society, Sint Antoniesbreestraat 69,
1011 HB Amsterdam, Netherlands
janine@streetchallenge.eu, meia@waag.org
[2] Knowledge Media Institute, The Open University,
MK76AA Milton Keynes, UK
lara.piccolo@open.ac.uk
[3] WWF Schweiz, Hohlstrasse 110, Postfach 8010 Zürich, Switzerland
christoph.meili@wwf.ch
[4] The Creative Cooperative, Amsterdam, Netherlands
andrew.bullen@orange.fr

Abstract. Changing behaviour related to energy conservation is not an emotionally neutral task. People have to deal with individual and group interests, contextual constraints, eventually trading-off between their values and effective actions in terms of savings. This paper presents a set of dynamics and artefacts for families to raise and share their energy awareness, and transform it into sustainable behaviour. This method based on human values was applied with 7 families to identify critical factors that must be in play when promoting energy conservation within a social group. Preliminary results confirmed that bringing families' values into discussion and establishing shared commitments and responsibilities are promising approaches for technology design with the purpose to raise awareness collectively and promote effective changes in behaviour towards protecting the natural environment.

1 Introduction

The potential of technology to mediate our relationship with the environment and gather people sharing similar interests has been increasingly explored for tackling contemporary social issues [1], such as the urgent need to review the way we explore the planet's natural resources. In line with that, this study aims at investigating how technology can be used to raise people's awareness of climate change and the energy issues, and how to turn awareness into active engagement.

Even in the current scenario where technology has been omnipresent, information is still a gap that needs to be bridged to transform energy awareness into behaviour change [2, 3]. Beyond dealing with habits, to make different choices in every day life that eventually impact comfort, people must be motivated. Not knowing what to do with the information they get, lack of peer support, sense of guilt, feeling manipulated,

© IFIP International Federation for Information Processing 2015
J. Abascal et al. (Eds.): INTERACT 2015, Part I, LNCS 9296, pp. 210–218, 2015.
DOI: 10.1007/978-3-319-22701-6_15

and resource constraints are examples of barriers that can prevent people to act in a more pro-environmental way [3, 4].

Climate change and behaviour are then considered *"complex subjects not emotionally neutral"* [5]. Promoting changes in behaviour cannot consider only users' rational choices, mostly driven by money of indirect or intangible benefits to the environment. Even when benefits are evident, environmental concern per se is rarely the main motivation for people reconsider their behaviour. Saving money, promoting health, sense of justice, or being seen favourably by others are sometimes concurrent or coexisting motivations [6]. A study in the UK, for instance, found that being part of a collective effort was more important to participants than the effectiveness of the action on the environment [7].

Different domains in science such as psychology, anthropology, sociology, and philosophy have put effort into understanding the forces that drive people's behaviour and decisions to be engaged with protecting the natural environment [8, 9]. Conceptualizing *human values* by referring to what people consider important, what guide their life [10] is one of these approaches. Considering the interplay between personal values and how people experience the world in their own context is crucial when targeting to promote a new way of thinking or acting [11], explaining then the raising interest around how values shape public engagement with a social issue [9].

In the HCI domain, the notion of human values has been applied for more than 15 years to inform technology design [12, 13]. The current scenario of technology shaping everyday behaviour, eventually mediating collective and individual interests, evidences the importance of keeping investigating methods and tools to elicit and inform design with the human values in play in different contexts.

This work-in-progress paper introduces a set of group dynamics and artefacts to identify families' values related to energy usage and map possible changes in behaviour. The study is part of a strategy to design interactive systems to promote collective behaviour change towards energy conservation informed by human aspects.

The method and its artefacts are described in the next section, followed by discussions around applying it with families in the Netherlands and Switzerland. We conclude listing preliminary resulting features and addressing future works.

2   Dynamics and Artefacts

Based on findings from literature on individual and social aspects that potentiate engagement and changes in behaviour (i.e. [3, 6, 7]), this study assumes that people need to feel personally involved and empowered to act. A set of group dynamics for families and physical artefacts were then created intending to engage emotionally by strengthening commitment and the sense of responsibility [14].

To capture human-values based factors with potential to instigate awareness and engagement and to transform it into changes in behaviour, the dynamics follow these 5 steps: (1) Make sense and record present behaviours; (2) Identify key behavioural factors (awareness); (3) Promote engagement; (4) Instigate changes in behaviour; (5) Sustain changed behaviour.

Two workshops, limited to 120 min each, cover these 5 steps. The first one introduces challenges and artefacts to map human values versus energy savings issues, while the second one targets on reflections and design of further solutions. The workshops should happen with an interval of several days between them, giving participants time to act in their household and reflect upon results. The audience targeted are families with a minimum of two children above the age of 6, ideally above 12 years old in order to be more engaged with the group discussions.

2.1   Workshop 1: Mapping Values X Energy Saving Issues

The workshop 1 (WS1) was designed to map the current energy usage situation in the households relating values and feelings. Reflection questions targeted in the WS1:

- What core values does your family unit embrace?
- How do these core values relate to the energy issue?
- Can you identify in detail the actual usage of energy in your family's home?
- How do you feel about the actual energy usage in your family's home? Good? Bad? Satisfactory?
- Can you reconcile this usage with your family values?
- How can you improve the situation in practical terms?
- Can you assume personal responsibility to practical change?

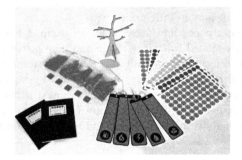

Fig. 1. The utility toolkit

A set of physical artefacts was designed to support the workshop activities. They compose the *Utility Toolkit* [15], Fig. 1, containing the Value Tree, Mood Tokens, an Energy Diary, Utility Labels and Personal Utility Stickers. The toolkit was conceived to be taken home by participants, extending the activities to the domestic environment. It can also be downloaded from [15].

The participant families are invited to follow this sequence of activities that starts in the workshop and continues at home: (1) Visualising the house routines (warming-up); (2) Identifying human values; (3) House mapping; (4) Mapping feelings; and (5) Homework: applying the Utility Labels. Between the activities, the participants present the results to be discussed by peer families.

(1) **Visualising the house routines.** The WS1 starts with families' members being asked to describe a typical day in their lives, focusing on their behavioural patterns in the house and the energy that might be used during these activities. Lego, paper, magazines, etc. can be used to support the visualisation, which is reported by every family member.

(2) **Identifying human values.** The families are asked to come up with at least five personal values regarding the environment and energy usage. Some examples of values can help participants, e.g. *health*, *"connectedness"*, *nature*, *family*, etc. First the family members define five values individually. Then, they form groups of two, which in turn define five values shared by both. In the case of a large family, all values need to be refined, step-by-step, until there are five values left agreed by the whole family. The family ranks and visualise these values by using the *Value Tree*, as illustrated in Fig. 2 (a) and (b). This exercise aims at linking personal emotions and commitment related to the environment and energy usage, creating also a shared understanding within the family.

(a) The downloadable Value Tree   (b) The Value Tree in use

Fig. 2. (a) The downloadable value tree (b) The value tree in use

(3) **House mapping.** Families' members are then invited to draw a map of the layout of their house. Each member starts with the room where he/she feels most comfortable. Everybody should draw a different room. During this exercise they try to consider all their appliances, energy points and their varying use of energy. The family members then combine their maps and add the rooms that have been omitted, such as washing room, pantry, corridor, etc. It results in a floor plan of the entire house, which does not need to be precise in terms of scale neither beautiful.

(4) **Mapping feelings.** Now the family members are asked to map their feelings about their energy usage in the house on top of their drawn map/floor plan. The *Mood Tokens* (Fig. 3a) are applied to represent the feelings ranging from very good (happy) to very bad (unhappy). A question mark is provided in case they cannot reach consensus. The families 'walk through' all the rooms and decide together where the Mood Tokens need to be placed (Fig. 3b). Once the entire house is mapped, the zero-measurement state is captured in a picture. This will be the reference for future activities towards implementing/evaluating changes.

(a) The set of Mood tokens

(b) Mood tokens on the house map

Fig. 3. (a) The set of mood tokens (b) Mood tokens on the house map

(5) **Applying the utility labels.** Once the 'unhappy spots' are identified with the Mood Tokens, the participants are ready to start the behavioural changes. Every 'weak spot' is then marked with a *Utility Label* (Fig. 4). There is one for energy, water, gas, and food, expanding the meaning of energy conservation beyond appliances usage.

Every family member is given his or her own *Utility Stickers* and can claim responsibility for a specific area of energy use. For example, one can be in charge of all the sockets verifying if there are no unnecessary phone or other chargers left in it. Another member looks after the waste disposal, and another checks the thermostat.

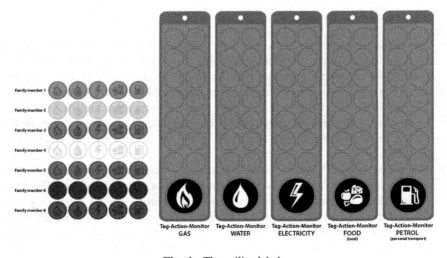

Fig. 4. The utility labels

The family discusses together, ideally in daily basis, additional possible improvements, which changes have been made, and who was responsible for these changes. If a change is deemed successful, the person responsible is allowed to place a sticker on the Utility Label in question.

The family records in a diary either the proposed changes and/or the effect of the changes on the household dynamics and the family's values. Regularly, the number of points and the stickers gained by each are added up and a 'Energy Champion' can be somehow rewarded, as established by the families themselves.

2.2   Workshop 2: Reflection on the Results

Workshop 2 (WS2) aims at instigating reflections on results and eventual changes in the household trigerred by the WS1. Reflection questions expected to be answered during this workshop are:

- What strategies and behaviour have you put in place in order to make the energy usage changes that were made durable?
- Which tools can you think of, that would support you more effectively in the implementation and monitoring of the changes in energy usage?
- Could you describe your role in this energy experiment?
- Could you think of ways to motivate friends and family to do the same?
- Could you give some examples of things that will motivate you to make the changes?

The WS2 is composed by this sequence of activities:

(1) **Value tree revaluation.** The Values Tree and the map with mood tokens resulting from WS1 are brought back for revaluation. Participants then discuss the process validity, the representation, consequent changes in behaviour, and the eventual need to reorder their values. Other families may suggest more improvements to the new plan of balancing value and energy use.

(2) **Reflection on using the toolkit.** WS2 reflection questions may be applied to guide a discussion among all participants. Families' members evaluate the past days (or weeks), how they made the changes, and how it has influenced the household. They can use photos of their houses and positioning of their tokens to guide their own evaluation.

(3) **Energy tool.** The families work on a design sketch for a specific energy solution in their home. This small invention can either be the installation of energy monitors, a personalized charting system to track the energy usage responsibilities of each family member, or even a small visualisation of each utility in the house. This solution is shared with other families expecting to receive their feedback.

(4) **Follow up.** For making the changes sustainable, the families are instructed to follow up their activities by using the Utility Toolkit. To motivate the family, new (game) mechanics can be introduced such as a daily "tombola" with a sustainable solution to be implemented, or the introduction of a challenge such as 'sweater-week' (when the heating is turned down, and people need to wear an extra sweater).

3 Execution

The workshops happened in a 2 months time (Jan–Feb 2014) engaging 3 families in Netherlands and 4 families in Switzerland, involving a total of 28 people. Parents age ranged from 37 to 52 years old, and children from 6–18 years old. It was essential that the families carried out the workshop process all together, as a unit.

The general feedback from the families was that the activities were effective in raising their awareness on energy usage, leading to changes in their behaviour. Some positive aspects reported by participants are summarized below according to the 5 steps to raise awareness and transform it into behaviour change.

(1) **Identifying values to make sense of current behaviour.** Defining and prioritising the families' core values was crucial to create an emotional and ethical basis. The values were often discussed not only in the workshops but also on a daily basis at home. Five out of the seven participant families decided to display the Value Tree as a reminder of their defined values. Value prioritisation was even changed by certain families in the course of the workshop period. *"I now like to think and share what is good for the family. It would be good to do this in other aspects of family life"*, said a mother in Zurich. *"Most important thing was for me to discuss about values with our teenaged son. We never do this normally"* father, Zurich.

(2) **House mapping to identify key behavioural factors.** This activity was perceived as decisive for raising awareness of the energy usage both in individual and familiar aspects. There was general consensus on the feeling of individual and group responsibility and engagement to change their behaviour. *"We've made the energy theme a topic of regular conversation. We've created some standards together that we can address together when somebody is being negligent. In that respect, energy has now become something that we can talk about without conflict"*, reported a father in Amsterdam.

(3) **Promoting engagement.** Keeping the discussion around energy was also reported as being a key factor in sustaining awareness and action. *"We have made it a tradition and ritual to sit together every evening to discuss the subject. In this way, we motivate each other's good behaviour. And particularly to stay active. We discuss our day, our energy behaviour, and what we still can do. This motivates us"* daughter, Amsterdam.

(4) **Instigating changes in behaviour.** The families reported the motivating effect of assigning individual and joint responsibilities to instigate changes. The peer pressure for daily discussions makes this force even stronger. *"The family sets its own goals and dates. This motivates us"*, father from Zurich. However, in line with stated in literature, the lack of information on how effectively change behaviour emerged: *"I'd like to read other people's journals for behavioural stimulation, for comparison and new ideas."* Mother, Amsterdam. *"I also like to be updated with tips and tricks to save energy. I guess this project will result in new kinds of behaviour that should be shared with the rest of the participants - and the world!"* said a father in Amsterdam.

(5) **Sustaining changes in behaviour.** The participants indicated the need to receive ongoing comparative information on their progress by monitoring consumption. Not only would such data foster engagement, but would also provide context and confirmation for their efforts. *"We talk about changes in our behaviour without really knowing what the actual effect is. We think we are doing better than before, but we have no objective standards or measurements to know exactly how much we did better or worse than (A) before (in our own household) (B) our neighbours (who have the same type of home) (C) the national average. Basically, we want to know what we are achieving"*, father from Amsterdam.

4 Preliminary Results and Conclusions

This paper presented a set of dynamics and artefacts for families to raise their energy awareness and transform it into behaviour change towards saving energy in domestic environment. The method proposed was designed shedding lights on human values by bringing them into discussion among the families, and considering them when mapping possibilities of savings.

Along the 5 steps from understanding patterns of behaviours to sustain behaviour changes, participants pointed out gaps and benefits of applying these dynamics. Creating shared awareness based on the values, and dealing with daily responsibilities and commitments to change their direct environment were pointed out by participants as positive factors, providing them a sense of empowerment and motivation to be engaged. The need for information, specially related to monitoring consumption, though, was evidenced as a gap to instigate and sustain behaviour change. Further research is needed into the practical use of energy usage monitoring devices complementing this approach, as well as to keep tracking the sustainability of changes in longer term.

Available for download with instructions to apply it [14], the Utility Toolkit is expected to be applied in different contexts, promoting direct contact across further communities to inspire and motivate changes on a wider social level. As examples, participants recommended it to be applied in schools and leisure centres.

This study with families represents a starting point for this research that has as a main goal the deployment of a collective awareness platform [1]. Results of this study have now been translated into software requirements aiming to design an online solution to empower and engage people within this climate change and energy issues. Providing an online space for negotiation among members in a community, sharing personal and contextualised energy saving hints, values identification, public commitment and bridging awareness with daily monitored behaviour at home are some of the features evidenced in this study that have been developed. As stated in [16], other user-centric studies have complemented the sociotechnical development.

Acknowledgments. This research is part of the project DecarboNet, funded by the FP7 program of the European Union, grant agreement 610829.

References

1. Arniani, M., et al.: Collective awareness platform for sustainability and social innovation: an introduction (2014) http://caps2020.eu
2. Abrahamse, W., et al.: A review of intervention studies aimed at household energy conservation. J. Environ. Psychol. **25**(3), 273–291 (2005)
3. Piccolo, L., et al.: Motivating online engagement and debates on energy consumption. In: ACM Web Science 2014, pp. 109–118. ACM (2014)
4. Moser, S.C., Dilling, L. (eds.): Creating a Climate for Change: Communicating Climate Change and Facilitating Social Change. Cambridge University Press, Cambridge (2007)
5. House of commons, science and technology committee. communicating climate change. Eighth Report of Session 2013–2014
6. Umpfenbach, K., et al: Influences on consumer behaviour. Policy implications beyond nudging. Final report. Ecologic Institute, Berlin (2014)
7. Motivations for pro-environmental behaviour, RESOLVE. Department for Environment, Food and Rural Affairs, Defra, London (2010)
8. Blunck, H., et al.: Computational environmental ethnography: combining collective sensing and ethnographic inquiries to advance means for reducing environmental footprints. In: Proceedings of e-Energy 2013, pp. 87–98. ACM (2013)
9. Corner, A., Markowitz, E., Pidgeon, N.: Public engagement with climate change: the role of human values. WIREs Clim Change **5**, 411–422 (2014)
10. Schwartz, S.H., Bilsky, W.: Toward a universal psychological structure of human values. J. Pers. Soc. Psychol. **53**, 550–562 (1987)
11. Parkhill, K.A. et al.: Transforming the UK energy system: public values, attitudes and acceptability. Synthesis report, UKERC, London (2013)
12. Hornung, H., Piccolo, L., Arpetti, A.: Human values: a gap between academia and industry. In: Proceedings XIII Brazilian Symposium on Human Factors in Computer Systems, pp. 449–445 (2014)
13. Friedman, B.: Value sensitive design. In: Schular, D. (ed.) Liberating Voices: A Pattern Language for Communication Revolution, pp. 366–368. The MIT Press, Cambridge, MA (2008)
14. Huizenga, J., Alani, H., Heerschop, S.: D1.2: social requirements specification. Technical report http://goo.gl/MHMvSs (2014)
15. WAAG society. utility toolkit. http://www.decarbonet.eu/2014/10/10/utility-toolkit/
16. Piccolo, L.S.G., Smith, C.: Designing to raise collective awareness and leverage energy savings. In: Proceedings of British HCI (2015, in press)

Gamification of Online Surveys: Design Process, Case Study, and Evaluation

Johannes Harms[✉], Stefan Biegler, Christoph Wimmer,
Karin Kappel, and Thomas Grechenig

INSO Research Group, Vienna University of Technology, Vienna, Austria
{johannes.harms, stefan.biegler, christoph.wimmer,
karin.kappel, thomas.grechenig}@inso.tuwien.ac.at

Abstract. Online surveys are an important means of data collection in marketing and research, but conventional survey designs are often perceived as dull and unengaging, resulting in negative respondent behavior. Gamification has been proposed to make online surveys more pleasant to fill and, consequently, to improve the quality of survey results. This work applied gamification to an existing survey targeted at teenagers and young adults. The gamified survey was evaluated in a study with 60 participants regarding the psychological and behavioral outcomes of gamification. Results indicate that gamification successfully increased the users' perceived fun, the average time spent, as well as their willingness to use and recommend the survey, without introducing a strong bias in survey results, albeit with a lower overall response rate.

Keywords: Gamification · Online surveys · Questionnaires · Evaluation

1 Introduction

Gamification of online surveys has been proposed to make questionnaire filling a more enjoyable experience and to improve the accuracy of survey results [6, 9]. This is an important goal because online surveys have been criticized for their dullness resulting in negative respondent behavior such as speeding, random responding, premature termination, and lack of attention [9, 17, 23]. In contrast to these negative effects, evaluations of gamified surveys have reported diverse benefits regarding user experience, motivation, participation, amount and quality of data [6, 8, 9, 23]. These prior works confirm the usefulness of gamified online surveys, but have remained unclear about suitable design processes. More recent work [13] has proposed (but not evaluated) a design process that unifies process models from the related disciplines of form design and gamification. This work employs and evaluates the process in a case study where two designers gamified a survey about sports and leisure activities amongst teenagers and young adults. The goals and contributions of this work are firstly, to document our application of the process and the resulting gamified design (Sect. 4). This will also provide qualitative results (Sect. 5) regarding the process's applicability and usefulness. And secondly, to evaluate the psychological and behavioral outcomes of the gamified design (Sects. 6–8) in an empirical study.

© IFIP International Federation for Information Processing 2015
J. Abascal et al. (Eds.): INTERACT 2015, Part I, LNCS 9296, pp. 219–236, 2015.
DOI: 10.1007/978-3-319-22701-6_16

2 Related Work

Gamification of online surveys builds on many disciplines [13]. The following section briefly discusses relevant backgrounds, concepts and methods.

Tradition and Innovation in Surveys. The use of forms for surveying information has a long historical tradition dating back to the 16th century when officers in Spanish provinces were equipped with questionnaires to standardize interviewing and observations [10]. These questionnaires enabled bureaucratic processes by abstracting individual life experiences into consistent, standardized representations [3, 10]. This characteristic is shared with today's digital forms and online surveys, albeit with a different purpose of enabling automated data processing. Understanding the history of online surveys provides ample opportunity for innovation, as demonstrated by related work that has linked today's forms with their historic predecessors in order to derive research goals for form design [12]. The goal of this work can be described accordingly: Gamification of online surveys seeks to avoid negative historical entailments of the 'form' UI metaphor (in particular, the connotations that forms are bureaucratic and dull [9]) by adding interactive game elements to the survey.

Form design. The discipline of form design is highly relevant to survey gamification because online surveys typically employ form-based UIs to enable data entry. Related work has captured best practices for form design in guidelines [2] and books [16, 28]. Relevant aspects have been structured into three *layers* of a form design process [16]. In the relationship layer, designers analyze the relationship with users, their tasks, and the usage context. In the conversation layer, designers seek to create interactions that make the conversations between users and the survey flow easily. The appearance layer describes detailed UI and graphical design.

Fig. 1. Gamification provides game elements as motivational affordances to produce psychological and behavioral outcomes [11, 13]. These outcomes are influenced by a priori factors such as context, tasks, user characteristics, and affect [11].

Gamification. Gamification has been defined as "the use of design elements characteristic for games in non-game contexts" [7]. In this definition, the "design elements characteristic for games" can more shortly be termed game elements. The MDA framework [15] provides a way to understand game elements as MDAs, i.e., as either game mechanics, dynamics, or aesthetics. Mechanics describe the basic building blocks (data representations, algorithms, rules, interactive elements) that make up a game. Dynamics refer to the resulting run-time behavior over time. Aesthetics characterize a player's emotional response and experience. The "non-game contexts" include business, education, health, many more listed in [11, 14], and online surveys, as examined in this work.

Gamified Online Surveys. As a potential benefit, gamification provides motivational affordances that produce psychological (e.g., user experience, emotion, fun) and behavioral (e.g., participation, performance) outcomes [11]. In Fig. 1, we additionally included a priori factors such as context of use, user characteristics, and affect because these have been shown to significantly influence the outcomes of gamification [11]. Related work has aimed at exploring possible designs for gamified surveys and at evaluating their impact [6, 8, 9, 23]. E.g., four designs have been compared in [9]: text-only, decoratively visual, functionally visual, and fully gamified. Evaluations have reported beneficial psychological outcomes such as a better user experience [8, 9] and increased motivation [6]. Beneficial behavioral outcomes have included more participation and engagement [6, 8], more feedback [23], and better data quality [8]. Despite these experienced benefits, not all gamified surveys have produced significantly positive results [9]. Furthermore, a recent literature review has shown benefits to be strongly influenced by users and context [11]. There is also a lack of comparisons of the required effort and subsequent benefits of specific game elements [11]. This calls for future studies to clearly describe the influence of survey domain and target user group(s), the game elements provided as motivational affordances, and the effort that was required for designing and implementing the gamified survey.

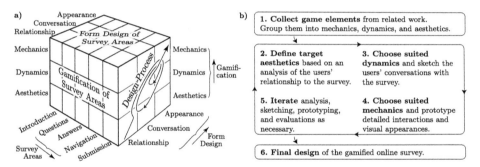

Fig. 2. Design process for gamifying online surveys. The process (a) unifies the disciplines of gamification and form design and applies them to the survey areas to be gamified, as originally proposed in [13]. Its iterations (b) follow the steps proposed in the MDA framework [15, 26] and in the "three layers of form design" [16].

3   A Design Process for Gamifying Online Surveys

To design a gamified online survey in this work, we chose to follow the process originally proposed in [13]. This process integrates and unifies the MDA (mechanics-dynamics-aesthetics) gamification framework [15, 26] and the three layers of form design [16], applying them to the various survey areas, as visualized in Fig. 2a. In addition to prior work, this work contributes a more detailed description of the process, complemented with examples (this Section), and a qualitative evaluation (Sect. 5).

1. Game Elements for Inspiration. Prior to starting with the gamification process, designers should collect game elements that can inspire their further design activities [13]. As a quick and easy starting point, they can use the pre-compiled catalogues of game elements suited for survey gamification from [23, 27]. Further game elements (not all of them necessarily suited for surveys) are provided in the "gamification toolkit" [26], "ingredients of great games" [24], game mechanics listed in [1], "motivational game design patterns" [19], "game flow criteria" [25], "playful experiences" in [18], and the aesthethics in [15]. The designers should familiarize themselves with the game elements so they can inspire the subsequent design steps.

2. Aesthetics and the Relationship Layer. As a first step of the proposed process, designers should analyze the intended users (i.e., the survey's target population), tasks (the form schema to be filled), and context, as described in the relationship layer of form design [16]. Based on this knowledge, they can set goals regarding intended aesthetics, i.e., the intended emotional responses and user experiences that shall be elicited by the survey. Designers may set different aesthetic goals for different survey areas (introduction, questions, answers, navigation, and submission, compare the "survey areas" dimension in Fig. 2a). Nonetheless, gamification should result in one coherent design; therefore a single process is proposed for all survey areas, see Fig. 2b. Aesthetics from the previously compiled catalogue of MDAs can serve as inspiration. Designers can rank and choose aesthetics as deemed suitable.

For example, designers may consider the aesthetics of challenge and sensation to be suited for a survey's target users, but may deem the fellowship aesthetic unsuited for an intended single-user experience. Regarding the various survey areas, they could aim at arousing curiosity and interest in a survey's introduction page. They could seek to provide visual and auditory sensation to enhance questions and answers, but refrain from making questions challenging to answer because perceived intellectual difficulty has been shown to adversely influence respondent behavior [17]. They could decide to design navigation with a target aesthetic of gameful exploration. The submission page could be designed to reward users for their effort. Note that the above aesthetics are provided as illustrative examples – other target aesthetics are of course possible.

3. Dynamics and the Conversation Layer. Designers can use the MDA framework [15] to reason about which game dynamics are suited for producing the intended aesthetics. This creative thinking can be inspired by the catalogue of MDAs. Note that since game dynamics refer to the run-time behavior of a gamified system [15], the considerations in this step of the process correspond to the conversation layer of form design [16], i.e., the flow of interactions that a user is going to have with the survey.

For example, the game dynamic of time pressure has been recommended for motivating users to provide lengthy free-text answers [23], but designers should avoid creating time pressure throughout the entire survey because this could motivate users to speed. Designers may also implement feedback loops, i.e., dynamics wherein user actions affect the overall state of gameplay [15]. Feedback loops may visualize concepts such as a user's progress, status, wealth, health, points, etc.

4. Mechanics and the Conversation and Appearance Layers. To produce the intended dynamics and aesthetics, designers can employ suitable game mechanics and playful elements. Again, they can use the catalogue of MDAs for inspiration. Since game mechanics are the detailed building blocks and rules that make up a game [15], this step relates to detailed design activities in the conversation and appearance layers of form design. As an overall goal, re-designed questions should still represent the construct of interest and the interactive UI elements should not bias the answers given by respondents.

For example, designers may choose to employ the mechanics of points and badges to implement the dynamic of feedback, which in turn can produce the aesthetic of challenge. They may further choose to visualize a stopwatch next to free-text fields to implement the dynamic of time pressure and the same aesthetic of challenge. They may choose to employ the avatar mechanic and allow users to freely move their avatar throughout the survey and thus produce an aesthetic of exploration.

5. Prototyping, Evaluation, and Iteration. As typical for creative design processes [5, 21], designers should work in a team, explore multiple designs in parallel, prototype, and evaluate prototypes. The overall gamification process will typically progress from deliberate vagueness during brainstorming, ideation, and sketching (primarily in steps 2–3) to increasing detail and specifity during prototyping and evaluation (primarily in step 4). Evaluations should consider both intended outcomes for the user (e.g., subjective experience) and outcomes for those who create the survey (e.g., completion rate, truthful answers). Formative evaluations can be performed with relatively few users, using test observation methods such as thinking-aloud [22]. In the authors' experience, paper prototyping and digital mockups have worked well in the first iteration, whereas later iterations have required digital, interactive prototypes. Three iterations have sufficed to create a pleasant design with good usability.

4   Case Study: Gamification of a Sports Survey

An existing online survey about sports and leisure activities amongst teenagers and young adults[1] was chosen as a case study because of its beneficial characteristics: The survey's questions are easy to understand and answer; therefore domain-specific knowledge amongst test users is unlikely to bias evaluation results. It employs state-of-the art survey design using survey-monkey's[2] default style and functionality. Furthermore, the survey addresses children and teenagers as target population; related work has shown this target group to react well to gamification [20].

4.1   Application of the Gamification Process

Methodologically, two designers (one senior with over five years in HCI and form design, one student in HCI) employed the design process presented in this work to

---

[1] http://jugendportal.at/befragung/bewegung-und-sport, Apr. 24th, 2015.
[2] http://surveymonkey.com/, Apr. 24th, 2015. Survey Monkey is a popular, commercial tool for creating and conducting online surveys.

gamify the sports survey. In summary, the designers held three workshops and took three iterations (each including prototyping and evaluation) to work through the different phases of the process, thus converting the conventionally-designed sports survey into a gamified one. In the first workshop, they discussed the *aesthetics* available in the catalogue in [27] and finally chose the three aesthetics of sensation, challenge, and exploration as suitable goals for the relationship layer of form design, i.e., for the intended relationship with teenage users. More specifically, they aimed at producing a design that elicits a rich *visual sensation* (in contrast to typical, text-only surveys), that includes small *challenges* in the form of micro-games (albeit without making questions too difficult to answer because this could potentially bias results), and that allows users to freely *explore and discover* the various survey areas. In the next workshop, they brainstormed possible designs using the catalogue of MDAs from [27] as inspiration. Their design activities iterated rapidly between explorative, abstract thinking (i.e., which dynamics and mechanics can produce the intended aesthetics) and specific, increasingly detailed design (i.e., sketching ideas and elaborating the conversation and appearance layers of form design). Regarding *dynamics*, they chose to implement feedback systems about the respondent's progress and about beneficial user actions. They further chose to implement the dynamic of time pressure to produce an aesthetic of challenge when users enter free-text answers. They sketched a design with the following *mechanics*: Users should steer an avatar through the survey. Feedback should be given using progress indicators and using coins as rewards for beneficial actions. In the third workshop, they produced mockups, thus addressing detailed UI design and the appearance layer of form design. An initial paper prototype was employed in an early, formative usability test and was subsequently replaced by a web-based prototypes and a final implementation.

4.2   Resulting Gamified Design

The resulting, gamified survey contains the same questions as the original sports survey, but features a novel design. The addition of many game elements resulted in a highly game-like appearance, as shown in Figs. 3 and 4.

Visual Design. The overall *theme* of the gamified survey was designed to reflect the survey's topic of sports. The *graphical appearance* was designed to remind of jump'n'run games (such as Super Mario) that members of the target population are likely to be familiar with from their childhood. Survey elements such as input controls were graphically decorated in order to produce the intended aesthetic of sensation. For example, radio buttons were re-designed to include the respondent's avatar along with pictures that each represent one possible answer, as shown in Fig. 4. All survey areas maintain a similar visual style but feature different interactions, as explained in the following subsections.

Avatar. In the first survey area, an avatar is automatically assigned to each respondent. The avatar's visual appearance depends on the demographic data that respondents provide about themselves, see Fig. 3a for an example.

a) Avatar creation

b) Map for navigating between survey areas

c) Soccer game for single choice questions

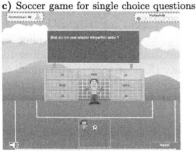

d) Javelin throwing for Likert questions

e) Long jump for Likert questions

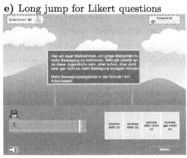

f) Sprint for free-text questions

g) Shop to spend rewarded coins

h) Medal ceremony as a thank-you page

Fig. 3. The gamified survey features multiple areas. Respondents (a) create an avatar, (b) freely navigate between survey areas, (c-f) play mini-games to answer questions, and (g) may buy accessories for their avatar in a shop using rewarded coins. Upon completion, they win the sports competition and are (h) rewarded a gold medal.

Free Exploration. The survey allows respondents to navigate freely between four sports disciplines that each represent a different survey area. Navigation is implemented through a map shown in the second survey area, see Fig. 3b. When respondents click on a sports discipline, their avatar walks to the specified place on the map and the according survey area is subsequently shown. Once they complete a survey area, they return back to the map.

Questions and Answers. The survey areas of soccer, javelin throwing, long jump, and sprint, see Fig. 3c–f, are micro-games that each afford and require different interactions through which respondents can answer questions. For example, the soccer game (Fig. 3c) instructs respondents to perform a penalty kick by dragging and then releasing their avatar. When released, the avatar kicks the ball in the specified direction into the goal and thus selects one of two options. The other survey areas are designed in similar ways. The javelin throwing and long jump games (Fig. 3d–e) map length (of jump or throw) unto answers. The sprint game (Fig. 3f) creates time pressure by visualizing a decreasing amount of time during which respondents shall provide a maximum of free-text answers. To avoid bias through unintentionally wrong answers, each survey area provides instructions about the required interactions. Furthermore, respondents are asked to practice and then demonstrate their skill by providing a pre-specified answer before they can start answering real questions. Respondents can correct every answer before confirming it by clicking a "next"-button that leads to the next question.

Feedback Mechanisms. Various mechanisms provide positive feedback about the respondents' progress. While filling the survey, they are awarded *coins*. The map allows respondents to enter a *shop* (Fig. 3g) where they can buy accessories such as sunglasses and hats for their avatar. The shop has no other purpose than to strengthen positive reward. The last survey area – shown upon completion of the entire survey – was designed as a *medal ceremony* (Fig. 3h) where each respondent is honored as winner of a sports competition.

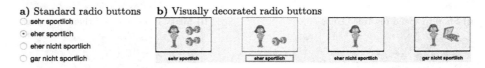

Fig. 4. Input controls were visually decorated as shown in the above example.

5   Lessons Learned About the Gamification Process

The two designers reported qualitative feedback regarding the applicability and usefulness of the gamification process, as experienced by them in the case study. Their overall opinion was positive. They both found the process served them as a *helpful guideline* about how to proceed with the gamification. This was especially important for one of them whose background was more in user interface design than in gamification. Both designers liked the *structure* provided by the process. They said they could follow the steps proposed in the process and found no need to deviate from its structure. We asked specifically if, in their experience, the structure of the process succeeded in combining the MDA-phases (aesthetics, dynamics, mechanics) with the layers of form design (relationship, conversation, appearance). They found that MDA-aesthetics fit very well with the relationship layer because both relate to setting design goals. One of them experienced the combinations of dynamics and mechanics with the conversation and appearance layers to be rather intermingled. Regarding the *first step of the process*, they found that using a *catalogue of MDAs* provided ideas and useful inspiration. They often consulted it during their design activities and wished for a more extensive catalogue. Regarding *subsequent steps*, they highlighted the need to carefully *avoid bias*. For example, they were aware that their chosen target aesthetic of challenge should not result in overly complex interactions that could bias answers. They had therefore decided to make questions easy to answer but to produce the aesthetic of challenge by designing a narration of sports competition. In a similar way, the designers reflected on their decision to include an avatar, expressing concerns that users taking on foreign roles are likely to bias survey results. They had therefore personalized the avatars based on respondent characteristics, thus communicating that the avatar represents the actual respondent, and not a fictitious role. Within this context, they stressed the need for *formative evaluations* and said they had discovered and fixed many usability problems through formative usability testing and subsequent design iterations. Both designers stated that iterative design and implementation of the gamified survey took a lot of *time and effort* – more than they had anticipated, and significantly more than the non-gamified variant, see Table 1 for a quantitative comparison. They found that – in addition to the gamification process – they could have used technical guidance and better development tools for their prototyping and implementation activities. They further suggested that future work should examine methods for reducing the implementation effort.

Table 1. Working time needed for design and implementation of the gamified vs. conventional survey. Note that since the designers gamified an already existing survey, the numbers do not include the time needed to plan and formulate survey questions.

Activity	Working hours:	Gamified	Conventional
Design & Meetings		57	1
Prototyping & Implementation		83	4
Testing		107	1
Total		247	6

6   Study Design

The gamified survey's psychological and behavioral outcomes were evaluated in a remote, comparative, between-subject usability test. Invitations were sent via Email and Facebook, asking to participate in a survey about sports activities. Since invitations could be forwarded without restriction, we had limited control over sample demographics. The invitations did not promise any extrinsic reward and did not disclose the study's true purpose of evaluating a gamified design. Participants were unaware of the existence of two different survey designs and were automatically assigned to one of two test conditions (gamified vs. conventional design) using a round-robin algorithm. After completing the survey, respondents were asked to also fill out a post-test questionnaire. Duplicate responses were prevented through technical measures, i.e., by setting a browser cookie. Respondent behavior and answers were logged into a database. The survey was completed after 60 participants, resulting in an equal distribution of 30 participants in both the conventional and gamified survey.

7   Results

A total of N = 60 participants accessed the sports survey. The participants' age distribution was higher than the intended target audience of the original sports survey, see Table 2. A total of 47 participants completed the survey (24 female, 23 male). A test session was considered complete if users finished the sports survey, no matter if they also filled (N = 40 out of 47) the subsequent post-test questionnaire. Quantitative results are shown in Tables 3–6, including means (M), medians (MD) and standard deviations (SD). Significant differences ($p < 0.05$), as tested using Mann-Whitney U-Tests, are highlighted in a bold font. Qualitative results are reported in Sect. 7.4.

Table 2. Age distribution of participants

What is your age?	0-14	14-17	17-21	22-24	> 24	Unknown
Gamified	0	3	0	5	13	9
Conventional	0	0	0	5	21	4

7.1   Respondent Behavior and Engagement

Respondent behavior was automatically logged during use. The gamified survey had a lower *response rate* of 70 % (21 out of 30 persons), as opposed to the conventional survey with a response rate of 86 % (26 out of 30 persons). We also measured the amount of time spent in the survey and the question where participants cancelled the survey. Amongst respondents who completed the survey, those working with the gamified design spent about *twice as much time* (19:20 ± 04:42) in comparison to those working with the conventional design (09:18 ± 04:39), see Table 3c. Amongst those who cancelled the survey, we found no significant differences regarding the *question after which participants cancelled* and the *time after which they quit*, as shown in Table 3a and b. Besides response rate and time spent, we took an additional measure of engagement by evaluating the *amount of plain-text answers* that respondents were willing to provide, but found no significant difference between the gamified and conventional survey, see Table 3d. We additionally investigated if respondent behavior was influenced by the following *demographic factors*: gender, age, self-rated health and sportiness, county, size of city, highest education and profession, relationship status, has children, living condition (i.e., lives with parents/friends/own family). None of these factors proved to have a statistically significant influence.

Table 3. Respondent behavior.

	N	M	MD	SD	Test statistic
a.) Amongst respondents who cancelled the survey: After how much time did they cancel?					
Gamified	9	02:22	02:23	02:05	U=70
Conventional	4	01:00	01:06	00:38	p=0.330
Total	13	01:57	01:41	01:51	
b.) Amongst respondents who cancelled the survey: After how many questions did they cancel?					
Gamified	9	7.56	6.00	6.54	U=110
Conventional	4	7.75	7.50	4.27	p=0.956
Total	13	7.62	6.00	5.75	
c.) Amongst respondents who completed the survey: How long did respondents take to complete it?					
Gamified	21	19:20	18:20	04:42	U=115
Conventional	26	09:18	07:52	04:39	**p=0.000**
Total	47	13:47	13:20	06:50	
d.) Amongst respondents who completed the survey: Did gamification increase the word counts of the plain text answers?					
Gamified	21	17.76	16.00	6.71	U=115
Conventional	26	15.46	15.00	10.40	p=0.120
Total	47	16.49	15.00	8.92	

7.2 Answers Given

We compared the answers given in response to the gamified versus non-gamified survey. For this purpose, all answers to the survey's 61 closed questions were numerically coded. The answers to 4 of 61 questions were significantly different between the two survey designs (Table 4); all other questions revealed no such influence. Interestingly, all four of these questions were negatively worded Likert questions, part of large blocks of radiobuttons in the text-only survey and part of the javelin-throwing survey area in the gamified design. All four questions got higher answers (i.e., "agree more fully") in the conventional survey. We further investigated the possibility of answers being systematically influenced by the gamified survey's microgames. The javelin-throwing micro game did produce significantly different answers, as compared between the gamified (2.50 ± 1.072) vs. conventional (2.65 ± 1.130) design. There were no significant differences any of the other micro-games.

7.3 Self-rated User Experience

Perceived usability and user experience were assessed upon completion of the sports survey through a post-test questionnaire that included System Usability Scale (SUS) [4] questions. It was filled out by an overall number of 40 respondents (21 gamified, 19

Table 4. Answers given. Amongst the survey's 61 closed questions, answers to the above four questions were significantly influenced by the survey's gamified vs. conventional design. All other questions showed no such influence.

	N	M	MD	SD	Test statistic	0: disagree ⇔ 4: fully agree
a.) Reasons for being physically active: My friends push me to do sports:						
Gamified	21	2.76	3.00	0.768	U=172.5	
Conventional	26	3.31	3.50	0.788		
Total	47	3.06	3.00	0.818	**p=0.020**	
b.) Reasons for not being physically active: I do not like when others watch me do sports:						
Gamified	21	2.86	3.00	1.014	U=151.5	
Conventional	26	3.62	4.00	0.852		
Total	47	3.28	4.00	0.994	**p= 0.003**	
c.) Reasons for not being physically active: I have made bad experiences:						
Gamified	21	3.33	4.00	0.913	U=200	
Conventional	26	3.73	4.00	0.724		
Total	47	3.55	4.00	0.829	**p=0.047**	
d.) Sports is being taken far too serious in our society:						
Gamified	21	2.57	3.00	1.076	U=178	
Conventional	26	3.23	3.00	0.765		
Total	47	2.94	3.00	0.965	**p=0.029**	

conventional). Pair-wise comparison of *individual SUS questions* (see Table 5) revealed that respondents were significantly more inclined to frequently use the gamified survey (2.81 ± 0.75), compared to the conventional version (1.16 ± 1.02). However, respondents felt significantly less confident using the gamified survey (3.1 ± 0.7), compared to the conventional version (3.79 ± 0.42). There was no significant effect of survey design on any other SUS question. *Overall SUS scores* for both survey versions were comparable as well, with the gamified survey scoring 77.98 points and the conventional survey scoring 79.08. Answers to further questions in the post-test questionnaire (Table 6) showed that respondents found the gamified survey (3.29 ± 0.56) significantly more *fun to use* than the conventional survey (2.32 ± 1.01). They were also significantly more inclined to *recommend* the gamified survey (3.38 ± 0.67), compared to the conventional survey (2.42 ± 0.96).

7.4   Qualitative Results

Qualitative comments were collected from respondents using open-ended questions in the post-test questionnaire. The comments were analyzed and grouped into structured categories (see Table 7). Of 21 respondents that finished the gamified survey, every single one answered the post-test questionnaire, while 19 of 26 respondents that finished the conventional survey answered the post-test questionnaire. Respondents were also much more inclined to provide comments (both positive and negative) for the gamified survey (N = 21 of 21) compared to the conventional survey (N = 9 of 26).

Respondents positively commented on the novelty (9), variety (4) and interactivity (2) of the gamified survey. They found it playful (4) and fun (3). Graphics and

Table 5. System Usability Scale (SUS) scores from the post-test questionnaire.

	N	M	MD	SD	Test statistic	0: disagree ⇔ 4:fully agree
Overall SUS Score:						
Gamified	21	78.21	77.50	11.10	U=112	
Conventional	19	79.20	77.50	10.67	p=0.851	
Total	40	78.69	77.50	10.77		
SUS 1: I think that I would like to use this system frequently.						
Gamified	21	2.81	3.00	0.75	U=140	
Conventional	19	1.16	1.00	1.02	**p=0.000**	
Total	40	2.03	2.00	1.21		
SUS 2: I found the system unnecessarily complex.						
Gamified	21	1.14	1.00	0.96	U=220	
Conventional	19	0.84	1.00	0.96	p=0.333	
Total	40	0.84	1.00	0.96		
SUS 3: I thought the system was easy to use.						
Gamified	21	3.05	3.00	0.81	U=230	
Conventional	19	3.53	4.00	0.51	p=0.078	
Total	40	3.28	3.00	0.72		
SUS 4: I think that I would need the support of a technical person to be able to use this system.						
Gamified	21	0.52	0.00	0.81	U=110	
Conventional	19	0.11	0.00	0.32	p=0.124	
Total	40	0.33	0.00	0.66		
SUS 5: I found the various functions in this system were well integrated.						
Gamified	21	3.29	3.00	0.56	U=110	
Conventional	19	2.68	3.00	1.16	p=0.124	
Total	40	3.00	3.00	0.87		
SUS 6: I thought there was too much inconsistency in this system.						
Gamified	21	0.86	1.00	0.73	U=230	
Conventional	19	1.16	1.00	1.12	p=0.469	
Total	40	1.00	1.00	0.93		
SUS 7: I would imagine that most people would learn to use this system very quickly.						
Gamified	21	3.14	3.00	0.66	U=110	
Conventional	19	3.32	4.00	1.15	p=0.117	
Total	19	0.11	0.00	0.32		
SUS 8: I found the system very cumbersome to use.						
Gamified	21	1.00	1.00	0.84	U=55	
Conventional	19	0.53	0.00	0.91	p=0.054	
Total	40	0.78	1.00	0.90		
SUS 9: I felt very confident using the system.						
Gamified	21	3.10	3.00	0.70	U=145	
Conventional	19	3.79	4.00	0.42	**p=0.003**	
Total	40	3.43	4.00	0.68		
SUS 10: I needed to learn a lot of things before I could get going with this system.						
Gamified	21	0.57	0.00	0.75	U=230	
Conventional	19	0.16	0.00	0.38	p=0.078	
Total	40	0.38	0.00	0.63		

animation also garnered positive comments (5), as well as the personalized and customizable avatar (4). Some respondents complained that the gamified survey took much longer to answer than a conventional survey might have taken (4). There also were complaints about the controls (4) and responsiveness of individual mini games

Table 6. Self-rated fun and likeliness of recommending the survey.

	N	M	MD	SD	Test statistic	0: disagree ⇔ 4:fully agree
a.) It was fun to answer this survey.						
Gamified	21	3.29	3.00	0.56	U=54	
Conventional	19	2.32	3.00	1.01	p=0.002	
Total	40	2.83	3.00	0.96		
b.) I would recommend this survey to other people.						
Gamified	21	3.38	3.00	0.67	U=55	
Conventional	19	2.42	2.00	0.96	p=0.001	
Total	40	2.93	3.00	0.94		

(3). Several respondents also commented that they would have liked to continue playing after finishing the survey (4), which is an interesting complaint insofar as it highlights the heightened level of engagement and joy compared to a conventional survey.

Comments regarding the conventional survey were less varied: Respondents found the survey easy to use (5) and easy to answer (3), while complaining about vague or ambigious questions (4) and boredom (3).

Table 7. Qualitative results. The table shows answers given to open-ended questions in the post-test questionnaire, structured into coded categories.

Gamified: Positive comments	N	Negative comments	N
Novelty	9	Duration	4
Graphics & animation	5	Inability to continue playing after survey	4
Playfulness	4	Controls	4
Rich in variety	4	Responsiveness of individual games	3
Customizable avatar	4	Complexity	1
Fun	3	Sound	1
Interactivity	2	Amount of textual instructions	1
Ease of use	1		
Anonymity	1		
Suitability for children	1		
No comment	0	No comment	6

Conventional: Positive comments	N	Negative comments	N
Ease of use	5	Vague or ambigious questions	4
Clarity and ease of answering	3	Boring	3
Broad theme	1	Missing progress indicator	1
No comment	12	No comment	12

8 Discussion

Results indicate that gamification successfully increased the users' perceived fun, the average time spent, as well as their willingness to use and recommend the survey, without introducing a strong bias in the survey results, albeit with a lower overall response rate. This improvement in user experience is in line with related studies on gamified online surveys [6, 9].

Quantitative results show that respondents found the gamified survey more fun and spent significantly more time. While an increase in time spent is in itself not necessarily a sign of heightened engagement, the fact that participants also found the gamified survey more fun and voluntarily spent more time suggests that the increased duration is the result of an improved user experience. This may prove beneficial for marketing surveys that aim at exposing users to a certain brand in a pleasant way. Furthermore, the respondents' higher willingness to use and recommend the gamified survey can be useful for viral marketing.

Given these positive outcomes, the lower overall *response rate* for the gamified survey was surprising and warrants further examination. Results provide two possible explanations. Firstly, higher engagement and positive feedback from those who did finish the gamified survey suggest that the gamified design may have caused polarized reactions among participants, turning those away who did not approve of the chosen design. This issue requires further examination in future work. Secondly, respondents stated they felt less confident using the gamified survey; the lack of familiarity with the novel design may have caused them to cancel. Future long-term studies are needed to investigate effects of novelty in gamified online surveys.

Overall, the gamified design barely influenced *answers given* by participants, as there was no significant effect of survey style for 57 of 61 questions. However, there was a significant difference for answers given in the javelin-throwing micro game that requires further examination. One interpretation is that the gamified survey successfully reduced negative respondent behavior and thus reduced bias – but the gamification may also have introduced new bias. To clarify the issue, we suggest that future work should develop automated measures of speeding, straightlining, random responding, lack of attention, conflicting and empty answers, compare [9, 17, 23], and use these measures to quantify negative respondent behavior in gamified and conventional surveys.

The *qualitative comments* given by respondents reaffirm our initial expectations and motivation: That conventional surveys are often perceived as somewhat dull and boring, and that gamification is a suitable approach to make surveys more fun and engaging. Some of the comments validate specific design decisions made during the gamification process, such as the use of a customizable avatar to represent survey respondents, as well as implementation details such as graphics and animation. However, other comments demonstrate the difficulty of getting every design detail right, as demonstrated by scattered complaints about controls or the responsiveness of individual micro-games. Additionally, the abrupt ending of the gamified survey drew a large number of complaints of users who would have liked to continue playing. While an abrupt ending might be appropriate for a conventional survey, it seems inappropriate for more playful, open-ended experiences, as in our gamified survey. Comparing the comments between the gamified versus conventional survey, it becomes apparent that the gamified survey garnered both a larger number as well as more varied comments. One possible explanation for this difference in quantity and quality of respondent's comments would be the novelty of the gamified survey raising awareness of specific survey design aspects, compared to the dull familiarity of a conventional survey spurring less reflection and comment.

9 Conclusion and Future Work

Gamification is a promising way of improving user experience and increasing engagement in online surveys. This work extends prior research by making the following two contributions.

Firstly, this work documents the successful application of a recently proposed design process for gamifying online surveys and describes the resulting design. The process was applied in a case study where two designers gamified a survey about sports and leisure activities amongst teenagers and young adults. The designers reported qualitative results supporting the practical usefulness and applicability of the process. This indicates that other survey gamification projects can benefit from the same or a similar process.

As a second contribution, the resulting gamified design was evaluated in a remote online study with 60 participants. The gamified survey achieved better psychological outcomes (respondents found the gamified survey more fun, they were more inclined to use and recommend the gamified design, and provided more, and more positive, qualitative feedback) and better behavioral outcomes (regarding engagement: respondents voluntarily spent more time in the gamified survey). These positive results are, however, accompanied by critical issues including a lower response rate in the gamified survey and possibly biased answers in one specific survey area. These issues warrant further empirical investigation.

Our future work in this area will continue in the following direction. Since a survey's gamification takes a lot of effort, we intend to examine ways of increasing benefits (e.g., by identifying best practices and by seeking ways of improving behavioral outcomes) and of reducing the required efforts (e.g., by creating re-usable design patterns and component libraries) in order to improve the return on investment of future survey gamifications.

References

1. Aparicio, A.F., Vela, F.L.G., Sánchez, J.L.G., Montes, J.L.I.: Analysis and application of gamification. In: Proceedings of the 13th International Conference on Interacción Persona-Ordenador, INTERACCION 2012, pp. 17:1–17:2. ACM, New York (2012)
2. Bargas-Avila, J., Brenzikofer, O., Roth, S., Tuch, A., Orsini, S., Opwis, K.: Simple but crucial user interfaces in the world wide web: introducing 20 guidelines for usable web form design. In: Matrai, R. (ed.) User Interfaces. InTech, Croatia (2010)
3. Becker, P.: Formulare als "Fließband" der Verwaltung? Zur Rationalisierung und Standardisierung von Kommunikationsbeziehungen. In: Collin, P., Lutterbeck, K.G. (eds.) Eine intelligente Maschine? Handlungsorientierungen moderner Verwaltung (19/20. Jh.). Nomos, Baden-Baden (2009)
4. Brooke, J.: SUS-a quick and dirty usability scale. Usability Eval. Ind. **189**, 194 (1996)
5. Buxton, B.: Sketching User Experiences: Getting the Design Right and the Right Design. Morgan Kaufmann Pub, Burlington (2007)
6. Cechanowicz, J., Gutwin, C., Brownell, B., Goodfellow, L.: Effects of gamification on participation and data quality in a real-world market research domain. In: Gamification 2013:

Proceedings of the First International Conference on Gameful Design, Research, and Applications, pp. 66–73. ACM, Stratford (2013)

7. Deterding, S., Dixon, D., Khaled, R., Nacke, L.: From game design elements to gamefulness: defining "gamification". In: Proceedings of the 15th International Academic MindTrek Conference: Envisioning Future Media Environments, MindTrek 2011, pp. 9–15. ACM, New York (2011)

8. Dolnicar, S., Grün, B., Yanamandram, V.: Dynamic, interactive survey questions can increase survey data quality. J. Travel Tourism Mark. **30**(7), 690–699 (2013)

9. Guin, T.D.-L., Baker, R., Mechling, J., Ruyle, E.: Myths and realities of respondent engagement in online surveys. Int. J. Mark. Res. **54**(5), 1–21 (2012)

10. Eisermann, F.: Zu den Anfängen des gedruckten Formulars (Gastbeitrag). In: Formulare. Von der Wiege bis zu Bahre…: Formulare im Corporate Design. Stiebner Verlag GmbH (2007)

11. Hamari, J., Koivisto, J., Sarsa, H.: Does gamification work? – a literature review of empirical studies on gamification. In: Proceedings of the 47th Hawaii International Conference on System Sciences (2014)

12. Harms, J.: Research goals for evolving the 'form' user interface metaphor towards more interactivity. In: Holzinger, A., Ziefle, M., Hitz, M., Debevc, M. (eds.) SouthCHI 2013. LNCS, vol. 7946, pp. 819–822. Springer, Heidelberg (2013)

13. Harms, J., Wimmer, C., Kappel, K., Grechenig, T.: Gamification of online surveys: conceptual foundations and a design process based on the MDA framework. In: Proceedings of the 8th Nordic Conference on Human-Computer Interaction: Fun, Fast, Foundational. pp. 565–568. ACM (2014)

14. Hsu, S.H., Chang, J.W., Lee, C.C.: Designing attractive gamification features for collaborative storytelling websites. Cyberpsychol. Behav. Soc. Netw. **16**(6), 428–435 (2013)

15. Hunicke, R., LeBlanc, M., Zubek, R.: MDA: a formal approach to game design and game research. In: Proceedings of the AAAI-04 Workshop on Challenges in Game AI, pp. 1–5 (2004)

16. Jarrett, C., Gaffney, G.: Forms that Work: Designing Web Forms for Usability. Morgan Kaufmann, Burlington (2008)

17. Kaminska, O., McCutcheon, A.L., Billiet, J.: Satisficing among reluctant respondents in a cross-national context. Public Opin. Q. **74**(5), 956–984 (2010)

18. Korhonen, H., Montola, M., Arrasvuori, J.: Understanding playful user experience through digital games. In: International Conference on Designing Pleasurable Products and Interfaces, pp. 274–285 (2009)

19. Lewis, C., Wardrip-Fruin, N., Whitehead, J.: Motivational game design patterns of 'ville games. In: Proceedings of the International Conference on the Foundations of Digital Games, FDG 2012, pp. 172–179. ACM, New York (2012)

20. Mavletova, A.: Web surveys among children and adolescents: Is there a gamification effect? Social Science Computer Review (2014)

21. Mayhew, D.J.: The Usability Engineering Lifecycle: A Practitioner's Handbook for User Interface Design. Morgan Kaufmann, Burlington (1999)

22. Nielsen, J.: Usability Engineering. Morgan Kaufmann, Burlington (1993)

23. Puleston, J.: Online research–game on!: a look at how gaming techniques can transform your online research. In: Proceedings of the 6th ASC (Association for Survey Computing) International Conference Shifting the Boundaries of Research, pp. 20–50 (2011)

24. Reeves, B., Read, J.L.: Total Engagement: Using Games and Virtual Worlds to Change the Way People Work and Businesses Compete. Harvard Business Review Press, Watertown (2009)

236   J. Harms et al.

25. Sweetser, P., Wyeth, P.: Gameflow: a model for evaluating player enjoyment in games. Comput. Entertainment **3**(3), 1–24 (2005)
26. Werbach, K., Hunter, D.: For the Win: How Game Thinking Can Revolutionize Your Business. Wharton Digital Press, Philadelphia (2012)
27. Wlaschits, B.: Gamifizierung von elektronischen Umfrageformularen: Design und Experten-Evaluierung. Master's thesis, supervised by Thomas Grechenig and Johannes Harms (2014)
28. Wroblewski, L.: Web Form Design. Filling the Blanks. Louis Rosenfeld, Brooklyn (2008)

Mind the Gap! Comparing Retrospective and Concurrent Ratings of Emotion in User Experience Evaluation

Anders Bruun[(⊠)] and Simon Ahm

Department of Computer Science, Aalborg University, Aalborg, Denmark
bruun@cs.aau.dk, x.simon@gmail.com

Abstract. User experience (UX) is typically measured retrospectively through subjective questionnaire ratings, yet we know little of how well these retrospective ratings reflect concurrent experiences of an entire event. UX entails a broad range of dimensions of which human emotion is considered to be crucial. This paper presents an empirical study of the discrepancy between concurrent and retrospective ratings of emotions. We induced two experimental conditions of varying pleasantness. Findings show the existence of a significant discrepancy between retrospective and concurrent ratings of emotions. In the most unpleasant condition we found retrospective ratings to be significantly overestimated compared to concurrent ratings. In the most pleasant condition we found retrospective ratings to correlate with the highest and final peaks of emotional arousal. This indicates that we cannot always rely on typical retrospective UX assessments to reflect concurrent experiences. Consequently, we discuss alternative methods of assessing UX, which have considerable implications for practice.

Keywords: User experience · Emotion · Memory-experience gap · Peak-end rule

1 Introduction

Emotion is considered a fundamental factor in determining user experience (UX) of interactive technologies [1, 2]. Forlizzi and Battarbee state: *"Emotion affects how we plan to interact with products, how we actually interact with products, and the perceptions and outcomes that surround those interactions"* [3].

The most frequent method to assess users' emotional states is subjective ratings where users fill in questionnaires such as the Self-Assessment Manikin (SAM) [1]. However, studies outside a UX context have shown a critical caveat in subjective ratings of emotions. Recently, Scherer argued that emotions are fleeting, i.e. they are short term, intensive peaks of experiences which may be difficult to recall at a later point in time [4]. This is supported by empirical observations of a discrepancy between overall retrospective ratings of an episode and the concurrent experiences during an episode [5]. This discrepancy is denoted the *memory-experience gap* and is verified by several studies in e.g. pain research. Notably, Redelmeier and Kahneman found retrospective ratings of pain to correlate with the highest and final intensities of pain

© IFIP International Federation for Information Processing 2015
J. Abascal et al. (Eds.): INTERACT 2015, Part I, LNCS 9296, pp. 237–254, 2015.
DOI: 10.1007/978-3-319-22701-6_17

experienced [6]. Those observations led to what is now known as the *peak-end rule*. Thus, studies outside a UX context suggest that retrospective ratings of emotions will likely not reflect concurrent experiences of an entire event.

This caveat also seems to be recognized within UX where studies measure emotions concurrently. SAM is typically filled in after completing each task in an interaction sequence, see e.g. [7–9]. However, very few studies within UX have been engaged with more detailed measurements of emotions [1]. Kujala and Miron-Shatz present initial insights on the presence of the memory-experience gap in a Human-Computer Interaction (HCI) context. The emphasis in [10] is on longitudinal assessments of emotions based on the Day Reconstruction Method (DRM). In DRM participants evaluate the set of experienced emotions by the ending of each day [10]. Given the fleeting nature of emotions, DRM suffers from a recall bias and is therefore well suited for longitudinal studies with an interest in estimating overall averages of emotional reactions [11]. It is, however, ill-suited for measuring emotions at specific time points, e.g. at specific points in an interaction sequence [12].

Consequently, we still know very little of the existence and extent of the memory-experience gap in an HCI context. Arguably, such a context is less extreme than Redelmeier and Kahnemans studies of pain.

This study contributes to the HCI community by showing that we cannot *always* rely on retrospective UX assessments to reflect concurrent experiences, even when they are assessed immediately after interacting with a system. This is critical as UX is primarily assessed retrospectively [1]. We discuss alternative approaches to assess UX, which provide more accurate accounts of concurrent experiences than, e.g. the Day-Reconstruction Method.

In the remainder of this paper we provide a theoretical overview introducing potential caveats of retrospective ratings as well as a set of hypotheses. We then present related work, experimental method and results. Finally, we discuss and conclude on our findings.

2 Theoretical Background

In this section we introduce theoretical stances dealing with the relationship between concurrent and retrospective ratings. We start by giving an account for the concept of emotions and how emotions can be measured. We then go through the theoretical background concerning the discrepancy between retrospective and concurrent ratings, i.e. the memory-experience gap and the peak-end rule. We conclude this section by presenting our hypotheses.

2.1 What Are Emotions?

In the classical theory of James-Lange from 1884, emotions are defined as the result of physical changes in autonomic and motor functions. Input from our senses creates a range of responses in our body, and our awareness of these changes is what constitutes an emotion [13]. Individual emotions are distinguished based on their unique bodily expression. The theory states that when an event happens in our environment (e.g. being attacked by a predator) we instantaneously get physiological reactions like muscle tension, increased sweat production etc. We interpret these unique combinations of physiological reactions as being a specific emotion [13].

Defining emotions is a topic of much debate and we do not attempt to provide an exhaustive walkthrough of the literature. However, basic assumptions behind the classical James-Lange theory are still supported after more than a century. Recently, Scherer described emotions as a mobilization and synchronization of five organismic subsystems as a response to a cognitive evaluation of external or internal stimulus events that are *"relevant to major concerns of the organism"* [4]. When an event happens that is of major concern, the event is evaluated through a comparison to innate prototypical responses, and a response (the emotion) is elicited through activation of the organismic subsystems [4]. It is important to note that this "evaluation" is not a time consuming and conscious process as is often associated with the term in HCI. Instead it relies on fast subconscious processes [4].

2.2 Measuring Emotions

Throughout research, two approaches have been used to elicit emotions: Subjective ratings and objective measurements.

Subjective Ratings. Subjective ratings of emotions are typically collected through questionnaires. These typically consist of standardized labels or pictograms representing emotions [4]. Most studies of emotions in UX are based on such subjective rating methods where the Self-Assessment Manikin (SAM) is the most widely applied technique [1]. SAM enables participants to assess their emotional states through graphical scales, cf. [14]. It is based on a dimensional model of emotion denoted PAD (Pleasure, Arousal, Dominance) that uses three dimensions to represent emotions:

- *Pleasure:* Indicates how pleasant an emotion is, i.e. its valence. It spans from negative to positive.
- *Arousal:* Indicates how intense an emotion. It spans from relaxed to excited.
- *Dominance:* Indicates how dominating an emotion is. It spans from low to high dominance.

Participants are asked to rate emotions based on these three dimensions. Thus, they assess the level of Pleasure, Arousal and Dominance, each on a 1-9 point Likert scale.

Objective Measurements. Psychological research has recently seen an advancement in applying physiological sensors to objectively assess emotions [4]. In doing this, participants do not rate emotions subjectively, but instead a sensor (or sometimes several) is attached on the body. A range of different sensors exist, each of which typically measures one dimension of the PAD model. As an example, Galvanic Skin Response (GSR) sensors have in particular been shown to correlate with arousal [15]. In essence, a GSR sensor reacts on changes in skin resistance (measured in mOhms) through varying levels of perspiration in sweat glands. A GSR sensor enables real-time measurements of arousal. Other sensors are Electromyography (EMG), Heart Rate

(HR) and Electroencephalography (EEG). For a more comprehensive overview of measurement sensors and their relative performances, see [16]. As noted by Scherer, it is currently not feasible to collect all types of measurements [4], and studies have also shown varying reliability of these in measuring emotions. However, GSR sensors are consistently correlated with arousal across different studies, this also includes the few studies of UX applying physiological sensors, see e.g. [17].

2.3 Memory-Experience Gap

According to Scherer, the purpose of emotions is to deal successfully with an event that is of direct concern to the organism, and the activation of physiological subsystems require lots of resources to do so [4]. Due to the level of intensity, which cannot be endured over a longer period of time, emotions are short-lived mental states. Furthermore, Scherer argues that emotions are always tied to a specific event [4]. So, if emotions are short-lived and tied to a specific event, what is then measured in retrospective ratings based on recall?

Several studies in psychology have demonstrated a discrepancy between the average of actual experienced emotions and the overall retrospective assessment of an experience [5]. Thus, there is a gap between concurrent emotions and the recollection of these after a given episode. This discrepancy is denoted the *memory-experience gap* [5]. Studies in psychology have shown that the memory-experience gap leads to overestimated retrospective ratings, i.e. that retrospective ratings reflect a higher emotional intensity compared to concurrent experiences [5].

It is argued that the memory-experience gap is present for both positive and negative stimuli [5]. However, a study conducted by Baumeister et al. indicated a larger memory-experience gap when experiencing negative stimuli compared to positive stimuli [18].

Transferring the above into an HCI context we could expect that 1) Retrospective ratings of UX are overestimated compared to concurrent ratings and 2) Retrospective ratings would especially be overestimated in episodes of negative experiences.

2.4 Peak-End Rule

The discrepancy between actual experienced emotions and retrospective ratings has also been studied in detail by Redelmeier and Kahneman. They made a striking discovery during their studies of how pain is experienced and recalled. They found that test subjects preferred a longer duration of pain over a shorter duration of pain [19]. In the condition with the longest duration, pleasantness was increased towards the end, although still being painful. In the other condition, the level of pain was kept constant, but the duration was shorter. Test subjects primarily recalled the experience of pain towards the end of the experimental conditions, i.e. they preferred the longest duration of pain with increasing pleasantness. In a later study it was found that test subjects retrospectively rated the entire experience based on the highest intensity of pain (the peak) and the pain experienced towards the end [6]. This has since become known as the *peak-end rule*.

In relation to HCI, it is plausible that retrospective ratings of emotions correlate with the highest peak of emotional intensity and the intensity measured towards the end of an interaction sequence.

2.5 Hypotheses

We have formulated the following hypotheses based on the above considerations of the memory-experience gap and peak-end rule:

H1   Retrospective ratings of emotions are higher than concurrent ratings of emotions.
H2   The memory-experience gap is larger for episodes of negative emotions than for episodes of positive emotions.
H3   Concurrent and retrospective ratings of emotions correlate following the peak-end rule.

3 Related Work

A recent literature survey confirmed that most UX assessments are conducted retro-spectively [1]. Based on the theoretical background above, this led us to question the extent to which retrospective ratings reflect an entire experience. As mentioned in the introduction of this paper, emotion is a key dimension in determining UX of interactive technologies. Therefore we emphasize this particular dimension and now provide an overview of previous UX studies of emotions.

Most studies of emotions in UX research are based on questionnaires, typically SAM, through which users provide subjective ratings [1]. From related work we primarily know that SAM ratings are affected by instrumental factors such as the level of usability, but we know very little of the discrepancy between concurrent and retro-spective ratings. Hassenzahl and Ullrich studied the effect of giving users predefined tasks versus open ended interaction [7]. SAM ratings were measured concurrently three times during interaction followed by a retrospective AttrakDiff rating. Primary findings showed that the type of tasks affected SAM and AttrakDiff ratings. As a byproduct of the entire experiment Hassenzahl and Ullrich found a correlation between concurrent SAM ratings and retrospective AttrakDiff ratings [7]. Mahlke and Thüring conducted a similar study in which they examined the effect of high/low usability and high/low aesthetics on emotional responses [9]. SAM ratings were taken three times during interaction followed by retrospective ratings of usability and visual aesthetics. Findings showed that concurrent SAM ratings differed significantly between high/low usability and to a minor extent between high/low aesthetics. In another study, Mahlke and Thüring studied the feasibility of measuring emotional states through a multiple components approach [20]. This was done by combining objective psychophysiolog-ical measurements and subjective ratings. In that study SAM was filled in after each task while collecting real-time physiological data. Findings also showed that concurrent SAM ratings differed significantly between the high/low usability versions of the system. Other UX studies of emotions apply SAM to extract emotions during use and with similar findings, see e.g. [2, 8].

Hassenzahl and Sandweg studied how concurrent experiences of mental effort related to retrospective assessments of perceived usability [21]. Participants were given seven tasks and the SMEQ questionnaire (for measuring mental effort) was filled in after each task. Findings showed significant correlation between the last rating of mental effort and the perceived level of usability. In their longitudinal study, Kujala and Miron-Shatz [10] applied the Day-Reconstruction Method (DRM) to elicit participant emotions of mobile phone usage. Participants were asked to report specific episodes at the end of each day and their related emotions over a five day period. On the sixth day, participants were asked to provide a summary rating of emotions. Findings showed that participants significantly overestimated the experienced positive emotion in their summary assessments.

From the above we know that ratings of emotions are affected by instrumental factors such as providing tasks or not, the level of usability and partly by the non-instrumental factor of aesthetics. It also seems that the potential memory-experience gap is recognized as participants are typically asked to provide SAM ratings concurrently rather than retrospectively. Yet, we know little of the potential discrepancy between retrospective and concurrent ratings. Notably, a single study showed that concurrent SAM ratings correlated with retrospective AttrakDiff ratings, cf. [7]. Findings from that study could indicate that the memory-experience gap is insignificant in an HCI context. Yet, this finding is contradicted in [10, 21]. Nevertheless, across all studies, we found that concurrent ratings were measured relatively few times, in some cases as few as three times per participant. Arguably, this may not reflect the whole set of short-lived emotions experienced during an entire interaction sequence. This critique has also been raised against DRM [12, 22], on which the study by Kujala and Miron-Shatz [10] is based. Thus, there is a critical need for more detailed studies of emotions in UX research, as is also stressed by Bargas-Avila and Hornbæk [1]. In the following section we describe how we studied the memory-experience gap and peak-end rule in an HCI context.

4 Method

The objective of our study was to examine the memory-experience gap and peak-end rule in subjective ratings of emotions. Therefore we needed participants to elicit several emotional states reflecting concurrent experiences, i.e. during interaction, as well as retrospective ratings. However, collecting concurrent ratings during interaction is not as straightforward as collecting retrospective ratings. Following related work, concurrent ratings can be collected after each task, this, on the other hand provides relatively few measurement points. We collected concurrent ratings based on the Cued-Recall Debrief (CRD) method as outlined below. This enabled a higher density in measurements while avoiding interruptions during interaction.

4.1   Cued-Recall Debrief

CRD is a method based on situated recall. The method was developed by Omodei et al. [23] to elicit emotional experiences while not interfering with participant behavior in naturalistic settings. The overall approach is to provide cues that enhance participants' ability to recall specific emotions after an event has occurred. This is done by re-immersing participants through replay of several snippets of video recordings, each showing a specific episode of an entire event [23]. To foster re-immersion, it is crucial that video recordings resemble a first-person point of view. In Omodei et al.'s study, video recordings were collected by head-mounted cameras positioned on helmets of firefighters [23]. CRD essentially builds on retrospection but several studies have validated the approach. In [23] it was found that CRD leads to considerably more detailed responses compared to retrospective ratings based on free recall [23]. Furthermore, Bentley et al. [24] found correlation between CRD ratings and real-time physiological measurements in an HCI context. Also, a more recent study published in the renowned TOCHI outlet applied CRD to elicit participants' emotions, cf. [25]. Thus, although CRD builds on retrospection, it has been shown to provide valid approximations of concurrent emotions. Furthermore, it does so without causing interference during interaction.

In practice CRD is conducted by selecting a set of video clips, each showing a specific episode of an entire event. Participants view one clip at a time for which they provide subjective ratings of emotions. This is then done for all video clips. In our case we selected video clips on the basis of real-time GSR data, i.e. we selected video clips surrounding peaks of arousal. Figure 1 illustrates this principle.

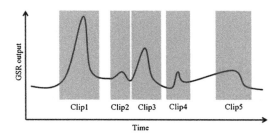

Fig. 1. Selecting video clips based on GSR peaks.

4.2   Experimental Conditions

Related work show that instrumental goals such as tasks/no-tasks and usability problems affect user emotions when interacting with technology, see e.g. [7, 9]. We were interested in studying the memory-experience gap and, based on previous studies, it was relevant to consider how this was affected by the level of usability.

We developed two versions of a software system (described in Sect. 4.4 "System"). The two versions differed as we in one version seeded a set of five usability problems into the user interface. The other version was developed to the best of our abilities. Thus we had two experimental conditions: (1) *Seeded* and (2) *Unseeded*.

4.3   Participants

A total of 20 university students participated (between subjects) with 10 in each condition. Ages ranged from 19-28 years (mean 22.85). In each condition we had 2 females and 8 males. All subjects were kept unaware of the actual premise of the experiment and none of them had previous experience in using the system.

4.4   System

We designed a system to create and edit posters which was specifically developed for the experiment. The functionality included simple text editing and styling for creating bold, italic and underlined text as well as a color picker. It was also possible to include images etc. The unseeded and seeded versions were built on the exact same platform and source code. Versions differed in the user interface only. In the seeded version we introduced the following five usability problems: (1) Standard buttons for text styling (known from typical word processors) were replaced with checkboxes, (2) no font preview was available, (3) font required for the task was unavailable, (4) color picker was based on text rather than actual colors and (5) inserting an image led to an incomprehensible error message.

4.5   Task

The task was to use the system to create an exact copy of a poster pictured on paper. Participants were informed that there was a 10 min time limit to solve the task. They could click a submit button at any time, if they felt the task had been solved before time the limit.

4.6   Setting and Data Collection

The experiment was conducted in a university classroom. The user was placed in front of a laptop with an external mouse, and given the paper describing their task as well as the poster to replicate. The student was alone in the room for the full duration.

We collected concurrent and retrospective ratings of emotions via the SAM questionnaire. All sessions were recorded using screen capture software. This was a picture-in-picture setup primarily showing participants' interaction with the system and a small picture of the face, which was recorded with a high-resolution webcam. The desktop recording resembled a first-person point of view, which is in line with the Cued-Recall Debrief (CRD) method outlined previously. Finally, a Galvanic Skin Response (GSR) sensor was placed in the palm of participants' non-primary hand. This was done in order to determine specific points in the interaction sequence where participants experienced peaks of arousal. That information was used to select video clips on which to base concurrent SAM ratings.

4.7 Procedure

This section describes the CRD procedure applied in the study:

1. *Introduction and Setup:* Participants were directed to the room where they received a piece of paper with the task and the poster to replicate using either the unseeded or seeded version of the software. The task was also described verbally by a researcher (one of the authors). The GSR sensor was then attached to their palm. Participants were not informed of the purpose of the study and the GSR sensor until they completed the experiment. After the user had confirmed that they understood the task at hand, the researcher started the software and left the room.
2. *Creating a Baseline:* Since the GSR sensor reacts on arousal we needed to identify the relaxed state of each participant, i.e. peaks of arousal are observed relative to a baseline. This baseline was measured by showing a blank screen for the first 4 min, while playing a relaxing piece of music. The song "Weightless" by Marconi Union was chosen. Previous studies have shown that this particular piece of music has a relaxing effect on participants [26].
3. *Completing the Task:* After the 4 min of relaxation, the user interface for the system appeared and the task could begin. Participants were allowed 10 min for this. All recordings were automatically stopped after 10 min and the researcher returned to the room.
4. *Retrospective SAM Rating:* Participants were asked to subjectively rate the overall emotion immediately after the 10 min.
5. *Concurrent SAM Ratings (*via *CRD):* The video of the users face was superimposed over the lower right corner of the screencast. The GSR data was visualized as a graph and superimposed over the timeline of the video player. This allowed for the researcher to visually identify peaks in the GSR data, and fast-forward to about 5 s before these points. The user was then shown this part of the video (screencast as well as their own facial expressions), and asked to freely describe their own thoughts as to what they may have reacted to, and how. If the user was able to deduce a reaction, the peak was noted along with their description of the event. They were also asked to rate the emotional state at the time using SAM.

5 Results

In this section we provide several measures, which will form the basis of our later discussion on whether to verify or falsify our three hypotheses.

5.1 Differences Between Retrospective and Concurrent Ratings

According to theory, the memory-experience gap should cause retrospective ratings to be overestimated in comparison to concurrent ratings (hypothesis H1). Below we compare the mean of concurrent and retrospective ratings in both experimental conditions, see Table 1.

Table 1. Mean SAM ratings distributed by condition and PAD dimensions. *= significant, n = No. of participants.

		Seeded (n = 10)	Unseeded (n = 10)
SAM - Pleasure	Retrospective	6 (1.6)*	5.6 (1.8)
	Concurrent	4.6 (1.8)*	5.7 (1.5)
	Overall mean	4.7 (1.8)	5.6 (1.5)
SAM - Arousal	Retrospective	4.6 (2.2)	3.3 (2.1)
	Concurrent	4.4 (1.8)	3.9 (2.1)
	Overall mean	4.5 (1.8)	3.8 (2.1)
SAM - Dominance	Retrospective	5.3 (2.1)*	5.5 (1.5)
	Concurrent	4.4 (1.7)*	5.4 (1.3)
	Overall mean	4.5 (1.8)	5.4 (1.4)

In the seeded condition the mean retrospective rating of Pleasure is 6 (SD = 1.6) while the mean concurrent rating is lower with 4.6 (SD = 1.8). A repeated measures Wilks' Lambda (.05 level) shows a significant difference as indicated by the * in Table 1 (Wilks' Lambda = .41, F = 11.3, p = .01). In the unseeded condition the retrospective rating of Pleasure is 5.6 (SD = 1.8), which is similar to the concurrent rating of 5.7 (1.5). This difference is not significant (Wilks' Lambda = .99, F = .008, p = .93).

In terms of Arousal, the seeded condition reveals a retrospective rating of 4.6 (SD = 2.2) and a similar concurrent rating of 4.4 (SD = 1.8). A Wilks' Lambda test reveals no significant difference (Wilks' Lambda = .99, F = .1, p = .77). In case of the unseeded condition we also observe comparable retrospective and concurrent ratings of Arousal with 3.3 (SD = 2.1) and 3.9 (SD = 2.1) respectively. No significant difference is found (Wilks' Lambda = .95, F = .44, p = .52).

Considering Dominance, we see that the retrospective rating in the seeded condition is 5.3 (SD = 2.1), which is higher than the concurrent rating of 4.4 (SD = 1.7). This difference is significant (Wilks' Lambda = .41, F = 11.3, p = .01). In case of the unseeded condition we see no significant difference between retrospective and concurrent ratings (Wilks' Lambda = .99, F = .008, p = .93).

In sum we found that all retrospective ratings in the seeded condition were higher than concurrent ratings. This was significant in terms of Pleasure and Dominance. In the unseeded condition we did not find significant differences between any of the retrospective and concurrent ratings. This indicates a larger memory-experience gap in the seeded condition.

5.2 Differences Between Conditions

Hypothesis H2 suggests that the memory-experience gap is larger for episodes of unpleasant emotions than for episodes of pleasant emotions. Below we seek to verify that the seeded condition leads to a worse experience compared to the unseeded condition. We do this by using two metrics: (1) Differences in ratings between conditions and (2) The level of emotional fluctuation experienced.

Differences in Ratings. In Table 1, the overall mean refers to the mean of retrospective and concurrent ratings combined. In the seeded condition the overall mean rating of Pleasure is 4.7 (SD = 1.8) while the overall mean is 5.6 (SD = 1.5) in the unseeded condition. An independent samples t-test at the .05 level reveals a significant difference between conditions (t = −4.1, df = 226, p = 0.0).

Participants rated the experienced level of Arousal to be higher in the seeded condition (overall mean = 4.5, SD = 1.8) than in the unseeded condition (overall mean = 3.8, SD = 2.1). An independent samples t-test indicates that this difference is significant (t = −2.4, df = 226, p = 0.02).

Finally, participants expressed a lower level of Dominance in the seeded condition (overall mean = 4.5, SD = 1.8) compared to the unseeded condition (overall mean = 5.4, SD = 1.4). This difference is also significant (t = −4.1, df = 226, p = 0.0).

In sum, emotions experienced in the seeded condition were more negative with a higher level of arousal compared to the unseeded condition. Emotions in the seeded condition were rated as less dominant than emotions in the unseeded condition.

Differences in Emotional Fluctuation. As mentioned in Sect. 2.2 "Measuring Emotions", GSR data shows fluctuations in arousal. Intuitively, the system version that was seeded with usability problems will lead to a higher level of fluctuation in arousal as the stress level increases when encountering a usability problem. Figure 2 shows two typical examples of GSR data obtained, one example from the unseeded condition (top) and one from the seeded (bottom). By visual inspection, the above examples appear to fluctuate differently with the seeded example having more peaks and a higher level of variance in arousal.

The number of peaks in the GSR graphs was counted on the basis of visual inspection by one of the researchers. Participants in the unseeded condition experienced a mean of 17.22 (SD = 3.8) peaks while participants in the seeded condition experienced 22.2 (SD = 5.6) peaks. An independent samples t-test revealed a significant difference between conditions (t = −2.21, df = 15, p = 0.042).

We also calculated the mean variance for both conditions. The mean variance for Pleasure is 1.58 (SD = 1.48) in the unseeded condition and 2.93 (SD = 0.77) in the seeded. An independent samples t-test reveals a significant difference in this respect (t = 2.31, df = 15, p = 0.034). The mean variance for Arousal is 1.63 (SD = 2.17) in the unseeded condition and 3.63 (SD = 1.1) in the seeded, which is also significant (t = 2.44, df = 15, p = 0.03). A similar pattern is observed in case of Dominance where the mean variance is 1.04 (SD = 1.24) and 3.02 (SD = 1.55) in the unseeded and seeded conditions respectively (t = 2.92, df = 15, p = 0.01).

Thus, we found significant differences in emotional fluctuations between the two conditions. In the seeded condition participants experienced significantly more peaks and the variance in ratings within this group was 2–3 times larger compared to the unseeded condition. Based on the overall mean ratings in Table 1 and differences in fluctuation of arousal, we find that the seeded condition leads to a worse experience compared to the unseeded condition.

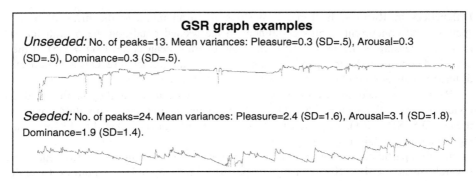

Fig. 2. Two examples of GSR graphs. Top: Unseeded condition, Bottom: Seeded condition

5.3   Peak-End Rule Correlations

In the following we consider the extent to which retrospective and concurrent ratings correlate with the peak-end rule (hypothesis H3). Table 2 shows the correlation table between retrospective, concurrent, highest peak and last peak ratings for the unseeded condition. This is based on computation of Pearson r correlation coefficients.

In the unseeded condition there is significant correlation between retrospective ratings of Pleasure and ratings of Pleasure made towards the end of the interaction sequence, i.e. at the last peak ($r = 0.642$, $n = 10$, $p = 0.045$). Additionally, we find significant correlation between retrospective ratings of Arousal and ratings of Dominance made at the highest peak ($r = 0.776$, $n = 10$, $p = 0.008$) and the last peak ($r = 0.9$, $n = 10$, $p = 0.000$). Finally, in the unseeded condition we see a significant correlation between retrospective and concurrent ratings of Arousal ($r = 0.774$, $n = 10$, $p = 0.009$).

In the seeded condition (not shown in Table 2) we observe significant correlation between retrospective and concurrent ratings of Pleasure ($r = 0.677$, $n = 10$, $p = 0.031$). Retrospective ratings of Pleasure also correlate with concurrent ratings of Dominance ($r = .688$, $n = 10$, $p = 0.028$).

Thus, in the unseeded condition we primarily see significant correlations between retrospective ratings and ratings given at the highest and last GSR peaks. This differs from the pattern in the seeded condition where we see correlations between retrospective and concurrent ratings.

6   Discussion

In the following we discuss our findings in relation to the three hypotheses and related work. Based on our findings we discuss how to apply retrospective ratings of user experience, which has high relevance for practice.

Table 2. Correlation table of retrospective and concurrent SAM ratings. Unseeded condition.
* = significant, n = No. of participants.

*= significant, n=No. of participants.

	SAM correlations *(Unseeded condition, n=10)*		**Pleasure** **(retrospective)**	**Arousal** **(retrospective)**	**Dominance** **(retrospective)**
Concurrent	**Pleasure**	Pearson	-.072	-.062	-.366
		Sig. (2-tailed)	.844	.866	.299
	Arousal	Pearson	-.249	.774*	.273
		Sig. (2-tailed)	.489	.009	.445
	Dominance	Pearson	-.359	.542	-.054
		Sig. (2-tailed)	.309	.106	.882
Highest Peak	**Pleasure**	Pearson	-.184	.593	-.187
		Sig. (2-tailed)	.611	.071	.604
	Arousal	Pearson	-.035	.268	.447
		Sig. (2-tailed)	.924	.454	.196
	Dominance	Pearson	-.103	.776*	.367
		Sig. (2-tailed)	.777	.008	.296
Last Peak	**Pleasure**	Pearson	.642*	.109	.555
		Sig. (2-tailed)	.045	.765	.096
	Arousal	Pearson	-.597	.545	-.161
		Sig. (2-tailed)	.068	.103	.657
	Dominance	Pearson	-.395	.900*	.058
		Sig. (2-tailed)	.259	.000	.873

6.1   Significant Memory-Experience Gap

Based on the theoretical background of emotions we formulated hypothesis H1: *"Retrospective ratings of emotions are higher than concurrent ratings of emotions"*. Looking across the two experimental conditions shows that we are able to verify hypothesis H1 in the case where the system had a relatively higher number of usability problems. Findings from our study revealed that retrospective ratings were higher than the mean of concurrent ratings. This finding applied to the system version that was seeded with five usability problems. This overestimation was especially apparent in terms of Pleasure and Dominance. In relation to this we also formulated hypothesis H2: *"The memory-experience gap is larger for episodes of unpleasant emotions than for episodes of pleasant emotions"*. We were also able to verify hypothesis H2. The seeded system version led to a relatively higher number of usability problems, which in turn caused users to experience more negative emotions compared to the unseeded version. We also found that the seeded condition led to a significantly higher level of fluctuation in arousal. The more negative ratings and higher level of arousal indicates that the seeded condition was experienced as the most unpleasant episode. As mentioned previously, we found that retrospective ratings of Pleasure and Dominance were significantly higher than concurrent ratings in this condition. Thus, there was a larger memory-experience gap in the seeded condition compared to the unseeded condition.

6.2   Retrospective Ratings Follow the Peak-End Rule

In terms of the peak-end rule we formulated hypothesis H3: *"Concurrent and retrospective ratings of emotion correlate following the peak-end rule"*. We validate H3 in the case where the system had a relatively lower number of usability problems. In the unseeded condition we identified significant correlations between retrospective ratings of Pleasure and ratings of Pleasure located at the last GSR peak measured. Furthermore, we found correlations between retrospective ratings of Arousal and ratings of Dominance at the highest and last peaks. This suggests that H3 could be verified. However, findings from the seeded condition show the opposite where e.g. retrospective ratings of Pleasure correlated with concurrent ratings. Thus, in the unseeded condition we primarily identified significant correlations following the peak-end rule while this was not the case in the seeded condition.

The difference between conditions can be explained by the level of emotional fluctuation experienced. In the seeded condition we observed significantly more peaks of arousal via the GSR sensor compared to the unseeded condition. The variance in SAM ratings in the seeded condition was also significantly higher on all Pleasure-Arousal-Dominance (PAD) dimensions. Consequently the highest and final peaks are interwoven with several other peaks of similar intensities. Arguably, such fluctuation obscures the peak and end experiences in the seeded condition. As a result, the most intensive and end experiences are evened out, hereby leading to correlations between retrospective and concurrent ratings. The opposite is the case for the unseeded condition where the lower level of fluctuation does not obscure peak and end experiences. Although the peak-end rule was not verified in the seeded condition we still stress that retrospective ratings were significantly overestimated in this case.

This is in line with the findings of Hassenzahl and Sandweg who found that the last concurrent rating of mental workload correlated with the retrospective rating of perceived usability [21]. Similarly, Kujala and Miron-Shatz found weekly ratings of emotions to be overestimated compared to the day-to-day ratings [10]. Thus, it seems that the peak-end rule is present for multiple UX dimensions. In contrast, Hassenzahl and Ullrich found correlations between concurrent SAM ratings and retrospective measurements of AttrakDiff [7]. This is in line with findings from our seeded condition, but contradictory of findings from the unseeded condition. As discussed above, peak-end correlation seems dependent on the level of fluctuation. Maybe the system applied in [7] led to a comparable variance in fluctuations as experienced by participants in our seeded condition. This brings us to discuss the main caveat of retrospective UX assessments.

6.3   Bottom Line: Mind the Gap in Current Practices

We found that participants significantly overestimated the level of Pleasure and Dominance in retrospective ratings, at least in the system with a relatively higher number of usability problems. Conversely, retrospective ratings were not overestimated in the system version with fewer problems. These findings show that retrospective assessments of emotions do not always reflect the concurrent experience and that this memory-experience gap depends on the level of usability.

Although we in this study emphasized the UX dimension specifically related to emotions, we believe that our findings also apply to more general assessments of UX. This is also supported by the findings in [21], which are based on measurements of mental workload. From related work we know that overall measurements of UX, e.g. AttrakDiff ratings, depend on emotions [7], and Forlizzi and Battarbee state: *"Emotion affects how we plan to interact with products, how we actually interact with products, and the perceptions and outcomes that surround those interactions"* [3].

Given that such overall ratings are primarily collected in retrospect [1], we now pose the following question: *How do we know when we can rely on retrospective UX assessments to provide accurate accounts of concurrent experiences?* In the unseeded condition we found no significant difference between retrospective and concurrent ratings. So an answer could be to apply current retrospective methods on a system with relatively few usability problems. This could e.g. be towards the end of a development process going into a phase of summative assessments. However, it is not trivial to decide when there are "few enough problems" such that retrospective ratings accurately reflect concurrent experiences.

Arguably, the current practice of applying questionnaires in retrospective UX assessment is defensible due to its simplicity. Others have justified this approach through the relative ease and low cost of use [20]. From previous studies we also know that people do not remember all their experiences, which lead to the memory-experience gap. Yet, retrospective evaluations are very important for people's later decisions, e.g. they buy products based on their memory of them [27]. Therefore, UX is not *only* about what happens concurrently but also how people remember their experience of products. However, the above discussion leads us to say that retrospective ratings (of emotions and overall UX alike) should be handled with care. Findings from this study have considerable implications for HCI practice and research, which we discuss in the following.

6.4   Moving Forward

As an alternative to retrospective questionnaire assessments we encourage practitioners to apply multiple methods in order to reflect concurrent experiences. In line with Scherer [4], we suggest to apply an approach relying on a combination of subjective ratings and objective psychophysiological measures. This is furthermore supported by Avila-Hornbæk who state that: *"In emotional psychology there are many established and validated ways of measuring emotions that provide more detailed and richer data… Future research might benefit from these to do in depth studies of affective sates in UX"* [1].

Psychophysiological measurements are widely used within emotional psychology and we believe that these can contribute in providing the detailed measurements suggested in [1]. As an example of an alternative method, our application of Cued-Recall Debrief (CRD) comprises a combination of subjective ratings (SAM) and objective psychophysiological measurements (GSR). We applied CRD by measuring real-time GSR data during interaction. We re-immersed users by showing video clips of their interaction at selected points, clips that were selected based on GSR peaks of arousal. Although ratings in CRD are retrospective in nature, CRD has been validated for measuring concurrent experiences [23–25]. Validity is also indicated through the verification of our initial hypotheses, i.e. we are able to explain our findings.

Our study also points to a more general implication for HCI research, which is in line with Karapanos et al. [28]. In [28] a highly relevant discussion of the reliability and veridicality of UX studies is brought up. Reliability in a temporal sense denotes the consistency with which people recollect emotional experiences while veridicality deals with the consistency between actual and recalled experiences. Within our study (and in using CRD in general) the aim is to increase veridicality. This is much more difficult to control in naturalistic and/or longitudinal studies such as the study by Kujala and Miron-Shatz [10]. In those types of studies, the emphasis should be on reliability. We believe the HCI community needs further discussions and studies to understand veridicality and reliability in UX assessments and the challenges herein. Being aware of the different challenges inherent in different methods will assist HCI researchers in selecting appropriate methods in relation to study aims.

6.5   Limitations

A clear limitation in our study is the sample size where we had 10 participants in each condition. Also, our study is based on a system for creating posters. A larger sample and more diverse systems would increase generalizability. However, as stated in the introduction, the contribution of this study is to show that we cannot *always* rely on retrospective UX ratings to reflect concurrent experiences. We found e.g. that retrospective ratings of pleasure were significantly higher than concurrent ratings, even on this relatively small dataset. This is sufficient to prove the point of the paper, but further studies are needed to make claims about the extent of the memory-experience gap across a wider population and other systems.

Another limitation is the artificial laboratory setting. Several UX studies are appearing based on "in the wild" methods as this reflects naturalistic system usage, e.g. the study by Kujala and Miron-Shatz [10]. However, the strength of the lab is its ability to control for outside interferences such as being startled by a ringing phone, being interrupted by a colleague, emails etc. Factors like these can impact physiological measurements. It was crucial for us that all measurements reflected the usage of the system and not the presence of confounding factors from the context.

A third limitation is the retrospective nature of the Cued-Recall Debrief method. We applied this to enable approximations of concurrent experiences as participants were asked to rate their emotions immediately after the interaction took place. Although not truly concurrent, we argue that the recall bias is considerably reduced compared to the Day-Reconstruction Method applied in other studies, e.g. [10].

7 Conclusions

The empirical study presented in this paper contributes to the HCI community by showing the existence of a memory-experience gap between concurrent and retrospective ratings of emotions. Findings showed that in the most unpleasant event, participants significantly overestimated retrospective ratings. In a more pleasant episode we found that retrospective ratings correlated with the highest and final emotional peaks of an entire experience. Thus, retrospective ratings do not always reflect concurrent experiences. This shows a potential caveat in current practices, which primarily are based on retrospection.

Alternatively we encourage practitioners to apply multiple methods to get insights on concurrent experiences. In the future it is critical to conduct further studies with larger sample sizes and different systems. This should be done in order to determine the extent of the memory-experience gap across other populations and systems.

References

1. Bargas-Avila, J.A., Hornbæk, K.: Old wine in new bottles or novel challenges. In: Procedings CHI, p. 2689. ACM, New York (2011)
2. Thüring, M., Mahlke, S.: Usability, aesthetics and emotions in human–technology interaction. Int. J. Psychol. **42**, 253–264 (2007)
3. Forlizzi, J., Battarbee, K.: Understanding experience in interactive systems. In: Proceedings DIS, pp. 261–268. ACM, New York (2004)
4. Scherer, K.R.: What are emotions? and how can they be measured? Soc. Sci. Inf. **44**, 695–729 (2005)
5. Miron-Shatz, T., Stone, A., Kahneman, D.: Memories of yesterday's emotions: does the valence of experience affect the memory-experience gap? Emotion **9**, 885–891 (2009)
6. Redelmeier, D.A., Kahneman, D.: Patients' memories of painful medical treatments: real-time and retrospective evaluations of two minimally invasive procedures. Pain **66**, 3–8 (1996)
7. Hassenzahl, M., Ullrich, D.: To do or not to do: differences in user experience and retrospective judgments depending on the presence or absence of instrumental goals. Interact. Comput. **19**, 429–437 (2007)
8. Mahlke, S., Lindgaard, G.: Emotional experiences and quality perceptions of interactive products. In: Jacko, J. (ed.) Human-Computer Interaction. Interaction Design and Usability SE – 19, pp. 164–173. Springer, Heidelberg (2007)
9. Mahlke, S., Thüring, M.: Studying antecedents of emotional experiences in interactive contexts. In: Proceedings CHI, pp. 915–918. ACM, New York (2007)
10. Kujala, S., Miron-Shatz, T.: Emotions, experiences and usability in real-life mobile phone use. In: Proceedings CHI, pp. 1061–1070. ACM, New York (2013)
11. Diener, E., Tay, L.: Review of the day reconstruction method (DRM). Soc. Indic. Res. **116**, 255–267 (2014)
12. Bylsma, L.M., Taylor-Clift, A., Rottenberg, J.: Emotional reactivity to daily events in major and minor depression. J. Abnorm. Psychol. **120**, 155–167 (2011)
13. James, W.: What is an emotion? Mind os-IX **9**, 188–205 (1884)

14. Lang, P.J.: Behavioral treatment and bio-behavioral assessment: computer applications. In: Sidowski, J.B., Johnson, J.H., Williams, T.H. (eds.) Technology in Mental Health Care Delivery Systems, pp. 119–137. Ablex, Norwood (1980)

15. Lang, P.J.: The emotion probe: Studies of motivation and attention. Am. Psychol. **50**, 372–385 (1995)

16. Andreassi, J.L.: Psychophysiology: Human Behavior and Physiological Response. Lawrence Erlbaum, Mahwah (2000)

17. Ward, R., Marsden, P.: Physiological responses to different WEB page designs. Int. J. Human-Computer Stud. **59**, 199–212 (2003)

18. Baumeister, R.F., Bratslavsky, E., Finkenauer, C., Vohs, K.D.: Bad is stronger than good. Rev. Gen. Psychol. **5**, 323–370 (2001)

19. Kahneman, D., Fredrickson, B.L., Schreiber, C.A., Redelmeier, D.A.: When more pain is preferred to less: adding a better end. Psychol. Sci. **4**, 401–405 (1993)

20. Mahlke, S., Minge, M., Thüring, M.: Measuring multiple components of emotions in interactive contexts. In: CHI EA, pp. 1061–1066. ACM, New York (2006)

21. Hassenzahl, M., Sandweg, N.: From mental effort to perceived usability: transforming experiences into summary assessments. In: CHI EA, pp. 1283–1286. ACM, New York (2004)

22. Dockray, S., Grant, N., Stone, A.A., Kahneman, D., Wardle, J., Steptoe, A.: A comparison of affect ratings obtained with ecological momentary assessment and the day reconstruction method. Soc. Indic. Res. **99**, 269–283 (2010)

23. Omodei, M.M., McLennan, J.: Studying complex decision making in natural settings: using a head-mounted video camera to study competitive orienteering. Percept. Mot. Skills **79**, 1411–1425 (1994)

24. Bentley, T., Johnston, L., von Baggo, K.: Evaluation using cued-recall debrief to elicit information about a user's affective experiences. In: Proceedings OzCHI, pp. 1–10. CHISIG Australia, Narrabundah (2005)

25. Gao, Y., Bianchi-Berthouze, N., Meng, H.: What does touch tell us about emotions in touchscreen-based gameplay? ACM Trans. Comput. Interact. **19**, 31:1–31:30 (2012)

26. Belford, Z., Neher, C., Pernsteiner, T., Stoffregen, J., Tariq, Z.: Music and physical performance: the effects of different music genres on physical performance as measured by the heart rate, electrodermal arousal, and maximum grip strength. In: JASS. 3 (2013)

27. Karapanos, E., Zimmerman, J., Forlizzi, J., Martens, J.-B.: Measuring the dynamics of remembered experience over time. Interact. Comput. **22**, 328–335 (2010)

28. Karapanos, E., Martens, J.-B., Hassenzahl, M.: On the retrospective assessment of users' experiences over time: memory or actuality? In: CHI EA, pp. 4075–4080. ACM, New York (2010)

Recognizing Emotions in Human Computer Interaction: Studying Stress Using Skin Conductance

Alexandros Liapis[1(✉)], Christos Katsanos[1,2], Dimitris Sotiropoulos[1], Michalis Xenos[1], and Nikos Karousos[1,2]

[1] School of Science and Technology, Hellenic Open University,
Parodos Aristotelous 18, 26 335 Patra, Greece
{aliapis,ckatsanos,dgs,xenos,karousos}@eap.gr
[2] Technological Educational Institute of Western Greece,
M. Alexandrou 1, 26 334 Patra, Greece

Abstract. This paper reports an experiment for stress recognition in human-computer interaction. Thirty-one healthy participants performed five stressful HCI tasks and their skin conductance signals were monitored. The selected tasks were most frequently listed as stressful by 15 typical computer users who were involved in pre-experiment interviews asking them to identify stressful cases of computer interaction. The collected skin conductance signals were analyzed using seven popular machine learning classifiers. The best stress recognition accuracy was achieved by the cubic support vector machine classifier both per task (on average 90.8 %) and for all tasks (Mean = 98.8 %, SD = 0.6 %). This very high accuracy demonstrates the potentials of using physiological signals for stress recognition in the context of typical HCI tasks. In addition, the results allow us to move on a first integration of the specific stress recognition mechanism in PhysiOBS, a previously-proposed software tool that supports researchers and practitioners in user emotional experience evaluation.

Keywords: Users emotional experience evaluation · Physiological data · Skin response conductance · Physiological signal analysis

1 Introduction

Evaluation of user emotional experience (UEX) is a topic with growing significance. Beyond traditional evaluation methods (e.g. questionnaires, interviews and observation etc.), the study of physiological signals has become increasingly important in human-computer interaction. Associations among emotions and physiological signals [1] have established innovative evaluation approaches [2, 3] which offer to researchers and practitioners new insights in UEX evaluation.

So far, existing methods for emotions induction rely on intense stimuli such as scary movie clips, favorite songs, major hardware/software failures, image datasets and gaming [4–7]. Such stimuli induce intense reactions, which may be depicted in facial expressions, body postures and physiological signals, and recognized by existing

© IFIP International Federation for Information Processing 2015
J. Abascal et al. (Eds.): INTERACT 2015, Part I, LNCS 9296, pp. 255–262, 2015.
DOI: 10.1007/978-3-319-22701-6_18

associated methods. However, recognition of emotions from subtle events [8], which are typically expected in most HCI tasks, remains challenging.

According to Lazar [9] the goal of an evaluation process is to identify system flaws which are often associated with negative emotions such as "stress" [10]. Thus, recognizing stress in typical HCI tasks is particularly important, and it is the object of this paper. Research shows [11, 12] that skin conductance, also known as Galvanic Skin Response (GSR) or Electro Dermal Response (EDR), is a reliable indicator of stress. Skin conductance is the physiological signal that was also selected and measured in this paper. To this end, 31 healthy participants performed five carefully selected stressful HCI tasks, and their skin conductance signals were monitored and analyzed using seven popular machine learning classifiers.

The purpose of this paper is twofold. First, it presents results from the first set of experiments aiming to create a publicly available dataset of physiological signals, which can be used for stress recognition in HCI. To the best of our knowledge, this is the first experimental approach in stress recognition that exclusively uses typical HCI tasks as stimuli. Second, the paper aims to investigate the performance of various algorithms in identifying stress from skin conductance. The obtained recognition results are going to guide the implementation of an automated stress identification algorithm in PhysiOBS, our previously-proposed software tool [13] aiming to support researchers and practitioners in UEX evaluation.

The rest of the paper is structured as follows. Section 2 presents the research-based approach followed for stimuli selection. In Sect. 3 the experimental general set-up and protocol, are described. Section 4 presents the used preprocessing techniques and recognition algorithms, along with their results. The paper concludes with a discussion of the implications of the presented work and directions for future research.

2   Research-Based Stimuli Selection (Stressors)

Eliciting emotions in a laboratory setting is challenging and needs a careful design. The appropriate stimuli should be plausible enough in order to induce a heightened level of physiological arousal. In addition, any stimuli selection method should be void of any bias introduced by researchers.

Stimuli selection process involved fifteen typical computer users (University employees, students, and colleagues) which participated in a face to face interview. Interviewees were asked to identify stressful tasks during interaction with a computer. All interviews were conducted in two phases by the same person. Each phase lasted from 15 to 20 min. First, demographics (e.g. age, skills in computer usage, profession, education etc.) were recorded. Next, participants were asked to describe at least five scenarios which stress them while interacting with a computer. Interviewees were neither informed nor participated in the stress monitoring experiment.

All the scenarios provided by the interviewees did not require any special experience or knowledge. Participants' answers were grouped and a frequency table was created. Answers analysis did not reveal any significant differences due to demographic parameters. Next, we pilot-tested the scenarios, starting from the most frequently mentioned. Although interaction scenarios related to financial transactions and viruses were commonly reported by interviewees, such tasks were not selected due to their requirements for being plausible enough to induce stress. For instance, a wrong charge in facilitators' credit card was not found to be stressful. In the end, the five most commonly reported scenarios were selected, excluding the aforementioned cases.

2.1   Scenario 1: Missing a File

Participants were asked to visit the website of the internal evaluation unit of the Hellenic Open University (http://meae.eap.gr). This website was selected because it was expected to be unfamiliar to participants. Next, they were asked to find and download a specific file from the website, save it to a network folder and log in a google email account to send the file at an email address. When participants shifted their attention from the network folder in order to create the email, experiment facilitators remotely deleted participants' downloaded file.

2.2   Scenario 2: Hardware Problems

Participants were asked to visit the website of a research group in our University (http://quality.eap.gr). Again, this specific website was selected in order to avoid any previous familiarity. Next, they were asked to find and copy the consortium list from one of the team's projects and then paste it in a text file. During the task, their mouse cursor speed was set in slow speed. The speed was remotely set using a custom-made software tool that had been previously installed in the testing computer.

2.3   Scenario 3: Slow Network Speed

In this scenario, participants visited a web portal that is popular in our country (http://www.in.gr) and were asked to find information about a specific movie. During the task, network connection was simulated at 56 Kbps in order to make interaction slower than the usual. The speed was manipulated through the Fiddler (http://www.telerik.com/) software.

2.4   Scenario 4: Web Advertisements (Popups)

Participants were asked to visit a popular online booking website (http://www.booking.com) in order to make a reservation for a predefined destination. Appropriately designed popup windows appeared in users' screen every 15 s while they were trying to complete the scenario. The popup window was relevant to both the website's content and visual appearance. The whole process was controlled remotely through a custom-made software tool that had been previously installed in the testing computer.

2.5   Scenario 5: Finding Information in Websites

Participants were instructed to visit the website of our University's library (http://lib. eap.gr) in order to find the authors of a specific book. In this scenario, no external action was applied. This website was chosen for this scenario because there was a plethora of complaints about its information architecture, which had been collected in a previous usability evaluation study.

3   Experiment

3.1   Setting and Equipment

The experiment was performed in our fully-equipped usability lab (http://quality.eap.gr). Skin conductance was recorded at 5 Hz using a Mindfield eSense sensor. Stimuli scenarios were presented randomly for each participant through the Tobii eye-tracker environment (i.e. Tobii Studio) which was also used to monitor participants' eye activity in real time (e.g. to delete participants' downloaded file in the first scenario while they were not looking at it). All scenarios were designed to require minimum typing effort in order to minimize participants' hand movements that may affect skin conductance measurements. Finally, external parameters such as testing room temperature were controlled in order to avoid noise in skin conductance recordings.

3.2   Process and Protocol

Thirty-one healthy participants (18 female), aged between 21 and 38 (Mean = 30.8, SD = 4.7) were recruited. The experiment lasted for six days.

First, participants were informed that they would interact with some websites in order to perform some tasks. Subsequently, they completed an appropriate consent form along with a questionnaire about demographic information. Next, the skin conductance sensor was placed on participants' non dominant hand in the middle and ring finger respectively. A short time of approximately five minutes was given to participants in order to familiarize with the sensor, while signals' transmission quality was checked. In addition, participants' body posture in front of the eye-tracker was also checked. During this short time, the facilitators were available to answer in any of the participants' question.

The experimental process started with a 1:30 min baseline recording [6, 14], during which participants were asked to relax. Subsequently, the five stress-inducing scenarios were presented to participants in a random order. At the end of each scenario, participants were asked to provide subjective ratings of their emotional experience both on a valence-arousal [15] and on a 1–7 rating scale; however analysis of these ratings is beyond the scope of this paper. Each session lasted approximately 40 min per participant including short breaks between scenarios. Skin conductance was not monitored during the breaks or the self-assessment process.

4   Analysis and Results

In this section, signal preprocessing and classification results are presented. All in all, 182 skin conductance signals were recorded from 31 participants involved in five interaction tasks and a baseline condition. In four cases (once in task 1, once in task 2 and twice in task 4), signal was not recorded successfully due to sensor malfunction or experimenter error.

The collected signals were smoothed using hanning window function. Smoothing window width for each signal was determined by experimentally adjusting the following root mean square error function:

$$\text{Error} = \text{SQRT}(\sum (X_i - X_{i-1})^2)/(2 * N)), \tag{1}$$

where Σ calculates the sum of first difference between sample values (X_i and X_{i-1}), and N is the total number of samples. This error value represents the signal's variability due to sampling rate frequency.

The smoothing process involved the following steps. First, an initial error value was calculated for each raw signal. Next, raw signals were smoothed using a five-point width hanning window, and the error value was recalculated. While the error correction value between raw and smoothed signal was below 76 %, the width of the hanning window was increased by five points and the raw signal was smoothed again. Some signals had to reach a window width value of 100 points or more to meet this error correction percentage, resulting in substantial signal degeneration. Thus, they were set to be auto-excluded from the feature extraction.

The smoothing window step was selected to be equal to the sampling rate (5 Hz). The error correction threshold was set to 76 % based on two criteria: (a) keep signals' crucial information, such as lows and peaks; Fig. 1 illustrates an instance of 200 samples (40 s) from a participant's skin conductance signal for 76 % and 90 % error correction, and (b) use the signals' majority in feature extraction; Fig. 2 illustrates that as the correction error gets higher than 76 %, significantly more signals are auto-excluded from the feature extraction process due to signal degeneration.

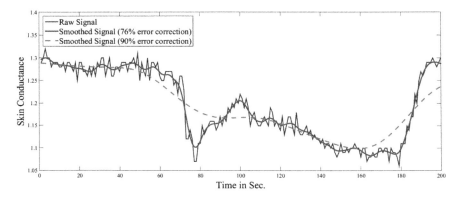

Fig. 1. Raw vs smoothed signal for 76 % and 90 % error correction.

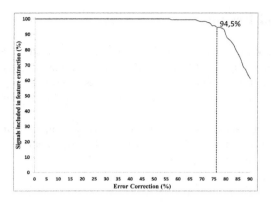

Fig. 2. Signals included in feature selection as a function of error correction.

After signal smoothing, 21 statistical features (e.g., mean, median, min, max, standard deviation, minRatio and maxRatio) [11] were extracted. The same statistics were extracted from the first and the second differences of signal.

The extracted features were used to train seven classifiers offered in the MATLAB R2015a Statistics and Machine Learning Toolbox v10.0: (a) Linear Discriminant Analysis (LDA), (b) Quadratic Discriminant Analysis (QDA), (c) Simple Decision Tree (S-Tree), (d) Linear Support Vector Machine (L-SVM), (e) Quadratic Support Vector Machine (Q-SVM), (f) Cubic Support Vector Machine (C-SVM), and (g) k-Nearest Neighbors (k-NN).

Table 1 presents classifier accuracies (%) for stress identification per task and for all tasks, using 100-times 10-fold cross validation for all tasks. C-SVM classifier had the best stress recognition accuracy both per task (Min = 89.6 %, Max = 91.6 %) and for all tasks (Mean = 98.8 %, SD = 0.6 %).

Table 1. Classifier accuracies (%) for stress identification per task and for all tasks. The last column presents results for the aggregated dataset of tasks, and not the cross-task mean.

	Task 1 Mean ± SD	Task 2 Mean ± SD	Task 3 Mean ± SD	Task 4 Mean ± SD	Task 5 Mean ± SD	All tasks Mean ± SD
LDA	90.5 ± 2.4	88.8 ± 2.7	88.8 ± 2.7	87.7 ± 2.0	88.0 ± 2.2	95.5 ± 0.4
QDA	83.8 ± 3.1	85.5 ± 3.6	83.0 ± 3.3	82.7 ± 3.9	82.5 ± 3.6	95.6 ± 1.0
S-Tree	88.6 ± 0.9	86.8 ± 1.7	87.9 ± 1.4	88.6 ± 1.5	86.4 ± 3.2	95.3 ± 0.9
L-SVM	88.4 ± 1.9	88.4 ± 1.3	88.2 ± 1.9	88.0 ± 1.2	89.3 ± 2.2	96.9 ± 0.4
Q-SVM	84.8 ± 3.0	84.5 ± 2.1	83.8 ± 3.6	83.6 ± 1.8	84.8 ± 1.5	95.2 ± 0.9
C-SVM	91.6 ± 2.2	89.6 ± 2.2	91.1 ± 1.7	90.5 ± 2.2	91.1 ± 2.2	98.8 ± 0.6
k-NN	90.2 ± 2.3	88.9 ± 2.5	88.9 ± 2.8	87.9 ± 3.1	89.8 ± 1.5	97.3 ± 0.8

5   Conclusion and Future Work

In this work a physiological dataset from 31 healthy participants involved in five stressful tasks and a baseline relax condition was created. A research-based approach was followed to produce the selected tasks. First, 15 typical computer users, not involved in the stress monitoring experiment, were asked to describe at least five stressful interaction experiences. Then, the ones mentioned most frequently were pilot-tested and five were selected for the stress monitoring experiment. The collected skin conductance signals were first preprocessed and then used to train seven popular machine learning classifiers to automatically detect the two emotional classes (stress – no stress) from skin conductance.

Results showed high identification accuracies, with the best being the one achieved by the Cubic Support Vector Machine (C-SVM) both per task (on average 90.8 %) and for all tasks (Mean = 98.8 %, SD = 0.6 %). This is an important finding that demonstrates the potentials of physiological signals in the study of subtle interaction events, which are typically expected in most HCI tasks, such as finding information in complex websites or being distracted by web advertisements while making an online booking. Our work makes a contribution towards this direction. In addition, the results allow us to move on a first integration of the specific automated stress recognition mechanism in PhysiOBS, our previously-proposed software tool [13] that supports continuous and multiple emotional states analysis by user experience practitioners.

One of our future aims is to replicate our findings by performing additional experiments following the same methodology using more peripheral physiological signals, such as blood volume pressure, respiration and temperature. In this way, we will also extend our emotionally-labeled dataset for stress recognition in typical HCI tasks, which we plan to make freely-available to the research community. Future work also includes investigating the effect (if any) of users' characteristics, such as gender, age and computer self-efficacy, on the stress recognition accuracy.

Acknowledgments. This paper has been co-financed by the European Union (European Social Fund – ESF) and Greek National funds through the Operational Program "Education and Lifelong Learning" of the National Strategic Reference Framework (NSRF) (Funding Program: "Hellenic Open University").

References

1. Chanel, G., Rebetez, C., Bétrancourt, M., Pun, T.: Emotion assessment from physiological signals for adaptation of game difficulty. IEEE Trans. Syst. Man Cybern. Part Syst. Hum. **41**, 1052–1063 (2011)
2. Vermeeren, A.P.O.S., Law, E.L.-C., Roto, V., Obrist, M., Hoonhout, J., Väänänen-Vainio-Mattila, K.: User experience evaluation methods: current state and development needs. In: Proceedings of the 6th Nordic Conference on Human-Computer Interaction: Extending Boundaries. pp. 521–530. ACM, New York (2010)
3. Ganglbauer, E., Schrammel, J., Tscheligi, M.: Possibilities of psychophysiological methods for measuring emotional aspects in mobile contexts. In: Proceedings of Mobile HCI (2009)

4. Mandryk, R.L., Atkins, M.S., Inkpen, K.M.: A continuous and objective evaluation of emotional experience with interactive play environments. In: Proceedings of the SIGCHI Conference on Human Factors in Computing Systems. pp. 1027–1036. ACM, New York (2006)

5. Scheirer, J., Fernandez, R., Klein, J., Picard, R.W.: Frustrating the user on purpose a step toward building an affective computer. Interact. Comput. **14**(2), 93–118 (2001)

6. Koelstra, S., Muhl, C., Soleymani, M., Lee, J.-S., Yazdani, A., Ebrahimi, T., Pun, T., Nijholt, A., Patras, I.: DEAP: a database for emotion analysis; using physiological signals. IEEE Trans. Affect. Comput. **3**, 18–31 (2012)

7. Lin, T., Omata, M., Hu, W., Imamiya, A.: Do physiological data relate to traditional usability indexes? In: Proceedings of the 17th Australia Conference on Computer-Human Interaction: Citizens Online: Considerations for Today and the Future. pp. 1–10. Computer-Human Interaction Special Interest Group (CHISIG) of Australia, Narrabundah, Australia (2005)

8. Ward, R.D., Marsden, P.H.: Affective computing: problems, reactions and intentions. Interact. Comput. **16**, 707–713 (2004)

9. Lazar, D.J., Feng, D.J.H., Hochheiser, D.H.: Research Methods in Human-Computer Interaction. Wiley, New York (2010)

10. Hernandez, J., Paredes, P., Roseway, A., Czerwinski, M.: Under pressure: sensing stress of computer users. In: Proceedings of the SIGCHI Conference on Human Factors in Computing Systems, pp. 51–60. ACM, New York (2014)

11. Healey, J.A., Picard, R.W.: Detecting stress during real-world driving tasks using physiological sensors. IEEE Trans. Intell. Transp. Syst. **6**, 156–166 (2005)

12. Lunn, D., Harper, S.: Using Galvanic skin response measures to identify areas of frustration for older web 2.0 users. In: Proceedings of the 2010 International Cross Disciplinary Conference on Web Accessibility (W4A), pp. 34:1–34:10. ACM, New York (2010)

13. Liapis, A., Karousos, N., Katsanos, C., Xenos, M.: Evaluating user's emotional experience in HCI: the physiOBS approach. In: Kurosu, M. (ed.) HCI 2014, Part II. LNCS, vol. 8511, pp. 758–767. Springer, Heidelberg (2014)

14. Drachen, A., Nacke, L.E., Yannakakis, G., Pedersen, A.L.: Correlation between heart rate, electrodermal activity and player experience in first-person shooter games. In: Proceedings of the 5th ACM SIGGRAPH Symposium on Video Games, pp. 49–54. ACM, New York (2010)

15. Russell, J.A., Weiss, A., Mendelsohn, G.A.: Affect Grid: a single-item scale of pleasure and arousal. J. Pers. Soc. Psychol. **57**, 493–502 (1989)

LEGO Pictorial Scales for Assessing Affective Response

Mohammad Obaid[1]([⊠]), Andreas Dünser[2], Elena Moltchanova[3],
Danielle Cummings[4], Johannes Wagner[5], and Christoph Bartneck[6]

[1] t2i Lab, Chalmers University of Technology, Gothenburg, Sweden
mobaid@chalmers.se
[2] Digital Productivity, CSIRO, Hobart, Australia
[3] Mathematics and Statistics Department, University of Canterbury,
Christchurch, New Zealand
[4] Texas A&M University, College Station, TX, USA
[5] Human Centered Multimedia, Augsburg University, Augsburg, Germany
[6] Human Interface Technology Lab New Zealand, University of Canterbury,
Christchurch, New Zealand

Abstract. This article presents the design and evaluation of novel types of pictorial scales for assessing emotional response based on LEGO Minifigures. We describe the creation of two pictorial scales (LEGO Face Scale and Stylized LEGO Face Scale) through the use of a semi-automatic process. We report on the results of two evaluation studies conducted to assess the validity of the proposed pictorial scales. The first study evaluated the rating of emotions expressed by other humans; the second focused on rating one's own emotional state when looking at expressive stimuli. We investigate the validity of the two pictorial scales by comparing them to ratings given on a conventional Likert Scale. Results show that assessing expressive faces using the proposed pictorial scales can differ from using a Likert scale; however, when rating one's own emotional state there is no difference. Finally, we assembled a physical version of the LEGO Face scale and discuss future work.

Keywords: LEGO minifigures · Evaluation · Pictorial · Emotion · Scale

1 Introduction

Emotional assessment plays an important role in the field of Human-Computer Interaction (HCI) as it provides an understanding of the user's state and emotional response when interacting with physical/digital content of a system. Capturing a person's emotion can be an important factor informing the design or re-design of a product. One of the main methods used to assess emotions is by having a person express them verbally or through a questionnaire. These questionnaires mostly ask the person to pick from a written set of emotions and rate the intensity, for example, on a Likert scale. This is supposed to capture the person's current emotional state, an experienced emotion, the emotion of somebody else or the emotional loading of an object. Text-based (non-pictorial) scales require a person to read through a list of possible

© IFIP International Federation for Information Processing 2015
J. Abascal et al. (Eds.): INTERACT 2015, Part I, LNCS 9296, pp. 263–280, 2015.
DOI: 10.1007/978-3-319-22701-6_19

answers and pick the most appropriate alternative. This can be accompanied by rating the intensity of their choice on a numeric scale. This approach has certain disadvantages such as being cognitively demanding and time consuming. Pictorial scales have been found to be less demanding with respect to time and effort. For example, Desmet et al. [11] found in their studies that "subjects are embarrassed when asked to express their emotional response to products. There are several explanations to this phenomenon. First, emotions are difficult to verbalize, especially the type of subtle, low intensity emotions by products". In addition, they explain it further stating that "asking users to describe their emotional responses will require cognitive involvement, which may influence the response itself". Moreover, Vastenburg et al. [30] state, "Most instruments [...] rely on verbal self-reports. Such questionnaires and scales tend to be rather demanding for the respondent."

Emotions can be difficult to verbalize, especially low intensity emotions [10]. Asking people to describe their emotions requires cognitive involvement, which could impact the response itself. Therefore, tools that let people express or rate emotions without the use of text can be preferable. The most efficient way of representing emotions is with facial features, because facial cues are used as a main means for judging emotional information even though other sources can provide more accurate information [13, 22]. Thus, in this paper we propose a novel assessment tool based on LEGO Minifigures. The goal and main contribution of this paper is the design and evaluation of a new tool that allows us to rate emotions by having people choose a specific Minifigure which best represents their emotional state or reaction.

There are nearly 6000 different Minifigures that have been designed since 1975 [3]. Whereas most other pictorial scales are based on a small number of drawings created for a specific purpose (e.g. [6, 7, 10, 31]), our approach was to select suitable facial expressions representing specific emotions from a large pool of LEGO Minifigures. This overcomes a potential shortcoming of other pictorial scales for which the initial sample of available drawings for each scale point might have been too small.

In the following sections we discuss related work, the development of the pictorial LEGO Minifigure scales, report on two experimental studies that evaluate the validity of the scales, and discuss our findings and future work.

2 Related Work

Although the perception of emotions has been shown to be culturally independent [14], words can be sensitive to different interpretations across cultures or across individuals from the same culture. Scales relying on written language rather than pictorial content require users to understand the language in order to be able to interpret the words correctly. Many verbal scales are not suitable for use across different cultures.

In addition, verbal scales may pose problems for people who cannot properly read written text, including young children. Age related lower levels of verbal fluency or development related variations in understanding of test questions are important factors to take into account [6]. Also, using numeric rating scales requires respondents to map their own concept of an emotion and its intensity onto another dimension. A judgment has to be made by translating the personal experience to numerical values, or a certain distance between end points represented by the scale.

Visser et al. [31] studied which graphic symbols are perceived by four-year olds as best representation of the four emotions: happy, sad, afraid, and angry. For each emotion they selected four graphic depictions of faces taken from three different sources (Picture Communication Symbols, PICSYMS, and Makaton; see [31]). They found that happy, the only positive or pleasurable emotion was a relatively easy emotion to represent in a graphic symbol. Angry was more difficult and sad and afraid were found to produce the least consensus in terms of expected responses to these emotions. This suggests that recognizing some emotions (e.g. angry) may be more susceptible to individual influences, as there is a variety of ways that different people in different contexts can express them.

The Self Assessment Manikin (SAM) is a pictorial scale to measure people's ratings of three independent affective dimensions: pleasure, arousal, and dominance. It is used to measure a person's affective reaction to situations, stimuli or events [7]. The SAM was developed to overcome issues with verbal scales such as the required time, effort and the need to be able to interpret written language. The scale uses graphical depictions of a Manikin to be rated by people. Each of the three dimensions has five figures representing different intensity levels. The pleasure dimension ranges from a happy to an unhappy figure. The arousal dimension ranges from an excited figure to a relaxed figure, whereas the dominance dimension changes the size of the manikin. Bradley et al. [7] compared people's responses to a set of 21 pictures (International Affective Picture system) using SAM (3 ratings) or a Semantic Differential (requiring 18 ratings). They found that correlations between the two rating methods were high for pleasure and arousal. Differences in the dominance dimension suggest that SAM may better track a person's response to an affective stimulus. They argue that SAM may lead to more consistent judgments because the figure is human-like.

Emocards [10] is a method that uses 16 cartoon faces showing eight different emotional expressions (one each for each gender). The expressions are combinations of two dimensions pleasantness and arousal. A pleasant emotion with high levels of arousal for example is euphoric, whereas an unpleasant emotion with high arousal is annoyed. The emotions depicted by the faces in Emocards are the ones most frequently elicited by products. Desmet et al. [10] argues that the method can be used as an aid to objectify emotional responses to a product and as an aid for starting conversation between participants and researchers or designers.

Isomursu et al. [22] presented a comparison of five self-report methods for measuring emotional responses to mobile applications. The comparison included SAM, Emocards, and three self-created tools (Experience Clip, Expressing Experiences and Emotions, and Mobile Feedback Application). They developed a comparison framework and showed that all of these methods can be successfully used for collecting emotional responses, all with certain advantages and disadvantages. SAM results, for example, correlated well with results obtained from other methods, however, they found that the SAM scales were not easy to interpret for participants. For some participants it was not clear whether to evaluate their own state or that of the application. Likewise for dominance, it is not clear whether the participant or application had to be judged. With Emocards some participants complained that they could not find a picture to represent their emotional state.

Pollak et al. [27] presented the Photographic Affect Meter (PAM), which is an affect tool that measures affect on the valence and arousal dimensions. It allows the user to select their mood from a set of pre-defined pictures that are obtained from the Flickr API. Based on several tests Pollak et al. identified the most common user-selected photos, and defined the arrangement of the tool in a 4 × 4 grid layout. Their results confirmed the validity of the proposed PAM tool.

Scales based on real faces often use actors for expressing the respective emotion. But actors might portray emotions differently and more intensively than non-professionals [18]. However, recent studies by Aviezer et al. [2] suggest that, in real world situations, people cannot distinguish between intense positive and intense negative emotions expressed through facial expressions alone but only in conjunction with body cues. Thus, for scales showing faces only, depicting exaggerated emotions might ensure better discriminability for low as well as highly intense emotions.

Another limitation of scales using photographs or drawings of faces that express emotions is that they can potentially introduce gender bias [10]. Authors can address this by generating both male and female faces, or by using gender natural faces.

We propose a measurement scale based on LEGO Minifigures that can be used by a range of different people; the nature and the wide use of LEGO allow it to be popular amongst both adults and children [32]. With pictorial scales, respondents still need the cognitive ability to match pictures of facial expressions with a specific emotion, but they do not need to be able to count or use numbers in a categorical way [20] or be able to express actual emotions and intensities in abstract entities (i.e. numbers). The ability to distinguish between facial patterns expressing basic emotions is developed by the age of 4 to 5 years [6]. Pictorial scales using faces are particularly suitable for children and preferred by children because they are concrete measures and easier to use [20]. In addition, the value of the proposed scale is to communicate the user's response on emotional stimuli and it is not limited to one context. Potential uses in HCI related contexts maybe evaluating emotional responses to new designs of physical artefacts and hardware interface as well as software interfaces.

We base our design on the well-established theory of Ekman [15] whose work identified six basic emotions. Other tools use a (slightly) different approach (e.g. SAM is based on pleasure, arousal and dominance; PAM measures affect on the valence and arousal dimensions; Emocards is based on pleasantness and arousal), providing arguably different angles on assessment. Thus, the main contribution of this work is the introduction of an orthogonal emotional evaluation scale using LEGO Minifigures that is based on the six expressions of Ekman and five intensities for each emotion. Our intention is to expand the toolbox for researchers interested in emotion assessment with a novel tool. In addition, the value of using LEGO Minifigures is that they are physically available and can introduce another dimension to an evaluation tool. Allowing people to pick a physical figuring that corresponds to an emotion is a unique and novel approach, which we intend to explore this in our ongoing work. In the following sections we describe how we have developed and evaluated two new pictorial scales for assessing emotions based on LEGO Minifigures.

3 Scale Development

The goal of this research is to develop a new measurement tool for emotions that will allow subjects to easily rate the emotional value of stimuli as well as their own emotional state. To accomplish this, we developed two scales based on the design of LEGO Minifigures. Our scales are based on a sample of 722 facial expressions available through the LEGO Minifigures. These expressions were rated in a previous study that investigated the change of emotional expression of 722 LEGO Minifigures released between 1975 and 2010 [4]. This study discovered that the variety of facial expressions increased considerably since 1989. Not surprisingly the two most frequent expressions were happiness and anger, however, the proportion of happy faces was decreasing over time. To collect this data we used Amazon's Mechanical Turk (MT)[1] for recruiting participants and administering the questionnaire.

The participants were shown one of the 722 LEGO Minifigure pictures at a time and the task was to rate the type and intensity of the expressed emotion from 1–5 (weak-intense). The emotional types to choose from were anger, disgust, fear, happiness, sadness, and surprise [12, 15]. For the scale development, 264 adult participants rated on average 82.05 faces each.

In a follow-up study [5], we evaluated the validity of gathered data via MT compared to gathered data via regular questionnaires. A subset of 96 faces was chosen and ratings received through MT, face-to-face questionnaire and online questionnaire respectively were compared. Our findings showed no substantial differences in the responses, suggesting that MT is a viable option for conducting experiments. These results served as a basis for choosing MT as a tool for rating emotion. We note, however, that although these ratings are based on subjective judgments from many people, this does not establish a "ground truth". This means that we cannot state that a particular face actually depicts a certain emotion, but that it was rated as showing a particular emotion with a certain frequency. However, this is similar to other scales that have been created based on people's subjective judgments.

Our results are in line with other research that has shown MT to be a viable option for conducting experiments of this type and that the quality of the results obtained were similar to conventional methods at much lower costs [8, 17, 26].

Based on our previous research we have developed a scale covering the emotions of 'Anger', 'Disgust', 'Fear', 'Happiness', 'Sadness', and 'Surprise' with 5 intensity levels each.

3.1 Item Selection

We used a semi automatic algorithm to find the most representative faces for each emotion type and intensity combination. For example, a participant can rate a LEGO Minifigure as 'anger' with intensity 5. At the same time the algorithm tries to maximize

---

[1] MT is a crowd-sourcing web service that enables distributing small tasks to a large anonymous workforce who receive micro-payments for completed tasks.

discriminability between categories. For example, a face that was frequently rated as "intense anger" but also often as "intense happy" would be a less suitable candidate than a face with similarly high number of "intense anger" ratings but less clear ratings on one or more particular other emotions.

For each LEGO Minifigure, two statistics were determined: the emotion-intensity category (for example, "intense anger") that is most frequently associated with the face, and the difference between the frequency of that association and the next most frequent association. For example, for the distribution shown in Table 1, the highest frequency is 9/30, for happiness-3, and the next highest frequency is 5/30 for happiness-1 and happiness-2, so the two statistics of interest are 9/30 and 9/30 − 5/30 = 4/30.

The two statistics are naturally correlated; the more often a face is associated with any particular emotion, the less often is it associated with any other, making the distance to the next most frequently selected emotion greater. A face which is consistently associated with a single emotion-intensity category will have values 30/30 = 1 and 30/30 − 0 = 1 respectively (the largest theoretically possible), whereas a face which has been associated equally with all the 30 emotion-intensity categories will have values 1/30 and 0 respectively (the smallest theoretically possible). For each emotion-intensity category, five candidate Minifigure faces were chosen to represent this category and no other. After that, the best option was selected manually from these candidates. Our choice was guided by two requirements: a face can only appear once in the whole scale and the faces should not be alien (i.e. animal or sci-fi like). Some faces were among the best five options for multiple scale points, in particular for low intensity emotions. A certain face might, for example, be equally suitable for sadness at the intensity level two or three. We selected the most suitable unique face for every scale point. From a design perspective, it is reasonable to give the entire scale a consistent look. Thus, we do not include faces of aliens or that have artefacts such as sunglasses.

Table 1. An example distribution of responses for a LEGO Minifigure image.

Intensity	1	2	3	4	5
Anger	2	1	1	2	1
Happiness	5	5	9	1	0

3.2 Stylization

Many LEGO Minifigure faces have certain features that might not be necessary for the communication of emotions, for example, slight shadows on the sides or slight variations in the color of the skin. Moreover, in certain situations it might not be advisable to present colorful faces. Reproducing color consistently across different devices such as screens, printers and projectors remains a difficult task requiring a full color synchronization process and color calibration for each device. To avoid these problems, we developed a stylized version of the LEGO faces that exclude unnecessary details and use gray scale colors. Moreover, transforming the LEGO faces to vector graphics enables users to scale the faces to any desired size without any loss of visual quality. A professional designer used the original LEGO faces as templates to draw stylized faces using a maximum of four gray scale colors: white, light gray, dark gray and black. The stylized faces were created using vectors rather than a bitmap and are therefore easily scalable. The vector graphics can be transformed to bitmap graphics at any desired size. Bitmap graphics are more commonly used in the World Wide Web, such as in the JPEG, PNG or GIF file format.

4 First Evaluation Study

We performed an experiment to evaluate the two new measurement instruments: LEGO Face Scale (LFS) and Stylized LEGO Face Scale (SLFS); examples are shown in Fig. 1(A) and (B) respectively. We investigated the validity of the two new instruments by comparing them to ratings on a 5-point Likert scale (Fig. 1(C)). In this first study we asked participants to rate the emotional expression of face portrait photographs selected from the Japanese Female Facial Expression (JAFFE) Database [25]. The following sections describe the methods and setup of the study.

(A) LEGO Face Scale (LFS)   (B) Stylized LEGO Face Scale (SLFS)

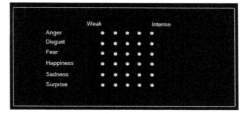

(C) Likert Scale

Fig. 1. The three measurement scales (A) LEGO Face Scale, (B) Stylized LEGO Face Scale, and (C) A five point Likert scale.

4.1 Stimuli

The 213 pictures of the JAFFE Database [25] were used as the stimuli for our experiment. All the faces were used for each of the three conditions, resulting in (213 × 50 × 3) 31.950 responses. In the LFS condition we used the images of the LEGO faces and in the SFLS condition we used the stylized LEGO faces. In the third condition, we used a five point Likert scale. Figure 1 shows the three scales, where the emotions presented in the scale's rows of Fig. 1(A) and (B) are (from the top) anger, disgust, fear, happiness, sadness, and surprise.

4.2 Method

A between-subject design was used to perform the experiment in which we used three different measurement tools as our three experimental scales: LFS, SFLS and Likert. We used MT to recruit participants and to execute the study. The participants were asked to rate what emotion each stimulus expressed using the measurement tools presented in Fig. 1. The experimenter posted the questionnaires as tasks within the MT environment, where the Mechanical Turk Users (MTU) could then answer as many questions as they desired. Fifty different participants rated each stimulus, where they could stop at any time. This means that it would have not been the exact same 50 participants rating each and every stimulus. This plays an important part in the selection of an appropriate statistical test, as described in the results section.

To protect the privacy of MTUs, we were not allowed access to demographic data; hence it is not available for this study. However, we can be relatively certain that all participants are adults since minors are not allowed as MTUs. Previous surveys on the population of MTUs reveal that MTUs from the US tend to be well educated, young, have moderately high incomes, and are roughly equally male and female [21, 28].

5   Second Evaluation Study

In this study we present standardized stimuli that are intended to induce physiological states that manifest themselves in physical reaction. Participants were asked to rate their reactions using the three measurement tools (LFS, SLFS, and Likert). For this study we directly recruited participants instead of using Amazon's MT. Section 4.1 describes how the stimuli images were selected and Sect. 4.2 outlines the method used to evaluate the proposed measurements tools.

5.1 Stimuli

In order to induce physical responses we used images from the standardized International Affective Picture System (IAPS) as stimuli [23]. The corpus of 1182 IAPS images comes with a table of ratings collected from a group of 100 college students (50 male, 50 female). These students were asked to rate the images based on the Self-Assessment Manikin (SAM); however, the images do not have an associated label that relates to one of the six basic emotions identified by Paul Ekman: happiness, surprise, fear, sadness, anger, and disgust combined with contempt [12, 15].

We reviewed the set of 1182 images and selected 50 that we believed to be the best candidates for eliciting the six emotions. We selected stimuli images with the highest arousal ratings (positive and negative) within their category and further edited the selection based on the content. We chose to limit our subset to 50 images based on the suggested limit in [9], in which 50 images was the approximate average number that participants were willing to evaluate in one sitting.

To verify the use of the 50 stimuli images and to ensure that we would obtain a sufficient variety of responses, we decided to perform a labeling pre-study to evaluate the reaction to the 50 images. We wanted to determine the overall feelings associated with our images as well as the level of intensity related to those feelings. The labeling pre-study involved 24 participants: 15 men and 8 women of ages 22-44 years, from eight countries. The labeling pre-study allowed participants to view each of the 50 images for a fixed time and then immediately presented them with an evaluation screen that allowed them to select one of six emotions and a level of intensity related to the emotion selected. The data obtained from this study verified that the 50 selected images consisted of a near equivalent number of positive and negative images with varying levels of impact as shown in Table 2.

In a follow-up interview, we asked participants about their overall emotional response to the images. Most stated that they were not overly disturbed or offended by the images shown. No one felt the need to end the study due to discomfort.

Table 2. Results from the image labeling pre-study.

Label	Number of Images (of 50)	Average Intensity
Sad	13	5.12
Scared	6	5.95
Disgusted	2	6.15
Surprised	5	4
Happy	22	5
Angry	2	7.1

27 positive labels; 23 negative labels; Overall intensity range: 3–8

5.2   Method

We developed a system to collect participants' responses on the set of stimuli images using the three different scales shown in Fig. 1. The system displays an image for five seconds; followed by a screen where the participant can identify one of the six emotions that they feel best describes their response to the image. A blank five-second countdown screen was used after each rating screen to prepare participants for the next stimulus image. Figure 2 shows the sequence of events when doing the study.

The study involved 14 participants: nine male and five female of ages from 23-35. For each participant, the set of 50 images was randomly divided into three subsets

(A, B, and C) as shown in Fig. 3; the number of images in the subsets were 16, 17, and 17 respectively. Each subset was then assigned to one of the three scale types of the study. We counter balanced the scale type-to-subset assignment for participants.

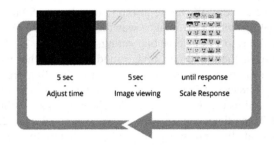

Fig. 2. Illustration of the trial sequence: five seconds break (black screen) followed by an image from the pool of 50 IAPS stimuli followed by one of the three scales (Likert, LFS, SLFS).

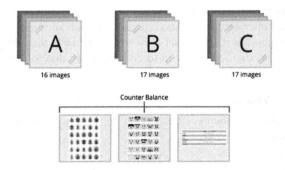

Fig. 3. Illustration of the setup for allocating each of the 50 IAPS into one of three sets and presenting the sets for evaluations using a counterbalanced order for each scale.

6   Statistical Methods

The emotion, selected by a participant to be associated with a given image, can be modeled as a categorical variable: Anger, Disgust, Fear, Happiness, Sadness and Surprise. Multinomial distribution is the common way to model such outcomes; however, it is difficult to summarize since it is, in effect, a multivariate distribution. In order to assess the consistency of scaling, the entropy statistic was calculated:

$$entropy = -\sum_{i=1}^{6} p_i \log(p_i)$$

where p_i is the proportion of respondents who have categorized the given image to emotion i. In our case, entropy equal to 1.79 would correspond to $p_i = 1/6 \forall_i$, i.e., a distribution obtained by random chance, and 0 corresponds to the case where all the 50 respondents have selected the same emotion. In order to explore pairwise agreement between scales, a sum of squared differences in proportions was calculated for each image, where p_{ki} is the proportion of respondents who have classified the image to emotion i on the scale k. This was selected rather than, for example, $x^2 - statistic$, which is inapplicable if zero-counts occur in any of the categories.

6.1 Mixed-Effects Multinomial Logistic Regression

To test for the effect of the scale on the frequency distribution of the emotions assigned by respondents to each image, a mixed-effects multinomial logistic regression model was fitted. This is a standard choice for nominal response data (e.g. [19]). We have chosen to implement the model within Bayesian framework, using the WinBUGS software [24]. The discussion of Bayesian inference is beyond the scope of this article and an interested reader may refer to, for example [16] for more information; it is, however, becoming more and more widely used due to its flexibility with regard to model formulation and assumptions.

To test if scale matters, the above model was fitted with/without the scale taken into account. The two models were then compared using the Deviance Information Criterion (DIC) [29]. DIC can be viewed as a Bayesian version of the Information Criterion (AIC), which is widely used in classical statistics to compare goodness-of-fit of non-nested models [1]. The smaller the value of DIC, the better the model, and, according to the authors, differences between 5 and 10 are substantial, while differences of more than 10 definitely rule out the model with the higher DIC^2. In addition, for the second evaluation study, a Bayesian mixed-effects multinomial logistic regression model was again implemented in WinBUGS (5000 burn-in and 5000 monitored iterations). The model structure accounted for the fact that each participant rated each of the fifty images, as well as for the order in which the images were presented. WinBUGSs was used to implement both models and. convergence was assessed visually.

7 Results

The distribution of observed entropy by scale and dominant emotion (defined here as the emotion most frequently selected by the respondents for a given image) is shown in Fig. 4. On average, respondents using the Likert scale tended to agree more than those using the other two. However, a large spread should be noted. For some images, the response distribution was not far from that obtained by responding at random. The plot of squared differences in estimated proportions in Fig. 5 shows that the distribution of responses obtained from using LFS and SLFS generally agreed across the emotion range, but both disagreed with the response distribution on the Likert scale.

---

2 http://www.mrc-bsu.cam.ac.uk/software/bugs/the-bugs-project-dic/#q9.

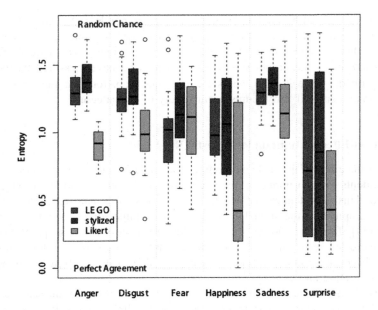

Fig. 4. Entropy by scale and mode emotion.

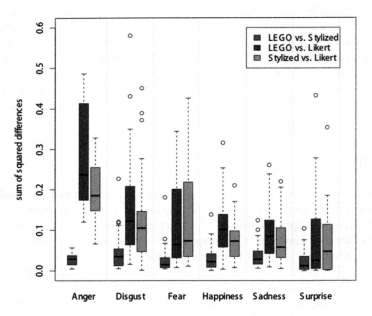

Fig. 5. Disagreement by scale and mode emotion.

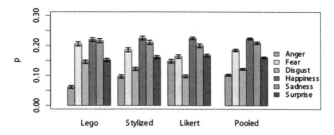

Fig. 6. For the first evaluation, the graphs represent the estimated posterior mean probabilities and the associated 95 % CIs (credible intervals) of categorizing a random photograph into each of the six emotions by scale, and pooled.

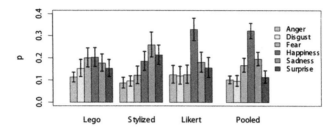

Fig. 7. For the second evaluation, the graph represents the estimated posterior mean probabilities and the associated 95 % CIs of categorizing a random image into each of the six emotions by scale, and pooled. Model adjusted for individual- and order- random effects.

The estimated multinomial probability distributions of assigning a random image to one of the six emotions under each scale in the evaluation studies one and two are shown in Figs. 6 and 7 respectively. These are adjusted for random and a pooled distribution is shown in each case as well. One can see a significant difference in the proportion of the images marked as 'angry' between the three scales, increasing from LFS to SLFS to Likert, with the opposite trend in 'disgust'.

For the second study, about 35 % of the images appear to have been assigned to the 'happy'-category with the rest of the probability mass being almost equally distributed between the other five emotions. The ΔDIC values expressing the possible scale-specific effects in evaluation studies one and two are shown in Table 3. In each case the model with scale-specific probabilities of emotion selection was compared to the model where scales were assumed to have identical probability distributions. A negative ΔDIC means that the pooled model was better than the scale-specific one and thus that no statistical evidence for the effect of scale has been found. The results for evaluation study one show that while for LFS and SLFS the distribution of responses, adjusted for random image-specific effects, is the same, there are significant pairwise differences between LFS and Likert as well as between SLFS and Likert scales. These differences are large enough to justify the scale-specific rather than pooled model overall (ΔDIC = 1315.00). For the second study, however, the pooled model was always found to be statistically better since the DIC was found to be always smaller for the pooled model (see Table 3). For the second evaluation study, the possible effect of the order in which the images were presented was also tested and the results are presented in Table 4. The smallest DIC is returned for the pooled model adjusted for order (DIC = 1763.52). The difference with the DIC of the pooled model not adjusted for order, however, is small (ΔDIC = 2.23) indicating only slight possible effect.

Table 3. DIC comparisons between the scale-specific and pooled models in studies 1 and 2. Large negative values indicate that the pooled model is better, i.e. no effect of scale on probabilities of assigning a photograph to an emotion-intensity categories. 'All' corresponds to testing the hypothesis of at least one of the scales being different from the rest.

Scales	Study 1: ΔDIC	Study 2: ΔDIC
LFS and SLFS	−580.28	−5.42
LFS and Likert	1628.03	−92.29
SLFS and Likert	1102.98	−49.11
All	1315.00	−79.85

Table 4. DIC comparisons between the models where order is taken into account and where it is not for the second evaluation data. Smaller DIC indicate a better model. There is therefore some evidence that order does have an effect on the assessment. Also, the pooled model has significantly smaller DIC values whether the ordering is taken into account or not, demonstrating lack of statistical evidence for the scale effect.

	DIC, with ord.	DIC, without ord.	ΔDIC
Style specific	1843.74	1849.09	−5.35
Pooled	1763.52	1765.75	−2.23

8 Discussion

We have conducted two studies to evaluate the proposed pictorial scales. First we compared the two pictorial scales to a Likert scale when judging emotions of others. The task was to judge images with facial expressions of different emotions with the three scales. This study was conducted using the Amazon Mechanical Turk service, which allowed us to gather a large amount of data for our evaluation purposes.

As a measure of reliability we calculated entropy, where the smaller the entropy, the better the respondents agree in their ratings of an emotion that a specific image depicts. This indicates that the respondents on average agree more when using the Likert scale than when using the pictorial scales. Happiness shows most agreement, however, the variation of the entropy measure for the different pictures that were rated as happy is rather large from almost perfect agreement to almost random ratings.

When comparing ratings of facial expressions between the three rating scales, our findings indicate that the judgments of facial expressions tend to agree between the two pictorial scales. On the other hand, the Likert scale ratings are likely to differ; this means that emotion might be rated differently with the Likert scale. Moreover, it indicates a lack of construct validity of the pictorial scales as measured against Likert-scale ratings. It should be noted that the Likert scale, although it is frequently used as a rating scale, it is not a baseline for rating emotions in a strict sense. Therefore, the finding that the ratings differ does not mean that the LFS and the SLFS scales are less suitable for rating emotional expressions. At this stage we cannot judge which of the three approaches generated more 'correct' emotional ratings.

One concern could be that, when rating the emotional expression of faces with pictorial scales, users might simply match the facial expression in the stimulus with an image in the scale that visually provides the best match. In principle, this visual matching could be done without actually judging the emotional expression. One then might argue that it is not necessary to actually judge the shown emotion. But this does not necessarily rule out the usefulness of such a pictorial scale. It could still give meaningful results when seen from the perspective that it allows users to just pick a face without having to go through an active cognitive interpretation process which for example requires verbalization of the otherwise just visually processed emotion. Brasley et al. [7] argue that the scale SAM may lead to more consistent judgments than a verbal scale (Semantic differential) because the stimulus material is human-like.

The translation of personal experience to numerical values, such as in Likert scales, can be somewhat problematic. While some might assume that the numbers represent equidistant categories for judging emotional intensity (e.g. the difference between level 1 and 2 is the same as between 2 and 3), others might interpret the same scale as ordinal (where the difference between levels is not necessarily the same). This must be taken into account in analyzing data from such scales. Equal intervals in a scale can ensure a higher level of discriminability in a sense that the categories are more or less distinct and do not measure the same quantity [6]. When designing our pictorial scales we developed a selection algorithm that was designed to find the best representative for each emotion and intensity level, while still aiming to achieve a high amount of discriminability. However, we cannot assume equidistance between the intensity levels. This should be taken into account by analyzing and interpreting data obtained with these scales.

In the second study, we took a slightly different approach compared to the first one. Instead of using pictures and having users judging these facial expressions, we used a set of images that were supposed to elicit an emotional reaction. The task was then to use one of the three methods to rate this emotional reaction. Therefore, instead of rating emotional facial expressions, the users' emotional state is of interest here. Furthermore, the above mentioned facial image matching could not take place because the stimulus material was more generic; not necessarily showing people's faces. Results of this experiment show that ratings made with all scales agree. This means that the two pictorial scales and the Likert scale produce very similar ratings for judging a user's emotional state elicited through pictorial stimulus material.

It would be desirable to first establish a ground truth to compare the ratings against. Taking our findings into account one might even argue that Likert scale based ratings, the most commonly used approach, might be less suitable for certain types of emotional rating as they require more cognitive effort. Therefore, trying to validate new methods with comparing them to Likert scale based ratings might not be the best approach. Thus, further studies are needed to investigate the scales' validity.

Our findings thus indicate that when judging emotion of faces, judgments based on the two pictorial scales that we have developed can in some instances be different from Likert scale based ratings. However, when rating one's own emotional state or reaction to a scene, there is no difference between these measures. Further investigations are needed to study these findings in more detail and to see, why the pictorial scales differ in the one instance but not in the other. One possible explanation for this could be found in the notion of pictorial matching. We could assume that having to interpret someone else's facial expression and having to verbalize this (i.e. finding the verbal expression that corresponds to the facial expression) requires more cognitive demand [11] and thus might introduce some bias in the emotion rating process. Using pictorial scales could be easier and quicker for completing the same task. When this easy matching process cannot be done (for example, when rating one's emotional response to a scene) there always has to be some interpretative step, which could explain why the three methods achieved more similar results in the second experiment.

Finally, the LEGO Minifigures are not only useful as a measuring tool, but there are other valuable uses. Similar to Desmet et al. [10] the Minifigures can be used as an aid to objectify emotional states and responses, which could be difficult for many people to express otherwise. Also, the Minifigures can be used to start a conversation on these responses between participant and researcher or designer.

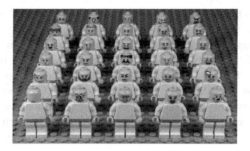

Fig. 8. A physical LEGO Face Scale named Emotion Rating Figurines (ERF).

9   Conclusion and Future Work

We describe the design and the evaluation a new measurement tool for rating emotions based on LEGO Minifigures. The measuring tool use Minifigures selected by responders to represent a respective emotion and intensity. As one step towards this tool, we chose to create two pictorial scales based on Minifigure images (LEGO Face scale and Stylized LEGO Face scale). The scales are based on images from a pool that consists of more than 700 Minifiguring faces. This allowed us to choose suitable facial expressions for the respective emotions and their intensities from a large amount of possible faces. This approach could overcome problems found by other researchers with tools based on a smaller selection of stimuli or designed stimuli.

Moreover, based on the results of our study we assembled a physical version of our facial scale (see Fig. 8). This version is now ready for further testing and we refer to it as the Emotion Rating Figurines (ERF). The ERF may enable people to indicate emotions by selecting an emotional figurine from our set of calibrated figurines. ERF may enable children to easily express their emotions, since they typically identify themselves with dolls during play already. Also other users who struggle with processing abstract categories of emotions could greatly benefit from this new measurement tool.

The ERF has a large potential for mental and other health assessments. An increasing number of children suffer from communication disorders, attention deficit hyperactivity disorder, Aspergers syndrome and autism. The ERF could enable them to communicate emotions even if their specific disorder impairs them from using language-based tools. Due to the potential toy-like design of the ERF, children may naturally be attracted to it. The great advantage of ERF over existing questionnaire based emotion measurement tools is the physical embodiment of the figurines.

In general, users could be more easily able to project themselves into the figurines compared to identifying themselves with a drawing on paper. The ERF might become useful for HCI researchers, psychologist, therapists, social workers and others who want to better communicate with their clients about emotions.

References

1. Akaike, H.: Information theory and an extension of the maximum likelihood principle. In: The second International Symposium on Information Theory, pp. 267–281 (1973)
2. Aviezer, H., Trope, Y., Todorov, A.: Body cues, not facial expressions, discriminate between intense positive and negative emotions. Science **338**(6111), 1225–1229 (2012)
3. Bartneck, C.: The Unofficial LEGO Minifigure Catalog. CreateSpace, Charleston (2011)
4. Bartneck, C., Obaid, M., Zawieska, K.: Agents with faces - what can we Learn from LEGO Minfigures. In: Proceedings of the 1st International Conference on Human-Agent Interaction. Hokkaido University, Sapporo, Japan, pp. III–2–1 (2013)
5. Bartneck, C., Duenser, A., Moltchanova, E., Zawieska, K.: Comparing the similarity of responses received from studies in Amazon's mechanical turk to studies conducted online and with direct recruitment. PLOS ONE **10**(4), e0121595 (2015)
6. Bieri, D., Reeve, R., Champion, G., Addicoat, L., Ziegler, J.: The faces pain scale for the self-assessment of the severity of pain experienced by children: development, initial validation, and preliminary investigation for ratio scale properties. Pain **41**(2), 139–150 (1990)
7. Bradley, M.M., Lang, P.J.: Measuring emotion: the self-assessment manikin and the semantic differential. J. Behav. Ther. Exp. Psychiatry **25**(1), 49–59 (1994)
8. Buhrmester, M., Kwang, T., Gosling, S.: Amazon's mechanical turk: a new source of inexpensive, yet high-quality data? Perspect. Psychol. Sci. **6**(1), 3–5 (2011)
9. Cummings, D.: Multimodal interaction for enhancing team coordination on the battlefield. Dissertation, Texas A&M University, College Station, TX, USA (2013)
10. Desmet, P., Overbeeke, K., Tax, S.: Designing products with added emotional value: development and application of an approach for research through design. Des. J. **4**(1), 32–47 (2001)

11. Desmet, P., Vastenburg, M., Van Bel, D., Romero, N.: Pick-A-Mood; development and application of a pictorial mood-reporting instrument. In: Proceedings of the 8th International Design and Emotion Conference, pp. 11–14 (2012)
12. Ekman, P.: An argument for basic emotions. Cogn. Emot. **6**(3), 169–200 (1992)
13. Ekman, P., Friesen, W.: The repertoire of nonverbal behavior: categories, origins, usage and coding. Semiotica **1**(1), 49–98 (1969)
14. Ekman, P., Friesen, W.: Constants across cultures in the face and emotion. Pers. Soc. Psychol. **17**(2), 124–129 (1971)
15. Ekman, P., Friesen, W.: Unmasking the Face. Prentice Hall, Englewood Cliffs (1975)
16. Gelman, A., Carlin, J., Stern, H., Rubin, D.: Bayesian Data Analysis. Chapman and Hall/CRC, Boca Raton (2004)
17. Goodman, J.K., Cryder, C.E., Cheema, A.: Data collection in a flat world: accelerating consumer behavior research by using mechanical turk. J. Behav. Decis. Making **26**, 213–224 (2013)
18. Grimm, M., Kroschel, K.: Evaluation of natural emotions using self assessment manikins. In: IEEE Workshop on Automatic Speech Recognition and Understanding, pp. 381–385 (2005)
19. Hedeker, D.: A mixed-effects multinomial logistic regression model. Stat. Med. **22**, 1433–1446 (2003)
20. Hicks, C.L., von Baeyer, C.L., Spafford, P.A., van Korlaar, I., Goodenough, B.: the faces pain scale - revised: toward a common metric in pediatric pain measurement. Pain **93**(2), 173–183 (2001)
21. Ipeirotis, P.G.: Demographics of mechanical turk. Technical report, New York University, (2010)
22. Isomursu, M., Tähti, M., Väinämö, S., Kuutti, K.: Experimental evaluation of five methods for collecting emotions in field settings with mobile applications. Int. J. Hum.-Comput. Stud. **65**(4), 404–418 (2007)
23. Lang, P.J., Bradley, M.M., Cuthbert, B.N.: International Affective Picture System (IAPS): Technical Manual and Affective Ratings (1999)
24. Lunn, D., Thomas, A., Best, N., Spiegelhalter, D.: WinBUGS – a Bayesian modeling framework: concepts, structure, and extensibility. Stat. Comput. **10**, 325–337 (2000)
25. Lyons, M.J., Akamatsu, S., Kamachi, M., Gyoba, J.: Coding facial expressions with Gabor wavelets. In: Third IEEE International Conference on Automatic Face and Gesture Recognition, 200–205. IEEE (1998)
26. Paolacci, G., Chandler, J., Ipeirotis, P.: Running experiments on amazon mechanical turk. Judgm. Decis. Making **5**(5), 411–419 (2010)
27. Pollak, J.P., Adams, P., Gay, G.: PAM: a photographic affect meter for frequent, in situ measurement of affect. In: Proceedings of the SIGCHI Conference on Human Factors in Computing Systems, pp. 725–734. ACM (2011)
28. Ross, J., Irani, L., Silberman, S., Zaldivar, A., Tomlinson, B.: Who are The crowdworkers? shifting demographics in mechanical turk. In: Proceedings of the SIGCHI Conference on Human Factors in Computing Systems, pp. 2863–2872. ACM (2010)
29. Spiegelhalter, D., Best, N., Carlin, B., Van der Linde, A.: J. Roy. Stat. Soc. Ser. B **64**(4), 583 (2002)
30. Vastenburg, M., Romero Herrera, N., Van Bel, D., Desmet, P.: PMRI: development of a pictorial mood reporting instrument. In: Proceedings of the SIGCHI Conference on Human Factors in Computing Systems, pp. 2155–2160. ACM (2011)
31. Visser, N., Alant, E., Harty, M.: Which graphic symbols do 4-year-old children choose to represent each of the four basic emotions? Augment. Altern. Commun. **24**(4), 302–312 (2008)
32. The LEGO Group: A Short Presentation (2011)

The Influence of Motivation on Emotional Experience in E-commerce

Samaneh Soleimani$^{(\boxtimes)}$ and Effie Lai-Chong Law

University of Leicester, University Road, Leicester LE1 7RH, UK
ss887@le.ac.uk, elaw@mcs.le.ac.uk

Abstract. To explore the notion of User Experience in regard to motivation and affect in the context of e-commerce, a preliminary research model was developed. According to this model, customers' motivations influence their experience of using e-commerce systems. A pilot study with 12 participants was designed to evaluate this hypothesis. The results suggested that customers' emotional experiences were associated with their motivation to visit an e-commerce website. Our future research will investigate the validity of this model with more thorough evaluation methods.

Keywords: User experience · Emotion · Motivation · E-commerce

1 Introduction

According to the Forrester research, e-commerce generated 112 billion Euros in sales for European retailers in 2012, and is expected to yield more than $191 billion Euros in 2017 [1]. These numbers imply the rapid growth of e-commerce technology. In addition, web-based retailing hinges crucially on the design and development of information and communication technology (ICT) [2], thus information systems and human-computer interaction (HCI) should support a variety of users' goals and needs. Until recently, research and practice in HCI has focused on improving usability qualities (e.g. effectiveness and efficiency) of interactive technologies (e.g. [3]). However, the limitations of the narrow focus of usability, which concerns more about work-related and instrumental qualities [4] and less about aesthetic or affective qualities [5], have been identified. Consequently, the notion of User Experience (UX) has emerged to go beyond the usability of such interactions and include the desirability and experiential quality of ICT services.

UX, as a phenomenon, is considered as subjective, dynamic and context-dependent [4]. Research [6] has described UX as a consequence of user's affect, emotions, needs, motivation (user's internal moods) and the characteristics of the context. In addition, [7] have discussed that UX is about user's feelings while they are interacting with a product or service and these feelings and expectations are anticipatory. Thus, it can be concluded that experience, which is described as inseparable from emotions [8] can be probed and investigated by asking the question "How do you feel?" [9].

© IFIP International Federation for Information Processing 2015
J. Abascal et al. (Eds.): INTERACT 2015, Part I, LNCS 9296, pp. 281–288, 2015.
DOI: 10.1007/978-3-319-22701-6_20

Since precedent conditions can influence users' affective and cognitive states and thus their appraisal of the service of interest, this paper's objective is to address the relationship between users' motivations, emotions and experience. To evaluate this assumption, we developed a research model to explore how customers' motivations can be linked to different affective states, which lead to different experiences.

2 Emotions in E-commerce

Emotions influence customers' cognition and their shopping behaviors in online environments [10] and they apperceive service or product quality based on their feelings [11]. For instance, it was suggested that affect mediates the perceived aesthetic quality of web-based stores [2]. Scholars have also argued that affective states can lead to different cognitive responses such as the perception of a website's effectiveness and informativeness [12]. As an example, [13] reported that positive emotions can contribute to the simple and default way of information-processing and negative emotions to the scrutinized analysis of information, which demands high cognitive involvement. Emotions can also cause changes on the current flow of interactions undertaken by the user [14]. For instance, if the user browses a website to identify certain information, and when the slow Internet connection impedes this goal, the user's frustration might lead him to search for information in another resource [14]. Consequently, research has attempted to explore affective features of the e-commerce environments. For instance, some studies have investigated the impact of interface design (e.g. [2, 15]) and atmospheric cues such as background color [16], text color, and music [11] to understand and evoke customers' emotions, which in turn have an influence on their cognitive states, decision making and their appraisal of the e-retailer [2].

3 Motivation and Experience in E-commerce

Research findings support the assumption that motivation plays a critical role in user's experience [17]. There are a number of studies that have reported two types of motivation for online shopping: recreational and task-oriented motivations (e.g. [17, 18]). There are situations that consumers shop because of the hedonic values such as fun, pleasure, fantasy, escapism or, in other words, the experiential goal of shopping. In this case, if the retailer could induce positive affect in customers by providing tailored content; this would lead to a positive perception of a company and its services [19]. On the other hand, task-oriented consumers shop based on their utilitarian goals; for example, to acquire items effectively and efficiently. Table 1 summarizes a few studies to show to what extent task-oriented and recreational motivations can result in different shopping outcome, shopping experience, consumer involvement and product browsing.

Table 1. Two shopping motivations and characteristics.

Objective	Shopping outcome	Shopping experience	Consumer involvement	Product browsing
Task-oriented	Consumers visit stores to purchase required products or obtain information [20].	Shopping is determined as a task or a rational and effective decision [21].	"Cognitive involvement", such as giving more attention to the product's features [11].	Task-oriented consumers probably browse fewer products than the recreational shoppers [22].
Recreational	Consumers visit stores to obtain gratification or pleasure from the visit per se [20].	Shopping is not a mission or boring task. It's based on experiential and emotional motives [21].	"Affective involvement", such as tendency to get pleasure of the shopping experience [11].	Recreational consumers probably browse more products than the task-oriented shoppers [22].

4 Modeling User Experience in E-commerce

4.1 S-O-R Model

Many studies have applied the Stimulus-Organism-Response (S-O-R) model of [23] to assess the effect of the web-based stimuli on the online customers' behaviors and consequently on their emotional states of pleasure and arousal (e.g. [11, 12, 24]). As stated by the S-O-R model, an environmental stimulus (S) incites user's internal affective appraisal (O), which in turn leads to the user's reaction or response (R). Within a website, signs, symbols, artefacts, ambient conditions, space and function are reported as stimuli [24]. Research has also observed that computer related events are not essentially different from other stimuli, they cause physiological changes and in turn these changes are expressed as level of arousal and manifest clues for valence [15].

4.2 Proposed E-commerce UX Model

According to [25], there are two types of characteristics in e-commerce: emotional thinking and rational thinking. For instance, looking for convenience and quickness in the process of searching, finding and shopping, accessibility of a variety of products and low prices [26] were regarded as the utilitarian attributes. Enjoyment and excitement resulting from online shopping, the searching process of new, unusual products and models, an experience of adventure, releasing stress and depression, and forgetting problems (e.g. [27]) were considered as the emotional aspect of e-commerce. Additionally, research has suggested that the motivation of shopping mediates the effect of arousal induced by the store environments on the pleasantness of the store visit [20].

Accordingly, we borrowed the theory of shopping motivation and its effects on shopping behaviors in stores and adopted the S-O-R model on web environments to propose that the motivations of e-commerce can influence user experience by inducing different emotional states. Our research model is presented in Fig. 1.

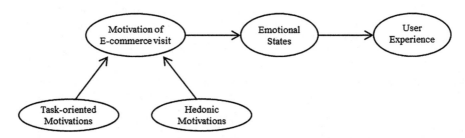

Fig. 1. The proposed research model

5   Exploratory Study

5.1   Method

Participants. To explore the relationship between customers' motivation and their affective state, we conducted 12 semi-structured interviews. Participants were recruited via personal email-invitation and they were asked to participate in this interview only if they have had a recent experience with an e-commerce website. All the participants volunteered to participate in this study and referred to their most recent experience within the past 10 days of the interview time. They were between 20–35 years old, 7 female and 5 male and all university educated (from bachelor to PhD degree).

Procedure. The interviews were carried out in English and performed through 8 face-to-face meetings and 4 Skype calls (one participant was from Australia and 3 of them were from the United States, therefore face-to-face meetings were financially not possible). In both cases (Skype and face-to-face) the same procedure was followed and the interview was audiotaped. The interviewees were asked to revisit the e-commerce website that they had used most recently, reflecting on their experience and repeating it retrospectively. Participants were asked to respond to the following questions:

- What type of product or service were you looking for?
- What was your motivation for this e-commerce visit and do you consider it as being recreational or task-oriented? (The interviewer gave examples of the two types of motivation to the interviewees.)
- What was your emotional status before and after entering the website?
- What was your emotional status after finishing your visit?
- Can you tell me what emotions you felt while you were visiting the website and the reasons behind them?

In addition, other information such as product price and participants' suggestions to improve the quality of their experience were collected during the interviews. The audio recordings were transcribed right after each interview.

5.2 Results and Discussion

To understand the relationship between emotion and motivation a list of emotion words that were verbalized by the interviewees during, before and after their e-commerce visit, was identified. Then according to each participant's motivation of their visit, each emotion word was linked to either hedonic or task-oriented. In addition, 5 HCI researchers rated each emotion word based on valence (being positive/negative) and on a 5-point-scale (ranging from calm to excited) to indicate the intensity of arousal. The average value of the arousal ratings was computed as the intensity of the emotion word. To analyze valence, each positive rating was assigned to 1 and negative rating to -1. If the average value was between -0.5 and 0.5, that emotion word was rated as Ambiguous. The only rated ambiguous emotion word was 'surprised'; a finding consistent with that of the previous research [28] (see Table 2 for details of the results). In addition, by looking at the emotion word list produced in this study, we observed that 9 emotion words were common in other similar research [28]. Moreover, a closer observation of the results suggested that those participants, who reported their motivation as hedonic, described their experience as emotional excitement (e.g. "impulsive shopping is exciting"), curiosity (e.g. "I wanted to experience the website and see what is my next step") and boredom (e.g. "looking for fun", "to improve my mood"). On the other hand, participants who wanted to do the purchase as quickly as possible and with straightforward actions (as a task and having no recreational goal) did not assess their experience with pleasure and evaluated it as neutral, confused (e.g. "seeing so many options") and stressed (e.g. "money is stressful"). This result implies that the motivation of the customer influences emotional experience, which is consistent with the literature [20].

5.3 Limitations

There are several limitations related to the results and implications of this work. First of all, this study was exploratory with the aim to verify the research question and to gain insight for the future work. Secondly, the number of participants is too small to draw a solid conclusion. Thirdly, studying memorized emotions and experiences is very challenging due to the reason that they are prone to change, fade or get rebuilt according to the characteristics of the situated context [29], which results in biased conclusions. Lastly, the reported emotions were the interviewees' subjective evaluation of their internal states. Thus the interpretation could be inaccurate because retrospective self-reported emotions differed from the emotions felt at the moment they were elicited. In addition, the data of this study were captured through semi-structured interviews whereas the validity and reliability of the implications should have been consolidated by applying other research methods such as qualitative and quantitative surveys.

Table 2. List of emotion words were verbalized by the interviewees when they repeated their last e-commerce experience.

Emotion word	Arousal (1–5)	Valence	Motivation	Time-slot of the emotion: Before/Within/After
Annoyed/Irritated	4	Negative	Goal/Hedonic	Within
Anxious/Distressed	3.8	Negative	Goal	Within
Bored	1.8	Negative	Hedonic	Before/Within
Comfort	2	Positive	Hedonic	Within
Confused	3.2	Negative	Goal/Hedonic	Within
Curious	3	Positive	Hedonic	Before/Within
Disappointed	2.6	Negative	Goal/Hedonic	Within
Excited	4.4	Positive	Hedonic	Before/Within/After
Frustrated	4.2	Negative	Goal	Within
Happy	3.6	Positive	Goal	After
Indecisive	2.2	Negative	Hedonic	Before
Insecure	2.8	Negative	Goal	Within
Liked	2.8	Positive	Goal	Before
Neutral	1.4	Neutral	Goal	Before/Within
Pleased	2.8	Positive	Goal	Within
Proud	3.2	Positive	Goal	Within
Relieved	3.4	Positive	Hedonic	After
Satisfied	3	Positive	Hedonic	After
Not satisfied	2.2	Negative	Hedonic	After
Secure	2.2	Positive	Goal	Before/Within
Stressed	3.6	Negative	Goal	Before/Within
Surprised	3.4	Ambiguous	Goal	Within
Trust	2.2	Positive	Goal	Within

6   Conclusion and Future Work

Empirical findings of our pilot study suggest that emotion as a factor of UX influences customers' online retail behaviors and the types of emotions experienced were mediated by customers' motivations. Therefore, it could be concluded that users' experience is mediated by users' motivation of their online commerce visit. In addition, according to [30] if we had a clearer understanding of how different motivational perspectives influence the use and appraisal of interactive products, we could create design rules for different circumstances without the need of knowing the details of the situation. Thus, in this study we endeavored to understand the effects of motivational orientation on the course of interaction by exploring the relationship between emotions and motivations. In addition, considering motivation as an antecedent of UX can help us obtain a more thorough understanding of this notion. Our future research will be carried out to substantiate our current findings by applying physiological measurements and subjective methodologies to evaluate users' affective states and motivations in live experiences.

References

1. European Online Retail Forecast (2012 –2017). https://www.forrester.com
2. Porat, T., Tractinsky, N.: It's a pleasure buying here: the effects of web-store design on consumers' emotions and attitudes. Hum.-Comput. Interact. **27**, 235–276 (2012)
3. Venkatesh, V., Agarwal, R.: Turning visitors into customers: a usability-centric perspective on purchase behavior in electronic channels. Manag. Sci. **52**, 367–382 (2006)
4. Law, E.L.C., Roto, V., Hassenzahl, M., Vermeeren, A.P., Kort, J.: Understanding, scoping and defining user experience: a survey approach. In: Proceedings of the SIGCHI Conference on Human Factors in Computing Systems, pp. 719–728. ACM (2009)
5. Zhang, P., Li, N.: The importance of affective quality. Commun. ACM. **48**, 105–108 (2005)
6. Hassenzahl, M., Tractinsky, N.: User experience-a research agenda. Behav. Inf. Technol. **25**, 91–97 (2006)
7. Petrie, H., Harrison, C.: Measuring users' emotional reactions to websites. In: CHI 2009 Extended Abstracts on Human Factors in Computing Systems. 3847–3852. ACM (2009)
8. McCarthy, J., Wright, P.: Technology as experience. J. Interact. **11**, 42–43 (2004)
9. Hassenzahl, M., Diefenbach, S., Görtiz, A.: Needs, affect, and interactive products–facets of user experience. Interact. Comput. **22**, 353–362 (2010)
10. Tucker, M.L., Sojka, J.Z., Barone, F.J., McCarthy, A.M.: Training tomorrow's leaders: enhancing the emotional intelligence of business graduates. J. Educ. Bus. **75**(6), 331–337 (2000)
11. Ding, C.G., Lin, C.H.: How does background music tempo work for online shopping? Electron. Commer. Res. Appl. **11**, 299–307 (2012)
12. Mazaheri, E., Richard, M.O., Laroche, M.: The role of emotions in online consumer behavior: a comparison of search, experience, and credence services. J. Serv. Mark. **26**(7), 535–550 (2012)
13. Clore, G.L., Schwarz, N., Conway, M.: Affective causes and consequences of social information processing. In: Srull, T.K., Wyer, R.S. (eds.) Handbook of Social Cognition, vol. 1, pp. 323–417. Erlbaum, Hillsdale (1994)
14. Stickel, C., Ebner, M., Steinbach-Nordmann, S., Searle, G., Holzinger, A.: Emotion detection: application of the valence arousal space for rapid biological usability testing to enhance universal access. In: Stephanidis, C. (ed.) Universal Access in HCI, Part I, HCII 2009. LNCS, vol. 5614, pp. 615–624. Springer, Heidelberg (2009)
15. Ward, R.D., Marsden, P.H.: Physiological responses to different web page designs. Int. J. Hum.-Comput. Stud. **59**, 199–212 (2003)
16. Cheng, F.F., Wu, C.S., Yen, D.C.: The effect of online store atmosphere on consumer's emotional responses–an experimental study of music and colour. Behav. Inf. Technol. **28**, 323–334 (2009)
17. O'Brien, H.L.: The influence of hedonic and utilitarian motivations on user engagement: the case of online shopping experiences. Interact. Comput. **22**, 344–352 (2010)
18. Bui, M., Kemp, E.: E-tail emotion regulation: examining online hedonic product purchases. Int. J. Retail Distrib. Manag. **41**, 155–170 (2013)
19. Holzwarth, M., Janiszewski, C., Neumann, M.M.: The influence of avatars on online consumer shopping behavior. J. Mark. **70**, 19–36 (2006)
20. Kaltcheva, V.D., Weitz, B.: A: When should a retailer create an exciting store environment? J. Mark. **70**, 107–118 (2006)
21. To, P.-L., Liao, C., Lin, T.H.: Shopping motivations on Internet: a study based on utilitarian and hedonic value. Technovation **27**, 774–787 (2007)

22. Novak, T.P., Hoffman, D.L., Duhacheck, A.: The influence of goal-directed and experiential activities on online flow experiences. J. Consum. Psychol. **13**, 3–16 (2003)
23. Mehrabian, A., Russell, J.A.: An Approach to Environmental Psychology. MIT Press, Cambridge (1974)
24. Froh, A., Madlberger, M.: The role of atmospheric cues in online impulse-buying behavior. Electron. Commer. Res. Appl. **12**, 425–439 (2013)
25. Yeh, L., Wang, E.M.-Y., Huang, S.-L.: A study of emotional and rational purchasing behavior for online shopping. In: Schuler, D. (ed.) HCII 2007 and OCSC 2007. LNCS, vol. 4564, pp. 222–227. Springer, Heidelberg (2007)
26. Ariely, D., Simonson, I.: Buying, bidding, playing, or competing? value assessment and decision dynamics in online auctions. J. Cons. Psychol. **13**, 113–123 (2003)
27. Arnold, M.J., Reynold, K.E.: Hedonic shopping motivations. J. Retail. **79**, 77–95 (2003)
28. Petrie, H., Precious, J.: Measuring user experience of websites: think aloud protocols and an emotion word prompt list. In: CHI 2010 Extended Abstracts on Human Factors in Computing Systems, pp. 3673–3678. ACM (2010)
29. Law, E.L.C., van Schaik, P.: Roto, V: Attitudes towards user experience (UX) measurement. Int. J. Hum.-Comput. Stud. **72**(6), 526–541 (2014)
30. Hassenzahl, M., Schöbel, M., Trautmann, T.: How motivational orientation influences the evaluation and choice of hedonic and pragmatic interactive products: the role of regulatory focus. Interact. Comput. **20**, 473–479 (2008)

The Presenter Experience of Canvas Presentations

Leonhard Lichtschlag$^{(\boxtimes)}$, Philipp Wacker, Martina Ziefle, and Jan Borchers

RWTH Aachen University, 52074 Aachen, Germany
{lichtschlag,wacker,ziefle,borchers}@cs.rwth-aachen.de

Abstract. Most presentations are given with supporting visuals and driven by specialized presentation software. Today, this software either follows the classic slideware metaphor, presenting a series of discrete screens—or it implements the more recent canvas presentation metaphor, using a zoomable free-form canvas to arrange information. Both paradigms were previously evaluated with presentation authors and audiences. In this paper, we extend our understanding to how they impact the presenter herself during delivery of a talk. In a lab study participants gave presentations with slideware and canvas tools, and we measured their emotional state through self-reporting. We find that a recommendation for a tool depends on the experience of the presenter or their spatial ability.

Keywords: Canvas presentations · Slideware · Zoomable user interfaces · Lab study

1 Introduction

Visual presentation support is prevalent in talks in research, industry, education, and many other areas. Most software, e.g., Microsoft's PowerPoint or Apple's Keynote, employs the slide metaphor, which originates from the technical restrictions of physical slides used on overhead projectors. Yet today, presentation visuals are usually displayed using a computer connected to a video projector. This removes the necessity to show a series of slides, one at a time, and this format has been criticized repeatedly for the limitations it imposes on authors and presenters [15, 20]. A recent alternative to the slide format are canvas presentations, which dismiss the slide metaphor in part or entirely. Instead, they place either the slides [7] or individual elements [11, 16] on an infinite canvas. Authors then define viewports and transition paths across the canvas to define the presentation sequence, or present ad hoc without a planned path.

It was previously studied how authors deal with the two paradigms when preparing for a talk [11, 13], and how audiences perceive talks given in the two formats [12], but the effect on the presenter herself has not been investigated, yet. The canvas format should be especially helpful for navigations that deviate from the planned presentation delivery, e.g., in response to a question [2, 7]. The presenter can quickly pan-and-zoom, thereby creating impromptu overviews and showing the macrostructure of the talk to the audience. However, we also hypothesize that the free format may be too

© IFIP International Federation for Information Processing 2015
J. Abascal et al. (Eds.): INTERACT 2015, Part I, LNCS 9296, pp. 289–297, 2015.
DOI: 10.1007/978-3-319-22701-6_21

demanding for a presenter who is preoccupied on talking. In this paper, we present a lab study with presenters who gave short talks in each format to investigate these issues. We measure the emotional state of the presenters during a presentation delivery in which several kinds of interruptions occur.

2 Related Work

Several tools have adapted the zoomable user interfaces paradigm [1, 2] specifically for presentation support [7, 11, 16]. CounterPoint [7] broke new ground by positioning PowerPoint slides inside a zoomable user interface. It lets authors place slides at varying distances from a virtual camera and create a spatial layout of slides. Fly [11] and Prezi [16] have no notion of slides at all and present content elements (text, figures, etc.) directly on a canvas. Without the limitations of the slide frame, authors adapt their approach to presenting content less linearly and incorporate good presentation behaviors such as overviews [11, 13]. Canvas presentations perform on par with slideware with regards to audiences' content recall and macrostructure understanding [12]. No studies investigated how presenters interact with canvas presentations.

Defining emotion is very difficult, and there are numerous attempts in the literature. A popular approach is to characterize emotion using a component model where expressions, bodily reactions, and the subjective experience have "long-standing status as modalities of emotion" [19]. There are different ways to combine these components; here we use a dimensional approach (e.g., [18]) with valence and arousal as the main components [19]. Valence dimension contrasts pleasure and displeasure, while the arousal describes intensity. The term *feelings* is defined in the component model as the subjective experience of an emotion and can occur separate from bodily reactions (e.g., [6]). As many people are anxious about public speaking, it is the presenter's feelings that we are interested in. Scherer [19] writes that these feelings can only be accessed through a person's self-reporting.

The *self-assessment manikin* (SAM) [4] (Fig. 1, right) is one way to elicit ratings from subjects. Each row represents change along one dimension of emotion as pictorial depictions of a person. In our study we used SAM without the dominance domain. While this method requires fewer ratings from a person, the two dimensional rating does provide little insight into the aspects that produced the emotion [19]. A more detailed technique is the *semantic differential* (SD) which measures the meaning of words [14] (Fig. 1). A semantic differential consists of point rating scales with bipolar word pairs on either end of the scale (e.g., good–bad). It has been used to measure attitude and feelings, for example in a classroom scenario [5]. A person rates a concept by indicating for each word pair where she places the concept between the limits.

3 Study Design

We conducted a lab study with every tester giving two presentations for about 7 min each (Fig. 1, left). One presentation was given with Apple's Keynote [10], representing slideware, and one with Prezi [16], representing the canvas condition (During

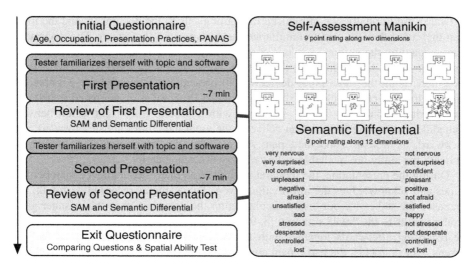

Fig. 1. *Left*: each participant presents two talks, after each she rates her feelings with the Self-Assessment Manikin (SAM) and the Semantic Differential (SD) described on the right. *Top Right*: One row changes from an unhappy person to a happy person (the valence dimension), one row from a person who has the eyes closed to a person experiencing intense feelings (arousal dimension). *Bottom Right*: SD dimensions used to quantify more precise feelings.

presentation delivery, the differences between the different canvas tools are negligible and we do not expect our choice of software to impact the study. Similarly for slideware). In this format, we were able to have comparable talks for all users and to include interesting tasks in the presentations as well as simulated technological problems. In each presentation, we first asked the tester to give their presentation normally by *stepping forward* through the presentation. Then we interrupted them and asked to *move to a well defined position* in the presentation (e.g., going back to a specific previous slide in response to a question) and then to *skip forward* towards the end (e.g., due to time constraints). Finally, we asked to *search for a loosely defined position* (e.g., the presenter has to find the slide to a question). One of the two talks also included simulated errors: a *misinterpreted input* (simulated by a step backwards on a forward command), and an *unresponsive program* (simulated by no action on the first command). We counterbalanced the order of conditions.

Our setup excludes many confounding variables (e.g., varying documents, audiences, stakes, presentation occasions, length, etc.) to build a baseline understanding in the lab with high control. As such, the results of this setup are limited until a field study can investigate their generalizability (cf. the approach taken by [11, 13]).

In both talks, testers presented the 2014 Soccer World Championship, a topic presented heavily in the media at the time, so that we could expect our testers to have at least some prior knowledge. The topic was also a good fit for a spatial layout by placing players on their actual position on the pitch. Therefore, the topic could be presented spatially in the canvas condition in a manner that was approachable to our testers (cf. [12] discussing of the problem of comparable documents between presentation software). Additionally, we introduced the participants to the documents and the tools, then they used the software to familiarize themselves with the matter. The documents were created by the authors; while is common to present foreign slides, this remains a limitation of the lab setup. All presentations were driven by an iPad carried by the presenter. Using the same input device for all presentations lowered the possible differences in interacting with the different software. Both software animated transitions, canvas with the inherent flyover, slideware with a slide-in from right to left between each slide. During the presentation delivery, the input modalities are step forward, step backward, as well as zoom and pan. All materials and presentation documents to replicate the study are available at http://hci.rwth-aachen.de/fly.

During the presentation, the moderator acted as an interested audience member that smiles and acknowledges the information given. Two cameras recorded each talk, this increased the stakes for our testers as playacting the presentation in this manner gives similar results to the "real" situation [8, 9]. Secondly, the cameras allowed us to watch the recording afterwards together with the presenter. Although memory of feelings lessens over time [17], the participant could relive the situation and assess her feelings, and we avoided interrupting the presentation. We used the self-assessment manikin with a nine-point rating scale [4] (Fig. 1) to measure the valence and arousal of the participant in the task situations. We also used the semantic differential [14] to ask her to rate twelve feelings on a nine-point rating scale to measure feedback on specific feelings. To find out which dimensions to use, seven weeks before our study, we had asked in an online survey which feelings presenters had experienced themselves or observed in others. We combined the reported emotions with directions from literature [7] and produced the dimensions in Fig. 1. Accounting for the possibility that underlying moods affect the feelings of the participants, we used the PANAS test, a reliable and valid method to measure mood over various periods of time [21]. Finally, in the exit questionnaire, we asked for informal feedback on the experience with the software, differences to their regular presentations, and how their feelings in the study related to feelings in real presentations. To see whether spatial ability influence the experience of presenting, we measured the participants spatial ability using a paper folding test [3]. We formulated these hypotheses:

H1: Feelings in canvas presentations are rated differently than feelings in slide presentations.

H2: Presentations with technical difficulties are rated differently than presentations without technical problems.

H3: Order of presentation and presence of errors does not influence ratings.

H4: Participants experience the same feelings during the study compared to a real world presentation.

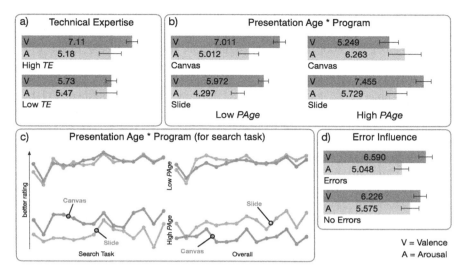

Fig. 2. (a) SAM ratings for technical expertise show significant difference. (b) Presentation experience influences emotional response. (c) SD ratings show experienced presenters rated the search task differently from the trend. (d) Arousal rating is influenced by presence of errors

4 Evaluation

We recruited 21 participants for the study with varying proficiency in presentation skills in general and technological skills in particular. The participants were 8 teachers, 7 students, 6 other professions, none familiar with the lab, aged 17–66 (mean = 37.09, SD = 16.02). To quantify the presentation experience we calculated a presentation age by subtracting the age at which a participant had given their first presentation from their current age. This *presentation age* (*PAge*) had a mean of 18.33 years and standard deviation of 11.73. The *technological expertise* (*TE*) was assessed by calculating the mean between how often the participant uses canvas tools and slideware respectively (rated on a five-point scale where higher values mean more often). *TE* had a mean of 1.33 and a standard deviation of 0.56. We also asked participants how much they *liked* to present (*L*) on a five-point rating scale (1–5, 1 = most enjoyment, mean = 2.19, SD = 0.93). Other gathered characteristics were *spatial ability* (*SA*, 0–20, number of correct solutions in the paper folding test; mean = 12.76, SD = 4.77) and mood (PANAS test, separated for *positive affect* (*PA*) (mean = 31.14, SD = 4.95) and *negative affect* (*NA*) (mean = 12.57, SD = 2.34)). A correlation of *PAge*, *SA*, *TE* and *L* showed that presentation age and spatial ability had a significant negative correlation. Hence we could not analyze them separately, and when we report on *PAge* below, *SA* can also be an explaining factor. For the evaluation we categorized the *PAge*, *TE* and *L* each into two groups.

As for the hypothesis of program influence (**H1**) we conducted two repeated-measures MANCOVAS with the valence/arousal ratings (SAM) and the semantic differential (SD) ratings as dependent variables respectively. *PAge*, *TE* and *L* were taken as between-subjects factors and positive affect *(PA)* and negative affect *(NA)* as covariates. For the valence/arousal ratings we found no main effect of the delivery method $(F(2,10) = 3.00,$ *ns*$)$ but a significant between-subjects effect of *TE* $(F(2,10) = 6.78,$ $p < .05)$ and a significant interaction effect of Program*$*PAge$ $(F(2,10) = 7.82, p < .01)$.

Between-subjects, *TE* had a significant effect on the valence ratings $(F(1,11) = 11.24, p < .01)$ with more *TE* leading to higher ratings (Fig. 2a). The interaction effect of Program*$*PAge$ was significant for the valence ratings $(F(1,11) = 14.66, p < .01)$. An analysis of the means showed that less experienced presenters gave higher valence ratings for the canvas presentation (5.97 to 7.01) while more experienced presenters gave higher ratings for the slideware presentation (5.25 to 7.46) (Fig. 2b). The results from the analysis of SD ratings indicated a main effect of the delivery method $(F(11,1) = 825.93, p < .05)$, an interaction effect of Program*$*NA$ $(F(11,1) = 1481.85, p < .05)$, an interaction effect of Program*$*PAge$ $(F(11,1) = 2249.68, p < .05)$ and an interaction effect of Program*$*TE$ $(F(11,1) = 349.55, p < .05)$. While the individual SD dimensions did not differ significantly between the programs, the overall trend was that the slideware presentation received more positive emotional response. The interaction effect of Program*$*PAge$ was significant for *pleasantness* $(F(1,11) = 8.4, p < .05)$, *positivity* $(F(1,11) = 10.11, p < .01)$, *afraid* $(F(1,11) = 14.67, p < .01)$, *satisfaction* $(F(1,11) = 20.38, p < .01)$, *stress* $(F(1,11) = 13.91, p < .01)$, *desperation* $(F(1,11) = 5.81, p < .05)$, *controlled* $(F(1,11) = 6.01, p < .05)$, and *lost* ratings $(F(1,11) = 16.83, p < .01)$. More experienced presenters gave positive ratings for slideware on all these dimensions, while less experienced presenters showed only minor differences. The interaction effect of Program*$*TE$ was significant for *surprise* $(F(1,11) = 9.99, p < .01)$, *unsatisfied* $(F(1,11) = 9.21, p < .05)$, and *lost* ratings $(F(1,11) = 5.47, p < .05)$. Presenters who had less *TE* gave higher ratings for slideware on all these dimensions while presenters with more *TE* showed only minor differences. In conclusion, we accept H1.

Exploring the data, we noted that the ratings for the search for a *loosely defined position* task showed a flipped behavior. An interaction effect Program*$*PAge$ occurred once again and valence values were significantly different for this task $(F(1,11) = 9.31, p < .05)$. Further analysis showed a great difference between slideware and canvas presentations for experienced presenters, with canvas presentations having a better rating, while no difference was found for less experienced presenters (Fig. 2c).

To explore the error hypothesis (**H2**) we conducted two repeated-measures MAN-COVAS with the valence/arousal ratings and the semantic differential (SD) ratings as dependent variables respectively. *PAge*, *TE* and *L* were taken as between-subjects factors and positive affect *(PA)* and negative affect *(NA)* as covariates. The analysis of valence/arousal ratings indicated a main effect of the error condition $(F(2,10) = 5.55, p < .05)$, an interaction effect of Error*$*PA$ $(F(2,10) = 6.62, p < .05)$ and an interaction effect of Error*$*TE$ $(F(2,10) = 5.88, p < .05)$. Arousal ratings were significantly different between the error conditions $(F(1,11) = 7.90, p < .05)$. Examination of means showed that arousal was rated higher in the no-error condition (Fig. 2d). The interaction effect of Error*$*PA$ was significant for the arousal ratings $(F(1,11) = 8.19, p < .05)$, and the plot indicated that while the positive affect rating had no effect on the arousal rating in the no-error condition, it had a positive effect on the arousal ratings in the error condition. The interaction effect of Error*$*TE$ was significant neither for valence nor for arousal ratings. The results from the analysis of SD ratings indicated between-subjects effects of *NA* on stress ratings and of *TE* on nervousness, pleasantness and positive-negative ratings. Further analysis showed that higher *NA* ratings correlated with more experienced stress, and that lower *TE* participants felt more nervous, more unpleasant, and more negative across both conditions. In conclusion, we accept H2.

Checking the quality of counterbalancing (**H3**), we compared presentations by order and found no differences between ratings for the programs (Canvas: $F(2,18) < 1$, *ns*; Slide: $F(2,18) < 1$, *ns*) or the errors (error: $F(2,18) = 1.73$, *ns*; no-error: $F(2,18) < 1$, *ns*). Thus, we accept H3.

As for **H4**, almost all (20) participants expressed that they felt similar to a real presentation. 14 mentioned that they felt less pressure since they had less stakes in the presentation, 10 mentioned an additional burden (e.g., the unfamiliarity of the topic), while 2 felt that the study was outright harder than their own presentations because of that. With this, we cautiously accept H4: the limitations of the lab study were manageable, and our setup was comparable to a real presentation.

5 Discussion and Summary

Our evaluation shows that presenters experience canvas and slide tools differently. More specifically, participants of our study that scored high on spatial ability or were less experienced preferred the canvas condition, while experienced or lower spatial ability presenters preferred classic slideware. Due to the strong overlap in our tester population between experience and lower spatial ability, we cannot attribute this effect to a single or a combination of these factors. We expected lower spatial ability to interact with the canvas condition due to its ZUI nature, but we could also explain that more experienced presenters are well versed in slideware and hence feel right at home. Interestingly, this difference is lessened in the *search for a loosely defined position*, a task that benefits particularly from the canvas format as the presenter can quickly zoom out to get an overview and pinpoint her target.

In summary, we have improved our understanding of canvas presentations and gained insight into who benefits from the format. Combined with the existing body of research [6, 8–10] we now have an understanding of all the actors involved in presentations. One may think of author and presenter as the same person, but the results of [11, 13] and this paper indicate opposing forces in the tools: The authoring work before the talk benefits from the freedom of expression of the canvas format. The same freedom of navigation while presenting comes with a drawback. Here, time and attention are limited and, as we have seen, a simpler linear format can be easier to handle for some presenters (cf. [7]). One could conclude to always limit the format during presentation delivery, but we have also shown that for some presenters this would be unfavorable. We suggest that during delivery, canvas tools should (1) allow the user to limit the navigation to the linear format until she needs the free format, and (2) offer her a simple way to get back to a safe place on the presentation path.

6   Limitations and Future Work

By design, our study was a lab study, and therefore is controlled situation that might not be representative of real-life use. A field study with presenters presenting their own presentations, with their own agendas on their own topic of expertise, and own audiences could corroborate the results of this paper. We were unable to attribute the interaction effect of program use to spatial ability or presentation age, as both independent variables correlated. A study with separated variables could investigate this issue further. Other limitations are the short nature of presentations and the novelty of the canvas condition. We invite replication of this study and the materials used in this experiment can be downloaded at http://hci.rwth-aachen.de/fly.

References

1. Bederson, B.B., Hollan, J.D.: Pad++: a zooming graphical interface for exploring alternate interface physics. In: Proceedings of the UIST 1994, pp. 17–26 (1994)
2. Bederson, B.B.: The promise of zoomable user interfaces. Behav. Inf. Technol. **30**(6), 853–866 (2011)
3. Ekstrom, R.B., French, J.W., Harman, H.H.: Manual for Kit of Factor-Referenced Cognitive Tests. Educational Testing Service, Princeton (1976)
4. Bradley, M.M., Lang, P.J.: Measuring emotion: The self-assessment manikin and the semantic differential. J. Behav. Ther. Exp. Psychiatry **25**(1), 49–59 (1994)
5. Evans, G.T.: Use of the semantic differential technique to study attitudes during classroom lessons. Interchange **1**(4), 96–106 (1970)
6. Frijda, N.H.: The psychologists' point of view. In: Lewis, M., Haviland-Jones, J.M., Barrett, L.F. (eds.) Handbook of Emotions, vol. 3, pp. 68–87. The Guilford Press, New York (2008)
7. Good, L., Bederson, B.B.: Zoomable user interfaces as a medium for slide show presentations. Inf. Visual. **1**(1), 35–49 (2002)
8. Higgins, R.L., Alonso, R.R., Pendleton, M.G.: The validity of role-play assessments of assertiveness. Behav. Ther. **10**(5), 655–662 (1979)
9. Kern, J.M., Miller, C., Eggers, J.: Enhancing the Validity of role-play tests: a comparison of three role-play methodologies. Behav. Ther. **14**(4), 482–492 (1983)
10. Apple Keynote. http://www.apple.com
11. Lichtschlag, L., Karrer, T., Borchers, J.: Fly: a tool to author planar presentations. In: Proceedings of the CHI 2009, pp. 547–556 (2009)
12. Lichtschlag, L., Hess, T., Karrer, T., Borchers, J.: Fly: studying recall, macrostructure understanding, and user experience of canvas presentations. In: Proceedings of the CHI 2012, pp. 1307-1310 (2012)
13. Lichtschlag, L., Hess, T., Karrer, T., Borchers, J.: Canvas presentations in the wild. In: Proceedings of the CHI EA 2012, pp. 537–540 (2012)
14. Osgood, C.E., Suci, G.J., Tannenbaum, P.: The Measurement of Meaning. University of Illinois Press, Urbana (1957)
15. Parker, I.: Absolute PowerPoint: Can a software package edit our thoughts? New Yorker **77** (13), 76–87 (2001)
16. Prezi. http://prezi.com

17. Robinson, M.D., Clore, G.L.: Belief and feeling: evidence for an accessibility model of emotional self-report. Psychol. Bull. **128**(6), 934–960 (2002)
18. Russell, J.A., Mehrabian, A.: Evidence for a three-factor theory of emotions. J. Res. Pers. **11** (3), 273–294 (1977)
19. Scherer, K.R.: What are emotions? and how can they be measured? Soc. Sci. Inf. **44**(4), 695–729 (2005)
20. Tufte, E.: The Cognitive Style of PowerPoint. Graphics Press, USA (2003)
21. Watson, D., Clark, L.A., Tellegen, A.: Development and validation of brief measures of positive and negative affect: the PANAS scales. J. Pers. Soc. Psychol. **54**(6), 1063–1070 (1988)

Using Online Reviews as Narratives to Evoke Designer's Empathy

Christiane Grünloh[(✉)], Åke Walldius, Gerhard Hartmann,
and Jan Gulliksen

[1] KTH Royal Institute of Technology, Lindstedtsvägen 3,
10044 Stockholm, Sweden
christiane.gruenloh@fh-koeln.de,
gulliksen@kth.se, aakew@nada.kth.se
[2] CUAS Cologne University of Applied Sciences, Steinmüllerallee 1,
51643 Gummersbach, Germany
gerhard.hartmann@fh-koeln.de

Abstract. Gathering health-related data is quite easy, but visualizing them in a meaningful way remains challenging, especially when the application domain is very complex. Research suggests that empathy can facilitate the design process and that narratives can help to create an empathic encounter between designers and the prospective users. We conducted an exploratory quasi-experiment in order to explore whether narratives in form of online reviews are able to evoke designer's empathy when developing an online platform for a direct-to-consumer genetic testing service. The results suggest that the narratives can help designers to engage with and take the perspective of the prospective user, who is then represented in more detail. Lacking narratives from real people leaves the designers to their own imagination, which can lead to the use of rather abstract stereotypes that do not enable an understanding of the user, but affect the subsequent design decisions.

Keywords: Human-Computer interaction · Empathy · Direct-to-consumer · Genetic testing · Health and wellbeing

1 Introduction

Consumer products with regard to health and wellbeing are on the rise. The increasing availability and affordability of self-tracking devices and apps enable people easier access to their health-related data. Recently Topol (2015) compared the smartphone to the Gutenberg press, in that it might help to break boundary in medicine, because patients today are able to take a more active role (e.g. accessing various information sources or using health apps) [33]. Data can be collected by the hardware itself (e.g. data related to physical activities like daily steps, heart rate, distance, speed, duration) or manually tracked by the individual (e.g. nutrition, mood), and shared with others (e.g. PatientsLikeMe[1]). Additionally, services like direct-to-consumer (DTC) genetic testing allow for easy access and exploration of personal genetic information. The

---

[1] http://www.patientslikeme.com/, (accessed: January 17, 2015).

© IFIP International Federation for Information Processing 2015
J. Abascal et al. (Eds.): INTERACT 2015, Part I, LNCS 9296, pp. 298–315, 2015.
DOI: 10.1007/978-3-319-22701-6_22

boundaries between services with regard to health and wellbeing on the one hand and medical issues on the other can easily become blurred. The very same app could be used as a tool for managing health and wellness, but also for medical purposes. Although the data collection is quite easy, it has to be processed and visualized in a way that helps the individual to understand them in order to generate meaning.

According to the ISO 9241-210 user experience includes "all the users' emotions, beliefs, preferences, perceptions, physical and psychological responses, behaviours and accomplishments that occur before, during and after use" [17]. Especially when it comes to services like genetic testing, the time span *after* the service has been used may become very important to consider. There are concerns that with "respect to asymptomatic individuals, [...] genetic testing may trigger an untoward psychological response, such as severe depression, anxiety, or even suicidal ideation" ([32], as cited in [15, p. 5]). Designing a system or service in this area can be very challenging, because it entails potentially complex data and addresses various customers with different motivations and backgrounds. Wright and McCarthy explored how empathy can facilitate the design process in terms of "knowing the user" [38]. Besides ethnographic approaches, which can be very time consuming, they considered also methods and techniques that involve empathic encounter without direct contact between designer and participant, e.g. the use of narratives.

In this paper we want to explore whether the reading of and the dealing with narratives in the form of online reviews is able to evoke or elevate the designer's empathy with the prospective users of their design. Furthermore we are interested whether the reading of the afore-mentioned material helps designers to identify important experiences, which should be considered and addressed in the design of a system or service. We tried to answer these questions by conducting an exploratory quasi-experiment, where students were asked to develop an online platform for a direct-to-consumer genetic testing service. We regarded this case of application appropriate, because the service provides complex information, which cannot clearly be categorized as health, wellness, or medical data. Therefore it offers great potential for multidimensional discussions and application of various perspectives, precisely because the testing can entail both innocent and very serious results. In order to reduce the distance to people and enable empathy and understanding, we used narratives and personal accounts that have been published by real people on the Internet.

2 Background

2.1 Empathy and Related Works

The value of empathy and the opportunities it provides as a useful tool has been discussed on several occasions (e.g. in ergonomics [30], HCI [38], participatory design [19], product design [28], design research [22]). Dandavate et al. even go so far to say that the success of products will depend upon the degree to which researchers and practitioners learn how to empathize with the product users early in the development process [8]. Keen defines empathy as a "vicarious, spontaneous sharing of affect" which can be provoked "by witnessing another's emotional state, by hearing about another's condition, or even by reading" [18, p. 208]. This can be referred to as the *affective* approach, which considers one's emotional response to the affective state of the other [2]. Empathy is also often understood as the ability to 'walk a mile in someone's shoes', i.e. to take the role of someone else or another's perspective, which can be seen as the *cognitive* approach of empathy [2].

Researchers and designers make use of specific methods like for example Experience Prototyping or autoethnography, which support them to take the perspective of the user. *Experience Prototyping* aims to support designers, users, and clients to understand existing user experience and future conditions by engaging with the prototypes themselves [4]. Buchenau and Suri describe as an example project the "Patient Experience", which addresses patients with chest-implanted automatic defibrillators. Due to the lack of first-hand experience by real patients, they wanted to recreate the essential elements of a personal experience, namely how it is like to be a defibrillating pacemaker patient. This was done by distributing pagers to the members of the design team as a proxy, where the pager represented defibrillating shocks at random times. The authors state that in this project empathy was promoted by the Experience Prototypes, but that this method should be seen as complementary to other design methods helping to understand other people's points of view [4, p. 432]. *Autoethnography* can be seen as related to Experience Prototyping. Here the researcher adopts the role of the participant as well in order to "understand and empathize with the experience mobile device user can face in difficult to access contexts" [25]. O'Kane et al. used this method to evaluate a wrist blood pressure monitor, because the non-routine situations they wanted to investigate were situations real users would be reluctant to disrupt for a study (e.g. holidays, festivities, etc.). They conclude that "for non-routine times it is an insightful method for challenging assumptions, gaining empathy with user experiences, and planning future user studies, including with mobile medical technologies" [25, p. 990].

Wright and McCarthy explore the relation between empathy and experience in Human-Computer Interaction (HCI) [38]. They see "empathic approaches as part of the broader pragmatist approach to experience", because from "the pragmatist perspective, understanding an other or more specifically, 'knowing the user' in their lived and felt life involves understanding what it *feels like* to be that person, what their situation is like from their own perspective. In short, it involves empathy" (emphasis in original) [38, p. 638]. Questioning whether an empathic encounter without direct contact is possible, the authors explore narrative approaches that have been created by HCI practitioners, e.g. ethnographic vignette, character-driven scenarios. They conclude: "Using these methods in the spirit of enquiry and responsive understanding in which they were intended to be used may be sufficient to provide empathic understanding." [38, p. 644].

Storyboards and narratives are a way to elicit empathy when direct contact to real users is not possible. McQuaid et al. used these as "customer surrogates" in order to understand their frustrating and pleasurable experiences with a national, public library and communicate those to stakeholders [23]. The storyboards were produced by user research specialists after they had acted as participants trying to fulfill a certain task. The authors consider these storyboards and narratives of select personas as effective techniques to help stakeholders to empathize with their customers. They believe that the stakeholders engaged more with the stories, because they were very realistic in the sense that they included real people and pictures, and that the process was very concrete and visual represented in the stories [23].

Cooper introduced personas as "hypothetical archetypes" of actual users which are defined by their goals and "with significant rigor and precision", although they are imaginary [7]. As concrete representations of target users, they help the design team to become more user focused by "putting a face on the user" and conveying information about the prospective users in ways that other artifacts cannot [27, p. 11]. These have been developed further by Pruitt and Grudin and used not only in the design team but for communication purposes to all project partners (i.e. developers, testers, writers, managers, etc.) [26]. Personas can help to make "assumptions and decision-making criteria equally explicit" and that without them certain decision are made routinely "without recognizing or communicating their underlying assumptions" about how the product will be used by whom [26]. However, already the process of creating the personas helped them to make the assumptions about the target audience more explicit [26]. Personas make use of images and the act of finding the right image for the persona can already stimulate empathy with users [37].

With regard to narrative approaches it is emphasized that abstract representations of the individuals are counterproductive, and that it is important for the designer to "engage with the characters" and understand "their background, personality, intentions, and motives" in order to explore "how that person might respond to new situations and new technologies" [38, p. 642]. According to Nielsen, describing "the user as a rounded character" helps the design team to engage with the user with empathy, but the description must be based on "knowledge of actual users"; i.e. on facts and not fiction [24, p. 104]. Golsteijn and Wright use a portraiture approach, in which the story of each interviewed or observed person is told in a separate individual portrait, "within the context of use and staying true to the real user" [16, p. 301]. The authors believe that their approach "minimizes the risks of stereotyping and oversimplifying users and their experiences" and that these holistic descriptions of real users should be imported directly in the ideation process (unlike personas which are more generalizing/summarizing and created *before* ideation has begun) [16, p. 301f].

Researchers aiming for improvement of quality of health care services and patients' experience developed the *experience-based co-design* (EBCD) approach, which also bases on narratives and personal stories [31]. This approach uses video narrative interviews with local patients and staff to identify opportunities for improvement from both perspectives. Due to the involved time and cost, this approach has been adapted to *accelerated experience-based co-design* (AEBCD), in which a national archive of patient narrative interviews[2] is used instead of interviewing and filming local patients [20]. Although national instead of local interviews were used, those films were considered "not perfect, but were 'good enough' to start the process of co-design" [20, p. 37f].

---

[2] The national archive is held by the Health Experiences Group in Oxford (HERG) and online available at http://www.healthtalk.org/ (accessed: January 17, 2015).

2.2   Genetic Testing

Due to the decreasing cost of testing and sequencing of genomes, genetic testing is becoming more and more popular. For example the Department of Health launched a project to sequence 100,000 whole genomes from NHS patients by 2017 [13]. However, genetic tests are also sold direct-to-consumer (DTC), which has been criticized due to ethical, legal, and social issues [5]. Depending on the information these tests provide, it is not easy to draw a clear line in categorizing the test as a medical product or an information product. Companies like 23andMe for example offer at the same time tests for harmless traits (e.g. eye and hair color) and serious diseases (e.g. Alzheimer's Disease, Breast Cancer, etc.). Packaging together trivial and potentially life-changing tests can be problematic, especially when this serves as a means to get around regulation when only the fun part is advertised [35]. The U.S. Food and Drug Administration (FDA) considers the service by 23andMe as "intended for use in the diagnosis of disease or other conditions or in the cure, mitigation, treatment, or prevention of disease, or is intended to affect the structure or function of the body" [34]. While the company is still waiting for an approval in the U.S., the service was approved in the UK, because the UK Medicines and Healthcare Products Regulatory Agency (MHRA) considered the service as an information product instead of a medical product [14]. A detailed discussion of the ethics involved in DTC genetic testing is beyond the scope of this article. For a more comprehensive discussion on the benefits and concerns regarding DTC genetic testing see for example [5, 29].

2.3   Doctor-Patient Relationship

Due to technology and other developments in healthcare the relationship between patients and the healthcare professional is changing. The more traditional relationship, also known as the "paternalistic model", assumes that the doctor can judge patients preferences, that both have the same goals, and that only the doctor has the expertise to determine how to proceed [9, p. 171f]. Moreover, this model also assumes that "the doctor will make the best treatment decision for the patient and can do so without eliciting personal information from the patient or involving him or her in the decision making process" [6, p. 781]. This has changed in that sense, that today the autonomy of patients is supposed be respected and some alternative models emerged, e.g. the *engineering model* (patient is the sole decision maker, physician only gives advice), the *collegial model* (recognizes the imbalance of knowledge and views between patients and providers; sees them as equal partners), the *contractual model* (shared decision making with contributions by both patient and physician) [36, as cited in 9, p. 172]. Emanuel and Emanuel outline four models of physician-patient interaction (paternalistic, informative, interpretive, and deliberative model) and compare them with regard to patient values, physician's obligation, conception of patient's autonomy, and conception of physician's role [10]. The authors recognize that different models may be appropriate under different clinical circumstances, but emphasize that the paternalistic model is justified in rather limited circumstances (i.e. emergencies), because "it is no longer tenable to assume that the physician and patient espouse similar values and views of what constitutes a benefit" [10, p. 2224]. Nowadays interventions for patient empowerment have been carried out, which aim to "increase the patient's capacity to think critically and make autonomous, informed decisions" [1, p. 279]. This is also supported by governments in Europe, which are promoting the "expansion of eHealth over the past years, arguing that this development enhances patient participation, empowerment and cost efficiency" [11, p. 1].

3   Method

In order to investigate whether the reading of narratives and reviews is able to evoke or elevate empathy for people, to the extent that it may change the design of a system or service, we conducted an exploratory quasi-experiment with a between-subject design. Two groups of students were asked to develop an online platform for publishing genetic test results for a direct-to-consumer genetic testing service. Since the students were not familiar with these services, we could assume that they were not aware of the controversies involved. The experiment considered as independent variable the material the groups were provided with, which for the experimental group additionally contained personal reviews written by actual customers of a direct-to-consumer genetic testing service. We regarded the dispositional empathy (i.e. empathy as a character trait) as a possible confounding factor. If for example the participants assigned to the control group are already very empathic and therefore don't necessarily need to read narratives as a means to empathize with a person. To control the confounding factor, we conducted a pretest in which the participants had to complete the Empathy Quotient (EQ), a self-assessment instrument developed by [2]. The results of the EQ served as a means to assign the participants to the two groups to achieve comparability.

3.1   Pilot Study

The initial experiment design was tested with two students, who didn't participate in the main study, in order to evaluate the feasibility of the study design and whether the material is comprehensible for the participants. It transpired that the task description and instructions had to be clearer and partly reworded. The students struggled when reading the English narratives. Therefore we decided to translate the customer reviews into German to make sure that they are fully understood.

3.2   Participants

The participants were recruited via student mailing lists and announcements on the University's wiki. The experiment comprised 14 advanced students of Media Informatics (8 male, 6 female; 10 Bachelor students, 4 Master students; age: 22–35 years). None of the participants have carried out a genetic test in the past.

3.3   Procedure

Due to the small sample (N = 14) random sampling was not appropriate. To reduce the effect of the confounding factor *dispositional empathy*, the groups were divided by help of matching. All participants completed the EQ questionnaire a few days prior to the study. We then assigned the individual participants to achieve comparable groups regarding the EQ (see Table 1). Both groups equally consisted of 7 participants and we also managed to have equal number of female/male, Bachelor/Master students in each group.

Table 1. Median, Means and Total EQ

Group	Median	Mean	Total
Control group	41	40.857	286
Experimental group	42	40.857	286

On the day of the study each participant received a consent form (and a personal copy), in which the process of the study was explained, as well as risks, advantages, how the study was recorded, how we deal with the data, and of course their right to withdraw from the study at any time. After the participants signed the informed consent, the study started with an introduction to the task and the procedure in general. We introduced the task description verbally and informed the participants, that we would separate them in two different groups, in which they then could work on the task. We then showed them four small video clips in order to make the participants familiar with the nature of genes, SNPs (Single Nucleotide Polymorphism), and phenotypes. The videoclips have been produced by 23andMe, published on youtube.com[3] and explain the topics in a rather playful and almost trivializing way. Taken the background music and the style (an animated cartoon) into account, these clips seem to target rather children than adults. However, it was important for us to adhere to the marketing strategy of those companies.

After showing the video clips, we separated the two groups and assigned them to two different rooms. Each group received a notepad for the group document and each participant also received a notepad for his/her individual notes. In addition every participant received a printed task description including the instructions, the procedure, and an excerpt of the diseases and conditions the service includes in its genetic analysis. This information was also taken from the 23andMe website[4], but shortened and included the categories: Ancestry Composition, Disease Risk, Drug Response, Traits, and Carrier Status. The material of the experimental group was supplemented by five personal reviews. In order to provide the participants in the experimental group with

---

[3] The videos are available at http://youtu.be/ubq4eu_TDFc?list=PLF9969C74FAAD2BF9 (last access: January 17, 2015). We showed the clips 1 to 4, but didn't view the first seconds where the company name is displayed.

[4] See https://web.archive.org/web/20130424163612/https://www.23andme.com/health/all/ (last access: January 23, 2015).

rich narratives that might enable the identification with the user of the service, we extracted real customer reviews from amazon.com[5]. Only little information was deleted or altered (e.g. we substituted the name of the company with a place holder). The reviews were chosen because they gave some hints regarding the motivation of using the service (e.g. one person was adopted and wanted to learn about diseases that run in the family or another wanted to know about the chances his kids develop schizophrenia). There were some negative comments within the reviews, but also some positive ones. As mentioned earlier, we translated the reviews into German to increase the comprehensibility. The experimental group got instructed that they would have to read all of the material, but they are not bound to use it in their design. We wanted to decrease the possibility that the participants regard the purpose of the material as something that they *have to* analyze in depth. After reading the instructions both groups were observed but not guided through their design process. Only questions regarding the procedure (e.g. how much time they have left) were answered by the observers. After approximately one and a half hours, the students were asked to stop their activities. After a short break, both groups presented their results to all participants. Finally we debriefed the participants and answered pending questions (e.g. regarding the purpose of the questionnaire they completed in advance).

3.4   Data Collection and Analysis

The data comprised video recordings of the group work (about 2 h per group) and the presentations, the group document written by the individual group secretary, individual notes of the participants, pictures from the group's output (e.g. from brainstorming, clustering) and observants' notes. Each group was recorded using the in-build camera and microphone of a MacBook Pro. The data was transcribed verbatim afterwards using MAXQDA11 for Mac[6]. The transcription was then analyzed using inductive Thematic Analysis as described in [3] to identify recurrent themes in the data; within and between the groups. After familiarizing with the data, 40 initial codes were generated by systematically working through the entire data set, one group at a time. The initial codes identified features like emotions, process (use of analogies, scope of the task), concerns (consequences, risks, comprehensibility for laypeople, legal issues, misuse, incorrect results, serious results), design (e.g. customer service, support, usability, functionalities, change of testing process, visualization of results), perspectives addressed (e.g. health insurance, physician, genetic testing company, design company, users, motivations), values (e.g. ethics and morals, freedom of choice, paternalism, data privacy, security). Afterwards the entire data set was reviewed with regard to the codes to examine coherence of the codes between the groups. Then the extracts were reviewed on code level, i.e. all extracts of both groups corresponding to a specific code were reviewed in order to analyze the codes. Due to the exhaustive set of data extracts and codes, extracts were exported from the software tool MAXQDA for

---

[5] See http://amzn.com/B002QPR852 (last access: January 23, 2015).

[6] For further information see http://www.maxqda.com/products/maxqda, (accessed: January 17, 2015).

further investigation and inspection, to collate the coded extracts within a code, and to "consider how different codes may combine to form an overarching theme" [3, p. 89]. In accordance to [3] this phase re-focuses the analysis at the broader level of themes rather than codes. Visual representations like mind maps and tables were very helpful to sort the codes into themes and to identify similarities and differences between the groups. By means of reading, categorizing and reviewing the codes and extracts for each theme repeatedly, the themes could be developed iteratively and will be described in detail in the next section.

4 Results

Our analysis showed that (I) the groups share deep concerns regarding the DTC genetic testing service; (II) the groups differ in how they represent the prospective users; (III) they differ in how they deal with their concerns with regard to their representation of users; (IV) the design decisions differ accordingly. These themes will be elaborated in detail in the following sections. For references to the data and quotations, the group is indicated as EG (experimental group) or CG (control group) and the number of the extract is added. The excerpts presented from the transcripts have been translated from German to English by the first author.

4.1 Shared Concerns

Both the experimental group (EG) and the control group (CG) shared several concerns with regard to the introduced DTC genetic testing service:

Revelation of Serious Results. Both groups identified early on that "for some people a genetic test is a very serious matter; for others it's more a gimmick" (EG:109). While the groups considered the rather harmless information (like Ancestry Composition, Drug Response, and Traits) to be revealed straightaway, information regarding Disease Risk and Carrier Status should be taken seriously and processed differently.

Both groups struggled with how to reveal such sensitive information and if the Genetic testing company is generally allowed to share such information with people. Both share their concern that the results might cause panic, psychic stress, or upset a person, when revealed via an online service. Both groups indicate on several occasions that they want to include some sort of psychological support, e.g. psychological counseling, reference to support groups, support by phone, or aftercare in general.

The groups share the concern with regard to undesired consequences, but the type of consequence differs between the groups. CG referred to rather extreme consequences due to how people would *react* after learning about the results (e.g. that a person would commit suicide, give up their child for adoption when the results are bad, or even perform an abortion). EG considered consequences in terms of what the results might *mean* for the person in their future (e.g. an unwanted result in a paternity test, or having a high probability regarding Alzheimer's or cancer).

Comprehensibility. Both groups identified that the information is quite complex and that laypeople probably need additional information and a comprehensible visualization. Both also realized that they as designers also struggle to understand the specific terms, which they feel is necessary in order to structure and cluster the data for laypeople. The experimental group went one step further in discussing that not only the lack of knowledge, but also the existence of prior knowledge (i.e. experts) should be addressed, because those "would probably rather understand professional jargon" (EG:314).

Data Access by Third Parties. The groups identified potential interests in the data by third parties, e.g. insurance companies, physicians, bone marrow database, or research (CG); employer, anyone else besides the donor (EG). In this regard, both groups also discussed the risk that an unauthorized person might send a sample of someone else.

4.2 Representation and Attitude Towards Users

The way the two groups talked about the users differed noticeably. The representation of users remained very abstract in the control group. When they discussed who would want to do such a genetic test, they referred to "people who panic to get sick" (CG:43); "curious" (CG:44, 179), "who have been adopted" (CG:45, 48), "who consult online docs" (CG:49), "overcautious" (CG:172), "doctors could use it for their patients" (CG:173), "hypochondriac" (CG:307,370), "parents who want to test the DNA of their children" (CG:503). The representations remained rather stereotypic without deep discussion regarding the characteristics of the person or further motivational aspects.

The experimental group didn't represent the users in such a stereotypic way. The discussions evolved here rather around the underlying motivations, interests, characteristics, and needs of people, e.g. "What would the customer, who doesn't know exactly why he actually makes the test... what could be important to him and what would he want to know" (EG:111). The discussions with regard to a person's background and characteristics were in all more detailed: "adopted child, who wants to know about their medical history and origin of the family" (EG:49); "in case a disease runs in the family, and one wants to know if one is affected" (EG:64), and with reference to a review: "Right here with schizophrenia. That he knows he does not have it so he's not schizophrenic. But he'd just like to know whether his children could get it." (EG:260); furthermore, a person might be interested only in certain information like origin of family - not more (EG:339); "people who have a serious disease" (EG:407); "users with shortcomings" which the student's would like to address (EG:313); people without specific domain knowledge ("laypeople"), and who might need some anecdotes (EG:314); and "experienced persons" who require professional jargon (EG:314).

Besides the identification of motivations in the reviews, the students of the EG also wanted to learn about the person's motivations, special needs, and disabilities (e.g. blindness) through some kind of pre-test, which would then lead to an individualized presentation (EG:308). Later in the process they also stepped back again: "We already started with the requirements, even though we didn't really address the users. Who are those people?" (EG:401), and further: what are their motivations (EG:403) and what additional information might be important to inquire up-front (EG:409) that could be used for individual representation (EG:414).

4.3   Paternalism vs. Autonomy

As already mentioned, the students struggled when it came to the revelation of serious results. The control group took quite early a rather paternalistic approach, in which the access to some results is denied. "I just had an idea… there are these online tests, so that you might ask some basic questions in advance… and then you say: No, sorry. You are not getting the results. Get in touch with our doctors or whatever. Something like that." (CG:26). Initial questions arose regarding the legal situation and if it is allowed to tell people their results "just like that" (CG:58), or whether some aspects would be excluded, a question which was met with the counter argument "How so? You always have a right to information" (CG:61). However, this wasn't considered further after a student used an analogy: "Yes, but for example I know with Parkinson tests, they have to go through [psychologic counseling] and so forth before they learn, if they have it or not. And if the psychologists detect that the person is too unstable to learn that, then they won't. That's why I can't imagine that all this information can be released just like that." (CG:62) The group then developed their idea further that the service would offer two packages, where the one with Disease Risk and Carrier Status would be only available in cooperation with a doctor. They planned to grant only the specific doctor access to this kind of data (CG:76).

Some of the students in the control group noticed, that this would change the company philosophy, because it is a *direct-to-consumer* service after all (CG:70,83) and that changing the process the process might be bad for their business (CG:110, 112). They raised concerns whether they were allowed to make these kind of decisions (CG:151). However, in the end they considered it as important and in the person's interest that the doctor is involved (CG:286): "the most important things that we really have in mind… what we are talking about the whole time, is to protect the user from himself and from the information he could get." (CG:264). Moreover, not only the design team is able to decide for the person, the doctor can do that as well: "Then the doctor can, … perhaps he knows his patient well… he can perhaps say directly: No, no, no, you don't want to know the disease risks" (CG:280).

When one student asked, "If this is the decision of the customer? […] who wants to get the results" (CG:288, 292), he was quickly overruled: "Well, bad luck, then go somewhere else" (CG:289); "Yes, but it's for his own safety." (CG:293). One student elaborated further on the protection with an analogy: "There are many things that are made for the protection of all of us, for example that we must fasten our seatbelt, etc. If I fast my seatbelt or not is still my own decision, but basically it is said you need to buckle up while driving, otherwise you could fly through the windshield." (CG:296) The argument that the person could sign an informed consent was also overruled, because "But then he can also be quite unstable or so… I think that one always believes: I can take it, I can manage it." (CG:300). The control group decided in the end that every person has to register and if they are interested in Disease Risk or Carrier Status, they have to cooperate with their doctor, who also has to sign a form.

The experimental group also had the idea to involve doctors or experts who might initiate psychological counseling (EG:115), identify the person (EG:117), or interpret certain test results: "bad news, yes… these diseases etc. that they are best interpreted by physicians" (EG:120). One group member early raised the concern that this would "depart from the business idea that they have" (EG:118). The group then changed the involvement of experts to be on a voluntary basis (EG:126) and that they would make recommendations who to contact (EG:131). The question if it is allowed or if someone is entitled to reveal such serious information in an automatized way (EG:132) and if this is ethical were met with "Yes, but he wants to know" (EG:133) and "He pays for it. He wants that." (EG:135). Unlike the control group they dismissed ideas with paternalistic tendencies for the sake of respecting the person's decision and gave the individual person and their perspective priority.

4.4   Design Decisions

Changes with Regard to the Testing Process. Although both groups considered to change aspects in the testing process of the DTC service, the underlying motivation differed and can be related to the previous theme. Both groups consider to include some kind of pre-test or application process. This was motivated in the CG in order to determine whether the person can handle this information. The pre-test was later obsolete, because according to their final design deliberations access to serious information was only granted through the doctor, who would then determine whether the person can handle it or not. The pre-test was considered in EG in order to determine an interest in specific information due to previous conditions (e.g. specific drug responses due to a certain disease) and to identify special needs of the person, which would then be addressed in the design; e.g. if the person is visually impaired.

Both groups considered to involve a doctor or an expert and mentioned that this could ensure the authenticity of the sample sender. However, this was not the initial motivation for the involvement, which differed between the groups. While the CG wanted to involve the doctor in order to reveal serious information in general, the EG wanted the doctor or expert to give *additional* information with regard to the results, interpret serious results, and initiate psychological counseling if necessary. Additionally, in the end only the control group kept the idea in their final design deliberations.

Usability. In line with the rather paternalistic approach, the CG tended to overload people with information in order to prevent them to sign up for this test thoughtlessly: "Rather put too much information than having the user click through it too easily" (CG:206); "I'd rather see to it that… that with the registration process, that in a sense scruple is generated" (CG:328). They recognized that it requires extra effort to undergo for example some sort of personal identification procedure (CG:329). They also considered that expressing additional consent that the person is aware of legal issues by an extra click might be contrary to usability, but they wanted to include that anyway "Just to make sure" (CG:438). The EG didn't mention usability aspects explicitly, but discussed that they want to provide individualized visualizations with regard to the specific needs (e.g. auditive, textual, graphical, or a personal contact) and according to the person's specific interests: "…not some kind of heap of graphics and data, but to say, well, this is something important or this may be of interest for you…" (EG:111).

Functionalities. The CG elaborated several design dimensions with regard to safety aspects. This addressed the system's security (restricted access, authentication, risk of having data online, ensure protection on a personal and data level). With regard to protection, the group wanted to make sure, that doctors will be involved, when health related results are to be revealed. Their solutions included an identification process and some kind of key encryption procedure to protect the data. The functionalities discussed in the CG dealt with Login, identification procedure, encryption, PDF export, anonymization, and verification. The EG focused not that much on technical solutions, although they also discussed some kind of personal identification procedure. Their design addressed functionalities like contact options for bi-directional communication with the company, the opportunity for ratings and reviews, provide communication platform between persons, filtering the results based on a person's interest and data.

Visualization. The main task for both groups was to develop a platform that should be used to publish the genetic testing results. The outcome with regard to the visualization differed noticeably. The CG excluded the two categories Disease Risk and Carrier Status completely and didn't discuss the visualization of the remaining categories in detail. They wanted to show certain information in a table on demand and if desired a person can get further information on a specific topic through hyperlinks. The EG discussed extensively how they want to visualize the information: e.g. visual and auditive, in a sensitive way, depending on the individual category (in a cheerful or serious manner), using some kind of color scheme (including the consideration of different cultural connotations), using different modalities (e.g. tree, table, list), using metaphors (e.g. traffic light, body parts, globe, maps).

4.5   Group Presentation

Due to the time constraints, the ill-defined character of the design task, and the consequential extensive discussions within both groups, the final presentation of their design focussed on specific aspects they would address when developing the platform. Table 2 gives an overview about the aspects the groups presented:

Table 2. Design aspects presented by the groups

	Control group (CG)	Experimental group (EG)
Access to results	Only access to • Ancestry composition • Drug response • Traits	Access to all categories
Doctor involvement	Mandatory for accessing • Disease risk	Optional, but recommended for serious results

(*Continued*)

Table 2. (*Continued*)

	Control group (CG)	Experimental group (EG)
	• Carrier status	
Visualization	• Visualization of results regarding Ancestry composition, Drug response, traits • Clear textual visualization • Hyperlinks with further information	• Visual and/or auditive • Sensitive way depending on category • Harmless results in a cheerful way • Address different user groups with special needs • Use of metaphors (maps for ancestry; use of colors; body parts; traffic light metaphor for drug response) • Comprehensible for laypeople and experts • Prevent misunderstanding • Use table, lists, hyperlinks
Other requirements/aspects	• Security • Data protection • Access restriction • Registration, unique ID, personal identification, • Export of data regarding disease risk and carrier status to doctor, who will discuss them with user • Provide extensive information up front about what the service offers in order to create confidence • Give information regarding counseling centers • Option to share data with research, bone marrow databases • Information regarding legal issues	• High priority for motivation of users • Customer service • Ensure transparency to create confidence • Trust • Data protection • User identification • Prevent data misuse • Dealing with consequences, offer a service to connect users to psychological counselor • Enable import of data from insurance company/doctor (e.g. allergies to drugs)

5   Discussion

Both groups started with the same concerns regarding the type of service they were asked to develop an online platform for. How the groups discussed and talked about the people they were designing for differed in that the CG remained abstract and used rather stereotypical description of the persons. And as Nielsen states: "As the stereotypes will function as a mental picture they will never enable an understanding of the user." [24, p. 104] The EG on the other hand described the users in more detail and took into consideration their background, interests, motivation, and needs. Although we can't 'measure' quantitatively whether empathy has been evoked or elevated by the narratives, this might be a strong indicator. Like Nielsen stated: "To describe the user as a rounded character brings a focus on the user into the design process. It helps the design team to engage with the user with empathy, thereby remembering the user all the way through and remembering that the design is for a user." [24]. The mental representation of the prospective users in the experimental group is likely to be influenced by the provided material (i.e. the narratives), because the EG referred to specific aspects of the narratives on several occasions.

The lack of empathy and/or the use of a rather stereotypical representation might have led the CG to follow a paternalistic approach, which then influenced the following discussions and design decisions. The stereotypical representation of the users can to some extent even be seen as preexisting individual bias (e.g. the "suicidal", the "unstable", the "hypochondriac"), which "has its roots in social institutions, practices, and attitudes" and "can enter a system either through the explicit and conscious efforts of individuals or institutions, or implicitly and unconsciously, even in spite of the best of intentions" [12, p. 333f]. The long tradition of the rather passive patient might have led to an unconscious bias in that they have to be protected and (in line with the paternalistic model) that it is appropriate to "spare patients the worry of decision making" [9, p. 172]. It is not our intention to imply that these systems should be build regardless of any concerns and that the user would themselves be responsible for any consequences. Rather to the contrary, we agree with Löwgren and Stolterman, that the "responsibility for what is created is fully in the hands of the creator - the designer" [21, p. 4]. However, we think that making decision for the prospective users (e.g. "protecting him from himself") without their involvement and hereby taking a paternalistic approach conflicts with recent attempts in terms of patient empowerment to increase the autonomy of people with regard to health and wellbeing.

We also noticed that the control group used analogies more often than then experimental group and lost themselves in discussions more often, whereas the EG managed to get back on topic faster. We cannot eliminate the influence of group dynamics, but one explanation could be that the EG had some material at hand, so that they did not need that much imagination and storytelling to get engaged in the task. This is in accordance to the work by Golsteijn and Wright, in which "the portraits acted to provide depth and focus, because rather than thinking about 'anything' we could think about the needs of one specific person – a real person – and what could be designed for this person" [16, p. 312].

6   Conclusions

In this paper we wanted to explore whether the use of narratives by real persons evokes or elevates the designer's empathy with the prospective users. Due to the sample size and the very design of the study (i.e. its explorative character, a design task as object of study within a restricted timeframe, and students as participants), the generalizability of the results is limited. However, based on the thematic analysis we conclude that providing additional material containing narratives from real people can help the design team to engage with and take the perspective of the prospective user, who is then represented during the discussions and in the design in more detail. Lacking narratives from real people leaves the designers to their own imagination, which can lead to the use of rather abstract stereotypes that affect the subsequent design decisions. However, it would be interesting to investigate, whether a study with professional designers with several years of experience would show similar results.

Although direct contact with real people is preferable for enabling an empathic encounter and to be able to "walk a mile in their shoes", this might not always be possible, e.g. due to time and budget constraints. However, today many people share their personal stories with others online; stories written by people in their very own words. These stories are therefore based on facts not fiction and might help designers to engage with the prospective users. Similar to other methods (e.g. experience proto-typing) using online reviews as narratives should be seen as a complementary activity, for example before and during the ideation process, to avoid an early oversimplification of users. Based on our results we believe that these stories help to look beyond the initial preconception and to get an idea what it might be like to be the other. Personal narratives can help to get rid of stereotypes, preexisting biases, and fixations in our heads, in order to make room for people's voices. Therefore, it would be interesting to explore further, whether this could even be enhanced when designers are giving the task to create personas based on these stories, because the creation process as such has been found to make assumptions about the target group more explicit. Furthermore it would also be interesting to not only make use of stories in a textual form, but for example published videos of real people. In the case of Genetic Testing videos from people talking about their DTC genetic testing results[7] or videos from the aforementioned archive of patient narrative interviews with regard to their experience with genetic testing[8] could be applicable.

Acknowledgements. We would like to thank all participants of the study for their time and commitment. Furthermore, we thank the anonymous reviewers for their detailed comments and thoughtful suggestions on our submission, which were very considerate and helpful.

References

1. Anderson, R.M., Funnell, M.M.: Patient empowerment: myths and misconceptions. Patient Educ. Couns. **79**(3), 277–282 (2010)
2. Baron-Cohen, S., Wheelwright, S.: The empathy quotient: an investigation of adults with Asperger syndrome or high functioning autism, and normal sex differences. J. Autism Dev. Disord. **34**(2), 163–175 (2004)

---

[7] for example https://www.youtube.com/watch?v=QqQpYEA9mpM (accessed: January 17, 2015).

[8] for example http://www.healthtalk.org/peoples-experiences/nerves-brain/carers-people-dementia/genetic-testing (accessed: January 17, 2015).

314   C. Grünloh et al.

3. Braun, V., Clarke, V.: Using thematic analysis in psychology. Qual. Res. Psychol. 3(2), 77–101 (2006)
4. Buchenau, M., Suri, J.F.: Experience prototyping. In: Proceedings of the 3rd Conference on Designing Interactive Systems: Processes, Practices, Methods, and Techniques, pp. 424–433. ACM, New York (2000)
5. Caulfield, T., McGuire, A.L.: Direct-to-consumer genetic testing: perceptions, problems, and policy responses. Annu. Rev. Med. 63(1), 23–33 (2012)
6. Charles, C., Whelan, T., Gafni, A.: What do we mean by partnership in making decisions about treatment? BMJ Br. Med. J. 319(7212), 780–782 (1999)
7. Cooper, A.: The Inmates are Running the Asylum. Macmillan, Basingstoke (1999)
8. Dandavate, U., Sanders, E.B.N., Stuart, S.: Emotions matter: user empathy in the product development process. Proc. Hum. Factors Ergon. Soc. Annu. Meet. 40(7), 171–176 (1996). Sage Publications
9. Deber, R.B.: Physicians in health care management: 7. The patient-physician partnership: changing roles and the desire for information. CMAJ Can. Med. Assoc. J. 151(2), 171–176 (1994)
10. Emanuel, E.J., Emanuel, L.L.: Four models of the physician-patient relationship. JAMA 267 (16), 2221–2226 (1992)
11. Erlingsdottir, G., Lindholm, C., Ålander, T.: eHealth services, patient empowerment and professional accountability-an empirical study on the changing patient-doctor relationship in the digital world. In: International EIASM Public Sector Conference, pp. 1–21 (2014)
12. Friedman, B., Nissenbaum, H.: Bias in computer systems. ACM Trans. Inf. Syst. (TOIS) 14 (3), 330–347 (1996)
13. Genomics England. http://www.genomicsengland.co.uk/the-100000-genomes-project/. Accessed 17 Jan 2015
14. Gibbs, S.: DNA-screening test 23andMe launches in UK after US ban. The Guardian (2014). http://www.theguardian.com/technology/2014/dec/02/google-genetic-testing-23andme-uk-launch. Accessed 17 Jan 2015
15. Goldman, J.S., Hahn, S.E., Catania, J.W., LaRusse-Eckert, S., Butson, M.B., Rumbaugh, M., Strecker, M.N., Roberts, J.S., Burke, W., Mayeux, R., Bird, T.: Genetic counseling and testing for Alzheimer disease: joint practice guidelines of the American college of medical genetics and the national society of genetic counselors. Genet. Med. 13(6), 597–605 (2011)
16. Golsteijn, C., Wright, S.: Using narrative research and portraiture to inform design research. In: Kotzé, P., Marsden, G., Lindgaard, G., Wesson, J., Winckler, M. (eds.) INTERACT 2013, Part III. LNCS, vol. 8119, pp. 298–315. Springer, Heidelberg (2013)
17. ISO 9241-210: Ergonomics of human-system interaction - Part 210: Human-centred design for interactive systems (2010)
18. Keen, S.: A theory of narrative empathy. Narrative 14(3), 207–236 (2006)
19. Lindsay, S., Brittain, K., Jackson, D., Ladha, C., Ladha, K., Olivier, P.: Empathy, participatory design and people with dementia. In: Proceedings of the SIGCHI Conference on Human Factors in Computing Systems, pp. 521–530. ACM, New York (2012)
20. Locock, L., Robert, G., Boaz, A., Vougioukalou, S., Shuldham, C., Fielden, J., et al.: Testing accelerated experience-based co-design: a qualitative study of using a national archive of patient experience narrative interviews to promote rapid patient-centred service improvement. Health Serv. Deliv. Res. 2(4), 1–122 (2014)
21. Löwgren, J., Stolterman, E.: Thoughtful Interaction Design: A Design Perspective on Information Technology. MIT Press, Cambridge (2004)
22. Mattelmäki, T., Vaajakallio, K., Koskinen, I.: What Happened to empathic design? Des. Issues 30(1), 67–77 (2014). MIT Press

23. McQuaid, H.L., Goel, A., McManus, M.: When you can't talk to customers: using storyboards and narratives to elicit empathy for users. In: Proceedings of the 2003 International Conference on Designing Pleasurable Products and Interfaces, pp. 120–125. ACM, New York (2003)
24. Nielsen, L.: From user to character: an investigation into user-descriptions in scenarios. In: Proceedings of the 4th Conference on Designing Interactive Systems: Processes, Practices, Methods, and Techniques, pp. 99–104. ACM, New York (2002)
25. O'Kane, A.A., Rogers, Y., Blandford, A.E.: Gaining empathy for non-routine mobile device use through autoethnography. In: Proceedings of the SIGCHI Conference on Human Factors in Computing Systems, pp. 987–990. ACM, New York (2014)
26. Pruitt, J., Grudin, J.: Personas: practice and theory. In: Proceedings of the 2003 Conference on Designing for User Experiences (DUX 2003). ACM, New York (2003)
27. Pruitt, J., Adlin, T.: The Persona Lifecycle: Keeping People in Mind Throughout Product Design. Morgan Kaufmann, San Francisco (2006)
28. Segal, L.D., Suri, J.F.: The empathic practitioner: measurement and interpretation of user experience. Proc. Hum. Factors Ergon. Soc. Annu. Meet. **41**(1), 451–454 (1997). Sage Publications
29. Su, P.: Direct-to-consumer genetic testing: a comprehensive view. Yale J. Biol. Med. **86**(3), 359–365 (2013)
30. Suri, J.F.: The next 50 years: future challenges and opportunities for empathy in our science. Ergonomics **44**(14), 1278–1289 (2001)
31. The King's Fund: Experience-based co-design. http://www.kingsfund.org.uk/projects/ebcd. Accessed 17 Jan 2015
32. Tibben, A., Stevens, M., De Wert, G., Niermeijer, M., Van Duijn, C., Van Swieten, J.: Preparing for presymptomatic DNA testing for early onset Alzheimer's disease/cerebral haemorrhage and hereditary Pick disease. J. Med. Genet. **34**(1), 63–72 (1997)
33. Topol, E.: The Patient Will See You Now: The Future of Medicine is in Your Hands. Basic Books, New York (2015)
34. U.S. Food and Drug Administration (FDA): Warning Letter to 23andMe, Inc. (2013). http://www.fda.gov/ICECI/EnforcementActions/WarningLetters/2013/ucm376296.htm. Accessed 17 Jan 2015
35. Udesky, L.: The ethics of direct-to-consumer genetic testing. Lancet **376**(9750), 1377–1378 (2010)
36. Veatch, R.M.: Models for ethical medicine in a revolutionary age. Hastings Center Report, pp. 5–7 (1972)
37. Visser, F.S., Stappers, P.J.: Mind the face. In: Proceedings of the 2007 Conference on Designing Pleasurable Products and Interfaces (DPPI 2007). ACM, New York (2007)
38. Wright, P., McCarthy, J.: Empathy and Experience in HCI. In: Proceedings of the SIGCHI Conference on Human Factors in Computing Systems, pp. 637–646. ACM, New York (2008)

AirDisplay: Experimenting with Air Flow as a Communication Medium

Omar Mowafi[1], Mohamed Khamis[1,2(✉)], and Wael Abouelsaadat[1]

[1] Computer Science and Engineering Department,
German University in Cairo (GUC), Cairo, Egypt
omar.mowafi@student.guc.edu.eg,
{mohammed.khamis,wael.abouelsaadat}@guc.edu.eg,
mohamed.khamis@ifi.lmu.de
[2] Media Informatics Group, University of Munich (LMU), Munich, Germany

Abstract. This paper presents a psychophysical experiment using a multi-fan device to communicate information to the user via air intensity and direction. We describe the implementation of a prototype, the AirDisplay. We identify the most effective configuration at which users can discern different air patterns by manipulating the fans' speed, the distance between the fans, and the different air patterns. Experiment results support the use of air to communicate information.

Keywords: Non-contact haptic feedback · Air streams · Multi-fan device

1 Introduction

Despite the variety of senses that humans possess, the vast majority of user interfaces target the human vision and hearing senses. This work examines the suitability of air streams to be used alongside personal computers to communicate information. Our prototype, the AirDisplay, utilizes the intensity and direction properties of air to exploit the human's ability to feel mechanical pressure (mechanoreception).

The use of air to communicate nonintrusive ambient information has a number of potential applications. For example, changes in the state of data (e.g. stock prices) can be mapped to the air flow intensity. Air streams can be used to enhance realism and immersion in games (e.g. on collisions, increasing speeds or in battle scenes). Furthermore, air streams can be used for untethered silent notifications. A message can be conveyed via an inaudible air stream, making it less noticeable by shoulder surfers.

These applications depend on the use of multiple air streams which the user can perceive separately. Our experiment sought to verify if this was possible and to determine the appropriate number of air sources and configuration of the device.

One of the earliest recorded uses of air to communicate information was by the cinematographer Morton Heilig. Heilig introduced Sensorama in the late 1950s, an "Experience Theater" targeting all human senses and using air to simulate wind [6]. Ishii et al. sought to use air to convey messages in the ambientROOM project [8], but controlling the flow of air proved challenging as reported in a later experiment [7].

© IFIP International Federation for Information Processing 2015
J. Abascal et al. (Eds.): INTERACT 2015, Part I, LNCS 9296, pp. 316–323, 2015.
DOI: 10.1007/978-3-319-22701-6_23

Suzuki and Kobayashi created a projection-based stereo display that used an air jet interface. The setup used air nozzles, 3D glasses, and a paddle that is to be held by the user [13]. The air nozzles created pressure on the paddle to simulate touching a 3D object. Unlike AirDisplay, it required wearing glasses and holding a paddle. Its maximum height range was 30 cm, while AirDisplay has a height range of 40 cm.

Most of the existing work that used fans was focusing on virtual reality applications. Previous work used big fans to simulate wind conditions in VR environments [3, 10]. Cardin et al. [2] developed a head mounted display with 8 fans to add realism in a flight simulator. Our approach, on the other hand, involves less bulky equipment and smaller fans that can be mounted on monitors. Air was also recently used to provide pneumatic feedback in in-car interaction [14].

Sodhi et al. demonstrated AIREAL [12], a haptic device that delivered tactile sensations in air. AIREAL used air vortices, directed by actuated nozzles. It provided tactile feedback of up to 8.5 cm resolution at a distance of 1 m from the device. Gupta et al. described AirWave [4], a stand-alone device intended to be placed in close proximity to computers. It provided at-a-distance haptic feedback using vortex generators. AirWave's resolution is 10 cm at a 2.5 m distance.

AirDisplay differs from AirWave and AIREAL in that it focuses on air streams rather than vortices. The usage of air streams emitted by fans is less expensive, and simpler to setup, operate, and manufacture than AIREAL. Unlike AirWave, AirDisplay uses small, flexible fans that can be integrated into the production of monitors.

Other works investigated haptic feedback through air suction [5, 9, 11, 14]. Unlike air streams, air suction has a rather limited range, making it more suitable for touch screens, but not for at-a-distance haptic feedback.

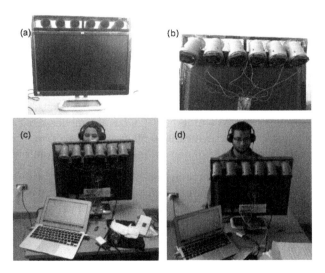

Fig. 1. (a) AirDisplay mounted on a monitor, (b) AirDisplay back view, (c) and (d) participants taking part in the experiment.

2 Design Issues

The human face has an abundance of Merkel's disks and Meissner's corpuscles, the two most sensitive Mechanoreceptors in the human skin [1]. Hence, we decided to position the AirDisplay around the monitor, to enable the output air to easily reach the user's face. We expect this to enable the user to differentiate between air streams. We decided to start with a single row of air sources mounted on the top of the monitor.

We decided that the device should communicate information to the user in two ways: whether the air source is on or off, and the intensity of the steady air stream coming from each source. By creating several distinct air streams at the same time, we could establish combinations of air streams that constitute a pattern. Each pattern would represent a meaningful piece of information to the user.

3 Evaluation

The goal of this experiment was to determine the most effective setup for the air sources. There are many parameters to be considered. Environment-specific parameters, like temperature and humidity, surely have an influence. However, in this study, we were interested to determine the most effective distance between adjacent air sources and the level of air intensity that would enable the user to distinguish different air patterns. An arrangement with essentially no space between fans enables us to increase the resolution of the display (number of air sources). However the user might find it difficult to discriminate between different air streams. Running a fan too slow might make its output unnoticeable, while running it too fast might disturb the user. We also wanted to investigate which air pattern can be most easily detected by users.

3.1 Apparatus

The hardware consisted of 6 fans aligned horizontally and placed inside a rectangular frame mounted on the top of the monitor.

Fan Selection. Directing air to the user's face raises concerns related to comfort, and to eye and skin irritation. The 259-1356-ND[1] fan has the moderate air flow, and minimal noise our project requires. It measures 50 mm L × 50 mm H × 10 mm and produces air flow up to 15.2 CFM (0.430 m^3/min) using 6100 rpm motor.

Physical Design. To ensure that there are no visual influences or distractions to the user, we had to conceal the fans. We installed each fan at one end of a curved plastic tube with diameter 45 mm, with the other end facing the user (see Fig. 1). The tubes add greater directionality to the air stream.

---

[1] KDE1205PFVX.11.MS.A.GN fan description manufactured by Sunon. http://www.digikey.com/product-detail/en/KDE1205PFVX.11.MS.A.GN/259-1356-ND/1021205.

Circuit. We used an Arduino Mega[2] to control the fans, since it has a high number of Pulse Width Modulation (PWM) pins. The Arduino chip cannot power the six fans to the maximum rpm, so an external power source was used. Transistors were used to control the current flowing to the fans with respect to the PWM signal.

Software. A custom desktop application was developed to control the fans and collect input from participants. In each trial, vertical buttons, each corresponding to the fan above, were displayed. The participant had to select the buttons corresponding to the fans from which she felt streams of air. When done with selection, the participant has to press the "done with selection" button. For each trial, the software records the time to complete the task, the actual fans in operation, and the participant selection.

Air Patterns. We picked 17 representative air patterns as unique trials to avoid having the participant do all the combinations. The patterns fall into 6 distinct groups: one fan at a time (P1), two adjacent fans (P2), left three and right three fans (P3), all fans (P4), alternating fans (P5) and no fans (Table 1).

Table 1. Air patterns

Fan1	Fan2	Fan3	Fan4	Fan5	Fan6
✓					
	✓				
		✓			
			✓		
				✓	
					✓
✓	✓				
	✓	✓			
		✓	✓		
			✓	✓	
				✓	✓
✓	✓	✓	✓	✓	✓
✓		✓		✓	
	✓		✓		✓
			✓	✓	✓
✓	✓	✓			

Air Flow. We picked a low speed (3050 rpm/6.8 CFM), a moderate speed (4575 rpm/11.5 CFM) and a relatively high speed (6100 rpm/15.2 CFM) to evaluate the user's ability to discern different air current intensities.

Interfan Distance. Overlap between air streams coming from adjacent fans could confuse the users about the source of air, making it impossible for them to discern the

---

[2] Arduino Mega 2560. http://www.arduino.cc/en/Main/arduinoBoardMega2560.

air pattern. Based on experiments with different interfan distances in addition to air intensities, we selected the following interfan distances: 1.0 cm, 2.5 cm and 5.0 cm.

3.2   Participants

Eight participants (15 – 34 years old) volunteered for the experiment. There were 4 males and 4 females. Participants were screened for skin conditions, and no issues were reported. Participants did not receive compensation for participation.

3.3   Procedure

The experiment was conducted in controlled environment. Room temperature was fixed at 22 °C to reduce the chance of sweating. The participants used the software to identify the tubes from which they felt a steady stream of air, thereby identifying the air pattern. Participants wore noise-cancelling earplugs to avoid identifying the working fans by the sound of the motors. All participants were positioned at approximately 40 cm away from the center of the AirDisplay (Fig. 1c and d).

3.4   Design

There were two experimentally manipulated conditions. First, we experimented with three interfan distances: 1.0 cm, 2.5 cm and 5.0 cm. Second, we investigated three air flow values: 6.8 CFM, 11.5 CFM and 15.2 CFM.

A randomized within participant repeated measures design was used. The 2 conditions were counterbalanced between the participants: 4 participants did the interfan distance condition first, followed by the air flow condition. The other group of 4 did the air flow condition first, followed by the interfan distance. The 17 air patterns were randomized among the users. Each participant performed 3 blocks, each consisting of 153 unique trials (17 patterns × 3 air flows × 3 interfan distances). Hence, each participant did 459 trials. The total number of trials in the experiment was 3672.

3.5   Results

We computed two dependent variables. First was the Success Rate, which is defined as the percentage of trials with a correct selection of a pattern. Second was the Response time, which is defined as the time from the moment the fans in a specific trial start until the user completes the identification of the pattern.

Success Rate. A repeated measures ANOVA was carried out on the data using SPSS. Significant main effects were found for air flow ($F(2, 14) = 113$, $p < .0001$) and interfan distance ($F(2, 14) = 6.3$, $p < .05$). This shows the identification of the air pattern depends on the air flow intensity and the distance in-between the fans. There was no interaction effect between distance and air flow.

Post hoc analysis was carried out to compare success rates for all air flow values. There was a significant difference in the success rate for 15.2 CFM (M = 6.6, SD = 1.3) compared to 11.5 CFM (M = 4.4, SD = .7); t(7) = 6.6, p < .0001. There was also a significant difference in the success rate for 15.2 CFM (M = 6.6, SD = 1.3) compared to 6.8 CFM (M = 2.3, SD = .7); t(7) = 13.4, p < .0001. The third pair also showed a significant difference for 11.5 CFM (M = 4.4, SD = .7) compared to 6.8 CFM (M = 2.3, SD = .7); t(7) = 11.5, p < .0001. Thus, 15.2 CFM had the highest success rate followed by 11.5 CFM, and finally 6.8 CFM.

We also used post hoc analysis to compare success rate for the different interfan distances. Two pairs showed significant differences; 5.0 cm (M = 5.3, SD = 1.4) compared to 1.0 cm (M = 3.5, SD = .6); t(7) = 3.3, p < .05, and 2.5 cm (M = 4.5, SD = 1.1) compared to 1.0 cm (M = 3.5, SD = .6); t(7) = 3.1, p < .05.

Table 2 illustrates the average success trials count for all participants with averages for each air flow intensity. The most effective configuration was at fastest (15.2 CFM) air flow since participants scored higher in that air flow value than the other two.

Table 2. Mean success rates (out of 17)

	6.8 CFM	11.5 CFM	15.2 CFM
1.0 cm	1.7	3.6	5.5
2.5 cm	2.3	4.5	6.8
5.0 cm	2.9	5.3	7.7
Avg.	2.3	4.5	6.7

To measure the effectiveness of each air pattern, we summed the success rate for each pattern across participants for each interfan distance and air flow (Table 3) Results show that using one fan at a time (P1) at the highest speed used (15.2 CFM) has the highest success ratio, followed by the moderate speed (11.5 CFM). The next best pattern was using two adjacent fans (P2) at the highest speed (15.2 CFM) followed by the moderate speed (11.5 CFM).

Table 3. Pattern success in percentage

Air flow (CFM)		6.8	11.5	15.2	6.8	11.5	15.2	6.8	11.5	15.2
Distance (cm)		1.0	2.5	5.0	1.0	2.5	5.0	1.0	2.5	5.0
Pattern	**P1**	8	27	25	50	48	54	60	69	65
	P2	13	5	13	20	23	28	38	40	43
	P3	6	19	6	13	6	38	25	31	13
	P4	13	0	0	0	0	13	0	0	0
	P5	0	0	0	6	6	6	13	19	0

Response Time. A repeated measures ANOVA was carried out on the data using SPSS. Prior to the analysis, all measurements greater than 2.5 standard deviation were excluded. Significant main effect was found for air flow (F(2,14) = 8.6, p < .05). Thus, the user response time taken to identify the emitted air pattern depends on the air flow intensity. However, the change of the interfan distance did not have an impact on the response time. Post hoc analysis was carried out to compare response time means for the different air flow values. There was a significant difference in the response time for the highest speed, 15.2 CFM, (M = 8.8, SD = 2.2) compared to the moderate speed, 11.5 CFM, (M = 10.6, SD = 2.9); t(7) = 2.6, p < .05. There was also a significant difference in the response time for the moderate speed, 11.5 CFM, (M = 10.6, SD = 2.9) compared to the low speed, 6.8 CFM, (M = 7.8, SD = 1.6); t(7) = 3.3, p < .05. Table 4 illustrates the average response time for all participants.

Table 4. Mean response time (sec)

	6.8 CFM	11.5 CFM	15.2 CFM
1.0 cm	7.3	5.4	7.9
2.5 cm	7.4	8.5	9.1
5.0 cm	8.7	11.2	9.5
Avg.	7.8	8.4	8.8

3.6   Discussion

Results show that the higher the air intensity and the farther the fans the better the success rate. Hence, there is a trade-off between the resolution of an AirDisplay and the pattern detection accuracy. Lower air flow values, such as 6.8 CFM and 11.5 CFM, greatly reduce the ability of the user to detect the air stream pattern correctly.

The pattern analysis shows that the participants were able to identify a single air stream source (P1) fairly accurately (approximately 70 % at 15.2 CFM and 2.5 cm). This creates an opportunity for associating information with a single fan at a time. The results for two adjacent fans (P2) were less encouraging as the best score was 43 % at 15.2 CFM and 5.0 cm. The same applies to P3 (three right and three left fans) and P5 (alternating fans) as the participants were not able to identify the majority of the patterns. This suggests that the air streams were overlapping. The worst case was all fans (P4) only two users could detect the pattern, at all, and each did so only once. We attribute this also to the air flow overlap in the output.

The increase in air flow caused an increase in the average response time. This suggests that increasing the amount of air pumped out by the fan confuses the participants, who then take more time to identify the pattern.

4   Conclusion and Future Work

In this work, we demonstrated that air could be used to deliver information. The distance between fans and air flow affect the ability to identify the air stream pattern. The most promising configuration, for an outlet tube of 45 mm diameter, is 15.2 CFM air flow and 2.5 cm interfan distance, at 40 cm distance from the user. Using this configuration, we achieved 70 % success ratio for single fan patterns. Further experimentation should utilize the identified configuration.

The AirDisplay's hardware can be extended to detect the user's face and direct air streams towards it. Another step would be using a multi row and column set of air sources that would surround the user monitor. Thus, we would be able to simulate air streams coming from 4 directions: top, bottom, left and right. This will also enable us to investigate the recognition of more complex (e.g. alternating) patterns, and determine the optimal fan placement.

Further research might also investigate pattern recognition and response time on different body parts, such as back of hands or arms. We also plan to try smaller tubes to direct airflow, and experiment with air nozzles to target a smaller area on the user face. Heating and cooling elements will change the temperature of air in future experiments. In addition to the applications suggested at the beginning of this paper, we plan to invest in learning the user preference of desired functionality of air-stream based systems through evaluations and surveys.

References

1. Afifi, A.K., Bergman, R.A.: Functional Neuroanatomy: Text and Atlas. McGraw-Hill (1998)
2. Cardin, S., Vexo, F., Thalmann, D.: Head mounted wind. In: Proceedings of CASA 2007, pp. 101–108 (2007)
3. Deligiannidis, L., Jacob, R.J.K.: The VR scooter: wind and tactile feedback improve user performance. In: Proceedings of 3DUI 2006, pp. 143–150. IEEE (2006)
4. Gupta, S., Morris, D., Patel, S.N., Tan, D.: Airwave: non-contact haptic feedback using air vortex rings. In: Proceedings UbiComp 2013, pp. 419–428. ACM Press (2013)
5. Hachisu, T., Fukumoto, M.: VacuumTouch: attractive force feedback interface for haptic interactive surface using air suction. In: Proceedings of CHI 2014, pp. 411–420. ACM (2014)
6. Heilig, M.L.: Sensorama simulator. US Patent 3,050,870. 28 August 1962
7. Ishii, H., Ren, S., Frei, P.: Pinwheels: visualizing information flow in an architectural space. In: Proceedings of CHI 2001, pp. 111–112. ACM Press (2001)
8. Ishii, H., Wisneski, C., Brave, S., Dahley, A., Gorbet, M., Ullmer, B., Yarin, P.: ambientROOM: integrating ambient media with architectural space. In: Proceedings of CHI 1998, pp. 173–174. ACM Press (1998)
9. Makino, Y., Shinoda, H.: Suction pressure tactile display using dual temporal stimulation modes. In: Proceedings of SICE 2005, pp. 1285–1288. IEEE (2005)
10. Moon, T., Kim, G.J.: Design and evaluation of a wind display for virtual reality. In: Proceedings of VRST 2004, pp. 122–128. ACM Press (2004)
11. Porquis, L.B.C., Konyo, M., Tadokoro, S.: Tactile-based torque illusion controlled by strain distributions on multi-finger contact. In: Proceedings of HAPTICS 2012, pp. 393–398. IEEE (2012)
12. Sodhi, R., Poupyrev, I., Glisson, M., Israr, A.: Aireal: interactive tactile experiences in free air. In: Proceedings of TOG 2013, vol. 32, no. 4, p. 134 (2013)
13. Suzuki, Y., Kobayashi, M.: Air jet driven force feedback in virtual reality. IEEE Comput. Graph. Appl. 25(1), 44–47 (2005)
14. Väänänen-Vainio-Mattila, K., Heikkinen, J., Farooq, A., Evreinov, G., Mäkinen, E., Raisamo, R.: User experience and expectations of haptic feedback in in-car interaction. In: Proceedings of MUM 2014, pp. 248–251. ACM (2014)

Experiencing the Elements – User Study with Natural Material Probes

Jonna Häkkila[1], Yun He[2], and Ashley Colley[2(✉)]

[1] Faculty of Art and Design, University of Lapland, Rovaniemi, Finland
jonna.hakkila@ulapland.fi
[2] CIE, University of Oulu, Oulu, Finland
{yun.he,ashley.colley}@cie.fi

Abstract. In this paper, we present the first systematic user study exploring the user experience and perceptions towards different natural materials – water, ice, stone, sand, fire, wind and soup bubbles. By trying out different materials, participants (n = 16) expressed their associations and perceptions, rated different qualities of the materials, and described their impressions through product reaction cards. Our findings reveal for example that light weight and ease of movement are perceived as central qualities when inspiring and fun elements are sought for. This exploratory study shines light on user experiences with natural elements, and provides an experimental grounding for naturalistic tangible user interface design. Material qualities in tangible user interface design create a subtle, but critical part of the user experience.

Keywords: Material qualities · User experience · Tangible user interfaces · Design · User studies

1 Introduction

In [1], Hassenzahl defines user experience (UX) as *"a momentary, primarily evaluative feeling (good-bad) while interacting with a product or service"*. User experience consists of both utilitarian and a hedonic aspect [2]. Whereas the utilitarian side typically dominates in the overall motivation for application design, in constructing the user interface, hedonic aspects are important to consider in order to create pleasurable and engaging user experiences. When designing tangible user interfaces, material qualities are an integral part of the holistic experience.

Material qualities of physical objects have been thoroughly considered in areas such as art, industrial design and mechanics, but research on the material's role in interactive systems has been quite sporadic, leaving much to explore. Especially, the use of natural materials has so far been little researched. As tangible user interfaces (TUIs) can make use of the human senses in a richer and more multidimensional way than conventional digital user interfaces (UIs) [3], it is of interest to explore the different qualities that are perceived and associated with different physical materials.

In this paper, we take steps towards systematic exploration of natural materials. We are especially interested of these because of the new possibilities they provide for the design for tangible user interfaces, aesthetics and rich user experiences, and offer

© IFIP International Federation for Information Processing 2015
J. Abascal et al. (Eds.): INTERACT 2015, Part I, LNCS 9296, pp. 324–331, 2015.
DOI: 10.1007/978-3-319-22701-6_24

potential for user interfaces and application linked with, e.g., sustainable values or interactive environmental installations.

2   Prior Art and Positioning of Our Work

Prior art has demonstrated the use of different natural materials in different types of interactive systems, often designed for playful purposes or as part of a larger, monumental installation. Döring et al. have demonstrated interaction with soap bubbles [4], Virolainen et al. have shown touch screen interaction with an ice wall [5] whilst water based input and output has been used e.g. in [6, 7]. Heavy stone based input [8], and air based haptic feedback [9] have also been demonstrated. Rydarowski et al. [10] present an installation, where individually controlled CPU fans are used to move paper clips with air pressure.

The user experience findings reflect the curiosity [7], aesthetics [5], and playful nature of the interaction [5, 8]. With water related interactive systems, the pleasant sensation the cool water creates against the skin has been highlighted by users [7, 8], and spilling water has been reported to offer a more powerful UI feedback than a virtual one [6].

Whereas examples of the use of natural materials in TUIs exist, differing from us, the earlier research has reported the user perceptions focusing each time on a single system without a systematic comparison between different tangible elements. Moreover, the focus of the prior art has been more on the proof-of-concept level installations rather than on explicit investigation of the user experience aspects. A few explorations of different material qualities exist, as in [11] in the context of fashion, fabric and shape-change, but to the best of our knowledge, not in the domain of natural materials.

3   Study Methodology

3.1   Material Probes

In our user study, we applied the material probes method introduced in [12]. Material probes for seven (7) natural materials were created. The materials were selected to have as wide a range of physical properties as possible, in order to elicit a full range of perceptions from our test participants when interacting with the probes. The material probes are shown in Fig. 1 and consisted of:

- *Water*, contained in a small bowl.
- *Stone* in the form of 3 smooth rocks.
- *Soap bubbles*, created as required from a soap solution container and wand.
- *Ice*, in the form of a tennis ball sized block.
- *Sand*, as a small pile on a plate.
- *Wind*, created as needed from a small desk fan.
- *Fire*, in the form of a candle flame.

Fig. 1. User study set-up.

3.2   User Study Procedure

Our user study included an open think-aloud method, subjective rating of qualities and two tasks that required users to associate the materials with objects or activities. Additionally we utilized the product reaction cards method adapted from [13]. Each study session lasted for approximately 60 min and the study procedure was as follows:

- Completing a background questionnaire.
- Interacting with each material probe in turn and giving a free form description of ideas, thoughts and associations the material created.
- Selection of a favorite material (see Fig. 2)
- Rating the materials on a 7-point Likert scale against the criteria: *Controllable, Calm, Inspiring* and *Overall preference.*
- Connecting each material with digital artifacts, e.g. such as an alarm clock. Here, multiple artifacts could be connected with each material, and participants could leave some material unused (see Fig. 5).
- Connecting each material with activities and thoughts, e.g. such as organizing files. Again, multiple activities could be connected with each material, and participants could leave some material unused (see Fig. 6).
- For each material, selecting 3 adjectives from a list of 20 that best describe the material. Here following a Product Reaction Cards (PRC) based methodology [13]. Table 1 contains the adjectives that were available.

The order in which participants interacted with the materials was counterbalanced to avoid any effects due to the presentation order.

Altogether 16 participants (5 female, 11 male) took part in the study. The age range of the participants was 18–24:13 %, 25–29:37 %, 30–39:44 % and 40–49:6 %. The participants were recruited through advertising on university email lists, and through personal networks. Although participants predominantly represented university

Table 1. Adjectives used in product reaction card method. Participants selected three (3) that best described each material.

Fast	Slow	Inconsistent	Consistent
Responsive	Rigid	Uncontrollable	Controllable
Fun	Serious	Unpleasant	Pleasant
Restful	Stressful	Boring	Exciting
Approachable	Unapproachable	Frustrating	Inspiring

students, they came from various backgrounds with several different nationalities being represented. No UX professionals or UI designers were included.

4 Results - Perceptions of Different Materials

4.1 Favourite Material

The materials the participants selected as favorite are shown in Fig. 2. Water was clearly the favorite material with almost half of the participants (7/16) selecting it as their favorite. Here, many of the participants highlighted the relaxing nature of water, for example, *"Water is comfortable and controllable to interact with. I can do it for a long time, just like swimming."* (User #3).

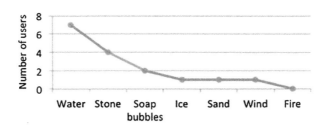

Fig. 2. Number of users preferring each material (n = 16)

4.2 Subjective Ratings and Product Reaction Cards

When asked to subjectively rate their perceptions of the materials (Fig. 3), users considered fire to be the least controllable and least calm material. Several users commented on the danger of fire, *"It is hot and untouchable. It hurts the hand. It is difficult to control and use."* (User #9). Water and Ice were perceived as two of the calmest and most inspiring elements. For both materials issues related to cleanliness and transparency were voiced e.g. *"Transparent and clean"* (User #9, water), *"Cold, beautiful and transparent"* (User #10, ice).

Examining the results from the Product Reaction Cards method (Fig. 4) provides congruent findings e.g. with fire and wind being considered uncontrollable by many

328   J. Häkkila et al.

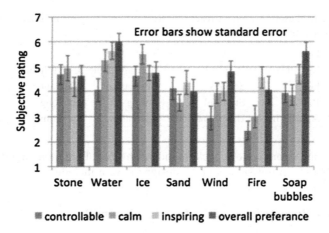

Fig. 3. Subjective ratings for each material

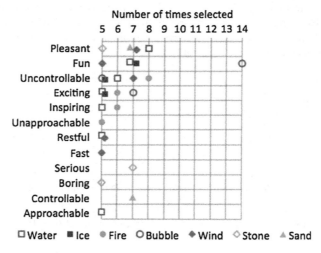

Fig. 4. Most frequently chosen adjectives for describing each material from Product Reaction Cards (N = 16 with 3 word selections per user).

users. Clearly soap bubbles are considered as fun, with all but 2 users (14/16) selecting this adjective.

4.3   Material Associations

The test participants associations between the materials and digital artifacts and activities are presented in Figs. 5 and 6 respectively. Whilst some of the strong associations are obvious, e.g. the association between the pairs ice - fridge and water -

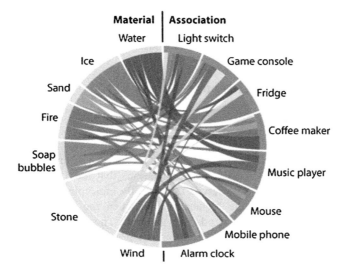

Fig. 5. Association between materials and digital artifacts. (The thickness of the base of each connection represents the number of users selecting that association).

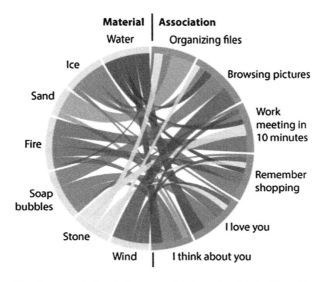

Fig. 6. Association between materials and activities/thoughts

coffee maker, other such as stone - mobile phone are less easily explained. Overall the high selection frequency of stone and low frequency of sand may be interesting to explore further.

In general the association of the given activities with materials is rather even, with most activities being associated to some extent with all of the materials. One clear exception is that of sand, which was almost exclusively associated with organizing files.

5 Discussion and Conclusions

5.1 Perceiving Materials

In this paper, we have reported the first user study seeking to systematically explore the user experiences perceived with different natural materials, investigated by using material probes. Based on the PRC results, it seems that lucid and light materials – water, wind and bubbles - are perceived as generally more playful, pleasant and fun. These materials also gained the highest ratings when the participants assessed in numerical scale how much they liked each material. Their light weight and ease of movement are perceived as central qualities when inspiring and fun elements are sought for. Although inspiring, fire was perceived uncontrollable and, based on the observations and comments, provoking reactions of respect and even fear.

Solid materials – stone, sand and ice – were perceived as more controllable and mostly pleasant. These were also the only materials that were associated with the task of 'organizing' (see Fig. 4). Whereas these associations are somewhat unsurprising, they confirm how materials that are quantifiable and behave less erratically are more easily associated with tasks that require control. This aligns with the findings reported by [8], where it is concluded that metaphors and interaction styles that match the physical characteristics of the interaction control should be utilized.

5.2 Limitations of the Study and Methodological Observations

In our study, we generally observed that people paid a lot of attention to each material - many spent a long time interacting with the materials in the tasks, and sometimes also came back to them. The test sessions generally took more time than we had first expected.

We acknowledge that our study is limited by the small sample size of participants. However, we believe that our research is valuable in its attempt to conduct a comparable study on different user experience qualities of natural materials. The laboratory type context was disconnected from any specific domains or use cases, and hence we believe provided a good environment for obtaining baseline results.

References

1. Hassenzahl, M.: User experience (UX): towards an experiential perspective on product quality. In Proceedings of IMH 2008. ACM, pp. 11–15 (2008)
2. Hassenzahl, M., Tractinsky, N.: User experience - a research agenda. Behav. Inf. Technol. 25(2), 91–97 (2006)

3. Ishii, H., Ullmer, B.: Tangible bits: towards seamless interfaces between people, bits and atoms. In: Proceedings of CHI 1997. ACM Press, pp. 234–241 (1997)
4. Döring, T., Sylvester, A., Schmidt, A.: Exploring material-centered design concepts for tangible interaction. Extended Abstracts CHI 2012. ACM Press, pp. 1523–1528 (2012)
5. Virolainen, A., Puikkonen, A., Kärkkäinen, T., Häkkilä, J.: Cool interaction with calm technologies - experimenting with ice as a multitouch surface. In: Proceedings of ITS 2010. ACM Press, pp. 15–18 (2010)
6. Geurts, L., Abeele, V.V.: Splash controllers: game controllers involving the uncareful manipulation of water. In: Proceedings of TEI 2012. ACM Press, pp. 183–186 (2012)
7. Pier, M.D., Goldberg, I.R.: Using water as interface media in VR applications. In Proceedings of CLIHC 2005. ACM Press, pp. 162–169 (2005)
8. Häkkilä, J., Koskenranta, O., Posti, M., He, Y.: City landmark as an interactive installation – experiences with stone, water and public space. In: Proceedings of TEI 2014. ACM (2014)
9. Sodhi, R., Poupyrev, I., Glisson, M., Israr, A.: AIREAL: interactive tactile experiences in free air. ACM Trans. Graph. (TOG) 32(4), 134 (2013)
10. Rydarowski, A., Samanci, O., Mazalek, A.: Murmur: kinetic relief sculpture, multi-sensory display, listening machine. In: Proceedings of TEI 2008. ACM, pp. 231–238 (2008)
11. Juhlin, O., Zhang, Y., Sundbom, C., Fernaeus, Y.: Fashionable shape switching: explorations in outfit-centric design. In: Proceedings of CHI 2013. ACM, pp. 1353–1362 (2013)
12. Jung, H., Stolterman, E.: Material probe: exploring materiality of digital artifacts. In: Proceedings of TEI 2011. ACM Press, pp. 153–156 (2011)
13. Microsoft Product Reaction Cards. http://www.microsoft.com/usability/UEPostings/ProductReactionCards.doc. Accessed 1 May 2015

PrintPut: Resistive and Capacitive Input Widgets for Interactive 3D Prints

Jesse Burstyn[1(✉)], Nicholas Fellion[1,2], Paul Strohmeier[1],
and Roel Vertegaal[1]

[1] Human Media Lab, Queen's University, Kingston, Canada
{jesse,paul,roel}@cs.queensu.ca,
nicholas.fellion@carleton.ca
[2] Creative Interactions Lab, Carleton University, Ottawa, Canada

Abstract. We introduce PrintPut, a method for 3D printing that embeds interactivity directly into printed objects. PrintPut uses conductive filament to offer an assortment of sensors that an industrial designer can easily incorporate into their 3D designs, including buttons, pressure sensors, sliders, touchpads, and flex sensors. PrintPut combines physical and interactive sketching into the same process: seamlessly integrating sensors onto the surfaces of 3D objects, without the need for external sensor hardware.

Keywords: 3D printing · Rapid prototyping · Printed sensors

1 Introduction

As computation becomes more ingrained into everyday objects, designers have a new responsibility to also consider how people interact with an object's digital aspects. As a result, it is increasingly important for industrial designers to start considering digital interactivity earlier in their design process.

When developing new artifacts, designers create prototypes to guide their design process about how an object should look, feel, and behave. These early designs might be digital, in the form of illustrations or rendered mock-ups, or they may be physical, for example, sculptures or 3D prints. On the one hand, physical prototyping is extremely useful for informing the aesthetic and ergonomic qualities of a product. But unlike their digital counterparts, the results of these prototyping methods are typically non-interactive.

To address this, there is an active research area surrounding augmenting physical prototypes with touch sensors [1, 2, 8, 9]. These solutions usually have a tradeoff between ease of use, resolution, and customizability. More importantly, designers must use these solutions *after* making a physical prototype. Wrapping a physical object with external sensors may disrupt the crafted shape that a designer is exploring, or may not be possible on complex geometries.

We introduce PrintPut, a process to create input sensors on 3D printed objects. With PrintPut, designing shape and interaction occurs together. In this paper, we present a collection of sensors that an industrial designer can easily incorporate into their 3D

J. Abascal et al. (Eds.): INTERACT 2015, Part I, LNCS 9296, pp. 332–339, 2015.
DOI: 10.1007/978-3-319-22701-6_25

designs, including buttons, pressure sensors, sliders, touchpads, and flex sensors. PrintPut enables a new category of objects with intrinsic touch sensing capabilities.

2   Related Work

A number of papers have explored the use of conductive inks to print flexible electronics. Rendl et al. [9] created PyzoFlex, a flexible sensor that detects touch, pen input, and hand proximity. Kawahara et al. [4] presented a method to create Instant Inkjet Circuits by modifying a consumer inkjet printer to print silver ink onto paper. They also demonstrated several capacitive sensors printed with this method. Olberding et al. [8] designed multi-layer topologies for flexible and cuttable multi-touch sensors. Gong et al. [1] extended this work with a printed sensor sheet that detects multi-touch and hand proximity with capacitive circuits, and folding and pressure with resistive circuits. With Resigraphs [2], Holman et al. demonstrated how designers can use resistive materials and paints to add touch sensing to non-planar objects.

There have also been a number of explorations using 3D printers for interactive prototyping and designing unique input and output methods. Ishiguro and Poupyrev presented methods to seamlessly integrate speakers into 3D printed objects [3]. Savage et al. demonstrated Sauron, a rapid-prototyping platform for physical user interfaces [10]. Sauron modifies 3D models such that, when printed, an internal camera can detect the motion of widgets such as push buttons, joysticks, and sliders. Leigh et al. [5] outlined the process they used to create custom conductive filaments. They also showed how the filament could be used to 3D print basic capacitive buttons and flex sensors. We extend their work by introducing a wider variety of sensors that can be directly integrated into objects and an automated workflow to do so.

3   Application Scenarios

Dome. Unlike sheet solutions, PrintPut sensors can be put onto non-developable surfaces: shapes that cannot be unfolded to flat. Figure 1 shows a touch pad printed onto a dome. A designer might use this shape to explore input on a globe, for example.

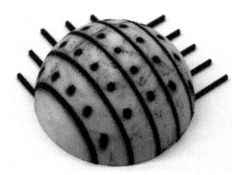

Fig. 1. X-Y touch pad integrated into a dome-shaped structure

Sound Wave Slider. Figure 2 shows a touch slider printed onto a decaying sine wave. Following this model, a musician could print the sound wave of their music track and tangibly scrub and mix through audio during a live performance.

Fig. 2. Slider printed onto a decaying sine wave

Multiple Sensor Toy. Figure 3 shows the exploration of a new toy design. A designer has created the model for a new interactive robot figure, with a combination of sensors placed around its body. The robot has a slider along its head and a pressure sensor on its belly.

Fig. 3. Toy design with multiple sensor types

4 PrintPut Implementation

4.1 Software

We created a series of scripts to help designers integrate sensors into complex three-dimensional geometries. We implemented the process in Rhinoceros 3D, a popular computer-aided-design (CAD) software package for industrial design. Specifically, our automation process operates within an official free plug-in, Grasshopper, a visual programming tool for algorithmic 3D modeling. Designers start the process by creating a base model of their 3D shape in either Rhinoceros or the CAD software of their choice. Next, they bring their model into Rhinoceros and define the points and curves for interactive areas. The script takes this user input and constructs the flat geometry for the desired sensors. The next step projects the sensor geometry onto the original model, such that it conforms smoothly to the surface. Then, the script extrudes the geometry into the surface and subtracts it from the base model. The result is two interlocking 3D models: the conductive circuits and the base model with hollows for these created paths (Fig. 4).

Fig. 4. Routing pattern for the printed toy design

4.2   Hardware

The critical component of PrintPut is a conductive ABS filament. Commercial solutions are now available and inexpensive: we used Maker Geeks Conductive ABS [6]. The filament has a high resistance and in our experience, a typical circuit has a baseline resistance in the $M\Omega$ range. PrintPut requires an ABS supported 3D printer with two extruders, such as a Makerbot 2X or Leapfrog Creatr. After a designer makes an object with sensor geometry, they import it into their 3D printer's build manager and assign the base and conductive geometry to standard and conductive filaments, respectively. Once the object is printed, sensor values can be easily read by connecting it to an Arduino or other microcontroller with alligator clips. For a lower profile, a designer can instead attach thin wires with conductive adhesives (e.g. copper tape or 3M Z-Axis conductive tape).

5   Sensing Methods

Capacitive Sensing. Capacitive sensors are made from a single terminal. They detect touch by repeatedly charging the terminal and recording the discharge time. When a finger is introduced, the sensor detects a larger capacitance.

Digital Resistive Sensing. Digital resistive sensors require two terminals, separated by a physical gap. The first terminal is connected to positive voltage (emitter), while the second connects to an input pin (receiver). Bridging the gap with a conductive material, such as a finger, allows current to flow, completing the circuit. A pull-down resistor is required at the emitter's pin.

Analog Resistive Sensing. Analog resistive sensors have a similar layout as digital sensors. In addition to detecting the presence of a bridge, the resistance of the bridge can modulate how much current is permitted.

6 Sensor Types

For clarity, Fig. 5 though 9 show the sensor types in their flat form factor. One of the primary benefits of PrintPut, however, is that it is not limited to flat surfaces.

Capacitive Buttons. One of the basic button types is a capacitive button, as originally presented by Leigh et al. [5]. They are made from a single pad of conductive filament, in any desired shape. Each capacitive button is directly connected to a unique input pin on the microcontroller.

Resistive Buttons. Another possible button type is a resistive button, which acts as a digital resistive sensor. To make a resistive button, a designer places a pad of conductive filament on an object, split down the middle (Fig. 5). When a user places their finger on a resistive button, it bridges the gap and completes the circuit. We recommend a 1 mm space between the two pads: close enough that a finger can create a bridge, but far enough to avoid unintended touch signals.

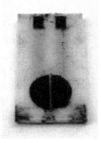

Fig. 5. Resistive button

Resistive Slider. With a resistive slider, a designer can detect the "linear" position of a finger along a surface. At their basic level, sliders are composed of a series of evenly spaced resistive buttons (digital resistive sensors). For simpler routing, the emitter halves of the buttons can be combined into a single line (Fig. 6). Although a resistive slider is made of discrete points, it is possible to perform some basic interpolation by noting when adjacent pads are simultaneously touched. Touching non-adjacent pads allows for multi-touch.

Fig. 6. Resistive Slider

Resistive X-Y Touch Pad. The touch pad extends the principle of the resistive buttons and sliders into two dimensions, by combing multiple touch sliders (Fig. 7). Aligning N vertical sliders in a row, each with M buttons, forms a touch pad with N × M touch points. This solution would require one combined emitter and N × M receivers. Rather than requiring one input pin per point, we take advantage of time-division multiplexing to combine the sliders. This is accomplished by maintaining one emitter per row and connecting each corresponding receiver pad underneath the surface of the printed object. The Arduino activates a single emitter, deactivates the others, and then reads values from each combined receiver. The process is repeated with each emitter to determine a touch location. By routing the touch pad in this way, a designer can significantly reduce the number of required input pins: it only requires M emitter pins and N input pins. For example, an 8 × 8 touchpad made with the first method would require 65 pins, but a multiplexed sensor would only need 16. In Fig. 7, the emitters are the odd rows and the receivers are the even columns.

Fig. 7. X-Y Touch Pad

GSR Pressure Sensor. PrintPut provides two methods to create pressure sensors. The first is made in the same way as a resistive button (Fig. 5), but treating it as an analog resistive sensor. A finger's galvanic skin response connects the two terminals by allowing current to pass through. Applying additional pressure lowers the resistance of the connection. In our experience, several other factors also contribute to the strength of the connection, including the size of the finger, sweat levels, ambient temperature, etc. [1]. As such, this type of sensor is more suited to detect relative changes in pressure.

Spring Pressure Sensor. The second method to create a pressure sensor is to make an analog resistive sensor where the physical space between the terminals is reduced when applying pressure. This is achieved by printing two pads, a thin one above another, with a small (0.4 mm) gap between the two. At rest, the gap is sufficiently large that little to no charge is passed. A small amount of force brings the two terminals in contact. The resistance of the bridge is reduced as further pressure is applied. Given that the contact between the two terminals results from the physical properties of the printed object and not a finger, this type of pressure sensor generally provides more consistent values (Fig. 8).

Fig. 8. Spring Pressure Sensor and exploded view

Flex Sensor. PrintPut also provides the ability to print flex sensors. To do so, a solid line of conductive filament is printed through a thin or hollow structure, along the axis of intended interaction (Fig. 9, top). Flex sensors are analog resistive sensors where one end of the filament acts as the emitter and the other is the receiver. When the structure is flexed, the carbon particles in the filament move further away from each other. As a result, the resistance of the circuit proportionally increases. One can also create a flex sensor using an elongated spring pressure sensor by taking advantage of the fact that its layers move closer as the structure is bent (Fig. 9, bottom).

Fig. 9. Flex Sensors. Top: Single line method. Bottom: Elongated pressure sensor method.

7   Limitations

We found that when dealing with a large amount of adjacent touch points, one should space them at least 3 mm apart. This recommendation ultimately limits PrintPut's touch resolution. One could overcome this with additional hardware or improved signal processing (such as with the touch pad), but such detailed resolution is likely unnecessary for the demands of a disposable prototype. In addition, the material properties of conductive filament and the process of printer extrusion results in slightly inconsistent conductivity for seemingly identical prints. Simply baselining sensor values or adjusting pull-down resistors can help resolve this behavior. Lastly, printing very large 3D models may be slower than desired for rapid-prototyping purposes (i.e. several hours). This could be addressed with techniques that print structures as wireframes with high-resolution sections, such as WirePrint [7].

8 Conclusion

In this paper, we introduced PrintPut, a category of 3D printed objects with a new dimension of interactivity. We presented a collection of interactive widgets that a designer can integrate into their models to help inform decisions when prototyping, including buttons, pressure sensors, sliders, touch pads, and flex sensors. PrintPut combines physical and interactive sketching into the same process, allowing sensors to be printed seamlessly onto 3D objects without external sensor hardware.

References

1. Gong, N.-W., Steimle, J., Olberding, S., et al.: PrintSense: a versatile sensing technique to support multimodal flexible surface interaction. In: SIGCHI Conference on Human Factors in Computing Systems, pp. 1407–1410. ACM Press, New York (2014)
2. Holman, D., Fellion, N., Vertegaal, R.: Sensing touch using resistive graphs. In: 2014 Conference on Designing Interactive Systems, pp. 195–198. ACM Press, New York (2014)
3. Ishiguro, Y., Poupyrev, I.: 3D printed interactive speakers. In: SIGCHI Conference on Human Factors in Computing Systems, pp. 1733–1742. ACM Press, New York (2014)
4. Kawahara, Y., Hodges, S., Cook, B.: Instant inkjet circuits: lab-based inkjet printing to support rapid prototyping of UbiComp devices. In: 2013 International Joint Conference on Pervasive and Ubiquitous Computing, pp. 363–372. ACM Press, New York (2013)
5. Leigh, S.J., Bradley, R.J., Purssell, C.P., Billson, D.R., Hutchins, D.A.: A simple, low-cost conductive composite material for 3D printing of electronic sensors. PLoS ONE 7(11), 1–6 (2012)
6. Maker Geeks: conductive ABS filament. www.makergeeks.com/co3dfi.html
7. Mueller, S., Im, S., Gurevich, S., Teibrich, A., Pfisterer, L., Guimbretière, F., Baudisch, P.: WirePrint: 3D printed previews for fast prototyping. In: 27th Annual ACM Symposium on User Interface Software and Technology, pp. 273–280. ACM Press, New York (2014)
8. Olberding, S., Gong, N.-W., Tiab, J., Paradiso, J.A., Steimle, J.: A cuttable multi-touch sensor. In: 26th Annual ACM symposium on User Interface Software and Technology, pp. 245–254. ACM Press, New York (2013)
9. Rendl, C., Greindl, P., Haller, M., Zirkl, M., Stadlober, B., Hartmann, P.: PyzoFlex: printed piezoelectric pressure sensing foil. In: 25th Annual ACM Symposium on User Interface Software and Technology, pp. 509–518. ACM Press, New York (2012)
10. Savage, V., Chang, C., Hartmann, B.: Sauron: embedded single-camera sensing of printed physical user interfaces. In: 26th Annual ACM Symposium on User Interface Software and Technology, pp. 447–456. ACM Press, New York (2013)

ReservoirBench: An Interactive Educational Reservoir Engineering Workbench

Sowmya Somanath[(✉)], Allan Rocha, Hamidreza Hamdi,
Ehud Sharlin, and Mario Costa Sousa

Department of Computer Science, University of Calgary, Calgary, Canada
{ssomanat, acarocha, hhamdi, ehud, smcosta}@ucalgary.ca

Abstract. *ReservoirBench* is an interactive workbench for educational geological science and engineering tasks. It is designed to facilitate education of
novice audiences to teach them basic concepts of reservoir modeling and simulation workflow. Traditional training using lectures and software practice can
lead to information overload, and retainability is questionable. As an alternative,
we propose a physical workbench that is coupled with digital augmentation for
the purpose of learning. We take advantage of the crucial role that spatiality and
3D representations play in petroleum reservoir modeling and allow basic
domain concepts to be introduced and explored in a tangible and experiential
manner. We describe the design of our prototype and reflect on the findings from
our preliminary design critique.

Keywords: Physical user interface · Education · Design · Reservoir
engineering

1 Introduction

The domain of petroleum engineering aims at studying the processes involved in the
exploration, production and extraction of oil and gas [8]. Introduction of domain
concepts via presentations and software tutorials can be difficult to grasp for novice
audiences such as first year geology undergraduates or non-domain experts who join
the industry (e.g. computer scientists). Generic slideshows can cause information
overload, and content retainability is questionable [16, 17]. On the other hand, simulation software packages such as Petrel[TM] [3] are designed for the expert user. Since the
goal is to become familiar with fundamental concepts and general modeling workflows
(engineering data integration, layer interpretation from seismic data, well modeling,
reservoir simulation and identifying challenging cost-benefit scenarios for well drilling), more suitable and interactive training methods are called for. The question then
becomes, "How can interactive interfaces be used to scaffold comprehension for novice
users?"

Modeling the petroleum reservoirs in 3D requires having the knowledge of spatial
configurations, structures and properties that are central to efficient data integration and
reservoir characterization. This was motivated before via cardboard box models used to
demonstrate the functionality of Petrel[TM], a commercial oil-and-gas software package
[2]. Interactive physical interfaces can help in automating this 3D spatial approach and

© IFIP International Federation for Information Processing 2015
J. Abascal et al. (Eds.): INTERACT 2015, Part I, LNCS 9296, pp. 340–348, 2015.
DOI: 10.1007/978-3-319-22701-6_26

can be designed to map interactions to varying visualizations to enhance the learning process [11]. We propose the use of a physical interactive workbench coupled with digital augmentation for teaching the basics of reservoir modeling workflows (Figs. 1 and 2). *ReservoirBench* is the first experiential learning reservoir engineering tangible user interface (TUI) for novice users and the uniqueness emerges from the application specific tasks.

2   Related Work

Physical and tangible user interfaces have been previously introduced for the purpose of teaching [9, 11, 14] and have contributed to develop ways to enhance learning [13, 21]. It has been noted that in situations where perception and cognition can be coupled [5], using physical materials in a learning task can change the nature of awareness gained relative to that gained through interacting with virtual materials [12].

Our workbench design supports experiential learning which encourages one to generate their own ideas about a phenomena while learning and prepares the individual for future learning [6]. More detailed knowledge could be developed as part of actual reservoir modeling tasks where the limitations of current software impede easiness and efficiency of implementing the various modeling and design scenarios. Our workbench can also be looked through the theoretical lens of boundary object's [18]. The structure of the interface is common enough to be recognized by the domain of oil and gas in general, but each sub-domain (i.e. geologist, reservoir engineer) can use it as a medium for different task explorations.

Within the realm of geology and reservoir engineering, TUI's [7, 10, 15], tabletop interfaces [19, 20] and a web-based interface [4] have been previously introduced. However, the focus in these instances of research has mainly been on data exploration. For instance, Snakey [10] is a TUI designed exclusively for expert users engaged in the particular task of well design in reservoir engineering. It is not an educational toolkit and does not attempt to address the breadth of essential reservoir modeling concepts that *ReservoirBench* is addressing.

3   ReservoirBench: Design and Implementation

3.1   Physical Interface

The physical interface is a simplified representation of an underground reservoir (Fig. 1). It consists of a wood frame structure (roughly 18 inch (l) × 18 inch (w)) with three slots on each of the vertical poles (Fig. 1a). The two vertical poles serve the dual purpose of being support structures as well as being representations of two already drilled oil wells used for seismic well-tie [8]. The top of the frame is sealed with a plane that represents the ground level. Three orthogonal planes, symbolic of seismic planes can be inserted into the empty slots using different configurations as seen in the Fig. 1a. The seismic planes define the boundaries between the different earth layers. Physical oil

(a) Inserting seismic planes   (b) Creating well trajectory

Fig. 1. *ReservoirBench* and workflow example.

well trajectories can be inserted between the planes using either the 3Doodler (hand-held fabrication tool [1]) or pipe cleaners (Fig. 1b).

The design rationale behind different configurations for the seismic planes comes from the fact that (in reality) the low resolution seismic volumes can impose a large uncertainty in defining the hydrocarbon producing layers. However, for the purpose of learning some options in terms of placements of seismic planes are sufficient to explore the concept of stratigraphic uncertainty in layers' thicknesses and their effects on calculation of volumetrics (e.g. initial hydrocarbon in place), reservoir performance and drilling plan of new infill wells for production optimization.

On the other hand, since the well trajectories are relatively more flexible in terms of design (i.e. can have configurations such as horizontal, vertical and multi-lateral [8]), we choose to test two different material options - the 3Doodler^{TM} and pipe cleaners. One of the fundamental constraints to input well trajectories is that the material should have the ability to retain shape and yet be malleable. Pipe cleaners are advantageous as they are flexible and afford for molding, but are limited as they do not afford the property to be easily molded back to their original state. In contrast, 3Doodle^{TM} is a step forward towards supporting free form sketching of 3D objects and thus, can better support quick iterative design explorations. However, it is important to note that accurate design of horizontal wells is rather difficult using the 3Doodler^{TM} due to gravity effect. In contrast to Snakey's [10] rigid and difficult to manipulate interface that is built from camera tripods, both the 3Doodler and the pipe cleaner afford further flexibility for free-form and iterative well design.

3.2   Digital Interface

The digital interface represents the visual feedback for the physical interactions (Fig. 2). The use of a monitor to display the visualizations was done keeping in mind the availabilities in a regular office setting. Placing the monitor above the physical interface was considered to be a better alternative to a side-by-side setup and can also work for demonstration purposes. In our current prototype the physical source object (Fig. 2a) can be digitally augmented in the four ways explained below. The visualizations are

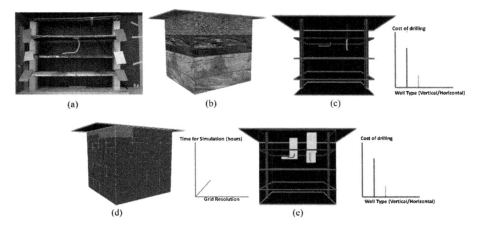

Fig. 2. Physical interface (a) and the corresponding mapped visualizations (b–e).

simplified reservoir modeling visualizations that professionals use during the regular workflow of examining seismic planes, gridding and well trajectories.

Figure 2b: shows the visualization of the geological layers of the earth mapped to the tracked physical seismic planes configuration that can be (re)arranged by the user. We use a Kinect to track the positions of the colored markers placed on the edge of the physical planes (Fig. 2a). The positions of the markers extracted from the Kinect image are converted into 3D coordinates to render the virtual seismic planes. A bounding box encompassing the virtual planes is computed and drawn to represent an approximate reservoir model. The purpose of this visualization is to provide contextual information regarding how a reservoir looks beneath the surface of the earth and helps identify in which layer oil is currently present and what is in the surrounding layers (e.g. aquifer, cap rock etc.).

Figure 2c: shows the visualization of the well trajectories input physically by the user. To reconstruct the virtual well we first compute the difference between the initial source image (before the well was inserted) and the current frame image (after the well was inserted) from the Kinect 2.0. Zhang-Suen thinning algorithm [22] is applied to the segmented image to extract the well trajectory skeleton. The skeleton and the depth image are then used in the calculations for 3D well reconstruction. The Kinect is placed at an angle as seen in Fig. 1 to capture maximum information. Our current prototype is limited by the use of a single Kinect camera and thus, occlusions cannot be resolved. However, since accuracy was not our primary concern when introducing basic concepts, we think this is a reasonable limitation. The well visualization is also coupled with a graph that shows the cost for drilling the infill well. From the vector direction of the well skeleton, the program automatically classifies the wells as either vertical (low cost) or horizontal wells (high cost), and the graph is updated to show the corresponding cost for drilling.

Figure 2d: shows the visualization of the gridded simulation model. The rendered grid is adapted to align according to the top and bottom of the seismic plane orientation allowing the viewer to learn about the variability in vertical thickness in each cell layer.

The resolution of the grid can be changed using a physical slider. The purpose for changing grid sizes is to allow the user to get a sense of how discretization is performed in real modeling cases and understand its effect on the time needed for completing a flow simulation run (which can be a very time consuming task based on the resolution of the grid). Thus, when the user interacts with the slider a graph showing the amount of time required for simulation is displayed.

Figure 2e: shows the intersection between the grid cells and the created well trajectories. In terms of learning, observing such intersections helps: (a) identify the cells with interesting heterogeneities, which might require further treatments in terms of nested local grid refinement and (b) identify the most and least contributing cells to the oil production rate.

3.3   Workflow Example and Presented Concepts

Figures 1 and 2 show the workflow of a user interacting with the *ReservoirBench*. The workflow is also a pointer to the various concepts that one can learn and explore. The typical workflow starts with positioning the interpreted (*Concept #1*) **seismic planes** configuration (obtained in actual workflow from 3D seismic data) [8] (Fig. 1a). Once the seismic configuration is in place (Fig. 1a), the user can explore the automatically generated (*Concept #2*) **geological layers** (i.e. between the seismic planes, Fig. 2b) and plan to (*Concept #3*) create a suitable **new well trajectory** to extract more oil from the reservoir. Figure 1b shows a user creating a new well trajectory using the 3Doodler^{TM}. Once the well is in position, the well is virtually reconstructed (Fig. 2c). The well trajectory can be positioned at any depth position of the plane. In practice, the well should be drilled starting from the ground surface, in the current prototype the user only needs to position the well in the target layer in which oil is found. This is also common practice in reservoir modeling software programs. The connection from the reservoir top to the ground surface is automatically computed by our program. Depending on the well created by the user, the program presents a graph of the (*Concept #4*) **drilling cost** of such a well (Fig. 2c). Finally, the user can (*Concept #5*) **grid** the reservoir model for simulation and understand the impact of the grid resolution on the (*Concept #6*) **time for the reservoir simulation** runs (Fig. 2d).

4   Preliminary Design Critique

To evaluate the limitations and advantages of the different components of our interface we conducted a preliminary design critique session with a domain and a non-domain (computer science graduate student) participant. The domain expert, a post-doctoral fellow in reservoir modeling with several years of experience in geoscience research and reservoir engineering, was involved in the iterative design and development of our interface. With the obvious limitations of our preliminary design critique (small number of participants, possible biases), it did provide interesting design reflection on *ReservoirBench*, including those of an expert reservoir engineer with considerable experience in this design space. Following we believe the insight we share below, while limited in scope, is still valid. We took a hands-on approach to design critique, asking both the participants to complete the following tasks: (a) arranging the seismic planes to the experimenter provided configurations, (b) creating a vertical and/or horizontal well to extract oil and (c) choosing the appropriate simulation model grid size and observe the costs and simulation time. At the end of the tasks we gathered qualitative feedback.

Domain Participant: In the opinion of the domain expert *ReservoirBench* can be useful for educating novices' about conceptual ideas, for example, what is a seismic plane? And, where is oil? He envisions that with increasing the complexity of the system and by combining the interface with an actual simulation program, the current interface can be used by the domain experts for testing out complex tasks i.e. reservoir characterization, economics calculations and well test design. *ReservoirBench* could also be used to design and/or to fine tune a 3D digital model and to explore various production scenarios for well placement. The domain expert found automatic reconstruction of physical well trajectories to be a useful feature for quick design iterations. Although the 3Doodler^{TM} is a flexible fabrication tool, it was difficult to use and found to be distracting due to its current limitations (speed of use, fat pen, gravity etc.) Therefore, the domain expert preferred the pipe cleaners, especially for designing horizontal wells. One of the noted limitations for the pipe cleaners was their length. Since the performance of a horizontal well depends on factors i.e. length and location within the layer, this was considered to be an important feature to keep in mind while choosing the right material.

Non-domain Participant: In addition to the hands-on tasks, the non-domain participant also answered the following eight questions: **(1)** what is a reservoir? **(2)** What is between the seismic planes? **(3)** What is a reservoir model? **(4)** What is the purpose of a reservoir model? **(5)** Which processes are involved in extracting oil? **(6)** When gridding the reservoir model, when do you think a low resolution grid (less number of cells) could be beneficial? **(7)** Similarly, when do you think a high resolution grid (more number of cells) could be beneficial? And finally, **(8)** rationalize the well trajectories you created in the well design task. The collected responses were all valid in terms of expected keywords (determined by domain-expert), pointing towards a positive outcome in terms of learning. From the discussions we learnt that lack of both, feedback during the tasks and prior knowledge, the participant felt less confident in answering the questions. The participant also mentioned that compared to the definition type questions (e.g. questions 1 and 2), she found the interface to be quite useful for answering task related questions (question 8). Beyond learnability, the participant found the interface to be fun, enjoyable and engaging. She mentioned, *"It was encouraging of curiosity, and made me want to learn more things. It was satisfying as I felt like it was doing something"*.

5 Discussion

Role of Spatiality and 3D representations: Spatiality and 3D representations play a crucial role in reservoir engineering. The benefit of having an associative and spatial system can help externalize traditional digital representations and present a physical view that people are familiar with [11] and is fundamental to geological entities [10]. Having working knowledge of oil and gas software tools the domain expert mentioned that practical learning with commercial software alone is rather difficult, specifically for non-domain audiences, since the software is designed for experts and not novices. Within this context, in the opinion of the domain expert our hybrid approach (physical-digital coupling) can be useful for training Novice users and arguably also be useful for domain experts to evaluate design choices for well placement tasks.

Control and Representation: Due to the meticulous nature of tasks conducted by reservoir engineers, interfaces such as ours will be limited in terms of the level of control that can be achieved. As mentioned by both the domain and non-domain participants', although the 3Doodler was a flexible fabrication tool for design iterations, it was difficult to use and found to be distracting due to the limitations of the current 3Doodler (speed of use, fat pen, gravity etc.). It was found to be lacking in precision and accuracy. Scaling is also a challenge. While part of the scaling issue can be mitigated by the use of digital representations, we need to be careful in our design considerations to ensure that the level of physical-digital coupling is not reduced to the point of creating disconnects in interaction behavior (a noted limitation of Snakey [10]). Alternatively, an advantage of interfaces such as ours is that the low-cost prototype production will allow users to quickly modify the design of the system. Readily available physical mediums can be added as interaction components to create representations that are meaningful to the users and programmatically coded as manipulatives.

Interactivity: Within *ReservoirBench's* context, externalizing geological concepts into easy to grasp physical representations presents a smart interaction alternative to the orthodox approach in which novice users are introduced to the domain (e.g. presentations and textbooks). The potential of systems such as ours lies in their ability to allow people to create and manipulate objects to support hands on learning. It can also function as a boundary object during interdisciplinary interactions. From a design perspective, *ReservoirBench* can be used not just for the purpose of learning the fundamental concepts but also in other design process such as designing rough 3D reservoir models. Active hands-on learning can also make the experience enjoyable and engaging as mentioned by the non-domain participant.

6 Conclusion and Future Work

We presented *ReservoirBench*, an interactive and educational TUI that facilitates learning about reservoir modeling workflow. Our preliminary critique highlights the usefulness of such systems for both learning and exploring reservoir modeling workflows. Efforts are underway to further improve our prototype to better facilitate instructional and smarter interactions. The design critiques point at promising benefits for such interfaces, but in future we will need to compare and contrast the *ReservoirBench* approach to training versus the existing traditional approaches. For long term future work we would like to explore the use of other physical manipulatives such as, grid meshes and fault constraints, to allow novice user's to gain added understanding on their effect on well planning and simulations. For example, the actual seismic planes combined with the complex 3D structures such as faults and folds can be efficiently used to represent the actual reservoir structures. The strategies to place wells can then be tested more realistically and better gridding strategies could be proposed. It will also be interesting to explore the possibilities of projection mapping and more advanced interaction techniques using 3D printed models.

References

1. Doodler. http://the3doodler.com/
2. Boxcut – Phil and Tyson Skit. https://www.youtube.com/watch?v=1_EYUtEp-oo/
3. Petrel E&P Software. http://www.software.slb.com/products/
4. Allen, G., Chakraborty, P., Huang, D., Lei, Z., Lewis, J., Li, X., White, C. D., Xu, X., Zhang, C.: A workflow approach to designed reservoir study. In: Proceedings of the 2nd Workshop on Workflows in Support of Large-Scale Science, pp. 75–79 (2007)
5. Barsalou, L.W.: Grounded Cognition. Ann. Rev. Psychol. **59**, 617–645 (2008)
6. Bransford, J.D., Schwartz, D.L.: Rethinking transfer: a simple proposal with multiple implications. Review of Research in Education **24**, 61–100 (1999)
7. Couture, N., Rivière, G., Reuter, P.: GeoTUI: a tangible user interface for geoscience. In: Proceedings of TEI 2008 (2008)
8. Dake, L.P.: Fundamentals of Reservoir Engineering. Elsevier, Amsterdam (1983)
9. Fjeld, M., Voegtli, B.M.: Augmented chemistry: an interactive educational workbench. In: Proceedings of ISMAR 2002, pp. 259–321 (2002)
10. Harris, J., Young, J., Sultanum, N., Lapides, P., Sharlin, E., Sousa, M.C.: Designing *Snakey*: a tangible user interface supporting well path planning. In: Campos, P., Graham, N., Jorge, J., Nunes, N., Palanque, P., Winckler, M. (eds.) INTERACT 2011, Part III. LNCS, vol. 6948, pp. 45–53. Springer, Heidelberg (2011)
11. Ishii, H., Ullmer, B.: Tangible bits: towards seamless interfaces between people, bits and atoms. In: Proceedings of SIGCHI 1997, pp. 232–241 (1997)
12. Klemmer, S. R., Hartmann, B., Takayama, L.: How bodies matter: fives themes for interaction design. In: Proceedings of DIS 2006 (2006)
13. Marshall, P.: Do tangible interfaces enhance learning? In: Proceedings of TEI 2007 (2007)
14. O'Malley, C., Fraser, D.S., et al.: Literature Review in Learning with Tangible Technologies. NESTA Futurelab, Bristol (2004)
15. Piper, B., Ratti, C., Ishii, H.: Illuminating clay: a 3-D tangible interface for landscape analysis. In: Proceedings of SIGCHI 2002 (2002)
16. Pugsley, K.E., Clayton, L.H.: Traditional lecture or experiential learning: changing student attitudes. J. Nurs. Educ. **42**(11), 520–523 (2003)
17. Specht, L.B., Sandlin, P.K.: The different effects of experiential learning activities and traditional lecture classes in accounting. Simul. Gaming **22**(2), 196–210 (1991)

18. Star, S.L., Griesemer, J.R.: Institutional ecology, translations' and boundary objects: amateurs and professionals in Berkeley's museum of vertebrate zoology. Soc. Stud. Sci. **19** (3), 387–420 (1989)
19. Sultanum, N., Sharlin, E., Sousa M.C., Miranda-Filho, D.N., Eastick, R.: Touching the depths: introducing tabletop interaction to reservoir engineering. In: Proceedings of ITS 2010 (2010)
20. Tateosian, L., Mitasova, H., et al.: TanGeoMS: tangible geospatial modeling system. IEEE Trans. Vis. Comput. Graph. **16**, 1605–1612 (2010)
21. Ullmer, B., Ishii, H.: Emerging frameworks for tangible user interfaces. IBM Syst. J. **39**(3–4), 915–931 (2000)
22. Zhang, T., Suen, C.Y.: A fast parallel algorithm for thinning digital patterns. ACM Commun. **27**(3), 236–239 (1984)

Shape-Change for Zoomable TUIs: Opportunities and Limits of a Resizable Slider

Céline Coutrix[1(✉)] and Cédric Masclet[2]

[1] CNRS-LIG, BP 53, 38041 Grenoble Cedex 9, France
Celine.Coutrix@imag.fr
[2] UJF-G-SCOP, 46 Avenue Félix Viallet, 38031 Grenoble Cedex 1, France
cedric.masclet@g-scop.eu

Abstract. Tangible sliders are successfully used as they do not need visual attention. However, users need to balance between opposite concerns: size and precision of the slider. We propose a resizable tangible slider to balance between these concerns. Users can resize the on-screen representation of the slider by resizing the tangible slider. Our aim is to benefit from both tangibility and flexible control, and balance between precision and minimum size. We measured the pointing performance of our prototype. We also assess the potential drawback (additional articulatory task for deformation) by evaluating the impact on precision of the additional articulatory task for deformation: for pursuing a target, we show that our resizable prototype supports better precision than its small counterpart as long as users do not need to resize it more often than around every 9 s.

Keywords: Resizable interfaces · Zoomable interfaces · Shape-changing interfaces · Tangible interaction · Distant interaction

1 Introduction

Tangible User Interfaces (TUIs) benefit users when the visual attention is not on the input interface but on a distant target thanks to their tangibility [10, 15]. As a consequence, TUIs have been extensively used. Example applications include lighting design with mixing tables and data visualization and manipulation on wall-sized displays [15].

When interacting with a distant target, users sometimes need to balance between opposite requirements: minimum size vs. precise manipulation of the TUI. Existing fixed-shaped TUIs are limited to a fixed and single compromise between these opposite requirements. For instance, mixing tables are very large and prevent their users from mixing at different location and e.g., get a different viewpoint on the scene. To overcome this limitation, we explore resizable TUIs. In particular, as tangible sliders are widespread, we focus on them for exploring the opportunities and limits of resizing for zoomable TUIs. For instance, to browse an on-screen timeline, a small tangible slider allows coarse browsing of the whole period, a medium tangible slider allows to browse days, and a long tangible slider allows to precisely browse minutes.

© IFIP International Federation for Information Processing 2015
J. Abascal et al. (Eds.): INTERACT 2015, Part I, LNCS 9296, pp. 349–366, 2015.
DOI: 10.1007/978-3-319-22701-6_27

An alternative solution would be to provide users with multiple sliders of different sizes. Sliders in the industry come in a large range of sizes. For instance, few millimeters long slider switches for mobile devices to 10 cm long sliders on mixing consoles. However, when size is critical, for instance when walking or craving for space on a table, multiplying the number of sliders is not an optimal solution. On the contrary, a resizable slider can give the user the opportunity to compromise on the precision in order to lessen the size.

In this paper we investigate the concept of resizable tangible sliders. We allow zooming up in motor and visual space when precision is critical, and zooming down when space is restricted. Users can enlarge the slider to get more definition and be more precise. Users can also shrink the slider to gain space and still interact, e.g. while seating at an encumbered desk. Doing so, users can benefit from both the physicality of tangible sliders and malleable control of digital sliders. We build proof-of-concept prototypes of such a resizable slider and integrated them in two example applications among our three envisioned scenarios of use. Beyond proposing a new tangible interaction technique, we measure its pointing performance and relate it to a second experiment assessing its possible flaw: the additional articulatory task and time needed for resizing. We show that the drawback of the resizable slider does not compromise its benefit: in our experiment, if the user does not need to resize more often than around every 9 s, our resizable tangible slider allows better precision compared to a small fixed-shaped tangible slider. In addition, the studies allowed us to identify how our particular proof-of-concept prototype can be improved for increasing the performance of such a novel tangible interaction technique.

After reviewing how previous research contributed to this work, we present our prototype and its applications. We then report user experiments evaluating its benefits and limitations, before concluding.

2   Related Work

We build upon the extensive related work in the area of multiscale interaction, shape-changing tangible user interfaces and interaction with sliders. We review the sub-area of work in these spaces that contributed to resizable tangible sliders for zoomable TUIs.

Interaction at Multiple Scales. The relationship between scale and performance has been studied for different tasks. All studies [1, 3, 12, 18] converge toward showing that the larger the scale, the better the performance. Recent work [7] demonstrated the importance of both motor and visual scale for the selection of small targets with a mouse [7]. We build on this work for the design of our zoomable tangible slider.

We found several techniques leveraging the idea of visual scale for improving performance, in particular within Graphical User Interfaces (GUIs). *Pad++* is a zoomable interface that allows navigation in a multiscale application [4]. The mouse's left button controls the cursor, the middle button zooms in and the right button zooms out. *Pointing lenses* [20] proposed to enlarged onscreen targets for selecting them with a pen on a tablet. *TapTap* [22] allows zooming on the area of a small target with a first tap with the thumb on a small touch-screen, and then select the enlarged target with a second tap. *Speed*, *Key* and *Ring* [2] introduced the coupling of motor and visual aspect in zoomable GUIs. However, these GUI techniques lack the benefit of tangibility. No zoomable tangible slider has been proposed yet, as it is not straightforward to design a shape-changing slider to be scaled in motor space.

Shape-Changing Tangible User Interfaces. Future challenges of Shape-Changing Interfaces have been explored [21]. However, the idea of shape-change to compromise between size and precision was not proposed. Shape-changing interfaces characterized in [23] aim at actuating the shape in order to change the grip and affordance. We extend this characterization by relating shape-change to control properties (scale and definition), and let the user initiate the change of shape. Resizable displays have been proposed through folding/rolling/coupling displays [16, 17, 19, 24, 25]. The authors explored resizing in two ways: first, to increase the display real estate; second, as an input technique itself. They do not leverage the change of shape for modifying control properties. Also, the widgets projected on these resizable surfaces lack the tangibility that was proven efficient in previous work [10, 15].

The change of control through the change of shape has been proposed in three previous works. First, stiffness-changing of the control has been explored [11]. However, this impact of the stiffness on the performance has not been evaluated yet. Second, with a different technology, *ForceForm* allows users to sculpt an interactive surface to create tangible controls [29]. Although promising, this technique requires users to carry a large surface and does not address the problem of size. Third, *TransformTable* [27] is a self-actuated shape-changing digital table with three predefined shapes: round, square and rectangle. It allows accommodating single and collaborative use of an interactive surface. This approach does not address tangibility and user-controlled continuous resizing.

Interaction with Tangible Sliders. Tangible sliders on the keyboard's side have been studied for interacting with scrollbars of GUIs [8]. We extend the knowledge on interaction with sliders by studying its resizable properties for zooming.

The performance of tangible sliders has been compared to digital sliders. A study [28] showed no significant difference in performance between tangible and untangible slider when the corresponding display is superimposed. However their tangible slider suffers from implementation problems. On the contrary, other comparative studies between digital and tangible sliders [15, 26] showed that tangible sliders help users focus on the distant targets. We build on this work by considering interaction with distant targets.

Zebra Sliders [6] allow the superposition of tangible sliders on a primary capacitive surface. Using this approach, a second fixed slider on top of another can alter its control properties. Although the performance can be improved, the multiplication of the number of sliders increases the size.

To conclude on previous research, the large body of work on multiscale interaction in the GUI paradigm showed that zoomable interfaces have a great potential for easing the selection of very small targets. However, none of this knowledge has been transferred to TUI. Shape-changing interfaces very recently started to explore the opportunities of shape-change. However, the potential for zoomable interfaces has not been explored yet. Finally, interaction with tangible sliders has been proven efficient when the target is distant. However, the balance between efficiency and size has not been addressed. We now present the design, prototype and applications of a resizable slider that aim at balancing size and performance in selecting distant targets.

3 Design, Prototype and Applications

Design. Figure 1 shows the design alternatives that we considered. In (a), the slider's thumb is fixed and the user simultaneously resizes to zoom and moves the slider's bounds to point. A drawback is that the space necessary to interact is large. In (b), the user only manipulates the thumb and the slider is resized by the system. A drawback is that it only suits a target-aware system. In (c), one bound is fixed and the user simultaneously zooms with the other bound and points with the slider's thumb. A drawback is that the user cannot freely place the slider. Figure 1(d) shows the design that we study in this paper: zooming is performed with two hands, one on each bound of the slider. We chose to study the efficiency of this design first, as it did not have the drawbacks of the others. Future work can compare the alternatives to find which offers the best compromise between performance, footprint and mobility.

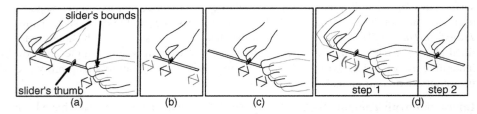

Fig. 1. Design alternatives for our resizable slider and the one we study in this paper (d). (Black/red) arrows show elements that can be moved (by the user/system) (Color figure online).

Prototype. Before addressing the technological issues for making such resizable sliders, we aim at studying the relevance of the concept. As resistive, capacitive, optical or magnetic embedded technologies currently used for tangible sliders are difficult to adapt for physically extension, we used external tracking to prototype a high-resolution proof-of-concept resizable tangible slider (Fig. 2). We used a retractable and rigid measuring tape as a smooth slide rail for the slider's thumb. For the bounds, we laser-cut two boxes. One of them hides the body of the measuring tape. The button to retract the measuring tape was made accessible to the user through a hole in the corresponding box. For resizing the slider, the user brings the bounds closer/further while pressing the button. For the slider's thumb, we laser-cut a piece to slide on the measuring tape. For better yaw stability, we (1) made the thumb 9 mm large and (2) made it to measure so that it perfectly fits the tape's shape and dimension. For better pitch stability, we added buttresses to the slider's thumb so that it stays horizontal when it slides. Buttresses were positioned far enough from the tape in order for them not to

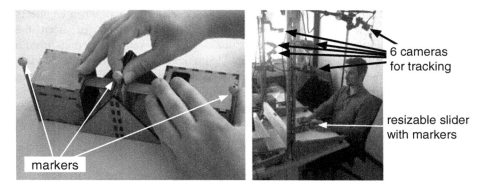

Fig. 2. (Left) Prototype of a resizable tangible slider. A rigid retractable measuring tape allows for the laser-cut thumb to slide on the slider's range. Three reflective markers are tracked by an infra-red tracking system with 6 cameras (right), detecting relative positions of the reflective markers placed on the bounds and the thumb (left).

prevent the slider's thumb to reach the bounds. This physical prototype ensures that the tangible interaction takes place smoothly and efficiently as expected by the users.

We track the position of the upper and lower bounds and of the thumb through three reflective infra-red markers and six cameras (OptiTrack Flex V100R2 infrared cameras from NaturalPoint). The tracking system is placed on a table to allow users to comfortably manipulate the slider with their elbows resting on the table. Cameras were placed as close as possible to the slider in order to maximize its resolution. Indeed, the resolution is a variable of the cameras, their number and their position. We measured the resolution of the slider as in [5] by four standard deviation of the sensed position of the static device. Throughout 500 measurements of the position of the static thumb (in fixed bounds), we found a resolution of 0.009 mm, i.e. 2822 dpi. The resolution was constant over all sizes of the slider. High-resolution mice are about 2000 dpi. As a consequence, we do not expect the resolution to limit the interaction, even in the smallest sizes like 2 cm long slider for instance.

Example Applications. Sliders are "a standard way to adjust continuously varying parameters" [26]. For most existing applications, users' needs for space and precision vary between uses or while using them. We illustrate the applicability of our approach through three example of these applications: our envision of future mixing consoles and two of our implementations (visualization and graphics edition).

Mixing consoles are widely used for sound, light or video in a variety of domains like public address systems, recording, film, broadcasting and television. First, users currently make a fixed performance/size compromise before use by selecting a particular console beforehand. Mixing consoles come in a wide range of sizes, with 20/30/45/60/100 mm sliders, depending on the size of the whole console. Our resizable sliders can be brought together to make a resizable console and help them make the best of each particular situation with one single console.

Second, users currently also change compromise during use: e.g., when engineers need to adjust mixes from the performers' positions on stage or from the front/back/edge rows of the venue, current solutions include verbal directions from a second engineer or non-tangible, less efficient [15] remote control of the console via a tablet[1]. Bringing the subset of necessary sliders to the particular location and resizing them to fit any support surface found on site would help improve performance during high-pressure (pre-)show setup. This would be an opportunity to keep the eyes-free ability to control multiples values simultaneously, make the best compromise between space and performance, and save time and human resources.

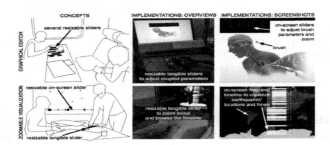

Fig. 3. Concepts (left) and implementations (center and right) of two applications of resizable sliders (black in concepts): (top) an illustrator works with sliders in a train to adjust brush parameters and (bottom) seismologists work around a table and zoom a timeline of earthquakes. The zoomable sliders are used to adjust to the available space and to the precision requirements.

Zoomable visualization currently rarely uses tangible sliders, but rather graphical sliders. However, previous work showed that visualization would benefit from tangible interaction [9, 15]. We build on this previous work and argue that it would further benefit from *zoomable* tangible interaction, as users need to explore data at different scales. In particular, some targets can be very small and their relative size cannot be changed as it conveys information.

To illustrate this (Fig. 3, bottom), we developed an application for seismologists to visualize past week's earthquakes on the world map. The application shows an earth map in full screen and a superimposed timeline, representing respectively place and time of earthquakes that occurred in the previous week. The prototype is mapped to the timeline. The slider's size allows for continuous zooming of the timeline. The slider's thumb allows selecting earthquake(s) on the timeline. In this continuous time dimension, both events and empty spaces convey relevant information to seismologists, through patterns or density, to gain insight and predict the future.

In our scenario, when Louis works with his team around a table in front of a wall-mounted screen, he can explore the earthquakes with the tangible slider on the table. He scales it up when in need to precisely select a single earthquake and scales it down when precision is less important than examining the documents lying on the table.

---

[1] https://synthe-fx.com/products/luminair, last retrieved April 30th 2015.

Graphical editors' interface includes a large number of graphical sliders for adjusting parameters, e.g., brush's size, softness, color. They are currently rarely used with tangible sliders. However, previous work showed that it would benefit from tangible interaction to more efficiently switch between parameters [10]. We build on this previous work and argue that it would further benefit from resizable tangible interaction: on the one hand, sometimes users' priority is not to be precise but they rather quickly draft many ideas, quickly switching between parameters. On the other hand, sometimes users' priority is to precisely adjust parameters to achieve high quality.

To illustrate this (Fig. 3, top), we developed a simple graphics editor that couples several resizable tangible sliders with corresponding zoomable graphical sliders among the most used: the zoom, and the brush's size, softness and color.

In our scenario, Helen works as a freelance medical illustrator. She meets with clients at their workplace, and never knows in advance the space available. She brings her tablet and her sliders as she can reduce them to minimum size for transport. When on site, she can use as many and as large sliders as possible to quickly switch between parameters and quickly draft ideas with the clients. On her way home, she often works on the train. Until the first stop, the train is almost empty so she takes advantage of the space and enlarges the sliders as much as possible for better performance. Then, a passenger sits next to her and she politely shrinks the sliders to share the table. Continuous resizing is here a high benefit. In general, continuously resizable sliders are promising for adapting to ad hoc interaction around a table: depending on the space available on the table and the task precision, users can reach the best compromise at any time through resizing. In the future, continuously resizable sliders can be coupled with resizable displays [17, 19, 25].

4   Pointing Performance of the Prototype

From [7], it is clear that larger sliders should perform better. However, it is not clear *how much* better our prototype is when larger, as [7] used a mouse. As we evaluate later in the paper the drawback of our system, it is important to compare its drawbacks to its benefits. Therefore, we conducted a preliminary experiment to measure the pointing performance of this slider at different scales.

Participants and Apparatus. Twelve right-handed participants took part in the study (6 female), aged from 21 to 42 years old (M = 30, SD = 6). The users seated 70 cm away from a 1600 × 1200 px (41.2 × 30.8 cm) display. The thumb of the prototyped slider (see Sect. 3) was manipulated on a table. The slider was prepared with a fixed size before each block and could not be resized during the block.

Experimental Design. We used a within subject design, with task's **Scale** and task's level of difficulty (**ID)** as independent variables.

We had three levels of Scale. The smallest scale, involving manipulation of the thumb with fingers only, consisted in a 2 cm long tangible slider and a 96 px long slider on the display. The medium scale was twice the smallest scale (4 cm/192 px) and involved manipulation with fingers and wrist. The largest scale was twice the medium scale (8 cm/384 px) and involved manipulation with fingers, wrist and elbow. The cursor size was 1 px large for all scales.

We had four levels of difficulty: Fitts' indexes of difficulty (ID) close to 2 (very easy), 3, 4 and 5 (very difficult): 2.00 and 2.12 were very easy, 2.81 and 3.09 were easy, 4.00 was difficult and 4.95 was very difficult. We used 2 distances between the starting position and the target (D) and, for each D, 4 corresponding target widths (W), given by ID = $\log2(D/W + 1)$. For the smallest scale (2 cm/96 px), D = {30, 60} px and W = {1, 2, 4, 10} and {2, 4, 9, 20} px respectively. For each D, the higher the ID is, the smaller the target's width is. For medium scale D and W were twice the value of the smallest scale and for the largest scale, D and W were twice the value of the medium scale.

Task and Procedure. Subjects were asked to be as fast and accurate as possible. Each block started with training, as long as the subject needed. Then, the trial started as soon as the subject pressed a key with their left hand on a keyboard below the display. A thin vertical white slider was displayed on the screen (Fig. 4). Users had to move the slider's thumb so that the white user's cursor coincides in the green target cursor. The error is shown in red between user's and target cursor. Like a typical computer pointing task, the task had to end successfully. Thus the error rate was forced to zero as in [7].

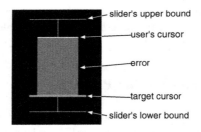

Fig. 4. Close-up screenshot of the experimental pointing task with the 8 cm/384 px slider (Color figure online).

When the task finishes, as soon as they correctly validated by pressing a key, the next target appeared at a predefined distance from the previous target.

A pseudo-random series of 80 trials (10 times each possible task) was build. This series was split into 2 blocks of 40 trials to allow a pause in the middle of the series. The two blocks were repeated for each Scale, making each participant perform 80 × 3 = 240 trials. The three scales were counterbalanced across the 12 participants through a Latin square. We collected 2880 trials, through 12 participants × 10 repetitions of each task × 3 scales × 4 widths × 2 distances.

Results. We considered the movement time (**MT**) and **error rate** as dependent variables. Error rate was computed as the number of times a validation occurred while

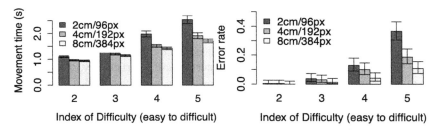

Fig. 5. Impact of task's ID and scale on the mean movement time (left) and error rate (right).

the cursor was not within the target. Figure 5[2] shows the impact of ID and scale on the mean movement time (MT) and error rate.

Movement Time. A Levene's test revealed that we could not assume the homogeneity of variances. As a consequence, we performed our analysis through a Friedman non-parametric test. The test revealed an impact on MT for ID ($\chi 2 = 1496$, $p < .001$) and scale ($\chi 2 = 464$, $p < .001$). Post hoc tests using Wilcoxon test with Bonferroni correction showed significant differences between all four IDs ($p < .001$) and between all scales ($p < .01$ between medium and large scales; $p < .001$ for all other scales). As shown in Fig. 5, for a very easy task (ID = 2), small and medium scales are significantly ($p < .001$), but little different: medium scale takes 0.87 × MT of small scale (i.e. 0.14 s gain). And medium and large scale are not significantly different. **For a very easy task, the slider's size has no to little impact.**

For ID = 3, large scale takes 0.95 × MT of medium scale (i.e. 0.06 s gain) ($p < .01$), itself taking 0.81 × MT of small scale (i.e. 0.30 s gain) ($p < .001$). For ID = 4, large scale takes 0.94 × MT of medium scale ($p < .01$) (i.e. 0.10 s gain), itself taking 0.74 × MT of small scale ($p < .001$) (i.e. 0.56 s gain). For ID = 5, large scale takes 0.87 × MT of medium scale ($p < .001$) (i.e. 0.27 s gain), itself taking 0.75 × MT of small scale ($p < .001$) (i.e. 0.70 s gain). **For these higher difficulties, the larger the slider, the bigger the size but the better the performance. It is then up to the user to compromise on one or the other.** We measured the strongest effect for the user for very difficult targets (ID = 5), where the large scale takes 0.65 × MT of the small scale (i.e. 0.98 s gain), for a device 1.75 larger (i.e. 6 cm). **The gain in size and performance are different, but their respective importance is up to the user.**

Error Rate. Pearson chi's square test for proportions shows an impact on the error rate of ID ($\chi 2 = 265$, $p < .001$) and scale ($\chi 2 = 55$, $p < .001$). More particularly, as shown in Fig. 5 (right), large scale leads to 0.42 times the errors of medium scale for ID = 4 ($\chi 2 = 5$, $p < .05$) (i.e. error rate 6 % lower). For ID = 5, large scale leads to 0.58 times the errors of medium scale ($\chi 2 = 5$, $p < .05$) (i.e. error rate 8 % lower), itself leading to 0.51 times the errors of small scale ($\chi 2 = 18$, $p < .001$) (i.e. error rate 18 % lower). **We measured the best benefit for the user in error rate for difficult targets (ID = 5)**

---

[2] In all figures, error bars show 95 % confidence intervals.

where the large scale leads to a third of the errors of the small scale (i.e. error rate 26 % lower) **for a device 1.75 larger** (i.e. 6 cm).

Discussion. Through this experiment, we measured the balance our prototype offers between size and pointing performance. For performance particularly, this experiment is not a strict, but a "conceptual" [14] replication of previous work [7]: it aimed at measuring earlier findings in different settings. Previous work [7] showed that motor and visual magnification at constant resolution (*Zoom* [7]) helps the acquisition of very small targets of a GUI with a mouse. In our experiment, we investigate the results of the same scaling method using a different device. D (2, 4, 8, 16 px [7]) and W (1, 2, 4, 8 px [7]) combinations are also different, as we wanted to allow for more representative range of manipulations of the slider and evaluate the slider with a wider range of targets' widths, even though including small targets (e.g., 1, 2, 4 px). In addition, they explored the scales of 1, 4, 16 and 64, but we preferred to focus on scales that are more likely to physically occur with TUIs: 1, 2 and 4. Keeping in mind these experimental differences and similarities, we compare[3] the results between scales 1 and 4: for MT, they (we) found that scale 4 leads to 1.33 (1.29) times faster selection than scale 1. For the error rate, they (we) found that scale 4 leads to 46 % (70 %) less errors than scale 1 with Zoom. Although the results for MT are comparable, the difference in error rate is more important in our experiment. As the resolution of our prototype was high (as in [7]), we hypothesize that the static friction of our prototype is responsible for this difference: we felt that very small corrections performed with the thumb of our prototype were slightly more difficult than with a mouse. Future improvement of the prototype will investigate ways of decreasing the force needed to start moving the thumb.

Another comparison with previous work can be done through standard Fitts' analysis [7]: ours lead to MT = 0.50 + 0.31 × ID (adjusted R2 = 0.98) for the small scale, MT = 0.44 + 0.25 × ID (adjusted R2 = 0.99) for the medium scale and MT = 0.46 + 0.23 × ID (adjusted R2 = 0.99) for the large scale. 95 % confidence intervals show that these regression lines only differ significantly between the small scale on the one hand and the medium/large scales on the other hand (for ID > 2). This is consistent with previous findings [7] (Sect. 5.3): they found the small scale to decreased their fit to a Fitts' model common to all scales.

We now present the evaluation of a main limitation of our resizable slider.

5   Impact of Resizing on Performance

The aim of the experiment is to answer the following question: how is the additional resizing task affecting the performance of the resizable slider compared to small and large sliders?

---

[3] We did not compare the effect sizes, as there is no straight way to compute the effect size of the non-parametric Friedman test that we had to use.

Participants and Apparatus. Nine right-handed participants took part in the study (5 female), aged from 21 to 49 years old (M = 31, SD = 8). The participants seated 70 cm away in front of a 1600 × 1200 px (41.2 × 30.8 cm) display. The prototyped slider (see Sect. 3) was manipulated on a table. The same resizable slider was either prepared with a fixed size before each block and could not be resized during the block; or resized by the user during the block.

Experimental Design. We used a within subjects design with the following independent variables:

- Three **Sliders:** Large (8 cm) fixed-size tangible slider (L), Resizable tangible slider (R), and Small (2 cm) fixed-size tangible slider (S).
- Four **Intervals** of difficulty change: every 3/9/18/30 s, the difficulty randomly changed between 3 levels of difficulty. The three levels of difficulty were 1, 2 and 4 px of target's widths when the slider was small (2 cm). When the slider was large (8 cm) then the three corresponding target's widths were 4, 8 and 16 px. In the case of the resizable slider, the user was asked to resize the slider when the difficulty changed so that the target's width reached 4 px.

The order of the Sliders was counterbalanced across the 9 participants through a Latin square and the four Intervals were randomized for each technique. We collected 5 h and 24 min of trials in 216 trials of 90 s (9 participants × 2 repetitions of each trial × 90 s long trial × 3 techniques × 4 intervals of difficulty change). From the collected data, we removed the first 3 s of each trial as participants had to first catch up with the continuous pursuit task. The experiment lasted 36 min (+ training) for each participant.

Task and Procedure. Participants were asked to follow a target cursor as in previous work with sliders [10, 15], as many higher-level tasks depend on it [15] like smooth adjustments of parameters in time. In Fig. 6, this task in presented on the right hand-side of the screen. Participants controlled the white cursor to follow the blue, moving cursor (target), i.e. to move the slider's thumb so that the white cursor coincides in the blue target cursor at all times. This allowed us to evaluate the impact of the additional articulatory task for resizing on this *continuous* pursuit task. The cost of resizing was then measured as the impact of the primary, resizing task on the performance of this secondary, pursuit task.

The error was highlighted in orange (Fig. 6). The participants were instructed to keep this error as small as possible at all times. The pursuit task was conducted with their right hand operating the tangible slider's thumb. As in [15], the target followed a pseudo-random path among three paths whose order was randomized between each block. The target moved at constant speed and darted off at pseudo random intervals (between 2 and 4 s). The slider's speed was 0.15 × the slider's size (in px per second). The dart-off distance was 0.3 × the slider's size.

With resizable slider (R) only, participants were asked to first reach the target size when the difficulty (i.e. the size of the target) changed, before pursuing the target cursor. Resizing the slider was conducted with both hands operating the bounds of the tangible slider. In Fig. 6, this task is presented on the left hand-side of the screen. The

360 C. Coutrix and C. Masclet

target size is green, the user's slider's size is white and the error is red. The aim of this resizing task is to reproduce in a controlled setting the fact that users will adapt the size of their interface to the space available and accordingly degrade their performance in order to keep interacting. As we aim at evaluating the consequence of this resizing on the secondary task, we controlled how participants performed the resizing task as accurately as possible: they could not perform the pursuit task, i.e. their white pursuit cursor was not displayed, as long as they did not reach the target size (± 50 px). In the case of fixed-size sliders (S and L), the left part of the screen (Fig. 6) was empty.

Subjects were asked to be as fast and accurate as possible throughout the experiment for both tasks. Each block started with training, as long as the subject needed. Then, as soon as the subjects pressed a key, the trial started. The task automatically finished after 90 s, avoiding the need for any key press validation from the subjects at the end of the trial. Subjects could then take a break and the second trial started after they pressed a key.

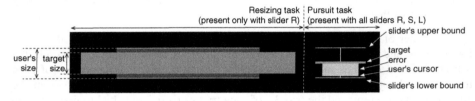

Fig. 6. Close-up screenshot of the experimental tasks during the resizing condition (R). On the left, the primary resizing task: the green rectangle shows the slider's size to reach. The size error is shown in red. On the right, the pursuit task: the thin white slider and the blue moving target to pursue. The pursuit error is shown in orange (Color figure online).

Results. As dependent variables, we considered the *resizing time* (in seconds), the *size* and *size error* (the distance between the size and target size, in cm) and the *pursuit error* (the distance between the cursor and the target, as a percentage of the slider size).

Resizing Time. Resizing time was computed from the analysis of the video recording of the experiment. We did not get this information from software logging. Indeed, we wanted to capture the duration between the resizing stimulus and the moment when the user was able to get back to pursuit. For the second, we observed that even though the pursuit task was displayed again on the screen, participants still had to place their hands correctly to be able to pursue again. As a consequence, only video analysis could help us identify the beginning of the pursuit movement.

We found that in average, the participants took 0.7 s to resize the slider with our prototype (SD = 0.5). We found no impact of the Interval on the resizing time. We also investigated the impact of the resizing distance (2, 4 or 6 cm) and of the direction (shrinking vs. stretching), but found no impact either.

We observed that most participants intertwined both tasks when they could, resizing while continuously keeping their grasp on the thumb to keep pursuing the target. This leads to think that the design of Fig. 1(c) is worth studying: it would have been easier if the upper bound of the prototype was fixed on the table, so that they would not need to leave the slider's thumb to use two hands to resize the prototype. We also observed that one participant manipulated the slider as shown in Fig. 1(b).

Size and Size Error. We confirm through this experiment that subjects were able to resize the slider as asked: size error was very close to zero (M = −0.03 cm, SD = 1.04 cm) for the resizable slider. The small and resizable sliders are the only sliders that could adapt to constrained space. They respectively freed more space or just the amount of space that was required. Considering the average size, R was measured 0.57 the size of L (i.e. 3.4 cm shorter), whereas S was a fourth of the size of the large slider (i.e. 6 cm shorter). R was measured 2.21 the size of S (i.e. 2.42 cm larger), whereas L was four times the size of S (i.e. 6 cm larger), i.e. almost twice the length of R.

Pursuit Error. Considering the pursuit error, we first examined its distribution (Fig. 7). As the distribution of the pursuit error is skewed, we considered the median pursuit error as it gives in this case a good measure of location. Figure 8 shows the impact of the interval of difficulty change on this median pursuit error.

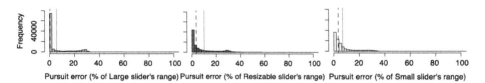

Fig. 7. Distribution of the pursuit error for each device condition (large, resizable and small). Dashed lines show the medians and red lines show the means (Color figure online).

A Levene's test revealed that we could not assume the homogeneity of variances (F(11,332628) = 1223.6, p < .001). As a consequence, we performed our analysis through Friedman non-parametric test. We found that Interval has an effect on pursuit error ($\chi2$ = 1678.887, p < .001) and that Sliders had an effect on pursuit error too ($\chi2$ = 28337.53, p < .001). In particular, post hoc tests using Wilcoxon test with Bonferroni correction showed significant differences between all four Intervals (p < .001) except between 18 and 30 s (Fig. 8). It also showed significant difference between all Sliders (p < .001). For all Intervals, all Sliders lead to significantly different pursuit error (p < .001 for all Intervals/Sliders, except p = 0.008 between R and S when the difficulty changes every 30 s). When the difficulty changes every 3 s, the pursuit error with the small slider is 5.53 times the pursuit error with the large slider (i.e. a loss in precision of 2.93 % of the slider's range). **The pursuit error with the resizable slider is far more important when the difficulty changes every 3 s:** 13.10 times the pursuit error with the large slider (i.e. a loss in precision of 7.82 % of the slider's range). **However, while the pursuit error of the small slider does not improve when the difficulty changes less often, the resizable slider gains in precision:** from 2.37 times the pursuit error of the small slider at every 3 s (i.e. a loss of precision of 4.89 % of the slider's range), the resizable slider becomes more precise than the small slider: its pursuit error is 0.68 times the pursuit error of the small slider at every 18 s (i.e. a gain in

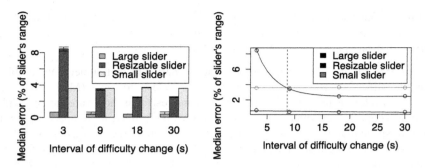

Fig. 8. Left: impact of Slider and Interval of difficulty change on the median error. Right: limit of difficulty change (around 9 s) for preferring R over S if space is an issue.

precision of 1.18 % of the slider's range). **To make the best of this result, users with space constraints can keep their slider small at fixed size if the difficulty is changing too often, and start resizing only if the difficulty does not change too often.**

We performed modeling of the medians of the pursuit error for each slider (Fig. 8) to find the limit of performance: if the difficulty changes less often than around every 9 s and space is an issue, then the resizable slider has to be preferred over the small slider. If space is not an issue, a large slider has to be preferred. If the difficulty changes more often than around every 9 s and space is an issue, then it is better to leave the resizable slider at a fixed, small size. This conclusion was confirmed by participants during interviews, as all agreed that 3 s was to fast for the resizable slider to be usable whereas 18 and 30 s was slow enough for the resizable slider to be usable. For 9 s, 3 participants could not decide if it was too fast or slow enough, while 2 found it too fast and 3 found it slow enough.

We can see in Fig. 7 that the difference between the mean (red) and the median (dashed) is larger in the case of the resizable slider. This is explained by the fact that the mean gives more importance to outliers and to the spread of a skewed distribution. Indeed, in the case of our resizable slider, the error can be higher than with a fixed slider when the user is resizing it. Whereas the error seldomly exceeds 30 % of the fixed slider's range (i.e. the target's dart off distance), the error exceeds this threshold in the case of the resizable slider when the user is resizing it. Very high errors occur when the difficulty changes and this increases the mean. As the video analysis showed, the participants sometimes could not control the location of the thumb when they needed two hands to resize the slider. Future improvement of the prototype will investigate ways for the system to control the location of the thumb while resizing the slider (Fig. 1 (a, c, d)).

As shown in Fig. 9, there is an impact on the percentage of time with pursuit error of Intervals ($\chi2 = 333.2468$, $p < .001$) and Sliders ($\chi2 = 29302.92$, $p < .001$). Figure 9 shows that the amount of time with error is very little impacted by the change of difficulty with small ($\chi2 = 17.1592$, $p < .001$, effect size $V = 0.01$) and large slider ($\chi2 = 64.6802$, $p < .001$, effect size $V = 0.02$)). However, the impact of Intervals is slightly higher in the case of the resizable slider ($\chi2 = 890.6538$, $p < .001$, $V = 0.09$).

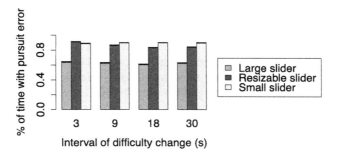

Fig. 9. Impact of Technique and Interval of difficulty change on the percentage of time with pursuit error.

Pursuit errors occurred around 2 s more in the 90 s trial with the resizable slider than with the small slider when the difficulty changes every 3 s ($\chi2 = 75.9095$, p < .001). **As the resizing occurred less frequently, the pursuit error occurred less often with the resizable slider than with the small slider:** as soon as the difficulty changes every 9 s, there is also a significant difference between S and R ($\chi2 = 152.2004$, p < .001). When resizing occurs every 9 s, users gain 3 s of precision with the resizable slider compared to the small slider during the 90 s trial and, when resizing occurs every 18 s, they gain 6 s in a 90 s trial). The large slider performs best ($\chi2 = 28919.3$, p < .001), at the cost of its larger size.

Discussion. Through this experiment, we measured the impact of the additional articulator task for resizing. Overall, participants reported that the manipulation of the prototype was easy. This is confirmed by comparison to previous work: our experiment is not a replication of previous work [15], but the task was identical, and, interestingly, our 8 cm slider lead to 6 % of mean pursuit error, achieving similar performance as previous 8 cm prototype [15]. Depending on the precision demand of the pursuit task, fixed-size or resizable sliders should be considered. If space is not an issue, then a large slider is better as it is more efficient. If space is limited or changing, then designers have to consider two cases:

- If the task demands to be as efficient as possible most of the time, then a resizable slider is better.
- If the task demands not to exceed a threshold of error, then the small slider, kept at fixed size, is better.

For example, for a mobile mixing console allowing to mix a performance from several viewpoint of the venue (e.g., performer, front row, back row, edges, etc.), engineers can face two different requirements: if the show is live, the engineer will prefer to avoid outliers, e.g., uncontrolled high levels. In this case, when the outliers have to be avoided, fixed-sized small sliders would prevent them to occur. On the contrary, if the show is recorded, the engineer would rather control the sliders as precisely as possible for best quality. In this case, when outliers will be cut during editing, a resizable slider is a better option to make the best out of each mixing location.

6 Discussion

We conducted both experiments with the same prototype in order to relate their results. From the second experiment, we found that the time needed to resize was 0.7 s ($\pm$0.5 s). As a consequence, in the worst-case scenario, resizing takes 1.2 s. In the first experiment, we measured the mean pointing MT when ID = 5(4), at 2.8 s(2.1 s) for the small slider. The corresponding MT for the large slider is 1.8 s(1.5 s). If the user has to perform at least two of such pointing tasks consecutively and space is not an issue during these interactions, it is better to first resize the slider. This would allow for a gain of 0.8 s(0.1 s) in this worst-case scenario - 1.8 s(1.1 s) in the best-case scenario. When a user, like Helen our illustrator, performs such pointing tasks for parameters adjustments hundreds of times a day, a resizable tangible slider can save a lot of her time over a small tangible slider, and save space over large tangible slider.

The benefits of our prototype for parameters adjustments (pointing and pursuit tasks) are promising. This paper validates the relevance of the concept and shows that further improvements are worth addressing in future work. In particular, several major challenges have to be addressed to improve the design and the prototype:

1. **Improving the Pointing Performance:** as reported, we felt that very small corrections performed with the thumb of our prototype were slightly more difficult than with a mouse due to static friction. One participant corroborated this hypothesis. In order to bring the pointing performance of our resizable slider to the one of a mouse [7], future improvement of the prototype will investigate ways of decreasing the force needed to start moving the thumb, e.g., decreasing its contact area on the support surface or decreasing its weight.

2. **Decreasing the Pursuit Error During Resizing:** we have two avenues to enable the control of the thumb while resizing. Pausing interaction during resizing is not considered for real-time interaction. First we plan to evaluate a resizable slider with a fixed bound in order for the user to resize with the left hand only and keep controlling the thumb with the right hand (Fig. 1c). We can limit the negative impact of this design on the mobility of the slider with an unobtrusive blocking mechanism between the slider's bound and the support surface (e.g., watch, smartphone, tablet, table, etc.). Second, if two hands are used for resizing, two stepper motors could actuate the thumb for the system to maintain its relative position during resizing.

3. **Improving Both Pointing and Pursuit Performance Through Reducing the Size of the Prototype:** future miniaturization needs to address two issues: slide rail and tracking. Current rigid, retractable tape can be shorten to fit in a smaller volume. Tracking can be done from the support surface [15, 28] or magnetic sensors at both ends, computing position and size. In longer term, our vision is addressed by nanotechnologies, which work towards reconfigurable and controllable material[4] that could be used for implementing such resizable sliders.

---

[4] see for instance www.cs.cmu.edu/~claytronics/.

7 Conclusion and Future Work

This paper presents a new tangible interaction technique, leveraging shape-change for the users to modify the control properties of a tangible slider: the larger the tangible slider, the more the visual and motor definition for better performance in target selecting and pursuit. Contrastingly, the smaller the tangible slider is, the less the footprint. Users can now balance between performance and size thanks to this resizable slider for zoomable TUIs. We show that the limit of this benefit resides in the frequency of resizing. If the interval between resizing of our proof-of-concept prototype is smaller than around every 9 s, the users should better keep the slider at fixed size. This advocates in favor of our interaction technique, as many situations of use do not require a change this frequent, as shown by our application scenarios.

Beyond being readily useful by the community, the outcome of this paper can be improved in follow-up work. The results of our studies pointed to several avenues for improving the design and the prototype. Future work should further study these alternatives to find their impact on users' performance and comfort. Doing so, we would further improve the performance of the resizable slider. Future extensions of this work include exploring if the users actually resize their sliders in an ecological experiment. Second, other tangible widgets, like knobs, could be resized. This raises new questions. For instance, how does the shape of a dial impact users' performance? Which tangible tool is best suited for which task? The presented slider is one concrete implementation of a broader concept that is yet to be investigated, where shape-changing TUIs are tightly coupled with digital information.

Acknowledgments. This work has been partially supported by the LabEx PERSYVAL-Lab (ANR-11-LABX-0025-01) and the DELight project (French government's FUI - Single Inter-Ministry Fund - program).

References

1. Accot, J., Zhai, S.: Scale effects in steering law tasks. In: ACM CHI, pp. 1–8 (2001)
2. Appert, C., et al.: High-precision magnification lenses. In: Proceedings of the SIGCHI Conference on Human Factors in Computing Systems. In: ACM CHI, pp. 273–282 (2010)
3. Balakrishnan, R., MacKenzie, S.: Performance differences in the fingers, wrist, and forearm in computer input control. In: ACM CHI, pp. 303–310 (1997)
4. Bederson, B., Hollan, J.: Pad++: a zooming graphical interface for exploring alternate interface physics. In: ACM UIST, pp. 17–26 (1994)
5. Bérard, F., Wang, G., Cooperstock, J.R.: On the limits of the human motor control precision: the search for a device's human resolution. In: Campos, P., Graham, N., Jorge, J., Nunes, N., Palanque, P., Winckler, M. (eds.) INTERACT 2011, Part II. LNCS, vol. 6947, pp. 107–122. Springer, Heidelberg (2011)
6. Chan, L., et al.: Capstones and zebrawidgets: sensing stacks of building blocks, dials and sliders on capacitive touch screens. In: ACM CHI, pp. 2189–2192 (2012)
7. Chapuis, O., Dragicevic, P.: Effects of motor scale, visual scale, and quantization on small target acquisition difficulty. ACM TOCHI **18**(3), 13:1–13:32 (2011)

8. Chipman, L., et al.: Slidebar: analysis of a linear input device. Behav. Inf. Technol. **23**(1), 1–9 (2004)

9. Dumas, B., et al.: Artvis: combining advanced visualisation and tangible interaction for the exploration, analysis and browsing of digital artwork collections. In: ACM AVI, pp. 65–72 (2014)

10. Fitzmaurice, G., Buxton, W.: An empirical evaluation of graspable user interfaces: towards specialized, space-multiplexed input. In: ACM CHI, pp. 43–50 (1997)

11. Follmer, S., et al.: Jamming user interfaces: programmable particle stiffness and sensing for malleable and shape-changing devices. In: ACM UIST, pp. 519–528 (2012)

12. Gibbs, C.: Controller design: interactions of controlling limbs, time-lags and gain in positional and velocity systems. Ergonomics **5**, 385–402 (1962)

13. Guiard, Y.: Asymmetric division of labor in human skilled bimanual action: the kinematic chain as a model. J. Mot. Behav. **19**, 486–517 (1987)

14. Hornbæk, K., et al.: Is once enough? on the extent and content of replications in human-computer interaction. In: ACM CHI, pp.3523–3532 (2014)

15. Jansen, Y., et al.: Tangible remote controllers for wall-size displays. In: ACM CHI, pp. 2865–2874 (2012)

16. Khalilbeigi, M., et al.: Foldme: interacting with double-sided foldable displays. In: ACM TEI, pp. 33–40 (2012)

17. Khalilbeigi, M., et al.: Xpaaand: interaction techniques for rollable displays. In: ACM CHI, pp. 2729–2732 (2011)

18. Langolf, G., et al.: An investigation of Fitts' law using a wide range of movement amplitudes. J. Mot. Behav. **8**, 113–128 (1976)

19. Lee, J., et al.: Foldable interactive displays. In: ACM UIST, pp. 287–290 (2008)

20. Ramos, G., et al.: Pointing lenses: facilitating stylus input through visual-and motor-space magnification. In: ACM CHI, pp. 757–766 (2007)

21. Rasmussen, M., et al.: Shape-changing interfaces: a review of the design space and open research questions. In: ACM CHI, pp. 735–744 (2012)

22. Roudaut, A., et al.: Taptap and magstick: improving one-handed target acquisition on small touch-screens. In: ACM AVI, pp. 146–153 (2008)

23. Roudaut, A., et al.: Morphees: toward high "shape resolution" in self-actuated flexible mobile devices. In: ACM CHI, pp. 593–602 (2013)

24. Spindler, M., et al.: Towards making graphical user interface palettes tangible. In: ACM ITS, pp. 291–292 (2010)

25. Steimle, J., Olberding, S.: When mobile phones expand into handheld tabletops. In: CHI EA, pp. 271–280 (2012)

26. Swindells, C., et al.: Comparing parameter manipulation with mouse, pen, and slider user interfaces. In: IEEE EuroVis, pp. 919–926 (2009)

27. Takashima, K., et al.: Transformtable: a self-actuated shape-changing digital table. In: ACM ITS, pp. 179–188 (2013)

28. Tory, M., Kincaid, R.: Comparing physical, overlay, and touch screen parameter controls. In: ACM ITS, pp. 91–100 (2013)

29. Tsimeris, J., et al.: User created tangible controls using forceform: a dynamically deformable interactive surface. In: ACM UIST Adjunct, pp. 95–96 (2013)

Eyes and Keys: An Evaluation of Click Alternatives Combining Gaze and Keyboard

Ken Neth Yeoh, Christof Lutteroth$^{(\boxtimes)}$, and Gerald Weber

Department of Computer Science, University of Auckland,
38 Princes Street, Auckland 1010, New Zealand
kyeo475@aucklanduni.ac.nz,
{christof,gerald}@cs.auckland.ac.nz

Abstract. With eye gaze tracking technology entering the consumer market, there is an increased interest in using it as an input device, similar to the mouse. This holds promise for situations where a typical desk space is not available. While gaze seems natural for pointing, it is inherently inaccurate, which makes the design of fast and accurate methods for clicking targets ("click alternatives") difficult. We investigate click alternatives that combine gaze with a standard keyboard ("gaze & key click alternatives") to achieve an experience where the user's hands can remain on the keyboard all the time. We propose three novel click alternatives ("Letter Assignment", "Offset Menu" and "Ray Selection") and present an experiment that compares them with a naive gaze pointing approach ("Gaze & Click") and the mouse. The experiment uses a randomized, realistic click task in a web browser to collect data about click times and click accuracy, as well as asking users for their preference. Our results indicate that eye gaze tracking is currently too inaccurate for the Gaze & Click approach to work reliably. While Letter Assignment and Offset Menu were usable and a large improvement, they were still significantly slower and less accurate than the mouse.

Keywords: Eye gaze tracking · Click alternative · Keyboard

1 Introduction

Pointing is a natural activity of the human eye: when we look at an object, this is a good indicator that the object is currently occupying our attention; this rule of thumb has become a core principle in research based on gaze tracking. As a result, gaze tracking is a promising technology for natural user interfaces. It does not require learning any new techniques. With eye gaze tracking devices entering the consumer market at prices similar to gaming mice, there is a growing interest among users as well as in the HCI community.

Gaze trackers hold promise for a variety of situations. They have become an established assistive technology for improving accessibility. While gaze tracking has yet to become a widely used technology, it holds promise for work away from the desk, especially with laptops. Laptops can provide a keyboard similar to desktop devices, but they have no adequate surface for a normal mouse, e.g. when used on the lap. Furthermore, the use of a mouse in typical productive work requires users to switch a hand

© IFIP International Federation for Information Processing 2015
J. Abascal et al. (Eds.): INTERACT 2015, Part I, LNCS 9296, pp. 367–383, 2015.
DOI: 10.1007/978-3-319-22701-6_28

between keyboard and mouse frequently, which incurs a time penalty. The use of gaze for pointing would allow users to keep their hands on the keyboard more persistently. In any case, users must identify a target visually before moving the mouse to click it, which means that eye gaze tracking could lead to more direct and fluent interaction. Gaze tracking technology may also mitigate some of the problems of repetitive strain injury (RSI) related to mouse overuse.

While pointing with the eyes may seem easy from a user's perspective, eye gaze tracking technology inherently suffers from inaccuracy. First, there are technical challenges of calibration, resolution, tracking volume, changing lighting conditions, variances in the anatomy of the face and eyes, and optical properties of visual aids such as glasses and contact lenses. All these factors make it difficult to achieve a good tracking accuracy for all users. Second, there are physiological limitations: involuntary eye movements such as jitter and drifts, blinks, and the size of our fovea which also provides clear vision of objects that are not exactly on the point of gaze. These challenges and limitations make it difficult to design methods for pointing and clicking UI elements based on gaze ("click alternatives") that are fast and accurate.

In this research we investigate click alternatives that make use of eye gaze tracking for pointing and a standard keyboard for clicking ("gaze & key click alternatives"). This fills a gap in the current literature, which mostly focuses on purely gaze-based or gesture-based click alternatives using techniques such as zooming, dwell time thresholds and confirm buttons. We propose three novel gaze & key click alternatives ("Letter Assignment", "Offset Menu" and "Ray Selection"), specify them formally using state machines and discuss their underlying design decisions. In an experimental study we compare the click alternatives with naive gaze-pointing and keyboard clicking ("Gaze and Click") and the mouse. We address the following research questions:

RQ1. How can fast and accurate gaze & key click alternatives be designed?
RQ2. How do gaze & key click alternatives compare with each other and the mouse?
RQ3. Are gaze & key click alternatives mature enough for everyday general use?

Our results shed light on the problems and opportunities of gaze & key click alternatives, providing guidance for interaction designers of gaze-based user interfaces. Furthermore, we share information and resources that will help other researchers perform realistic click alternative evaluations. In summary, this paper makes the following contributions:

- Three novel gaze & key click alternatives with formal state machine specifications.
- An experimental comparison of gaze & key click alternatives, with insights into the interaction design and general usability of such technologies.
- An experimental procedure for the evaluation of click alternatives and an open-source implementation of the aforementioned gaze & key click alternatives.

Section 2 summarizes related work about gaze-based click alternatives. Section 3 describes the design of the proposed gaze & key click alternatives. Section 4 describes the experimental methodology used. Section 5 gives an overview of the results, and Sect. 6 discusses them. Section 7 summarizes conclusions and points out future research directions.

2 Related Work

Eye gaze tracking as a pointing device currently lacks the accuracy required to be used as a simple point & click device [1–5], for a number of different reasons. Firstly, the fovea of the eye, which is responsible for sharp central vision, covers about one degree of visual angle [4, 6]. This relatively large angle means that it may be difficult for the eye gaze tracker to accurately pinpoint what the user is looking at on the screen, especially if the target is small such as an icon or text. At a distance of 65 cm from the screen, the eye can view an area of about 1.1 cm diameter clearly. Furthermore, our gaze subconsciously drifts or jumps to other points of interest. As a result, it takes a conscious effort from the user to hold the gaze in an area for a length of time [5]. These eye gaze tracking inaccuracies cannot be solved by simply upgrading the hardware; therefore different software solutions have been built to increase the accuracy in pinpointing the user's gaze.

Zhang et al. [7] proposed techniques to improve the stability of an eye gaze cursor, using force fields, speed reduction and warping to a target's center. Force fields act as a kind of magnet for the cursor: the algorithm attempts to deduce the user's intent and tries to prevent the cursor from veering off target. Cursor speed reduction was found to increase speed and accuracy when using the eye gaze pointer for medium-size targets. Such techniques are useful, but do not improve the accuracy of eye gaze cursors sufficiently for general use.

The most obvious and natural purely gaze-based click alternative is "dwell", which clicks a target after the gaze dwells on it for a certain time. For simple object selection tasks, dwell can be significantly faster than the mouse [8]. However, while it has been successfully used for specialized UIs such as carefully-designed menus [9, 10], dwell alone is generally insufficient as a general click alternative because it is not accurate enough for small targets. Hardware buttons for clicking seem slightly faster than simple dwell with a typical 0.4 s dwell threshold, but less accurate as people tend to click before the gaze has fully settled on the target [11]. The accuracy can be improved by taking into account system lag and delaying triggers accordingly [12].

One approach to address the lack of accuracy is to enlarge or zoom in on the general area of the user's gaze. EyePoint [13] magnifies the area around the gaze when a hotkey is pressed, and performs a click at the point of gaze in the magnified view when the hotkey is released. The reported click times are fast (below 2 s), but there are problems with accuracy (error rate exceeding 10 %). There are similar techniques relying only on gaze: Zoom Navigator [3] continuously magnifies the area the user is looking at, until it is clear what the target is and the target is automatically clicked. If correcting movements are made, Zoom Navigator zooms out for a short period before continuing to zoom in again.

Most zooming techniques overlay the area under the cursor with a magnification, so context is lost. There are techniques to mitigate the loss of contextual information, such as fish-eye lenses and offset magnifying glasses. Ashmore et al. [14] investigated a dwell-activated fish-eye lens with a continuous fish-eye zoom, which preserves but distorts the context around the target. FingerGlass [15] employs an offset magnifying glass which never covers the zoomed-in area for touch-based interaction. However, when applying offset techniques in gaze-based interaction, one must consider that the offset content will immediately attract the user's gaze.

Bates et al. [4] investigated gaze clicking with zooming and found a clear relationship between the target size and the level of magnification used by a user when targeting a small area. Participants would zoom in until the target is just larger than the pre-test measured pointing accuracy of the eye gaze tracker. It was also found that the participants had difficulty maintaining focus on a target during the selection process. The time spent correcting the cursor position on targets was the largest portion of non-productive time spent carrying out the tasks. This emphasizes the need for additional techniques to address the inaccuracy of gaze cursors.

ceCursor [2] uses transparent directional buttons located around the area the user is looking at. The buttons, which are activated by dwelling on them, can be used to move a cursor. This technique is accurate (even for small targets) but slow, taking on average 11.95 s. Using a keyboard, it would be straightforward to use the directional keys in a similar manner. But while accurate, this would be slow compared to the speed of gaze.

The gaze-based WeyeB browser [1] uses a combination of dwell and eye gestures for link navigation. Once the user is looking at the desired target, they must flick their eyes upwards and then back downwards to click a link. If multiple links are under the general area of the cursor, a large secondary drop down menu with the different link options is displayed – an alternative to zooming. The combination of dwell and eye gestures solved the "Midas touch" problem, i.e. inadvertent clicking that can occur when using dwell alone. Gaze & key click alternatives generally do not suffer from the Midas touch, as a key can be used to clearly signal a click.

Another method of improving the accuracy of pointing with eye gaze is to use facial movements to refine the cursor position [16]. Four electrodes are placed on the user in order to capture electromyogram (EMG) signals from muscles in the face. The user first looks at the approximate target location, then uses facial movements to incrementally move the cursor, and finally performs click actions using other facial movements. While this increased accuracy to near mouse levels, it was still about four times slower (more than 4 s per click).

Some approaches combine gaze tracking with a physical pointing device. MAGIC [17] moves the pointer quickly to the gaze position to speed up pointing, using the mouse for finer movements and clicking. The Rake Cursor [18] shows a grid of multiple mouse pointers simultaneously, moving the whole grid with the mouse and selecting the active pointer in the grid by gaze. It successfully reduces mouse movements as the pointer closest to a target can be used. The Gaze-enhanced User Interface Design (GUIDe) [19] combines gaze with keyboard and mouse to improve various common tasks.

3   Click Alternative Design

Four gaze & key click alternatives were designed and implemented as follows. The Ray Selection alternative is included here, but was not used in the experiment for reasons outlined later in this section. All click alternatives are designed with a web browser as the basis, so the targets in the following examples are hyperlinks. The click alternatives can also be applied to other types of targets. All click alternatives were implemented in Java using the Webkit[1] web browser engine as a basis. They are freely available as open-source software[2].

3.1 Gaze & Click

This is the simplest of the four click alternatives: gaze is used for pointing and a hotkey (we chose the 'F' key) is used for clicking. If the hotkey is pressed while the recorded gaze position is directly on a link, then the link is clicked. Otherwise, no link is clicked. Figure 1 shows a screenshot of the implementation. Figure 2 illustrates the overall interaction in a state machine diagram, using the notation from [20]. Its modeless nature is clearly expressed in the presence of a single state.

As indicated by the related work, it is very hard to use this click alternative, and this was confirmed in our pilot study. In particular, it was simply too difficult for the users to know if a link is currently underneath the recorded gaze position. It was necessary to add a visual gaze cursor, an orange dot representing the user's current gaze position. While it may be possible to hide the gaze cursor for larger targets, most textual hyperlinks are simply too small given the typical inaccuracy of gaze tracking. With a visible gaze cursor users are at least aware of the gaze tracking error and can compensate for it by adjusting their gaze.

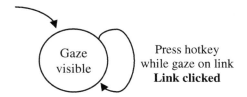

onic engineering deals with the study of sm
ing computers and integrated circuits. Alterr
usually concerned with using electricity to tr

Fig. 1. Screenshot of the Gaze & Click implementation (note the gaze cursor after "integrated")

Gaze
visible

Press hotkey
while gaze on link
Link clicked

Fig. 2. State machine of the Gaze & Click alternative

3.2 Letter Assignment

The main idea of the Letter Assignment alternative is to assign letters to links close to the gaze and allow the user to choose between them by pressing the corresponding key. This is similar to hotkeys, with the difference that assigned letters are shown near the

---

[1] http://www.webkit.org/.

[2] http://github.com/aucklandhci/gazebrowser.

gaze and both gaze and keys are used for disambiguating targets. The use of gaze ensures that all visible links are clickable with a single keystroke even on crowded pages. Figure 3 shows a screenshot of the implementation. Figure 4 shows the state machine diagram. After gazing at an area with at least one hyperlink, a unique capi-talized letter is drawn slightly above all hyperlinks within a radius around the gaze position. The letter shown for each hyperlink is chosen as the first available character in the label of the link, making it easier for users to anticipate the letter for a link. If there is no unique character in the hyperlink's label, the next available letter in the alphabet is used instead. To click the hyperlink, the user presses the corresponding key.

A white rectangle is drawn behind the overlaid letter to allow easier reading of the letter; since the hyperlinks are often quite close to other text, the overlaid letters could otherwise be hard to make out. A drop shadow is drawn behind the overlaid letters, on top of the white rectangle, to give the illusion of layering; the overlaid letters are on top and the web browser is the background. The user will naturally want to interact with the top-most layer. The color of the letters is kept black (the same as most of the text on the page) to make them less distracting, so they can be ignored more easily if clicking hyperlinks is not the user's intention.

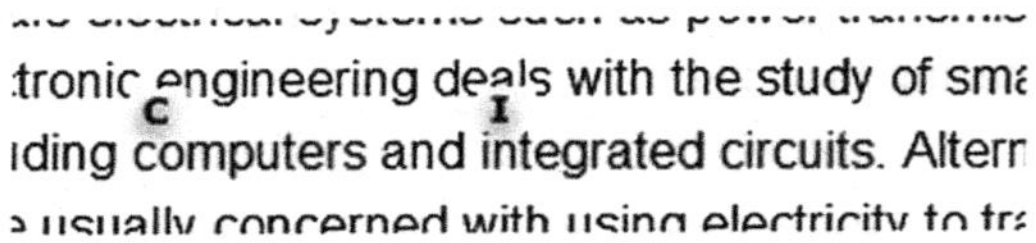

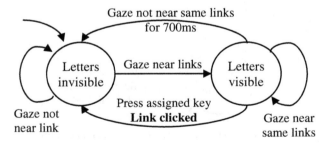

Fig. 3. Screenshot of the Letter Assignment implementation

Fig. 4. State machine of the Letter Assignment click alternative

3.3 Offset Menu

The main idea of the Offset Menu is similar to that of confirm buttons [20], i.e. buttons that are used to confirm a click action after pointing with gaze. Instead of dwell-activated confirm buttons in a page margin, a menu with buttons is activated with a hotkey (we chose the 'F' key again). Because the menu cannot appear accidentally, as with the dwell-activated confirm buttons, the menu can be placed at an offset to the

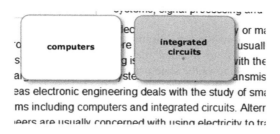

Fig. 5. Screenshot of the Offset Menu implementation (Color figure online)

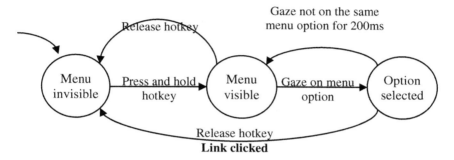

Fig. 6. State machine of the Offset Menu click alternative

gaze position without disruption. A screenshot of the implementation is shown in Fig. 5 and the state machine diagram in Fig. 6. When the user presses and holds the hotkey, a menu is displayed at an offset above the current gaze position. If the offset menu would be cut off by any screen edge, it is shifted to display correctly. The menu contains an entry for each hyperlink within a radius of the reported gaze, i.e. the same set of hyperlinks as in Letter Assignment. If there are no hyperlinks in the vicinity, no menu is drawn. While still holding down the hotkey, the user can shift their gaze to one of the menu options, and the menu option will turn green to show it is currently selected. The user can then release the hotkey, and whichever menu option is currently selected will be clicked. If no menu option is selected when the hotkey is released, no hyperlink will be clicked. There is a de-selection threshold of 200 ms, to prevent jitter in the gaze coordinates from unintentionally de-selecting an option.

A drop shadow is again drawn behind the menu options to create the illusion of layering; the menu options are on top and the web page is in the background. The selected option is green because the color green affords "going forward", much like a traffic light. The size of the menu options is large enough to allow for some inaccuracy and imprecision in gaze tracking. The text is centered, drawing the user's attention to the center of the menu option to make it easier to select.

3.4   Ray Selection

The main idea of this alternative is to disambiguate links by selecting the direction of the intended target, similar to a radial menu. Figure 7 shows a screenshot of the implementation. Figure 8 shows the state machine diagram. When the user presses and holds the hotkey (we chose the 'F' key again), a ray is drawn from the recorded gaze point at the time the hotkey was pressed (the start point) towards the current gaze point. This ray is redrawn as the current gaze point changes. The ray may intersect with hyperlinks. The intersected hyperlink closest to the current gaze point is the selected hyperlink; it is highlighted with a red border and its name is drawn at the end of the ray, at the user's current gaze position, to let the user know which hyperlink is currently selected. When the user releases the hotkey, the selected hyperlink is clicked. If no hyperlink intersects the ray, no link is clicked.

The selected hyperlink's name is drawn on a semi-opaque white background, so it is possible to read the name even against background text. A drop shadow creates the illusion of layers, similar to Letter Assignment and Offset Menu. The selected hyperlink is highlighted with a red border to make it clear to the user which hyperlink is selected, even if the user is not looking at it directly.

ᴇlᴇctrical ᴏystᴇms ᴏucʜ aᴏ powᴇr traʜᴏmioᴏioʜ aʜᴅ motor ᵗ

ʜic engineering deals with the study of small-scale electroɴ

g computers and integrated circuits. Aᴸₜₑᵣₙₐₜᵢᵥₑₗᵧ, electricᴀ
                                       **integrated
                                       circuits**

ᴜally concerned with using electricity to transmit energy, ᴡ

ᴀers are concerned with using electricity to transmit informᴀ

Fig. 7. Screenshot of the Ray Selection implementation (Color figure online)

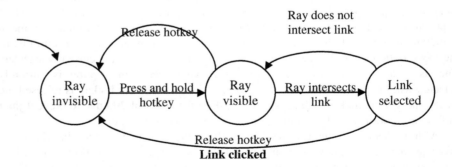

Fig. 8. State machine of the Ray Selection click alternative

During our pilot study, it became clear that this alternative exhibited several clear disadvantages, to a degree that it was clearly not worth to include it into the main study. We present this alternative in the interest of reporting also negative results, so that others can learn from our experience. Users often found it very difficult to click the desired hyperlink as they were unsure where to look to select a target. In particular, they found it difficult to change the currently selected hyperlink if it was not the desired one. The start point would typically already be close to the target (as in Fig. 7), forcing users to look beyond the target to make the ray point into the right direction despite gaze tracking inaccuracy. Our experience with this alternative illustrates the problems of separating gaze from intention, i.e. of making users look at anything that is not clearly a target.

4 Methodology

The usability study was conducted using a within-subjects design to reduce error variance stemming from individual performance differences. The independent variable is the click alternative used to complete the given tasks. The dependent variables measured are "time taken to click link" (click time) and "number of incorrect clicks" (inaccuracy). Ease of use was measured using the System Usability Scale (SUS) [21].

A 30 inch 144 Hz LCD monitor with a resolution of 1920×1080 pixels, a standard QWERTY keyboard and standard mouse with the default Win7 configuration were used. A Tobii X2-30 W eye gaze tracker with a refresh rate of 30 Hz was mounted on a tripod below the monitor in a non-intrusive space. A fully adjustable chair with headrest and armrests allowed participants with various heights to be well within the tracking volume of the gaze tracker, helped keep their head still and be overall comfortable for the duration of the experiment. The room was lit by fluorescent lights, and the blinds were closed to block sunlight from interfering with the eye gaze tracker.

After filling out a pre-experiment demographics questionnaire, the participants were comfortably seated and the chair adjusted to best fit the eye gaze tracker's usable parameters. Before each click alternative was started, the eye gaze tracker was calibrated using Tobii's EyeX software, which took 20–30 s. Additional calibration was provided if the participant moved around too much or found the calibration to be too inaccurate. Calibration was then measured using a custom program which logged how close the gaze tracker coordinates were to each of nine on-screen calibration points.

A generic clicking task was used to measure click time and accuracy, in a series of 40 hyperlinks pseudo-randomly chosen from Wikipedia. We chose Wikipedia because it is one of the most visited websites and all the participants had used it in the past. An offline Wikipedia[3] was used to ensure all the pages were static and consistent. For each click alternative, participants were allowed as much "free-play" time as they wanted, so they could learn how the click alternative worked properly and get used to navigating Wikipedia pages.

Participants were told to click the target hyperlinks as fast and accurately as they could. Before each click, a brief countdown was shown, and then the target link was highlighted with a thick black rectangle (Fig. 9) until a click was performed. The series of target hyperlinks was the same for each participant, as the same starting seed was

---

[3] http://schools-wikipedia.org/.

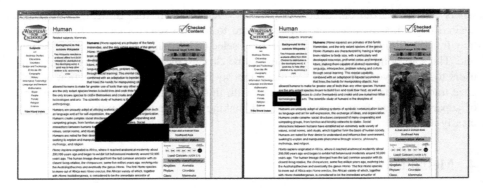

Fig. 9. Screenshots of the task: a brief countdown (left) followed by highlighting of the click target (right)

used. When a participant accidentally clicked the wrong target, the browser would still navigate to the correct target for consistency. For each click alternative the first 10 clicks were training trials; only the following 30 clicks were used for later analysis. The order in which participants used the click alternatives was permuted to mitigate order bias and training effects.

All clicks were logged in a CSV file together with fine-grained events, such as the time the target was found and the time a button was pressed. After each click alternative was tested, a post-task questionnaire was filled out by the participant, which contained the ten SUS questions answered on a five-point Likert-scale. After completing the tasks using all four click alternatives, a post-experiment questionnaire was filled in, which asked the participants to rank the click alternatives from one to four, with one the best. An optional comment section allowed participants to explain their rankings and express their thoughts on each of the click alternatives.

5   Results

The experimental data set is available on the web[4]. 20 participants successfully took part in the main experiment (16 men and 4 women). There was one other participant for whom we were unable to calibrate the eye gaze tracker. The unsuccessful calibration was most likely due to a very high difference in his glasses' strength between the left and right eye. The participants were all aged between 19 and 45, with a variety of ethnicities and a range of disciplines including Computer Science, Engineering and Psychology. Participants indicated reading between 2 and 12 h a day (median 5.5), and using the computer between 3 and 12 h a day (median 8.0). Nine participants wore either glasses or contact lenses of varying strengths. In total, 2400 clicks were measured, recorded and analyzed (600 for every condition). Table 1 summarizes the results.

---

[4] http://github.com/aucklandhci/gazebrowser/tree/master/datasets/.

5.1 Performance

A one-way within-subjects ANOVA was conducted to test the effect of the click alternative on click time, showing a very significant effect ($F(3, 1797) = 46.97$, $p < 0.0001$). Paired samples t-tests with Holm correction were used to make post hoc comparisons between the conditions. There were significant differences between the click times of all conditions ($p < 0.001$) except for Letter Assignment and Offset Menu ($p = 0.13$). It is clear that Gaze & Click is the slowest and the mouse is the fastest click alternative. This is illustrated in more detail in the click time distributions in Figs. 10, 11, 12 and 13. The red line shows the cumulative percentage over all measured clicks.

Another one-way within-subjects ANOVA was conducted to test the effect of the click alternative on the number of correct clicks, showing a very significant effect ($F(3, 72) = 9.97$, $p < 0.0001$). Paired samples t-tests with Holm correction were used to make post hoc comparisons between the conditions. Similar to click time, there were significant differences between the numbers of correct clicks of all conditions ($p < 0.01$) except for Letter Assignment and Offset Menu ($p = 0.10$). It is clear that Gaze & Click is the least accurate and the mouse is the most accurate click alternative.

Participants clearly had problems clicking the correct links with Gaze & Click, and also some problems with Letter Assignment and Offset Menu. The click time distributions indicate that the gaze & key alternatives suffer from a fairly large number of outliers compared to the mouse. However, Letter Assignment and Offset Menu are a large improvement over Gaze & Click. Some of the typical comments on performance from the participants are as follows:

- "Letter assignment was quick and easy to use. Mouse beats the other two because it was far more accurate"
- "Mouse is the one I'm used to. Offset Menu was quick and accurate. Letter Assignment required whole keyboard. Gaze and click was super inaccurate"
- "Gaze & click with very accurate eye tracker would outperform the other two"
- "Offset: had to literally search the alternatives $\rightarrow$ cumbersome. Gaze and click: sometimes hard to hit target. Letter assignment: good but change of focus between keyboard and screen not ideal. Mouse: slow movement speed".

Table 1. Summary of results (click time in seconds)

	Gaze & Click	Letter Assignment	Offset Menu	Mouse
Click time mean	4.28	2.71	3.03	1.26
Click time std. dev.	7.17	3.94	3.24	0.47
Click time median	2.07	1.79	2.00	1.16
Click time median 95 % CI	[1.84, 2.31]	[1.70, 1.88]	[1.92, 2.09]	[1.14, 1.20]
Incorrect clicks	35.33 %	10.17 %	6.5 %	0.5 %
SUS score mean	53.7	71.6	77.1	91.5
SUS score std. dev.	14.4	14.9	13.5	9.2
Rank mean	3.85	2.48	2.38	1.3

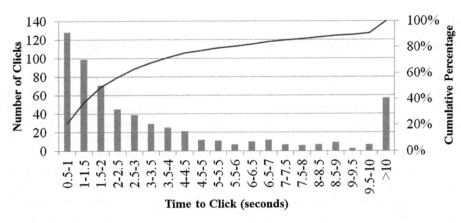

Fig. 10. Click time distribution for the Gaze & Click alternative (Color figure online)

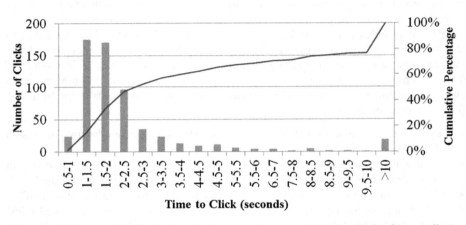

Fig. 11. Click time distribution for the Letter Assignment alternative (Color figure online)

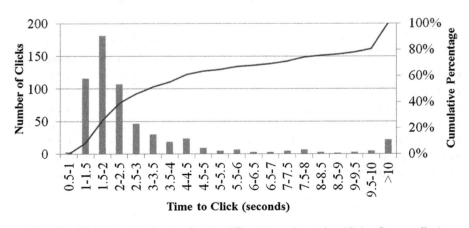

Fig. 12. Click time distribution for the Offset Menu alternative (Color figure online)

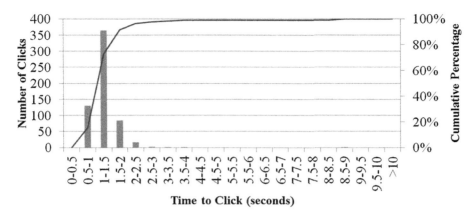

Fig. 13. Click time distribution for the mouse (note the beginning of the time-to-click axis at 0 s as opposed to 0.5 s in the previous figures) (Color figure online)

5.2   Usability

Figure 14 shows the mean SUS scores of the click alternatives. A one-way within-subjects ANOVA was conducted to test the effect of the click alternative on SUS score, showing a very significant effect ($F(3, 57) = 39.13$, $p < 0.0001$). Paired samples t-tests with Holm correction were used to make post hoc comparisons between the conditions. Similar to the performance results, there were significant differences between the SUS scores of all conditions ($p < 0.001$) except for Letter Assignment and Offset Menu ($p = 0.20$). It is clear that Gaze & Click has the lowest and the mouse the highest SUS score.

Figure 15 shows a histogram of the click alternative rankings. A Friedman rank sum test was conducted to test the effect of the click alternative on rank, showing a very significant effect ($\chi 2 = 39.74$, $df = 3$, $p < 0.0001$). Paired Wilcoxon signed-rank tests with Holm correction were used to make post hoc comparisons between the conditions. Consistent with the SUS scores, there were significant differences between the ranks of all conditions ($p < 0.01$) except for Letter Assignment and Offset Menu ($p = 0.82$). It is

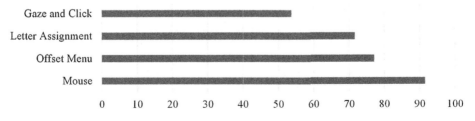

Fig. 14. Mean SUS scores of the click alternatives

clear that Gaze & Click is ranked the worst and the mouse is ranked the best. Some typical comments on usability from participants are as follows:

- "Letter assignment was a little troublesome actually having to wait for and read the assigned letter, which is annoying when it's not the first letter"
- "Offset menu is predictable and lots of visual feedback"
- "Offset menu was easy to use but still seemed like a strain on the eyes with continuous use".

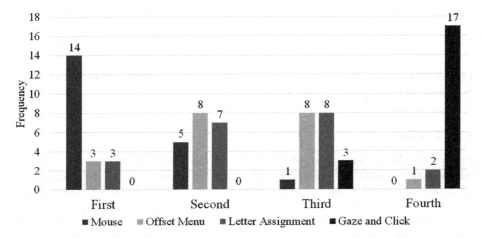

Fig. 15. Histogram of click alternative rankings (Color figure online)

6   Discussion

As expected, the mouse was the fastest and most accurate click alternative, with the best SUS score. This may be in part due to every participant being heavily used to it and its easy learning curve. Gaze & Click has no support for helping users click links accurately; therefore we expected it to be the least accurate click alternative, but not necessarily the slowest. Interestingly, participants often went for one of two different approaches. One was to click links quickly regardless of whether they were sure their gaze position was on top of the right link, and the other was to spend a long time getting their gaze position to be stable on top of the right link before clicking the hotkey. The first approach was very quick, often being faster than the mouse, but the second approach sometimes took upwards of 10 s. Participants were told to "click links as fast and as accurately as possible", so participants had to decide whether to be fast or to be accurate, as it was clearly not possible to do both.

From observation, participants had trouble deactivating the Offset Menu if none of the options given were correct. There were two causes for this. First, the 200 ms de-selection threshold was not explicitly explained to users beforehand. Second, some users looked too far off-screen, breaking the line of sight with the gaze tracker. This often caused the gaze position to freeze on a menu option. In both cases, the option would still be selected when the user released the key.

From observation, Letter Assignment proved to be difficult for participants because the assigned letter for a link was not always the one they were expecting. For example, two links "Citizenship" and "Countries" were often next to each other and both assigned a letter. "Citizenship" would be assigned the 'C' key and "Countries" would be assigned 'O'. Participants would often click 'C' if they wanted to go to "Countries". Most of the time the assigned letter was the one the participants were expecting, so it would trip them up when it was not.

For both Letter Assignment and Offset Menu, the speed was quite close to the mouse if the target link was among the first links selected (either by displaying the letters or showing the menu). However, if the target link was not immediately selected for whatever reason, then this would at least double the click time: the user would need to de-select and then re-select the options. This was not an issue for Gaze & Click or the mouse, as both of them are modeless and do not need a selection/de-selection process.

How do the presented gaze & key click alternatives compare to other gaze-based click alternatives? It is difficult to compare the results of studies with different methodologies. However, some studies use hyperlink clicking tasks similar to the one presented here, so at least a discussion is possible. The purely gaze-based Multiple Confirm click alternative [20] seems slower than Letter Assignment and Offset Menu, which is not surprising considering that no hardware buttons are used. Interestingly, Multiple Confirm also seems more accurate, probably because it is harder to click incorrect (and correct) links. EyePoint [13], which is another gaze & key click alternative, seems faster than Letter Assignment and Offset Menu, but less accurate than Offset Menu. This could be because Offset Menu – in contrast to EyePoint – gives clear feedback about the target that will be clicked.

7   Conclusion

Eye trackers may well be one of the next types of computer peripherals going mainstream. However, it is still a challenge to create added value off these devices in everyday computing. Using them as a pointing device seems natural, and combining them with a keyboard to create a point-and-click interface may have advantages in situations where the use of a mouse is inconvenient or impossible.

We designed and implemented novel gaze & key click alternatives combining eye gaze tracking and keyboard input (Letter Assignment and Offset Menu), allowing users to click targets on the screen without the mouse. These click alternatives are able to mitigate some of the inaccuracies of eye gaze trackers and the eye, resulting in an improved accuracy when compared to a naive click alternative based on direct gaze pointing and a physical button (Gaze & Click). They are still significantly slower and less accurate than the mouse, however, we believe that with more work they could become realistic mouse replacements for certain situations.

One major issue found during the experiments was calibration: it was frequently necessary to recalibrate the gaze tracker, and many participants found this tiring and time-consuming. As a consequence, the use of methods for automatic or simplified calibration should be considered. Furthermore, there are problems of the proposed click alternatives that should be addressed, e.g. the assignment of unintuitive letters to targets in Letter Assignment and difficulties with the de-selection of potential targets in Offset Menu.

Finally, there are some open questions. For example, in how far did touch typing skills affect the performance of Letter Assignment? What are the long-term effects of using gaze & key click alternatives? How do such click alternatives compare to other pointing devices such as trackpads and touchscreens? We hope to answer some of these questions in future work.

Acknowledgements. We would like to acknowledge Abdul Moiz Penkar for his work on the web browser implementation, and all our participants without whom this study would not have been possible.

References

1. Porta, M., Ravelli, A.: WeyeB, an eye-controlled web browser for hands-free navigation. In: Proceedings of the Conference on Human System Interactions (HSI), pp. 210–215. IEEE (2009)
2. Porta, M., Ravarelli, A., Spagnoli, G.: ceCursor, a contextual eye cursor for general pointing in windows environments. In: Proceedings of the Symposium on Eye-Tracking Research & Applications, pp. 331–337. ACM (2010)
3. Skovsgaard, H.: Noise challenges in monomodal gaze interaction. Ph.D. thesis, IT University of Copenhagen, Köpenhamn (2012)
4. Bates, R., Istance, H.: Zooming interfaces! enhancing the performance of eye controlled pointing devices. In: Proceedings of the Fifth International ACM Conference on Assistive Technologies, pp. 119–126. ACM (2002)
5. Penkar, A.M., Lutteroth, C., Weber, G.: Designing for the eye: design parameters for dwell in gaze interaction. In: Proceedings of the Australian Computer-Human Interaction Conference (OzCHI), pp. 479–488. ACM (2012)
6. Wandell, B.A.: Foundations of Vision. Sinauer Associates, Sunderland (1995)
7. Zhang, X., Ren, X., Zha, H.: Improving eye cursor's stability for eye pointing tasks. In: Proceedings of the SIGCHI Conference on Human Factors in Computing Systems (CHI), pp. 525–534. ACM (2008)
8. Sibert, L.E., Jacob, R.J.K.: Evaluation of eye gaze interaction. In: Proceedings of the SIGCHI Conference on Human Factors in Computing Systems (CHI), pp. 281–288. ACM (2000)
9. Ohno, T.: Features of eye gaze interface for selection tasks. In: Proceedings of the Asia Pacific Conference on Computer Human Interaction (APCHI), pp. 176–181. IEEE (1998)
10. Urbina, M.H., Lorenz, M., Huckauf, A.: Pies with eyes: the limits of hierarchical pie menus in gaze control. In: Proceedings of the Symposium on Eye-Tracking Research and Applications (ETRA), pp. 93–96. ACM (2010)
11. Ware, C., Mikaelian, H.H.: An evaluation of an eye tracker as a device for computer input. In: Proceedings of the SIGCHI/GI conference on Human Factors in Computing Systems and Graphics Interface (CHI), pp. 183–188. ACM (1987)

12. Kumar, M., Klingner, J., Puranik, R., Winograd, T., Paepcke, A.: Improving the accuracy of gaze input for interaction. In: Proceedings of the Symposium on Eye Tracking Research and Applications, pp. 65–68. ACM (2008)
13. Kumar, M., Paepcke, A., Winograd, T.: EyePoint: practical pointing and selection using gaze and keyboard. In: Proceedings of the SIGCHI Conference on Human Factors in Computing Systems (CHI), pp. 421–430. ACM (2007)
14. Ashmore, M., Duchowski, A.T., Shoemaker, G.: Efficient eye pointing with a fisheye lens. In: Proceedings of Graphics Interface (GI), pp. 203–210. Canadian Human-Computer Communications Society (2005)
15. Käser, D.P., Agrawala, M., Pauly, M.: Fingerglass: efficient multiscale interaction on multitouch screens. In: Proceedings of the SIGCHI Conference on Human Factors in Computing Systems (CHI), pp. 1601–1610. ACM (2011)
16. Chin, C.A., Barreto, A., Cremades, J.G., Adjouadi, M.: Integrated electromyogram and eye-gaze tracking cursor control system for computer users with motor disabilities. J. Rehabil. Res. Dev. 45(1), 161–174 (2008)
17. Zhai, S., Morimoto, C., Ihde, S.: Manual and gaze input cascaded (MAGIC) pointing. In: Proceedings of the SIGCHI Conference on Human Factors in Computing Systems (CHI), pp. 246–253. ACM (1999)
18. Blanch, R., Ortega, M.: Rake cursor: improving pointing performance with concurrent input channels. In: Proceedings of the SIGCHI Conference on Human Factors in Computing Systems (CHI), pp. 1415–1418. ACM (2009)
19. Kumar, M., Winograd, T.: GUIDe: gaze-enhanced UI design. In: Proceedings of the SIGCHI Conference on Human Factors in Computing Systems - Extended Abstracts (CHI EA), pp. 1977–1982. ACM (2007)
20. Penkar, A.M., Lutteroth, C., Weber, G.: Eyes only: navigating hypertext with gaze. In: Kotzé, P., Marsden, G., Lindgaard, G., Wesson, J., Winckler, M. (eds.) INTERACT 2013, Part II. LNCS, vol. 8118, pp. 153–169. Springer, Heidelberg (2013)
21. Brooke, J.: SUS: a 'Quick and Dirty' usability scale. In: Jordan, P.W., Thomas, B., Weerdmeester, B.A., McClelland, A.L. (eds.) Usability Evaluation in Industry, pp. 189–194. Taylor & Francis, London (1996)

Interactions Under the Desk:
A Characterisation of Foot Movements
for Input in a Seated Position

Eduardo Velloso[1(✉)], Jason Alexander[1], Andreas Bulling[2],
and Hans Gellersen[1]

[1] Infolab21, School of Computing and Communications, Lancaster University,
Lancaster LA1 4WA, UK
{e.velloso,j.alexander}@lancaster.ac.uk,
hwg@comp.lancs.ac.uk
[2] Perceptual User Interfaces Group, Max Planck Institute for Informatics,
Campus E1 4, 66123 Saarbrücken, Germany
andreas.bulling@acm.org

Abstract. We characterise foot movements as input for seated users. First, we built unconstrained foot pointing performance models in a seated desktop setting using ISO 9241-9-compliant Fitts's Law tasks. Second, we evaluated the effect of the foot and direction in one-dimensional tasks, finding no effect of the foot used, but a significant effect of the direction in which targets are distributed. Third, we compared one foot against two feet to control two variables, finding that while one foot is better suited for tasks with a spatial representation that matches its movement, there is little difference between the techniques when it does not. Fourth, we analysed the overhead caused by introducing a feet-controlled variable in a mouse task, finding the feet to be comparable to the scroll wheel. Our results show the feet are an effective method of enhancing our interaction with desktop systems and derive a series of design guidelines.

Keywords: Foot-based interfaces · Fitts's law · Interaction techniques

1 Introduction

Computer interfaces operated by the feet have existed since the inception of HCI [1], but such devices remained restricted to specific domains such as accessible input and audio transcription, being largely overshadowed by hand-based input in other areas. However, this overshadowing cannot be put down to lack of dexterity, as we regularly accomplish a wide variety of everyday tasks with our feet. Examples include the pedals in a car, musicians' guitar effect switches, and typists' use of transcription pedals. Recent technological advances renewed interest in foot-based input, be it for interacting with a touch-enabled floor [2], for hands-free operation of mobile devices [3], or for adding more input channels to complex tasks [4]. Despite this, we still lack a thorough understanding of the feet's capabilities for interacting in one of the most common computing setups—under the desk.

© IFIP International Federation for Information Processing 2015
J. Abascal et al. (Eds.): INTERACT 2015, Part I, LNCS 9296, pp. 384–401, 2015.
DOI: 10.1007/978-3-319-22701-6_29

In particular, unlike previous work that used trackballs [5], pedals [6], and foot mice [7], we wished to explore unconstrained feet movements. This removes the need for a physical device (as well as the related foot-to-device acquisition time) and provides a wide range of interaction possibilities (analogous to the ones available from a touch-screen over a mouse).

We envision numerous applications to arise from this greater understanding. These include using your feet to scroll a page while the hands are busy with editing the document, changing the colour of a brush while moving it with the mouse, or manipulating several audio parameters simultaneously (using both the hands and the feet) to create novel musical performances.

To address this gap we conducted a series of experiments exploring different aspects of foot-based interaction. In the first, we recorded 16 participants performing 1D and 2D pointing tasks with both feet to build the first ever ISO 9241-9 Fitts's Law models of unconstrained foot pointing for cursor control. This first study provided some evidence that side-to-side movement is faster than backwards and forwards. To confirm this hypothesis, we conducted a second experiment in which participants performed 1D serial pointing tasks in each direction. In the third experiment, we investigated the manipulation of multiple parameters using one and two feet. In the fourth and final experiment, we evaluated the use of the feet together with the hand.

In summary, (1) we built 1D and 2D ISO 9241-9 compliant movement time models for unconstrained foot pointing; (2) we found that unconstrained foot pointing is considerably slower than mouse pointing, but comparable to other input devices such as joysticks and touchpads; (3) we found no significant difference in performance between the dominant and non-dominant foot; (4) we found that left and right movement is easier than backwards and forwards; (5) the most comfortable movement for desktop foot interaction is heel rotation; (6) techniques that have a direct spatial mapping to the representation outperform the others; (7) when variables are shown separately, two feet work better than one; (8) we show that the feet perform similarly to the scroll wheel in tasks where the feet are used in conjunction with the mouse; and (9) we provide design guidelines and considerations based on our findings.

2 Related Work

Foot-Operated Interfaces: Early prototypes of foot-based interfaces aimed at reducing the homing time between switching from the keyboard to the mouse. Examples for such interfaces include English et al.'s knee lever [1] and Pearson and Weiser's moles [8]. Other works employed the feet for a variety of tasks including cursor control [1, 8], mode selection [9], spatial navigation [10], mobile phone control [3], command activation [11], gaming [12, 13], tempo selection [14, 15], user identification [16] and text input [6].

Tracking the Feet: Feet interfaces appear in the literature in different forms. Peripheral devices include foot mice, pedals, and switches. Wearable devices obtain input from sensors embedded in users' clothing [12], footwear [17] or mobile devices [3]. For tracking motion, inertial measurement units (accelerometer, gyroscopes and magnetometers) are commonly employed [3, 12], whereas pressure sensors [17] and textile switches [10] are used to detect button pressings and gestures such as heel and toe clicking. Wearable tracking systems are usually more mobile and individualised than remote ones, but require some user instrumentation.

Conversely, remote tracking approaches rely on augmenting the environment where the system is going to be used, which usually means less instrumentation on the user and more versatility in cases where multiple users share the same system at different points in time. Sensing may be performed by conventional colour cameras [13], depth cameras [4, 16], optical motion capture [18], audio [15] and smart floors [2].

Quantitative Evaluations of Foot Interfaces: Analyses of feet performance date back to Ergonomics work by Drury [19] and Hoffman [20], who asked participants to tap on physical blocks on the floor. Springer and Siebes compared a custom-built foot joystick to a hand-operated mouse in an abstract target selection task [21]. Pakkanen et al. investigated the performance of trackballs operated by the feet and by the hand in common graphical user interface tasks [5]. Dearman et al. compared foot switches on a pedal to screen touch, device tilt, and voice recognition in text editing tasks [6]. Garcia et al. looked at how performance evolves as users learn to operate a foot joystick and a hand trackball [7]. Table 1 summarizes the results of these studies.

Table 1. Previous studies on the performance of hand and feet pointing for seated users, summarising number of participants (N) and the ratios of task completion times and error rates between the feet and hands.

Foot device	Hand device	N	$\frac{\text{Foot Time}}{\text{Hand Time}}$	$\frac{\text{Foot Error}}{\text{Hand Error}}$	Ref.
None	None	10	1.95[a]	–	[20]
None	None	10	1.7[b]	–	[20]
Joystick	Mouse	17	2.32	1.56	[21]
Trackball	Trackball	9	1.6	1.2	[5]
Pedals	Tilt	24	1.05[c]	1.20[c]	[6]
Pedals	Touch	24	0.98[c]	1.87[c]	[6]
Joystick	Trackball	16	1.58[d]	–	[7]

[a]Ratio between the reported coefficients of the ID for *visually controlled* movements.
[b]Reported ratio for *ballistic* movements.
[c]Ratio between reported means for selection time and error rate in the text formatting task.
[d]Mean ratio between reported task completion times for the foot joystick and the mouse.

These works evaluated several different foot interfaces, but the wide variety of experimental designs makes comparing results difficult. Further, these studies have only looked at 1st order devices (i.e. devices that control the rate of change of a value, rather than the value directly, such as the joystick and the pedals) and relative input devices (i.e. devices that sense changes in position, such as the mouse and the trackball) [22]. Hoffman investigated unconstrained absolute positioning, but with users tapping on physical targets rather than using the foot for cursor control. However, modern devices that take input from the feet, such as depth cameras [4] and interactive floors [2] use absolute positioning, sometimes without physical proxies, making it important to study this kind of interaction.

3 Study 1: Fitts's Law Performance Models

To fill this gap, we conducted an experiment in which 16 participants performed 1D and 2D pointing tasks with both feet, to build the first ever ISO 9241-9 Fitts's Law models of unconstrained foot pointing for cursor control. This allows us to compare our model to those of other input devices based on the same standard using the mean throughput for each condition. We also tested for effects of task and foot on user performance.

We recruited 16 participants (11 M/5F), aged between 20 and 37 years (median = 27), with foot sizes ranging from 23 to 30 cm (median = 26 cm). Participants were inexperienced with foot interfaces and half of them were regular drivers. All participants were right handed, but one was ambidextrous. All participants were right footed.

The experiment was conducted in a quiet laboratory space, on a laptop with an 18-inch screen and 1920×1080 resolution. To track the feet, we used an implementation of Simeone et al.'s tracker [4]. This system uses a *Kinect* sensor mounted under the desk and a MATLAB program that subtracts the background, converts the coordinate system from the camera plane to the floor plane, isolates the feet and fits ellipses to the remaining data. The ellipses' foci are then used to approximate the position of the toes and heels. The tracker worked at 26 frames per second. We made sure that only one foot was visible to the camera at any point in time, by asking participants to keep the opposite foot under the chair, and that the cursor control was assigned to the toes of whichever foot was in view. Mouse clicks were performed using a conventional mouse with disabled movement tracking. The tracker was calibrated with a 1:1 CD gain, so that the cursor and foot movements matched exactly.

Participants performed 1D and 2D Fitts's Law tasks, for which we used Wobbrock et al.'s *FittsStudy* tool, an ISO-9241-9-compliant C# application to "administer conditions, log data, parse files, visualize trials and calculate results" [23]. The tool was configured to administer nine different combinations of A (amplitude) $\times$ W (width) defined by three levels of A {250, 500, 1000} crossed with three levels of W {20, 60,130}, yielding nine values of ID {1.55, 2.28, 2.37, 3.12, 3.22, 3.75, 4.14, 4.7, 5.67}.

We recorded all sessions using additional cameras pointed at participants' faces and feet, as well as the screen using the *Open Broadcaster Software* (see Fig. 1).

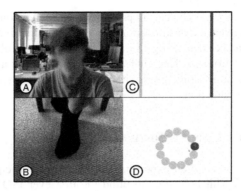

Fig. 1. We recorded participants faces (A) and feet (B), synchronized with the 1D (C) and 2D (D) tasks.

3.1 Procedure

Participants first signed a consent form and completed a personal details questionnaire. The tasks were conventional ISO 9241-9 pointing tasks, in which targets appeared in blue on the screen. Participants selected targets by moving their feet so the cursor was above the target and by left-clicking the hand-held mouse. We chose this technique rather than foot tapping as we were interested in the time it takes to move the feet and the gesture time might delay the task unnecessarily.

Participants performed both a 1D task (with vertical ribbons on either side of the screen) and a 2D task (with circular targets in a circular arrangement), with both their dominant and non-dominant foot. The order of tasks was randomized, but we ensured that the same foot was not used twice in a row. Each task comprised 9 *IDs* and was repeated in 13 trials (the first 3 discarded as practice). To summarize, each participant performed 2 feet × 2 tasks × 9 *IDs* × 13 trials = 468 movements. To make the friction with the floor uniform across all users, we asked them to remove their shoes and perform the tasks in their socks.

After completing the tasks we asked participants to fill in a questionnaire adapted from the ISO 9241-9 standard for the use with the feet (see Fig. 2(B)). We also conducted an open-ended interview about participants' experience using the foot interface, what they liked and disliked about it, what strategies and movements they used to reach targets, etc. All interviews were transcribed and coded accordingly.

3.2 Results

Our analysis had two objectives: to build a Fitts's Law performance model for each task and each foot and to check whether there was any difference in performance—as measured by the throughput—for different feet and tasks.

To build the performance models, we computed the mean movement time (*MT*) and the mean 1D and 2D effective indices of difficulty (*IDe*) for each participant and for each combination of $A \times W$. We then built the performance models using linear

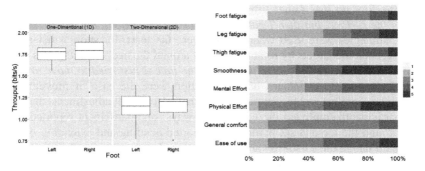

Fig. 2. Study 1 Results: (A) Mean throughput for each task and foot and (B) Subjective reactions to the interaction technique (1-Low, 5-High)

regression on these data, using the formulation described by Soukoreff and MacKenzie [24]. Table 2 summarizes the movement time models, as well as the R-squared and the mean throughput averaged over the individual mean throughputs for each participant. To test for differences in performance for each condition, we compared the mean throughput (see Fig. 2(A))—a metric that takes into account both speed and accuracy of the movement performance [24]—using a factorial repeated-measures ANOVA. We found a significant main effect of the task on the average throughput ($F_{1,15}$ = 391, $p < .001$), with an average *TP* of 1.75 for the 1D task and 1.15 for the 2D task, but not of the foot ($F_{1,15}$ = .75, $p = .09$) or the interaction between foot and task ($F_{1,15}$ = .41, $p = .12$) (see Table 2). Participants' subjective ratings covered the whole scale (see Fig. 2(B)), suggesting that some people like it, whereas other people hated it.

After transcribing and coding the interviews, some consistent patterns of users' opinions emerged.

Table 2. Performance model for each condition with its corresponding r-squared, mean throughput and error rate

Condition	Movement time (ms)	R^2	TP (bit/s)	Error (%)
1D right	$99 + 561 \times ID$	0.88	1.75	8.43
1D left	$-56 + 609 \times ID$	0.96	1.75	8.49
2D right	$423 + 739 \times ID$	0.85	1.16	7.64
2D left	$372 + 789 \times ID$	0.75	1.14	8.60

Movement Behaviours: In general, participants preferred to move around their hips and knees as little as possible, leaving as much of the movement as possible to the ankle joints. Participants reported five strategies for reaching targets on the screen: dragging the foot, lifting the foot, rotating the foot around the heel, rotating the foot around the toes and nudging the toes. At the beginning of the tasks, participants often started by dragging the foot across the floor, but quickly realized that this was tiring (*"was a bit uncomfortable"*, *"I could instantly feel my abs working"*, *"more taxing and not really natural"*). Four participants reported lifting the foot across the floor, but found that keeping the foot up was rather tiring (*"I'd have more control and I don't have the friction of the surface, but then I got very fatigued from keeping my whole leg up"*).

These strategies were used when targets were far apart; for shorter distances participants reached the targets by rotating the foot around the heels with the toes up, what they often referred to as "pivoting" (*"most of the time, I just tried to move around my heel"*). The reported advantages of heel rotation were the ease of movement, less fatigue, higher comfort and higher precision. Finally, for small adjustments and smaller targets, participants employed the toes in two ways: one participant reported rotating the foot around the toe and six participants reported bending and extending their toes, which would nudge the cursor towards the target (*"when I wanted to do a fine grained, on the smaller targets, I would crunch my toes"*).

Differences between Tasks: All participants but one found the one-dimensional task easier than the two-dimensional one, which is reflected in the quantitative difference in throughput. This can be explained by the fact that moving left and right could be accomplished with heel rotation (the easiest movement, as participants reported), whereas back and forth movements required knee flexion and extension, either by dragging the foot on the floor or lifting it above it, both strategies that were reported as being tiring.

Challenges: The biggest challenges reported by participants were the cognitive difficulty in reaching small targets (*"when the targets are smaller you need more precision so you need to focus"*) and in coordinating the hands and feet (*"it was weird starting, because you'd have to coordinate your thought process, your clicking and your feet, but I think as you went on, It was pretty quick to adapt"*), fatigue (*"a little fatigue influenced the outcome"*), friction with the floor (*"I don't like this kind of rubbing with the floor"*), and overshooting (*"I knew that I was going to overshoot, so I just overshot and tried to click at the same time"*).

3.3   Discussion

Our regression models are in line with previous work as our one-dimensional model is very similar to Drury's ($MT = 189 + 550 \times ID$) [19]. Hoffman found a much lower coefficient ($MT = -71 + 178 \times ID$) [20], but both him and Drury conducted experiments with physical targets rather than cursor control. As Drury noted, this effectively increases the sizes of the targets by the size of the participant's shoe [19]. Also, whereas we use the Shannon formulation of *ID*, Drury used Fitts's original formulation and Hoffman used the Welford formulation.

Since our model is compliant with the ISO standard, we can compare our throughputs with other studies reported in literature. The typical range of throughput for the mouse is between 3.7 and 4.9 bit/s, considerably higher than the 1.2–1.7 range we found for the feet, but expected given users' experience and practice with it [24]. The values we found, however, fall into the range for other input devices such as the isometric joystick (1.6–2.55) [24], the touchpad (0.99–2.9) [24] and video game controllers (1.48–2.69) [25].

By allowing participants to choose how to reach the targets, we obtained valuable insights into the most comfortable ways of using the feet. Although heel rotation was perceived as the most comfortable movement, most foot-operated interfaces do not use this movement (an exception is Zhong et al.'s *Foot Menu* [26]). Our results are also in line with Scott et al.'s in which users also reported that heel rotation was the most comfortable gesture, followed by plantar flexion, toe rotation and dorsiflexion [3]. The use of heel rotation is suitable for radial and horizontal distributions of targets. This kind of interaction could be used in a discrete (e.g. for foot activated contextual menus) or in a continuous fashion (e.g. controlling continuous parameters of an object while the hands perform additional manipulations).

We investigated foot performance for seated users so our results apply to foot-only (e.g. mice for people with hand disabilities), and foot-assisted (e.g. driving simulators, highly-dimensional applications) desktop interfaces. It remains to be seen how these results apply to standing users (e.g. using a touch-enabled floor). A second limitation is that our participants were not familiar with this kind of input device, which might affect the predictive power of our models if the device is used more frequently.

4   Study 2: Effects of Foot and Direction of Movement

One possible use for the feet in a seated position is to provide one-dimensional input, be it discrete (e.g. selecting an option in a menu) or continuous (e.g. changing the music volume). To better understand how to design such interfaces, it is important to understand if there is a significant difference in the movement times and comfort between different directions of movement. In this study, we tested the effects of the direction in which the targets were distributed (horizontal vs. vertical) and the foot (dominant vs. non-dominant) on the movement times and error rates.

For this experiment, we recruited 12 participants (8 M/4F), aged between 19 and 31 years (mean 27), with posters on campus and adverts on social networks. All participants were right handed and one was left footed; seven participants were car drivers. Foot sizes ranged from 22 cm to 33 cm (mean 27.1 cm). None of the participants had ever used a foot mouse or similar foot-operated pointer before. The experimental setup was the same as in Study 1.

4.1   Procedure

To begin, participants signed a consent form and filled in a questionnaire. The task in our experiment was analogous to other Fitts's Law experiments. The user was presented with a green and a red bar, in either horizontal or vertical orientation, with a certain width (W) and separated by a certain distance (A) on the screen. For each trial, the user had to select the green bar, at which point the colours of the bars switched.

To select a target, participants used their feet to position an on-screen cursor over the green bar and press the space bar. We selected 14 combinations of W and A to yield exact indices of difficulty from 1 to 7, using the Shannon formulation. Each ID combination was executed with each foot in both horizontal and vertical configurations.

We balanced the order of the feet and the direction of the bars among participants but and ensured the task was not repeated with the same foot twice in a row so as to reduce fatigue. The order of difficulty was randomised. The complete procedure was repeated ten times. To summarise, each participant performed 2 feet × 2 directions × 14 ID combinations × 10 repetitions = 560 movements.

The system continually logged the position of the feet and cursor and a video camera placed under the desk recorded participants' leg movement. At the end of the experiment participants filled in another questionnaire on the perceived difficulty and speed of the target selection on the top, right, bottom, left and centre of the screen for each foot. We also asked for suggested applications of foot-operated interfaces.

4.2   Results

To compare the conditions we computed the mean of means of the throughput of each case. We compared the throughputs using a factorial repeated-measures ANOVA. We found that horizontal movements had a significantly higher throughput (2.11 bit/s) than vertical ones (1.94 bits/s), $F_{1,11} = 14.06$; $p < .05$, but dominance of the foot used had no significant effect, $F_{1,11} = 4.62$, $p = .055$, on the task completion time. We also found no significant interaction effect between the foot and the direction of movement, $F_{1,11} = 4.72$, $p = .052$, indicating that both feet perform roughly the same in both directions.

4.3   Discussion

The results from this study confirm our hypothesis that it does not matter which foot is used, but moving it horizontally is faster than moving it vertically. We attribute this phenomenon to the possibility of pivoting the foot when moving it horizontally and the necessity to drag or lift the foot when moving it vertically.

Suggestions for tasks that could be improved by the use of the feet together with traditional input modalities pointed to the fact that it is not suitable for fine positioning, but it would be useful for **mode switching** ("switching tasks", "switching between colours when drawing", "changing tabs in a browser"), **navigation** ("scrolling", "game exploration", "Google maps", "navigating a document"), and **selection between a reduced number of options** ("anything where you have a limited number actions to do", "two or three big buttons", "if there were large quadrants, it would be useful").

For real-world use, one participant said that he "(…) would not want the tracking to be always on. To toggle this mode, I would suggest holding down a key".

5   Study 3: Simultaneous Manipulation of Two Parameters

The previous experiment focused on how the feet can be used to control one parameter. However, the feet have a greater bandwidth than one parameter as their positions and orientations in space can have meaning for input. In this experiment, we aimed to understand how people can use their feet to control two parameters at the same time. Is it better to use one foot to control multiple parameters or distribute these parameters across the two feet? Further, does the visual representation of the control of parameters affect the interaction?

For this experiment, we recruited a group of 12 participants (8 M/4F), aged between 19 and 42 years (mean 28) using posters on campus and adverts on social networks. Two of the participants were left handed and footed and nine were drivers. Foot sizes ranged from 22 cm to 32 cm (mean 26.7 cm). None of the participants had ever used a foot mouse or similar foot-operated pointer. The experimental setup was the same as for the previous experiment.

5.1   Procedure

Participants were first asked to sign a consent form and complete a personal infor-mation questionnaire. They were then given time to familiarise themselves with the interface. The goal of the study was to investigate how interaction technique and visualisation influence task completion time and error rate. To this end, participants were asked to manipulate two variables, within a certain threshold, while we varied the following two factors: *Interaction Technique* (3 levels): The two input values were manipulated by (1) XY position of 1 foot (1F); (2) X position of both feet (XX) and; (3) X position of one foot and Y position of the other (XY); and *Visualisation* (2 levels): Rectangle resizing and slider adjustment (described below).

In the first visualisation, the task was to fit the dimensions of an adjustable rectangle to those of a target rectangle (see Fig. 3(A)). The target values were the width and height of the destination rectangle while the threshold was represented by the thickness of the rectangle's stroke. In the second visualisation, participants were asked to set two sliders along a scale to different target values marked by red tags (see Fig. 3(B)). Here, the target values were the centres of the tags and the threshold was represented by their thickness. We chose these two visualisations because in the first the two degrees of freedom are integrated (as the corner of the rectangle) while in the second they are independent (as separate sliders). We hypothesised that these different visualisations might influence the performance depending on the number of feet used in the inter-action. For each task, we measured the task completion time and error rate.

5.2   Results

We computed the mean task completion time and error rates for each condition (see Table 3). We considered an error when users clicked the mouse outside the target bounds. We compared the task completion times using a factorial repeated-measures ANOVA, testing the assumption of sphericity with Mauchly's test where appropriate. All effects were reported as significant at $p < .05$. There was a significant main effect of the technique, $F_{2,22} = 14.82$, and of the visual representation, $F_{1,11} = 50.46$, on the task completion time. There was also a significant interaction effect between the technique and the visual representation, $F_{2,22} = 34.10$, indicating that the interaction technique influence on participants' speed was different for the rectangle and slider representa-tions of the task.

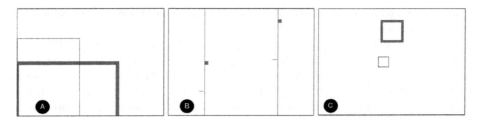

Fig. 3. Tasks in Study 2: (A) Resizing a rectangle and (B) Setting sliders and (C) task in Study 3

Table 3. Time to select a target and error rate for each technique and visualization in Study 3

	Rectangle			Sliders		
	1F	XX	XY	1F	XX	XY
Time (ms)	3428	5068	4161	9098	4625	4902
Error (%)	5.5	3.7	8.0	8.2	8.1	8.0

Bonferroni post hoc tests revealed that using one foot is significantly different than all other conditions in the slider representation ($p < .05$), but not in the rectangle one, as in this condition, it was not significantly different than using one foot horizontally and the other foot vertically ($p = 0.38$). The two conditions in which participants used both feet were not significantly different in any combination of techniques and representations at $p < .05$.

We also compared accuracy using a factorial repeated-measures ANOVA. Mauchly's test indicated that the assumption of sphericity had not been violated neither by the effects of the technique ($W = 0.86$, $p = 0.47$) nor by the effects of the interaction between technique and visual representation ($W = .91$, $p = .72$). Our results showed no significant effect of the technique, of the visual representation or the interaction between them.

5.3   Discussion

Our results show that when manipulating multiple variables with the feet the visualisation strongly affects performance. The best performances amongst all conditions were interaction techniques 1F and XY in the rectangle representation, which were not significantly different at $p < .05$. In these two conditions, there was a direct spatial mapping between the technique and the task, since in technique 1F, the foot moved together with the corner of the rectangle and in technique XY, the feet moved together with its edges.

Users were confused when this spatial mapping was broken. The worst performing condition was using technique 1F for the slider task. Even though the underlying task was exactly the same, the change in visualisation caused the mean completion time to increase over twofold. This can be explained by how users would complete the task. In the slider task, participants would often set one slider at a time and in technique 1F, this meant moving the foot in one direction and then in the other. The problem is that users find it hard to move the foot in only one direction at a time. As we discovered in our previous study, when moving the foot horizontally, users tend to pivot their feet, rather than drag them, and this movement causes the cursor to move in both directions at the same time, resulting in users setting one slider, then setting the second one and having to go back and forth between them to make final adjustments. This was not a problem when controlling each value by a different foot. Regardless of whether the user tried to set both values at the same time or in sequence, moving one foot did not affect the other, so the visual representation was not an issue when using two feet.

An interesting effect we observed was in technique XY in the rectangle representation. Even though only one axis of the movement of each foot was being used to control the size of the rectangle, some participants would move both feet diagonally and symmetrically. One participant was even conscious of this, but kept on using this strategy: "I knew that each foot controlled only one dimension, but I found myself moving each one in both directions." This suggests that symmetrical movements might be more comfortable than independent ones when using two feet.

6   Study 4: Parallel Use of Feet and Hands

The previous experiments investigated interactions using the feet alone. In this experiment we wanted to investigate the overhead caused by using the feet in parallel with one hand. More specifically, we wanted to test whether there is an effect of resizing technique (scrolling with the mouse wheel, the position of one foot, or the distance between two feet) on the completion times and accuracy of the task, while the hand repositions the same square.

For this experiment, we recruited a group of 12 participants (10 M/2F), aged between 19 and 32 years (mean 26), with posters on campus and adverts on social networks. Two participants were left-handed and -footed while 10 participants were drivers. Foot sizes ranged from 22 cm to 34 cm (mean 28 cm). None of the participants had ever used a foot mouse or similar foot-operated pointer. The experimental setup was exactly the same as the one for the previous experiments.

6.1   Procedure

Upon arrival, participants signed a consent form and completed a personal information questionnaire. They were then given some time to familiarise themselves with the interface. The task consisted of resizing and positioning a square to match a destination square at a different place on the screen. In all experimental conditions, the positioning was done with the mouse but the size of the square would be manipulated by one of three controls: the scroll wheel of the mouse, the horizontal coordinate of one foot or the horizontal distance between the two feet. We chose the scroll wheel as it is widely used for manipulating continuous variables. When the size and position of the two squares were matched, the user would click with the mouse and the button would reappear in the centre of the screen. We considered an error when users clicked the mouse outside the target bounds. Each participant repeated this task 40 times for each condition, with the target square in different positions and with different sizes. We measured the task completion time and the error rate. In the end of the study participants were asked to rank their preference of interaction techniques.

6.2   Results

The mean task time was similar across all conditions: 2.50 s for the scroll wheel, 2.63 for the two feet condition, and 2.95 for the one foot condition. We first compared the task completion times in each condition with a one-way repeated measures ANOVA. Mauchly's test indicated that the assumption of sphericity had not been violated, $W = 0.55$, $p = 0.05$. Our results showed a significant effect of the technique used for resizing on the task completion time, $F_{2,22} = 5.08$, $p < .05$. Post hoc tests showed that using one foot was significantly slower than the other two conditions ($p < .05$), but no significant difference was found between using two feet and scrolling ($p = .062$).

We also computed the error rates for each technique: 0.15 for the scroll wheel, 0.089 for the two feet and 0.081 for the one foot. We then compared the error rates for the conditions using a one-way repeated measures ANOVA. Mauchly's test indicated that the assumption of sphericity had not been violated, $W = 0.96$, $p = 0.86$. Results show a significant effect of the technique on the error rate, $F_{2,22} = 20.03$, $p < .05$. Bonferroni *post hoc* tests showed that using the scroll wheel was significantly more accurate than the other two conditions ($p < .05$), but no significant difference was found between using one or two feet ($p = 1.00$).

The most preferred technique was the scroll wheel, chosen as the top technique by 85 % of participants. Participants were divided between the feet techniques, with eight preferring two feet and four preferring one foot.

6.3   Discussion

We chose an increment value for each step of the scroll wheel so that users would not overshoot the thickness of the stroke of the target rectangle, but it also caused the scroll wheel to be slower, so it might have fared better with adjustments in its sensitivity. In terms of task completion times, the feet performed similarly to the hands, showing little overhead for the task being performed, but with a significant decrease in accuracy. Taking into account that users are more familiar with the scroll wheel and none of our participants had any experience with foot-operated interfaces, from these results we speculate that with training, the feet could match (if not outperform) the scroll wheel as a means of providing continuous input to applications.

Our results show that using two feet was significantly faster than using one. We suggest two explanations for this. First, because what mattered was the relative distance between the feet, users could place their feet wherever they felt most comfortable within the tracked area. Because in the one foot condition, what mattered was the absolute position of the foot, depending on how the user was seated, this position might not have been ideal, causing a decrease in performance. Second, as both conditions used the same calibration, moving two feet simultaneous would cause a twofold change in the size of the rectangle, as compared with moving just one foot, increasing the overall speed of the interaction. Despite being faster, almost 40 % of participants still preferred one foot, citing that moving two feet was more tiring than moving just one.

7 Guidelines and Design Considerations

Based on previous work, the quantitative and qualitative results from our experiments and our own experience while investigating the subject, we suggest a set of guidelines and considerations for designing desktop interactive systems that use feet movements as input.

Resolution: Our findings confirm the observations of Raisamo and Pakkanen that pointing with the feet should be limited to low fidelity tasks, in which accuracy is not crucial [5]. For example, when compared to using only the hands in experiment 3, the feet were significantly less accurate.

Visibility and Proprioception: In a desktop setting, the desk occludes the feet, which prevents the direct manipulation of interfaces, such as the floor-projected menus in Augsten et al. [2]. Moreover, foot gestures suffer from the same problems as other gestural interactions (see Norman [27] for a discussion of such problems), which are amplified by this lack of visibility of the limbs. Our second study showed that when designing such interactions, on-screen interfaces should provide a direct spatial representation of the movement of the feet. However, the lack of visibility of the feet is somewhat compensated by the user's proprioception: the inherent sense of the relative positioning of neighbouring parts of the body. Therefore, even though users are not able to see their feet they still know where they are in relation to their body.

Fatigue: Similarly to mid-air gestures, users report fatigue after extended periods of time using leg gestures. In all of our studies, participants reported that, in order to minimise fatigue, they preferred pivoting the foot around the heel to dragging the feet across the floor. Fatigue must also be taken into account when designing interactions where any foot is off the floor. In our experiment, when moving the feet across the floor, users preferred dragging the foot to hovering it over the floor.

Balance: Foot gestures performed whilst standing up only allow for one foot to be off the floor at the same time (except when jumping). While sitting down, the user is able to lift both feet from the floor at the same time, allowing for more complex gestures with both feet. To prevent fatigue, such complex gestures should be limited in time and potentially also space. In this work, even though we tracked the feet in three dimensions, we only took into account their two-dimensional position in relation to the floor. It remains an open question how adding a third dimension could affect the interaction.

Chair and Spatial Constraints: The kind of chair where the user is seated may influence the movement of the feet. For example, the rotation of a swivel chair might help with moving the foot horizontally. Further, when both feet are off the floor, swivel chairs tend to rotate as the user moves which may hamper interaction. The form factor of desks, chairs and clutter under the desk also affect the area in which the user can perform gestures. This also offers opportunities for interaction, as physical aspects of the space can help guide the movement of the feet or serve as reference points. Another aspect that needs to be taken into account are the properties of the floor, which might influence the tracking (shiny floors will reflect the infra-red light emitted by the Kinect, creating additional noise) and interaction (floors covered in carpet or anti-slip coating may slow down feet movements, while smooth flooring may speed them up).

Rootedness: Mid-air gestures often suffer from the problem of gesture delimiters, similar to the classic Midas touch problem, as it is hard to tell specific actions and gestures from natural human movement [28]. This is less of a problem for feet gestures in a seated stance, because when sat down, most leg and foot movement consists of postural shifts, reducing the number of movements that might be recognised as false positives in gesture recognition systems. We addressed this problem in our studies by defining an area on the floor where the feet would provide input for the system, but in applications where it would be desirable to track the feet at all times, it is necessary to pay special attention to designing gesture delimiters that are not part of users' normal lower limb behaviour.

Footedness: In the same way that people favour one hand they also favour one foot and, even though they are often correlated, there are exceptions to this rule, with approximately 5 % of the population presenting crossed hand-foot preference [29]. Our findings indicate there is no significant difference between the dominant foot and the non-dominant one. These results, however, reflect the performance of users with no experience with feet-based interfaces. It is not clear if this similarity in performance still holds for experienced users. Further, it is necessary to consider which foot will be used in the interaction, as crossing one foot over the other to reach targets on the opposite side might be too uncomfortable.

Hotspot: Touch-based interfaces, despite suffering from the phenomenon of 'fat-fingers', can still provide a high resolution of input due to the small relative size of the contact area between the finger and the touch-sensitive area. Feet, however, provide a large area of contact with the floor. The designer can then opt for reducing the foot to a point or using the whole contact area as input. The former has the advantage of providing high resolution input, but users' perceptions of the specific point on the foot that should correspond to the cursor is not clear, as demonstrated by Augsten et al. [2]. Using the whole of the foot sole makes it easier to hit targets (as shown by Drury's modification of Fitts's Law [19]), but increases the chance of hitting wrong targets. Hence, if using this approach, the designer needs to leave enough space between targets as to prevent accidental activation.

8 Limitations

In this work, we described four experiments that attempt to characterise some funda-mental aspects of the use of foot movements for interacting with desktop computers. These experiments, however, have some limitations. We collected data from a relatively small number of participants, so more precise estimates of the real value of the times and error rates presented here can certainly be achieved in experiments with larger pools of participants. Also, our participant pool was not gender-balanced in every study and did not cover a wide age range. We present results using only one tracking system that has several limitations of its own. For example, our prototype was implemented in Matlab, achieving a frame rate of 25 fps, but the tracking speed could be improved by porting the system to a faster language, such as C ++. While our results are in line with the ones in related work, further work is necessary to assess whether they translate to other foot interfaces.

9 Conclusion

In this work we took a bottom-up approach to characterising the use of foot gestures while seated. We implemented a foot tracking system that uses a Kinect mounted under a desk to track the users' feet and used it to investigate some fundamental characteristics of this kind of interaction in three experiments.

First, we presented ISO 9241-9 performance models for 1D and 2D foot pointing in a sitting position. Our results suggest little difference in performance between the dominant and non-dominant foot and that horizontal foot movements are easier to perform than vertical ones. We identified five strategies that participants used to reach targets and found that the preferred one was rotating the foot around the heel. We also found that the biggest challenges for foot-based interaction in a desktop setting are difficulties in reaching small targets, hand-feet coordination, fatigue, friction with the floor, and overshooting targets. These findings are important because they help us complete our understanding of the potential of foot-operated interfaces and provide guidance for future research in this emerging domain.

Second, we studied the performance of each foot in controlling a single parameter in a unidimensional task. Our results showed no significant difference between the dominant and non-dominant foot, but it showed that horizontal movement on the floor is significantly faster than vertical. Also, users showed a preference for pivoting their feet rather than dragging them. Third, we looked at controlling two variables at once, comparing the use of one foot against the use of two (each foot using the same movement axis or different ones). Our results showed that the visual representation of the variables do matter, with the performance for techniques that have a direct spatial mapping to the representation outperforming the others. It also showed that when the variables being manipulated are shown separately (such as in independent sliders), it is preferable to use two feet rather than one. Fourth, we analysed the use of the feet in parallel to the hands, showing that the feet perform similarly to the scroll wheel in terms of time, but worse in terms of accuracy, suggesting that with training and more accurate tracking systems, the feet could be used to support hand based interaction in a desktop setting.

Future work will focus on using these insights to design and implement techniques that can possibly enhance the interaction by supporting the hands in everyday computing tasks. While we provide some guidelines for design, it is still an open question as to which tasks can effectively be supported by the feet and the size of the cognitive overhead of adding such an interactive modality.

References

1. English, W.K., Engelbart, D.C., Berman, M.L.: Display-selection techniques for text manipulation. Trans. Hum. Factors Electron. **HFE-8**, 5–15 (1967)
2. Augsten, T., Kaefer, K., Meusel, R., Fetzer, C., Kanitz, D., Stoff, T., Becker, T., Holz, C., Baudisch, P.: Multitoe: high-precision interaction with back-projected floors based on high-resolution multi-touch input. In: UIST, pp. 209–218. ACM (2010)
3. Scott, J., Dearman, D., Yatani, K., Truong, K.N.: Sensing foot gestures from the pocket. In: Proceedings of the 23nd Annual ACM Symposium on User Interface Software and Technology, pp. 199–208. ACM, New York (2010)
4. Simeone, A., Velloso, E., Alexander, J., Gellersen, H.: Feet movement in desktop 3D interaction. In: Proceedings of the 2014 IEEE Symposium on 3D User Interfaces (2014)
5. Pakkanen, T., Raisamo, R.: Appropriateness of foot interaction for non-accurate spatial tasks. In: CHI 2004 EA, pp. 1123–1126. ACM (2004)
6. Dearman, D., Karlson, A., Meyers, B., Bederson, B.: Multi-modal text entry and selection on a mobile device. In: Proceedings of Graphics Interface 2010, pp. 19–26. Canadian Information Processing Society (2010)
7. Garcia, F.P., Vu, K.-P.L.: Effects of practice with foot- and hand-operated secondary input devices on performance of a word-processing task. In: Smith, M.J., Salvendy, G. (eds.) HCI International 2009, Part I. LNCS, vol. 5617, pp. 505–514. Springer, Heidelberg (2009)
8. Pearson, G., Weiser, M.: Of moles and men: the design of foot controls for workstations. In: Procedings of CHI, pp. 333–339. ACM, New York (1986)
9. Sellen, A.J., Kurtenbach, G.P., Buxton, W.A.: The prevention of mode errors through sensory feedback. Hum.-Comput. Interact. **7**, 141–164 (1992)
10. LaViola, Jr., J.J., Feliz, D.A., Keefe, D.F., Zeleznik, R.C.: Hands-free multi-scale navigation in virtual environments. In: Proceedings of the 2001 Symposium on Interactive 3D graphics, pp. 9–15. ACM (2001)
11. Carrozza, M.C., Persichetti, A., Laschi, C., Vecchi, F., Lazzarini, R., Vacalebri, P., Dario, P.: A wearable biomechatronic interface for controlling robots with voluntary foot movements. Trans. Mechatron. **12**, 1–11 (2007)
12. Han, T., Alexander, J., Karnik, A., Irani, P., Subramanian, S.: Kick: investigating the use of kick gestures for mobile interactions. In: Proceedings of the 13th International Conference on Human Computer Interaction with Mobile Devices and Services, pp. 29–32. ACM Press, New York (2011)
13. Paelke, V., Reimann, C., Stichling, D.: Foot-based mobile interaction with games. In: Proceedings of the 2004 ACM SIGCHI International Conference on Advances in computer entertainment technology, pp. 321–324. ACM (2004)
14. Hockman, J.A., Wanderley, M.M., Fujinaga, I.: Real-time phase vocoder manipulation by runner's pace. In: Proceedings of the International Conference on New Interfaces for Musical Expression (NIME) (2009)
15. Lopes, P.A.S.A., Fernandes, G., Jorge, J.: Trainable DTW-based classifier for recognizing feet-gestures. In: Proceedings of RecPad (2010)
16. Richter, S., Holz, C., Baudisch, P.: Bootstrapper: recognizing tabletop users by their shoes. In: Proceedings of the SIGCHI Conference on Human Factors in Computing Systems, pp. 1249–1252. ACM (2012)

17. Paradiso, J.A., Hsiao, K., Benbasat, A.Y., Teegarden, Z.: Design and implementation of expressive footwear. IBM Syst. **39**, 511–529 (2000)
18. Kume, Y., Shirai, A., Sato, M.: Foot interface: fantastic phantom slipper. In: ACM SIGGRAPH 1998 Conference Abstracts and Applications, p. 114 (1998)
19. Drury, C.G.: Application of Fitts' Law to foot-pedal design. Hum. Factors J. Hum. Factors Ergon. Soc. **17**, 368–373 (1975)
20. Hoffmann, E.R.: A comparison of hand and foot movement times. Ergonomics **34**, 397–406 (1991)
21. Springer, J., Siebes, C.: Position controlled input device for handicapped: experimental studies with a footmouse. Int. J. Ind. Ergon. **17**, 135–152 (1996)
22. Hinckley, K., Jacob, R., Ware, C.: Inputoutput devices and interaction techniques. In: Tucker, A.B. (ed.) CRC Computer Science and Engineering Handbook, pp. 1–32. CRC Press LLC, Boca Raton (2004)
23. Wobbrock, J.O., Shinohara, K., Jansen, A.: The effects of task dimensionality, endpoint deviation, throughput calculation, and experiment design on pointing measures and models. In: Proceedings of the SIGCHI Conference on Human Factors in Computing Systems, pp. 1639–1648. ACM (2011)
24. Soukoreff, R.W., MacKenzie, I.S.: Towards a standard for pointing device evaluation, perspectives on 27 years of Fitts' law research in HCI. Int. J. Hum Comput Stud. **61**, 751–789 (2004)
25. Natapov, D., Castellucci, S.J., MacKenzie, I.S.: ISO 9241-9 evaluation of video game controllers. In: Proceedings of Graphics Interface 2009, pp. 223–230. Canadian Information Processing Society (2009)
26. Zhong, K., Tian, F., Wang, H.: Foot menu: using heel rotation information for menu selection. In: 2011 15th Annual International Symposium on Wearable Computers (ISWC), pp. 115–116. IEEE (2011)
27. Norman, D.A., Nielsen, J.: Gestural interfaces: a step backward in usability. Interactions **17**, 46–49 (2010)
28. Benko, H.: Beyond flat surface computing: challenges of depth-aware and curved interfaces. In: Proceedings of Multimedia, pp. 935–944. ACM (2009)
29. Dargent-Paré, C., De Agostini, M., Mesbah, M., Dellatolas, G.: Foot and eye preferences in adults: relationship with handedness, sex and age. Cortex **28**, 343–351 (1992)

Life in the Fast Lane: Effect of Language and Calibration Accuracy on the Speed of Text Entry by Gaze

Kari-Jouko Räihä[(✉)]

School of Information Sciences, University of Tampere, Tampere, Finland
kari-jouko.raiha@uta.fi

Abstract. Numerous techniques have been developed for text entry by gaze, and similarly, a number of evaluations have been carried out to determine the efficiency of the solutions. However, the results of the published experiments are inconclusive, and it is unclear what causes the difference in their findings. Here we look particularly at the effect of the language used in the experiment. A study where participants entered text both in English and in Finnish does not show an effect of language structure: the entry rates were reasonably close to each other. The role of other explaining factors, such as calibration accuracy and experimental procedure, are discussed.

Keywords: Text entry · Gaze input · Performance · Entry speed · Error rate · Comparative evaluation · Longitudinal study

1 Introduction

Augmentative and alternative communication techniques are crucial for a considerable share of the world's population. Without such techniques they would, for instance, not be able to use many of the services that are increasingly being offered through the internet. Techniques that have been developed include speech synthesis and Braille printers for the vision impaired, and speech-to-text solutions for the hearing impaired.

A particularly challenging user group is those with severe motor-neuron diseases, such as the locked-in syndrome or ALS. In such situations the cognitive abilities are intact, but the ability to control the muscles deteriorates and eventually disappears. The eyes are often the last muscle that works. Techniques that allow communication using just the eyes have been developed and studied extensively [6].

Here we focus on using the eyes for text entry. This, too, is an actively studied field; see [4, 8] for reviews. However, as will be discussed in the next section, the results concerning the text entry speed that can be reached by using the eyes vary a lot. We will tackle one possible explanation: the difference in the language used in the experiments, and study it systematically. In addition, we will look at a number of other factors that might explain the results.

Why is it important to know the limits of text entry by gaze? By understanding the subtle differences in the implementation details of a technique we can produce better tools for the people that need the software. Sufficiently fast text entry can, for instance,

© IFIP International Federation for Information Processing 2015
J. Abascal et al. (Eds.): INTERACT 2015, Part I, LNCS 9296, pp. 402–417, 2015.
DOI: 10.1007/978-3-319-22701-6_30

in the future enable the development of applications where one partner enters text on a mobile phone with the eyes, the phone uses text-to-speech to transmit it to a hearing partner at the other end, who can then respond. To carry out a real conversation the process cannot take too long. Therefore "How fast can one type with the eyes?" is an equally interesting and important research question as "How fast can one type with the typewriter" was for decades.

2 Previous Work

Results from past experiments with text entry by gaze have been collected in Tables 1 (experiments with a soft keyboard) and 2 (experiments with other techniques). We have included only longitudinal experiments where the participants came back to the lab on several days and thus had a chance to improve their performance through experience. The data in the tables is teased out from the publications. For [17] the exact numbers were not reported and are therefore estimated from the graphs in the paper. The same holds for the MSD rate in [9].

Table 1. Data from experiments on text entry by gaze with soft keyboards

Reference	Tracker	Participants	Session length	Sessions	Dwell threshold	WPM	MSD
[5]	Tobii 1750	11	15 min	10	adjustable	19.89	0.36 %
[17]	Tobii 1750	8	8 phrases	14	330 ms	>8	<0.01 %
[10] lp	Tobii T60	10	15 min	10	adjustable	18.45	0.58 %
[10] ap	Tobii T60	10	15 min	5	420-250 ms	18.98	0.46 %
[11] e1	Tobii P10	9	10 min	9	1000 ms	6.0	2.20 %
[11] e2	Tobii P10	12	15 min	9	adjustable	7.0	4.00 %

Several papers reported on more than one studies. For [10], there were results for the learning phase (denoted by lp in Table 1) and the advanced phase (denoted by ap). In [11] there were two experiments, denoted by e1 and e2. Pedrosa et al. [9] carried out a number of experiments; two longitudinal studies with able-bodied participants, followed by individual trials with users with motor disabilities. Here we report the numbers from their second longitudinal study that produced the fastest text entry rates.

The WPM column shows the standard metric for measuring text entry speed: words per minute (WPM), where "word" means five letters (including spaces and punctuation). In other words, WPM is the number of characters entered in a minute divided by 5. MSD indicates uncorrected errors, i.e. errors that remain in the text that was entered. It is computed as the mean string distance of the entered phrase and the model phrase [16].

Since all the experiments included in Tables 1 and 2 consisted of several sessions, the numbers reported indicate the averages of all participants for the best session in the series (typically the last one). Individual participants could reach better performance in some sessions. The best reported single session text entry rate was 23.10 WPM for soft keyboards [10] and 23.11 WPM for Dasher [14].

Table 2. Data from experiments on text entry with novel techniques

Reference	Tracker	Participants	Session length	Sessions	Technique	WPM	MSD
[17]	Tobii 1750	8	8 phrases	14	EyeWrite	> 6	<0.01 %
[15]	SR-Research Eyelink2	9	3 sayings	20	pEYEwrite-WoDyn	13.47	0.01 %
[14]	Tobii 1750	12	15 min	10	Dasher	17.26	0.57 %
[11] e1	Tobii P10	9	10 min	9	Dasher	12.4	1.70 %
[11] e2	Tobii P10	12	15 min	9	Dasher	14.2	3.30 %
[9]	Tobii REX	6	20 min	6	Filteryedping	15.95	<0.3 %

It is understandable that for different interaction techniques there is high variation in the performance, but it is surprising that for the same basic technique (soft keyboards in Table 1 and Dasher in Table 2) the results vary so much. There are a number of factors that are not shown in the tables and that do affect the efficiency; we will discuss them extensively later. However, one aspect that stands out is that all the fastest results [5, 10, 14] were achieved with Finnish as the language of the phrases that were entered. In all the other studies the language was probably English (the language is not reported in [15] and it could also be German).

Could it be that language has such a drastic effect on the text entry speed? We cannot really say based on the results quoted above, because, e.g., different participants took part in each experiment. To shed light on this issue, we carried out an experiment where the same participants entered text using gaze both in English and in Finnish. Longitudinal studies are laborious and we were only able to do the experiment for soft keyboards, but there the difference in past results is anyhow the largest.

3 Method

We followed a similar experimental design as has become the norm (with small variations) in studies of text entry by gaze. The details are presented next.

3.1 Participants

Eight participants (5 male, 3 female) were recruited for the experiment. Seven of them had participated in a previous experiment where eye tracking was used passively just to follow participants' eye movements while viewing a set of images. None had previously used gaze as an input technique. Two participants wore eyeglasses. Selection of participants was based on their demonstrated ability to be tracked by the eye tracker, and on their self-reported knowledge of written English. Six participants reported their skill level as excellent ("mistakes in grammar and vocabulary are rare") and two reported it as good ("I can communicate but I make mistakes"). All had Finnish as their mother tongue.

Each participant was paid €15 for each one hour test session. In addition, a bonus of €70 was paid both to the participant that reached the highest text entry rate, and to the participant that showed the biggest improvement in text entry rate over the sessions.

3.2   Apparatus

A Tobii T60 eye tracker with a 17-inch TFT color monitor with 1280 × 1024 resolution was used to track the gaze. A PC running Windows XP was used for the experiment. The software for text entry was an in-house application based on a soft keyboard. The application window filled the screen, as shown in Fig. 1.

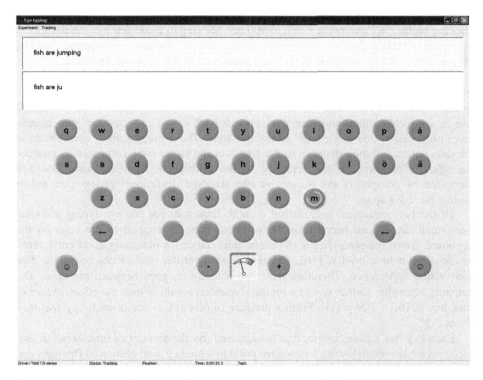

Fig. 1. A screenshot of the application used in the experiment. The QWERTY keyboard shows the Scandinavian layout used (Color figure online)

The top frame of the window is used to display the model phrase that the participant must enter. The text entered is shown in the next frame in red. These are later referred to as the source and target frames, respectively.

The layout of the keys follows the layout on a standard Scandinavian qwerty keyboard. The letters on the keys are displayed in 18 pt Arial bold. There is no shift key, since the phrases that had to be entered did not have upper case letters. Similarly, the punctuation marks are missing for the same reason. On the row below there are five space keys and two backspace keys. The motivation for multiple keys with the same function was to provide a short path to these frequently used keys, as suggested in [10].

When a key is gazed at, a red curve starts to grow on the key, as shown for the letter "m" in Fig. 1. Once the curve has made a full circle, the letter gets selected: a sharp clicking sound is played and the letter appears in the target frame.

The bottom left and right corners hold "ready" keys (smileys) to be selected when the participant has finished entering the model phrase. This causes the next phrase to appear in the source frame and the target frame to be cleared.

The time needed for a key to be selected can be adjusted by the participant at any point during the experiment. This is done using the two gaze-controlled keys on the bottom row; the speedometer between them is an indicator of the selected threshold. Clicking on the "+" key increases speed, i.e., shortens the dwell time. The decrement depends on the current level of the dwell threshold. At 1000 ms (the initial setting), clicking on the "+" lowers the dwell to 900 ms. Moving to faster settings the decrement decreases, so that at 260 ms and below, clicking on "+" shortens the required dwell by 20 ms. The "−" key works with similar increments in the opposite direction.

In addition to the experimental text entry software, the TraQuMe application [1] was used to measure calibration accuracy in the beginning and end of each test session. In our experiment TraQuMe was used in a mode where it displayed five targets (much like in a typical calibration procedure), each for 1.5 s, and collected the gaze coordinates produced by the eye tracker during that time. The average x and y coordinates of the data points and their distance to the center of the target were computed to produce the *offset*, a measure for the accuracy of the calibration. Similarly, precision was measured by computing the *dispersion* (the standard deviations) of the gaze points during the 1.5 s span.

Of the two measures, small offset is more important for our eye typing software than small dispersion, because of the way that gaze is mapped to the keys on the keyboard. Since the algorithm is of crucial importance for obtaining good entry rates, we describe it here briefly. First, the expansion algorithm makes objects larger than their visual appearance. Therefore there are actually no gaps between the keys. The mapping algorithm further works with this expanded layout, where the effective size of each key is 100 × 100 pixels. From a distance of 60 cm the side of each key was thus about 2.5°.

Each key has a time counter that is increased (by the amount of time between two successive gaze points) when a new gaze point hits the key, and decreased (by the same amount of time) otherwise. With each sample only one key increases its counter, all others decrease their counters or keep them at 0. Once a counter exceeds the dwell time, the corresponding key becomes selected, and all counters are reset. The dwell time progress circle is shown on the key that has the greatest counter value at the moment.

3.3   Procedure

Each participant first came to the lab for a briefing of the software and the experiment. The functionality of the software was explained and the procedure to be followed in the test sessions was described. The participant then had a chance to try out the software. Each participant first entered in Finnish two phrases with a 1000 ms dwell threshold. They were then instructed to try decrementing the threshold with one or two notches and to enter two phrases in English. They were further offered the chance to experiment with two more phrases, but only two participants made use of that opportunity; in general everyone got the hang of it during the first four phrases. Finally the experimenter stepped in the user's role and showed with two phrases how text entry looks like when the dwell threshold is in the order of 300 ms.

The participants were instructed that the goal of the experiment was to find out how fast they can enter correct text. They were advised to correct errors that they spotted immediately, but not to back up long stretches of already entered text if they noticed an error in the beginning.

The actual sessions took place on consecutive working days. Each participant was requested to carry out the test on at least five and at most eight consecutive days. All eight participants came back for at least six days, meaning that everybody had a weekend in between the sessions at some point. One participant did the experiment for seven days and four participants for eight days.

Each day of the experiment consisted of two 15-minute sessions with a 10-minute break in between. One session was in English and the other in Finnish. The order of the languages was swapped each day. Half of the participants started with Finnish, the other with English in the first day.

In the first session the participants were asked to use the initial dwell threshold setting of 1000 ms for the first phrase, and after that to adjust the threshold at will. At the end of the first day (Sessions 1 and 2), the rules of how to get the bonus were revealed. In particular, the metric to be used (entered words per minute minus error percentage) was explained.

The participants were seated at a distance of about 60 cm from the screen. In each of the two sessions the eye tracker was first calibrated for the participant using a 9-point calibration. The calibration procedure was repeated until the result looked adequate in the calibration window of the ETU driver [13] that was used by the software. Then TraQuMe [1] was used to quantitatively measure the quality of the calibration. The measurement was repeated at the end of the 15 min session.

3.4   Task

The participant's task was to transcribe the model phrases as quickly and accurately as possible. The English phrases came from the 500-phrase collection [3] that is customarily used in such experiments. The upper case letters in the phrases were replaced by lower case letters for this experiment. The Finnish phrases mostly came from the Finnish translation [2] of the English corpus. However, some English phrases that were lines in song lyrics (e.g., "starlight and dewdrops" from *Beautiful Dreamer*) did not make sense as direct translations, since the lyrics were not translated literally for the Finnish version of the song. In such cases popular Finnish songs were used instead as a source of phrases.

The text entry application chose the model phrases at random. It logged the text entered and full gaze data. It also kept time, so that when 15 min had passed, it allowed the participant to finish entering the current phrase but at the click of the ready key a save dialog would pop up. The experimenter then stepped up to an adjacent display, saved the log and carried out the calibration quality measurement.

4   Results

Altogether 114 text entry sessions took place. In them a total of 5 338 phrases and 146 607 letters were entered. In addition, in 38 cases the participant unintentionally clicked the ready key while entering the phrase, and these (0.7 % of all cases) were removed from the data.

Figure 2 plots the average text entry speed over the sessions. The graph shows the data from all participants over six days (12 sessions) and separately the data from those four participants that continued for the full eight days.

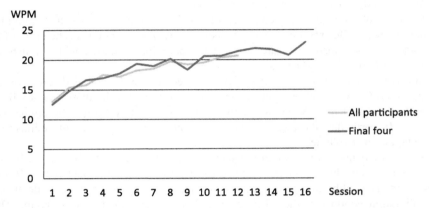

Fig. 2. Text entry rate as a function of session number (Color figure online)

For easier comparison with previous research, the entry rates in Fig. 2 and elsewhere in this paper are expressed in WPM without taking into account the errors in the remaining text. The participants were extremely conscientious in correcting the errors they spotted. On average, the error rate (measured as string edit distance, MSD) was 0.39 % – that is, approximately one incorrect character for every 260 correct characters. The errors decreased from 0.58 % in the beginning to 0.28 % in the last session. Their effect is so negligible that the speed metric that takes errors into account follows very closely the same pattern as the WPM metric in Fig. 2.

The best average session rate, 25.6 WPM, was achieved by participant P5 in Session 12. He stopped then and did not continue for the final two days. In that session the resulting text had 4 errors, meaning an error rate of 0.06 %. His data is shown in Fig. 3 as an example of how experience affected the measures.

Figure 3 also plots the keystrokes per character (KSPC), a common metric to measure how many errors were made and corrected during a session [16]. P5 was one of the participants who moved quickly to very short dwell times. That backfired in Session 3, where poor calibration created a need to backspace often, as Fig. 3 shows. High KSPC correlates strongly with lower WPM rates.

Figure 3 indicates that for P5, results for Finnish were somewhat better than for English. Figure 4 shows for the first six days, and for all participants, the text entry

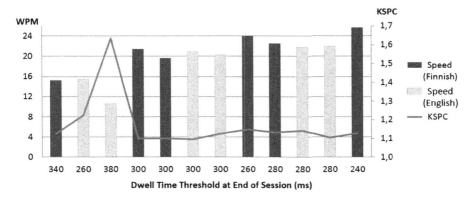

Fig. 3. Development of text entry rate (as bars) and keystrokes per character (as line graph) for participant P5. Blue bars denote sessions with Finnish, striped red bars with English (Color figure online).

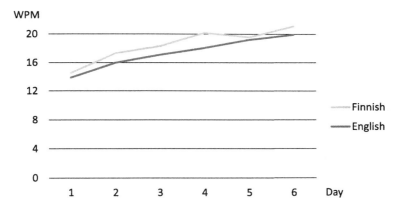

Fig. 4. Text entry rates for Finnish and English as a function of day of experiment (Color figure online)

speed separately for Finnish and English. Each day each participant carried out one session in each language.

A two-way ANOVA with language and day as within-subject factors revealed a significant effect of day on WPM ($F_{7,5} = 17.48$, $p < .0001$). Although the graph for Finnish stays above the one for English for every day, the difference is not big enough to be statistically significant ($F_{7,1} = 5.25$, ns).

On average, calibration accuracy remained on the same level throughout the sessions. The average offset at the beginning of sessions was $0.6°$ (with SD of $0.06°$), and the average dispersion was $0.3°$ (SD $0.05°$). The figures are low and as good as can be expected from the eye tracker used in the experiment. However, although the variation between sessions, taken over all participants, was thus low, there was higher variation for individual participants. The WPM rate for each session is plotted in Fig. 5 for each

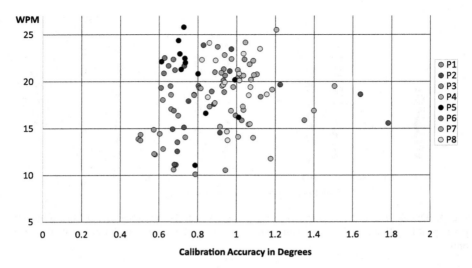

Fig. 5. WPM vs. quality of calibration at start of session for each participant (Color figure online)

participant against the calibration quality at the beginning of the session. For simplicity, the sum of offset and dispersion was used as the combined quality measure.

We also measured the calibration accuracy at the end of each session. However, those measurements are less reliable, since some participants had the tendency to relax at the end of the session and change their posture considerably. Therefore the measurements are not reported here.

Another factor that directly affects text entry rate is the dwell time threshold. We recorded it at the start and end of each session. Figure 6 plots text entry rate against the

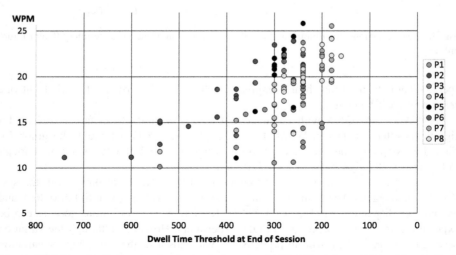

Fig. 6. WPM vs. dwell time threshold at end of session for each participant (Color figure online)

dwell time threshold at the end of each session; note that a faster or slower pace can have been used at some point during the session. However, with the exception of the first day, the within session adjustments of the threshold were moderate.

The time taken to transcribe the model phrases is affected by how easy it is to recall them and their spelling. The number of glances back to the source and target frames at the top of the window are plotted in Fig. 7 for each participant. The first graph shows the overall number for the two frames, whereas the second graph focuses on the glances to the source frame only and shows the numbers for English and Finnish phrases separately.

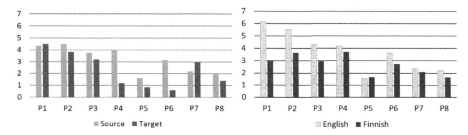

Fig. 7. On the left the average number of glances to the source and target frames per phrase and participant. On the right the average number of glances to the source frame for the English and Finnish phrases (Color figure online).

A two-way ANOVA with language and day as within-subject factors revealed a significant effect of language on glances both to the source ($F_{7,1} = 15.24$, $p < .01$) and target ($F_{7,1} = 7.62$, $p < .05$) frames, with English giving rise to more glances than Finnish per phrase (4.0 vs. 2.7 for source, 2.7 vs. 2.2 for target). Day did not have a significant effect, nor was there interaction between language and day.

5   Discussion

5.1   Speed of Text Entry

This study did not provide with convincing evidence of the effect of language on the speed of text entry by gaze one way or the other. The trends in Fig. 4 appear clear on the surface, but the ANOVA analysis did not show a statistically significant difference (although it was fairly close with $p = .056$).

How much difference can one expect between the participants' mother tongue and another language that they know well? In a similar study that used a regular keyboard instead of eye gaze as the input technique, Isokoski and Linden [2] found a bigger difference: 49.7 WPM for Finnish vs. 41.8 WPM for English, a difference of about 16 %. In this light the difference of the average rates in the participants' best sessions, 22.8 WPM for Finnish and 20.9 WPM for English, i.e. a difference of about 8 %, is considerably smaller than expected.

Text entry by gaze is in many ways different from using a keyboard, even if the layout of the keys is similar. With a hard keyboard the typist can use at least two hands, if not all ten fingers. In text entry by gaze the process is strictly sequential, with the same "device" (eyes) used to select in succession all the keys one by one. Then the distance to be covered when moving from one key to the next can come into play. Could it be different for the two languages?

To analyze this, we computed the bigram frequency matrices for both corpora. A bigram is a pair of letters that appear in succession in the text, and the frequency matrix gives the number of occurrences of each bigram in the corpus. A similar matrix was created for the distance between the letters in each bigram on the soft keyboard. Multiplying these matrices gives us a bigram distance matrix weighted with the frequencies, and taking the average over all bigrams then tells us whether we can expect an effect that is caused by the bigram frequencies being different.

Table 3 summarizes the key characteristics of the corpora.

Table 3. Characteristics of the corpora.

	Finnish	English
Phrases	500	500
Words	1834	2713
Characters	13878	14310
Distinct bigrams	352	389
Double letters	1027	324
Average weighted bigram distance	324.9	304.4

There is a difference of 304.4 pixels vs. 324.9 pixels (about 6.5 %) in average weighted bigram distance in favor of English, which can be expected to affect the text entry speed. Adding this to the observed speed difference of 8 % brings us closer to the findings in [2].

Another factor that, however, works in the opposite direction, is the proportion of double letters (the same letter appearing twice in succession) in the two languages. Double letters are more frequent in Finnish than in English. To enter the double letters with our text entry software the user can simply keep looking at the letter. After the first of the pair of letters is entered, there is a fixed threshold of 150 ms before the dwell time counter is restarted. This is both quick and convenient, making the entry of double letter bigrams faster than entering the other bigrams: the average time to move the gaze from one character to the next was typically more than 200 ms. The share of double letter bigrams in the corpora is 7.4 % for Finnish and 2.3 % for English.

Finally, it should be noted that Fig. 2 indicates that the entry speeds were still improving after the 6th day (12th session). Our analysis was based on the first six days only to have a sufficient number of participants.

In addition to learning from day to day, one may ask if there was difference between the two daily sessions. Indeed, the overall grand mean of text entry speed was slightly higher for the second daily session (18.5 WPM vs. 17.4 WPM). However, the difference was not statistically significant ($F_{7,1} = 5.39$, ns).

In summary, there are factors that have an adverse influence on the expected text entry speed: the mother tongue (other than English) puts English to a disadvantaged position, but the characteristics of the language can have features that affect the entry speed in both directions.

5.2 Errors

The extremely low level of errors in the text entered, 0.28 % in the last sessions, may come as a surprise. It is largely explained by the feel of text entry with a low dwell threshold. Typing then becomes essentially an activity of moving the gaze from one letter to the next, with a very short time for waiting for the letter to get selected. The typist hears the click and realizes if the gaze was on the intended letter or not. If not, it feels natural to click on the backspace and correct the error immediately. In fact, a large portion of the remaining errors are not caused by entering a letter that the typist did not intend, but rather by recalling the model phrase incorrectly.

With a low dwell threshold it becomes easier to get into a regular typing rhythm. The importance of rhythm has been noted before [4]. In our study one participant (P8) voluntarily commented on this; even if correcting the errors is an almost automatic activity, it still interferes with the typing rhythm, which she considered crucial for fast text entry.

Compared to typing with a conventional keyboard, the sequential nature of text entry by gaze has a positive effect on the level of errors. The two hands can be in action at the same time and may arrive at their target keys in the wrong order without the typist noticing this before looking at the text entered. With gaze such a competition situation is not possible and the typist can trust the order of letters to be correct.

This becomes evident also in analyzing the glances to the source and target frames. Figure 7 (left) shows that most participants looked more at the source frame than the target frame. The two participants for which this does not hold (P1 and P7) had to struggle in many sessions with calibration that deteriorated during some sessions. The number of glances is particularly low for the overall fastest typist, P5. The formula for fast text entry speed seems to be a combination of a suitably small dwell threshold combined with trust in the correct letters getting entered, and thus no need to check the text frames frequently.

Trust is, of course, affected by calibration accuracy and thereby the software behaving "as expected". Nevertheless, Fig. 5 indicates that people can learn to adjust their gaze position to compensate for poorer calibrations as well. Participant P7, in particular, who was often struggling with a lower quality calibration, still put up respectable entry speed numbers, and reached even the second best result of all in spite of the calibration accuracy in that session being as poor as $1.2°$.

Getting back to the glances, Fig. 7 (right) shows that the source phrase is glanced at more often for English than for Finnish. This is understandable for people who don't have English as first language. In addition to some rare words with difficult spelling that might give problems even to native speakers (e.g., "conscience", "exasperation", "dewdrop"), the problem is compounded by the different spellings in dialects of English (e.g., "favourite" vs. "favorite"). No such problems exist with Finnish, which is written as pronounced. It is understandable that participants rechecked the source phrase in such cases to make sure that they got the spelling right.

In summary, the participants took many means to ensure the correctness of their entered text: correcting errors immediately and checking the spelling of words when in doubt. Excluding from the analysis errors that were the result of memory lapses would have further improved the correctness rate substantially.

5.3   Why Are the Findings Across Studies So Different?

If the language of the phrases does not explain the difference in the results obtained in different experiments, what does? Perhaps most importantly, even if the basic techniques are the same, they may differ significantly in important implementation details. This holds for the experiments with Dasher [11, 14], and the same is true for soft keyboards. For instance, feedback modes have a significant effect on text entry speed [7]. The dwell time threshold similarly affects both the efficiency and the experienced workload [10].

The fact that the user is in control of adjusting the dwell time threshold during a session, as pioneered in [5], is of crucial importance. In [11], the dwell time was also adjustable, but the paper does not give details on how this was done. Judging from the screenshot of the interface in [11], this was only possible between the sessions. It is understandable that users are not eager to jump to big decrements in the dwell threshold if they are unsure of how it affects them. When they have the tool to increase or decrease the threshold at will, they can experiment with shorter dwell times to see if it works for them.

The briefing given at the beginning of the experiment is also important. We showed ourselves what text entry with a short dwell time threshold looks like before the participants were engaged in the first session. This presumably caused them to move to short thresholds much faster than in any previous experiments. As Fig. 6 shows, a clear majority (71 %) of the sessions ended with the threshold being in the 200–300 ms range. In 8 % of the sessions it was below 200 ms and in 21 % of the sessions above 300 ms. Only one participant used higher than 300 ms thresholds after the third day of the experiment.

It should be emphasized again that a short threshold not only enables fast text entry, but it gives a very different feeling to the user. Text entry changes from interacting with icons that represent keys to selecting letters that one wants to enter. In other words, interacting with the interface as an artefact fades to the background and the user can focus on the task at hand.

One obvious factor affecting the results is the corpus used [12]. Especially in our case, when we decided to use only lower case letters to limit any confounding factors, it can be expected that the results are better than in previous studies. Comparing our best single session average (25.61 WPM) and overall last session average (20.36 for the 12th session with all participants, 22.66 WPM for the 16th session with final four participants) to the results quoted in Sect. 2 (23.10 WPM and 19.89 WPM, respectively), we see that this is indeed the case.

The apparatus used in the experiments is another significant factor. Most experiments reported in the literature have been carried out with Tobii eye trackers. Trackers with a higher sampling rate would provide an interesting comparison. Importantly, the algorithm for mapping gaze points to keys of the keyboard plays a central role. We suspect that the algorithm described in Sect. 3.2 contributes greatly to achieving high text entry rates, and it may explain much of the differences in the results of other soft keyboard experiments. This, of course, requires further experimentation.

Finally, the choice of participants and their motivation are also important factors. In most studies cited here the participants were compensated for their participation and often rewarded for best performance, so this should not be a major cause of variation. Our participants were native speakers of Finnish and fluent with English. The participants in [11] were also fluent in English, but the paper does not tell if this means that they were natives. Participants having English as their mother tongue can be expected to get even better results than those in our study, even if the spelling controversies discussed in Sect. 5.2 still remain to some extent.

6 Conclusion

We have carried out a controlled experiment where the participants entered text using a soft keyboard with their gaze from three to four hours (12 to 16 sessions of 15 min each), half of it in English and the other half in Finnish. No statistically significant difference was found between the languages. For reasons discussed in Sect. 5.3, our participants reached somewhat higher entry rates than has been reported in the literature before. In particular, the speed of text entry in English (best single session rate of 22.31 WPM, and overall average rate of 19.95 WPM for the sixth day and 21.07 WPM for the eighth day) is much higher than has been reported before.

We don't intend to claim the superiority of one technique over the other. Instead, we want to underline the importance of the many factors that affect the results in such experiments. To compare two designs with each other it is important to control as many of the experimental variables as possible: same participants, same briefing, same goal setting, same compensation, comparable calibration quality and same tracker. Without control over such factors the results are not fully commensurate.

Finally, it should be noted that our experiment (as most similar experiments) was carried out with able bodied users. The users that really need the technology of text entry by gaze can develop into very fast eye typists, as evidenced e.g. by some videos on the Internet for English[1] and Finnish[2]. To trace the world record speed in text entry by gaze, the experiment should involve such users who use the technique not for hours, but for days, weeks and months.

Acknowledgments. I am grateful to Per Ola Kristensson for suggesting this experiment and to Päivi Majaranta, Poika Isokoski, Saila Ovaska and Oleg Špakov for discussions and comments

---

[1] http://www.eyegaze.com/eye-tracking-assistive-technology-device/.

[2] http://www.iltalehti.fi/iltv-doc/201411070115600_dc.shtml (text entry e.g. at 01:00 and 03:48).

on the manuscript. In particular, Oleg Špakov implemented the soft keyboard and the gaze tracking algorithm used in the experiment. The statistical analysis was done using I. Scott MacKenzie's Java tools (http://www.yorku.ca/mack/RN-Anova.html). Finally, the participants in the experiment were committed and responsible – thank you very much!

This work was supported by the Academy of Finland (project MIPI).

References

1. Akkil, D., Isokoski, P., Kangas, J., Rantala, J., Raisamo, R.: TraQuMe: a tool for measuring the gaze tracking quality. In: Proceedings of the Symposium on Eye Tracking Research and Applications (ETRA 2014), pp. 11–18. ACM, New York (2014)
2. Isokoski, P., Linden, T.: Effect of foreign language on text transcription performance: Finns writing English. In: Proceedings of the Third Nordic Conference on Human-Computer Interaction (NordiCHI 2004), pp. 109–112. ACM, New York (2004)
3. MacKenzie, I.S., Soukoreff, R.W.: Phrase sets for evaluating text entry techniques. In: CHI 2003 Extended Abstracts on Human Factors in Computing Systems (CHI EA 2003), pp. 754–755. ACM, New York (2003)
4. Majaranta, P.: Text entry by eye gaze. Dissertations in Interactive Technology 11, University of Tampere (2009)
5. Majaranta, P., Ahola, U.-K., Špakov, O.: Fast gaze typing with an adjustable dwell time. In: Proceedings of the SIGCHI Conference on Human Factors in Computing Systems (CHI 2009), pp. 357–360. ACM, New York (2009)
6. Majaranta, P., Aoki, H., et al. (eds.): Gaze Interaction and Applications of Eye Tracking: Advances in Assistive Technologies. IGI Global, Hershey (2012)
7. Majaranta, P., MacKenzie, I.S., Aula, A., Räihä, K.-J.: Effects of feedback and dwell time on eye typing speed and accuracy. Univ. Access Inf. Soc. 5, 199–208 (2006)
8. Majaranta, P., Räihä, K.-J.: Text entry by gaze: utilizing eye-tracking. In: MacKenzie, I.S., Tanaka-Ishii, K. (eds.) Text Entry Systems: Mobility, Accessibility, Universality, pp. 175–187. Morgan Kaufmann, San Francisco (2007)
9. Pedrosa, D., da Graça Pimentel, M., Wright, A., Truong, K.N.: Filteryedping: design challenges and user performance of dwell-free eye typing. ACM Trans. Accessible Comput. 6(1), 37 (2015). Article 3
10. Räihä, K.-J., Ovaska, S.: An exploratory study of eye typing fundamentals: dwell time, text entry rate, errors, and workload. In: Proceedings of the SIGCHI Conference on Human Factors in Computing Systems (CHI 2012), pp. 3001–3010. ACM, New York (2012)
11. Rough, D., Vertanen, K., Kristensson, P.O.: An evaluation of Dasher with a high-performance language model as a gaze communication method. In: Proceedings of the 2014 International Working Conference on Advanced Visual Interfaces (AVI 2014), pp. 169–176. ACM, New York (2014)
12. Sanchis-Trilles, G., Leiva, L.A.: A systematic comparison of 3 phrase sampling methods for text entry experiments in 10 languages. In: Proceedings of the 16th International Conference on Human-Computer Interaction with Mobile Devices and Services (MobileHCI 2014), pp. 537–542. ACM, New York (2014)
13. Špakov, O.: iComponent – device-independent platform for analyzing eye movement data and developing eye-based applications. Dissertations in Interactive Technology 9, University of Tampere (2008). http://www.sis.uta.fi/~csolsp/downloads.php
14. Tuisku, O., Majaranta, P., Isokoski, P., Räihä, K.-J.: Now Dasher! Dash away! longitudinal study of fast text entry by eye gaze. In: Proceedings of the Symposium on Eye Tracking Research and Applications (ETRA 2008), pp. 19–26. ACM, New York (2008)

15. Urbina, M.H., Huckauf, A.: Alternatives to single character entry and dwell time selection on eye typing. In: Proceedings of the Symposium on Eye Tracking Research and Applications (ETRA 2010), pp. 315–322. ACM, New York (2010)
16. Wobbrock, J.O.: Measures of text entry performance. In: MacKenzie, I.S., Tanaka-Ishii, K. (eds.) Text Entry Systems: Mobility, Accessibility, Universality, pp. 47–74. Morgan Kaufmann, San Francisco (2007)
17. Wobbrock, J.O., Rubinstein, J., Sawyer, M.W., Duchowski, A.T.: Longitudinal evaluation of discrete consecutive gaze gestures for text entry. In: Proceedings of the Symposium on Eye Tracking Research and Applications (ETRA 2008), pp. 11–18. ACM, New York (2008)

Cognitive Accessibility for Mentally Disabled Persons

Stefan Johansson[✉], Jan Gulliksen, and Ann Lantz

KTH Royal Institute of Technology,
CSC – School of Computer Science and Communication, Stockholm, Sweden
stefan.johansson@funkanu.se

Abstract. The emergence of various digital channels, the development of different devices and the change in the way we communicate and carry out various types of services have quickly grown and continues to grow. This may offer both new opportunities for inclusion and risks for creating new barriers in the society. In a recent study we have explored the questions: Is the society digitally accessible for persons with mental disabilities? How do persons with mental disabilities cope with their situation? What are the benefits and obstacles they face? Based on the answers to these questions we wanted to explore if there is a digital divide between the citizens in general and the citizens with mental disabilities. And if so; what is the nature of this divide? Methods used in the study were Participatory action research oriented with data collection via research circles. In total over 100 persons participated. The results show that a digital divide is present. Persons with mental disabilities differ from citizens in general in how they have access to digital resources. The result also indicates that services and systems on a societal scale do not deliver the expected efficiency when it comes to supporting citizens with mental disabilities. And finally the results indicate that the special needs this group might have are often not identified in wider surveys on the citizen's use of Internet, digital services and use of different technical devices. Several of the participants describe this as being left outside and not fully participate in a society where digital presence is considered a prerequisite for a full citizenship.

Keywords: Mental disability · Mental problems · Cognitive accessibility · Digital society · Inclusion

1 Introduction

The ambition to fully include persons with disabilities in the society is manifested in the UN-declaration of human rights and in international and national legislation. The ambition is to include persons with different kinds of disabilities in all aspects of life. The example presented in this paper is located in Sweden, a country with high ambitions in this field.

In the study described in this paper we have explored the questions: Is the society digitally accessible for persons with mental disabilities? It is likely that the fast development of devices, services and techniques open up opportunities for a better life but it is also likely that different kind of obstacles may occur. So, is the digital society

© IFIP International Federation for Information Processing 2015
J. Abascal et al. (Eds.): INTERACT 2015, Part I, LNCS 9296, pp. 418–435, 2015.
DOI: 10.1007/978-3-319-22701-6_31

accessible for persons with mental disabilities provided they live in a highly developed welfare state? What are the digital needs of people with mental disabilities in the society? How do persons with mental disabilities cope with this situation? - What are the benefits and obstacles they face? Based on the answers to these questions we wanted to explore if there is a digital divide between citizens in general and citizens with mental disabilities. And if so; what is the nature of this divide?

1.1 Mental Health Problems

Mental health is defined by WHO as "a state of well-being in which an individual realizes his or her own abilities, can cope with the normal stresses of life, can work productively and is able to make a contribution to his or her community". Furthermore WHO defines a mental disorder in the following way: *"Mental disorders comprise a broad range of problems, with different symptoms. However, they are generally characterized by some combination of abnormal thoughts, emotions, behavior and relationships with others"* [1]. Mental problems are by WHO pointed out as global problems [2].

The absence of mental health is described in different ways. In this text we use the terms mental problems or mental disability and by that we include any kind of mental problem that are disabling a person in the everyday life.

The National Institute of Mental Health (NIMH) publish statistics[1] on mental health in the United States saying that 26.2 % of the US population experience some form of mental disorder each year and 46.4 % will experience a mental problem in their lifetime. Of all US adults 4.1 % are estimated to have serious mental problems.

Persons with mental disabilities are often described as at risk from being excluded from the mainstream society. In the public debate this group is often described as "vulnerable" or "socio-economic weak". It is known that a long period of mental problems increase the risk of being unemployed and of dying earlier than the average population [3, 4].

The empirical study presented in this paper is based on cases from Sweden and we will therefore present some data concerning mental problems among Swedish citizens.

1.2 Background on the Case of Mental Health Problems in Sweden

As an example of a state with a highly developed society with a comprehensive public welfare, we have decided to look at the case of Sweden. According to the OECD,[2] the Swedish tax-to-GDP ratio was 44.3 % in 2012. The highest rate in the world is in Denmark, 48.0 and the U.S rate is 24.3.

Sweden has a relatively large geographic area (449 964 km^2) with a relatively small population (9.7 million in 2014).

---

[1] http://www.nimh.nih.gov/Statistics/index.shtml

[2] http://www.oecd.org/ctp/tax-policy/revenue-statistics-ratio-change-previous-year.htm

Sweden is a highly digitized country. A very large proportion of the population is using the Internet and has access to fast broadband[3]. Broadband coverage is high even in remote parts of the country[4]. Commercial and public services have quickly built up a digital presence. In most cases the digital presence is added to traditional channels for information and communication, but there are also examples where access to the net is the only, or a much cheaper, way to perform certain services.

A few examples:

- 67 % of Swedes' income declarations 2014 are done digitally[5]
- Application for a place at upper secondary school must be done via the Internet[6]
- 62 % of Sweden's municipalities communicate with citizens through social media (2014)[7]
- The majority of Swedish banks will no longer handle cash. They push for the clients to use cards[8]

In Sweden it is The National Board of Health and Welfare (Socialstyrelsen)[9] or the Public Health Agency of Sweden (Folkhälsomyndigheten)[10] who publishes statistics on mental health. In surveys 20–40 % of the population state that they suffer from mental problems and 5–10 % is estimated having so severe problems that they need treatment but only 3–4 % is in an active treatment.

The Swedish government has assigned The Swedish Post and Telecom Authority (PTS)[11] to monitor if any problems emerge, especially for persons with disabilities. As a part of this monitoring effort, we have been commissioned to carry out a study on "Electronic communication for persons with mental disabilities".

PTS has also given us a mandate to carry out two literature studies "Accessibility to electronic communication for people with cognitive disabilities: a systematic search and review of empirical evidence" [5] and "Accessibility to electronic communication for people with cognitive disabilities: a review of grey literature" [6]. Both studies display great gaps of knowledge in this field.

1.3   Digital Society

In this paper we use the term digital society to cover the broad and diverse use of technical devices, services and technologies that has changed the way we communicate and interact with both persons and systems. This development has come to include both

---

[3] http://en.soi2014.se/.

[4] http://bredbandskartan.pts.se/.

[5] www.skatteverket.se.

[6] www.gyantagningen.se.

[7] www.skl.se.

[8] http://www.dn.se/ekonomi/kontanterna-forsvinner-fran-bankerna/.

[9] http://www.socialstyrelsen.se/psykiskhalsa.

[10] http://www.folkhalsomyndigheten.se/about-folkhalsomyndigheten-the-public-health-agency-of-sweden/.

[11] www.pts.se.

how we interact with friends and acquaintances as well as businesses and government agencies. This is an ongoing process and the changes have occurred over a short period of time. All societies are subject to these changes but differ in how far progress has gone. In a specific society it is likely that there are differences between how different citizens and groups of citizens embrace this development.

In this study we have explored how persons with mental disabilities in a highly developed society with a comprehensive public welfare cope with this situation. The overall question is if the society can be described as digitally accessible for persons with mental disabilities.

2 Method

The overall research approach follows the tradition of Action Research [7] More specifically the method is heavily influenced by the tradition of Participatory Design [8, 9] or the more Scandinavian version of Cooperative Design [10, 11] and we have therefore used an adapted form of Participatory Action Research [12]. We have in the past seen many problems to actually manage to work well with user participation [13] and the traditional methods for user participation are not sufficient when users have mental problems. In this project we have explored and developed methods adapted to perform better for persons with mental problems. This work is presented in a paper called "User participation when users have mental and cognitive disabilities" (manuscript) [14].

We have used a concept called study circles [15]. Study circles have a long tradition in the Nordic countries. A study circle is a group of adults that meet and discuss a specific topic. It is done by free will and in a democratic way. There is no teacher; instead a study circle has a leader who facilitates the discussions.

The concept of study circles has been further developed to so called research circles as a way for researchers and practitioners to work together to produce knowledge and gain deeper understanding [16]. The practitioners formulate problems and try to resolve them. The basic idea is that researchers and practitioners meet and learn about each other's knowledge and experiences. In a structured process this will lead to actions, reflection and to new knowledge.

2.1 Basic Study Setting

In the study over 100 persons (aged 15–75) with a mental disability participated. Activities have been implemented in major cities, smaller towns and rural areas. The participants have various diagnoses such as bipolar disorder, depression, schizophrenia, panic disorder or other mental disorders. They have had their problems for a long time. In addition to different kind of mental problems most of the participants can also describe a number of different types of cognitive difficulties. Participants are members in an organization for persons with mental problems, called RSMH.

The study went on between October 2013 and February 2014.

Groups of 8–12 persons where formed and each group met at least three times with at least one week in between each meeting. A meeting lasted for three hours. Every meeting was documented with text and important discussions and important findings were documented with illustrations, so called Mock-up Visualizations [14].

In three cities we arranged half-day activities as a onetime occasion. The activity lasted for 4–5 h. Having only one opportunity to discuss created a lot of frustration among participants. So in comparison; the three time approach was considered far better.

For most of the participants accessibility was equivalent with thresholds in the physical environment. So each set of meetings started with a short presentation on the topic "What is accessibility in the perspective of mental disabilities".

This was followed by a session where the participant could prioritize what to discuss during the rest of the meetings. The initial question was "What is it in your life that creates the biggest obstacles?" Initially, there was no connection to the digital society. This connection was made later in the process. During 10–15 min the participants individually was asked to write down issues on post-it notes. Notes with similar issues were grouped together and in the next phase each participant was given 5 points. They were asked to use the points to prioritize what they wanted to discuss. They could go "all in" and place all five on one single item or they could spread them. By using this procedure silent participants can have as much influence on what to discuss as more talkative participants. In each group there were some participants who initially were silent and a few that remained silent almost to the end of the third session. The result was a prioritized list of topics. We went back to the list of topics during the whole process to check that prioritized issues were discussed but sometimes new topics emerged.

Initially the study circle leader has no influence at all on what to discuss. The researcher's role is to act as a the circle leader. Later in the process the researcher connects the discussion with questions about electronic communication, design and accessibility.

3 Analysis

During each session two assistants were present with the task of taking notes. The researcher and a coordinator from RSMH also took notes and all notes where consolidated into minutes. The minutes were distributed by mail or by post to all participants with a call for comments. Some discussions were visualized with so called MockUp Visualizations [14]. The visualizations were made by the researcher.

Minutes, Post-it notes and other material produced during different sessions was organized into groups of related subjects; How I am treated, Economy, Health Care and Medication, Work, Information, Housing, Light and sound, Memory and Assistance. In next step the material was analyzed and organized into different subjects such as Mobile phone, Internet, Computer, Online services. Participants were included also in analyzing the collected material mainly by discussing the MockUp Visualizations.

One example of a MockUp is shown below (Fig. 1):

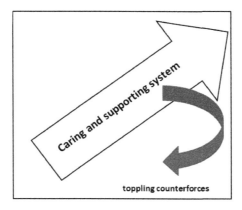

Fig. 1. This picture was produced to visualize that in every caring and supporting system, invented to help, there are counterforces that work in another direction. For example; a good system can be damaged by forcing the user to fill in too complex forms or use to complex web services. This picture has become a powerful tool to pinpoint counterproductive elements in systems, organizations and services.

4   Results

Mental disabilities often leads to a variety of cognitive difficulties [17]. When facing different kind of practical problems it is often fruitful to analyze them as cognitive accessibility problems.

Participants in this study describe problems with: execution abilities, memory, concentration and focus. They also describe how persistent mental problems gradually affect such as: self-confidence, self-esteem, trust and security.

The cognitive difficulties the participants describe can often be linked to ICF, International Classification on Functioning, Disability and Health[12] in the following areas (numbers indicate the code of the ICF system):

- Sustaining attention, b1400
- Shifting Attention, b1401
- Short-term memory, b1440
- Organization and planning, b1641
- Time management, b1642
- Problem-solving, b1646
- Experience of Time, b1802
- Undertaking a complex task, d2101
- Completing multiple tasks, d2201
- Handling stress, d2401

---

[12] http://www.who.int/classifications/icf/en/

The picture emerging from the stories told by the participants is that they face a number of accessibility problems but it is also possible to see that digital devices and digital services can play very important roles in the everyday life for a mentally disabled person.

4.1   Mobile Phones – A Hub and a Lifeline

Every participant in the study had a mobile phone. They described their mobile phone as a hub and a precious commodity. Many of the participants use the mobile phone just as a phone. They used it to talk and to send text messages. Some used it for surfing on the Internet and for e-mail but talking and texting is the most common use. For many the mobile phone works as a center for communication with friends, caregivers, authorities and colleagues (for the minority that had a work). The majority did not have a regular phone and many did not have a computer of their own.

A reason for not surfing and using e-mail was that many had old mobile phones or new cheap models that could not be classified as smartphones. In comparison to Swedes in general persons with mental disabilities seems to have less access to smartphones. 65 % of the Swedes use a smart phone and when discussing this with the participants they described a situation where a majority of them can't afford buying a smartphone.

Some of the older models could use e-mail but only a few of the participants knew how to configure this to work. Many of the participants are trying to use different features they have in their mobile phone. The most common seems to be some kind of notes. They also sometimes use the clock to get reminders of important things to do. Even if there is a calendar function and often other functions in the phone, there are few persons who use them. They seem to be too cognitively difficult to use and participants describe that it is a too big step to start using a feature even if you would benefit a lot from using it in the long run.

Only a small group of the participants have any experience of the more advanced features that can be found in smartphones. As a consequence they have not tested apps that could be used as cognitive support. Some participants have heard about apps for time managing, task planning, feedback and reminders on the market. They have also heard about apps for cognitive behavioral therapy and information management. Many participants call for opportunities to test and learn more.

Text Messages as a Personal Archive. Many participants described that incoming text-messages works as an archive. It is much easier to search among those messages in a phone than trying to find a letter that was delivered by the postal service. Several participants described difficulties with postal messages. They often get lost and it happens that they do not open letters at all. Many described that they wanted more electronic communication with caregivers, government agencies and other important contacts. Over time many persons stored large number of messages in their phones and it becomes difficult to find information and sometimes they have experienced insufficient room for storage. Participants lack simple ways to save and move text messages.

Important Information Gets Lost. Almost all participants had experienced losing important information when changing mobile phone, upgrading their phone or upgrading or changing a subscription. Several participants describe this as a huge calamity. Stored contacts, stored SMS-messages and notes turned out to be the most troublesome information to loose. *"You get those questions whether you want to save to SIM-card or the phone, but it always ends up with me losing important stuff. I do not know how to do"*, one person said.

Flat Rate for Mobile Phone Calls. Having a flat rate is one of the most important measures to achieve increased accessibility to the society for a mentally disabled person. A person in the study expressed it this way: *"The biggest accessibility-thing that happened to us with mental disabilities is flat rates for mobile phones."* As the mobile phone is central for persons with mental disabilities a low or predictable cost for subscriptions and calls is very important. When these costs vary it creates uncertainty and insecurity. Either *"How high will the bill be?"* or *"How long can I talk before the prepaid card is empty?"* A flat rate eliminates those concerns.

Flat Rate for Mobile Surfing. It is a large group in this study who do not surf with their phone. Their mobile phone cannot handle it, or they have no subscription. Among the persons who surf via the mobile phone cost control is very important and they are looking for low cost or flat rate subscriptions. It is however very difficult to predict the actual cost of a subscription and comparing different subscriptions is considered very difficult.

Let's Talk You Through the Night. An example where flat rate makes a truly vital difference is when persons with mental disabilities help each other through the night. Most suicide attempts are done during the night, especially when night turns to dawn. And almost everyone in the study could tell of friends committing suicide. Spontaneously organized groups are formed where persons with mental problems help each other and establish phone connections with a friend on the brink of committing suicide. It works like a relay and different persons take turns on speaking to the person at risk. As one participant said *"Nowadays you don't need to think about the cost, thanks to flat rate. It was really frustrating when you ran out of money and you had to hook up leaving a desperate friend all alone in the middle of the night. Some friends did not make it"*.

Parallel Mobile Phone Subscriptions. Several of the people we met during the study have experienced having parallel mobile phone subscriptions. Without really understanding, they have signed up for a new subscription that also means that they will continue to pay on an old one. It also happens that they pay for Internet surf although they use phones with no Internet capability.

This seems to be the result of aggressive marketing in combination with poor impulse control and difficulties in understanding information about subscriotions.

4.2 Postal Address and Letters Is not the Safest Way to Get in Touch

Handling officers in the health and social care and other authorities usually just recognize your formally registered address as a contact point and they are forced to do so due to legislation. If the authority wants to provide you with information or a call for action from you they will send a letter to the address where you are registered. The participants describe several problems connected with addresses and letters.

The most common problem is that a person simply does not open letters; to open a letter is associated with great discomfort and anxiety. Other problems are that persons for various reasons choose not to live at the address they stated, are homeless or voluntarily or forcibly admitted to a mental health care institution.

Participants in the study told us that you very well know that you should do something about received letters, but the ability is simply not there. Rather the knowledge of what needs to be done builds more anxiety and worries.

4.3 When a Person Is Institutionalized for Care Contact Channels are Broken

People with severe mental disabilities can be hospitalized for periods of time. This may be both through free will and through force. During this period the mobile phone often is the only channel for communication alongside with personal visits from friends or relatives. Several of the persons in the study testify that they or others have got into difficulties because letters sent to their home address is not re-distributed to the clinic and you have to organize that someone drops by your home and collect the mail. Psychiatric clinics do not seem to have clear procedures for how this issue should be dealt with.

It is the clinic who decides whether you should be allowed to use a phone or not. Participants describe restrictions in phone usage is a common disciplinary tool. They regard it as a major assault being deprived of their phone and without it they have no channels of communication open.

4.4 Meetings with Caregivers and Other Authorities

The study shows that there are significant problems related to meetings. Persons with mental disabilities may be called to a large number of meetings. In some cases, there are over 100 meetings a year. There are various actors who call for such meetings. Often they represent different county and municipality organizations, but sometimes also a government agency. Also private actors invite to meetings.

Many participants describe this as a major problem. You are supposed to manage all this by your own and remembering calls, remembering what is being discussed and remembering to carry out different tasks between meetings is described as troublesome.

One of the participants drew the picture below. It shows different organizations you may have contact with (Fig. 2).

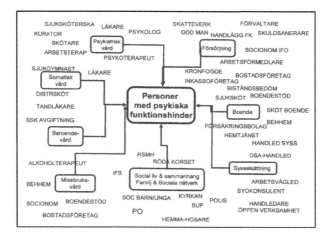

Fig. 2. The person with mental problems is represented by the box in the middle. The boxes that are connected to this person represent different types of societal actors. Every word around these squares represents an organization/person that the person has contacts with.

Taking this one step further we discussed how many meetings it can be under a specific period of time. Schematically, it can be described as follows (Fig. 3):

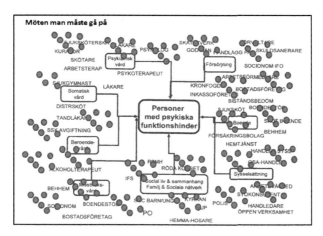

Fig. 3. Each dot represents a meeting. Different actors often do not coordinate their activities. It can easily be up to 100 meetings a year.

The Consequence of Missing a Meeting. In many cases, if you miss an appointment, you will be billed with a penalty. The various organizations have rules for how a cancellation should be done. If a person is absent or cancels too late a cancellation fee will be charged. So do many psychiatric clinics in Sweden. The purpose of this is to discipline patients so that they do attend at meetings.

Several persons in the study have testified that invoices sent from the county council psychiatric clinics eventually lead to payment defaults. It seems to happen like this: Periodically you feel so bad that you simply cannot attend at meetings. Depression, anxiety, or other conditions make it impossible to take off for the meeting, and also impossible to cancel in time. The county council's computer system records this as a case for a cancellation fee and sends an invoice by letter. As mentioned earlier it is common that letter remains unopened and this will eventually end up with a payment default.

Participants point out that they find it difficult to understand why the clinic that is supposed to support them put them into trouble when acting precisely as expected from a person with a mental and cognitive disorder. The participants want both calls for meetings and documentation to be handled in digital channels. The also call for online connections between home and clinic.

4.5   Computers

According to the participants many persons with mental disabilities do not have access to a computer at home. But many also do not have a work so they do not get access to computers through their work either. If they do have access to computers, the computers are often old with poor performance and frequent malfunction and with software that are no longer supported or functioning well.

Several of the participants in the study inform us that public authorities nowadays require modern computers and software to manage their services online. An actual recent example is the Swedish national agency for unemployed. Participants in our study have been told that they are expected to log in daily to report on their level of job-seeking activity. One participant in our study reported that she on a daily basis must log in and apply for jobs and report these activities in the system. At the same time as she was engaged by the same agency in work practices with a company. She informed the agency that she did not have access to a computer at home. She finds it problematic to do these tasks at her work practice, since she is anxious to show that she is able to follow the rules and do a good job. Consequently, they suggest her to come to the agency office to enter the information. But to do that, she would have to leave the work place during working time. She felt caught in a trap.

Computers at the Local RSMH Associations. As a member in RSMH you can often use computers and occasionally also get help with for example paying bills or sending e-mails at their local meeting places. These computers are often very old with frequent malfunction.

The recent development trend with simplification of computers and software has not yet reached the target audience for our study. Many of the participants report on loosing important information due to frequent computers breakdowns. Having important data "in the cloud" and thereby protect it from disappearing is not yet a common solution.

Accessing Computers in Public Libraries. A smaller group of participants visit libraries where they can use public computers for free that often work well but have a variety of restrictions that can cause trouble.

Often there are time limits on how long a person can use a library computer. The rule exists to provide access to as many people as possible. But this creates stress.

The computers are often located in open areas where groups of people sit together and use them. There may be both advantages and disadvantages from this. For some users, it creates a sense of security, for others it is a concern. If you use the library's computer to pay bills, for example, you may not want to be completely open and transparent with this information. There may also be privacy issues relating to people "looking over ones shoulder".

4.6   Tablets

In the study, we intended to discuss the participant's experiences of using tablets. None of the participants in the study has had their own tablet. Some had occasionally tried one, but in general the experience of tablets among the participants was marginal. According to the national survey[13] "The Swedes and the Internet 2014", 45 % of the population sometimes uses a tablet and 25 % use a tablet on a daily basis.

4.7   The Internet and Web Accessibility

Every person in the study uses Internet to some degree. Several persons could describe difficulties with the use of web pages. Most troublesome are pages with:

* Unwanted movements or flickering
* Cluttered design
* Evil design (when design is used to persuade or trick you to do something)
* Functions and services with login
* Lack of logic and consequence in concept and design
* Lack of trustworthiness

The participants were not aware of the existence of a standard for web accessibility [18]. They did not connect problems they experience using web pages with poor accessibility rather they regarded the difficulties as personal shortcomings. Many expressed a lack of confidence in their own abilities to understand and use resources on the web. In some cases the self-esteem was affected by repeated failures. It is common that persons with mental disabilities call for help from friends or relatives to carry out tasks online. Some described this as an invasion of privacy but they really could not see any alternative. One example is paying bills online, since online banking is considered difficult. Other example where help often is needed is buying tickets or online shopping.

---

[13] http://en.soi2014.se/

Public and Commercial Services Online. The participants have little experience of using online services provided by municipalities, counties and state. An increasing amount of services has gone online the last years but they are not commonly used by the participants.

Many of the participants have bought tickets online and some have tested online shopping but when asked about preferences a majority says they rather would do this by interacting with a person rather than a machine. Some participants argue that many probably would change opinion if they were given the opportunity to learn more and to try and test devices and services.

Captcha, eID and Other Login Methods. According to the participants in the study there is no really good way to "prove who you are" on the Internet. Most persons in the study did not use eID. Overall, there are severe problems with login procedures. Several participants seem to directly avoid any solutions that require login. Many of the participants in the study talked about the difficulties to manage passwords and other codes. Many also specifically mentioned CAPTCHA (acronym for Completely Automated Public Turing test to tell Computers and Humans Apart) as an obstacle that they cannot manage to pass. CAPTCHA was even described as "evil design" by one person.

4.8   Direct Debit (Autogiro)

Many of the participants in the study tell us that the direct debit is a very important function. It is an example of a function which compensates for periods of problems with undertaking complex tasks or problems with planning. Bills registered for direct debt is automatically paid every month.

Persons, who have lived with their mental problems for a long time, often advice newcomers to arrange for direct debt as soon as possible. You can get that help from the society, but often first after that you got a payment default.

4.9   Fixed Time Slots, Telephone Queues and Automatic Responses

A majority of the participants are strongly opposed to what we might call modern PBX (Private Branch Exchange) technology. Several participants said that they hang up immediately if they hear an automated voice that begins urge to "press 1 if you ...". They are not even listening to the options.

Systems with music played during periods of waiting are regarded as disturbing by many and totally inaccessible by some. For some, music, recurring information from an automated voice and waiting is so disturbing that they lose the reason why they initially called.

Another problem is fixed time slots for incoming calls. Some participants gave almost the same story: If you start every day with medication the medicine can as a side effect make it impossible for you to make telephone calls for a period of time. This means you cannot call someone in the morning and if someone only answers on fixed hours at that period you basically cannot phone them. Waiting in telephone queues is also described as very problematic.

4.10 Little Use of Assistive Tools

In the study, there were several participants who probably would have found various IT-based assistive devices very useful. No one had access to any such tools. One of the participants had tried to get support for a memory supporting aid called Comai but it was rejected. The solution was considered too expensive for her needs. Previous studies have also shown that persons with mental disabilities find it very difficult to get assistive tools [19].

5 Discussion

Since the dawn of the "information society" in the 1990s there has been an interest in exploring who is included and who is excluded from using the emerging new devices and the new services. The use of computers and the use of the Internet were of particular interest. It soon became clear that age, level of education, work presence, and level of income is key factors in this dynamic and rather complex context [20]. Disability is another, sometimes forgotten, factor. Early studies on how persons with disabilities used the Internet or had access to computers revealed a "digital gap" [21, 22]. An important question was if this gap would close or widen over time? Was it a question of late adopters who lagged behind but soon would keep up with the rest of the population or was it a question of a more permanent exclusion?

The early studies included persons with vision and hearing impairment, limitations in mobility and sometimes reading and writing difficulties. Gradually persons with dyslexia, attention disorders, autism spectrum disorders and learning difficulties have been included in digital accessibility research but it is still hard to find studies exploring how accessible the digital society is for those groups and it is still harder to find anything about persons with mental disabilities.

What we can see is that in any given point in time when someone ask the question "Is there a digital divide between people with disabilities and people without disabilities" the answer is "yes". Key factors for this exclusion seems to be fewer opportunities to get in contact with new technology, lack of competence and low incomes. Often a person with a disability reports a significant desire to increase their use of, what for the time of the study is regarded as, modern technology [23]. This indicates that being outside the digital society is not a self-selected choice, rather a consequence of poor accessibility.

Our study shows a similar pattern. We have focused on persons with mental disabilities since little is known about how this group copes with today's digital society. We started out by asking the questions: Is the society digitally accessible for persons with mental disabilities? How do persons with mental disabilities cope with this situation? What are the benefits and obstacles they face? Based on the answers to these questions we wanted to discuss if there is a digital divide between the citizens in general and the citizens with mental disabilities.

We have explored a broad range of devices, services and situations and the conclusion is that a digital divide clearly exists. The society is not digitally accessible for persons with mental disabilities. The participants in this study can describe numerous situations supporting this conclusion. Most of the problems the users face are of a cognitive nature. It is difficult to learn, understand, remember and recall how devices and interfaces work.

Having said that, they can also describe numbers of situations where modern technology work in their favor, especially the mobile phone and the decreasing costs for communication for both telephone calls and for using mobile Internet connections. For many participants their mobile phone is a highly valued property. The consequences of losing it or lose information stored in it can be disastrous.

5.1   Weak Digital Support in Caregiving Processes

When facing mental problems and the consequences thereof a person gets in contact with a number of actors; health and care services, social care services, enforcement and police authorities, special housing services etc. The communication between individuals and those actors do not make use of modern tools for communication. Information is delivered on paper by traditional postal service; the disabled person is often supposed to remember and accurately retell oral information given by one instance when visiting another, making the quality of information heavily depending on the disabled person's own capability to remember, recall and retell the information.

A specific caregiver acts as they are the only one in contact with the person with a mental disability. They seem unaware of the problems the large amount of meetings creates. There is little coordination between different operators so a person can get calls for several meetings during a short period of time, even the same day. Better and coordinated booking systems, better communication and exchange of information would create major opportunities for improvement in this field.

It seems that many times the development of IT support for specific caregiving situations is optimized from the caregiver's perspective and from the singular situation it is supposed to support, not taking a holistic perspective from the person seeking treatment or support.

5.2   Low Experience of Using Modern Technology

A majority of the participants use old mobile phones and old computers. Besides the hassles that the use of older systems brings, it also means that most of the participants do not know the potential of modern technology. As an example, there is a variety of software and apps that could serve to support people with mental and cognitive disabilities, but these do not work on the older equipment that they are using.

Smartphones and tablets have a potential to improve the access to different kinds of services and to make it easier to communicate and to be integrated in the digital society. The participants in our study describe a wish to be more included in the society and an increased digital presence is considered important. They call for activities where they can learn more and try devices and applications that could help them in different aspects of life.

5.3   Future Research

As the research needs in this field and the knowledge gap is so big we intend to pursue more research with this user category. In a project in cooperation with the social service in Stockholm, starting early 2015, we will explore and test how modern technology can be used to improve the communication between homeless persons with mental disabilities and the social care services.

The knowledge on how persons with mental problems experience the web needs to be deepened but the results so far indicates that standards such as the web content accessibility guidelines (WCAG) [16] do not fully support the needs of persons with mental disabilities.

6   Conclusions

Increasing the cognitive accessibility for persons with mental disabilities is a very important challenge. When we survey the field we find very few published scientific studies to support the development of ICT for this group.

In short, we want to point out the following points as the most important discoveries we have made

- The important role of the mobile phone
- The importance of flat rates, both for phone and internet
- The low use and experience of smartphones and tablets
- The use of old, decommissioned, computers and old software
- The low use of public and commercial services online
- The reluctance to use login functions
- The problems with protecting important information in mobile phones
- The lack of connection between IT-systems used by caregivers and the personal devices used by persons with mental disabilities
- The struggle to keep up with the introduction of new digital devices and digital services as they emerge
- The great interest to acquire further training and competence to better cope with the digital society

Working with users with mental and cognitive disabilities does not only give us insights into their lives and needs, but we also learn a lot about ourselves, our prejudice and lacking knowledge about this group and their needs. We strongly believe that research into cognitive and mental accessibility needs to expand, and the knowledge gained may not only be used to improve the design of ICT support for this group, but improve the accessibility and usability for all users. Some of our findings needs to be addressed to social science or other research fields. What can be done in the field of HCI then? At this stage we can see a number of interesting issues:

- Making the complicated and complex more intuitive, easy and cost effective
- Making the consequences of errors and mistakes less ominous
- Design for trust, self-esteem and self confidence
- Design login and identification techniques accepted by all users

- Better communication between social- and health care systems/staffs and the personal devices used
- Implementation of assistive technology features into standard devices and services

Acknowledgements. We want to thank all participants from RSMH and all central and local organizers of the meetings. We also want to thank The Swedish Post and Telecom Authority (PTS) for funding this project. We are grateful for valuable comments provided by the reviewers.

References

1. WHO: Mental Health Action Plan 2013–2020. http://www.who.int/mental_health/publications/action_plan/en/
2. WHO: Mental Health Action Plan (2013). http://www.who.int/mental_health/action_plan_2013/en/
3. OECD: Making Mental Health Count (2014). http://www.oecd.org/els/health-systems/Focus-on-Health-Making-Mental-Health-Count.pdf
4. OECD: Factsheet Highlights from OECD's Mental Health and Work Review (2011). http://www.oecd.org/els/soc/49227189.pdf
5. Borg, J., Lantz, A., Gulliksen, J.: Accessibility to electronic communication for people with cognitive disabilities: a systematic search and review of empirical evidence. Universal Access in the Information Society, pp. 1–16 (2014)
6. Lantz, A., Borg, J., Johansson, S., Hildén, A.,Gulliksen, J.: Accessibility to electronic communication for people with cognitive disabilities: a review of grey literature. Unpublished manuscript (submitted)
7. Lewin, K.: Action research and minority problems. J. Soc. Issues 2(4), 34–46 (1946)
8. Schuler, D., Namioka, A.: Participatory Design: Principles and Practices. L. Erlbaum Associates Inc., Hillsdale (1993)
9. Muller, M.J.: Participatory design: the third space. In: HCI: Human-Computer Interaction: Development Process, vol. 4235 (2003)
10. Kyng, M., Greenbaum, J.: Design at Work: Cooperative Design of Computer Systems. Lawrence Erlbaum Associates, Incorporated, Hillsdale (1991)
11. Ehn, P.: Work-Oriented Design of Computer Artifacts, vol. 78. Arbetslivscentrum, Stockholm (1988)
12. Whyte, W.F. (ed.): Participatory Action Research. Sage Publications Inc., Newbury Park (1991)
13. Gulliksen, J., Lantz, A., Boivie, I.: User Centered Design in Practice-Problems and Possibilities, vol. 315, p. 433. Sweden, Royal Institute of Technology (1999)
14. Johansson, S., Gulliksen, J., Lantz, A.: User Participation When Users Have Mental and Cognitive Disabilities (manuscript). Royal Institute of Technology, Sweden
15. Larsson, S.: Seven aspects of democracy as related to study circles. Int. J. Lifelong Educ. 20(3), 199–217 (2001)
16. Rönnerman, K., Olin, A.: Research circles. In: Rönnerman, K., Salo, P. (eds.) Lost in Practice, pp. 95–112. SensePublishers, The Netherlands (2014)
17. McGurk, S., Mueser, K., Pascaris, A.: Cognitive training and supported employment for persons with severe mental illness: one-year results from a randomized controlled trial. Schizophr. Bull. 31(4), 898–909 (2005)

18. ISO/IEC 40500:2012.: Information technology – W3C Web Content Accessibility Guidelines (WCAG) 2.0 (2012)
19. Adolfsson, J.: Kognitiva hjälpmedel Nationell uppföljning av hjälpmedelsförsörjningen för personer med kognitiva funktionsnedsättningar (Assistive aids for persons with cognitive disablities. Only available in Swedish) (2012)
20. Van Dijk, J., Hacker, K.: The digital divide as a complex and dynamic phenomenon. Inf. Soc. **19**(4), 315–326 (2003)
21. Kaye, H.S.: Computer and Internet Use Among People with Disabilities. Disability Statistics Report (13). U.S. Department of Education, National Institute on Disability and Rehabilitation Research, Washington, DC (2000)
22. Dobransky, K., Hargittai, E.: The disability divide in Internet access and use. Inf. Commun. Soc. **9**(3), 313–334 (2006)
23. Ennis, L., Rose, D., Denis, M., Pandit, N., Wykes, T.: Can't surf, won't surf: the digital divide in mental health. J. Ment. Health **21**(4), 395–403 (2012)

Design and Evaluation of Mobile Learning Applications for Autistic Children in Pakistan

Muneeb Imtiaz Ahmad[1](✉) and Suleman Shahid[2]

[1] MARCS Institute, Human Machine Interaction Group,
Department of Computing, University of Western Sydney, Sydney, Australia
muneeb06@gmail.com
[2] Tilburg Centre for Cognition and Communication, Department of Information
and Communication Sciences, University of Tilburg, Tilburg, The Netherlands
S.Shahid@uvt.nl

Abstract. In this paper, we present the design and evaluation of culturally specific mobile learning applications, designed as a tool to encourage social interaction in autistic children. These applications were designed for Pakistani children keep their cultural context in mind. We performed longitudinal evaluation (around eight weeks) of these applications at an autistic school in Pakistan. Our initial results, based on pre and post evaluation questionnaires and video analysis of social interactions, showed that the applications had a positive effect on the development of socio-emotional skills of children and were appreciated not only by children but also by the teachers.

Keywords: Culture · Autism · App · Tablet · Social skills

1 Introduction

Autism Spectrum Disorder (ASD) is a persistent behavioral and neurodevelopment disorder manifesting in children at an early age. Over the last decade, researchers have designed and evaluated numerous digital solutions (e.g. games, learning applications, tabletop applications and robotic solutions) for assisting autistic children of different age groups. Earlier studies have shown that factors like cultural background and mother language significantly affect the development of behavioral, emotional, social and communication skills of children. Despite an immense amount of research on autism, the role of culture while designing rehabilitation applications has relatively been understudied. Similarly, most of the research on ASD is limited to group of children from western countries and relatively, less attention has been paid on the children belonging to non-western countries especially from South Asian counties where the prevalence of autism is quite high [1].

Culture can be defined as a way of living for a certain group of people. Recent studies on cross cultural comparisons have shown that social behaviors are affected by religion, socio-economic situation, parent's way of upbringing, parent's expectations and level of education [2]. It also shows that socialization practices are influenced by culture [3]. Studies on ASD therapy have also shown that ASD interventions should

© IFIP International Federation for Information Processing 2015
J. Abascal et al. (Eds.): INTERACT 2015, Part I, LNCS 9296, pp. 436–444, 2015.
DOI: 10.1007/978-3-319-22701-6_32

take into account the customs of the individual society in order to improve behavior and social skills of individuals diagnosed with autism [4].

A variety of digital solutions have been designed for autistic children to address their difficulties with verbal and non-verbal communication and social skills. Picture Exchange Communication System (PECS) is famous example, in which pictures are used as a tool for teaching verbal and non-verbal communication skills [5]. Toby Playpad [6], Proloquo2Go, iComm, and TapToTalkis are also good examples of Speech generating devices which support communication through images and text to voice conversion features. The Let's Face It! program has been used as a game to teach non-verbal skills including the face recognition skill to autistic children [7]. Avatars have been used in a study to enable autistic children develop understanding about human emotions and expressions. [8]. Touch Story shown [9] is computer game software that deals with development of social understanding in children with autism. Graphical Social Scenarios [10] is another system inspired from social stories and comic strip conversation. However, these applications have been designed primarily for western countries and without keeping cross-cultural differences and similarities in mind. These 'one size fit all applications might not work well in all cultures because socio-emotional experiences are derived by cultural norms and these applications primarily address these experiences. In this paper, we present the design and of a mobile learning application that is customized based on the local cultural norms in order to improve social and emotional skills of autistic individual from Pakistan. We also present the results of the longitudinal evaluation of these applications performed at an autistic school in Pakistan.

2   Design of Our Applications

The design of our applications is based on the user research and literature review. We conducted a user study focused on observing children, interviewing teachers and parents to gather the user requirements. We observed 8 children in different situations during for about 8 weeks. We also interviewed, 8 teachers, 2 psychologists, and 'that many' parents. In addition, we evaluated existing mobile applications for 6 weeks, designed for improving the non-verbal communication and social skills, with a group of autistic children. However, results suggested that children in general, were not able to understand the avatars showing different emotions. In addition, stories used in the applications to depict different social situations were also found to be irrelevant. Based on the observations, feedback from parents and teachers and results of the evaluation sessions with existing applications, we designed two different simple and easy to use tablet applications, (1) Learning Emotions, and (2) Social Learning.

2.1   Learning Emotions and Expressions

Our application, Learning Emotions and Expressions consists of two games. (1) Emotion Finder and (2) Guess Expressions. 'Emotion Finder' is a simple game, which enables children with autism to find a particular emotion from a scene. Children were exposed to various emotions in a scene. Later, they were asked to tap/select the asked emotion. 'Guess Expressions' is another simple game, which uses natural and spontaneous human facial expressions, elicited in a proper experimental setting, to help autistic children in understanding these expressions. In this game, children are required to choose the correct option from the multiple choices of different expressions.

Keeping in mind the cultural context, actual facial expressions of Pakistani children and elders were used in these games. In case of emotion finder, we used culture-specific backgrounds. The goal was to improve children's non-verbal communication skills and help them in improving their understanding of basic and complex emotions and expressions (Fig. 1).

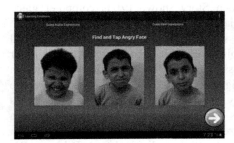 

Fig. 1. Learning emotions and expressions (left) and social learning (right)

2.2   Social Learning

Social learning consists of a simple game that asks children to guess the missing link from a social scene. The design of the app is based on the concept of comic books in which different situations are described with the help of sequence of different images. In addition, the design is also inspired by the core concept of the Touch story [9]. However, the stories designed for our application are according to the cultural norms of Pakistan. Children doing mischiefs story presents a scenario of mischief performed in the cultural settings of Pakistan. Similarly, Saying hello story presents a scenario of how we greet people in Pakistan e.g. shaking hands and hugging. Moreover, it's a common practice in Pakistan to throw garbage on the road. We designed a story (names as throwing dust story) to help children in realizing that throwing garbage on road is a bad idea.

3   User Evaluation

We designed our applications to address different difficulties faced by autistic children. Our objective was to investigate whether our applications were able to address the problems children face in everyday lives i.e. unable to understand emotions and responding intelligently in different social situations. Past research has shown that autistic children lose interest in therapy applications and do no cooperate. We wanted to see how our game based activities enhanced the engagement of autistic children?

How do they socially interact with each other? How understanding about different emotions and expressions was improved? Were they able to understand and connect with different social scenarios presented in the game? Finally, we intended to measure the difference between the app and no app version to justify the need of mobile version of the activities.

Our evaluation approach was to perform one to one and group sessions with autistic children using our applications. The idea was to engage these children socially with each other while they interact with our applications. Furthermore, in order to measure if the application fulfilled the research objective, we implemented a web based feedback system for teachers. At the end of each week, we requested the teachers to give feedback about each child. We asked them about a child's progress and behavioral adaptions after the sessions. Our approach was inspired by this study [11].

We performed the evaluation at one of the schools at Lahore, Pakistan. The age of the participants was between 8 to 12 years. The sample size of our group was 8 children. All 8 children were high functioning individuals. We designed a longitudinal evaluation plan of 2 months with these applications. We performed a session of 25 to 30 min with pairs of children. We performed a pre and post evaluation questionnaires session with all children at the start and end of evaluations. The 'Super Skills Profile for Social Discovery' was used at the start and end of evaluation to measure the difference for various fundamental social and behavioral skills. The teachers were requested to rate these skills on the scale of 0 being "Poor" to 6 being "Excellent". In order to compare our apps with the non-digital intervention, we designed paper-based apps, equivalent to that of tablet apps. We printed expressions and stories on the cards.

We began to evaluate our applications at a school in Lahore, Pakistan from Monday afternoon starting at the mid of August till the end of second week of October. We conducted activities with a pair of two children on daily basis. Each pair had to work with evaluator and teachers; evaluator was required to conduct a session and we requested teachers to record videos. The role of the researcher was to help individuals understand the applications and to support them performing the activity when required. The children were asked to play the Emotion Finder or Guess the Expression and Social Learning activities in pairs. They were asked to complete the activity by taking turns. They were also encouraged to work together closely to finish the activity.

We performed one activity per day with all eight children. Each session was video recorded. These videos were later used for the analysis to measure the amount of social interaction. We performed a within-subject study. The media type i.e. paper vs. computer was used as an independent variable during the evaluation. We began with the completion of the pre-evaluation questionnaires. After these questionnaires, we began our evaluation with the mobile app for two weeks and then paper-based version of all the activities was used for four weeks. After that, we shifted to the tablet apps for another two weeks. This design helped us in observing the changing behavior of individuals over time and also enabled us to compare the results of independent variables (paper, and tablet). In addition, it enabled us to measure amount of social interaction while using the similar apps in different environments.

4   Evaluation Results

4.1   User Evaluation Feedback Results

The results of the 'Super Skills Profile for Social Discovery' questionnaire (See Fig. 2), used at the start and end of evaluation, show that each parameter showed a slight improvement for each child.

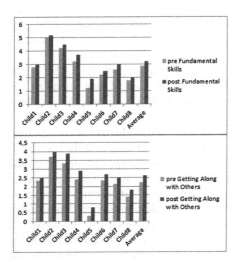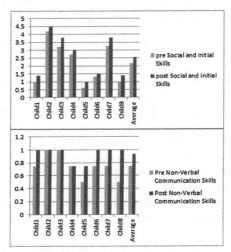

Fig. 2. X-axis shows pre and post results for fundamental skills, social skills, getting along with others and non-verbal communication skills of all children and y-axis shows the value parameters.

The results of two 'Learning Emotions and Expressions' apps showed that overall children were able to understand different emotions. At the end of our evaluation, teachers were very positive about the app and gave very positive feedback. For example one teacher said, "He has been able to understand the new emotions i.e. fearful, disgusted and surprised. He has also been able to imitate them properly". Another teacher mentioned, "Children's understanding of the emotions has been greatly improved. He has been able to express and identified all emotions". Another said, "He has responded very well, initially he did not show any response but as weeks passed, he started imitating the emotions and were able to understand them."

The overall results for social learning activity were also promising. For example, one teacher said, "He has been learning new words used during each social learning activity session and later repeating them in other activities." Teachers were also happy that students are applying the knowledge, learnt using the applications, outside the class "He has understood the stories for mischief, dust cleaning, and banana peel. He also uses them outside the class". Another teacher said, "When i asked him to act out social stories like making the queue, he started doing it without hesitation." Finally all teachers mentioned "Storytelling app has positive effects on students and we would like to continue with it."

4.2   Video Analysis Results

All the recorded videos (child's behavior while performing different activities during each session) were coded for verbal interaction, physical interaction, supportive and discouraging comments. These constructs were coded as numbers. We tested whether the data was normally distributed using Kolmogorov-Smirnov's (K-S) test. If normal distribution was found, which the case was, we compared activities with app and no app using paired t-test. Two researchers were involved in video coding process. One of the researchers did not take part in the evaluation process.

We focused on coding for social interaction among pairs of children. The videos were coded manually for the following parameters: (1) Verbal Interaction: We counted one verbal interaction when a child spoke during the activity, or repeated after the researcher, (2) Supportive comments: We counted one supportive comment when a child communicated to support during the task, pointed to the characters in the story, asked questions about the story, or depicted the shown emotion or expression, (3) Discouraging comments: We counted one discouraging comment when a child did not like something about the activity or stood up and started moving. In addition, when a child was not comfortable with the partner and verbally expressed displease, and (4) Physical interaction: We counted one physical interaction when child was able to perform turn taking or when a child participated during other child's turn or when the child imitated the evaluator.

We transcribed all the sessions. We use these transcripts to measure the total number of sentences. All videos were of different length, so we normalized the occurrence of above-mentioned parameters per minute.

Tests showed significant differences between app and no app for no of sentences used ($p < .001$), for richness of verbal interaction ($p < .01$), for the use of supportive comments ($p < 0.01$), for the physical interaction ($p < 0.01$) and for the use of discouraging comments ($p < 0.05$). The results can be seen in Fig. 3(a). In all cases, the usage of App had a much better impact than the usage of paper-based intervention. We also used questionnaire to measure differences between level of interaction, likability and involvement between activities performed on paper and tablet. We asked teachers to rank parameters like attention, involvement, likeability, interaction, and enjoyment on a scale from 1 to 5. We calculated the mean value for the app and no app for all these parameters. The results are shown in Fig. 3(b). Again, the app versions performed much better than the no app versions.

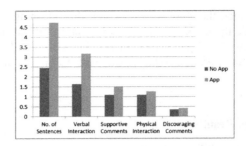

Fig. 3a. (left) Left: X-axis represents the mean value of all children; y-axis represents the minimum and maximum value parameters app and no app

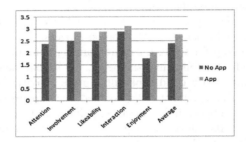

Fig. 3b. (right) Right: X-axis represents the mean value of all children for app and no app versions; y-axis represents the minimum and maximum value parameters

5   Discussions and Limitations

In general, these early results show a very positive and encouraging trend. The result generated by the teacher's feedback system also gave an indication that children were able to understand complex emotions. Similarly, the understanding about the new social scenarios was also developed. In addition, the transfer of knowledge from the digital environment to the real world i.e. imitating the emotional expressions and stories indicated that social learning, and learning emotions and expressions activities were quite effective. The results of video analysis showed a clear support for the app version because children's social interaction and communication was significantly improved while performing the activities on a tablet. The results also showed that the level of interaction, involvement and enjoyment was higher in the app version as compared to the paper version. Finally, the higher number of sentences uttered and rich verbal interactions indicate that children showed better interaction skills during these activities. In addition, the higher amount of supportive comments also indicated that children showed interest in the activities.

We think the reason that the app-based intervention worked better than the paper-based intervention is that the children found the digital intervention novel, structured and organized. We know that autistic children feel anxiety when they have to deal with uncertain and unpredictable events. The teachers informed us that interacting with tablets is more predictable and controllable than manual interaction because that much heavily relied on people, which brings more uncertainty and affects the overall structure. This is study is one of the first studies of its kind conducted in the Pakistani context. The evaluation methodology we used for this study is in line with previous studies but unlike previous applications [10], we believe that our design approach is different. We focused on a number of contextual factors while designing emotion training apps and social learning apps and we believe that due to this reasons our Apps worked quite well in this new context.

One of the limitations of this study is the number of participants who participated in this study. In future we would like to run another study with similar apps with more children. Furthermore, we would like to run between-subject design experiment in order to avoid any prior learning effects.

6 Conclusion and Future Work

In this paper, we presented the design and evaluation of two mobile learning applications, which were used as a tool to improve the socio-emotional skills of autistic children. These applications specifically incorporated a number of culture-specific design elements in their design to make them more suitable for Pakistani children. The results indicated that our applications were able to engage children in positive social interactions and their socio-emotional skills were improved after two months. Verbal and physical interaction among children was significantly higher when they used the digital app version of activities as compared to the no app version. The school management also endorsed the effectiveness of our design and they also requested copies of our software, which are currently being used at the school.

References

1. Daley, T.C.: The need for cross-cultural research on the pervasive developmental disorders. Transcult. Psychiatry **39**(4), 531–550 (2002)
2. Trembath, D., Balandin, S., Rossi, C.: Cross-cultural practice and autism. J. Intellect. Dev. Disabil. **30**(4), 240–242 (2005)
3. Habash, M.: Emotion Recognition and Social Skills in Virtual Environments for People with Autism (2014)
4. Boujarwah, F.A., Nazneen, N., Hong, H., Abowd, G.D., Arriaga, R.: Cross-Cultural Comparisons of Social Expectations of Individuals with Autism. https://imfar.confex.com/imfar/2011/webprogram/Paper9264.html. Accessed 25 Dec 2013
5. Charlop-Christy, M.H., Carpenter, M., Le, L., LeBlanc, L.A., Kellet, K.: Using the picture exchange communication system (PECS) with children with autism: Assessment of PECS acquisition, speech, social-communicative behavior, and problem behavior. J. Appl. Behav. Anal. **35**(3), 213–231 (2002)

6. Venkatesh, S., Phung, D., Duong, T., Greenhill, S., Adams, B.: TOBY: early intervention in autism through technology. In: Proceedings of the SIGCHI Conference on Human Factors in Computing Systems, pp. 3187–3196. ACM, April 2013
7. Tanaka, J.W., et al.: Using computerized games to teach face recognition skills to children with autism spectrum disorder: the let's face it! program. J. Child Psychol. Psychiatry 51(8), 944–952 (2010)
8. Konstantinidis, E.I., et al.: Using affective avatars and rich multimedia content for education of children with autism. In: Proceedings of the 2nd International Conference on PErvasive Technologies Related to Assistive Environments. ACM (2009)
9. Davis, M., Dautenhahn, K., Nehaniv, C., Powell, S.: Towards an interactive system eliciting narrative comprehension in children with autism: a longitudinal study. In: Clarkson, J., Langdon, P., Robinson, P. (eds.) Designing Accessible Technology, pp 101–114. Springer, London (2006)
10. Riedl, M., Arriaga, R.I., Boujarwah, F.A., Hong, H., Isbell, J., Heflin, J.: Graphical social scenarios: toward intervention and authoring for adolescents with high functioning autism. In: AAAI Fall Symposium: Virtual Healthcare Interaction, October 2009
11. Hourcade, J.P., Williams, S.R., Miller, E.A., Huebner, K.E., Liang, L.J.: Evaluation of tablet apps to encourage social interaction in children with autism spectrum disorders. In: Proceedings of the SIGCHI Conference on Human Factors in Computing Systems, pp. 3197–3206. ACM, April 2013

Exercises for German-Speaking Children with Dyslexia

Maria Rauschenberger[1](✉), Silke Füchsel[2], Luz Rello[3,4],
Clara Bayarri[4], and Jörg Thomaschewski[2]

[1] OFFIS – Institute for Information Technology, Oldenburg, Germany
maria.rauschenberger@offis.de
[2] University of Applied Sciences Emden/Leer Emden, Emden, Germany
sfuchsel@gmx.de, joerg.thomaschewski@hs-emden-leer.de
[3] Change Dyslexia Foundation, Madrid, Spain
luz@changedyslexia.org
[4] Cookie Cloud Barcelona, Barcelona, Spain
clara@cookie-cloud.com

Abstract. In this work-in-progress we present a computer-based method to
design German reinforcement exercises for children with dyslexia. From different schools, we collected more than 1,000 errors written by children with
dyslexia. Then, we created a classification of dyslexic errors in German and
annotated the errors with different language specific features, such as phonetic
and visual features. For the creation of the exercises we took into account the
linguistic knowledge extracted from the analyses and designed more than 2,500
word exercises in German that have been integrated in a game available for iOS.
The game and the resource of dyslexic errors are available online (https://itunes.
apple.com/us/app/dyseggxia/id534986729?mt=8) and they are, to the best of our
knowledge, the first contributions of this kind for German.

Keywords: Dyslexia · iOS · Spelling · German · Children · Gamification

1 Introduction

Dyslexia is a specific learning disability with neurological origin. It is characterized by
difficulties with accurate and/or fluent word recognition and by poor spelling and
decoding abilities. These difficulties typically result from a deficit in the phonological
components of language that is often unexpected in relation to other cognitive abilities.
Secondary consequences may include problems in reading comprehension and reduced
reading experience that can impede growth of vocabulary and background knowledge
[1]. Dyslexia is frequent: Worldwide, 10 % of the population and from 5 to 12 % of the
German students have dyslexia [2].

In Germany, only 25 % of the poor spellers achieve average spelling performance
during the period of primary school [3]. In a longitudinal study Esser et al. [4] showed
that children with diagnosed dyslexia at the age of eight achieved less school performance and a higher rate of unemployment, than the control group measured afterwards
at the age of 25. Schulte-Körne et al. [5] showed that it takes longer for children with

© IFIP International Federation for Information Processing 2015
J. Abascal et al. (Eds.): INTERACT 2015, Part I, LNCS 9296, pp. 445–452, 2015.
DOI: 10.1007/978-3-319-22701-6_33

dyslexia to achieve school grades that are comparable to the others, even if these children have a socio-economic condition above the average.

Overcoming dyslexia means a great effort for children and requires doing language exercises regularly [6]. Traditionally, these exercises are done using pen and paper. In the case of dyslexia, exercises on paper introduce an added difficulty for some students due to the fact that dysgraphia[1] is comorbid with dyslexia [7].

More recently, it was shown that computer games are a convenient medium to provide exercises in an engaging way to significantly improve the reading performance [10, 11] and the spelling performance [12] of children with dyslexia. These methods cannot simply be extended to other languages because manifestations of dyslexia depend on the different orthographies of the languages [13].

In this paper, we present a game for children with dyslexia for German. To make the training exercises, this method uses real errors found in texts written by children with dyslexia. To the best of our knowledge, this is the first time that error-based exercises targeted for people with dyslexia are done for German.

The structure of the paper is stated as follows: Sect. 2 details related work while Sect. 3 presents how we created the content design of the application. Finally, we draw conclusions and describe our future work in Sect. 4.

2   Related Work

There are several approaches of assistive technology for dyslexia [14]. Following, we only present related games to support and train specific issues of dyslexia.

Lernserver is a tool to diagnose dyslexia in German, define the level of support the child needs, and provide support exercises [15]. An evaluation with the Landesinstitut für Schule found out that 78, 2 % of the students (N = 3798) improved their writing using this tool [16]. Similarly, *Klex 11*[2] helps to practice vocabulary in German adapted to a certain school degree. These tools only use correct-based exercises in the game. Likewise, *CESAR schreiben 2.0*[3] is a strategy and educational game, which includes listening, spelling and vocabulary.

Kyle et al. [10] compared two computer-assisted reading interventions for English inspired by the Finnish *GraphoGame* [17]: *GG Rime* and *GG Phoneme*. They conducted a user study with 31 children of 6 and 7 years old. While the results show that both games may benefit decoding abilities, no significant effects were found, probably due to an insufficient number of participants or not enough training time. The closest work to us is *Dyseggxia* or *Piruletras* for iOS [18], a game composed of error-based exercises to support writing in children with dyslexia in English and Spanish. During eight weeks, the authors carried out a within-subject experiment with 48 children from 6 to 11 years old. Children who played *Dyseggxia* for four weeks in a row had

---

[1] Dysgraphia refers to a writing disorder associated with the motor skills involved in writing, handwriting and sequencing, but also orthographic coding [7].

[2] http://www.legasthenie-software.de.

[3] http://www.ces-verlag.de/deutsch/Schreiben2_0/schreiben2_produktinfo.php5.

significantly less writing errors in the tests than after playing the control condition for the same time [12]. Our game differs from previous work in being the first tool for German based on written dyslexic errors.

3 Game Content Design

In this section we explain the steps we followed to create the exercises to be integrated in the application. We decided to use errors written by people with dyslexia as the starting point because they can be used as a source of knowledge. Regarding dyslexia, the errors that people with dyslexia make are related to the types of difficulties that they have [19].

3.1 Collecting Texts from Children with Dyslexia

We collaborated with two schools to gather anonymous texts written by students with dyslexia. We collected 47 texts (homework exercises, dictations and school essays) written by students from 8 to 17 years old. A total of 32 texts came from children who have been diagnosed with dyslexia. Teachers collected the remaining texts from children with a high spelling error rate. The children attended primary school, comprehensive school *(Gesamtschule)*, high school *(Gymnasium)* or a special school *(Förderschule)*.

3.2 Classification of German Dyslexic Errors

We analyzed the errors and defined an error classification for German. Except from the categorie capital letter, the rest of the error types are consistent Pedler's classification of dyslexic errors [21][4]:

- **Substitution:** change one letter by another, *grümeln (krümeln, 'crumble')*.
- **Insertion:** insert one letter, *muttig (mutig, 'bravely')*.
- **Omission:** omit one letter, *zusamen (zusammen, 'together')*.
- **Transposition:** reversing two letters, *Porblem (Problem, 'problem')*.
- **Multi-errors:** more than one letter different, *Stag (stark, 'strong')*.
- **Word boundary errors:** They are run-ons and split words. A run-on is the result of omitting a space, such as *nichtärgern (nicht ärgern, 'don't tease')*. A split word occurs when a space is inserted in the middle of a word, such as *Vogel futter (Vogelfutter, 'bird food')*.
- **Capital letter:** in German nouns are written with capital letters, while other kinds of words like verbs, adjectives or articles are not. This leads very often to spelling errors frequently based on the lack of attention [22]. For example *geschichten (Geschichten, 'stories')* or *Glücklich (glücklich, 'happy')*.

---

[4] Examples with errors are preceded by an asterisk '*'. We use the standard linguistic conventions: '<>' for graphemes, '/ /' for phonemes and '[ ]' for phones.

3.3 Annotation of Dyslexic Errors

We annotated each of the word-error pairs with linguistic features [23]. Each of the word-error pairs was enriched with specific phonological and visual features derived from the analysis of the errors and some examples:

- **Visual information:** for each of the target and the error graphemes we annotate the letters involved in the error with the following visual information, considering handwritten text. As a guideline we chose the *Lateinische Ausgangsschrift* [24] because it is commonly used in schools where the texts were collected. The tags use for visual information are: (a) the presence of mirror letters (<d> and <b> or <m> and <w>), (b) rotation letters (<d> and <p>.) or fuzzy letters, that is, similar visual letters but not due to rotate or mirror, such as <s> and <z>.
- **Phonetic information:** Each of the error words was tagged using a classification inspired by the error analysis of the *DRT* [20]. This classification is based on traditional articulatory phonetic features [25] and is divided into the following categories: (a) sound distinction, (b) sound sequence, (c) combination of consonants, words with <v>, (d) umlaut, (e) double consonant/false double consonant, (f) lengthening, (g) words with <s/B>, and (h) derivation. For instance, in (h) derivation, related words are often written the same way or similar but pronounced different. To write these words in the right way, one possibility is to have a look at the plural form so that the right writing can be derivate, e.g. *Walt (Wald [valt]; Wälder [vɛldɒ], 'forest')*. We took these features into account to design the exercises (see next Section).

3.4 Exercise Design

First, we analyzed statistically the features of the errors and created a set of linguistic patterns for designing the exercises. Then, we manually created 2,500 exercises for German. The types of exercises were defined according the kind of errors found in our resource. These are:

- **Insertion:** A missing letter is shown and the child need to insert a letter from a set of possibilities displayed on the screen, e.g. **Geburstag, (Geburtstag, 'birthday')*.
- **Omission:** The child is given a word with an extra letter and is asked to identify and remove it, e.g. **Abennd, (Abend, 'evening')* (Fig. 1, right).
- **Substitution:** A word with a wrong letter is displayed and the user is asked to identify and substitute the wrong letter by another letter from a set of possibilities displayed on the screen, e.g. **Muntag, (Montag, 'monday')* (Fig. 1, left).
- **Separation:** A set of words, normally composed of a lexical word and a small word or/and functional word are displayed on screen without spaces. Lexical words (e.g. *Hund, 'dog'*) form the basic elements of a language's lexicon. They have a lexical meaning which is less ambiguous than the grammatical meanings expressed by functional words e.g. *zu, bei ('at, by')*. The user is asked to separate the character chain into different words, e.g. **ausVersehen, (aus Versehen, 'by mistake')*.

- **Transposition:** The child needs to rearrange the letters or the syllables of a word, e.g. *Zugbürcke, (Zugbrücke, 'drawbridge').*

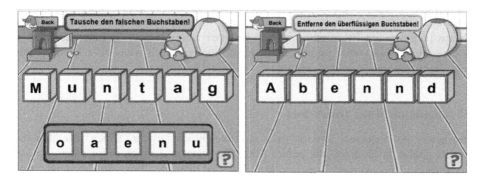

Fig. 1. Exercises of Substitution (left) and Omission (right).

The amounts of types of exercises per class are defined according the real errors percentages found in our error list. For instance, omission errors were the more frequent type in dyslexic texts (28.14 %), therefore were created more **Insertion** exercises to target this kind of error. The other types of errors were substitution (21.03 %), capital letter (10.61 %) and no capital letter (7.21 %) for **Substitution** exercises, addition (21.03 %) for **Omission** exercises, run-on (0.29 %) and split in (2.73 %) errors for the **Separation** exercises, and transposition (0.88 %) for the **Transposition** exercises. We used the multi-errors (18.31 %) for higher levels.

3.5 Target Word Selection

To assure that the exercises are useful for the children, we used (1) only valid words in German language, (2) a set of the most frequent words of German,[5] (3) words used in books in school in Germany,[6] (4) and words from our error list. The final list of words is the intersection of these criteria.

For selecting the words we took into consideration specific difficulties of dyslexia. German words can be very long e.g. *Straßenbahnhaltestelle ('tram stop').* Since people with dyslexia have difficulties with very long words [26] we included long words but not longer than 20 letters. For the **Separation** we chose functional words because of the same reason, people with dyslexia tend to have more errors with small and functional words [27].

---

[5] http://www.lsa.umich.edu/german/hmr/Vokabeln/frequent_words.html.

[6] http://bildungsserver.berlin-brandenburg.de/fileadmin/bbb/unterricht/faecher/sprachen/deutsch/
Grundschule/2011_11_25_GWS_1_WEB.pdf.

3.6   Modification of the Target Words

For the exercises that are not derived directly from the incorrect words in the corpora, we apply the linguistic patterns extracted from the errors to the most frequent words or schoolbook words. For instance, when the sound /a:/ is represented by the letters <ah> *(Wahl, 'election'),* <a> *(Tal, 'valley')* or <aa> *(Haare, 'hair'),* these three groups of letters are frequently mistaken between themselves or by other letters such as <e>. By applying these patterns to the most frequent words we cover relevant words that might not appear in our corpora.

3.7   Selection of the Distractors

Distractors are incorrect options in a multiple-choice answer, which resemble the correct option to 'distract' the player [28]. We selected distractors for each exercise word taking into account linguistic features. For instance, the most frequent errors involve letters which the one-to-one correspondence between graphemes and phones is not maintained, such as in <sch> pronounced as only on phone [ʃ]. Another example is similar letters representing similar sounds, such as the occlusive consonants [t, d, b, p, g]. We used as distractors the letters that tend to induce more errors.

3.8   Difficulty Levels

The game has five difficulty levels: *Initial, Easy, Medium, Hard*, and *Expert*. The levels of the exercises were designed considering the difficulties of people with dyslexia. They have more difficulties with less frequent and longer words [26, 29] and words with complex morphology [27]. Hence, in higher difficulty levels, the target word is less frequent, longer and has a more complex morphology. For instance, only words in *Hard* and *Expert* levels have prefixes and suffixes.

People with dyslexia also struggle with phonetically and orthographically similar words [30]. Phonetically similar words are presented in all levels; orthographically similar words are used in all levels except from *Initial* level.

3.9   Implementation

The application was done in Objective-C by using the Model-View-Controller pattern and a high level abstraction to make it easily portable from iOS to Android and later to any other platform if needed. Since text presentation has a significant effect on reading performance of dyslexic readers, the interface of the game implements the guidelines that – according to the latest findings in accessibility research [8, 9].

4 Conclusions and Future Work

In this paper we have presented a method for creating exercises in German to support the spelling of children with dyslexia. The exercises were created on the basis of the linguistic analyses of errors written by children with dyslexia (from 8 to 17 years old) and can easily be transferred to other languages, because it relies on little language-dependent resources. The tool with the German exercises integrated will be soon available in the App Store.[7] Also, the resource with the German errors and all the annotations is freely available.

The creation of this tool is the first step of a work-in-progress. Our next and final step for future work is to conduct a longitudinal evaluation to measure the efficiency of the tool in a German school with children with diagnosed dyslexia. We also plan to create more types of exercises, adapt the levels, automatically create exercises and improve the application by tailoring the exercises on the basis of the child's performance.

References

1. Lyon, G.R., Shaywitz, S.E., Shaywitz, B.A.: A definition of dyslexia. Ann. Dyslexia 53(1), 1–14 (2003)
2. Gesundheitsforschung – BMBF - Genetische Ursache für Legasthenie entdeckt. http://www.gesundheitsforschung-bmbf.de/de/1271.php
3. Remschmidt, H., von Aster, S.: Kinder- und Jugendpsychiatrie: Eine praktische Einführung: 177 Tabellen. Thieme, Stuttgart [u.a.], 4., neu bearb. und erw. aufl edition (2005)
4. Esser, G., Wyschkon, A., Schmidt, M.: Was wird aus achtjährigen mit einer Lese- und Rechtschreibstörung? Ergebnisse im alter von 25 Jahren. Zeitschrift für Klinische Psychologie und Psychotherapie 4, 235–242 (2002)
5. Schulte-Körne, G., Deimel, W., Jungermann, M., Remschmidt, H.: Nachuntersuchung einer Stichprobe von Lese-Rechtschreibgestörten Kindern im Erwachsenenalter. Zeitschrift für Kinder und Jugendpsychiatrie und Psychotherapie 31(4), 267–276 (2003)
6. Hornsby, B.: Overcoming dyslexia. Martin Dunitz, London (1986)
7. Nicolson, R.I., Fawcett, A.J.: Dyslexia, dysgraphia, procedural learning and the cerebellum. Cortex 47(1), 117–127 (2011)
8. Gregor, P., Newell, A.F.: An empirical investigation of ways in which some of the problems encountered by some dyslexics may be alleviated using computer techniques. In: Proceedings of ASSETS 2000, pp. 85–91. ACM Press, New York (2000)
9. Rello, L., Baeza-Yates, R.: Good fonts for dyslexia. In: Proceedings of ASSETS 2013, Bellevue, Washington, USA, October 2013
10. Kyle, F., Kujala, J., Richardson, U., Lyytinen, H., Goswami, U.: Assessing the effectiveness of two theoretically motivated computer-assisted reading interventions in the United Kingdom: Gg rime and gg phoneme. Read. Res. Q. 48(1), 61–76 (2013)

---

[7] https://itunes.apple.com/us/app/dyseggxia/id534986729?mt=8.

11. Lyytinen, H., Ronimus, M., Alanko, A., Poikkeus, A.-M., Taanila, M.: Early identification of dyslexia and the use of computer game-based practice to support reading acquisition. Nordic Psychol. **59**(2), 109 (2007)

12. Rello, L., Bayarri, C., Otal, Y., Pielot, P.: A computer-based method to improve the spelling of children with dyslexia using errors. In: Proceedings of ASSETS 2014, Rochester, USA, October 2014

13. Goulandris, N. (ed.): Dyslexia in Different Languages: Cross-Linguistic Comparisons. Whurr Publishers, London (2003)

14. Petrie, H.L., Weber, G., Fisher, W.: Personalization, interaction, and navigation in rich multimedia documents for print-disabled users. IBM Syst. J. **44**(3), 629–635 (2005)

15. Höinghaus, A., Schönweiss, F.: Ampelsignale zeigen Förderbedarf – bundesweite Lisa-Bildungskampagne, 28 July 2010

16. Flug, L.: Projekt-Evaluation Bremen: Erprobungsphase des Lernservers an bremischen schulen, 11.2007

17. Lyytinen, H., Erskine, J., Kujala, J., Ojanen, E., Richardson, U.: In search of a science-based application: a learning tool for reading acquisition. Scand. J. Psychol. **50**(6), 668–675 (2009)

18. Rello, L., Bayarri, C., Gorriz, A.: What is wrong with this word? Dyseggxia: a game for children with dyslexia. In: Proceedings of the 14th International ACM SIGACCESS Conference on Computers and Accessibility. ACM (2012)

19. Sterling, C., Farmer, M., Riddick, B., Morgan, S., Matthews, C.: Adult dyslexic writing. Dyslexia **4**(1), 1–15 (1998)

20. Grund, M., Naumann, C.L., Haug, G.: Diagnostischer Rechtschreibtest für 5. Klassen: DRT 5; Manual. Deutsche Schultests. Beltz Test, Göttingen, 2., aktual. aufl. in neuer Rechtschreibung Edition (2004)

21. Pedler, J.: Computer Correction of Real-word Spelling Errors in Dyslexic Text. Ph.D. thesis, Birkbeck College, London University (2007)

22. Stang, C.: Duden, Deutsche Rechtschreibung. Praxis kompakt. Dudenverl, Mannheim and Leipzig and Wien and Zürich (2010)

23. Rello, L., Baeza-Yates, R., Llisterri, J.: DysList: an annotated resource of dyslexic errors. In: LREC 2014: The 9th International Conference on Language Resources and Evaluation. Reykjavik, Iceland, pp. 26–31, May 2014

24. Topsch, W.: Grundkompetenz Schriftspracherwerb: Methoden und handlungsorientierte Praxisanregungen, Volume Bd. 5 of Beltz Pädagogik. Beltz, Weinheim and Basel, 2., überarb. und erw. aufl edition (2005)

25. International Phonetic Association: Handbook of the International Phonetic Association: A Guide to the Use of the International Phonetic Alphabet. Cambridge University Press, Cambridge (1999)

26. Rello, L., Baeza-Yates, R., Dempere-Marco, L., Saggion, H.: Frequent words improve readability and short words improve understandability for people with dyslexia. In: Kotzé, P., Marsden, G., Lindgaard, G., Wesson, J., Winckler, M., (eds.) INTERACT 2013, Part IV. LNCS, vol. 8120, pp. 203–219. Springer, Heidelberg (2013)

27. Patterson, K., Marshall, J.C., Coltheart, M.: Surface Dyslexia: Neuropsychological and Cognitive Studies of Phonological Reading. Lawrence Erlbaum Associates, London (1985)

28. Mitkov, R., Ha, L.A., Varga, A., Rello, L.: Semantic similarity of distractors in multiple-choice tests: extrinsic evaluation. In: Proceedings of EACL Workshop GeMS 2009, pp. 49–56 (2009)

29. Coltheart, M.: Phonological dyslexia: past and future issues. Cogn. Neuropsychol. **13**(6), 749–762 (1996)

30. Ellis, A.W.: Reading, Writing and Dyslexia. Erlbaum, London (1984)

Serious Games for Cognitive Training in Ambient Assisted Living Environments – A Technology Acceptance Perspective

Jan Wittland, Philipp Brauner$^{(\boxtimes)}$, and Martina Ziefle

Human-Computer Interaction Center (HCIC) Chair of Communication Science,
RWTH Aachen University, Campus-Boulevard 57, 52074 Aachen, Germany
{wittland,brauner,ziefle}@comm.rwth-aachen.de

Abstract. Two technology trends address the rising costs of healthcare systems in aging societies: Serious Games for Healthcare and Ambient Assisted Living Environments. Surprisingly, these concepts are rarely combined and the users' perception and use of Serious Games in Ambient Assisted Living environments is insufficiently understood. We present the evaluation of a serious game for stimulating cognitive abilities for elderly with regard to technology acceptance (based on the UTAUT2 model), performance and preference for an interaction device (tablet, table, wall). The results suggest that acceptance of serious games is independent of gender, technical expertise, gaming habits, and only weakly influenced by age. Determinants for acceptance are perceived fun and the feeling that the users can make playing the game a habit. Performance within the game is explained by age and previous gaming experience. All investigated interaction devices were rated as useful and easy to learn, although the wall-sized display had lower approval levels. The article concludes with guidelines for successfully introducing serious games for healthcare to residents in ambient assisted living environments.

Keywords: Serious games for healthcare · Ubiquitous computing · Ambient assisted living · Technology acceptance · Design for elderly

1 Introduction

Increased life expectancy and declining birth rates in many western societies lead to a demographic change that has a tremendous impact on the healthcare system. The share of people aged 65 years and older is projected to rise from 17 % in 2008 to 30 % in the year 2060 [1]. This influences the financing of the healthcare systems, as the number of jobholders who cover dependent elderly persons is declining from 3.2:1 to 1.85:1 within the next 40 years. Additionally, the number of people 80 + is expected to nearly triple within the same period. As chronic illnesses and diseases increases with age [2] the declining number of jobholders need to cover even higher expense for geriatric care. In contrast, the per capita expenses in the healthcare system is declining in OECD countries [3] and therefore less money is available for caregiving and offering therapy for older, handicapped or chronically ill persons.

© IFIP International Federation for Information Processing 2015
J. Abascal et al. (Eds.): INTERACT 2015, Part I, LNCS 9296, pp. 453–471, 2015.
DOI: 10.1007/978-3-319-22701-6_34

Two solutions address the rising costs of the healthcare systems: Ambient Assisted Living (AAL) environments and Serious Games for Healthcare (SG4HC). The former aim at enhancing the quality of life of elderly or handicapped people through supportive technology in the living environment, while the latter harnesses the ludic drive to make physical and cognitive exercises for training and rehabilitation fun and desirable. Serious games can easily be offered in AAL environments. Yet, these games can only unfold positive effects on mental or physical health and well being, if they are used frequently and periodically. This adherence depends on a number of system factors (e.g., feedback accuracy, latency, usability, ...), as well as personality factors (e.g., age, gender, expertise, trust, ...) that are not sufficiently understood. To address this void, this work evaluates a prototypic serious game for ambient assisted living environments that aims at improving cognitive functioning. This summative user study investigates the interrelationship of user diversity and system design on performance, perceived usability and acceptance of serious games for healthcare.

2   Related Work

This section gives an overview about current approaches for Ambient Assisted Living, Serious Games for Healthcare, and Technology Acceptance research.

2.1   Ubiquitous Computing and Ambient Assisted Living

In 1991 Marc Weiser predicted a future in which computers shrink in size and grow in number, capacity, and capability. Weiser envisioned "smart environments" in which numerous computers are seamlessly integrated into physical environments and eventually converge with everyday objects [4]. He envisioned that computers will work unnoticeable and enhance the quality of work and life and that using them will be "as refreshing as taking a walk in the woods".

Ambient Assisted Living (AAL) takes up the idea of ubiquitous and smart environments to support elderly, handicapped or chronically ill people: Smart information and communication technology integrated in personal home environments is designed to support an independent and self-determined life style [5–7]. AAL can support people in various ways: First, they can offer emergency assistance by preventing or detecting acute situations (e.g., strokes, heart attacks, when a persons falls, ...). Second, they can enhance the autonomy of a person by supporting cleaning, medication or even shopping, or by offering trainings and rehabilitation measures. Third, they can increase comfort through home automation or by infotainment offerings.

Although AAL is increasingly recognized from politics and research institutions as a humane and viable solution to meet the challenges caused by the demographic change [8], many fundamental ethical, social and legal questions have not yet been sufficiently answered: The social implications of these technologies at home and the user's requirements regarding privacy and trust are insufficiently understood issues [9, 10]. Nevertheless, understanding the user's thoughts, concerns, and requirements is a significant research domain and critical for the success of AAL [11, 12].

To understand how people would live in and use these technology-enhanced supportive environments and to capture their requirements, prototypic living labs are constructed and innovative technologies and services are evaluated. The present study was carried out in RWTH Aachen University's *eHealth Lab* [13]. The specifications of the lab are given in the description of the experiment.

2.2 Serious Games

Serious Games are not primarily focused on entertainment, but on other goals such as to train or educate [14]. Michael and Chen define a "serious game is a game in which education (in its various forms) is the primary goal, rather than entertainment" [15]. The effectiveness of serious games build upon the Premack principle [16]: The occurrence of an unlikely activity will increase if coupled with a likely activity. Hence, unlikely and inconvenient activities, such as regular physical or cognitive training, can be linked with likely and pleasant activities such as playing games. Playing games is part of the human nature and many people play on a regular basis [17], hence they are suitable to link with exercising or training which are often undesired activities.

In the healthcare domain best-known examples of serious games are Exergames (exercise games) that use the users' body movements as input. Exergames are already successfully used in rehabilitation [18] or to promote physical fitness [19, 20].

Yet, the field of cognitive training is still insufficiently explored. Although the suitability, effectiveness and necessity of game-mediated cognitive training is often cited from the medical point of view [21, 22] and commercial games for cognitive training are readily available at video game stores (e.g. *Brain Boost: Beta Wave* for Nintendo DS, *Body and Brain Connection* for Microsoft Xbox 360 or *Smart As...* for Sony PlayStation Vita), little is known about how these games can be successfully integrated in AAL environments and how they should be designed to be accepted and used by a diverse population of users.

2.3 Technology Acceptance Research

The goal of technology acceptance research is to predict if users will adopt and adhere to a technology – such as eHealth technology or Serious Games for Healthcare – and to identify the factors that influence this process. It has its roots in the Ajzen and Fishbein's *Theory of Reasons Action (TRA)* [23] and *Theory of Planned Behavior (TPB)* [24]. These theories state that an individual's behavior is based on his or her intention to perform the behavior. This *behavioral intention* is formed by the individual's attitudes, subjective beliefs, and (in TPB) self-efficacy towards the behavior. Based on these models from behavioral psychology, Davis developed the well-known *Technology Acceptance Model (TAM)* that predicts the usage intention and later use of software applications [25]. In TAM *perceived usefulness*, *perceived ease of use*, and the *attitude towards using* the software determines the intention to use the software. As in TRA and TPB, the intention to use the software is closely related to the later actual use. Hence, factors contributing to usage intention also explain later use.

Davis' Technology Acceptance Model – originally designed to predict software usage in professional environments – continuously evolved to describe software and technology adoption processes in different contexts (e.g., for consumer electronics or voluntary software use) or with a refined set of explaining variables. A prominent example that this study builds on is the *Unified Theory of Acceptance and Use of Technology 2 (UTAUT2)* by Venkatesh et al. [26]. UTAUT2 is designed to predict the adoption of technologies outside work environments, i.e., in situations where the use is voluntary and not driven by work requirements. In UTAUT2 seven factors predict the (voluntary) adoption of a technology: *Performance expectancy* models the user's perceived benefit from using the technology through increased performance or richer possibilities. *Effort expectancy* addresses a persons' perceived effort in learning how to use the technology. *Facilitating conditions* captures the individual's perception of whether he or she is able to acquire help by others, if obstacles hinder using the technology. *Social influence* meters the influence of family, friends and colleagues on the adoption process, e.g. if using the technology is encouraged or admired by others. *Hedonic motivation* refers to the fun and pleasure the individual perceives while using the technology. *Price-value* models the tradeoff between the individual's financial investment in the technology and the perceived benefit from using it. *Habit* captures the user's perception whether he or she can make using the technology a routine. Overall, the UTAUT2 model can predict about 75 % of the variance of behavioral intention and over 50 % of variance of later use of a technology. UTAUT2 is therefore a suitable model to predict the adoption of technologies where the use is voluntary and not required by superiors or – in the case of medical technology – physicians.

2.4   Combination of These Domains

The combination of the three domains Serious Games for Healthcare, Ambient Assisted Living, and Technology Acceptance Research is mainly unexplored and a rich and challenging research domain.

A serious exercise game for enhancing the physical fitness and independence of elderly residents in AAL environments was analyzed in [27]. Central findings of the study with 64 participants are that the intention to use the game is explained only by gaming frequency, meaning that people who like to play games have a higher intention to use exercise games to improve their fitness. Usage intention was independent of age, gender, or need for achievement, although these were the best predictors for performance within the game. Regarding the UTAUT2 model, all explaining variables were positively related to the intention to use exercise games. Strongest predictors for an adoption were a person's feeling of making exercising a habit and social inclusion and social encouragement.

It is unclear if these findings from an exercise game are transferable to other game domains. Hence, a game that addresses the cognitive functioning of elderly (retention and planning capabilities) will be evaluated using the same research methodology. The next section outlines the game design, followed by the experimental setup.

3 Game Design and Development

This section outlines the needs of elderly regarding usability and game design, the game design process, and the actual game.

3.1 Game Design Considerations

Facing the growing aging population, one of the major challenges for healthcare systems in the 21st century is to master the demands of an aging society [28, 29]. Healthcare-related technologies become increasingly important. Supporting older adults in keeping an independent life style at home is achievable only by technology that fit into the individual's living spaces, that respects the specific needs and demands of people and their willingness to use and integrate devices into their personal spaces and their personal lives [30]. Currently, most technical interfaces are designed neglecting the needs and abilities of aged users. Aging is connected to a number of changes in sensory, physical, psychomotor and cognitive functioning over the life span [31]. Beyond visibility problems and a decreasing psychomotor ability, one major characteristic of aging is the deceleration of executive functions, i.e., working memory, information processing, and planning of complex tasks [32–34]. Planning competence comprises many cognitive sub skills that have to be executed in parallel and/or consecutively. For example, for preparing meals, users have to memorize the recipe, know which food products are necessary, anticipate the order of food products to be used one after another, and anticipate potential problems and the way they could be solved. Especially in all-day situations, the decreasing planning ability is a serious issue that could be supported in computer-assisted trainings. On the other hand, older users have greater difficulties in handling technical devices [35–37] and face difficulties in learning and using new computer applications. Contrary to current stereotypes, according to which older users are unable or unwilling to learn new technologies, older users are interested in becoming acquainted with novel technology. However, older users do have higher demands on usable interface designs [38].

To build a game that is accepted and used by older adults, the game environment must be designed in line with the wants and needs of this target group. De Schutter has identified three elemental aspects that games must provide to address their interests and preferences [39]: *Connectivity*, *cultivation*, and *contribution*. Connectivity describes that people prefer games in which they can connect with others, friends and family. Hence, games should support multiplayer modes or high-scores. Older adults not only want to be consumers of video games, but also want to cultivate themselves. Despite their age, they are still interested in seeing new places, learning, and gaining knowledge. Contribution is the desire of many people to contribute their knowledge to others. This may be new game content or shared knowledge or personal experiences. Possible game concepts identified by De Schutter include a chef cook game, but also games such as a fashion designer, a travel game, or guessing games.

3.2   The Game Concept

We identified cooking as a promising game scenario because nutrition is an important concern of everyday life and cooking requires certain cognitive skills to produce an enjoyable outcome. In particular it requires good retention capabilities to remember the preparation steps already done and to be done next. In addition a vital executive function in form of planning skills is essential to be able to organize the cooking process. This concept becomes manifest in the name of the game: "Cook It Right".

In the game players select recipes from a list that he or she wants to reproduce in a virtual kitchen. Before the preparation of meal starts, the player needs to memorize the instructions, as these will not be available later on. The user then starts to produce the outcome on a virtual kitchen worktop, where all the ingredients and required tools are presented. The visual representation of the playing area changes according to the users interactions, which he or she can choose from popups after selecting an ingredient or kitchenware (e.g. after a bread is selected a popup appears that offers to put butter on the bread). Finally, if the user decides that the meal is completed and served on a virtual dish, a result view is shown which contains a rating depending on the time required for the preparation.

Cook It Right fulfills De Schutters three criteria of games for older adults: *Connectivity* is realized in a multiplayer scenario in which two players prepare the meal together. *Cultivation* is accomplished as new recipes can be learned within the interactive game. *Contribution* is satisfied with a recipe designer, where users can provide and design their own favorite recipes that then get played by other users.

3.3   Development Process and Interaction Design

The design and development of the game strictly followed a user-centered and participatory design approach with several iterations of implementation and evaluation phases [40]. The development started with storyboards (see Fig. 1, left) and paper prototypes (see Fig. 1, center) to generate basic ideas of the user interface, its elements and interactions [41]. During these phases fundamental design changes along with a number of minor corrections were made based on the feedback of usability experts and elderly users. In the game the user must combine several ingredients (e.g., water, salt, and flour) and use tools (e.g., blender) to prepare meals or parts of a meal (e.g., pastry). The user selects visible ingredients and tools on the display surface using touch interaction and a context-sensitive menu offers possible actions (e.g., put flour into bowl). For each preparation step a specific time is allocated and multiple parallel tasks had to be synchronized (e.g., dough had to stay in the oven for 2 min, then tomato sauce must be ready; comparable to [33]). The users disliked this timed concept, found it too stressful, and too little game like. Following user's suggestions, it was changed to be purely turn based and users can interact with the game in their own pace. After the preparation of a meal is finished, a feedback score is presented based on completion time and correctness.

Fig. 1. Stages of the iterative development of *Cook It Right*: Storyboard of the basic game interactions (left), interactive paper prototype (center), game's functional prototype (right)

The overall positive feedback supported the decision to continue the development as a high fidelity and functional software prototype. First, the logic for handling recipes and an extendable recipe pool was developed. We analyzed several recipes and identified a tree-like structure with three entities: *Ingredients*, *tools* and *containers*. In every possible interaction (which we name transitions since a state traversal occurs) a container is involved (e.g., a bowl or a pan). In each step a tool or ingredient is combined with a container. There can be several possible interactions in a certain state for a container: For example, to produce pastry one has to blend water with flour in a bowl and there are two possible paths: First, water can be put into the bowl, then flour is added and the ingredients are blended. Second, flour can be added first, then water is added and both ingredients are blended. Also, some transitions are idempotent, i.e. actions can be executed repeatedly without changing the visual outcome. For example, salt can be added repeatedly without changing the outcome of the dish (contrary to reality were a soup can actually be over salted). These interactions were modeled with an attributed XML structure. The inner vertices of this tree represent containers in a certain state. The leafs represent ingredients or tools, which can be combined with its container. Within the application, this tree structure is used to check possible transitions and to construct the popup menus for presenting possible actions for combining the ingredients. It is also used for checking for completeness and for calculating a final score as performance feedback, once the user has finished cooking by pressing the button "Serve Dish".

The visual design of this iteration is related to the early paper prototype of the game, as hand-drawn images from the prototyping sessions we used as sprites in the game (see Fig. 1, right).

3.4   The Game's Context: AAL Living Environment

The game is developed as one of several applications in our university's Ambient Assisted Living lab [13]. It resembles a prototypic living room of 25 m^2 with two comfortable couches, a coffee table, bookshelves, and wall pictures. However, the lab is designed for chronically ill or frail elderly people and is equipped with various sensor technology for measuring the residents vital parameters (e.g., blood pressure, temperature, coagulation, and weight) and its attentive sensory floor is able to detect falls.

The living room provides various forms of support to the resident's life. For example, a large display wall can be used as a video link to communicate with friends, relatives, or medical staff, the lights and heating can be controlled via several different devices and from different positions within the room, and music, personal pictures, and videos are easily available.[1]

People can interact with the room through various different devices, ranging from a Kinect-based gesture detection system, through a touch surface embedded in the couch. This allows us as researchers to explore novel interaction devices and interaction techniques together with prospective users in a realistic living context. Within this study, the game *Cook it Right* was delivered and evaluated on three different touch-based interaction devices: A large multitouch wall (4.8 × 2.4 m^2, see Fig. 2, left) realized using rear projection on the surface elements, a multitouch display embedded in a off-the-shelf coffee table from a Swedish furniture store (47.5 × 29.9 cm^2, see Fig. 2, right), and on a multitouch tablet device (18 × 28 cm^2). The users' perception of these input devices was measured within the evaluation of the game, though the devices differed in size, resolution, and latency. Still, this evaluation will reveal whether there are utterly unsuitable devices for interacting with the game or whether the game is usable regardless of the interaction media.

Fig. 2. Cook It Right on the wall-sized multitouch display (left) and on the table (right).

4   Evaluation

The following study explores how older adults interact with serious games in ambient assisted home environments, taking the presented game "Cook It Right" as an example. To understand the factors that contribute to game performance and to acceptance (i.e., intention to use the game and later adherence) we carried out a controlled experiment with prototypic elderly users, a younger control group and different interaction devices. The voluntary participants were all in full possession of their cognitive and motor skills, and had normal or corrected-to-normal vision. As none of the participants was

---

[1] An in-depth presentation of the room is available online: http://vimeo.com/31951636.

living in a (technology) assisted living environment, they were introduced to the vision of ambient assisted living and the potential of a serious game for cognitive training. The investigated measures were captured using questionnaires before and after the game intervention. Log files captured all user interactions with the game. The experiment took about 45 to 60 min. for each participant.

The following research questions guided this study: First, what are the key determinants that explain acceptance of the game? Second, what are the key determinants that explain performance within the game? Third, which interaction device is most suitable to support older adults in terms of performance and acceptance?

4.1   Independent Variables

We controlled and manipulated the independent variables *age*, *gender* and *device type* for the sample. It consisted of 50 % male and 50 % female and 50 % younger and 50 % older users. *Device type* is a between- subjects variable and the participants interacted with one of three devices *tablet*, *table*, *wall* available in the AAL environment.

Level complexity: The game's complexity increases with each level. Participants started with the easiest level (*scrambled egg*) that requires at least 6 interaction steps (Fig. 3, left, illustrates the recipe tree). This level was played as a guided tutorial: The subjects learnt the interaction principles and optional help was provided by the investigator. The second recipe (*pancake*) is of medium complexity and requires at least 14 steps (see Fig. 3, center). The last recipe (*steak and roast potatoes*) has the highest complexity, though it also requires 14 steps (see Fig. 3, right). This illustrates that complexity is more than the number of elements, as the increased complexity is a result of the wider recipe tree (see [42]).

4.2   Control Variables

The control or explanatory variables cover individual factors that were measured during the study, but not specifically used for constructing the sample.

Gaming frequency: We measured the subjects' inclination towards playing games as the playing frequency across a wide set of different games and activities (from card games to outdoor games).

Technology expertise: The users' technology expertise is captured as usage frequency and perceived ease of use across different electronic devices and the self-efficacy in interacting with technology using a standardized scale by Beier [43].

Health-related behavior: Participant's health related behavior is captured by the health sub-scale of the Domain Specific Risk-Taking scale (DOSPERT [44]).

Cooking self-efficacy: To understand the relationship between domain knowledge and rating of or performance in the cooking-related game, we measured the users' perceived ease of cooking, cooking frequency and cooking self-efficacy. These cooking scales are congruent with the technology scales.

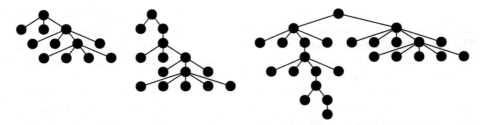

Fig. 3. Illustrations of the recipe trees for simple (left), medium (center), and hard (right) levels.

4.3 Dependent Variables

The dependent variables in this experiment fall into three categories: First, the variables capturing the acceptance of the used input devices. Second, variables that measure the overall acceptance of the game. Third, variable that measures the performance and completion of each level.

To understand which input devices are suited best for interacting with this serious game, the participants furthermore rated their interaction devices with regard to (perceived) *suitability*, *input precision*, and *learnability*.

As dependent variables, the seven dimensions from the UTAUT2 [45] model were measured: *Performance Expectancy, Effort Expectancy, Facilitating Conditions, Habit, Social Influence, Price Value,* and *Hedonic* were measured through 3 items each on 6 point Likert scales (see below). *Behavioral Intention* captures the users' intention to use the technology in the future was also assessed by 3 items. According to UTAUT2 and related models, there is a strong relationship between *Behavioral intention* and the later *use* of the technology (that cannot be captured at this development stage).

Furthermore, *efficiency* (time on task for each level in *s*) and *effectivity* (number of executed steps, and completed/not completed) is measured for each level.

We used a similar design to evaluate an exercise game within the AAL lab. A more verbose description of the lab, the measured variables and details about the reliability measures of the scales can be found in [27].

4.4 Statistical Methods

All subjective measures were measured on 6-point Likert scales and then analyzed with statistical methods, such as Person's χ^2, uni- and multivariate analyses of variance (ANOVA/MANOVA) and multiple linear regression analysis. Type I error rate (significance level) is set to $\alpha = .05$. Spearman's ρ is used for reporting bivariate correlations, Pillai's V is reported for the omnibus effect of the MANOVAs. For multiple linear regressions the step-wise method was used and models with high variance inflation (VIF $\gg$ 1) were excluded. Parametrical tests are robust against small violations of assumptions. Hence, non-parametrical tests were used to validate the findings, but results from the parametrical tests are reported. Further, a Kolmogorov-Smirnov test confirmed that both key variables *Performance* and *Behavioral Intention* are normally distributed ($Z = .693, p > .723; Z = .837, p > .485$) and that using parametrical methods is admissible.

4.5   Description of the Sample

64 people have participated in the study (34 male, 30 female) and the age ranged from 16 to 84 years (avg. 41.6 years, SD 18.4). To investigate age-related effects using factorial methods, the sample was split into a *young* (M = 25.6, SD = 4.3) and *old* (M = 56.7, SD = 12.9) group at the median age. These groups were not associated with gender ($\chi^2(1, N = 64) = .071$, p = .790 > .05, ns.).

   Age has a strong negative influence on gaming frequency ($\rho(64 - 2) = -.731$, p < .01, sig.) and older participants play less than younger participants. Furthermore, older participants report a healthier lifestyle than younger participants ($\rho(64 - 2) = -.323$, p < .01). As in previous studies, age has strong negative influence on perceived ease of using technology, usage frequency and self-efficacy in interacting with technology ($\rho(64 - 2) = -.399$, p < .01). Perceived ease of cooking, cooking frequency and cooking self-efficacy is independent of age ($\rho(64 - 2) = .108$, p = .394 > .05).

   Gender is only marginally related to gaming frequency ($\rho(64 - 2) = -.234$, p = .063 > .05) with men being more inclined to games than women. Within this sample, gender is unrelated to the attitude towards health ($\rho(64 - 2) = .079$, p = .535 > .05). Also in line with previous findings, gender influences a person's self-efficacy in interacting with technology ($\rho(64 - 2) = -.376$, p < .01). Men have higher self-efficacy in interacting with technology than women. Interestingly, gender influences perceived ease of cooking, cooking frequency and cooking self-efficacy ($\rho(64 - 2) = .293$, p = .019 < .05) with women being more inclined to cooking than men.

   Surprisingly, participant's gaming frequency and health related behavior are connected ($\rho(63 - 2) = .281$, p = .026 < .05), with gamers being less anxious about their health than non-gamers.

5   Results

The results section is structured as follows: First, the factors contributing to performance within the game are presented. Second, the determinants for acceptance and presumed later use of the serious game are shown. Finally, the comparison of the three different input devices is presented.

5.1   Determinants for Performance

Only one participant had difficulties solving the given tasks. All others completed all tasks perfectly and with or near the minimum number of required steps in each level. Hence, the following section only addresses the individual differences regarding the time for completing each level.

The time for completing a level increases significantly with the level's difficulty and the player's age $\left(V = .300, F_{2,37} = 7.915, \eta^2 = .300\right).^2$ As illustrated in Fig. 4, older players are on average 27 %–33 % slower than younger players. Corresponding, a multiple linear regression with performance as dependent variable and independent and explanatory variables as independent variables reveals that *age* is the strongest predictor for performance ($r^2 = .278$). The second contributing factor *gaming frequency* explains additional $\delta r^2 = .100$ of variance in performance ($r^2 = .366$) and people who play games often are also faster in the game. The model's parameters are given in Table 1a. Surprisingly, neither gender, nor attitude towards health, nor technical self-efficacy, nor cooking self-efficacy significantly influences performance within this sample, if controlled for age and gaming frequency.

Table 1. Regression tables for *Performance* (r^2 = .366) (left) and *Usage Intention* based on UTAUT2 (r^2 = .633) (right).

Model	B SE B	β	T	Model	B SE B	β	T
(constant)	.000 .000		– 8.614	(constant)	-.437 .360		– -1.214
Age	.000 .000	-.886	-5.003	Hedonic	.635 .091	.594	6.992
Gaming freq.	.000 .000	-.466	-2.634	Habit	.464 .114	.345	4.061

5.2 Determinants for Acceptance

Regarding the personality factors none of the dependent and control variables has an influence on behavioral intention. Specifically, neither *gender*, previous *gaming frequency*, *technical self-efficacy*, *cooking self-efficacy*, nor the *attitudes towards health* influences the *intention to use* the game and the relationship between *age* and *intention* is above the level of significance ($\rho(62 - 2) = .229$, p = .069 > .05, n.s.).

Five of the seven dimensions from the UTAUT2 model are strongly related to the intention to use the game (*Performance Expectancy, Habit, Social Influence, Price Value*, and *Hedonic*). Only the two dimensions *Effort Expectancy* ($\rho(62 - 2) = -.113$, p = .373 > .05, n.s.) and *Facilitating Conditions* ($\rho(62 - 2) = .052$, p = .686 > .05, n.s.) are not related to usage intention.

To disentangle the interrelationship between the variables from the UTAUT2 model and the personality factors a multiple linear regression analysis was calculated. Intention to use is used as dependent variable and the independent, control and UTAUT2's model variables, as well as average performance are used as independent variables. The regression reveals a significant model with the two explaining factors *hedonic* and *habit* that explains $r^2_{adj} = .633$ of the variance. Table 1 (right) shows the regression model.

---

^{2} Due to technical difficulties with the performance log files the evaluation of game performance is based on 45 of the total 64 cases (70 %).

Table 2. Relation of independent, explanatory, UTAUT2 variables, and Behavioral Intention (BI) (n = 64), Note:' p < .1, * p < .05, ** p < .01. Gender dummy coded (1 = male, 2 = female).

	PERF	PE	EE	FC	HA	SO	PV	HE	BI
Performance Expectancy (PE)		–	-.434**		.537**	.487**	.628**	.487**	.499**
Effort Expectancy (EE)	.249+		–	.490**			-.264*		
Facilitating Conditions (FC)				–					
Habit (HA)					–	.544**	.476**	.453**	.578**
Social Influence (SO)						–	.430**	.611**	.612**
Price Value (PV)							–	.318*	.413**
Hedonic (HE)								–	.718**
Age	-.675**	.407**	-.269*			.222'	.334**	.477**	.229'
Gender			-.289*			.358**			
Health-related behavior	.367*								
Gaming Frequency	.373*	-.335**		.304*		-.250*	-.350*	-.317*	
Cooking Self-efficacy									
Technical self-efficacy	.495**	-.342**	.290*			-.257*			-.283

The interrelationships between independent and explanatory variables and the dimensions from the UTAUT2 model are given in Table 2.

5.3   Device

Each participant interacted with one of three devices available in the AAL environment (tablet, table, wall) and none of the participants had severe difficulties interacting with his or her device.

The general *task suitability* was rated high for all investigated input devices (M_{all} = 4.1 ± 1.2, M_{tablet} = 4.4 ± 1.5, M_{table} = 4.5 ± 0.7, M_{wall} = 3.5 ± 1.2). Although the ratings differ significantly across the three devices $\left(F_{2,61} = 4.738, p = .012 < .05\right)$, a post hoc Tukey-HSD test shows that the difference is only significant between the ratings of the wall-sized display and the table (p = .015 < .05). Neither the ratings of the wall sized-display and the tablet (p = .061 > .05), nor the ratings between the tablet and the table (p = .926 > .05) differ significantly.

Contrary, the perceived *input precision* was rated as less good (M_{all} = 3.2, ± = 1.8) and only slightly above the scale mean (2.5). Yet, no sig. differences were found between the three devices $\left(F_{2,60} = 2.079, p = .134 > .05\right)$.

The perceived *learnability* of the three input devices was rated high (M_{all} = 4.4, ± = 0.8) and did not differ across the three devices $\left(F_{2,61} = 1.512, p = .229 > .05\right)$. Figure 5 illustrates the findings.

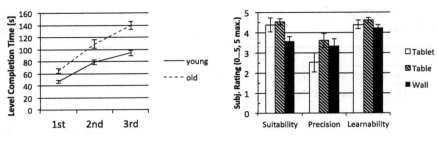

Fig. 4. Performance.   **Fig. 5.** Device ratings.

6 Discussion

We designed, implemented, and evaluated a prototypic serious game for ambient assisted living environments. The game aims at training the cognitive abilities (specifically remembering and planning competencies) of the residents and runs on several of the interaction surfaces available in the prototypic living environment. The study with older adults and a younger control group reveals findings in line with our expectations and some surprising aspects.

6.1 Evaluation of the Game

First, the study showed that every but one participant completed all asks of the user study. Hence, the participants were able to read, remember, and replicate the three given recipes on one of the three interaction surfaces. Most of our prototypic users were acquainted with tablet devices, but none of the older participants had experiences with the tabletop device or the wall-sized device. Still, they had no difficulties to learn and use this touch-based technology successfully. Overall, the study showed that serious games for healthcare in ambient assisted living environments were usable by older and younger players and that a successful integration is possible. Furthermore, some elderly participants stated after the experiment that they enjoyed the seamless integration of technology in the room and that the playful application would encourage them to perform training activities regularly, while they refrain from learning to interact with current notebooks or tablets due to their high complexity (see also [28]).

Second, though this study revealed differences in the perception of the three utterly different interaction surfaces (wall, table, tablet), there is no clear "winner". Within this study, the table has received the highest overall rating, closely followed by the two other interaction surfaces. Still, none of the devices was rated unsuitable and the participant's had little difficulties completing their tasks regardless of the device.

Third, according to our expectations (and the companion study presented in [27]), *age* is the strongest predictor for game *performance* and performance decreases with age. The second strongest predictor is gaming frequency, meaning that people who are inclined to games and play games frequently were faster in *Cook it Right* than people who are less inclined towards games. Contrary to the companion study (see Sec. 2.4), neither gender, nor need for achievement influences the performance. Also, domain expertise (measured as cooking frequency, ease of cooking and cooking self-efficacy) does not influence performance. Surprisingly, self-efficacy in interacting with technology is unrelated to game performance if controlled for age. This contrasts innumerable studies in which people with lower technical self-efficacy suffered from lower performance (efficiency) and lower completion rates (effectivity). We speculate that the triad of a game-based environment, touch based interaction surfaces, and the hand-drawn appearance of *Cook it Right* lowers the perceived and actual barriers to a successful use and adoption of ICT-based medical technology. Besides completion time the number of interaction steps was also considered, but almost all participants completed the levels with the minimum number of steps. Hence, they did not use the trial-and-error method and they were not rapidly testing all possible combinations. We think that this is caused by the rather strong visual cues the game offers, e.g., it is easy to see when a steak is placed in a pan and none of the participants tried to add steaks multiple times. A follow up study with more difficult levels will need to investigate the influence on user factors on the number of interaction steps and their influence on the usage intention. We assume that if people "feel lost" in more complex recipe trees the number of non-functional interaction steps will increase and the usage intention will derogate. Similar findings were already observed for interacting with menu trees on small screen devices [46] and the transferability of these findings must be investigated in the context of games and AAL.

6.2 Guidelines for the Successful Introduction of Serious Games for Healthcare

Intention to use the game is mostly explained by the factors within the UTAUT2 model and not by personality factors. Only *age* mildly influences the intention to use the game, with older players being more inclined towards the game. The nature of this effect is still unidentified and requires further investigation. A possible explanation for the higher usage intention of older participants may be that they can better relate to the concept of cognitive trainings. Alternatively, younger participants may have a lower usage intention as they are spoiled by current game titles. Strikingly, the evaluation of the game is independent of the achieved performance. Hence, even people who do not perform well due to cognitive or technical difficulties enjoyed the game. Regarding the UTAUT2 model's variables the study showed that neither *effort expectancy*, nor *facilitating conditions* influence the intention to use the game. Hence, the participants believe that the presented game-based technology is easy to learn and that they do not need to rely on support by others to successfully use the game. All other constructs from UTAUT2 have a strong positive influence on the usage intention. Designers and developers of games for healthcare, as well as medical professionals accompanying the introduction of these games, should closely pay attention to these constructs, as they are crucial for a successful introduction of serious games for healthcare in ambient assisted living environments.

Guidelines for an effective introduction of serious games for healthcare can be formulated based on the determinants of usage intention. A high hedonic value is the strongest lever for later use. Hence, designers must carefully craft games that are enjoyable by the target audience. Furthermore, it is advisable that potential players are included in the design process from the beginning, to ensure a fun game play and an interesting game scenario. The second-strongest aspect is a persons' believe of making playing the game a habit. Thus, a successful integration of serious games for healthcare depends on accompanying measures that strengthen this feeling. Bandura's self-efficacy theory [47] suggests role models that successfully use the games in their daily life or social support by friends and family members. The latter also relates to the social influence dimension from UTAUT2, which also has a positive influence on the usage intention. Although a reasonable price-value tradeoff is of lower priority within this study, the financial investments still have an influence on the acceptance. As health insurance companies will profit from a widespread and frequent use of healthcare games, they should invest in these to support their diffusion.

7   Limitations and Outlook

The presented results reflect the users' short-term evaluation of the game. Therefore, a long-term evaluation must address the interrelationship between behavioral intention and actual behavior (i.e., adherence to the game) over time. Also, this evaluation relates to the design of the game and may change with games addressing a different domain or different interaction styles. We think, however, that the findings presented here are transferable to serious games in general, as we have similar results on an exercise game [27].

The data presented here was aggregated from separate studies for each input device and the evaluation of these is only briefly discussed here and the evaluation was carried out in context of the game and the environment. Hence, the findings might be inter-mingled with influences therefrom. A follow-up study should more closely address the barriers and benefits of the different input devices. A within-subject experiment focusing solely on the user's perception, performance, and effectivity with the three devices should reveal which device is suited best for delivering the game or whether a bouquet of input devices can and should be provided in AAL environments.

It is a necessity to understand the user's wishes and demands on serious games for healthcare. Not only regarding the objectives and themes of the games, but also regarding the possible interaction interfaces. The present study presents a glance on these questions; nevertheless further studies will need to explore the design space of input devices in AAL environments and its relationship with serious games for healthcare.

Acknowledgements. We thank all subjects for their willingness to participate and to share their thoughts about the game with us. Furthermore, we thank Markus Gottfried and Dirk Netteln-breker for support during experiment and evaluation. We also thank RWTH Aachen University's eHealth team for collaboratively building the lab in which the study was carried out and espe-cially Felix Heidrich and Kai Kasugai for crafting the input devices used in this study. The precious comments of the anonymous reviewers are highly acknowledged.

References

1. Giannakouris, K.: Ageing characterises the demographic perspectives of the European societies (2008)
2. Ho, K.K.L., Pinsky, J.L., Kannel, W.B., Levy, D.: The epidemiology of heart failure: the framingham study. J. Am. Coll. Cardiol. **22**, A6–A13 (1993)
3. Health at a Glance: Europe 2012. OECD Publishing (2012)
4. Weiser, M.: The computer for the 21st century. Sci. Am. **265**, 94–104 (1991)
5. Kleinberger, T., Becker, M., Ras, E., Holzinger, A., Müller, P.: Ambient intelligence in assisted living: enable elderly people to handle future interfaces. In: Stephanidis, C., (ed.) UAHCI 2007 (Part II). LNCS, vol. 4555, pp. 103–112. Springer, Heidelberg (2007)
6. Mukasa, K.S., Holzinger, A., Karshmer, A.: Intelligent User Interfaces for Ambient Assisted Living. Fraunhofer IRB Verlag, Stuttgart (2008)
7. Raisinghani, M.S., Benoit, A., Ding, J., Gomez, M., Gupta, K., Gusila, V., Power, D., Schmedding, O.: Ambient intelligence: changing forms of human-computer interaction and their social implications. J. Digit. Inf. **5**(4) (2004)
8. Röcker, C., Ziefle, M.: Current approaches to ambient assisted living. In: International Conference on Future Information Technology and Management Science & Engineering, pp. 6–14 (2012)
9. Lahlou, S.: Identity, social status, privacy and face-keeping in digital society. Soc. Sci. Inf. **47**, 299–330 (2008)
10. Wilkowska, W., Ziefle, M.: Privacy and data security in e-health: requirements from the user's perspective. Health Inf. J. **18**, 191–201 (2012)
11. Mynatt, E.D., Rogers, W.A.: Developing technology to support the functional independence of older adults. Ageing Int. **27**, 24–41 (2001)
12. Meyer, S., Mollenkopf, H.: Home technology, smart homes, and the aging user. In: Schaie, K.W., Wahl, H.-W., Mollenkopf, H., Oswald, F. (eds.) Aging Independently: Living Arrangements and Mobility, pp. 148–161. Springer, Heidelberg (2003)
13. Ziefle, M., Röcker, C., Wilkowska, W., Kasugai, K., Klack, L., Möllering, C., Beul, S.: A multi-disciplinary approach to ambient assisted living. In: Röcker, C., Ziefle, M. (eds.) E-Health, Assistive Technologies and Applications for Assisted Living: Challenges and Solutions, pp. 76–93. Hershey, IGI Global (2011)
14. Abt, C.C.: Serious Games. Reprint. University Press of America, Lanham MD (1987)
15. Michael, D., Chen, S.: Serious Games: Games That Educate, Train, and Inform. Thomson Course Technology, Boston (2006)
16. Premack, D.: Toward empirical behavior laws: I. Positive reinforcement. Psychol. Rev. **66**, 219–233 (1959)
17. Huizinga, J.: Homo Ludens: A Study of the Play-Element in Culture. Pantheon, New York (1939)
18. Lewis, G.N., Rosie, J.A.: Virtual reality games for movement rehabilitation in neurological conditions: how do we meet the needs and expectations of the users? Disabil. Rehabil. **34**, 1880–1886 (2012)
19. Macvean, A., Robertson, J.: Understanding exergame users' physical activity, motivation and behavior over time. In: CHI 2013 Proceedings of the SIGCHI Conference on Human Factors in Computing Systems, pp. 1251–1260 (2013)
20. Tanaka, K., Parker, J., Baradoy, G., Sheehan, D., Holash, J.R., Katz, L.: A comparison of exergaming interfaces for use in rehabilitation programs and research. Loading. **6**, 69–81 (2012)

21. Ball, K.K., Wadley, V.G., Vance, D.E., Edwards, J.D.: Cognitive skills: training, maintenance, and daily usage. Encycl. Appl. Psychol. **1**, 387–392 (2004)
22. Heyn, P., Abreu, B.C., Ottenbacher, K.J.: The effects of exercise training on elderly persons with cognitive impairment and dementia: a meta-analysis. Arch. Phys. Med. Rehabil. **85**, 1694–1704 (2004)
23. Fishbein, M., Ajzen, I.: Belief, Attitude, Intention and Behavior: An Introduction to Theory and Research. Addison-Wesley Publishing Company Inc., Reading (1975)
24. Ajzen, I.: The theory of planned behavior. Organ. Behav. Hum. Decis. Process. **50**, 179–211 (1991)
25. Davis, F.D.: Perceived usefulness, perceived ease of use, and user acceptance of information technology. MIS Q. **13**, 319 (1989)
26. Venkatesh, V., Davis, F.D.: A theoretical extension of the technology acceptance model: four longitudinal field studies. Manage. Sci. **46**, 186–204 (2000)
27. Brauner, P., Holzinger, A., Ziefle, M.: Ubiquitous computing at its best: serious exercise games for older adults in ambient assisted living environments – a technology acceptance perspective. EAI Endorsed Trans. Serious Games **15**, 1–12 (2015). doi:10.4108/sg.1.4.e3
28. Arning, K., Ziefle, M.: Different perspectives on technology acceptance : the role of technology type and age. HCI Usability Inclusion **5889**, 20–41 (2009)
29. Rogers, Y.: The changing face of human-computer interaction in the age of ubiquitous computing. In: Holzinger, A., Miesenberger, K. (eds.) USAB 2009. LNCS, vol. 5889, pp. 1–19. Springer, Heidelberg (2009)
30. Ziefle, M., Rocker, C., Holzinger, A.: Medical technology in smart homes: exploring the user's perspective on privacy, intimacy and trust. In: IEEE (2011)
31. Fisk, A.D., Rogers, W.A.: Handbook of Human Factors and the Older Adult. Academic Press, San Diego (1997)
32. Kliegel, M., McDaniel, M.A., Einstein, G.O.: Plan formation, retention, and execution in prospective memory: a new approach and age-related effects. Mem. Cogn. **28**, 1041–1049 (2000)
33. Craik, F.I., Bialystok, E.: Planning and task management in older adults: cooking breakfast. Mem. Cogn. **34**, 1236–1249 (2006)
34. d'Ydewalle, G., Bouckaert, D., Brunfaut, E.: Age-related differences and complexity of ongoing activities in time- and event-based prospective memory. Am. J. Psychol. **114**, 411–423 (2001)
35. Arning, K., Ziefle, M.: Effects of age, cognitive, and personal factors on PDA menu navigation performance. Behav. Inf. Technol. **28**, 251–268 (2009)
36. Goodman, J., Gray, P., Khammampad, K., Brewster, S.: Using landmarks to support older people in navigation. Mob. Hum. Comput. Interact. - MobileHCI **2004**, 38–48 (2004)
37. Marquié, J.C., Jourdan-Boddaert, L., Huet, N.: Do older adults underestimate their actual computer knowledge? Behav. Inf. Technol. **21**, 273–280 (2002)
38. Tuomainen, K., Haapanen, S.: Needs of the active elderly for mobile phones. In: Stephanidis, C. (ed.) Universal Access in HCI: Inclusive Design in the Information Society, pp. 494–498. Lawrence Erlbaum Associates Inc., Mahwah (2003)
39. De Schutter, B., Vandenabeele, V.: Meaningful play in elderly life. In: 58th Annual Conference of the International Communication Association "Communicating for Social Impact" (2008)
40. Nielsen, J.: Usability Engineering. Morgan Kaufmann Publishers Inc., San Francisco (1993)
41. Snyder, C.: Paper Prototyping: The Fast and Easy Way to Design and Refine User Interfaces. Morgan Kaufmann, Elsevier Science, San Francisco (2003)
42. Kieras, D., Polson, P.G.: An approach to the formal analysis of user complexity. Int. J. Man Mach. Stud. **22**, 365–394 (1985)

43. Beier, G.: Kontrollüberzeugungen im Umgang mit Technik [Locus of control when interacting with technology]. Rep. Psychol. **24**, 684–693 (1999)
44. Blais, A.-R., Weber, E.U.: A Domain-Specific Risk-Taking (DOSPERT) scale for adult populations. Judgment Deci. Making J. **1**, 33–47 (2006)
45. Venkatesh, V., Morris, M.G., Davis, G.B., Davis, F.D.: User acceptance of information technology: Toward a unified view. MIS Q. **27**, 425–478 (2003)
46. Arning, K., Ziefle, M.: Understanding age differences in PDA acceptance and performance. Comput. Hum. Behav. **23**, 2904–2927 (2007)
47. Bandura, A.: Self-efficacy: toward a unifying theory of behavioral change. Psychol. Rev. **84**, 191–215 (1977)

Continuous Mental Effort Evaluation During 3D Object Manipulation Tasks Based on Brain and Physiological Signals

Dennis Wobrock[1,2], Jérémy Frey[2,3,4], Delphine Graeff[1],
Jean-Baptiste de la Rivière[1], Julien Castet[1], and Fabien Lotte[2,3(✉)]

[1] Immersion SAS, Bordeaux, France
dennis.wobrock@ensc.fr,
{delphine.graeff,jb.delariviere,
julien.castet}@immersion.fr
[2] Inria Bordeaux Sud-Ouest, Talence, France
{jeremy.frey,fabien.lotte}@inria.fr
[3] LaBRI, Talence, France
[4] Université de Bordeaux, Bordeaux, France

Abstract. Designing 3D User Interfaces (UI) requires adequate evaluation tools to ensure good usability and user experience. While many evaluation tools are already available and widely used, existing approaches generally cannot provide continuous and objective measures of usability qualities during interaction without interrupting the user. In this paper, we propose to use brain (with ElectroEncephaloGraphy) and physiological (ElectroCardioGraphy, Galvanic Skin Response) signals to continuously assess the mental effort made by the user to perform 3D object manipulation tasks. We first show how this mental effort (a.k.a., mental workload) can be estimated from such signals, and then measure it on 8 participants during an actual 3D object manipulation task with an input device known as the CubTile. Our results suggest that monitoring workload enables us to continuously assess the 3DUI and/or interaction technique ease-of-use. Overall, this suggests that this new measure could become a useful addition to the repertoire of available evaluation tools, enabling a finer grain assessment of the ergonomic qualities of a given 3D user interface.

Keywords: 3D user interfaces · Evaluation · Passive Brain-Computer interfaces · Physiological signals · Electroencephalography · Mental workload

1 Introduction

3D User Interfaces (UI) and systems are increasingly used in a number of applications including industrial design, education, art or entertainment [3, 11]. As such, 3DUI and interaction techniques can be used by many different users with many varying skills and profiles. Therefore, designing them requires adequate evaluation tools to ensure good usability and user experience for most targeted users [2, 11]. To do so, a number of evaluation methods has been developed including behavioral studies, testbeds,

© IFIP International Federation for Information Processing 2015
J. Abascal et al. (Eds.): INTERACT 2015, Part I, LNCS 9296, pp. 472–487, 2015.
DOI: 10.1007/978-3-319-22701-6_35

questionnaires and inquiries, among others [3, 8, 11]. This resulted in the design of more relevant, efficient and easy-to-use 3DUI.

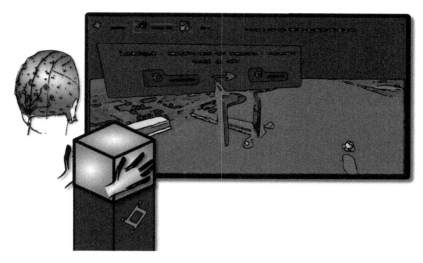

Fig. 1. Schematic view of a user performing 3D manipulations tasks with the CubTile input device. His/her mental effort are monitored based on brain signals (ElectroEncephaloGraphy).

Nevertheless, there is still a lot of room for improvements in the currently used evaluation methods. In particular, traditional evaluation methods could either be ambiguous, lack real-time recordings, or disrupt the interaction [8]. For instance, although behavioral studies are able to account in real-time for users' interactions, they can be hard to interpret since measures may not be specific, e.g., a high reaction time can be caused either by a low concentration level or a high mental workload [10]. Questionnaires and other inquiry-based methods such as "think aloud" and focus group all suffer from the same limitation: resulting measures are prone to be contaminated by ambiguities [19], social pressure [23] or participants' memory limitations [13].

For instance, a useful UI evaluation measure is the user's mental workload, i.e., the pressure on the user's working memory, which is typically measured using the NASA-TLX post hoc questionnaire [10]. Even though it can be used to assess users' preferences regarding UI [12], NASA-TLX being a post-experiment measure, this is only a subjective and global measure that cannot inform on where and when the user experienced higher or lower workload. There is therefore a need for more objective (or more precisely "exocentric", as defined in [8]) and continuous measures of the usability qualities of 3DUI that do not interrupt the user during interaction.

In order to obtain such measures of the user's inner-state during interaction, a recent promising research direction is to measure such states based on brain signals – e.g., from ElectroEncephaloGraphy (EEG) – and physiological signals – e.g., from heart rate measurements or skin's moisture – acquired from the user during interaction [8]. Indeed, there are increasing evidence that the mental states that can be relevant for

3DUI evaluation, like mental workload [17], can be estimated from brain and physiological signals [8, 20]. Interestingly enough, some recent works have started to use brain signal based measures of workload to compare 2D visual information displays [1, 22]. However, to the best of our knowledge, estimating mental workload from both brain and physiological signals has never been explored to evaluate 3DUI, although it could provide relevant evaluation metrics to complement the already used ones. Indeed, previous works were focused on evaluating workload levels based on brain signals during 2D visualizations, thus with more passive users [1, 22]. 3D interaction tasks are more complex for the user since (1) the user is actively interacting with the application, and not as passively observing it, and as such should decide what to do and how to do so, and (2) perceiving and interacting with a 3D environment is more cognitively demanding than perceiving and interacting with a 2D one, since it required the user to perform 3D mental rotation tasks to successfully manipulate 3D objects or to orientate him/herself in the 3D environment. Therefore, as compared to existing works which only explored passive 2D visualizations, monitoring mental workload seems more relevant during 3D manipulation tasks, since the user is more likely to experience pressure on his/her cognitive resources. Therefore, evaluating the resulting changes in workload levels seems even more necessary to ensure the design of usable 3DUI. Moreover, the active role of the user during 3D interaction tasks (as compared to more passive visualizations) and the higher cognitive demand as well as the richer visual feedback resulting from the use of a 3D environment means that EEG and physiological signals will be substantially different and more variable as compared to those measured during 2D visualization tasks. Finding out whether they can still be used to estimate workload levels in this context is therefore a challenging and relevant question to explore.

Therefore, in this paper, we propose to assess the mental effort (i.e., the mental workload) made by the user during 3D object manipulation tasks, based on brain (EEG) and other physiological signals. We notably propose a method to estimate workload levels from both EEG, ElectroCardioGram (ECG) and Galvanic Skin Response (GSR) signals, and we study mental workload levels during a 3D docking task in a pilot study (see Fig. 1). Our results show that this approach can provide useful information about how users learn to use the 3DUI and how easy-to-use it is.

2   Methods

To continuously monitor workload levels during 3D interaction, we first propose an approach to estimate such workload levels from EEG, ECG and GSR signals, described hereafter. We then present how to use the resulting workload estimator to evaluate 3D object manipulation tasks and the corresponding study we conducted.

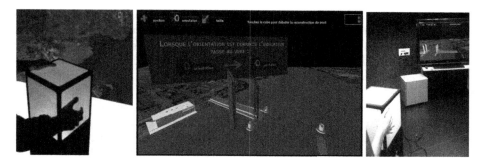

Fig. 2. *Left:* The CubTile interaction device. *Center:* The bridge building application. *Right:* The bridge building application controlled with the CubTile and used to analyze workload levels during 3D docking tasks.

Measuring and Estimating Workload Levels. Estimating workload levels from EEG, ECG and GSR signals first requires a ground truth data set with such signals labeled with the corresponding user's mental workload, in order to calibrate and validate our workload estimator. Based on this ground truth signal data set, we propose signal processing and machine learning tools to identify the user's workload level. They are described hereafter.

Inducing Mental Workload to Calibrate the Estimator. To obtain a ground truth signal data set to calibrate and validate our workload estimator, we induced 2 different workload levels in our participants. To do so, we had them perform cognitive tasks, the cognitive difficulty of which being manipulated using a protocol known as the N-back task, a well-known task to induce workload (see, e.g., [17]). With such a task, users saw a sequence of letters on screen, the letters being displayed one by one, every 2 s. For each letter the user had to indicate whether the displayed letter was the same one as the letter displayed N letters before or was different, using a left or right mouse click respectively. Each user alternated between "easy" blocks with the 0-back task (the user had to identify whether the current letter was the letter 'X') and "difficult" blocks with the 2-back task (the user had to identify whether the current letter was the same letter as the one displayed 2 letters before). Each block contained 60 letters presentations and each participant completed 6 blocks, 3 blocks for each workload level (0-back vs 2-back). Therefore, 360 calibration trials (i.e., one trial being one letter presentation) were collected for each user, with 180 trials for each workload level ("low" versus "high").

Measuring Brain and Physiological Signals. During all experiments, EEG signals were acquired using 30 electrodes located all over the scalp (positions C6, CP4, CPz, CP3, P5, P3, P1, Pz, P2, P4, P6, PO7, PO8, Oz, F3, Fz, F4, FT8, FC6, FC4, FCz, FC3, FC5, FT7, C5, C3, C1, Cz, C2, C4), using a 32-channels g.USBAmp (g.tec, Austria). ECG and GSR were measured using a BITalino acquisition card [28]. 3 ECG sensors were placed on the user's torso, and 2 GSR sensors on the user's index and middle fingers from the active hand. All EEG and physiological sensors were acquired using the OpenViBE platform [25].

Signal Processing Tools to Detect Mental Effort. In order to estimate mental workload from brain and physiological sensors, we used a machine learning approach: the measured signals were first represented as a set of descriptive features. These features were then given as input to a machine learning classifier whose objective was to learn whether these features represented a low workload level (induced by the 0-back task) or a high workload level (induced by the 2-back task). Once calibrated, this classifier can be used to estimate workload levels on new data, which we will use to estimate mental effort during 3D object manipulation tasks. From the signals collected during the N-back tasks described above, we extracted features from each 2-seconds long time window of EEG and physiological signals immediately following a letter presentation, as in [17]. We used each of these 2-seconds long time windows as an example to calibrate our classifier. Note that a classifier was calibrated separately for each participant, based on the examples of brain and physiological signals collected from that participant. Indeed, EEG signals are known to be very variable between participants, hence the need for user-specific classifiers to ensure maximal EEG classification performances [5, 17].

We used the EEGLab software [4] to process EEG signals. We filtered the signals in the Delta (1–3 Hz), Theta (4–6 Hz), Alpha (7–13 Hz), Beta (14–25 Hz) and Gamma (26–40 Hz) bands, as in [17]. For each band, we optimized a set of 6 Common Spatial Patterns (CSP) spatial filters (i.e., linear combinations of the original EEG channels that lead to maximally different features between the two workload levels) [15, 24]. For each frequency band and spatial filter, we then used as feature the average band power of the filtered EEG signals. This resulted in 30 EEG features (5 bands × 6 spatial filters per band). Note that high frequency EEG is likely to be contaminated by muscle activity (ElectroMyoGraphy - EMG) from the user's face or neck [6, 9]. As such, we explored EEG-based workload estimation based on low frequencies only (Theta, Delta, Alpha) and both low and high frequencies (Theta, Delta, Alpha, Beta, Gamma).

This signal processing approach is the one we used to discriminate workload levels from EEG signals between 0-back and 2-back tasks, i.e., within the same context on which the workload estimator was calibrated. However, it is known that EEG signals change between different contexts, due, e.g., to the different user's attention and involvement that the context triggers or to different sensory stimulations (e.g., different visual inputs) that change brain responses and thus EEG signals. This means that a workload estimator calibrated in a given context will have poorer performances (i.e., will estimate an erroneous workload level more often) when applied to a different context [17]. In our experiment, the final application context, i.e., 3D objects manipulation, is very different from the calibration context, i.e., the N-back tasks. Indeed, during the N-back tasks the user is moving very little as he/she is only performing mouse clicks, and exposed to very little visual stimulations as the N-back task only involves the display of white letters on a black background. On the contrary, manipulating 3D objects means that the user will be moving more and would be exposed to very rich visual stimulations. As such, a workload estimator simply calibrated on the N-back tasks and applied to the 3D object manipulation tasks is very likely to give very poor results or even to fail. Therefore, we modified the above mentioned signal processing approach to make it robust to EEG signal changes between the two contexts. In particular, rather than using basic CSP spatial filters, we used regularized CSP spatial filters [14] that are robust to changes between calibration and use contexts. To do so, based on [27], we estimated the EEG signal covariance matrix from the calibration context (N-back tasks) and from the use context[1] (3D object manipulation tasks), and computed the Principal Components (PC) of the difference between these two matrices. These PC represent the directions along which EEG signals change between calibration and use. These directions are then used to regularize the CSP spatial filters as in [27], to ensure that the obtained spatial filters are invariant to these EEG signals changes.

From ECG signals we extracted the Heart Rate (HR) and 2 features from the Heart Rate Variability (HRV), namely the low frequency HRV (< 0.1 Hz) and the Root Mean Square of Successive Differences, as in [16], using the Biosig Matlab toolbox [29]. From GSR signals we also extracted 3 features: the mean GSR amplitude, skin conductance responses (SCR, here band power between 0.5 Hz and 2 Hz) and the skin conductance level (SCL, 0.1–0.5 Hz) [7].

We then used a shrinkage Linear Discriminant Analysis (sLDA) classifier [15] to learn which feature values correspond to a high or low workload level.

Note that since both ECG and GSR analyses rely on low frequencies, we had to extend the time windows from 2 s to 10 s when we studied those physiological signals (for instance, for HRV at 0.1 Hz, 10 s are needed to observe a single cycle). As such the number of trials per condition (0-back vs 2-back) in these particular scenarios were reduced from 180 down to 36.

Estimating Mental Effort During 3D Manipulation. Once we have a classifier that can estimate workload levels from brain and physiological signals, we can use it to study mental effort during 3D objects manipulation tasks. With this objective in mind, we designed an experiment in which participants, equipped with the sensors described previously (EEG, ECG and GSR), had to manipulate 3D objects using an interaction device known as the CubTile [26]. In particular, participants had to perform 3D docking tasks in order to build a bridge in 3D by assembling together its different parts (see Fig. 2). The following sections describe the participant population used for this experiment, the CubTile input device and the protocol of the bridge building application.

Population and Apparatus. 8 participants (2 females, age from 16 to 29) took part in this study. They were all first-time users of the bridge building application and the CubTile (except for one participant who has used the CubTile before for another application). These participants completed 3D manipulation tasks using the CubTile. The CubTile is a multi-touch cubic interface consisting in a medium-sized cube where 5 out of 6 sides are multitouch. It can sense several fingers, offers interaction redundancy and lets a user handle 3D manipulation thanks to single handed and bimanual input [26]. In particular, with the CubTile, translations can be performed by moving symmetrically two fingers each on opposite sides of the cube. Scaling can be performed by connecting or disconnecting two fingers. Finally, rotations can be performed either

---

[1] Note that this is only possible here because we perform an offline evaluation, after the 3D manipulation tasks have been performed and the corresponding EEG signals collected. It would not be possible to use the exact same algorithm for a real-time estimation of workload during 3D objects manipulation tasks as the covariance matrix of EEG signals during these tasks is not yet fully known.

by rotating symmetrically several fingers each set on opposite sides of the cube or by translating asymmetrically two fingers each on opposite sides of the cube.

Protocol. The experiment took place in a dedicated experimental room, in a quiet environment. When the participant entered the room, he/she was told about the experiment and then equipped with the different sensors. Then he/she participated into 6 blocks of the N-back task (except S6 who only completed 3 blocks due to technical issues), on a standard computer screen, in order to obtain calibration data to setup the workload classifier. This took approximately 15 min. The participant also participated in two other calibration sessions (about 15 min each), to calibrate two other mental states that were not used nor analyzed for this study. Once the calibration sessions were completed, the participant was asked to sit in front of the CubTile which was itself in front of a 65 inches Panasonic TX-P65VT20E screen.

The participant then had to construct the 3D bridge by assembling the bridge parts (e.g., the 4 supporting pillars and the road) one by one. In particular, the participant had to perform docking tasks, by translating, rotating and scaling the bridge parts, in order to put them at the correct location. The correct location was indicated to the user with proper 3D feedback, integrated to the 3D scene, in the form of text and color indicating how close he/she was from the correct position, scale and orientation. All the translations, rotations and scaling were controlled by the CubTile. The participant had to perform a set of 7 docking tasks:

1. Positioning the 1st pillar, by controlling rotation, translation and scaling – repeated 3 times for different angles, sizes and positions
2. Positioning the 2nd pillar, by controlling 2 translations, 1 rotation and scaling, while the pillar was being continuously and automatically translated along the vertical axis – repeated 4 times for different angles, sizes and positions
3. Positioning the lower half of the 3rd pillar by controlling a crane carrying the pillar part, along 1 rotation and 1 translation (up/down) – repeated 3 times for different angles and heights
4. Positioning the upper half of the 3rd pillar by controlling a crane along 1 rotation and 1 translation, seen from a different angle than the previous task – repeated 3 times for different angles and heights
5. Positioning the 4th pillar by controlling 2 translations and 1 rotation. Without warning the users, **the gestures for rotation and translation were inverted**, e.g., moving symmetrically two fingers on opposite sides of the cube triggered a rotation instead of the usual translation. Controls were only inverted for this task.
6. Positioning the road joining the first two pillars to the river bank with 2 translations and 1 rotation - repeated 3 times for different angles and starting position.
7. Positioning the road joining the four pillars with 1 translation, 3 rotations and scaling.

These different tasks enable us to observe how users get to learn how to use the CubTile for 3D objects manipulation tasks. Task number 5, with inverted control commands, enables us to observe mental workload while using voluntarily difficult and counter-intuitive interaction techniques. During the whole duration of the experiment, the participant brain and physiological signals were recorded.

3 Results

For each user, we first setup a workload level classifier based on the signals collected during the calibration session (N-back tasks). The next section describes the performances achieved for each participant and each signal type. Then, using the best workload classifier, we could estimate the workload level over time during the 3D docking tasks. This work was done offline, after the experiment.

Accuracy of Mental Effort Detection. First, based on the data collected during the calibration session (N-back tasks), we could estimate how well low workload could be discriminated from high workload based on EEG, ECG and GSR. To do so, we used 2-fold cross-validation (CV) on the calibration data collected. In other words, we split the collected data into two parts of equal size, used one part to calibrate the classifier (CSP filters and sLDA) as described in Sect. 2, and tested the resulting classifier on the data from the other part. We then did the opposite (training on the second part and testing on the first part), and averaged the obtained classification accuracies (percentage of signal time windows whose workload level was correctly identified). This CV was performed by using each signal type (i.e., EEG, ECG and GSR) either separately or in combination. Table 1 displays the obtained classification accuracies.

Table 1. Cross-validation classification accuracies (%) to discriminate workload levels from EEG, ECG and GSR on the calibration session data. A "*" indicates mean classification accuracies that are significantly better than chance (p < 0.01 according to [18])

Participant	S1	S2	S3	S4	S5	S6	S7	S8	Mean
EEG (Delta, Theta, Alpha)	74.0	76.2	76.5	80.2	84.9	81.9	81.7	75.4	78.9*
EEG + EMG (Delta, Theta, Alpha, Beta, Gamma)	85.0	93.1	81.7	87.6	94.8	97.3	84.8	84.3	88.6*
ECG	37.3	50.7	45.3	58.7	42.6	55.3	54.9	61.2	50.7
GSR	77.3	52.1	60.0	70.6	74.7	68.4	58.6	54.6	64.5
EEG + EMG + ECG + GSR	44.0	53.3	44.0	61.5	54.8	52.6	54.6	61.2	53.3

Classification results highlight that workload levels can be estimated in brain and physiological signals, even though the large inter-participant performance variability suggests that workload levels can be estimated more clearly for some users than for some others.

As can be first observed, it appears that EEG can discriminate workload levels with an accuracy higher than chance level, for all participants. In other words, the classification accuracies obtained are statistically significantly higher than 50 % for a 2-class problem, i.e., more accurate than flipping a coin to estimate the workload level. Indeed, according to [18], for 160 trials per class, the chance level for p < 0.01 and a 2-class problem is an accuracy of 56.9 %. Note that 180 trials per class were available with EEG in our experiment, meaning that the chance level is actually even slightly lower.

Regarding the GSR, it led to a better-than-chance classification accuracy only for some participants, but not for all. Indeed, we had 36 trials per class with GSR (due to the use of longer time windows as mentioned previously), which means a chance level of about 65 % for p < 0.01 according to [18]. ECG signals could not lead to better-than-chance performances for any participant.

Overall, EEG seems to be the signal type the best able to discriminate workload levels reliably. Moreover, when EEG features include high frequency bands – i.e. when Delta, Theta and Alpha bands are combined with Beta and Gamma bands – and thus when EEG measures potentially contain EMG activity as well, the performances are the highest, close to 90 % on average.

The poor performances of the system when all physiological signals are combined (EEG + EMG + ECG + GSR) may be explained by too important disparities in the features for the classifier to handle them correctly. On a side note, we also tested ECG and GSR on 2 s time windows with adapted features – HR for the former, mean value and SCR for the latter. Despite the increased number of trials in training and testing phases, the results were very similar to those already described in Table 1. Altogether, the relatively poor performances obtained with ECG and GSR are likely due to the short time windows (2 s or 10 s long) used. Much better performances should be expected with larger windows, e.g., with 30 s-long or even 2 min-long time windows [16], at the cost of a coarser temporal resolution.

Since we already obtained a classification accuracy close to 90 % through the sole use of EEG recordings (which possibly include EMG activity as well), we did not push further our investigations about a multimodal (multiple signals) approach to mental effort estimation. Such method would necessitate longer time windows, strong synchronization between signals and extra classification steps, with little benefit to expect considering that a classifier based on GSR hardly reaches 65 % of accuracy in our protocol.

We then calibrated the workload classifier on EEG signals from both low and high frequency bands (i.e., combining EEG and possibly EMG), and used it to analyze workload variations during the 3D manipulation tasks.

Mental Effort During 3D Object Manipulation. While the participants were performing 3D docking tasks to build the 3D bridge, their brain signals were recorded. By using the workload level classifier obtained offline, such classifier being able to estimate whether the current 2-seconds long time window of signals corresponds to a low or high workload for the user, we could notably continuously estimate the workload levels during the tasks. This gave us unique insights into how much mental effort the participants were devoting to each task, and how this mental effort evolved over time.

Due to the large between-user variability in terms of workload level estimation accuracy, and since these estimations are not 100 % accurate, we studied average workload levels to obtain a robust and reliable picture of the mental workload level associated with each task. To do so, we first normalized between -1 and +1 the output that was produced by the classifier for each participant during the virtual bridge construction. As such, a workload index close to +1 during the 3D object manipulation represents the highest mental workload a participant had to endure while performing the 3D docking tasks. It should come close to the 2-back condition of the calibration phase. In a similar manner, a workload index close to -1 denotes the lowest workload (similar to that of the 0-back condition).

Because there was no time constraint regarding task completion – users made as many attempts as needed to complete each one of them – we could not compare directly workload indexes over time. Some participants took more than 13 min to complete all the tasks while others finished in less than 5 min (mean: 7.7 min, SD: 2.9 min). This is why we averaged the workload index per task. Note that due to technical issues, for some participants the beginning and end of a couple of tasks were not accurately recorded or missing. If it was the case, the workload indexes for this task and participant were not included in the analysis to ensure unbiased results. Altogether, out of the 56 tasks (8 participants × 7 tasks per participant), 13 tasks were not included in the analysis to ensure clean results. More precisely, 1 task was missing for participant S3, 2 tasks were missing for participants S2 and S5, 3 tasks for participant S8, and 5 tasks for participant S4. No tasks were missing for the remaining participants. We followed a rather conservative approach (i.e., we discarded a task in case of doubt), to ensure only clean and meaningful results are presented.

Figure 3 displays the workload levels averaged over all participants and over the duration of each docking task. This thus provides us with the average mental workload induced by each 3D object manipulation task.

To ensure that the observed workload levels were really due to some information and structure in the data that are detected by the workload classifier, and not just due to chance or to some artefacts that are unrelated to workload levels, we performed a permutation analysis. In particular, we performed the exact same analysis described previously except that we used random classifiers instead of the real workload classifiers trained on the N-back task data. This aimed at estimating the type of workload

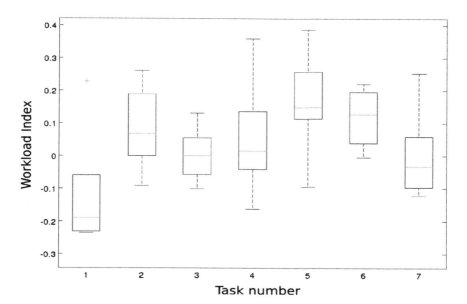

Fig. 3. Average workload levels (averaged over participants and task duration) measured for the different 3D docking tasks.

level indexes we could obtain by chance on our data. To do so, for each participant, we shuffled the labels of the N-back task data, (i.e., the EEG signals were not labelled with the correct workload level anymore), and optimized the spatial filters and classifier described in Sect. 2 based on this shuffled training data. In order words, we built random classifiers that would not be able to detect workload levels. Then using these random classifiers for each participant, we computed the mean normalized workload level indexes for each 3D manipulation task, as described previously. We repeated this process (workload labels shuffling, then random classifier training, and testing of the classifier on the 3D manipulation task data) 1000 times, to obtain the distribution of the mean workload level indexes for each task that can be obtained by chance (see Fig. 4). More precisely, we estimated the multivariate normal distribution of the vectors of mean workload level per class (i.e., a vector with 7 elements, the ith element being the averaged workload level over participants for task i) obtained for each of the 1000 permutations. This multivariate distribution thus represents the mean workload levels per task that can obtain by chance. We finally compared the actual mean workload levels per task that we obtained using the real workload classifiers (i.e., those optimized on the unshuffled training data, whose output is displayed on Fig. 3) to this chance multivariate distribution obtained with the random classifiers. This helped us estimate whether the obtained mean workload levels per task were due to chance or not. Results showed that the observed real workload levels are statistically significantly different from that obtained by the chance distribution with $p < 0.001$, i.e., they are not due to chance. This suggests that our workload classifier does find a work load level information during the 3D docking tasks that cannot be found by chance.

In order to sense whether or not the workload index fluctuated along tasks completion, we conducted a second analysis. Using the same normalized index, we compared the workload level between the first quarter and the last quarter of every task –

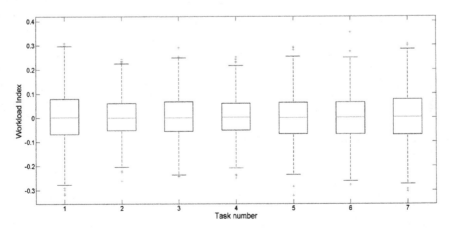

Fig. 4. Average workload levels obtained with a permutation test (see text for details), i.e., with random classifiers, for the different 3D docking tasks. The real workload levels we observed (i.e., those displayed in Fig. 3) significantly differ from those random workload levels, i.e., they are not due to chance.

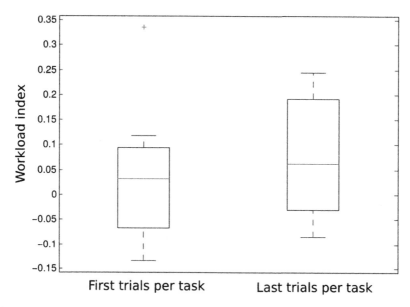

Fig. 5. Average per subject of the workload index during the first quarter of every task (left) compared to the last quarter (right).

average across tasks for each participant (Fig. 5). A Wilcoxon Signed-rank test showed that there was no significant difference.

4 Discussion

First, the fact that the observed workload levels during 3D manipulation tasks are not due to chance on the one hand and that our workload classifiers are calibrated on the N-back task, which is a widely used and validated workload induction protocol [21] on the other hand, strongly suggests that our approach may be used to observe how workload levels vary during 3D manipulation tasks. Indeed, our workload classifiers identified a specific EEG + EMG signature of workload levels thanks to the use of the N-back task, which then enabled us to estimate a non-random sequence of workload levels for each task. Naturally, if the variations of another mental state (or artefact) are highly correlated to that of the workload levels, and have a similar EEG + EMG signature as workload so that these variations are picked-up by our classifiers, then the observed variations of workload may be due to variations of another mental state. Therefore, the influence of a confounding mental state or artefacts cannot be completely ruled out without exploring how all possible mental states vary, which is of course impossible. However, the fact that our classifiers are specific to workload variations (since they are calibrated with the N-back task which specifically makes workload levels vary) and that the observed variations are not due to chance makes the influence of a such confounding factor rather unlikely. Based on this interpretation, we can now analyze how the workload level changes during the different 3D manipulation tasks and why.

The observed workload levels suggest that despite the novelty and the complexity of the interaction – handling at the same time rotation, translation and scaling of elements in a 3D environment right from the beginning – the participants did not make an important mental effort to complete the first task. That could be due to the practicality of the CubTile, which may ease 3D interaction thanks to its additional degrees of freedom compared to a traditional input device such as a mouse.

When a constraint appeared concurrently with the second task – pillars were "falling" continuously from the sky and had to be positioned quickly before they touched the ground – the workload index increased substantially. This is consistent with the sudden pressure that was exerted on users. As one could expect, the mental workload lowered and settled in tasks 3 and 4, during which there was no more time pressure – but still more complex manipulations compared to task 1.

We purposely inverted the commands during the fifth task to disorientate participants. As a matter of fact, this is the moment when the workload index was the highest on average among all participants. Then, after this sudden surge of mental stress, once again the measured workload has been reduced in the two subsequent tasks. Interestingly enough, for task 6, in which the control commands were inverted back to normal, the workload indeed decreased as compared to that of task 5, but was still higher than for the other tasks. This probably reflects the fact that users had somehow integrated the counterintuitive manipulation technique and had to change again the gestures they used to manipulate the 3D object, thus being forced to forget what they had just learned in task 5 which resulted in a high workload. Since the new control scheme was the one they had already used during the previous tasks though, the workload was not as high as in task 5.

Overall, the mental workload that was measured with EEG and EMG along the course of the interaction matches the design of the tasks. Workload increased when a sensitive element of the interaction was deprived – e.g. time or commands – which can be explained by the need to overcome what participants have learned previously and re-learn how to handle the new environment. Afterward, when going back to the previous scheme, the workload goes back to a low level, as could be expected.

The absence of differences in the workload index between the beginning and the end of the tasks could be due to their durations. We expect to observe a learning effect when the CubTile – or any other input device – is operated during a prolonged period of time in steady conditions; i.e., the workload index would be lower in the end.

Overall, these results suggested that continuous mental workload monitoring was possible and could provide us with interesting insights about how cognitively easy-to-use a given 3D interaction technique can be. As compared to previous works, our results show that it is possible to monitor mental workload based on brain and physiological signals, even when the user is actively interacting (and not passively observing as in previous works), moving, and performing more complex and more cognitively demanding 3D manipulation tasks, in a visually rich 3D environment.

The approach we proposed here enabled us to perform continuous mental workload monitoring, but only with an offline analysis. Indeed, our algorithm required computing the covariance matrix of EEG signals recorded during the context of use (i.e., here during 3D object manipulation tasks), which would not have been possible if mental workload was to be estimated in real-time during these manipulation tasks. The covariance matrix was estimated on all the EEG data collected during the manipulation tasks, and thus could only be estimated once the tasks were completed. In the future, it would be interesting to design a continuous workload estimator that can also be used in real-time. To do so, our algorithm could be adapted in two ways: (1) the covariance matrix of the EEG signals recorded during 3D manipulation tasks could be estimated on the first task - or couple of tasks - only, to enable workload estimation in real-time on the subsequent tasks; (2) the differences between the calibration context and the use context are likely to be the same across different participants [27]. As such, the EEG signals directions that vary between contexts can be estimated on the data from some users, and used to estimate robustly the workload on the data from other users, hence without the need to estimate these variations for a new user, as done in [27] for the classification of EEG signals related to imagined hand movements. We will explore these options in the future, which would potentially open the door for robust continuous mental effort estimation during 3D interaction, in real-time.

5   Conclusion

In this paper, we have explored a new way to evaluate 3DUI in a more continuous, objective/exocentric and non-interrupting way. In particular we proposed to continuously monitor the mental effort exerted by users of a given 3DUI based on the measure of their brain signals (EEG). We first proposed a method to estimate such level of mental effort from EEG, EMG, ECG and GSR signals. We then used the resulting mental effort estimator to study mental workload during a pilot study involving 3D object manipulation tasks with a CubTile. Monitoring workload enabled us to continuously observe when and where the 3DUI and/or interaction technique was easy or difficult to use. In the future, it could potentially be used to also study how users learn to use the 3DUI, possibly in real-time. Overall, this suggested such approach can be a relevant tool to complement existing 3DUI evaluation tools.

Future works will consist in using the proposed workload estimator to assess other 3D interaction tasks such as navigation or application control. We will also explore other mental states that could be measured from brain and physiological signals, such as error recognition (to measure how intuitive a 3DUI can be) or emotions (to measure how pleasant and enjoyable a 3DUI can be). It would also be important and interesting to estimate whether and how wearing different sensors affects the way the user interacts with the 3DUI. Overall, we aim at designing a comprehensive evaluation framework based on brain and physiological signals that could be a new evaluation tool in the repertoire of UI designers.

References

1. Anderson, E.W., Potter, K.C., Matzen, L.E., Shepherd, J.F., Preston, G.A., Silva, C.T.: A user study of visualization effectiveness using EEG and cognitive load. Eurographics 30(3), 791–800 (2011)
2. Bowman, D., Gabbard, J., Hix, D.: A survey of usability evaluation in virtual environments: classification and comparison of methods. Presence 11(4), 404–424 (2002)
3. Bowman, D., Kruijff, E., LaViola Jr., J., Poupyrev, I.: 3D User Interfaces: Theory and Practice. Addison-Wesley/Pearson Education, Boston (2005)
4. Delorme, A., Makeig, S.: EEGLAB: an open source toolbox for analysis of single-trial EEG dynamics including independent component analysis. Journal of neuroscience methods (2004)
5. van Erp, J., Lotte, F., Tangermann, M.: Brain-computer interfaces: Beyond medical applications. IEEE Comput. 45(4), 26–34 (2012)
6. Fatourechi, M., Bashashati, A., Ward, R., Birch, G.: EMG and EOG artifacts in brain computer interface systems: A survey. Clin. Neurophysiol. 118(3), 480–494 (2007)
7. Figner, B., Murphy, R.O.: Using skin conductance in judgment and decision making research. In: A handbook of process tracing methods for decision research, pp. 163–184. (2011)
8. Frey, J., Mühl, C., Lotte, F., Hachet, M.: Review of the use of electroencephalography as an evaluation method for human-computer interaction. In: Proceedings of PhyCS (2014)
9. Goncharova, I., McFarland, D., Vaughan, T., Wolpaw, J.: EMG contamination of EEG: spectral and topographical characteristics. Clin. Neurophysiol. 114(9), 1580–1593 (2003)
10. Hart, S., Staveland, L.: Development of NASA-TLX (Task Load Index): Results of empirical and theoretical research. In: Human Mental Workload (1988)
11. Jankowski, J., Hachet, M., et al.: A survey of interaction techniques for interactive 3D environments. In: Eurographics 2013-STAR (2013)
12. Karnik, A., Grossman, T., Subramanian, S.: Comparison of user performance in mixed 2D-3D multi-display environments. In: Winckler, M., (ed.) INTERACT 2013, Part I. LNCS, vol. 8117, pp. 260–277. Springer, Heidelberg (2013)
13. Kivikangas, J.M., Ekman, I., Chanel, G., Järvelä, S., Cowley, B., Henttonen, P., Ravaja, N.: Review on psychophysiological methods in game research. In: Proceedings of 1st Nordic DiGRA (2010)
14. Lotte, F., Guan, C.: Regularizing common spatial patterns to improve BCI designs: Unified theory and new algorithms. IEEE Trans. Biomed. Eng. 58(2), 355–362 (2011)
15. Lotte, F.: A tutorial on EEG signal-processing techniques for mental-state recognition in brain–computer interfaces. In: Miranda, E.R., Castet, J. (eds.) Guide to Brain-Computer Music Interfacing, pp. 133–161. Springer, London (2014)
16. Mehler, B., Reimer, B., Wang, Y.: A comparison of heart rate and heart rate variability indices in distinguishing single task driving and driving under secondary cognitive workload. In: Proceedings of Driving Symposium on Human Factors in Driver Assessment (2011)
17. Mühl, C., Jeunet, C., Lotte, F.: EEG-based workload estimation across affective contexts. Front. Neurosci. 8, 114 (2014)
18. Müller-Putz, G., Scherer, R., Brunner, C., Leeb, R., Pfurtscheller, G.: Better than random: a closer look on BCI results. Int. J. Bioelectromagnetism 10(1), 52–55 (2008)
19. Nisbett, R.E., Wilson, T.D.: Telling more than we can know: Verbal reports on mental processes. Psych. Rev. 84(3), 231–260 (1977)

20. Nourbakhsh, N., Wang, Y., Chen, F.: GSR and Blink Features for Cognitive Load Classification. In: INTERACT 2013 (2013)
21. Owen, A.M., McMillan, K.M., Laird, A.R., Bullmore, E.: N-back working memory paradigm: A meta-analysis of normative functional neuroimaging studies. Hum. Brain Mapp. **25**(1), 46–59 (2005)
22. Peck, E.M.M., Yuksel, B.F., Ottley, A., Jacob, R.J., Chang, R.: Using fNIRS brain sensing to evaluate information visualization interfaces. In: Proceedings of CHI, pp. 473–482 (2013)
23. Picard, R.W.: Affective computing. Technical report 321, MIT Media Laboratory (1995)
24. Ramoser, H., Muller-Gerking, J., Pfurtscheller, G.: Optimal spatial filtering of single trial EEG during imagined hand movement. IEEE Trans. Rehabil. Eng. **8**(4), 441–446 (2000)
25. Renard, Y., Lotte, F., Gibert, G., Congedo, M., Maby, E., Delannoy, V., Bertrand, O., Lécuyer, A.: OpenViBE: an open-source software platform to design, test, and use brain-computer interfaces in real and virtual environments. Presence: Teleoperators and Virtual Environ. **19**(1), 35–53 (2010)
26. de la Rivière, J.B., Kervégant, C., Orvain, E., Dittlo, N.: CubTile: a multi-touch cubic interface. In: Proceedings of ACM VRST, pp. 69–72 (2008)
27. Samek, W., Meinecke, F.C., Müller, K.R.: Transferring subspaces between subjects in brain–computer interfacing. IEEE Trans. Biomed. Eng. **60**(8), 2289–2298 (2013)
28. da Silva, H.P., Fred, A., Martins, R.: Biosignals for everyone. IEEE Pervasive Comput. **13**(4), 64–71 (2014)
29. Vidaurre, C., Sander, T.H., Schlögl, A.: BioSig: the free and open source software library for biomedical signal processing. Comput. Intell. Neurosci. **2011**, 12 (2011). doi:10.1155/2011/935364. Article ID 935364

Continuous Tactile Feedback
for Motor-Imagery Based Brain-Computer
Interaction in a Multitasking Context

Camille Jeunet[1,2]([✉]), Chi Vi[3], Daniel Spelmezan[3],
Bernard N'Kaoua[1], Fabien Lotte[2], and Sriram Subramanian[3]

[1] Laboratoire Handicap and Système Nerveux, University of Bordeaux,
Talence, France
camille.jeunet@inria.fr, bernard.nkaoua@u-bordeaux.fr
[2] Project-Team Potioc, Inria Bordeaux Sud-Ouest/LaBRI/CNRS,
Talence, France
fabien.lotte@inria.fr
[3] Bristol Interaction and Graphics (BIG) Group,
University of Bristol, Bristol, UK
{vi,sriram}@cs.bris.ac.uk,
daniel.spelmezan@bristol.ac.uk

Abstract. Motor-Imagery based Brain Computer Interfaces (MI-BCIs) allow users to interact with computers by imagining limb movements. MI-BCIs are very promising for a wide range of applications as they offer a new and non-time locked modality of control. However, most MI-BCIs involve visual feedback to inform the user about the system's decisions, which makes them difficult to use when integrated with visual interactive tasks. This paper presents our design and evaluation of a tactile feedback glove for MI-BCIs, which provides a continuously updated tactile feedback. We first determined the best parameters for this tactile feedback and then tested it in a multitasking environment: at the same time users were performing the MI tasks, they were asked to count distracters. Our results suggest that, as compared to an equivalent visual feedback, the use of tactile feedback leads to a higher recognition accuracy of the MI-BCI tasks and fewer errors in counting distracters.

Keywords: Brain-Computer interaction · Tactile feedback · Multitasking

1 Introduction

Brain-Computer Interfaces (BCIs) are communication and control systems allowing users to interact with their environment using their brain activity alone [27]. BCIs based on ElectroEncephaloGraphy (EEG, i.e., recording neurons' electrical activity on the scalp) are increasing in popularity due to their advantages of having high temporal resolution while being non-invasive, portable and inexpensive compared to BCIs based on other brain sensing techniques (e.g., functional Magnetic Resonance Imaging). In particular, sensorimotor rhythms (SMRs), i.e., oscillations in brain activity recorded from cortical somatosensory and motor areas (detectable in the 8–30 Hz frequency

© IFIP International Federation for Information Processing 2015
J. Abascal et al. (Eds.): INTERACT 2015, Part I, LNCS 9296, pp. 488–505, 2015.
DOI: 10.1007/978-3-319-22701-6_36

band) [22], are most frequently used. BCIs based on SMRs allow users to send commands to the system without moving, just by doing so-called "Motor-Imagery" (MI) tasks. Indeed, these rhythms are modified while doing a movement, but also while preparing or imagining this movement. Thus, for instance, some applications enable a wheelchair to turn left by doing a specific MI task, such as imagining a left hand movement [18]. BCIs based on this paradigm are known as Motor-Imagery based BCIs. MI-BCIs are not time-locked, which means that users can send commands to the system without waiting for and focusing on stimuli. As no stimulus is required, users can focus their visual attention on another task or on the environment. Consequently, MI-BCIs are attractive to many interactive applications.

Fig. 1. A participant receives tactile feedback while controlling the MI-BCI. Vibrations from the motor on the right hand represent the current feedback provided by the MI-BCI system.

However, MI-BCIs have had limited uptake outside laboratories [27] due imperfect classification algorithms and the difficulty for users to learn to control MI-BCI based systems. Indeed, previous studies have shown that around 20 % of users are unable to control an MI-BCI (so called "BCI illiteracy/deficiency"), while the remaining 80 % have relatively modest performances [2]: their mental control commands (MI tasks) are correctly recognised by the system less than 75 % of the time on average.

One utmost important aspect (while not much considered) of MI-BCI performance is the user's ability to acquire the skills necessary to control the system. Indeed, in order to improve the system's performances, i.e., its capacity to correctly recognise the MI tasks the user is performing, the latter should be able to (1) generate specific and stable brain activity patterns when performing an MI task, and (2) make these patterns well distinguishable from other MI tasks. Thus, studies have shown that the feedback design was important to favour this skill acquisition, and so to improve users' performance [16]. To date, most MI-BCI studies involved visual feedback to inform the user about the MI task recognised by the system. Yet, this visual feedback is difficult to assimilate when integrated with the visual layout of the primary interactive application that it supports [9]. Indeed, the visual channel is often overtaxed in interactive environments [15]. Thus, integrating the visual feedback into the application increases the number of visual search tasks. This is a typical *branching* condition [1] where users have poor performance in searching for visual objects [11].

On the other hand, tactile feedback, although popular in other areas of HCI, has not received much attention for MI-BCI despite its advantages such as: (a) freeing the visual channel in order to reduce cognitive workload [15], (b) maintaining a certain amount of privacy, as it is more difficult to be perceived by the surroundings than the visual or auditory ones, and (c) the possibility to be used in a wide range of interactive tasks, such as in gaming conditions. Using tactile feedback will separate the application channel (visual) from the MI-BCI feedback channel (tactile), thus potentially improving the branching condition of the application. This should consequently increase the user's performance and system's efficiency.

In this paper we explore the benefits of providing a continuously updated tactile feedback (i.e., updated at 4 Hz -see Sect. 3.1) to improve MI-BCI users' performance (i.e., their ability to do MI tasks correctly recognised by the system) in an environment containing visual distracters (Fig. 1). Indeed, BCIs are inherently developed to promote interaction. Yet, most MI-BCI studies test their feedback efficiency (1) in a laboratory context, i.e., with no distracters and (2) with no side task, while in real applications such as games users would have to perform multitasking. Thus, the efficiency of these feedbacks cannot be guaranteed in an interaction and multitasking context. This is why we study our tactile feedback's efficiency by comparing it to an equivalent visual feedback, (1) in a context including visual distracters (to mimic an interaction environment) and (2) by adding a counting task (to evaluate the cognitive resources needed to process each kind of feedback). Our tactile system is in the form of a wearable glove that integrates five vibrotactile actuators for each hand to provide continuous tactile feedback to the user regarding the BCI output. This expands the user's feedback bandwidth while reducing the visual cognitive load. Through a first user-study we calibrated the device to the users' feedback preference while matching the visual feedback fidelity to this tactile feedback (so that both feedbacks can be rigorously compared). In a second study we compared the tactile and visual feedback in an environment containing distracters and found that users obtained significantly better MI-BCI performances with tactile feedback. Our results suggest that tactile feedback is a powerful modality for MI-BCI in an HCI context.

The main contributions of this paper are: (1) design and implementation of a glove that provides continuously updated vibrotactile feedback to the user's hands with a fidelity comparable to standard visual feedback; (2) evaluation of our tactile feedback glove in an environment including visual distracters and in a multitasking context: our results suggest that users have better MI-BCI performances and better scores at counting distracters with continuous tactile feedback than with visual feedback.

2   Related Work

2.1   Visual Feedback for MI-BCIs

Usually in MI-BCI training protocols, a visual feedback is provided (Fig. 2). It gives information to the user about the classifier output (for more details, see Sect. 5.5): the label (i.e., which MI task was recognised by the classifier, e.g. left-hand MI), and the confidence value (e.g., the probability estimate for the selected MI task). Standard

MI-BCI training protocols display this feedback visually as an extending bar [22]. The direction of the bar depends on the classifier label (e.g., left direction if a left-hand MI is recognised) and its length is proportional to the BCI output. The visual appearance of the bar has been varied in many studies, but the principle did not change [20]. While simple to implement and very intuitive, visual feedback is often boring [16] and may result in decreased motivation and bad user-experience. In a bid to maintain motivation, some researchers have designed gamified MI-BCI training protocols: [17] proposed two simple games based on the ball-basket paradigm and on a spacecraft avoiding bombs. Other studies, reviewed in [14], went even further and integrated virtual reality in MI-BCI training protocols. The gamification of the protocols appeared to be efficient since these studies revealed a better user performance compared to standard protocols.

However, these protocols have two weak points: (1) they propose a feedback which is specific to the MI-BCI training protocol: thus, will the learned skills be transferable to another MI-BCI task? (2) All these feedbacks involve the visual channel, which is often overtaxed in interaction situations. Nevertheless, using a visual feedback independent from the interactive application (e.g., the game or navigation task) would force the user to split his attention between different visual information (the game and the MI-BCI feedback), thus demanding more cognitive resources [15].

This led the BCI-community to investigate other feedback modalities. Several studies explored auditory feedback, in which the different classifier output values were represented as variations of frequency [6], intensity [17] or pitch [12, 21]. Auditory feedback has been shown to be efficient for patients in a locked-in state as they often suffer from visual impairment and sensory loss [13]. However, as the auditory channel is also much demanded in interaction contexts, auditory feedback does not seem to be more relevant than visual feedback.

We argue that haptic feedback could present many advantages. First, the tactile channel is usually less overtaxed than the visual and auditory ones in situations of interaction. Thus, multimodality could make the information processing easier by avoiding the cognitive overload due to the visual channel overtaxing [25]. Second, tactile feedback is more personal than visual and auditory feedbacks as it is difficult to perceive for other people (which can be appreciated, e.g., for multiplayer games).

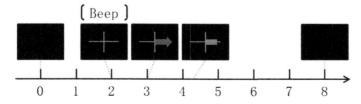

Fig. 2. Timing and visualisation of a standard MI-BCI training protocol

2.2   Tactile Feedback for MI-BCIs

On the one hand, tactile feedback for MI-BCIs has been mainly used in a medical context. Indeed, [26] explored lingual electro-tactile stimulation, as the tongue provides an excellent spatial resolution, and its sensitivity is preserved in the case of spinal cord injuries; while [8, 23] focused on proprioceptive feedback (i.e., information about the limbs' position and about the strength developed while performing a movement) and show that proprioceptive feedback allows increasing BCI performance, indicating that these alternative feedback are very promising for patients. However, these kinds of tactile feedback are quite invasive and expensive. Thus, they do not seem to be relevant for HCI applications targeting the general public.

However, a few studies explored tactile feedback for general public applications. Most of these studies in which haptic feedback has been chosen to inform the user about the classifier output used vibrotactile feedback with either a variation of the vibration patterns (e.g., different motor activation rhythms according to the classifier output) [4] or variations in spatial location [5, 17].

Results show benefits when coupled with visual feedback, but only when the vibrotactile feedback maps the "stimulus" location (i.e., the MI task the participant has to perform). This relationship is known as "control-display mapping" [24]. For example, when a right-hand MI is recognised, tactile feedback provided to the right part of the body will be more efficient (i.e., associated with better performance and user experience) than tactile feedback provided to the left side. Results also show similar performances between visual and tactile feedback, and the participants reported that tactile feedback was more natural than visual feedback, although negative feedback due to a misclassification of the mental task can be annoying. Nevertheless, [5, 15] suggest that although it is disturbing, negative vibrotactile feedback has no impact on classification (i.e., it does not affect the brain patterns used by the system to recognise the MI tasks). A few studies already attempted to use continuous vibrotactile feedback [5, 9, 15]. For instance, concerning [5] a continuous tactile feedback is proposed in one of their studies. However, their set up is different from ours: feedback is provided on the neck (as opposed to the palm of the hand), only updated every 2 s (as opposed to every 0.250 s) and more importantly, the feedback has not been tested in a BCI control context. In [9], a comparison between visual and tactile feedback was proposed, and the findings showed that they are associated with equivalent performances in a BCI context. In [15], visual and tactile feedback were compared in the context of a visual attention task performed using a BCI. In the latter study, tactile feedback was shown to be associated with better performances than the visual one. Unfortunately, these studies present some limitations. First, the samples are small: 6–7 subjects. Second, and most importantly, as they used within subject comparisons and that the conditions were not counterbalanced (the visual feedback was always tested before the tactile feedback), one cannot rule out that these results are due to an order effect. Finally, while the feedbacks were tested in presence of distracters [15], it is not a multitasking context as the visual attention task and the MI-BCI control task have been performed sequentially. In our paper, we propose to overcome these limitations with a larger sample (18 participants), a counter-balanced between-subject paradigm and an MI-BCI control task combined with a counting task requiring supplementary cognitive resources.

3 Design of Visual and Vibrotactile Feedback

The main goal of our work is to compare the standard visual feedback with an equivalent tactile feedback in a context of multitasking and in an environment containing distracters in order to mimic possible interaction situations in which MI-BCIs could be used, e.g., a video game. Thus, in this section we first explain how we designed our vibrotactile and corresponding visual feedback. Then we describe the developed hardware prototype and the design of the glove for providing this tactile feedback at the hand, as well as the mapping between visual and tactile stimuli.

3.1 Temporally Continuous Tactile Feedback

As pointed out earlier, the MI-BCI classifier output, which is usually provided as feedback to the user, is the combination of the label of the recognised MI task and the confidence value of the classifier in the recognition of this task. These two elements can be presented as a value in the range of $[-0.5, 0.5]$. Negative values correspond to a left hand MI recognition while positive values correspond to right hand MI recognition. The closer these values are to the end of the range, the higher the confidence level of the classifier (e.g., for right hand MI the value 0.45 represents a higher confidence level than 0.16). Our goal was to represent this output via the tactile channel as closely as possible to the standard visual feedback (in which the output is represented as a bar varying in length and direction).

The MI-BCI system relies on left- and right-hand MI. Thus, we decided to give tactile feedback to the hands to maintain the control-display mapping [24] between the intended user actions (MI) and the sensory information perceived by the user (the tactile feedback). Indeed, control-display mapping has been shown to be necessary so that tactile feedback is efficient [24]. The large surface of the palm (the average width is 74 mm for women, 84 mm for men) makes it possible to create a tactile display suitable for representing the MI-BCI classifier output (Fig. 2). Indeed, considering the two-point threshold of the palm ($\sim$ 8 mm [7]), the width of the actuators, 8 mm, and the fact that we wanted our design to be suitable for most of the users (and thus narrower than the average palm width, 74 mm), we determined that we could put 5 motors maximum on each hand. Thus, we divided the classifier output range of $[-0.5, 0.5]$ into 10 discrete levels, with 5 levels on the left and 5 levels on the right hand. Vibrations on the left/right palm corresponded to the recognition of a left/right hand MI by the classifier, respectively. With the palms being facing upwards, vibrations near the thumbs corresponded to high confidence levels (close to $|0.5|$) while vibrations near the little finger corresponded to low confidence levels (close to 0).

Standard MI-BCI update rates, i.e., 16 Hz (62.5 ms), can be difficult to achieve with tactile feedback as a stimulus should be provided for at least 200 ms to be easily recognisable over the tactile channel [7]. Consequently, we chose an update rate of 4 Hz (every 250 ms), to ensure a perceivable tactile feedback.

3.2   Visual Feedback

Standard visual feedback corresponds to a continuous bar varying in length and direction. To make both the visual and tactile feedback as similar as possible, and because the tactile feedback has been spatially discretised (classifier output range of [-0.5, 0.5] divided into 10 discrete levels), we also discretised the standard bar in the same way (Fig. 3). Thus, the feedback was displayed as a red cursor on a cross, with 5 ticks on the left and 5 ticks on the right side (Fig. 2). The cursor was on the left/right side of the cross when a left/right hand MI was recognised, respectively. Moreover, the cursor moving to the extremities of the cross represented high confidence values. Finally, we also reduced the standard update rate of 16 Hz to 4 Hz so that it fits the tactile feedback update rate.

Fig. 3. Visual feedback with current feedback symbolising the recognition of a right hand MI, at level 3/5.

3.3   Hardware Design

To provide the user with tactile feedback, we designed a glove for the left and the right hand in which 5 vibrotactile actuators were embedded (Fig. 4). The actuators were cylindrical vibration motors (model 307-100 by Precision Microdrives, Fig. 4, left). Each motor is 8.0 mm wide and 25 mm long. The motors were connected to a custom-built motor shield and were controlled by pulse-width modulation using an Arduino Due. The ten motors were powered from an external supply (2 V).

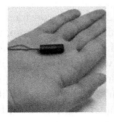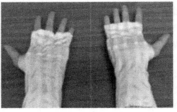

Fig. 4. Left: A vibration motor. *Right:* Our gloves with 10 embedded motors (5 per hand). In the tactile feedback condition, individual motors are activated to represent the classifier output.

4   STUDY I - Determining the Intensity and the Pattern of Activation of the Motors for the Vibrotactile Feedback

Some previous studies have explored continuously updated feedback for MI-BCIs [5, 9, 15], but not much work has been led in order to evaluate the optimal parameters for this feedback modality. For instance, should the vibration pattern be encoded as localised vibration from a single motor, or as simultaneous vibrations of multiple neighbouring motors to represent a specific classifier output? Another question concerns the tactile stimulus intensity. Indeed, the vibration should be strong enough to be perceived but not too intense, as it could distract the user and be uncomfortable. In the next section, we describe the user study conducted to investigate these issues.

4.1 Experimental Design

The aim of this study was to determine the pattern and intensity of vibration which provide the user the most pleasant and distinct feedback. We investigated two designs of vibration patterns for representing the classifier output. One design implemented localised vibration, i.e., only one of the vibration motors was active at a given time (e.g., the third motor of the right hand if a right-hand MI was recognised with a confidence value in [0.2, 0.3]). The other design implemented simultaneous vibration of neighbouring motors. The latter pattern entailed activating all motors of the hand corresponding to the recognised MI task whose index value was smaller or equal to the current classifier level (e.g., the first, second and third motors of the right hand, from left to right, if a right-hand MI was recognised with a confidence value in [0.2, 0.3]). The rationale between these two designs was to (1) maintain the spatial mapping between the visual and tactile feedback and (2) to indicate the relative change in the classifier's output.

Our first informal test of the motors (2 V) revealed a strong unpleasant tactile stimulus (the normalized vibration amplitude of the motor was 3G relative to a 100 g mass). In order to design more subtle tactile stimuli, we adjusted the voltage used to control the motors (pulse-width modulation), which implicitly changed the motor's vibration frequency and vibration amplitude. The experiment followed a 2×4 within-participant design with the factors:

- Pattern: *localised* vs. *simultaneous* vibration;
- Intensity: [0.1, 0.3, 0.5, 1] G with corresponding frequencies of [10, 40, 60, 85] Hz.

4.2 Participants

Ten volunteers (4 women, with age 28.8 ± 8.2) from the local university participated in this study. Some participants had previous experience with vibrotactile feedback but none of them had participated in this experiment before.

4.3 Task and Procedure

At the beginning of the study the experimenter informed the participants about the goal of the study and asked them to sign a consent form which was approved by the University's Ethics Committee. The participants were then asked to put on the gloves and to place their hands on the table in front of them in a supine position (palms facing upwards, as in Fig. 4-right).

We designed 8 vibration sequences which simulated vibrotactile feedback. As in a real scenario, these sequences were provided for 4 s, during which 16 tactile stimuli appeared (4 Hz update rate). We varied the factors Pattern and Intensity to compare:

a. Localised to simultaneous vibrations with the same intensity level (4 possibilities);
b. Localised vibration at 2 different intensity levels (6 possibilities);
c. Simultaneous vibration at 2 different intensity levels (6 possibilities).

We considered both presentation orders for the patterns in (a), i.e., first localised then simultaneous and vice versa, and for the intensities in (b, c), i.e., first intensity 1 then intensity 2 and vice versa. Overall, we tested (4 + 6+6)*2 = 32 combinations. We randomly assigned one of the eight sequences at each of the combinations (so that they are not associated with the same combination for the different participants). For each combination, we asked the participants their favourite feedback, i.e., localised or simultaneous for (a) and intensity 1 or intensity 2 for (b, c). Thus, we evaluated the quality of the different patterns and intensities according to the number of times they were selected as the favourite one. This paradigm allowed us to find the best pattern*intensity association, which was the most often chosen as the favourite one.

4.4 Results

Figure 5 reveals a Pattern x Intensity interaction [$F_{(3,72)} = 8.785$, $p < 0.001$, $\eta2 = 0.268$], a main effect of the pattern [$F_{(1,72)} = 10.184$, $p < 0.005$, $\eta2 = 0.124$], and a main effect of the intensity [$F_{(3,72)} = 6.071$, $p < 0.005$, $\eta2 = 0.202$]. Participants preferred the localised vibration over the simultaneous vibrations. Moreover, they preferred the lowest intensity in the case of simultaneous vibrations (the other ones being perceived as too strong). For the localised vibration, however, the lowest intensity (0.1G, 10 Hz) was barely noticeable and did not allow the participants to clearly perceive the tactile feedback. The highest frequency was associated with a very strong and uncomfortable sensation. Thus, they preferred the middle intensity (0.3–0.5G).

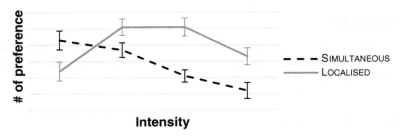

Fig. 5. Average number of times that a pattern was preferred as a function of its intensity.

4.5   Discussion

The results of this study suggest that the participants preferred a localised vibration at the palm, with only one vibration motor being active at a given time. Our findings also suggest that either 0.3G (40 Hz) or 0.5G (60 Hz) is appropriate for providing tactile feedback at the palm using the developed tactile feedback system.

These findings provide first guidelines on how to design tactile feedback for stimulating the palm in an MI-BCI context. In addition, these results can inform the design of feedback for other interactive tasks in HCI which require a similar presentation of feedback to the user.

5   STUDY II – Comparing Visual and Tactile Feedback in a Multitasking Context

5.1   Training Environment

BCIs are developed to be used in interactive applications (e.g., video games or navigation tasks), i.e., in a context including distracters and requiring multitasking abilities. Thus, it seems irrelevant to test the efficiency of a feedback outside this kind of context, i.e., in laboratory conditions by doing only a MI-BCI task. This is why we designed a training environment including visual distracters and asked the participants to perform a counting task at the same time they were performing the MI-BCI task (Fig. 6, right).

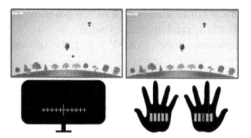 

Fig. 6. Two feedback types representing the recognition of a right-hand MI, at level 3 out of 5. *Left:* Visual feedback was displayed as a red circle moving along the axis and vibrotactile feedback at the palm was encoded as a vibration of the corresponding motor; *Right:* Environment visualisation with all elements: an enemy (top right), the spacecraft (centre), and visual feedback (lower centre, below the spacecraft); three distracters: missile (top left), cloud (top centre), and rabbit (bottom centre) (Color figure online).

By adding these elements, we were able to compare the cognitive workload required to process each kind of feedback in an interactive situation and to evaluate how cognitive multitasking (branching [1]) influences the efficiency of each feedback.

In order to include the distracters and the counting task to the MI-BCI task in a consistent environment, we modified the standard MI-BCI training protocol [22]. The standard arrows pointing left or right to inform the user he has to perform a left or right-hand MI have been replaced by a spacecraft the goal of which was to protect its planet by destroying bombs coming from the left or right (controlled by performing left- or right-hand MI, respectively) (Fig. 6).

Besides, the distracters were appearing randomly in the form of (1) a missile, which was launched in a vertical direction from a tank, (2) a rabbit crossing from the left to the right, or (3) a cloud crossing from the right to the left (Fig. 4). Each distracter appeared for a similar amount of time (approximately 2.5 s).

5.2 Participants

Eighteen healthy volunteers (5 women; aged 27.6 ± 4.8) participated in the study. Some of them had previously experienced vibrotactile feedback. However, none of them had previous experience with MI-BCI.

5.3 Experimental Design

After they completed the informed consent form and were notified about the progress of the experiment, the participants have been randomly assigned to one of the two groups: visual or tactile feedback. Consequently, nine participants were provided with visual feedback, and the other nine participants were provided with vibrotactile feedback during the whole experiment. The experiment was divided into 6 runs, each of 7 min duration. The first run was used to train the MI-BCI classifier. The remaining 5 runs were used for the user training and data recording. Each run was composed of 40 trials: 20 left-hand MI and 20 right-hand MI trials, randomly distributed.

Thus, the experiment followed a 2×5 between-subjects ANOVA with the factors:

- Feedback Condition: *visual* or *tactile*;
- Runs: *1–5*.

During the experiment, the participants had to control a spacecraft (shown at the centre of the screen in Fig. 4) by performing left- or right-hand MI tasks to make it move left or right, respectively. The goal of this spacecraft was to protect the planet against bombs falling down on the planet. Thus, when a bomb was falling off the left/right side of the screen, participants had to perform left/right-hand MI in order to make the spacecraft move left/right, face the bomb and destroy it. The application was developed in C# using Microsoft/XNA 4.0.

Each trial was lasting around 8 s and had the same structure, described hereafter and depicted in Fig. 7. At the beginning, the spacecraft was in the middle of the screen for 3 s. Then the instruction was given to the participant as a bomb appearing either at the top left or right of the screen and moving vertically towards the planet (at a speed of one pixel/frame). This instruction informed the participant about the command to perform: a right-hand or a left-hand MI, in order to move the spacecraft to the right or to the left, respectively, face and destroy the enemy. 1.25 s after the appearance of the bomb, the MI-BCI classifier output was provided to the participant continuously for a duration of 3.75 s, either in the form of a moving cursor on a visual cross at the lower centre of the screen, or as vibrotactile feedback at the palm. At the end of the feedback period, the mean classifier output was calculated and the spacecraft was moving to the left or right based on this value (e.g., to the left if the mean classifier output was in [−0.5,0) and to the right if the mean classifier output was in (0, 0.5]). If the correct MI task was recognised, the spacecraft aligned its position with the bomb and shot to destroy the bomb. Otherwise, the bomb speeded up (20 pixels/frame) and exploded when it reached the planet.

Furthermore, as explained in the previous section, during each trial, one or more distracters were appearing between the moment when the enemy was displayed and the moment when the spacecraft started to move in order to destroy the enemy. Each distracter type appeared at most once during each trial. In each run, which consisted of 40 trials, each distracter type appeared at least 15 times and at most 25 times. At the beginning of each run the participants were asked to count how many distracters of a specified type appeared, and to report this number at the end of the run.

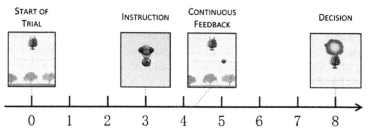

Fig. 7. Timing of a trial.

5.4   Score Calculation

At the end of the trial, the score was updated according to the following formula:

$$\text{New Score} = \text{Current Score} + \text{Class Label} * \text{Classifier Output} * 200$$

The CLASS-LABEL was {−1} if a left-hand MI was recognised and {+1} if a right-hand MI was recognised. The CLASSIFIER-OUTPUT was the **mean** classifier output value calculated at the end of the trial: in [−0.5,0) if a left-hand MI was recognised, and in (0,0.5] if a right-hand MI was recognised. Therefore, after each trial, the score was increased or decreased by 100 points **maximum**, given that to obtain 100 points at one trial, the mean classifier output value of the trial had to be 0.5, which means that the classifier output had to be 0.5 for each of the 15 time windows (the feedback being updated at 4 Hz for 3.75 s). This value of 0.5 thus means that the classifier was 100 % sure that the participant was performing a right-hand MI for each of the 15 time windows. This never happens in MI-BCI. Besides, while the mean classifier output is positive, it means that the trial has been correctly classified. Thus, to take an extreme case, a score of 40/4000 at the end of the run (e.g., 1/100 at each of the 40 trials of the run) could be associated with a classification accuracy of 100 % (as each mean classifier output was positive, it means that all the trials have been correctly classified). The MI score corresponded to the sum of the scores obtained in each trial. Furthermore, at the end of each run, the participant was asked to report the number of distracters (rabbits, clouds or rockets) he counted. If this number was correct, the participant was rewarded with 200 points being added to the MI score. If the error was in the order of ± 1, the score remained unchanged. Otherwise, 200 points were subtracted from the MI score. The final score corresponded to the sum of the MI scores for the 40 trials of the run and the counting task score. While arbitrary, this metric enabled to consider and give a significant weight to both the MI score and the counting task which allowed to evaluate the feedback relevance for both these aspects.

5.5   EEG Recordings and Signal Processing

The EEG was recorded from a BrainVision actiCHamp amplifier from Brain Products, using 30 scalp electrodes (F3, Fz, F4, FT7, FC5, FC3, FCz, FC4, FC6, FT8, C5, C3, C1, Cz, C2, C4, C6, CP3, CPz, CP4, P5, P3, P1, Pz, P2, P4, P6, PO7, PO8, 10–20 system), referenced to the right mastoid and grounded to AFz. Such electrodes cover the sensori-motor cortex, where EEG variations due to MI can be measured. EEG and data were sampled at 256 Hz. First, EEG signals were band-pass filtered in 8–30 Hz (containing the SMR rhythms) [22]. At the end of the first run, which served for training the classifier, a Common Spatial Pattern algorithm [19] was used for each user on the collected data, to find 6 spatial filters whose resulting EEG power was maximally different between the two MI tasks. The spatially filtered EEG signals power (computed on a 1 s time window, with 250 ms overlap between consecutive windows) was used to train a linear Support Vector Machine (SVM) [19]. The SVM was then used online to differentiate between left- and right-hand MI during the 5 user-training runs. The SVM classifier provided a probability value in [0, 1] indicating which of the two classes the signal belongs to. For convenience, we subtracted the value 0.5 to the classifier output so that negative values, in [−0.50–0.00), corresponded to left-hand and positive values, in (0.00–0.50], to right-hand MI recognition.

5.6   Results

The main measurements of interest are (1) the final score (the sum of the MI task and the counting task scores), (2) the MI score alone, and (3) the absolute value of the difference between the counted and the actual number of distracters. These measures were analysed using three two-factor (independent) ANOVAs. We performed a 2-way ANOVA so that we can analyse the interaction between both variables. However, given the low number of participants per condition (8 and 9) it was not possible to test the prerequisites for this analysis. Thus, we computed the effect sizes to ensure the robustness of our results. Analyses have been performed on 17 participants: 8 in the visual condition and 9 in the tactile condition. The data from one outlier participant have been removed as his final score (1628.8 ± 630.5) differed considerably from his group mean final score (183.0 ± 559.5).

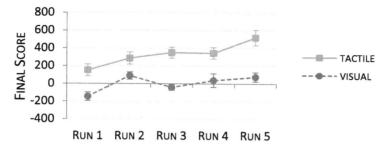

Fig. 8. Average of the final scores (with standard error): sum of the MI task score and the distracter counting task score (reward and penalty).

The two-factor ANOVA on the final score shows a main effect of the Feedback-Condition (visual vs. tactile) [$F_{(1,15)} = 6.327$, $p < 0.05$, $\eta^2 = 0.291$], a main effect of the Run [$F_{(1,15)} = 3.961$, $p < 0.01$, $\eta^2 = 0.457$] but no Run * Feedback-Condition interaction [$F_{(1,15)} = 1.476$, $p = 0.243$, $\eta^2 = 0.09$]. The Feedback Condition effect is due to participants in the tactile feedback group having significantly better results than participants in the visual feedback group. Furthermore, concerning the Run main effect, post hoc analysis shows a significant increase of performance between Run 1 and Run 5 ($p < 0.005$) (Fig. 8) which reveals the learning effect of the performed motor-imagery task, as indicated by the large effect size.

The two-factor ANOVA on MI scores (Fig. 9, left) shows strong tendencies towards a Run main effect [$F_{(1,15)} = 3.961$, $p = 0.065$, $\eta^2 = 0.209$] and towards a Feedback Condition effect [$F_{(1,15)} = 4.063$, $p = 0.062$, $\eta^2 = 0.213$], as well as no interaction between these two factors [$F_{(1,15)} = 1.207$, $p = 0.289$, $\eta^2 = 0.074$]. These results indicate a strong tendency towards a better MI score with tactile feedback than with visual feedback and a tendency towards an improved MI score across the Runs.

The two-factor ANOVA on the counting task (Fig. 9, right) shows a main effect of the Run [$F_{(1,15)} = 9.806$, $p < 0.01$] but no main effect of the Feedback Condition [$F_{(1,15)} = 2.860$, $p = 0.111$] and no Run * Condition interaction [$F_{(1,15)} = 0.000$, $p = 0.990$]. Thus, the participants improved their performance across the Runs for the

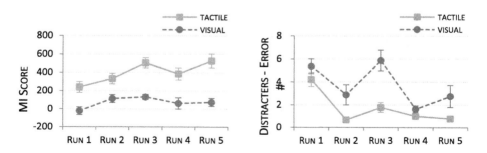

Fig. 9. Left: Average of the MI scores (with standard error) without the counting task (reward and penalty). **Right:** Average of the distracter errors (difference between the counted and the actual number) for the counting task as a function of Run number and Feedback Condition.

counting task. Indeed, post hoc analysis shows a significant difference between Run 1 and Run 4 ($p < 0.001$) and Run 1 and Run 5 ($p < 0.005$) performances.

5.7   User-Experience Results

As no adapted BCI user-experience questionnaire exists, we proposed a custom-ised one, designed to measure four dimensions of usability: learnability/memorability (LM), efficiency/effectiveness (EE), safety, satisfaction. The 1 fac-tor ANOVA did not reveal any differences between the visual and tactile feedback conditions: LM   [$\bar{X}_{visual} = 60.47 \pm 10.52, \bar{X}_{tactile} = 56.53 \pm 13.46 - F_{(1,17)} = 0.444, p = 0.515$], EE [$\bar{X}_{visual} = 67.86 \pm 13.72, \bar{X}_{tactile} = 56.19 \pm 19.95 - F_{(1,17)} = 1.921, p = 0.186$], Satifaction [$\bar{X}_{visual} = 67.50 \pm 13.42, \bar{X}_{tactile} = 58.70 \pm 20.39 - F_{(1,17)} = 1.071, p = 0.317$], Safety [$\bar{X}_{visual} = 61.25 \pm 18.08, \bar{X}_{tactile} = 55.56 \pm 23.51 - F_{(1,17)} = 0.307, p = 0.588$].

5.8   Discussion

Results and Ecological Validity: While the participants did not find the MI-BCI training easier or more satisfying with the tactile feedback (cf. user-experience ques-tionnaire), results suggest that continuous tactile feedback can significantly improve users' MI-BCI performances as compared to an equivalent visual feedback (same timing & update rate), in an interactive context. We believe that testing these equivalent feedbacks in a multitasking context increases the ecological validity of the results. *Branching Effect:* Results suggest that vibrotactile feedback can support branching tasks better than visual feedback in this context. *Learning Effect:* Results reveal a learning effect for the MI tasks for both feedback modalities. It seems that both feedback types are equally effective for the investigated task.

6   Discussion

Our study suggests that it is possible to provide MI-BCI users with a relevant con-tinuous vibrotactile feedback while they are performing MI tasks, and that this tactile feedback can improve BCI control reliability in a multitasking context (as compared to an equivalent visual feedback). It suggests that providing feedback through another modality than the visual one, but with the same content has advantages: it tends to improve users' BCI control, frees the visual channel and thus some cognitive resources to perform other tasks. For some BCI users, it may be difficult to pay attention to both the visual feedback and the MI task. Naive BCI users often report this issue informally. This difficulty is drastically increased when the MI has to be performed in a multi-tasking environment (e.g., a game). Indeed, in this kind of environment, the visual channel is overtaxed de facto. Thus, providing a visual feedback concerning the MI-BCI tasks being performed in addition to environment related information forces the user to split his attention and use more cognitive resources. Besides, receiving a continuous tactile feedback consistent with the motor imagery tasks being performed is probably more natural and intuitive than a visual feedback.

Furthermore, from an MI-BCI based application point of view, our study showed that a continuous tactile feedback enabled the user to be better at performing multitasking. Indeed, most interactive applications (e.g., games) rely heavily on the visual modality, and users are often asked to split their visual attention between different tasks and events. As such, our study suggests that further increasing the visual workload by adding visual BCI feedback is actually detrimental to the BCI reliability. Yet, although BCI-based gaming has been rather extensively studied [14], all the BCI/game studies used only the visual modality. Our study suggests that continuous vibrotactile feedback is more appropriate. In the future, we could imagine designing BCI based game control pads that can provide tactile feedback. Since real-life contains a lot of visual distractions (like it is the case in video games), we could expect that our tactile feedback improves BCI performances even outside a gaming context.

Overall, tactile feedback for BCI has been mostly studied so far with discrete feedback and targeted at patients. Only a few studies explored continuous tactile feedback for BCIs [5, 9, 15]. Results suggested that, at best, tactile feedback was as good as visual feedback [5] for MI-BCI control. In our study, when using a continuous tactile feedback with the same content as the visual one, and in a multitasking context, a different picture emerged: tactile feedback seems to improve user performance, both for MI-BCI control and side tasks (counting the distracters). However, in our study, tactile feedback was continuously updated (at 4 Hz) but not spatially continuous. This is due to the technical difficulty of providing a good motion illusion to the users. One study [5] addressed this point and obtained encouraging results using motion illusion for MI-BCI feedback. This difficulty added to the fact that we could only embed 5 motors per glove explains why we had to divide the classifier output into 10 intervals, thus provide a non-spatially continuous feedback. Overtaking this technical issue would lead to spatially and temporally continuous feedback, which would increase the level of precision. However, no study has been conducted yet in order to determine which level of precision was associated with the best MI-BCI performance. One could argue that a good precision can allow users to increase their performance, but also that too much information could increase the workload, and thus decrease performance.

To summarise, our study reinforces the idea that tactile feedback combined with MI-BCI has potential to enrich a wide range of interactive applications for the general public, such as gaming. However, using tactile feedback for interactive applications in general, and gaming settings in particular, requires the designer's attention and creativity to use it.

7   Conclusion and Future Work

Our results showed that it is possible to provide MI-BCI users with an intuitive and efficient continuously updated vibrotactile feedback. A first user study allowed us to determine the parameters of this tactile feedback:

- *Tactile feedback location*: we chose the hand palms for their high spatial accuracy and the consistency with the MI tasks (left- and right-hand movement) [24].
- *Tactile feedback update rate*: we used a 4 Hz feedback update rate so that each feedback is well perceived by the user [7].
- *Pattern of vibration*: our first user study suggested that a tactile feedback based on localised stimulation (one motor at the time) is more pleasant and distinguishable than simultaneous vibrations.
- *Intensity of vibration*: our first study suggested that vibration intensities between 0.3G (40 Hz) and 0.5G (60 Hz) were best: lower intensities did not allow users to perceive the feedback clearly, whereas higher intensities were uncomfortable.

This tactile feedback was associated with better MI-BCI performances and better scores at the counting task than visual feedback in a multitasking context, thus suggesting that it could be an effective means to support users for a wide range of interactive applications.

In the future, different elements should be considered in order to increase the validity of this study. First, more participants should be included. Moreover, as long-term use of continuous tactile feedback could result in a palm desensitisation and thus a decrease of performance, It would be important to determine when the feedback is useful or not so that performance can be optimised. Finally, in this study, only the feedback form is discussed. Yet, much work has to be done on feedback content so that it can be really relevant. Among others, it should be explanative, supportive and meaningful [16].

References

1. Afergan, D., Shibata, T., Hincks, S.W., Peck, E.M., Yuksel, B.F., Chang, R., Jacob, R.J.K.: Brain-Based Target Expansion. ACM, UIST (2014)
2. Allison, B., Neuper, C.: Could Anyone Use a BCI?. Springer, London (2010)
3. Carter, T., Seah, S.A., Long, B., Drinkwater, B., Subramanian, S.: UltraHaptics: Multi-Point Mid-Air Haptic Feedback for Touch Surfaces. ACM, UIST (2013)
4. Chatterjee, A., Aggarwal, V., Ramos, A., Acharya, S., Thakor, N.: A brain-computer interface with vibrotactile biofeedback for haptic information. J. NeuroEng. Rehabil. 4(1), 1–12 (2007)
5. Cincotti, F., Kauhanen, L., Aloise, F., Palomäki, T., Caporusso, N., Jylänki, P., Mattia, D., Babiloni, F., Vanacker, G., Nuttin, M., Marciani, M.G., Millán, J.d.R: Vibrotactile feedback for BCI operation. Intell. Neurosci. **2007**, 7 (2007)
6. Gargiulo, G.D., Mohamed, A., McEwan, A.L., Bifulco, P., Cesarelli, M., Jin, C.T., Ruffo, M., Tapson, J., van Schaik, A.: Investigating the role of combined acoustic-visual feedback in one-dimensional synchronous brain computer interfaces, a preliminary study. Med. Dev. **5**, 81–88 (2012). (Auckland, N.Z.)
7. Gescheider, G.A., Wright, J.H., Verrillo, R.T.: Information-processing channels in the tactile sensory system: a psychophysical and physiological analysis. Taylor & Francis, New York (2010)

8. Gomez-Rodriguez, M., Peters, J., Hill, J., Schölkopf, B., Gharabaghi, A., Grosse-Wentrup, M.: Closing the sensorimotor loop: haptic feedback facilitates decoding of motor imagery. J. Neural. Eng. **8**(3), 036005 (2011)
9. Gwak, K., Leeb, R., Millán, J.d.R., Kim, D.-S.: Quantification and reduction of visual load during BCI operation. In: Proceedings IEE SMC (2014)
10. Hamada, K., Mori, H., Shinoda, H., Rutkowski, T.: Airborne ultrasonic tactile display brain computer interface paradigm. In: Proceedings of International BCI Conference (2014)
11. Han, S.H., Kim, M.S.: Visual search does not remain efficient when executive working memory is working. Psychol. Sci. **15**(9), 623–628 (2004)
12. Hinterberger, T., Neumann, N., Pham, M., Kübler, A., Grether, A., Hofmayer, N., Wilhelm, B., Flor, H., Birbaumer, N.: A multimodal brain-based feedback and communication system. Exp. Brain Res. **154**(4), 521–526 (2004)
13. Laureys, S., Pellas, F., Van Eeckhout, P., Ghorbel, S., Schnakers, C., Perrin, F., Berre, J., Faymonville, M.E., Pantke, K.H., Damas, F., Lamy, M., Moonen, G., Goldman, S.: The locked-in syndrome what is it like to be conscious but paralyzed and voiceless? Prog. Brain Res. **150**, 495–511 (2005)
14. Lécuyer, A., Lotte, F., Reilly, R.B., Leeb, R., Hirose, M., Slater, M.: Brain-computer interfaces, virtual reality, and videogames. Computer **41**, 66–72 (2008)
15. Leeb, R., Gwak, K., Kim, D.S., Millán, J.d.R.: Freeing the visual channel by exploiting vibrotactile BCI feedback. In: Proceedings IEEE EMBC, pp. 3093–3096 (2013)
16. Lotte, F., Larrue, F., Mühl, C.: Flaws in current human training protocols for spontaneous BCI: lessons learned from instructional design. Front. Hum. Neurosci. **7**, 568 (2013)
17. McCreadie, K.A., Coyle, D.H., Prasad, G.: Is sensorimotor BCI performance influenced differently by mono, stereo, or 3-D auditory feedback? IEEE Trans. Neur. Syst. Rehab. **22**(3), 431–440 (2014)
18. Millán, J.d.R., Ferrez, P.W., Galan, F., Lew, E., Chavarriaga, R.: Non-invasive brain-machine interaction. Int. J. Pattern Recognit. Artif. Intell. **22**, 959–972 (2008)
19. Müller, K.R., Tangermann, M., Dornhege, G., Krauledat, M., Curio, G., Blankertz, B.: Machine learning for real-time single-trial EEG-analysis: from BCI to mental state monitoring. J. Neurosci. Methods **167**(1), 82–90 (2008)
20. Neuper, C., Pfürtscheller, G.: Neurofeedback Training for BCI Control. Springer, London (2010)
21. Nijboer, F., Furdea, A., Gunst, I., Mellinger, J., McFarland, D.J., Birbaumer, N., Kubler, A.: An auditory brain-computer interface (BCI). J. Neurosci. Methods **167**(1), 43–50 (2008)
22. Pfürtscheller, G., Neuper, C.: Motor imagery and direct brain-computer communication. Proc. IEEE **89**(7), 1123–1134 (2001)
23. Ramos-Murguialday, A., Schürholz, M., Caggiano, V., Wildgruber, M., Caria, A., Hammer, E.M., Halder, S., Birbaumer, N.: Proprioceptive feedback and brain computer interface based neuroprostheses. PLoS ONE **7**(10), e47048 (2012)
24. Thurlings, M.E., van Erp, J.B., Brouwer, A.M., Blankertz, B., Werkhoven, P.: Control-display mapping in BCIs. Ergonomics **55**, 564–580 (2012)
25. Wickens, C.D.: Processing resources in attention, dual task performance, and workload assessment. Defense Technical Information Center, Fort Belvoir (1981)
26. Wilson, J.A., Walton, L.M., Tyler, M., Williams, J.: Lingual electrotactile stimulation as an alternative sensory feedback pathway for brain-computer interface applications. J. Neural Eng. **9**(4), 045007 (2012)
27. Wolpaw, J., Wolpaw, E.W.: Brain-Computer Interfaces: Principles and Practice. Oxford University Press, Oxford (2012)

Towards Brain Computer Interfaces
for Recreational Activities: Piloting a Drone

Nataliya Kosmyna[1(✉)], Franck Tarpin-Bernard[1,2],
and Bertrand Rivet[3]

[1] LIG-IIHM, BP 53, Grenoble Cedex 9, France
natalie@kosmina.eu, f.tarpin@sbt.fr
[2] Scientific Brain Training, Bat. CEI, 66 Bd. Niels Bohr CS 52132,
69603 Villeurbanne Cedex, France
[3] Gipsa-Lab/Grenoble INP, 11 Rue des Mathématiques,
38400 Saint Martin d'Hères, France
bertrand.rivet@gipsa-lab.grenoble-inp.fr

Abstract. Active Brain Computer Interfaces (BCIs) allow people to exert voluntary control over a computer system: brain signals are captured and imagined actions (movements, concepts) are recognized after a training phase (from 10 min to 2 months). BCIs are confined in labs, with only a few dozen people using them outside regularly (e.g. assistance for impairments). We propose a "Co-learning BCI" (CLBCI) that reduces the amount of training and makes BCIs more suitable for recreational applications. We replicate an existing experiment where the BCI controls a drone and compare CLBCI to their Operant Conditioning (OC) protocol over three durations of practice (1 day, 1 week, 1 month). We find that OC works at 80 % after a month practice, but the performance is between 60 and 70 % any earlier. In a week of practice, CLBCI reaches a performance of around 75 %. We conclude that CLBCI is better suited for recreational use. OC should be reserved for users for whom performance is the main concern.

Keywords: Brain computer interface · Engagement · Replication · Drone

1 Introduction

Active Brain Computer Interfaces (BCIs) allow people to exert direct voluntary control over a computer system: their brain signals are captured and the system recognizes specific imagined actions (movement, images, concepts). Active BCIs and their users must undergo training (between 10 min and 2 months). This skill is also known as BCI training. This makes the signals easier to recognize by the system. This acquisition can take from 10 min up to 2 months. BCIs can thus be applied to many control and interaction scenarios of our everyday lives, especially in relation to entertainment [1].

BCIs have mostly been used in laboratories and in medical applications (e.g. spellers for locked-in syndrome patients [1]). A few dozen people at most use BCIs at home, as exhibited by the BNCI FP7 roadmap report [2]. Moreover, as an emerging

© IFIP International Federation for Information Processing 2015
J. Abascal et al. (Eds.): INTERACT 2015, Part I, LNCS 9296, pp. 506–522, 2015.
DOI: 10.1007/978-3-319-22701-6_37

and new interaction technology, they offer a good prospect of inspiring people's imaginations and of providing a new and enjoyable way of interaction [3].

For example, personal drones are a popular phenomenon that takes an increasing role in our daily lives. There are "selfie drones"[1] that take off from a user's wrist to take a "selfie" photo, such drones can be controlled by BCIs. Recent press coverage of a BCI system that controls a drone quadcopter [4] has shown a strong interest in the general public of experiencing BCI control.

In this particular drone piloting application, the training protocol for the BCI is called Operant Conditioning (OC), needs to teach users to harness their brain signals and adapt them so that they can be recognized by the computer, which requires one to two months of rigorous training. Alternatives to OC for BCIs are training protocols based on machine learning that record typical brain signals for a set of mental actions or states and build classifiers to recognize those actions or states. Although training is shorter (10–20 min sessions [5]), the process requires a continuous focus and concentration from users, is more error-prone than OC and involves feedback to users [6] that is not appealing.

None of the two training paradigms are entirely adequate to let people test the technology in a way that would make them want to try again or even adopt it for enjoyment.

In this work we want to gauge the possibility of producing a BCI trained interactively in short sessions and that provides a viable alternative to OC and standard training protocols.

We introduce a "Co-learning BCI" (CLBCI) that reduces the initial amount of training required before the BCI is functional and that allows an incremental and interactive training process. We want to know if it is better to do one long training session with OC before using the BCI altogether or to have a short training session with CLBCI before every use of the BCI (a balance of quality versus time versus degree of control). We are particularly interested in what happens in the long run by evaluating whether OC and CLBCI are compatible with an overly positive user experience. Moreover, we want to know when OC should be favored over CLBCI and vice versa.

To that end, we perform an experiment over three training durations: 1 day, 1 week, 1 month. We train users in two groups, for all training durations: one group with CLBCI and the other using OC training. We want to see whether CLBCI reaches an acceptable performance for shorter training periods while maintaining the effect of signal variability to a minimum. We also asked users to fill informal questionnaires to share their experiences.

With this experiment we want verify the following hypotheses:

- (H.1): For duration of below one month, using CLBCI leads to better task performance compared to OC.
- (H.2): Beyond the one month duration, OC leads to better task performance.

---

[1] http://lightbox.time.com/2014/11/03/selfie-drone-camera/

a) The drone before takeoff.   b) The drone through the right ring.

c) The drone flies towards the left ring.

Fig. 1. The experimental environment with two rings four meters apart. The subject is in-stalled in front of a table in between the targets. The drone must pass through the hoops following an "8" trajectory during 5-minute piloting sessions.

- (H.3): Despite the better performance for OC after a month training, users prefer to train for a shorter period whenever they want to use the BCI, rather than spend a full month training once.

For the evaluation, we apply our system to the drone piloting task used in LaFleur et al. [4] to pilot an AR.Drone (Fig. 1) and we evaluate the task performance of CLBCI compared to OC. The task and the OC implementation are a replication of LaFleur et al's experimental protocol. We use the same evaluation measures and training protocols.

We first present background information on BCIs and their application and then some related work pertaining to control applications and co-adaptive BCI learning. Then, we present the CLBCI system and continue with the experimental protocol and the analysis and discussion of the results.

2   Background Information and Related Work

In this section we will present background information about BCI systems and then go on to study the state of the art and relevant BCI research for human computer inter-action and control applications.

2.1   Brain Computer Interfaces

A BCI system B must assign a brain signal S_t of a fixed duration (an epoch; e.g. 1 s) at time t, to a class Cl_i from a set of N classes Cl, that correspond to a set of brain activity states BS_i to recognize. A machine learning classifier C is trained to that effect with a set of training examples $T(Cl_i)$ for each class Cl_i. A training example is a signal epoch of the same duration as S_t that was recorded when the user was in the desired state BS_i for class Cl_i (Training or Calibration phase). The recording of such a training example and the associated protocol is called a training trial. For general matters on the processes associated with BCIs, we refer the reader to the state of the art presented by Nicolas-Alonso et al. [7]. A recent and extensive survey on BCI classification techniques is presented by Lotte et al. [8].

There is a further distinction between synchronous and asynchronous systems. In synchronous systems, stimuli are always shown to the user at fixed intervals of time during training, given that activations in the brain usually occur with a consistent delay after the stimulus onset. During online use (after training) one must wait for stimulation time, before the BCI generates an output command [8]. In an asynchronous system, there is no synchronization of the stimuli during online use and the BCI can be used at any moment without having to wait for the stimulus to begin. The additional difficulty lies in separating the target activity from all the rest of the brain activity [9]. There are many BCI paradigms, however in this work we use Motor Imagery (MI). MI requires users to imagine a motor action (moving their arm left/right, tapping their feet, etc.) without actually moving. This elicits similar activations as though they had moved and can be detected by a BCI. MI is an appropriate modality that can be applied to direct control applications, as the imagined actions match with the directions of the control (left/right hand for turning left/right, tapping feet to go down, etc.) [1] and thus with the inherent semantics of the control task.

2.2 BCIs for Control and Recreational Applications

The first area of application of BCIs was to use them for direct control in HCI systems [1], but also to combine them in a multimodal setting [10], with more common interaction modalities (e.g. Eye-tracking [11]). There are many practical applications: video games, e.g. World of Warcraft, serious games [12–14], robotics & prosthetics [15, 16]; virtual reality applications [17, 18].

There are two types of possible control paradigms: event-based control, where the BCI is used to trigger discrete events in an interface; continuous control, where the BCI is used to directly control the movement of an object or element of the interface (e.g. the movements of a pointer).

One particular continuous control application for BCIs of interest for this article is 3D navigation for the purpose of piloting a drone. Royer et al. [19] first evaluate the feasibility of the 2D control of an helicopter in a virtual environment, followed by Doud et al. for 3D control [20] with the motivation of achieving a means for telepresence. Finally LaFleur et al. [4] apply this technique for the 3D control of a real AR. Drone, with good success by using an Operant Conditioning training for 2 months on 5 users. More recently, a practical 2D control BCI system was demonstrated [21, 22]. The system allows to control an AR.Drone and that is operational within minutes (turning left/right or taking off and landing). This type of system is asynchronous and uses co-adaptation techniques between the classifier and the user, which are the main current focus of research efforts that aim at bringing BCIs out of the lab. The system presented in this work also falls in the category and we will thus review some of the related work on BCI co-adaptation.

2.3   Co-adaptation for Asynchronous BCIs

Scherer et al [23] propose an asynchronous BCI for the control of a virtual environment with three MI classes + a non-control state. They found it difficult to obtain a reliable classification in the asynchronous context. To remediate this problem several approaches have been proposed. One is to add a form of feature selection process to the BCI by performing co-adaptation from the EEG signals, for example the work of [24, 25] that extends Scherer et al. An initial synchronous calibration phase captures artifact free trials from each class whereby one feature out of six possible features is selected to train a classifier. Subsequently during the online phase, feedback is provided to enable periodical recalibrations when new artifact-free trials become available.

To the contrary of other state of the art approaches, in our system, CLBCI, the co-adaptation is driven by the user through a feedback loop rather than by the system through automatic adaptation (we call this co-learning rather than co-adaptation). Given the BCI also relies on machine learning and the feedback is based on incrementally capturing new training examples for the classifier from the user's signal. As such CLBCI lies at the intersection of BCI co-adaption and interactive machine learning [26], where the interaction drives the training of a classifier. The motivation for this approach is to provide a more engaging training period to users, as a long monotonous session of merely following instructions at fixed intervals lead to boredom and to a loss of attention and concentration. This view is inspired by the application of educational science research to BCIs [12] and in improving training protocols for BCIs [6].While other state of the art co-learning approaches tackle the reduction of training time and the minimization of errors the user still remains passive: they do not rely on the ability of the human to learn to use the BCI.

In light of the fact that what we want to evaluate in the experiments is the human learning component, we chose not to make a comparison to these methods in our experiment.

3   CLBCI System and Architecture

The architecture of the CLBCI system is based on minimum distance classification. The Minimum Distance Classifier (MDC) is a simple classification technique that stems from the pattern recognition literature, where it is used extensively (e.g. image recognition) [27]. It was among the first classifiers applied for BCIs but was mostly supplanted by classifiers such as LDA Linear Discriminant Analysis (LDA) or Support Vector Machine (SVM) [8]. The weakness of MDCs is that they are sensitive to noise and when signal sources are not well separated, however they were successfully applied to BCIs in combination with divergences based on Riemannian geometry and was shown to reach state of the art performance [28]. In this work we use Independent

Component Analysis (ICA) in its FastICA implementation to separate signal sources in an unsupervised setting and then apply the distance measures on the identified independent components [29].

3.1   Signal Processing and Acquisition

We applied the following signal processing pipeline in the raw signals in order:

- The Butterworth filter allows selecting the appropriate frequencies for Motor Imagery and discarding unwanted frequencies. We selected a 8–25 Hz pass band with a filter of magnitude 4 and with a ripple of 0.5 db.
- We make 1 s epochs from the band passed signals with a .75 s overlap (.25 s sliding window), we average them 5 by 5 so as to obtain 2 average epochs/s.
- Then FastICA is computed on each average epoch in an unsupervised manner in order to separate noise from target activity and make the distance-based classifier's job easier. The FastICA [29] algorithm projects the signal data in a space where data points are maximally independent, essentially separating task related sources from noise sources and other interference. The difference with other ICA algorithms is that FastICA uses a fast algorithm based on fixed-point calculations. We applied the variant of FastICA with symmetric orthogonalization and using a hyperbolic tangent contrast function. We computed 10 components. We used a GPL Java implementation of the original algorithm as described by Hyvärinen and Oja [29].
- We then produce average epochs that allow us to smooth the signal and remove some of the variability. The system thus produces an average epoch every second, which is then used for feature extraction and for classification. Thus, the classifier will yield one classification per second. Given that ICA is rather costly to compute, anything less than one second led to sub real-time performance on the machine we performed the processing on (2012 MacBook Air, i7@2.9 GHz).
- Given the sensitivity to noise and to variability in minimum distance based classification, ICA or other similar processes separate noise source from authentic signals and make it easier for the distance measure to accurately capture relevant differences in EEG patterns. Our classifier only requires minimal training data to start functioning, as our aim was to reduce that training time to a single calibration trial per class. In our system, reference average epochs are captured for each BCI class.

3.2   Feature Extraction and Classification

For each classification, we take the current average epoch and compute the distance between this current epoch and the reference signals for each of the class references. The classification outcome is where the distance to the current epoch is the shortest. However our distance measures are not stable under a noisy signal. Right after calibration, there is a single reference signal per class, however when feedback is given, more reference signals are added for each class. When there are several references per class, there will be several distance measurements, in which case the classification will be decided by a majority vote on classification outputs resulting from the individual distance measurements.

Similarly, given that several EEG channels are used, if we use single variable distance measures (as opposed to multivariate measures), we obtain one distance value per channel, which is handled the same way as in the multiple reference setting. In fact, when there are more than one distance measurements, the minimum distance classifier becomes similar to a k nearest neighbors (kNN) classifier. We can also consider using several different distance measures at the same time, much to the same effect. This work extends the work [30]. All the details about the system, its interface and its implementation are available in [30].

4   Experiments

The objective of the task is of user to fly an AR.Drone and make it pass through large rings continuously in a 5 min session (Fig. 2). We want to reproduce the experiments of LaFleur et al. [4] in order to compare the performance of OC (good performance, slow training) to CLBCI. We want to observe how user learning and performance evolve over increasingly long training durations (1 day, 1 week, 1 month) for both approaches to training. We consider that flying a quadcopter, all the more so with a BCI, is an entertaining activity that is appreciated by users as shown by the affluence to previous demos and exhibitions [21, 22].

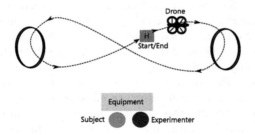

Fig. 2. The experimental environment.

4.1   Experimental Setup

We used a g.tec USBAmp EEG amplifier[2] with 16 electrodes over the motor cortex, with an acquisition rate of 512 Hz. The electrodes were placed over the channels: FCz, C5, C3, C1, Cz, C2, C4, C6, CP5, CP3, CP1, CPz, CP2, CP4, CP6, Pz (Fig. 3). We used the TOBI TiA[3] signal server on a Win. XP VM and then connected into our java BCI application trough our own Java implementation of the TiA protocol.

---

[2] http://www.gtec.at/Products/Hardware-and-Accessories/g.USBamp-Specs-Features

[3] http://sourceforge.net/projects/tools4bci/

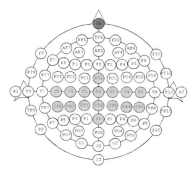

Fig. 3. Electrode placement for Motor Imagery according to the extended 10–20 electrode placement system.

We keep the same BCI paradigm based on Motor Imagery used LaFleur et al. [4], with the same controls:

- Rise up/Top Target (for 1D/2D cursor tasks): Both hands imagined movement;
- Go down/Bottom target: Both Feet imagined movement;
- Go Left/Left Target: Left hand imagined movement;
- Go Right/Right Target: Right hand imagined movement;
- Resting state: constant forward motion.

For left and right turns, the drone was programmed to make a 90 degree turn while moving forward at constant speed (to achieve a smooth turn).

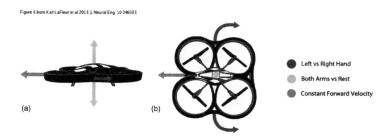

Fig. 4. The motor imagery drone control scheme (Color figure online)

The operator makes the drone takes off at the start of the experiment and land at the end of the experiment. Figure 4 illustrates the commands for the drone[4].

---

[4] The figure is taken from the Minnesotta paper by Lafleur et al. 2012 [4] and is made available in the open access article under a Creative Commons Attribution 3.0 license.

4.2   Protocol

We compare user learning (progression in performance over multiple sessions) for both an OC training setting inspired by LaFleur et al [4] and our CLBCI architecture over three different durations: 1 day, 1 week and 1 month. As such we are not precisely replicating the experiments of LaFleur et al. [4] as we are considering shorter durations.

With this experiment we want verify the following hypotheses:

- (H.1): For duration of below one month, using CLBCI leads to better task performance compared to OC.
- (H.2): Beyond the one-month duration, OC leads to better task performance.
- (H.3): Despite the better performance for OC after a month training, users prefer to train for 5 min prior to every time they pilot the drone rather than spend a full month before being able to pilot the drone for the first time.

We made groups of users who follow the same training protocol over three different durations for OC and CLBCI (6 groups). 24 healthy subjects aged between 23 and 44 and novices with BCIs participated in the experiments, and thus we distributed them in groups of 4 for each Duration x System pair:

- 1 day training (1.d): (1.d.CLBCI) CLBCI – 4 subjects; (1.d.oc) OC – 4 subjects;
- 1 week training (1.w): (1.w.CLBCI) CLBCI – 4 subjects; (1.w.oc) OC – 4 subjects;
- 1 month training (1.m): (1.m.CLBCI) CLBCI – 4 subjects; (1.m.oc) OC – 4 subjects.

In their paper, for operant conditioning, LaFleur et al. followed a precise training protocol. First users performed 1D cursor tasks for the left/right directions and the top down directions, until they could achieve a performance of at least 80 %. Then users performed a 2D cursor task for left, right, top and down combined until 80 % performance was achieved. Then their users were performed training sessions on a drone simulator, before actually flying the drone. Their training sessions were spread over 2 months and could last up to 50 min. The rationale for choosing 80 % is that it is a task performance that clearly lies above the performance and acceptable task performance of 60 %. The rationale for 60 % being considered as usable is that it is well above the empirical random classification performance by at least 10 % (45 % for 4 classes, like in this paper, Müller-Putz et al. [31]).

For our experiment, for the OC condition, we replicate the same type of training sessions where users must complete 1D Left/Right cursor (1D L/R) and Up/Down cursor (1D U/D) sessions, 2D cursor sessions, drone simulator sessions (DS) and a drone piloting session through a ring course (RS).

With CLBCI, instead of following the progressive training paradigm for OC, we ask users to perform a single training session over 4 trials for all classes at once and then follow with a test session. The test session is the phase that directly includes user involvement:

- We explain to the user how to cycle through the three distance measures: so that they can determine the measure that leads to the largest amount of perceived self-control by informally evaluating the resulting classification accuracy.

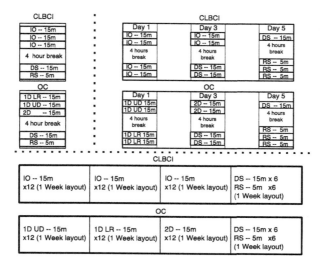

Fig. 5. Experimental schedule

- We offer the possibility of adjusting the decision margin of the classifier in the same fashion to find equilibrium between classification speed and accuracy.
- If some of the training trials are faulty (the users report they were distracted or that they moved), we can remove the individual training trails in real-time.

Once these settings are determined in the first few sessions, users remember them and start off with a customized BCI.

After the training sessions, the users still perform the simulator sessions (DS) and the ring course sessions (RS). We fixed all session lengths to 15 min and the piloting session length to 5 min. Within the experimental durations (1 day, 1 week, 1 month) we distributed each session type evenly with equal numbers of sessions, following the order: 1D L/R, 1D U/B, 2D, DS, RS for OC and the interface only session for CLBCI followed by DS and RS. The exact schedule for the experimental sessions is presented in Fig. 5.

4.3 Evaluation

We evaluate the performance of each user intrinsically like La Fleur et al. through task related measures: Number of rings acquired (number of rings the drone has successfully passed through) – **RA**; Number of wall collisions, when the drone collides with the walls of the rooms or with objects other than the rings – **WC**; Number of ring collision, **RC**; Flight time, the time between ring acquisition – **FT**; Session length, the total flight time during a session – **SL**. From the above measurements we can derive several performance indices that will allow us to evaluate different aspects of task performance.

Table 1. 10-fold cross-validated accuracy of our BCI system on two subjects over 10 sessions for Motor Imagery with three different distance measures: Mahalanobis Distance (Maha.), Riemannian Distance (Riem.) and Spearman rank correlation distance (Corr.).

Dist. Measure	Accuracy Subject A	Accuracy Subject B
Maha.	**71.24% (2.54%)**	70.35% (1.42%)
Riem.	70.45% (1.51%)	**71.26% (2.97%)**
Corr.	69.92% (2.10%)	**72.34% (1.23%)**

- Average Rings per maximum flight or **ARMF**, the average number of rings acquired during one session by users. This allows us to measure the absolute task performance without directly considering errors. The higher the ARMF the better.
- Average ring acquisition Time or **ARAT** in ms, the average of FT across a group. The lower the ARAT, the better the performance.
- Percent Total Correct or **PTC**, the percentage of ring acquisition compared to the sum of the number of ring collisions, the number of wall collisions and the number of ring acquisitions. **PTC** = RA/(RA + RC + WC).
- Percent Valid Correct or **PVC**, the percentage of Ring Acquisition compared to the sum of the number of wall collisions and ring acquisitions. Thus a valid ring acquisition is a ring acquisition that was not directly preceded by a wall collision. **PVC** = RA/(RA + WC).
- Percent Partial Correct or **PPC**. Here we consider that a ring collision is a partial ring acquisition, and thus PPC is the percentage of the sum of the number of ring acquisition and of ring collisions over the sum of the number of ring collisions, wall collisions and ring acquisition. **PPC** = (RA + RC)/(RA + RC + WC).

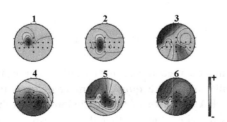

Fig. 6. Averaged IC activation map

4.4 BCI Validation

We performed a simple validation that consisted classifying a set of unlabeled signals and comparing them to a set of reference signals for each class using 10-fold cross-validation. We used the three distance measures that can be used with our system

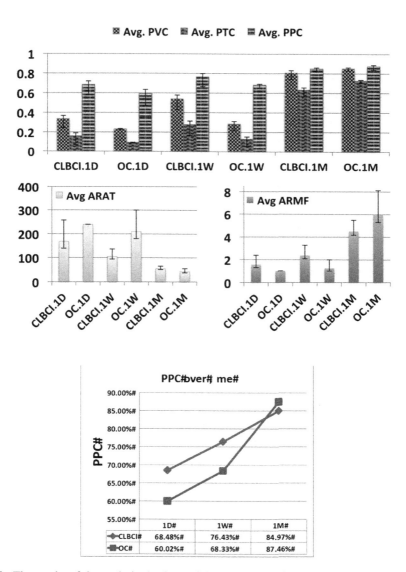

Fig. 7. The results of the study in the form of the 5 indicators for CLBCI and OC for all three durations (1D = 1 day; 1 W = 1 week; 1 M = 1 month. Group differences are all significant (ANOVA) as well as pairwise post hoc tests with a student t-test with p < 0.05. The equality of variance and normality preconditions were both met.

in order to see what is the best distance, if there is one. The analysis was done over the signals of two subjects captured over the course of 10 sessions. We can now look at the cross-validation results from the off-line analysis to validate the BCI system depending on the distance measure used in Table 1. In bold is the best result for each measure and each subject. We did not find that any of the distances had an absolute advantage over the others: it varies from subject to subject. Thus we decided to add a control that allows dynamically switching the distance measure used during the online phase so that it could be easily adapted to each user.

Moreover, we compute ICA dipole activation maps for the ICA components that explained 99 % of the variance, to check that activations are not due to artifacts (Fig. 6). We can see that components 1–2 correspond to left-hand MI, while 4–6 correspond to right-hand MI, although components 5 and 6 seem slightly contaminated by eye movement artifacts, however the cumulative percentage of variance explained for both of the is only 5 %.

4.5   Results

Given the number of subjects for each condition, we used the Shapiro-Wilk test and found a p value of $p = 0.234$, which means there is insufficient evidence to accept that the null hypothesis of the normality of the distribution of the data is valid. Consequently, we use the Kriskal-Wallis test to measure for significant group effects and then use the Mann-Whitney-U test for post hoc pairwise analysis with an FDR p value adjustment for multiple comparisons.

Figure 7 shows the results in the form of a bar chart for each of the five indicators. The error bars represent the sample standard variance. The general trend for all three percentage indicators is that CLBCI is better than OC. Overall for training durations of one day and one week CLBCI was better by about 8 %. However, OC performs better after a one-month training (~ 3 % difference, 87 % for OC and 84 for CLBCI). Although the difference is small, more training (e.g. 1–2 months) could give edge to OC, however, it is likely that performance will not increase significantly. We observe a similar trend for ARAT (lower ARAT for CLBCI for 1D and 1 W and then a lower ARAT for OC) and ARMF. A single day of training leads to low PVC and PTC but acceptable PPC for CLBCI. This means that the system is not very usable. After one week of training the performance improves for OC and CLBCI by the same amount, so that they maintain an 8 % difference. With above 75 % task performance, CLBCI is already usable after a week.

We asked our users informally what their impression of the experience was. Most found the experiment and experience interesting and enjoyable: it made them very motivated to perform well. One user said: "It was really a lot of fun! The control was not perfect, but even the part where I bumped into things was quite entertaining and thrilling to say the least." The main concern raised is that the BCI classification rate is slow and makes a smooth movement of the quadcopter difficult to achieve, moreover due to the automatic balancing systems of the drone user felt that the lateral movements of the drone were sometimes sudden, "the drone acted strangely sometimes". Users from the OC groups complained that the training tasks were somewhat boring and that they would have liked to be able to pilot the drone sooner. They found it very difficult to concentrate towards the end of training sessions. On the other hand users from the CLBCI group were quite surprised that they could pilot the drone so quickly and pointed out that it motivated them to go further and to improve their performance.

5   General Public CLBCI Demonstration

The CLBCI system has been demonstrated publicly and tested by over 60 people during several events with the objective of introducing new technologies and inter-action modalities to users. The session performed by each user was around 10–15 min in total (explanation, installation, training, piloting). Most people achieved control and enjoyed themselves greatly even for those that had performed the test several times. Even users who did not achieve control had a lot of fun trying to control it and understand how it works. This attracted media attention and showed that people are inclined to having access to this sort of technology.

6   Discussion

According to all indicators, CLBCI performs better for training durations up to a month (H1), while the OC training slightly outperforms CLBCI after a month of training (H2). This validated both hypotheses 1 and 2 within the confines of our experimental setting. However, in a broader scope of actual usage by users, we do not have sufficient evidence to suggest whether for longer training periods, the performance of OC is likely to remain better than with a continuous use of CLBCI or whether CLBCI overtakes OC for much longer durations. This means that only a very long-term study in situ is required to really ascertain the best training practices.

CLBCI reaches a usable performance after about a week of use on average, however, by increasing the amount of training for each session when the user starts using the system, we can achieve a better performance for immediate use.

In consequence, we can further hypothesize that over time, if we are satisfied with the classification performance for a particular application, we can reduce the training time proportionally to the increase in performance in order to obtain a constant per-formance with an increasing comfort use due to the shortening of the training times. In this regard, the integration of implicit error potential detection from other state of the art co-adaptation techniques would be beneficial and complimentary with our own approach. Naturally, we can never go below a single training trial, which amount to a few seconds of training. This point is fundamental because it implies that CLBCI and OC could potentially converge towards the same signal modulation in users. The difference of course lies in the long training period, where CLBCI would allow having a usable system already whereas with OC the user would have to wait until the end of the long period.

In critical application areas (reeducation, prosthesis control, etc.) it would be unacceptable to have anything less than the best achievable performance, and thus a system such as CLBCI would not be robust before it converged to the same level of modulation in users as with OC. However for non critical tasks where user experience, comfort and enjoyment are criteria, then systems like CLBCI are doubtless preferable. Based on informal user feedback from both CLBCI and OC groups, we have some evidence that our third hypothesis (H.3) is true, however a definite proof of its correctness would have required a within-subjects experimental design and a formal questionnaire evaluation, that are incompatible with a between-subjects design aimed at evaluating the temporal evolution of performance.

7   Limitations and Future Work

The main limitation is signal variability. With CLBCI we need supplemental filtering to minimize noise: our training is shorter than for supervised systems. The processing is costly: we can classify twice per second, which is limiting for continuous control. The limitation on training time constrains us to around four actions for realistically usable systems. Additionally, the low count of electrodes is not ideal for ICA, further studies should have a full 10–20 electrode coverage are required to better perform the validation of the CLBCI system.

Building signal databases (database of EEG signals built offline from a large number of subject for a given paradigm that can serve to produce training-free BCIs) [32] may help to obtain BCI systems that require no training.

Moving on from technical limitations, we have discussed that this work is preliminary in the sense that the evaluation is in vitro (controlled environment) and over a relatively short duration. Experiments in situ over long periods of time are required in order to truly determine whether the hypothesis of the convergence of CLBCI and OC training is actually possible. Another limitation is the absence of the study of the quantitative user experience through a formal questionnaire. Follow-up in situ studies should include a detailed questionnaire to precisely gauge how users perceive the training protocols. Finally, recruiting more subjects and a comparison to synchronous supervised systems would be beneficial in future experiments.

8   Conclusion

We propose a "Co-learning BCI" (CLBCI) that reduces the initial amount of training and makes BCIs more suitable for recreational applications. We replicate an existing experiment where the BCI controls a drone and compare CLBCI to their protocol (OC) over three durations of practice (1 day, 1 week, 1 month). We find that OC works at 80 % after a month practice, but the performance is between 60 and 70 % any earlier. In a week of practice, CLBCI reaches a performance of around 75 %. We conclude that CLBCI is better suited for recreational use. OC should be reserved for users for whom performance is the main concern. The experiment is performed in a controlled environment over a relatively short-term period, we need to carry out further studies in situ in the long term (1+ years) in order to have a more accurate picture. Given our observations, it is likely that CLBCI (but more generally co-adaptive asynchronous BCIs) and OC eventually converge to the same performance where users have learned to modulate their signals correctly. In summary, the challenges and approaches presented and discussed in this paper show that there are many opportunities for further research. We have identified promising directions and actionable ideas (shorter initial training, co-learning) for researchers in this field. We thereby hope to inspire work that will unlock the full potential of BCIs in everyday applications.

References

1. Wolpaw, J.R., Birbaumer, N., McFarland, D.J., Pfurtscheller, G., Vaughan, T.M.: Brain-computer interfaces for communication and control. Clin. Neurophysiol. **113**, 767–791 (2002)
2. Future BNCI: A Roadmap for Future Directions in Brain/Neuronal Computer Interaction Research. Future BNCI Program under the European Union Seventh Framework Programme, FP7/2007–2013, grant 248320 (2012). http://future-bnci.org/images/stories/Future_BNCI_Roadmap.pdf
3. Mancini, C., Rogers, Y., Bandara, A.K., Coe, T., Jedrzejczyk, L., Joinson, A.N., Price, B.A., Thomas, K., Nuseibeh, B.: Contravision: exploring users' reactions to futuristic technology. In: Proceedings of the SIGCHI Conference on Human Factors in Computing Systems, pp. 153–162. ACM, New York (2010)
4. LaFleur, K., Cassady, K., Doud, A., Shades, K., Rogin, E., He, B.: Quadcopter control in three-dimensional space using a noninvasive motor imagery-based brain-computer interface. J. Neural Eng. **10**, 046003 (2013)
5. Blankertz, B., Losch, F., Krauledat, M., Dornhege, G., Curio, G., Müller, K.R.: The Berlin brain - computer interface: Accurate performance from first-session in BCI-naïve subjects. IEEE Trans. Biomed. Eng. **55**, 2452–2462 (2008)
6. Lotte, F., Larrue, F., Mühl, C.: Flaws in current human training protocols for spontaneous brain-computer interfaces: lessons learned from instructional design. Front. Hum. Neurosci. **7**, 568 (2013)
7. Nicolas-Alonso, L.F., Gomez-Gil, J.: Brain computer interfaces, a review. Sensors **12**, 1211–1279 (2012)
8. Lotte, F., Congedo, M., Lécuyer, A., Lamarche, F., Arnaldi, B.: A review of classification algorithms for EEG-based brain-computer interfaces. J. Neural Eng. **4**, R1–R13 (2007)
9. Nooh, A., Yunus, J., Daud, S.: A review of asynchronous electroencephalogram-based brain computer interface systems. Int. Conf. Biomed. Eng. Technol. **11**, 55–59 (2011)
10. Nijholt, A., Reuderink, B., Oude Bos, D.: Turning shortcomings into challenges: brain-computer interfaces for games. In: Nijholt, A., Reidsma, D., Hondorp, H. (eds.) INTETAIN 2009. LNICST, vol. 9, pp. 153–168. Springer, Heidelberg (2009)
11. Kosmyna, N., Tarpin-Bernard, F.: Evaluation and comparison of a multimodal combination of BCI paradigms and eye tracking with affordable consumer-grade hardware in a gaming context. IEEE Trans. Comput. Intell. AI Games **5**, 150–154 (2013)
12. Kos'myna, N., Tarpin-Bernard, F., Rivet, B.: Towards a general architecture for a co-learning of brain computer interfaces. In: 2013 6th International IEEE/EMBS Conference on Neural Engineering (NER), pp. 1054–1057. IEEE (2013)
13. Sung, Y., Cho, K., Um, K.: A development architecture for serious games using BCI (brain computer interface) sensors. Sensors (Basel) **12**, 15671–15688 (2012)
14. Wang, Q., Sourina, O., Nguyen, M.K.: EEG-based "serious" games design for medical applications. In: 2010 International Conference on Cyberworlds, pp. 270–276 (2010)

15. Bell, C., Shenoy, P., Chalodhorn, R., Rao, C.: Control of a humanoid robot by a noninvasive brain-computer interface in humans. J. Neural Eng. **5**, 214–220 (2008)
16. Hochberg, L.R., Serruya, M.D., Friehs, G.M., Mukand, J.A., Saleh, M., Caplan, A.H., Branner, A., Chen, D., Penn, R.D., Donoghue, J.P.: Neuronal ensemble control of prosthetic devices by a human with tetraplegia. Nature **442**, 164–171 (2006)
17. Lécuyer, A., Lotte, F., Reilly, R., Leeb, R.: Brain-computer interfaces, virtual reality, and videogames. Comput. (Long. Beach. Calif) **42**, 66–72 (2008)
18. Guger, C., Holzner, C., Groenegress, C.: Brain computer interface for virtual reality control. In: Proceedings of the 7th European Symposium on Artificial Neural Networks, pp. 443–448 (2009)
19. Royer, A., Doud, A., Rose, M., He, B.: EEG control of a virtual helicopter in 3-dimensional space using intelligent control strategies. IEEE Trans. Neural Syst. Rehabil. Eng. **18**, 581–589 (2010)
20. Doud, A., Lucas, J., Pisansky, M., He, B.: Continuous three-dimensional control of a virtual helicopter using a motor imagery based brain-computer interface. PLoS One **6**, e26322 (2011)
21. Kosmyna, N., Tarpin-Bernard, F., Rivet, B.: Bidirectional feedback in motor imagery bcis: learn to control a drone within 5 min. In: CHI 2014 Extended Abstracts on Human Factors in Computing Systems, pp. 479–482. ACM, New York (2014)
22. Kosmyna, N., Tarpin-Bernard, F., Rivet, B.: Drone,your brain, ring course – accept the challenge and prevail! In: UBICOMP 2014 ADJUNCT, pp. 243–246. ACM, New York (2014)
23. Scherer, R., Lee, F., Schlogl, A., Leeb, R., Bischof, H., Pfurtscheller, G.: Toward self-paced brain-computer communication: navigation through virtual worlds. IEEE Trans. Biomed. Eng. **55**, 675–682 (2008)
24. Faller, J., Scherer, R., Costa, U., Opisso, E., Medina, J., Müller-Putz, G.R.: A co-adaptive brain-computer interface for end users with severe motor impairment. PLoS ONE **9**, e101168 (2014)
25. Faller, J., Vidaurre, C., Solis-Escalante, T., Neuper, C., Scherer, R.: Autocalibration and recurrent adaptation: Towards a plug and play online ERD-BCI. IEEE Trans. Neural Syst. Rehabil. Eng. **20**, 313–319 (2012)
26. Fails, J.A., Olsen Jr., D.R.: Interactive machine learning. In: Proceedings of the 8th International Conference on Intelligent User Interfaces, pp. 39–45. ACM, New York (2003)
27. Duda, R., Hart, P., Stok, D.: Pattern Recognition, 2nd edn. Wiley-Interscience, Hoboken (2001)
28. Barachant, A., Bonnet, S., Congedo, M., Jutten, C.: Multiclass brain-computer interface classification by Riemannian geometry. IEEE Trans. Biomed. Eng. **59**, 920–928 (2012)
29. Hyvärinen, A., Oja, E.: A fast fixed-point algorithm for independent component analysis. Neural Comput. **9**, 1483–1492 (1997)
30. Kosmyna, N., Tarpin-Bernard, F., Rivet, B.: Adding human learning in brain computer interfaces (BCIs): towards a practical control modality. ACM Trans. Comput. Interact. ACM SIGCHI (2015, to appear)
31. Müller-Putz, G.R., Scherer, R.: Better than random? A closer look on BCI results. Int. J. Bioelectromagn. **10**, 52–55 (2008)
32. Congedo, M., Goyat, M., Tarrin, N., Varnet., L., Rivet, B., Ionescu, G., Jrad, N., Phlypo, R., Acquadro, M., Jutten, C.: "Brain Invaders": a prototype of an open-source P300-based video game working with the OpenViBE platform. 5th International BCI Conference, Graz, Austria, 280–283 (2011)

A Human Cognitive Processing Perspective in Designing E-Commerce Checkout Processes

Marios Belk[1]([⊠]), Panagiotis Germanakos[1,2], Argyris Constantinides[3], and George Samaras[1]

[1] Department of Computer Science, University of Cyprus, 1678 Nicosia, Cyprus
{belk, cssamara}@cs.ucy.ac.cy,
panagiotis.germanakos@sap.com
[2] Suite Engineering UX, Products and Innovation SAP SE,
Dietmar-Hopp-Allee 16, 69190 Walldorf, Germany
[3] Department of Computer Science, University College London, London, UK
argyris.constantinides.14@ucl.ac.uk

Abstract. Designing a usable checkout process is of paramount importance for both E-Commerce and M-Commerce success. Aiming to understand human-computer interactions during checkout and improve the usability and user experience of checkout tasks, this research work investigates the relation among users' cognitive styles, and alternative checkout designs in terms of user preference and task performance. A controlled user study with 38 participants was conducted which entailed a psychometric-based survey for highlighting the users' cognitive styles, combined with a real usage scenario with two variations of checkout designs that were deployed on standard desktop computers and mobile touch-based devices. Results suggest that human cognitive differences could play an important role in designing E-Commerce and M-Commerce checkout processes, and particularly users' cognitive styles may affect the way users perceive and perform during such tasks.

Keywords: Human cognitive factors · E-Commerce · Usability · User study

1 Introduction

The checkout process has become widely known over the years in online commercial environments, and making purchases on the World Wide Web has become a fairly standard process, with clear steps and expected outcomes [1]. Nevertheless, recent research has shown that a high number of E-Commerce and M-Commerce environments entail usability issues, from the user's conceptual understanding of commercial Web-sites, to how users interact with form fields [2–5]. In addition, studies revealed that usability issues of M-Commerce Web-sites as well as the small screen displays discourage users from accessing M-Commerce Web-sites [6].

In this realm, research has shown that both E-Commerce and M-Commerce Web-sites should satisfy the needs and preferences of users via the visual and interaction design of the system aiming to improve the shopping experience of users [7]. Thus, it is necessary to understand human-computer interactions in such realms and

© IFIP International Federation for Information Processing 2015
J. Abascal et al. (Eds.): INTERACT 2015, Part I, LNCS 9296, pp. 523–530, 2015.
DOI: 10.1007/978-3-319-22701-6_38

follow user-centered design approaches when designing checkout processes, by incorporating the unique needs, characteristics and preferences of users. Taken into consideration that users do not necessarily share common cognitive backgrounds in which online purchase decisions are required to be taken, we suggest that individual differences in cognitive processing should be investigated and integrated in the user interface design process of checkout environments.

Accordingly, the work presented in this paper aims to understand and investigate whether individual differences in cognitive processing styles (Wholist/Analyst) affect user preference and task performance in different checkout designs that are deployed on alternative interaction device types (standard desktop vs. touch-based devices). The work is primarily motivated by existing research and theory that relates the Wholist/Analyst cognitive style to the way individuals navigate within hypermedia environments and the way hypermedia content is structured [8–10].

The rest of the paper is structured as follows: we present the underlying theory of this work in the next two sections. Thereafter we describe the context of a controlled user study and methods. Finally, we analyze and discuss the findings of the study and outline the implications of the reported research.

2 Individual Differences in Cognitive Styles

Research on individual differences in cognitive styles aims to understand how individuals differ in mental representation and processing of information. Among various theories on cognitive styles [8, 11, 12], we have utilized the Wholist/Analyst cognitive style [8] since it is considered a widely accepted and accredited cognitive style dimension. The Wholist/Analyst cognitive style distinguishes individuals as *Wholists* that prefer and tend to structure incoming information as a whole to get the big picture, and experience surroundings of the environment in a relative passive and global manner, or as *Analysts* that prefer and tend to structure the incoming information in detail, and experience surroundings in an active manner and with an internal perspective.

A high number of studies which investigated the effect of cognitive styles on users' task usability and interaction patterns within Web environments, revealed implications of cognitive styles on users' performance and preferred ways of using different navigation tools and display options [13–15]. On the contrary, various studies concluded that cognitive styles do not have a main effect on users' task performance and preference within hypermedia environments [16].

3 Checkout Designs

We investigated the checkout designs of the most popular commercial Web-sites [4, 5], and concluded that the majority of them utilized two broad checkout designs that could be categorized as follows: (i) a single one-page checkout process that contains all the necessary information for performing the purchase in a single page; and (ii) a guided step-by-step checkout process in which users have to fill out their information in multiple steps, usually across multiple pages.

Based on theory of cognitive styles, the single one-page checkout design could be related to the analytical approach that Analysts follow since it enables users to freely access all sections of the checkout process in a single page. On the other hand, the guided step by step design could be related to the Wholist dimension of cognitive styles since it presents content through a constrained and guided environment. In this respect, this work investigates the following research questions:

– Do users with different cognitive processing styles prefer a particular visual and interaction design of checkout processes?
– Do users with different cognitive processing styles perform differently in terms of task completion efficiency in different visual and interaction designs of checkout processes?
– Is there an observable interaction effect between cognitive processing styles of users and device type towards user preference and task performance of different checkout designs?

For the purpose of this study, we utilized different checkout designs of two existing commercial Web-sites: nordstrom.com (Nordstrom) and amazon.com (Amazon). Nordstrom checkout design follows a simple top-down navigation style in which users can freely enter the required information for performing the checkout process (Fig. 1). All required information (shipping information, payment information, etc.) is visible in one single Web-page.

Amazon illustrates content in a guided horizontal step-by-step navigation style in which users can only enter information of a particular section, and then proceed to the next section (Fig. 2). In the desktop version, a horizontal menu is utilized illustrating the active section of the checkout process.

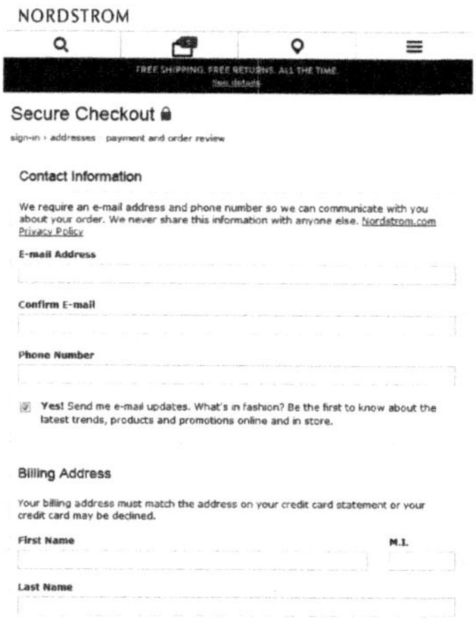

Fig. 1. Nordstrom checkout process design.

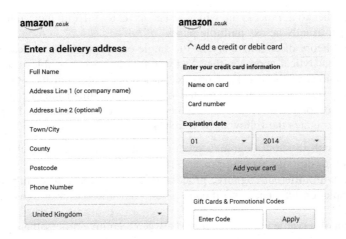

Fig. 2. Amazon checkout process design.

4 Method of Study

4.1 Sampling and Procedure

A total of 38 undergraduate Computer Science students (18 female and 20 male, age 20–25) participated voluntarily in a controlled user study held at the laboratory of the researchers. Controlled laboratory sessions were conducted with a maximum of two participants in each session and were held at times convenient to the students. Participants initially interacted with a psychometric instrument aiming to classify each user to the Wholist or Analyst cognitive style class. Depending on the cognitive style classification of each participant, a mixed design (within-subjects and between-subjects) was followed in which all participants navigated in two different commercial Web-sites; Nordstrom and Amazon, and were assigned to complete an online purchase in each checkout setting (within-subjects). Half of the participants interacted with standard input/output (IO) devices (keyboard and mouse) on desktop computers (IBM Thinkcenter M73, 21″ monitor), and the other half interacted with mobile touch-based devices (Apple iPad 3) (between-subjects). The allocation of checkout designs' sequence as well as the device types used for interaction was balanced across users depending on their cognitive styles' classification.

The instructions provided to the participants for both navigation scenarios were as follows: (i) select a product of their choice and add it to the shopping basket of the system; and (ii) start the checkout process until buying the product with a virtual credit card that was provided to them at the beginning of the study. A client-side logging tool measured the total time spent for completing the checkout process, aiming to compare the usability of each checkout process in terms of task efficiency. At the end of the study, focus group sessions were conducted and questionnaires were provided in order to elicit the users' subjective preference and perception of each design.

4.2   Cognitive Style Elicitation

Users' cognitive styles where elicited by exploiting Riding's Wholist/Analyst Cognitive Style Analysis test (CSA) [17]. As reported in Peterson et al. [18], the reliability of the test is $r = 0.81$, $p < 0.01$. The psychometric test highlights individual differences in Wholist/Analyst cognitive style by requiring from users to respond to 40 questions as true or false. In particular, 20 of the questions ask whether a pair of geometric shapes is identical or not (*"Is shape X the same as shape Y?"*), and the remaining 20 questions ask whether a single geometric shape is part of another complex geometric figure (*"Is shape X contained in shape Y?"*). It is assumed that Wholists respond faster in the task that involves the comparison of two figures than Analysts, whereas Analysts respond faster in the task that requires dis-embedding the simple geometric shape from the complex one than Wholists. Depending on the response time and provided answer to each of the stimuli type, users are classified as Wholists or Analysts.

5   Analysis of Results

Users were grouped as follows based on their responses to the psychometric test: Wholists ($N = 21$, $f = 55$ %), Analysts ($N = 17$, $f = 45$ %).

5.1   Task Efficiency

A Repeated Measures Analysis of Variance (ANOVA) test was conducted using cognitive styles (Wholist or Analyst), device type (standard desktop or touch-based), and environment (Nordstrom or Amazon) as independent variables and the time spent to complete the checkout process as the dependent variable. Table 1 illustrates the mean of time to complete the process per checkout design and cognitive style group.

Table 1. Means of task performances (in seconds).

	Wholists		Analysts	
	Desktop	Touch	Desktop	Touch
Nordstrom	140.00 (36.15)	159.66 (57.39)	100.75 (24.28)	151.00 (18.74)
Amazon	118.16 (50.81)	135.73 (32.99)	127.33 (31.30)	164.60 (14.53)

The analysis revealed that, the effect of checkout design on time needed to complete the checkout process is not significant ($F(1,34) = 0.032$, $p = 0.860$). In contrast, there was a statistically significant interaction between cognitive styles and checkout design on the time to complete the checkout process ($F(1,34) = 7.525$, $p = 0.01$, *partial eta^2* = 0.181). Furthermore, there was no interaction effect between cognitive styles and device type on the time to complete the checkout process ($F(1,34) = 0.232$, $p = 0.633$, *partial eta^2* = 0.007). Pairwise comparisons between checkout designs for each cognitive styles group and device type revealed that Analysts were significantly more efficient in completing the single page checkout design (Nordstrom) when this was deployed on desktop computers (MD = -26.583, SE = 12.583; $F(1,34)$ = 4.463, p = 0.042). Furthermore, when the interaction was performed on touch-based devices, again, Analysts were faster in completing the single page checkout process but with no statistical significant differences (MD = -13.600, SE = 19.494; $F(1,34)$ = 0.487, p = 0.490). On the other hand, Wholists were significantly more efficient in completing the guided step-by-step checkout process (Amazon) when this was deployed on touch-based devices (MD = 23.933, SE = 11.255; $F(1,34)$ = 4.522, p = 0.042), whereas no significant differences where observed when the interaction took place on desktop computers (MD = 21.833, SE = 17.795; $F(1,34)$ = 1.505, p = 0.288). Furthermore, a comparison between the two cognitive style groups revealed that Analysts were significantly faster than Wholists when interacting in Nordstrom ($F(1,38)$ = 7.056, p = 0.012). On the other hand, no significant differences were observed between Wholists and Analysts in Amazon ($F(1,38)$ = 0.422, p = .520).

5.2   User Preference

Focus-group sessions were concentrated around the participants' subjective preference and perception of the different checkout designs. The focus groups followed a semi-structured process based on predetermined questions that lasted approximately 15 min. The participants were asked to rank the checkout designs based on their preference. In particular, participants ranked the checkout designs with 1 and 2 to represent their first and second choice. Table 2 lists the number of participants who chose a specific design as their first choice.

Table 2.   User preference of checkout design.

	Wholists		Analysts	
	Desktop	Touch	Desktop	Touch
Nordstrom	2	7	8	6
Amazon	7	5	2	1

A Chi square test revealed that there is statistical significant association between cognitive styles and checkout design preference in desktop computers (*Chi square value* = 6.343, df = 1, p = 0.012). For interactions that took place on desktop computers, Analyst users significantly preferred the single one page design, whereas Wholists preferred the guided step-by-step approach. On the contrary, in cases where users interacted with touch-based devices, no significant association between cognitive styles and checkout design has been revealed (*Chi square value* = 1.534, df = 1, p = 0.216) since the majority of participants preferred the single page checkout design (Nordstrom). Based on comments, this might be based on the fact that users preferred to have all information in a single page due to size and interaction limitations. In the case of Wholists, although the task efficiency analysis revealed that they were significantly faster when interacting in a guided step-by-step checkout design (Amazon), they preferred the other type of checkout given the limitations of the touch-based device.

6   Conclusions

Designing a usable checkout process is of paramount importance for both E-Commerce and M-Commerce success. Thus, supporting users that are engaged in such tasks with more efficient decision-making and information processing is of critical importance. Aiming to understand how individual differences in cognitive processing styles affect users' interactions in different checkout designs, a controlled user study was conducted that explored the impact of the Wholist-Analyst cognitive style on user preference and task performance of different checkout designs within E-Commerce and M-Commerce settings. We primarily intended to focus on the Wholist/Analyst dimension since it highlights differences in the way individuals view the structure presented by their visual field as well as react and behave in various situations triggered by their contextual surroundings (e.g., desktop vs. touch-based interactions). Analysis of results suggests that cognitive styles affect users' task completion across device types (desktop computers and mobile touch-based devices). In particular, Wholist users have performed more efficiently in checkout processes that followed a guided approach, whereas Analyst users were more efficient and preferred a single page checkout design which did not follow a guided approach and provided more flexibility while entering information.

Results of the study suggest that personalizing the checkout process based on intrinsic cognitive characteristics could support the users in terms of usability and improve the users' buying experience, and eventually benefit the providers since personalized tasks improve user acceptance of their services, and thus gain a competitive advantage. Nonetheless, the practical feasibility of such an approach entails a number of issues and challenges that need closer attention. An important challenge relates to the prior knowledge required by the system, about the users' cognitive characteristics in order to provide personalized checkout designs without engaging users in a psychometric test. Given the complexity of cognitive styles' research, implicit elicitation methods of cognitive styles without engaging users in a psychometric test is still at its infancy. In this context, existing noteworthy works could be used for implicitly eliciting the users' cognitive styles based on the users' navigation behavior [9, 10]. Another point relates to practitioners adopting the cognitive style elicitation process since the current paradigm of interactive systems might limit the proposed approach of applying cognitive style as a user profile and personalization factor. In view of our long-term goal of personalizing checkout tasks based on cognitive differences, this work aims to point out the importance of personalizing such tasks. In this respect, findings of this research build on the promise that human cognitive factors could offer an alternative perspective to the current one-size-fits-all paradigm of checkout processes.

Limitations of the study relate to the rather small sample size and non-varying user profiles (e.g., age, experience). Furthermore, the study did not control possible influencing factors such as content, images, etc., since different commercial Web-sites were used. On the other hand, we aimed to initially investigate the accumulated experience of users in real life settings aiming to increase the ecological validity of the study. Future work entails investigating different combinations of content presentation and navigation within such tasks, and recruiting participants with varying profiles in order to increase our understanding about the effects of cognitive styles on users' checkout process behavior and thus increase the external validity of this research.

Acknowledgements. The work is co-funded by the Cyprus Research Promotion Foundation project PersonaWeb (ΤΠΕ/ΠΛΗΡΟ/0311(ΒΙΕ)/10) and EU project Miraculous-Life (#611421).

References

1. Nielsen, J.: Ecommerce Usability. NNGroup 2014
2. Kukar-Kinney, M., Close, A.G.: The determinants of consumers' online shopping cart abandonment. Acad. Mark. Sci. **38**(2), 240–250 (2010)
3. Close, G.A., Kukar-Kinney, M.: Beyond buying: motivations behind consumers' online shopping cart use. Bus. Res. **63**, 986–992 (2010)
4. Appleseed, J., Holst, C.: E-Commerce Checkout Usability: Exploring the Customer's Checkout Experience. Baymard Institute, Denmark (2013)
5. Appleseed, J., Holst, C.: M-Commerce Usability: Exploring the Mobile Shopping Experience. Baymard Institute, Denmark (2013)
6. Shim, J.P., Bekkering, E., Hall, L.: Empirical findings on perceived value of mobile commerce as a distributed channel. In: Proceedings of Information Systems, pp. 1835–1837 (2002)
7. Bellman, S., Lohse, G.L., Johnson, E.J.: Predictors of online buying behavior. Commun. ACM **42**(12), 32–38 (1999)
8. Riding, R., Cheema, I.: Cognitive styles – an overview and integration. Educ. Psychol. **11** (3–4), 193–215 (1991)
9. Chen, S., Liu, X.: An integrated approach for modeling learning patterns of students in web-based instruction: a cognitive style perspective. ACM Trans. Comput.-Hum. Interact. **15**(1), 1–28 (2008)
10. Belk, M., Papatheocharous, E., Germanakos, P., Samaras, G.: Modeling users on the world wide web based on cognitive factors, navigation behavior and clustering techniques. Syst. Softw. **86**(12), 2995–3012 (2013)
11. Kozhevnikov, M.: Cognitive styles in the context of modern psychology: toward an integrated framework of cognitive style. Psychol. Bull. **133**(3), 464–481 (2007)
12. Peterson, E., Rayner, S., Armstrong, S.: Researching the psychology of cognitive style and learning style: is there really a future? Learn. Individ. Differ. **19**(4), 518–523 (2009)
13. Chan, C., Hsieh, C., Chen, S.: Cognitive styles and the use of electronic journals in a mobile context. Documentation **70**(6), 997–1014 (2014)
14. Lo Storto, C.: Subjective judgment, cognitive style and ecommerce website evaluation: a non-parametric approach. Adv. Sci. Lett. **20**(10–12), 2073–2077 (2014)
15. Belk, M., Germanakos, P., Asimakopoulos, S., Andreou, P., Mourlas, C., Spanoudis, G., Samaras, G.: An individual differences approach in adaptive waving of user checkout process in retail ecommerce. In: Proceedings of HCI International, pp. 451–460 (2014)
16. Brown, E., Brailsford, T., Fisher, T., Moore, A., Ashman, H.: Reappraising cognitive styles in adaptive web applications. In: Proceedings of World Wide Web, pp. 327–335 (2006)
17. Riding, R.: Cognitive Styles Analysis - Research Administration. Learning and Training Technology, Birmingham (1991)
18. Peterson, E.R., Deary, I.J., Austin, E.J.: The Reliability of Riding's Cognitive Style Analysis Test. Personality Individ. Differ. **34**(5), 881–891 (2003)

Bilingual Reading Experiences: What They Could Be and How to Design for Them

Clément Pillias$^{(\boxtimes)}$ and Pierre Cubaud

Conservatoire National des Arts et Métiers, CÉDRIC,
292 rue Saint Martin, Paris, France
`{clement.pillias, cubaud}@cnam.fr`

Abstract. We introduce the idea of *bilingual reading*, where a document comes in two languages and the reader can choose at will on which language to focus during the reading. Between the complete ignorance of a language (where translation is the only option) and bilingualism (where translation is useless), there exists a variety of contexts of partial bilingualism where bilingual reading interfaces would prove highly useful. We first study through interviews and reviews how the bilingual reading experience is understood today. We provide an analysis framework and highlight design challenges for the design of bilingual reading appliances. We then describe a taxonomy of the different approaches available to address these challenges, analyze them in the light of our framework and show how they can be derived to sketch future bilingual reading interfaces.

Keywords: Bilingual reading · Mechanisms of reading · Nexus of attention · E-book · E-reader · Parallel text · Text morphing · Text animation

1 Introduction

"Cognitive, social, personal, and economic benefits accrue to the individual who has an opportunity to develop a high degree of bilingual proficiency when compared with a monolingual counterpart." This is how Tucker presented in 1999 the definitive conclusions of 30 years of research on multilingualism [39]. This observation calls for the promotion of language education, but also calls for more exposure to foreign-language medias. Novels, for instance, can meet various individual interests: a reader's desire to better appreciate the author's work and culture; the need to practice a foreign language; social recognition, etc. Reading a text written in a foreign language is however difficult for people who are not fluent with the language. To alleviate this difficulty, one can bind a foreign-language text with a high-quality translation of it in the reader's mother tongue. The binding uses an *alignment structure* that links each part of the original text to the corresponding part in the translated text and reciprocally, resulting in a *bitext* (see Fig. 1). One expected benefit of this solution is to ease the transition between the two versions of the text. This paper discusses *bilingual reading experiences* based on bitexts and studies interaction designs for such experiences.

People are already bilingual (at various levels of proficiency) in most parts of the world, and have accepted e-books as viable alternatives to paper books [31]. Publishing

© IFIP International Federation for Information Processing 2015
J. Abascal et al. (Eds.): INTERACT 2015, Part I, LNCS 9296, pp. 531–549, 2015.
DOI: 10.1007/978-3-319-22701-6_39

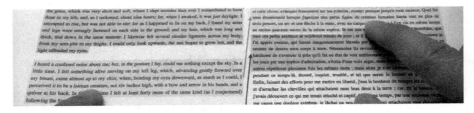

Fig. 1. *Gulliver's Travels* by Jonathan Swift is available in many languages for free on the Gutenberg Project (http://www.gutenberg.org). In this picture, we show extracts of the original English version (left) and of a French translation (right). Note the differences in the layout of paragraphs and construction of sentences. Natural Language Processing techniques can now automatically find the corresponding parts of each version to create an *alignment structure*. Here, this structure is represented at the level of paragraphs with arrows and color-coding.

industry is familiar with translation processes and already distributes many resources in multiple languages: successful books are translated to reach an international market and old books and their translations have been massively digitalized. Natural language processing techniques are being developed to ease the creation of alignment structures at a massive scale [38] and individuals can already create such structures at reasonable costs.

With such an economical and societal importance and so little technical barriers, it is striking how little HCI works address bilingual reading. Reading has been studied many times in HCI, highlighting the variety of reading purposes and reading styles [27] and the importance of supporting activities [32, 37]. More general views have also been suggested about what digital reading could be [33]. All of these works are relevant for bilingual reading, but none of them mention bilingual reading as an opportunity.

The central question of the research agenda on bilingual reading is: *How could the reader benefit the most from both the original text and its translation?* It is therefore essential to understand what it actually means for readers to benefit from each version of the text. Each version can satisfy different goals, e.g., the translated text is easier to read, but reading the original version allows one to practice the language. But how does the reader deal with conflicting goals such as "learning new foreign words and expressions" vs. "staying in the flow of the story"? More questions arise if one can switch at will and seamlessly between the two versions: What is the cost of language-switching decisions? What strategies inform them? What are the resulting switching patterns?

Answering these questions raises two methodological issues: First, existing materials support bilingual reading very poorly, so observing people using them might only provide limited knowledge about bilingual reading. Second, it is difficult to collect readers' memories of past bilingual reading experiences or to rely on their ability to imagine themselves having such experiences. Indeed, most potential users of bilingual reading appliances are *experts* in reading in their mother tongue: they have spent many years learning how to do it and they practice their reading skills everyday (without even noticing it), up to the point that whole areas of their brain have become dedicated to reading [11]. Reading is for them an activity that relies mostly on unconscious processes, and this holds true even for reading in a foreign language once they have mastered its writing system. These readers tend therefore to focus on remarkable events in their previous foreign-language reading experiences, which are mainly frustrating situations such as having to stop reading because of an unknown word. They have therefore a strongly biased understanding of what a bilingual reading experience could be and researchers need to find methods that let potential users reflect on their own or fictive experiences in an unbiased way.

This understanding of bilingual reading is necessary to discover what would be a *right thing to design*, but the complementary problem of *getting the design right* also brings its own challenges. Indeed, designers are also experts in reading and are therefore subject to the same biases than potential users. Moreover, text display technologies seem to have reached a stable and mature form after centuries of evolution, it is thus difficult to think out of the box and discover innovative ways of displaying text and interacting with it. In this context, proposing and evaluating a simple proof-of-concept prototype appliance might impede the discovery of alternative techniques, by focusing designers and researchers minds on the design of this prototype or some variant of it. Opening the design space to bring some room for unconventional techniques is therefore one of the main concerns that guided this work.

We describe in this paper our approach for the study of bilingual reading and discuss some early results. We focus on addressing two issues: avoiding biases in users' examinations of their experiences, and providing support for designers while keeping the design space open. We narrow these research questions by focusing first on reading for pleasure [9] and especially on reading novels. We also focus on a pair of languages that share the same writing system while having both common roots and strong differences: French and English.

After setting the technical and scientific background for bilingual reading, we introduce in Sect. 3 the method that we used to investigate what a bilingual reading experience could be, and some preliminary observations. We provide in Sect. 4 a framework to describe how a bitext is displayed and read. In Sect. 5, we report on a set of design challenges that were highlighted during our interactions with potential users and analyze these challenges in the light of the previous framework. We also consider solutions proposed in other domains that address some of these challenges, and show that they follow three different approaches. Finally, we give hints about how to adapt these approaches for bilingual reading.

2 Background

2.1 Current Support for Bilingual Reading

Printed Materials. Bilingual printed books often assign a different language to the left and right side of the book, so that facing pages display corresponding parts of the text. These so-called *parallel texts* use a coarse granularity for the alignment: when the reader encounters an unknown word, finding its translation can be difficult as it might require to scan a big part of the facing page. Establishing a visual match at a finer granularity (e.g. paragraphs or lines) could raise the publishing costs and would still require the aligned text elements to follow the same ordering in both languages. This can be a problem with non-literal translations, where parts of text can be swapped or removed, or where sentences can be grouped differently to form paragraphs. Printed parallel texts therefore rely often on dedicated or adapted translations.

Digitalized Materials. Reading a digitalized parallel text with a standard e-reader is cumbersome, as parallel texts have specific requirements for navigation between pages. Bederson et al. designed a smart-phone application to address related navigation issues in digitalized children books (including multi-lingual ones) [3]. While their interaction techniques can be used to access and read text boxes corresponding to different languages, it does not allow the reader to quickly switch its focus of attention from one language to the other. Another solution could be to use dual-display readers such as *Codex* [19], dedicating a display to each language.

Interactive Digital Materials. Web-based machine translation services like *Google Translate* are the best known and most used interfaces to read a web page originally written in a foreign language. When these tools are used to translate a full web page, hovering a translated sentence with the mouse triggers the display of a tool-tip showing the original version of this sentence. *Doppel Text*[1] provides a similar interface for reading classical novels as e-books, but exchanges the roles of the two languages (tool-tips show the translation). Its use of professional translations certainly allows for a better reading experience but reduces the number of available books (only 32 at the time of writing). Much more content could be made available to readers with the use of natural language processing tools that compute a (sentence-level) alignment structure. These interfaces only use very simple interactions and have ergonomic issues, such as the tool-tips being hard to distinguish from the original document. More advanced interaction techniques allow disclosing supporting materials [7] but have not been tested for bilingual reading. Users' reception of these techniques being highly varied [42], they require a fine-tuning of the design and there is room to explore more design options.

2.2 Related Work

Monolingual Digital Reading. Reading with digital tools has been studied for a long time: many studies have investigated the effect of display and text parameters on reading performance [36], or the benefits of pagination over scroll layout (which is supposed to involve lower levels of mental workload [40] and to make a better use of spatial memory [28, 29]), or of other visualization techniques [20]. Other studies have investigated the role of paper and the physicality of printed books, to find that they better support navigation [24, 35] and recall of the text [25] than e-books.

Enhanced Foreign-Language Reading. Some techniques have been proposed to facilitate the reading of a text in a foreign language without relying on a bi-text. For

---

[1] http://www.doppeltext.com/

example, *Jenga* splits and indents sentences to make their grammar easier to grab [41]. *iDict* uses eye-tracking techniques and algorithms to identify the foreign language words that cause difficulties to the reader, and automatically displays in a side pane the corresponding entry in a bilingual dictionary [21]. Han et al. discuss the benefits of using pictures instead of bilingual dictionaries entries to avoid reading in multiple languages [18]. In the context of written conversations, people better understand machine-translated messages when the sender highlights the key words in the message [16]. These helping techniques and other similar ones could be used for bilingual reading, however we will argue that bilingual reading cannot be reduced to the availability of such help tools.

Generalization to Multi-representational Reading. Studies of interest can be found in the context of multiple representations. For example, a document written in a markup language such as HTML has two natural representations: the textual one with markup code, and the graphical one displayed in the browser. The rendering process binds these representations together, defining links between elements of each representation in a similar way than the alignment structure does for languages. This kind of links has been generalized to other relations between documents such as: an original document and its annotations; successive or concurrent versions in the document edit history (the link is then obtained by a kind of *diff* operation); etc. [26]. Animation has been used in such settings to help in understanding the differences between successive edits of wiki pages [8] or to help in understanding how a source file is compiled into a graphical representation [12]. The later also allow graphical picking of source code, which eases the document edition and avoid disruptive searches in the code. Understanding how some text has been translated and searching the translation of some part of text are similar tasks in bilingual reading.

3 Understanding Bilingual Reading Experiences

Methodology. To understand what a bilingual reading experience could be, we have conducted informal interviews with people who showed interest in this question: novel reading amateurs, foreign language teachers, professional translators and their students, linguists, and researchers in natural language processing. We interviewed around 20 people individually or in groups of less than 10, in sessions of one to four hours, with some people interviewed multiple times. The goal of these interviews was as much to get insights about bilingual reading experiences than to test methods that could be used to get such insights.

These interviews made obvious the tendency of interviewees to focus on the negative aspects of their past experiences of reading in a foreign language. They also immediately suggested solutions to their problems, and all following discussions revolved around these solutions. Almost all interviewees mentioned, for instance, the following idea: *"if I encounter a word that I don't know, I could press a button and get its translation."* None of the interviewees realized that parallel texts provided a different solution to this problem, although most of them had previous experience with this kind of material. So we had to tell them: such interventions seemed necessary to get more useful insights, and we were interested in finding what kind of intervention would be the most useful and if it could become part of a more formal collaborative design method.

The most useful interventions were the ones that allowed the interviewees to re-examine their concerns in the light of a different, familiar past experience. We used first the metaphor of subtitles in movies, which could be introduced like this: *"As non-native English speakers, we like to watch Hollywood movies subtitled in our native language. This way, the actors' voices seem more natural and we can better appreciate their acting and the director's work. Our English is good enough to understand most of the dialogs, but we are sometime lazy or the characters use slang or have a strong accent that we cannot understand. We can then easily have a look at the subtitles to understand what is going on. Moreover, it clearly makes us practice our English speaking skills, adding the pleasure of improving ourselves to the enjoyment of being immersed in a good movie. We want to create for novels what subtitles are to movies."* This metaphor was useful to communicate a vague idea of what could be a bilingual reading experience, as well as in triggering memories about particular situations where the interviewee would switch its attention from the subtitles to the audio or conversely. However, the metaphor was not strong enough that the interviewees would spontaneously refer to it during the whole interview – movies probably seemed too far away from reading.

We also asked interviewees to analyze their concerns in the light of existing materials such as parallel texts or *Doppel Text*. It helped in highlighting the benefits and drawbacks of these materials and to find other ways to use them than simply looking for the translation of unknown words. We finally introduced and tested *reading traces*, a more formalized approach where a group is asked at the beginning of the session to read a short novel printed in the parallel text format. The reading takes less than 30 min and the sheets of the document can be detached to let the readers adopt the configuration of printed materials that they judge the most satisfying. Participants are asked to annotate the document with a pen, using their own marks, to create *"a trace of what and how they read, that they could use in the following discussion, and that we could use in a later analysis"*. They also write at the end of the document a description of the mark system that they used and other comments. A round table follows the reading session with each participant commenting on her experience. A group discussion ends the session. We found that asking participants to write traces of their reading activities incited them to reflect on their actions both during the reading and during the discussion.

What We Have Learned. The first lesson is that bilingual reading should not be confused with an enhanced form of foreign-language reading, but encompasses it. For example, another important aspect of bilingual reading is to satisfy the reader's curiosity, e.g. when she asks herself *"how can one translate that pun?"* or *"did they translate the double entendre?"* These examples show other punctual and opportunistic needs for the translation, but bilingual reading experiences can rely on a much intensive use of the two texts, in a way that redefines the reader's engagement with the novel. We experienced this while reading parallel texts: at some point the reading turned into a game where we tried to predict how each sentence had been translated.

In our experimentation with reading traces, we observed a great variety of reading behaviors: reading the whole original text first and then the translation (or the opposite); reading each sentence or paragraph in both languages before reading the following one; switching language at each new paragraph; having a quick overview of one text to pick interesting words or expressions that the reader were interested in knowing the translation; being so immersed in the story as to forget to switch back to the first language; trying to improve the translation; marking corresponding paragraphs to ease language switching; etc. This variety of strategies reflects the diversity of readers' skills and interests. It also highlights the role of the medium: the participants generally judged parallel text as providing a poor support for bilingual reading. It however supports reading strategies that would be hard to sustain with other techniques such as tool-tips.

4   Describing Reader's and System's Behaviors

While the bilingual reading experience still has to be invented, it will necessary follow a few principles imposed by the mechanisms of human visual attention and display resources manipulation. We recall these principles here and put them in the context of bilingual reading. We believe that these principles provide a common language and knowledge basis that can be used at all stages of the design process: They can be used to describe observed behaviors, whether it is to understand the bilingual reading activity or to test design solutions. They can also be used during the design phase to explore different strategies and design solutions.

4.1   Visual Selective Attention and Associated Spaces

Visual selective attention is a fundamental mechanism of human vision that is used extensively to read. It can be defined broadly as a selection mechanism, where one "object" in the visual field of the reader is selected and other objects are ignored. We will call this selected object the *focus* of attention, while the position of this object in the visual field or world will be called the *locus* of attention.[2] While often used as synonyms, these concepts actually refer to elements that belong to different spaces. We will also introduce another notion, the *nexus* of attention, as something that connects two "objects", permitting or calling for an attention shift from one to the other.

Locus of Attention and Display Resources. When reading, the locus of attention is a point on a *display surface* where the text in focus is displayed. For our concerns, it is important to consider the diversity of possible display surfaces and their properties: sheets of paper or electronic paper, LCD screen, desktop or whiteboard surfaces where something is video-projected, etc. The notion of a display surface has become very rich and also includes virtual surfaces such as windows or coherent arrays of displays [5]. It should not be confounded with the close notion of *work surface*, which is a surface in

---

[2] Our definitions could conflict with other works in HCI or in other fields that are more legitimate to define these notions, such as cognitive sciences.

the workspace that can host display surfaces, such as a desktop or wall. Both display and work surfaces will be described as *display resources*.

Focus of Attention and the Representation Space. The representation space is the space of all possible focuses of attention. It has therefore 3 axes corresponding to the properties of the object in focus, which belongs to one version of the text defined by its *language*, has a *position* in this text version, and corresponds to a *linguistic level* such as the word, the sentence or the paragraph. By adding a language axis, the representation space generalizes the space-scale diagrams used to discuss information spaces visualization techniques [15], but it uses the position in the text and the linguistic level instead of continuous axes for space and scale.

Nexus of Attention and Links in the Representation Space. A nexus of attention connects two possible attention focuses, and can thus be understood as a bidirectional link between two points of the representation space. There are three natural kinds of nexuses: First, consecutive words, sentences and paragraphs are connected by *positional links*, i.e. links between points of the representation space that differ only along the *position* dimension. Second, elements are connected to their containers at the upper linguistic level by *hierarchical links*. And finally, the translation defines *alignment links* between points that differ along the *language* dimension (and potentially also along the other dimensions, e.g. a word can sometime be translated as a full sentence). The text itself can contain links between points that have the same language but can differ along the other dimensions, like footnotes, figures and references. The notion of a nexus of attention can also be extended to include links to elements in other documents, such as hyperlinks or the entry corresponding to a word in a bilingual dictionary.

4.2   Using These Spaces in the Design Process

Analyzing Readers' Behavior. To analyze readers' behavior, it can be useful to know how the focus of attention changes during the reading, which can be visualized as a path in the representation space. Such information can be hard to obtain, however some works suggest that it can be usefully approximated by the parameters of the rendering process, such as the amount of scrolling [6, 20]. They can also be used to compute quantitative values that can be directly compared, such as the proportion of reading time during which a given element was visible.

Defining the Interaction. Displaying bilingual texts consists basically in rendering some text elements taken from the representation space at some location in a display surface. It thus requires the definition of a *composition mapping* between the display surfaces and the representation space (see Fig. 2). Interaction can take advantage of the different nexuses of attention, which define possible tasks, as we will see later. In particular, these nexuses can be used to identify opportunities for interactive elements in the displayed text, like the hyperlinks used in *Doppel Text*.

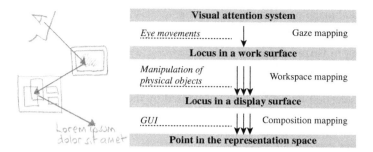

Fig. 2. The pipeline of visual attention. Gray boxes represent limited resources, and the arrows represent one-to-one mappings between elements of each type of resource. These mappings are defined or controlled by the mechanisms on the left.

4.3   Manipulating Limited Resources

In most situations, there is much more text to read than what can be displayed on the available display surfaces and made visible on the available work surfaces: these display resources should then be considered as limited. Visual attention can also be considered as a limited resource since there is only one focus of attention. This limitation in resources motivates the reader's need to interact with the text, including the physical manipulation of printed books. (The *way* one interacts, however, should be tailored to the readers' tasks) The management of limited resources (and particularly their reuse) has generic methods, and we discuss how they apply to attention and display resources. These methods can be used to describe observed readers' behavior in terms of strategies used, but can also be used for a design space as we will see later.

Reuse of Work Surfaces. Taking into account the need to reuse workspace allows one to highlight the function of some design elements that could otherwise be over-looked. For example, a book binding could be seen as only useful to maintain the sheets together, but it is also a mechanical guidance that eases the reuse of work space: when turning a page, the binding forces the new page to take the place of the previous one on the work surface. Similarly in GUIs, dragging is constrained to a single dimension to implement scrolling, while page flipping animations help in understanding how the surfaces are reused.

Spatial and Temporal Multiplexing. Visual attention implies a chain of one-to-one mappings depicted in Fig. 3. Attention is bound to a locus on a work surface by eye movements (*gaze mapping*); this locus on a work surface is bound to a locus in a display surface by the physical manipulation of the display surfaces (*workspace mapping*); and then this locus in a display surface is bound to a point in the representation space by the *composition mapping*, which is controlled through the graphical user interface. Moreover, the composition mapping can itself be defined as a chaining of multiple mappings as it can use split panels, each of which correspond to a viewport in a virtual space where another composition process is held. When a space (virtual or real) is split so that a different mapping is used in each sub-space, we refer to *spatial multiplexing*. On the other hand, *time multiplexing* describes a mapping that changes in time. The total mapping must change in time to reuse resources, therefore at least one of the three mappings must change in time.

Multiplexing in Gaze Mapping. In *free attention*, eye movements define the locus of attention: the gaze mapping changes in time. The remaining mappings can be fixed, allowing for spatial multiplexing strategies. In *directed attention*, the reader does not control the selection process, which is imposed by the rendering process. Eyes do not have to move (the gaze mapping is fixed), but the remaining mappings evolve in time. Rapid Serial Visual Presentation epitomizes this temporal multiplexing approach [30], although other variants are possible.

Multiplexing in Composition Mapping. The printed book uses spatial multiplexing: each page, as a display surface, displays a fixed part of the representation space. On the other hand, the screen of an e-reader relies on temporal multiplexing: it displays different parts of the representation space at different times. However, e-readers use a text container metaphor such as a pagination metaphor that reproduces the pages of a printed book or a scroll metaphor. Their composition mappings are then better described as chains of two mappings: First, the screen is bound to a specific virtual display surface (a virtual page or a viewport on a virtual scroll) using temporal multiplexing. Then, text is placed in this virtual display surface using spatial multiplexing (different parts of the virtual display surface are bound to different words in the text). Fluid documents [7] and fish-eye lenses use a similar mixed strategy, however the time-multiplexed mapping introduces a geometrical deformation in addition to defining a viewport. Temporal and spatial multiplexing can also be used to describe other features: a display surface can be split using spatial multiplexing so that one part of it displays the text at another level of detail (creating an overview) or at another position (e.g. to display footnotes).

5 Designing for Bilingual Reading

5.1 Four Challenges Highlighted by the Interviews

The bilingual reading mechanisms presented in the previous section offer a complex yet incomplete model of this activity: it ignores emotional aspects and important cognitive mechanisms such as working memory, and oversimplifies user input mechanisms. This framework is however sufficient to describe the following challenges for the design of bilingual reading appliances, which were all derived from an analysis of the concerns spontaneously expressed by the people we have interviewed.

Secondary Tasks. The main task in reading is to acquire the text meaning by focusing sequentially on (most of the) successive words. This task only uses one type of nexus corresponding to positional links. Other tasks can involve other types of nexuses and they can also be very important to make the reading experience rich and diversified. Obviously, language links are particularly important for bilingual reading. Hierarchical links are used to define the context, as we learned from some participants of the reading traces experiment: they marked where translated paragraphs should be split to match the original ones. Links to glossaries or to the first occurrence of a proper name were frequently requested, as well as links to external references such as dictionaries or encyclopedias.

Bi-focal Tasks. Some tasks require considering simultaneously two elements, which imply to focus alternatively on them with frequent focus switches. An obvious example of such a task would be a comparison task, e.g. comparing the syntaxes used in a sentence and its translation. A more straightforward example for our concerns is a task where the information provided by the focus of attention is better understood in the light of another element, which becomes a second possible focus. The necessity to support this general class of tasks has been recognized for a long time in HCI: many *focus + context* techniques have been designed to deal with situations where the context helps to understand the focus [14] and compared using the notions of spatial and temporal multiplexing [10]. These techniques use mainly the hierarchical links to define the context, but language links can also be used for bilingual reading. For instance, the translation of a sentence provides a context that can help understand the meaning of an unknown word in that sentence. We have accordingly observed people using their two index fingers to keep track of the two focuses of attention. Using our framework, we define *bi-focal tasks* as tasks where two points from the representation space need to be accessed quickly from one to the other and back. These two points can be connected by any kind of link defined in the document, e.g. by features such as footnotes, references and figures. They can also be defined on the fly by the reader, e.g. to support lightweight navigation such as *"looking ahead in the text to preview or anticipate"* [24].

Staying in the Flow. Many interviewees stressed the fact that when they had to pause their reading because they could not understand a word or sentence, they felt very unsatisfied. The resulting loss of context and the non-satisfaction of their desire to advance in the story cause this feeling, but it may just be a special case of the frustration that arises when somebody's flow of thoughts is interrupted. The challenge of creating interfaces that allow *staying in the flow* (as defined by Csikszentmihalyi) is well known in HCI. Bederson, for example, advise to make interfaces that encourage users to develop their skills; that reduce the need for users to consciously make connections between different interface states; that give users the feeling of being in control; and that let users set clear goals and have feedback on their progression [2]. Reading is considered as a good example of activity that can create a state of flow, and it is easy to see how a book, taken as an interface, follows Bederson's advices. Reading is mostly a navigating in the text: instead of using commands to follow the positional links, the reader rather sets the display resources in a state that allows her to follow these links visually and unconsciously. This principle also appears in the lightweight navigation techniques used by people who read paper magazines [24].

The secondary tasks discussed earlier are often supported explicitly by specific commands such as clicking on a hyper-link. Instead of providing such direct support for some tasks, a strategy that keeps the reader in the flow could then be to let her *navigate* in a continuous space defined by the rendering process. This way, the number of controls required is reduced and the user only needs to manipulate the view until she reaches a setting that allow her to accomplish her task. We thus see an excellent design opportunity in a more pervasive use of navigation as an interaction scheme. Relying on navigation in continuous spaces brings another opportunity, with the design of inter-action techniques that change the position of the view simultaneously along multiple dimensions. Such an *integral navigation* has been studied for the dimensions of space and scale, with expected and measured benefits for long-range navigation [1, 15].

Breaking the Container Metaphor. If we do not want the expression "bilingual reading" to be a paraphrase for "mostly monolingual reading where a different lan-guage is sometime used", we probably need to escape from the box-like container metaphor. It is indeed possible to display some text without making it look like being part of a page or scroll. For instance, RSVP departs strongly from such layouts [30]. The presentation tool *Prezi*[3] has been cited during the interviews because of its non-conventional text flow: it puts all slides in an unbound 2D zoomable space so that they can intersect with or contain other slides. And while these slides are not otherwise different from paper ones, transitions between slides are animated like navigation in the zoomable space, which makes viewing them a quite different experience. In our framework, container metaphors make use of the particular combination of temporal and spatial multiplexing described in Sect. 4.3. From this, a clever designer can devise other strategies by slightly modifying the bindings and spaces involved. For example, *content-aware scrolling* [22] works in a similar way than a scroll metaphor, but defines a continuous path in the document and allows the viewport's size to change to adapt to the document's content. The *horizontal scroll* [4] uses the spatial multiplexing strategy already used in multi-column layouts and mixes it with the temporal multiplexing strategy used by classical scrolling. These techniques illustrate how our framework opens a design space for new text display methods, which need to be explored in search of efficient techniques to display bitexts.

5.2 Analysis of Existing Approaches

To better understand the space of solutions to the previous challenges, we have additionally conducted an extended review of the HCI literature, looking for works that addressed at least one of these challenges. These works can be described as using one of three different approaches that we introduce and describe in the following sections and Fig. 3. We discuss the potential benefits and drawbacks of each approach, as well as some related technical issues that need to be addressed.

Switch on Demand. Techniques belonging to the *switch on demand* approach use a single display surface. The ones that display text on this surface do it with a standard container metaphor. The techniques support bi-focal tasks by letting the user explicitly select the link between the two focuses, e.g. by clicking on a special element such as a hyper-link. A view that contains the destination of the link is then displayed in a tooltip-like transient visualization, which uses temporal multiplexing for the compo-sition mapping. Another command allows closing that tool-tip and getting back to the original view. This use of transient visualizations is believed to "bring the user into

---

[3] http://prezi.com/

direct and instant involvement with the information representation", use display resources economically, and provide fast access to the information because of its closeness [23]. The drawbacks of this approach are related to its use of an explicit selection of the link that defines the target focus element. Indeed, selecting the link by its source element can be a difficult task for some types of content or interfaces (e.g., using a touch screen). A second problem comes from the fact that a single element may involve multiple nexuses of attention, calling for different targets: this is the "secondary tasks" design challenge. Altogether, this approach might require carefully designed interaction techniques to select at the same time a focus of attention and the type of nexus (or command) to use.

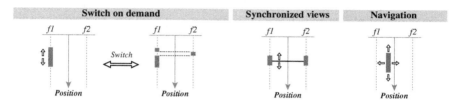

Fig. 3. Position-focus diagrams for the three discussed approaches. For bilingual reading, the two focuses f_1 and f_2 are two different languages and these diagrams are a projection of the representation space where the linguistic level is not represented. The blue rectangles represent the set of points displayed on some display surface at a given time. Arrows represent possible navigation actions (Color figure online).

Synchronized Views. This approach consists in having one display surface by focus (spatial multiplexing), which are synchronized so that they always display corresponding parts: when the user changes the position or level of detail in one surface, the other one is automatically updated (temporal multiplexing). This approach replaces an explicit selection of the nexus involved in a bi-focal task by a continuous use of similar nexuses, allowing using navigation instead of explicit commands. On the other hand, the approach can only be applied with nexus types that define a correspondence for each subset of the document (which is the case for language nexuses). This approach can also make it difficult to analyze the alignment structure as it is used indirectly in the rendering process. And obviously, it uses more display resources.

Spatial multiplexing can be done in two ways for this approach. First, the two display surfaces can be laid out next to each other, as a split screen or using different devices. This is the strategy used for *parallel texts*: considering the virtual display surfaces formed by a book's open pages, each side corresponds to a different focus. Second, a surface can be laid on top of another, and render the second focus associated with the area hidden below. For instance, *magic lenses* and *magnification lenses* use a lens as the second focus surface; *mobile augmented reality* uses a display surface belonging to a different object hold between the original display and the user's eyes.

A major drawback of parallel texts is their low granularity, as seen in Sect. 2.1. It makes it hard to locate in the second view the part corresponding to some known element of the first view, e.g. a single word. The searched part being unknown, it can only be identified using the context, which requires some interpretation and often many eye movements back and forth the two views. All techniques using synchronized views suffer from similar issues unless there is a geometrical correspondence between the two views (which is usually the case with mobile AR, but not for bilingual reading). This drawback can however become a benefit if the reader needs to access frequently the second view, as she will memorize the structure and spatial position of previously visited elements.

The approach also has a rendering issue, which is to maintain a coherent second view when the first one is scrolled (see Fig. 4). Indeed, the different ordering of elements can cause some elements that are not relevant anymore to stay in the second view. This view may also have to display more elements than it can contain. Solutions to these problems may need to break the container metaphor by dynamically changing the size of displayed elements and hiding some, e.g. using ellipsis. Techniques inspired by other properties of paper such as folding could be used, as *Melange* did for bifocal tasks that use positional or hierarchical links [13].

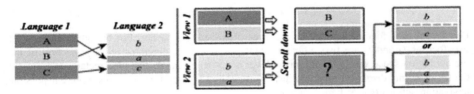

Fig. 4. Coherence issues with synchronized views. Left: paragraph boxes for two versions of a same text in different languages with the corresponding alignment structure. Center: initial views for each language. Right: after scrolling down in view 1, paragraph *a* becomes irrelevant in view 2, but paragraph *c* should be displayed. Two possible renderings for view 2 are provided, with global rescaling (bottom) or ellipsis (top).

Magic lenses and Mobile AR provide another opportunity, as they can be used in two ways: Either the display surface of the second view is kept in a static position and scrolling in the first view triggers updates for the second view, or the display surface is moved (and eventually resized) relatively to the first view, which will also trigger updates. The second option allows the reader to specify what part of the first view she is interested in by using a spatial navigation scheme. The corresponding manipulations of the magic lens or hand-held device are however rather cumbersome and might require new developments.

Animated Transition Between Focuses. With this approach, a single view is used. An element displayed in this view can be selected and, on demand, the whole view content is replaced by another content so that the view now displays the second focus associated to the selected element. Like synchronized views, this approach requires a type of nexus that can be defined on any subset of the document, but uses a temporal rather than spatial multiplexing scheme. When the two focal elements only differ in position or linguistic level, the transition can use animated panning and zooming. Otherwise, there might be no natural way of animating the transition. *Diffamation* [8] and *Gliimpse* [12] are notable examples showing that efficient animated transitions can however be devised for some types of textual data. These works use apparition, removal and displacement of text blocs, text lines and other graphics to animate the transition. We refer to this approach as *morphing* as it uses the shapes and positions of visual elements and their hierarchical relations to define the animation. These works highlight the need for advanced techniques such as animating paragraphs reflow, using curved trajectories and stabilizing the view vertically on focal elements. The benefit of these methods is to allow the user to memorize the two documents layouts, and to quickly switch from one document to the equivalent position in the other one. Because animations are deterministic, they can also be memorized to make afterward animations easier to follow. However, animations can also confuse the user if she cannot keep track of what is moving where, so the flow of animation has to be carefully tuned.

5.3 Adapting These Approaches to Bilingual Reading

Switch on Demand. For bilingual reading, this approach might be the most obvious one and is actually used by current software (see Sect. 2.1). Because selecting text is difficult when done with the usual techniques, one may want to reduce the set of possible selections to full words, full sentences, full paragraphs, etc., taking advantage of the small number of linguistic levels. Yet, the hierarchical organization of such elements prevents the use of simple selection techniques like picking. Existing materials thus only allow the selection of sentences, reducing the granularity of the alignment structure. There is therefore room to design more efficient selection techniques. One possibility would be to reify the various linguistic levels into new in-page interactive elements that do not overlap. Such elements are already used in pop-up books to make elements appear, hide, transform or move in response to user actions. They could be used in similar ways for bilingual reading, e.g. to reveal the translation of a paragraph by raising the (virtual) flap on which it is printed. Simulations of paper folding and bending could also add realism to the space distortions introduced by techniques like fluid documents.

Synchronized Views. The synchronized views strategy used by lenses and mobile augmented reality might be inefficient for bilingual reading, as the original and translated texts can have very different layouts. The other strategy offers however many possibilities that are worse exploring, considering the diversity of behaviors that they support (as observed in the reading traces experiment). Notably, using a second device like the reader's smartphone for the second view provides another interaction surface and opens a new space for simple gestures based on the proximity and orientation of this device.

Finally, it is possible to mix the two strategies. For instance, the two views could be defined by splitting a screen along the vertical dimension rather than along the horizontal one like parallel texts do. The top and bottom view would use different languages, and the bottom view would display the text that corresponds to what immediately follows the text displayed in the top view. The reader can then get the translation of what she just read in the bottom view simply by scrolling down, which would move the text read toward the top view where its translation would appear.

Navigation Between Languages. Morphing text from one language to another is more complicated than what *Diffamation* and *Gliimpse* have done, because there may be no common visual element between the start and final views. There are however many opportunities to create such a morphing: Elements can be morphed differently according to their linguistic level, in the spirit of distinguished visual transitions [34]. The morphing can better use the structure of the document by using successive steps that each address a lower linguistic level. For the animation of changes in abstract trees, this approach allows to easily understand what elements are transformed and how [17]. The last morphing step can then replace words from the first language with their translation.

We also suggest exploring the idea of letting the user control the morphing evolution instead of following a time-controlled animation. This could bring the feeling of navigating between languages. Midway positions could also be valuable, as they expose the linguistic structure of the text, which is sometime enough to relieve ambiguities. The reader can control the animation speed, skip it entirely or go backward, depending on her needs. By coupling in a single gesture this morphing control together with the initial selection of a word to stabilize, we could get similar benefits than with the "switch on demand" approach: a precise selection of the element whose translation is wanted, at the right linguistic level. On the other hand, the interleaving of words belonging to two distinct languages could also be a source of problems for specific readers (e.g. dyslexic ones) or purposes (e.g. language teaching).

Mixing Approaches. These approaches are not necessarily incompatible: they could be used together, or the reader could switch softly from one to another. For example, a tooltip created in a "switch on demand" approach could be turned into a permanent synchronized view. Interactions techniques developed to select text in a "switch on demand" approach could still work for synchronized views, highlighting the part of the second view corresponding to the selection. Similarly, the animation techniques developed for the "navigation between languages" approach could be used to solve the display coherence issues appearing when synchronized views are scrolled.

6   Future Work

In our future work, we will follow two parallel tracks. The first one is the continuation of our reflection on the design methods required to better understand how to design for bilingual reading. The second one concerns the realization of prototypes. We hope that the two tracks will converge in the longer term, e.g. in the form of technological probes.

For the realization of prototypes, the three approaches presented in Sect. 5 revealed the usefulness of three types of operations that can be used in combination: advanced text selection operations required for the "switch on demand" approach, space distortion techniques required for the "synchronized views" approach, and structured morphing strategies required for the "navigation between languages" approach. We have already started the development of a framework that provides these operations and helps exploring new solutions.

More importantly, the creation of design methods will require complementing, formalizing and evaluating the design methods that we have started to use, such as the reading traces experiment. One question that we want to answer is whether presenting to potential users the approaches introduced in Sect. 5.3 would trigger their imagination and allow them to provide even more insights about their bilingual reading experiences? Finally, the question of evaluating interfaces for bilingual reading is complex and will need further developments.

Acknowledgments. This work has been funded by the ANR CONTINT Transread project. We would like to thank Delphine Soriano for her useful and much appreciated help, as well as all the people we interviewed.

References

1. Appert, C., Fekete, J.D.: OrthoZoom scroller: 1D multi-scale navigation. In: Proceedings of CHI 2006. pp. 21–30. ACM, New York (2006)
2. Bederson, B.B.: Interfaces for staying in the flow. In: Ubiquity 2004, September 2004
3. Bederson, B.B., Quinn, A., Druin, A.: Designing the reading experience for scanned multi-lingual picture books on mobile phones. In: Proceedings of JCDL 2009, pp. 305–308. ACM (2009)
4. Braganza, C., Marriott, K., Moulder, P., Wybrow, M., Dwyer, T.: Scrolling behaviour with single- and multi-column layout. In: Proceedings of WWW 2009, pp. 831–840. ACM (2009)
5. Bucher, P., Chatty, S.: Qu'est-ce qu'une surface d'affichage?: une analyse rétrospective. In: Proceedings of IHM 2009, pp. 3–12. ACM, New York (2009)
6. Buscher, G., Biedert, R., Heinesch, D., Dengel, A.: Eye tracking analysis of preferred reading regions on the screen. In: CHI EA 2010, pp. 3307–3312. ACM, New York (2010)
7. Chang, B.W., Mackinlay, J.D., Zellweger, P.T., Igarashi, T.: A negotiation architecture for fluid documents. In: Proceedings of UIST 1998, pp. 123–132. ACM, New York (1998)
8. Chevalier, F., Dragicevic, P., Bezerianos, A., Fekete, J.D.: Using text animated transitions to support navigation in document histories. In: Proceedings of CHI 2010, pp. 683–692. ACM, New York (2010)
9. Clark, C., Rumbold, K.: Reading for pleasure: a research overview. National Literacy Trust (2006)
10. Cockburn, A., Karlson, A., Bederson, B.B.: A review of overview+detail, zooming, and focus+context interfaces. ACM Comp. Surv. **41**(1), 2:1–2:31 (2009)
11. Dehaene, S.: Reading in the Brain: The New Science of How We Read. Penguin Group, New York (2009)
12. Dragicevic, P., Huot, S., Chevalier, F.: Gliimpse: animating from markup code to rendered documents and vice versa. In: Proceedings of UIST 2011, pp. 257–262. ACM (2011)
13. Elmqvist, N., Henry, N., Riche, Y., Fekete, J.D.: Melange: space folding for multi-focus interaction. In: Proceedings of CHI 2008, pp. 1333–1342. ACM, New York (2008)
14. Furnas, G.W.: A fisheye follow-up: Further reflections on focus + context. In: Proceedings of CHI 2006, pp. 999–1008. ACM, New York (2006)
15. Furnas, G.W., Bederson, B.B.: Space-scale diagrams: understanding multiscale interfaces. In: Proceedings of CHI 1995, pp. 234–241. ACM Press/Addison-Wesley Publishing Co., New York (1995)

16. Gao, G., Wang, H.C., Cosley, D., Fussell, S.R.: Same translation but different experience: the effects of highlighting on machine-translated conversations. In: Proceedings of CHI 2013, pp. 449–458. ACM, New York (2013)

17. Guilmaine, D., Viau, C., McGuffin, M.J.: Hierarchically animated transitions in visualizations of tree structures. In: Proceedings of AVI 2012, pp. 514–521. ACM, New York (2012)

18. Han, C.H., Yang, C.L., Wang, H.C.: Supporting second language reading with picture note-taking. In: CHI EA 2014, pp. 2245–2250. ACM, New York (2014)

19. Hinckley, K., Dixon, M., Sarin, R., Guimbretiere, F., Balakrishnan, R.: Codex: a dualscreen tablet computer. In: Proceedings of CHI 2009, pp. 1933–1942. ACM, New York (2009)

20. Hornbæk, K., Frøkjær, E.: Reading patterns and usability in visualizations of electronic documents. ACM ToCHI 10(2), 119–149 (2003)

21. Hyrskykari, A., Majaranta, P., jouko Räihä, K.: Proactive response to eye movements. In: Proceedings of INTERACT 2003, pp. 129–136. IOS Press (2003)

22. Ishak, E.W., Feiner, S.K.: Content-aware scrolling. In: Proceedings of UIST 2006, pp. 155–158. ACM, New York (2006)

23. Jakobsen, M.R., Hornæk, K.: Transient visualizations. In: Proceedings of OZCHI 2007, pp. 69–76. ACM, New York (2007)

24. Marshall, C.C., Bly, S.: Turning the page on navigation. In: Proceedings of JCDL 2005, pp. 225–234. ACM, New York (2005)

25. Morineau, T., Blanche, C., Tobin, L., Guéguen, N.: The emergence of the contextual role of the e-book in cognitive processes through an ecological and functional analysis. Int. J. Hum Comput Stud. 62(3), 329–348 (2005)

26. Nelson, T.H.: Xanalogical structure, needed now more than ever: parallel documents, deep links to content, deep versioning, and deep re-use. ACM Comput. Surv. 31(4es) (1999). Article No 33

27. O'Hara, K.: Towards a typology of reading goals. Technical report, Xerox RXRC (1996). http://www.xrce.xerox.com/content/download/16322/117657/file/EPC-1996-107.pdf

28. O'Hara, K., Sellen, A., Bentley, R.: Supporting memory for spatial location while reading from small displays. In: CHI EA 1999, pp. 220–221. ACM, New York (1999)

29. Piolat, A., Roussey, J.Y., Thunin, O.: Effects of screen presentation on text reading and revising. Int. J. Hum.-Comput. Stud. 47(4), 565–589 (1997)

30. Potter, M.C.: Rapid serial visual presentation (RSVP): A method for studying language processing. In: Kieras, D.E., Just, M.A. (eds.) New Methods in Reading Comprehension Research, pp. 91–118. Erlbaum, Hillsdale (1984)

31. Rainie, L., Zickuhr, K., Purcell, K., Madden, M., Brenner, J.: The rise of e-reading, April 2012. http://libraries.pewinternet.org/2012/04/04/the-rise-of-e-reading/

32. Schilit, B.N., Golovchinsky, G., Price, M.N.: Beyond paper: Supporting active reading with free form digital ink annotations. In: Proceedings of CHI 1998, pp. 249–256. ACM Press/Addison-Wesley Publishing Co., New York (1998)

33. Schilit, B., Price, M., Golovchinsky, G., Tanaka, K., Marshall, C.: The reading appliance revolution. Computer 32(1), 65–73 (1999)

34. Schlienger, C., Dragicevic, P., Ollagnon, C., Chatty, S.: Les transitions visuelles différenciées : principes et applications. In: Proceedings of IHM 2006, pp. 59–66. ACM (2006)

35. Shibata, H., Omura, K.: Effects of paper on page turning: comparison of paper and electronic media in reading documents with endnotes. In: Harris, D. (ed.) Engin. Psychol. and Cog. Ergonomics, HCII 2011. LNCS, vol. 6781, pp. 92–101. Springer, Heidelberg (2011)

36. Subbaram, V.M.: Effect of display and text parameters on reading performance. Ph.D. thesis, The Ohio State University (2004)

37. Tashman, C.S., Edwards, W.K.: Active reading and its discontents: The situations, problems and ideas of readers. In: Proceedings of CHI 2011, pp. 2927–2936. ACM, New York (2011)
38. Tiedemann, J.: Bitext alignment. In: Hirst, G. (ed.) Synthesis Lectures on Human Language Technologies, vol. 14. Morgan & Claypool Publishers, San Rafael (2011)
39. Tucker, G.R.: A global perspective on bilingualism and bilingual education. In: Georgetown University Round Table on Languages and Linguistics 1999, p. 332 (2001)
40. Wästlund, E., Norlander, T., Archer, T.: The effect of page layout on mental workload: a dual-task experiment. Comput. Hum. Behav. **24**(3), 1229–1245 (2008)
41. Yu, C.H., Miller, R.C.: Enhancing web page readability for non-native readers. In: Proceedings of CHI 2010, pp. 2523–2532. ACM, New York (2010)
42. Zellweger, P.T., Regli, S.H., Mackinlay, J.D., Chang, B.W.: The impact of fluid documents on reading and browsing: an observational study. In: Proceedings of CHI 2000, pp. 249–256. ACM, New York (2000)

Dynamic Workload Adjustments in Human-Machine Systems Based on GSR Features

Jianlong Zhou[1(✉)], Ju Young Jung[1,2], and Fang Chen[1]

[1] National ICT Australia (NICTA), Eveleigh, NSW 2015, Australia
{jianlong.zhou,fang.chen}@nicta.com.au, jjun3170@uni.
sydney.edu.au
[2] The University of Sydney, Sydney, NSW 2006, Australia

Abstract. Workload is found to be a critical factor driving human behavior in human-machine interactions in modern complex high-risk domains. This paper presents a dynamic workload adjustment feedback loop with a dynamic cognitive load (CL) adaptation model to control workload adjustment during human-machine interaction. In this model, physiological signals such as Galvanic Skin Response (GSR) are employed to obtain passive human sensing data. By analyzing the obtained sensing data in real-time, the task difficulty levels are adaptively adjusted to better fit the user during working time. The experimental results showed that SVM outperformed other methods in offline CL classifications, while Naïve Bayes outperformed other methods in online CL level classifications. The CL adaptation model 1 (average performance is 87.5 %) outperformed the adaptation model 2 during the dynamic workload adjustment.

Keywords: Cognitive load · GSR · Dynamic adjustment · Machine learning

1 Introduction

Cognitive load (CL, also known as workload) refers to the amount of mental demand imposed on a user by a particular task, and has been associated with the limited capacity of working memory and the ability to process novel information [1, 2]. The cognitive load experienced by a user in completing a task has a major impact on her/his ability to acquire information during the task, and can severely influence the overall productivity and performance. High levels of cognitive load are known to decrease effectiveness and performance of users, as well as their ability to learn from their tasks [1]. On the other hand, if a task is very easy and routine, only inducing a low level of cognitive load, it may cause boredom and loss of focus, ultimately resulting in lower performance. In this way, the concept of an optimal range of cognitive load levels is developed, outside of which a subject's ability to learn, perform, and complete a task is likely to be negatively affected [2]. It is crucial to maintain the cognitive load experienced by a user within this optimal range to achieve the highest productivity. Cognitive load measurement (CLM) therefore plays an important role in applications involving human-machine interface. Furthermore, Galvanic Skin Response (GSR) is a

© IFIP International Federation for Information Processing 2015
J. Abascal et al. (Eds.): INTERACT 2015, Part I, LNCS 9296, pp. 550–558, 2015.
DOI: 10.1007/978-3-319-22701-6_40

measure of conductivity of human skin, and can provide an indication of changes in human sympathetic nervous system [3]. GSR has attracted researchers' attention as a prospective physiological indicator of cognitive load [3].

In order to keep the user in an optimal state and improve user's engagement and performance, dynamic workload adjustment (DWA) systems automatically modulate the difficulty of tasks and other factors related to tasks in human-machine systems in real-time. By monitoring user's state and adapting the task difficulty levels, a dynamic workload system improves user's performance and helps users maximize their capacity for productive work. However, there are still challenges in utilizing CLM in dynamic workload adjustment. For example, there is no effective model allowing the system to effectively adjust task elements dynamically.

This paper presents a dynamic workload adaptation model to control how workload can be adjusted during human-machine interaction. In this model, physiological modalities such as GSR are employed to obtain passive human sensing data. By analyzing the obtained sensing data in real-time, we adapt task difficulty levels in order to optimize workload in real-time, which allows the system to better fit the task to the user during working time. The dynamic workload adaptation feedback loop helps to balance the task performance and workload levels.

2   Related Work

Shi et al. [4] evaluated users' stress and arousal levels with GSR. The results showed that mean GSR significantly increases when task cognitive load level increases. Moreover, users' GSR readings are found to be lower when using a multimodal interface, instead of a unimodal interface. Son and Park [5] estimated driver's cognitive load using driving performance and skin conductance level as well as other measures in a driving simulator. The results showed that the skin conductance level provides clear changes associated with difficult level of cognitive workload. Nourbakhsh et al. [3] also indexed cognitive load with GSR features of accumulative GSR and GSR power spectrum in arithmetic tasks. Wang et al. [6] indexed cognitive load with GSR features such as mean-difference. GSR data were also tested by the Boosting algorithm with Haar-like features for cognitive load classifications. Furthermore, Afergan et al. [7] used functional near-infrared spectroscopy (fNIRS) to detect task difficulty and optimize workload with a dynamic adaptation. However, few researches use GSR features to index cognitive load dynamically in an adaptive feedback loop. This paper investigates the use of GSR in a dynamic workload adaptation feedback loop in order to improve task performance.

3   Experiment

3.1   Dynamic Workload Adaptation Feedback Loop

We propose a dynamic workload adaptation feedback loop as show in Fig. 1. In this feedback loop, physiological signals such as GSR are recorded when the user is performing a task. The recorded signals are then analyzed and classified as different CL

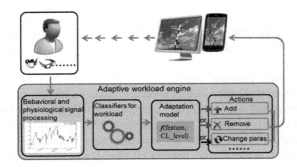

Fig. 1. Diagram of feedback loop of dynamic workload adaptation.

levels. The classified CL levels are input into the adaptation model in order to modulate task elements. A new task session is then performed based on the adaptation in order to keep task difficulty on an optimal level for the participants.

3.2   Task Design

Arithmetic addition task is used in this study. Each task is designed to stimulate a particular CL level from the participant based on the difficulty of the task. An "X" is shown at the beginning on a computer LCD display followed by four numbers in succession, where each number and "X" are displayed for 3 s. The participant is required to add these numbers up in his/her head during the task, and must choose one answer from the four options. At the completion of each task, the collected data are analyzed by the system. A new task is followed with a particular CL level controlled by the adaptation model. CL levels are designed as in Table 1 based on [3], where the number in each of the columns represents how many of the particular category of number (binary, 1-digit, 2-digit, 3-digit) are shown in the task.

Table 1. Cognitive load level definitions.

CL	Binary	1-Digit	2-Digit	3-Digit
0	4	0	0	0
1	3	1	0	0
2	2	2	0	0
3	1	3	0	0
4	0	4	0	0
5	0	3	1	0
6	0	2	2	0
7	0	1	3	0
8	0	0	4	0
9	0	0	3	1
10	0	0	2	2
11	0	0	1	3
12	0	0	0	4

3.3   Procedures

The experiment is carried out with the following procedures: (1) A computer is firstly setup with the GSR sensor connected and the corresponding drivers installed. (2) The participant is seated facing the LCD display of the computer. The tips of the index and fourth fingers of the left hand of the participant are connected to the GSR sensor, and the right hand of the participant is used to navigate the mouse to engage with the program. (3) The experiment begins by launching the experiment program. (4) The training stage firstly runs for a total of 8 tasks. (5) After training is completed, 6 testing stages are run, and each testing stage has a total of 20 tasks. Table 2 illustrates the different testing stage scenarios. The numbers displayed for the arithmetic tasks are all randomized, and the difficulties of tasks are controlled by the adaptation model. GSR devices from ProComp Infiniti GSR of Thought Technology Ltd were used in the experiment. 10 participants of university students and research staff were recruited in this experiment.

Table 2. Testing stage scenarios.

Testing stage	Initial CL	Adaptation model
1	0	1
2	6	1
3	12	1
4	0	2
5	6	2
6	12	2

The scenarios of testing stages are as follows:

- The testing stages starting from an initial CL level of 0 and 12 are designed to test how effective the adaptation model is in allowing the difficulty level to shift from one extreme to a more desirable state.
- The testing stages starting from an initial CL level of 6 is designed to test the robustness of the adaptation model, and observe its effectiveness in keeping the CL level stable at the desirable state.
- Two different adaptation models are used for comparison resulting in 6 experiment scenarios.

4   Cognitive Load Classification

4.1   Signal Processing

The raw GSR signals are firstly calibrated in order to account for variations of GSR between individuals and time intervals. As mentioned in Sect. 3.2, an "X" is shown at the beginning before the actual arithmetic task begins. This period is used as the reference point on which the rest of the data can be calibrated. The calibration is achieved using the relationship: $G_T = \frac{G_t - G_X}{G_X}$, where G_X is the average GSR value during the X-displaying period, and G_t and G_T are the raw and calibrated GSR signals during the task time respectively. Signal smoothing is achieved using a Hann window function as a low pass filter to remove high frequency noise.

4.2   Feature Extraction

Time domain features and frequency domain features are extracted in this study. For the time domain features, we focus on analyzing the nature of the major peaks in the data. In order to normalize the magnitudes of these peaks across all participants, the processed GSR signal for each task is divided by the mean value of all tasks of the particular participant:

$$G_N(i, k, t) = \frac{G_T(i, k, t)}{\frac{1}{m} \sum_{j=1}^{m} \sum_{t=1}^{T_{ij}} G_T(i, j, t)},$$

where $G_T(i, k, t)$ is the result from signal processing and $G_N(i, k, t)$ is the normalised GSR value at time t of task k of subject i.

The significance of each peak i is quantified using the duration of the peak S_{d_i}, magnitude S_{m_i}, and area $S_{a_i} = S_{d_i} S_{m_i}$. The time domain features include: (1) Sum of peak durations $S_d = \sum S_{d_i}$; (2) Sum of peak magnitudes $S_m = \sum S_{m_i}$; (3) Sum of peak areas $S_a = \sum S_{a_i}$; (4) Number of peaks S_f; and (5) Time taken to choose answer T_c.

For frequency-domain feature extraction, Z-score normalisation is firstly applied:

$$G_{Z(i,j)} = \frac{G_T(i,j) - \mu_{G_T(i,j)}}{\sigma_{G_T(i,j)}},$$

where G_T is the calibrated and smoothened GSR signal and G_Z is the normalised signal of task j of subject i. μ and σ are the mean and standard deviation of $G_T(i,j)$. Since each task is normalised in this way using its own mean and standard deviation, the magnitudes and range of G_Z of each task become standardised, thus the frequency features can be isolated more effectively. The power spectrum is extracted using:

$$P(\omega) = \frac{1}{N} Y(\omega) Y^*(\omega),$$

where P is the power spectrum, ω is frequency, N is the length of the signal, and Y and Y^* are the frequency spectrum and its complex conjugate respectively. The average power below 1 Hz was calculated for each task, as this frequency region contained the most non-zero values.

4.3   Offline Cognitive Load Classifications

Using all of the features mentioned above, three different machine learning (ML) methods were used to classify CL levels: SVM, Naïve Bayes, and Random

Forest. Data was collected from 12 participants who performed an offline variation of the experiment with no real-time adaptation, using the same task design. For each participant, equal number of tasks were performed for CL levels {0,4,8,12}. Leave-one-out cross-validation across the participants was used to evaluate ML performance. For the collected offline GSR signals, SVM slightly outperformed the other two with the accuracy of 78.1 % compared to 71.9 % for Naïve Bayes and 76.0 % for Random Forest for the 2-class classification. For the 4-class classification, SVM also outperformed the other two ML methods (49.0 %), compared to 40.6 % and 36.5 % for Naïve Bayes and Random Forest respectively. Therefore, SVM was chosen as the ML method during the dynamic workload adaptation.

4.4   Online Cognitive Load Classifications

The online cognitive load classification during the dynamic workload required a slightly different cross-validation method compared to the offline classifications. In the online cognitive load classifications, the ML model was trained using a calibrated and therefore *personalized* version of the same static data used in the offline cross-validation. After extracting the features from the data, they were calibrated using the mean and variance of the features extracted from a short training stage conducted by the particular subject. In this way, the participant did not have to run an extremely long training stage, and the classification model would still take into account the subjective differences between participants to a certain extent.

Correctness and therefore *accuracy* of the classifications also need to be more clearly defined for online classifications as the CL levels are all integer values ranging from 0–12 for the tasks, but classifications are only made from the set of {0,4,8,12}. *Correctness* in the online 4-class classification is defined as follows: for any CL level that falls between two of {0,4,8,12}, a classification is considered *correct* if it matches one of these two *neighboring* values. For example, if the CL level is 3, a classification of either 0 or 4 is considered *correct*. For a 2-class problem, it is difficult to use a similar logic, thus a *correctly* classified value was defined to be within 6 levels of the true CL level. The *correctness* of classification for the online analysis was purposely defined more loosely due to issues that arise with stricter definitions given the nature of the task design. As a consequence of the inherent randomness presented in the tasks, the CL level can only be used as a good indicator of the difficulty rather than an exact metric. This is especially more relevant for the online classification problem involving 13 different CL levels as the margins between each level are not as distinguished. For the offline case which only involved levels {0,4,8,12}, this issue is minimized as the margins between levels are less disputable.

Table 3 shows the comparison of classification accuracy between offline classifications and online classifications. The results show that all ML methods have similar or even better performance in online CL classifications as in offline CL classifications. All three ML methods can effectively classify CL levels of tasks in real-time.

Table 3. Accuracy of offline classifications vs. online classifications.

Algorithm	2-Class (%)		4-Class (%)	
	Offline	Online	Offline	Online
SVM	78.1	81.7	49.0	44.0
Naïve Bayes	71.9	89.2	40.6	63.6
Random Forest	76.0	88.4	36.5	56.6

5 Dynamic Workload Adjustment

5.1 Adaptation Models

The objective of the adaptation model is to keep the CL level within the range 4–8 (middle range of CL levels) during the dynamic workload adaptation. Two adaptation models are designed in this study.

- Adaptation model 1:
  - If classified CL level CL_t at time t is to be 8 or 12, decrease the CL level by 1;
  - If CL_t is classified to be 0 or 4, increase CL level by 1.
- Adaptation model 2:
  - If CL_t is classified to be 12, or CL_t and CL_{t-1} are both classified to be 8 or above, decrease CL level by 1;
  - If classified level is 0, or CL_t and CL_{t-1} are both classified to be 4 or below, increase CL level by 1.

Adaptation model 1 can be regarded as the more *dynamic* variation model, while the adaptation model 2 is clearly more *stable* as it has to meet slightly more strict criteria to change levels. The design of both adaptation models is also kept consistent with their objective by ensuring that their behaviors are symmetrical about the mean value of the desired range, i.e. the level 6.

5.2 Performance Evaluation of Adaptation Models

Performance of the adaptation model is defined as the percentage of tasks which have $4 \leq CL \leq 8$ out of all tasks performed during a testing stage. It is regarded as the *desirable* range in the dynamic workload adaptation. Figure 2 shows the changes of average CL levels during dynamic adaptation process. Each point (n, CL) on a curve represents the average CL level for the corresponding task number (n) of a particular testing stage scenario, differentiated by their initial CL and the adaptation model used. In Fig. 2, it is clear to see that all adaptation models were able to successfully drive and maintain the CL level within the desired range, and only minor differences are observed between the two adaptation models. For a quantitative comparison, the mean performances for each scenario are summarized in Table 4.

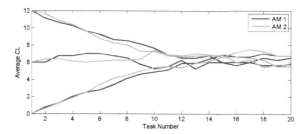

Fig. 2. CL Changes throughout testing stages.

Table 4. Average performance of adaptation models.

Initial CL	AM1 (%)	AM2 (%)
0	53.1	56.9
6	87.5	86.3
12	41.9	51.5

Significant differences are only observed for $CL_{initial} = 12$, where adaptation model 2 achieved around 10 % higher performance than adaptation model 1. Reasons for poorer and more disparate performance levels for this scenario could be attributed to the subjectivity inherent in the experiment that could not be completely removed from the task design. Subjectivity is a more significant issue for higher difficulty level tasks, as the GSR responses are likely to show greater variations between participants due to differences in arithmetic ability. With this increased diversity, accurate classification becomes more challenging, and translates to poorer performance.

6   Conclusions and Future Work

This paper investigated the use of GSR features in dynamic workload adjustment. Both time domain and frequency domain features were extracted and used for CL level classifications. The experimental results showed that SVM, Naïve Bayes, and Random Forest were all able to provide reasonable accuracies of CL level classifications. The classification results could be used as inputs to CL adaptation models for a dynamic workload adjustment environment, where the CL level is driven and maintained around an optimal level. Future work will focus on designing more complex adaptation models as well as the generalization of the dynamic workload adjustment on a wide variety of real working environments.

Acknowledgements. NICTA is funded by the Australian Government as represented by the Department of Broadband, Communications and the Digital Economy and the Australian Research Council through the ICT Centre of Excellence program. The authors thank Lucas Mattos for help in setting up the experiment.

References

1. Chandler, P., Sweller, J.: Cognitive load theory and the format of instruction. Cogn. instr. **8** (4), 293–332 (1991)
2. Paas, F., Tuovinen, J.E., Tabbers, H., Va n Gerven, P.W.M.: Cognitive load measurement as a means to advance cognitive load theory. Educ. Psychol. **38**(1), 63–7 1 (2003)
3. Nourbakhsh, N., Wang, Y., Chen, F.: GSR and blink features for cognitive load classification. In: Kotzé, P., Marsden, G., Lindgaard, G., Wesson, J., Winckler, M. (eds.) Human-Computer Interaction – INTERACT 2013, pp. 159–166. Springer, Berlin (2013)
4. Shi, Y., Ruiz, N., Taib, R., Choi, E., Chen, F.: Galvanic Skin Response (GSR) As an Index of Cognitive Load. In: Extended Abstracts on Human Factors in Computing Systems CHI 2007, pp. 2651–2656. New York, NY, USA, ACM (2007). doi:10.1145/1240866.1241057
5. Son, J., Park, M.: Estimating cognitive load complexity using performance and physiological data in a driving simulator. In: Proceedings of Automotive UI 2011. Austria (2011)
6. Wang, W., Li, Z., Wang, Y., Chen, F.: Indexing cognitive workload based on pupillary response under luminance and emotional changes. In: Proceedings of the 2013 International Conference on Intelligent User Interfaces, pp. 247–256 (2013)
7. Afergan, D., Peck, E.M., Solovey, E.T., Jenkins, A., Hincks, S.W., Brown, E.T., Jacob, R.J. K.: Dynamic difficulty using brain metrics of workload. In: Proceedings of the SIGCHI Conference on Human Factors in Computing Systems, pp. 3797–3806. New York, NY, USA ACM (2014)

Text Touching Effects in Active Reading: The Impact of the Use of a Touch-Based Tablet Device

Hirohito Shibata[1](✉), Kentaro Takano[2], and Shun'ichi Tano[3]

[1] Research and Technology Group, Fuji Xerox Co. Ltd.,
430 Sakai, Nakai, Kanagawa 259-0157, Japan
hirohito.shibata@fujixerox.co.jp
[2] Research and Technology Group, Fuji Xerox Co. Ltd.,
6-1 Minatomirai, Nishi-ku, Yokohama, Kanagawa 220-8668, Japan
kentaro.takano@fujixerox.co.jp
[3] Graduate School of Information Systems,
The University of Electro-Communications,
1-5-1 Chofugaoka, Chofu, Tokyo 182-8585, Japan
tano@is.uec.ac.jp

Abstract. This paper describes experiments examining the effect of touching interaction with text in active reading through evaluating the impact of the use of a touch-based tablet device. The first experiment compared the performance of proofreading when using paper and when using a touch-based tablet device. Results showed that participants detected more errors when reading from paper than when reading from the tablet device. During reading, when using paper, participants frequently performed the interaction of text touching, such as pointing to words and sliding their fingers or pens along sentences. This fact suggests that touching interaction with text plays an important role in proofreading tasks. To verify this hypothesis, we conducted a second experiment in which participants proofread documents with constrained interaction with paper. Results showed that they detected more errors when they were allowed to interact with text freely than when they were not allowed to interact with text. Considering these results, we discuss practical implications to effectively support active reading with a touch-based tablet device.

Keywords: Active reading · Proofreading · Touch-based tablet devices · Digital reading devices · Text touching · Pointing to text · Sliding a finger or a pen

1 Introduction

Tablet devices have rapidly gained widespread use recently. People use them for various purposes in a variety of situations [22]. They are also used in work situations such as checking email, searching the Web, and giving presentations [8]. However, they are not frequently used for knowledge-intensive reading activities such as reading academic papers critically or proofreading technical reports thoroughly [14]. According

© IFIP International Federation for Information Processing 2015
J. Abascal et al. (Eds.): INTERACT 2015, Part I, LNCS 9296, pp. 559–576, 2015.
DOI: 10.1007/978-3-319-22701-6_41

to Muller's diary study [22], viewing documents that seems to include such reading accounted for merely 1.3 % of all activities for which tablet PCs were used.

Such knowledge-intensive reading, which includes critical thinking or learning, is called *active reading* [25]. Active reading involves not merely reading itself but also underlining a text, annotating, finding information within a text, and summarizing. Our interest in this paper is how touch-based tablet devices affect active reading.

To clarify the motivation of this research, we begin with a description of our experience. After the release of the first version of iPad, one of the authors started to read academic papers using an iPad. However, he found it difficult to read papers using it. When he touched the display panel during reading, the documents were often moved or expanded against his wishes and this interfered with reading. He had to touch the panel carefully or give up touching documents so that the presentation of documents would not be changed. He realized for the first time that he often pointed to text or slid his finger along text while reading and restricting these actions made him uncomfortable.

From this experience, we inferred that these actions, which are performed almost unconsciously, played a cognitively important role in understanding documents. For example, people can impress a certain word on their minds by pointing to the word. By pointing to two words, they can easily compare distant information in documents. By sliding a finger on sentences, they can control the speed of reading to avoid skipping words or sentences unconsciously. We have noticed that touch-based tablet devices would not promote such interaction with text and wondered whether this might degrade reading performance.

To discuss the issue more precisely, we classify readers' behavior performed during reading. Interaction with paper documents is divided into two types: *interaction with sheets* and *interaction with contents*. The former includes moving documents, arranging documents, and turning or flipping pages, which we call *document manipulation* in this paper. For the latter, i.e., interaction with contents, we divide them into two types. One is *annotation* that includes underlining text, drawing symbols such as circles or asterisks, and writing text in the margin area. It remains permanent information in the document. The other is a touching gesture for contents without leaving any permanent information, which we call *text touching*. It includes pointing to text and sliding a finger or a pen along text.

The issue of unexpected behavior of a touch-based tablet device in active reading is caused by the interaction of text touching. However, the effect of text touching for active reading is not investigated as far as we know. Therefore, in this paper, we examine how text touching affect reading performance in active reading.

2 Related Work

Previous studies that compared reading from paper and reading from screens have mainly dealt with sequential reading in which readers read documents from beginning to end while turning pages one-by-one [4, 5, 7]. However, in a work situation, people often skim a document, move back and forth between pages repeatedly, move and organize documents by laying out multiple documents spatially during reading [1, 18,

26]. In the following, we overview studies dealing with such work-related reading, whose characteristics are closely similar to active reading, and we describe how interaction with contents affects reading.

Regarding document manipulation, O'Hara et al. [23, 24] reported that paper documents are easy to handle in moving or arranging documents and this effectively supports reading. Paper as a physical artifact allows such easy document manipulation [21]. In other words, in some cases, awkward manipulability of electronic media sometimes degrades the performance of reading in such reading. In fact, some experiments have shown that reading from paper is superior to reading from electronic media in reading for learning [13], reading to organize or select relevant documents [2], cross-reference reading for multiple documents [27], reading with frequent moving among pages [28], and reading for discussion [29].

Regarding annotations, Marshall [16, 17] investigated how annotations are used and how they support reading based on observational studies. O'Hara et al. [23, 24] observed that annotating is integrated with reading more smoothly when using paper. Johnson [12] experimentally showed that annotations are more frequently performed when reading from paper than when reading from screens, and that annotations help to develop spatial memory of text. In addition to these studies, the effect of annotation for reading has been widely recognized. In fact, many systems to support active reading pay much attention to the support of annotation [3, 6, 9, 10, 19, 25]. Most of them provide a feature of free-form ink annotation like paper and a pen. Morris et al.'s [21] report, based on their experiment, that current computer environments including tablet PCs do not sufficiently support easy quick annotation.

Regarding text touching, very little research has addressed the effect of text touching for reading. According to microscopic analysis of actions performed during actual reading in a work situation, people were frequently performing pointing to text [11, 27, 30]. Additionally, based on an informal observation, Kirsh [13] pointed out that people explicitly pay attention to a certain part of text by using a finger. These facts bring us an inference that pointing to text supports reading. However, no study has assessed how pointing to text affected reading performance quantitatively, as far as we have found. Moreover, the effect of sliding a finger or a pen has not been addressed even from the perspective of observation.

Considering these facts, we aim at assessing the effect of text touching in active reading. If we can understand its role, we expect that we can provide promising design implications to support active reading in tablet devices.

3   Text Touching Effects

As we described before, very little research has addressed the effect of text touching for reading. However, we do not think the reason is because text touching does not play an important role in reading. At the least, we consider text touching has the following cognitive effects for reading on theoretical grounds:

- *Paying attention to a certain part.* By pointing to a word or a sentence, readers can pay attention to its position explicitly [13]. This spatial cue helps strengthen readers' experience and memory for that part of the text [20].
- *Keeping a reading position.* Readers sometimes put their finger or hand at the start of a line or a paragraph where they are reading [11, 13]. In doing so, they can easily move back to the start position of the line. Moreover, they can also easily move to the next line without losing their place in the text.
- *Comparing different parts.* By putting fingers or a pen on different words or sentences, readers can readily compare them located in different positions. In this case, the finger or the pen can function as a navigational guide to direct the eye.

Sliding a finger or a pen on text brings about the following cognitive effects:

- *Reading while devoting attention to each word.* By sliding a finger or a pen along text, readers can check words one-by-one carefully. Readers can explicitly devote attention to a certain part.
- *Controlling the reading speed.* Readers sometimes make haste unconsciously, especially when they read a document they already know. Sliding a finger or a pen visualizes the speed of reading and helps a reader to avoid skipping words or sentences.

Additionally, by touching text constantly, readers are apparently able to continue concentrating on reading activities [20]. These cognitive effects seem to support reading documents carefully. If text touching is constrained, readers cannot leverage these cognitive effects, which might degrade the reading performance.

When using touch-based tablet PCs, documents might be moved or expanded against readers' wishes. Therefore, readers might think that they must not touch the panel while reading. Additionally, they might refrain from touching the panel frequently because the panel surface is too smooth and glassy. They might think that they are reluctant to leave a fingerprint on such a glassy surface. So, the use of touch-based tablet devices might restrain the interaction of text touching, which might lower the reading performance.

To verify this initial hypothesis, in the first experiment, we compare reading from paper and reading from a touch-based tablet device. We measure the number of text touches that are performed while reading. In the second experiment, to verify the effects of text touching, we examine how the restriction of text touching affects the reading performance.

4 Basic Framework

In our experiments, we require readers to read a document and detect errors as much as possible. Independent variables are reading media (paper or a tablet PC) or reading conditions. Dependent variables are error-detection rate and reading speed.

As a first step to examine the effect of text touching in active reading, we select cognitively demanding reading as an experimental task. According to our preliminary observational study, readers performed text touching frequently in cognitively demanding reading. Typical examples of this were reading difficult technical documents or documents written in a foreign language. Therefore, we require readers to detect semantic errors such that the term "a cat" must be replaced by "a dog" or the term "increased" must be replaced by "decreased." Classical experiments that compare reading among media have mainly required participants to detect alphabetical errors during a reading task [4, 7]. However, readers can detect alphabetical errors with superficial reading and, technically speaking, they do not have to understand the meaning of the document. However, in our task, readers must understand the context of documents accurately to detect contextual inconsistencies. Moreover, we require readers to detect errors within a limited time to make them concentrate on proofreading with great caution.

To concentrate on assessing the effect of text touching for reading, we need to isolate text touching from document manipulation. We use one single-page single document at a time to avoid the operations of arranging documents or turning pages.

Readers usually hold a pen during proofreading. Therefore, we allow readers to annotate while reading of the experiments. However, we analyze text touching and annotation separately and assess the effect of them for reading performance separately.

In an experiment using a tablet PC, i.e. in Experiment 1, we tried to minimize the effect of different writing tools and different writing manners for the reading performance. When reading from a tablet PC, we attached a transparent film on the panel of the tablet PC and allow participants to write anything on the film with an oil-based pen in the same way as the use of paper as shown in Fig. 1. The ink does not smear on the hand during reading because the pen is oil-based. The transparent film is similar to a protective film of display panels that many people use. Therefore, we think this film apparently does not change the participants' usual panel-touching behavior for the tablet PC.

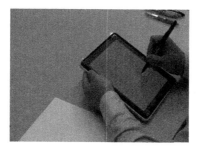

Fig. 1. Annotating on the panel of a tablet PC.

In all experiments, we required readers to report the positions of errors orally without correcting them. If we require them to check the error positions using special marks such as underlines or circles, then readers must use other notations to give their own annotation and this might change their annotating behavior. Therefore, we adopted the method of oral reporting to avoid giving any restriction for annotation.

5   Experiment 1: Paper vs. Tablet PC

In the first experiment, we compare reading from paper and reading from a touch-based tablet PC during proofreading to detect semantic errors. In this experiment, we examine the following two hypotheses.

First, we expect that reading from a touch-based tablet device would be inferior to reading from paper in reading with frequent text touching. Unexpected behavior of digital documents caused by touching the panel would become a factor in degrading the reading performance. In addition, if the tablet device constrained the interaction of text touching, then readers would not make use of the effectiveness of text touching by devoting attention to each word or comparing multiple words or sentences easily.

Second, we expect that people would perform text touching more frequently when reading from paper than when reading from the tablet device. Most current tablet devices are hard and heavy. Therefore, people less frequently hold these devices during reading and manual interaction with tablet devices would not be promoted. Moreover, touching of panels might cause unexpected document operations such as expanding, shrinking, or turning pages. Such operations might deter readers from touching panels while reading. Additionally, most panels of tablet devices are a glossy surface. Some users might hesitate to touch the panel because fingerprints can stain the surface when they are touched. Consequently, surface materials might not encourage touching of the panel.

5.1   Method

Design and Participants. The experimental design was a one-way within-participants design. The factor was the medium (paper and a tablet device). Each participant performed all conditions of tasks and performed two trials in each condition. The order of the media used in the participants' trials was counterbalanced to cancel the overall effects of the trial order.

Participants were 24 Japanese people (12 men, 12 women). Their ages were 23–40 years (avg. 31.3). Each had three or more years' experience using PCs. The vision of each, after correction, was better than 0.7. Among them, 12 people had their own touch-based tablet PCs or smart phones; 3 people were using these devices in business on a daily basis.

Materials. We created documents for the experiment based on columns of a Japanese-language newspaper. We eliminated columns related to current events because the level of understanding differs widely depending on background knowledge related to these events. Additionally, we eliminated metaphorical columns or prosy columns because the understanding of them differs widely among individuals.

Each document had five semantic errors. Participants were unable to detect these errors without checking the semantic context of the text carefully, although they were able to detect typographical errors while checking text at a surface level.

The average length of the four documents was 660.0 characters.

Task. The experiment task was to detect as many semantic errors as accurately as possible. The time limit was four minutes. For the report of error positions, we required them to read aloud at least five characters around errors to judge the position of errors in the text. The task trials were terminated when participants detected all five errors or when the time limit was reached.

Environments. We used the following two media in the experiment.

- **Paper:** The documents were printed in black and white on one side of B5 paper. They were written horizontally in 14 point font. Regarding the margin of the documents, the side margins were 2.8 mm, the top margin was 2.1 mm, and the bottom margin was 2.4 mm. Each document had 26 lines, each with 34 characters. The line spacing was 22 point.
- **Tablet PC:** As a typical example of touch-based tablet PC, we selected an iPad (WiFi 16G model; Apple Computer Inc.), which is widely used. The documents were converted to PDF files and were presented on an iPad. We used i-Bunko HD (ver. 1.07) as a PDF viewer, which is widely used as a Japanese e-book reader. We adjusted the electronic document character size to be equal to that of characters on the paper.

In both conditions, we allowed participants to annotate using the same oil-based pen. As we described before, in the Tablet PC condition, the panel of the PC was covered by a transparent film (Fig. 1). We provided the same manner of annotation among media so that the difference of the mode of writing among media does not affect the reading performance. We used new transparent films for every trial.

In i-Bunko HD, the change of document representation is caused by the following interaction. A document is expanded or shrunk when users pinch out or pinch in the document using two fingers. When the document is expanded, the display area of pages is changed when users drag the document. The display page of a document is changed when users swipe the panel or when users tap the side area of the panel. A menu and a slider are displayed when users tap the bottom area of the panel. Interaction of these types is common and broadly used in touch-based tablet PCs and smart phones. However, because the documents used in the experiment were all one-page, page-turning is not performed to complete the task of the experiment. Moreover, these functions do not work by contact with the oil-based pen.

Procedure. Before the experiment, participants engaged in training and became accustomed to using the iPad and performing the task. They also adjusted the brightness of the devices according to their preferences.

In performing the task, we allowed participants to hold the paper or the device freely. While performing the task, we displayed the count of error-detection that they had found using a paper board. We did not give feedback to participants related to whether the detected errors were correct or not while performing the task.

After the experiment, we conducted a questionnaire survey and an interview.

5.2   Results and Discussion

Figure 2 presents a comparison of the error-detection rate, which is the percentage of answers that participants had detected correctly. The error bar shows the standard error of the mean. It is the same throughout this paper.

A paired t-test revealed a significant difference among media [$t(23) = 2.51, p < .05$]. Participants detected 17.2 % more errors in the Paper condition than in the Tablet PC condition. Regarding the task completion time, no significant difference was found among media [$t(23) = 1.96, p > .1$] (the average times were, respectively, 218.5 s and 225.4 s in the Paper condition and the Tablet PC condition).

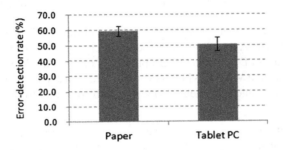

Fig. 2.   Error-detection rate in each medium.

Participants detected fewer errors when using the tablet device. This result supports our first hypothesis: reading from touch-based tablet devices is inferior to reading from paper in this cognitive demanding reading.

In the post-task survey, for four statements (Q1 You were able to concentrate on the proofreading task, Q2 You were able to detect many errors, Q3 You were able to perform the task quickly, Q4 You felt little fatigue), we required participants to evaluate two conditions (Paper and Table PC) using a 5-point rating (1 = strongly disagree, 2 = disagree, 3 = neither agree nor disagree, 4 = agree, and 5 = strongly agree). Figure 3 presents the average of the ratings given for each question item.

A paired t-test was conducted for each question. Results show that significant difference was found for Q1 [$t(23) = 4.05, p < .001$], Q3 [$t(23) = 2.50, p < .05$], and Q4 [$t(23) = 3.09, p < .01$]. Participants felt that they were able to concentrate on the task when using paper. They were also able to perform the task quickly and felt little fatigue when using paper.

Next, why was reading from the tablet device inferior to reading from paper? One possible reason for this result is a factor of presentation quality of documents. However, it has been verified experimentally that reading performance does not differ between paper and computer displays when using high-performance displays [4, 7, 23]. These experiments were conducted from the late 80s to the early 90s. However, the iPad used in this experiment provided higher-quality presentation than the computer displays used in the earlier experiments. Therefore, it seems that the presentation quality of media did not affect the error-detection rate of reading.

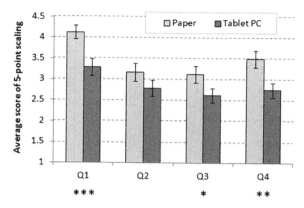

Fig. 3. Subjective evaluation of each media (***, **, and * denote significance at 0.1 %, 1 %, and 5 % levels respectively).

The next possible reason is a factor of document manipulation and interaction with the content. However, because we used single-page single documents in this experiment, there was no document manipulation such as moving documents, arranging documents, and turning pages. This allowed us to specifically analyze interaction with the content.

Figure 4 presents a comparison of the frequency of interacting with the content per minute. The interaction is divided into three types: annotating the document (Annotating), sliding a finger or a pen along the text (Sliding), and pointing to the text (Pointing). The latter two correspond to text touching. The type of interaction with text was judged visually by one of the experimenters by referring video data. On judging the type of interaction, sliding and pointing are discriminated based on whether participants move a finger or pen on the media surface. On counting the interaction with the text, every time participants' finger or pen was released from the panel, we considered that a new interaction occurred. We observed several times that participants' finger or pen hovered over the text without touching the panel. Such interaction can be also considered as interaction with text. However, we did not count such actions because it is difficult to judge whether participants are hovering or just moving their finger or pen in the air and it is also difficult to determine the start and the end of each hovering action. Therefore, we can say that the interaction with text was performed more in actual than the figures of Fig. 4.

We conducted a paired t-test among media for every type of interaction. Results show that, for annotating, no significant difference was found among media [$t(23) = 1.40$, $p > .1$]. Regarding text touching, a significant difference was found regarding the pointing [$t(23) = 4.00$, $p < .001$] and the sliding [$t(23) = 2.17$, $p < .05$]. Therefore, participants performed pointing to text and sliding a finger or a pen along text more when reading from paper than when reading from the tablet.

From this result, we discuss the following two points. First, participants performed text touching more frequently when using paper than when using the tablet device. This supports our second hypothesis: people perform text touching more frequently when

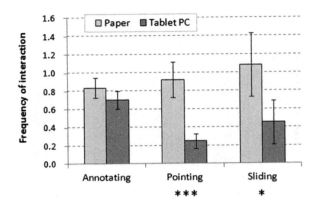

Fig. 4. Frequency of interacting with text (*** and * denotes significance at 0.1 % and 5 % level respectively).

reading from paper than when reading from a tablet device. In the post task interview, one participant reported that when putting their hand on the panel during the training session, a document was expanded unintentionally; thereafter, the person devoted special attention to the hand when touching the panel. Another participant reported that the person hesitated to touch the panel because it was so glassy and smooth. We think that these were main reasons why people performed text touching less frequently when using the tablet device.

Second, no significant difference was found in the amount of annotation among media. Previous studies revealed that people annotated more on paper than on electronic media [12, 21]. However, in this experiment, the amount of annotation did not differ among media, probably due to the following two reasons. First, participants did not have to re-read documents later in this task. Therefore, they did not have to extract information for the next reading. In fact, most of the annotation that participants made in this task was underlining or circling error positions. Second, the documents used in the experiment were all single-page documents. Participants were able to view a whole document at one time and they did not have to compare information from different pages. Therefore, placing permanent information in the document might not have produced any important benefit in this task.

Considering these results, we developed a new hypothesis: the frequency of text touching affects reading performance. In other words, reading from a tablet device is inferior to reading from paper in cognitive demanding reading because the interaction of text touching is constrained when using the tablet. In fact, a positive correlation was found between the error-detection rate and the amount of text touching. Pearson's product-moment correlation coefficient was 0.451, which is significantly different from zero [$p < .05$]. Therefore, those who frequently performed text touching made a high score in the error-detection rate. If people are unable to point to text, they might forget to devote attention to a certain part, or it might become difficult to compare distantly positioned parts of text. If they are unable to slide a finger or a pen on text, people might skip words or sentenced during reading. It is possible that such inconvenience lowers reading performance. To verify our new hypothesis, we conduct another experiment, as explained in the next section.

6 Experiment 2: Restricting Interaction with Paper

This experiment examines how reading performance varies when text touching was constrained. The following hypotheses in this experiment are tested with this experiment. Even if people read documents using paper, we expect that reading performance would be degraded when the interaction of text touching is restricted.

6.1 Method

Design and Participants. The experimental design was a one-way within-participants design. The factor was the task condition (Untouchable, Touchable, and Writable). Each participant performed all conditions and performed two trials in each condition. The order of the task condition in the participants' trials was counterbalanced to cancel the overall effect of the trial order.

Participants were the 24 people who participated in Experiment 1.

Materials. We created documents for the experiment in the same way as Experiment 1. For the six documents used in this experiment, the average length of text was 661.0 characters.

Task. The task of this experiment was identical to that of Experiment 1. In each trial, participants were required to detect semantic errors to the greatest extent possible within four minutes. We did not reuse the documents used in Experiment 1.

Task Conditions. Each task environment was identical to the Paper condition of Experiment 1. The documents were printed on one side of B5 paper in black and white. We gave the following three conditions related to the interaction with contents.

- **Untouchable:** Participants cannot touch paper documents at all except for setting the initial position of the documents.
- **Touchable:** Participants can touch paper documents but cannot write anything on the documents.
- **Writable:** Participants can touch paper documents and can write anything on the documents.

Procedure. Before the experiment, participants engaged in training and became accustomed to each task condition.

After the experiment, we conducted an interview.

6.2   Results and Discussion

Figure 5 presents a comparison of error-detection rates among the three task conditions. One-way repeated measures analysis of variance revealed that the main effects of the task condition were significant [$F(2, 46) = 5.38$, $p < .01$]. We conducted a multiple comparison using the Fisher's LSD (Least Significant Difference) method. Results show that the error-detection rate in the Untouchable condition was significantly lower than that of the Touchable condition and the Writable condition [$p < .05$]. No significant difference was found between the Touchable condition and the Writable condition [$p > .1$].

The error-detection rate was degraded when text touching was prohibited. This fact supports the hypothesis that reading is deteriorated when the interaction of text touching is restricted, which indicates that text touching is an important factor affecting the reading performance.

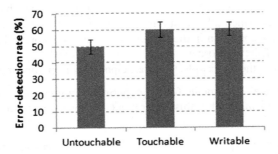

Fig. 5.   Error-detection rate in each condition.

Many studies support the effectiveness of annotation to understand and re-read text documents [16, 23, 24]. However, in this experiment, writing (i.e., annotating) did not improve the reading performance. As we described in Experiment 1, the reading task of this experiment did not require heavy annotation to perform the task of this experiment. We think that participants were unable to make use of the benefits of annotation in this task. In fact, most annotations that participants made were underlining or circling the positions of errors that they found.

Regarding the effects of pointing to text, many participants reported that they were able to devote attention consciously to a certain part. One participant reported "I was able to remember the rough positions of errors by pointing to them. Therefore, I do not need to check them again in a second reading." This statement indicates that pointing to text strengthens spatial memory for a certain part within a page. Additionally, one participant found it easy to compare distantly positioned parts by pointing to a certain word. The person reported "this part is about China, but that part describes Japan. I checked whether this correspondence was correct or not."

Regarding the effect of sliding a finger or a pen along the text, two participants reported that they were able to read text intentionally slowly. One participant reported "I am apt to hurry up in reading. By sliding a finger, I can avoid this problem." In particular, when people proofread a document that they wrote by themselves, they tend to skip reading because they already know the contents of the document. Sliding a finger along text would help to read text intentionally slowly without skipping each word.

Many participants reported that they were able to concentrate on the reading task better when reading with text touching than when reading without text touching. One participant reported "(in the Untouchable condition) I felt frustrating because I could not touch a document. I felt a sense of distance from the document. I felt as if I was looking at a bulletin board." Reading without text touching seems to give participants a feeling of looking at a document from a distance. Text touching might bring about a psychological effect that removes a distance or boundary between a reader and a document and which compels a reader to concentrate on reading.

After the experiment, two participants explicitly reported that they realized that they were usually pointing to text or sliding a finger on text unconsciously. One reported "Today, for the first time, I realized that it was quite difficult to read documents without touching them." The other reported "I realized that I had been frequently performing text touching during reading. I had not been aware of it until I participated in this experiment." These statements indicate that text touching is performed almost unconsciously and that people realize the importance of text touching when it is restricted.

7 General Discussion

Experiment 1 revealed that in a certain type of reading, at least when proofreading to detect semantic errors, people detected fewer errors when reading from a touch-based tablet device than when reading from paper. Additionally, people performed less text touching when using the tablet device than when using paper. We hypothesized that the use of the tablet degraded the reading performance because it did not promote the interaction of text touching during reading. To confirm this, in Experiment 2, we examined how reading performance varies when text touching was restricted. As a result, when text touching was prohibited, reading performance was degraded. This means that text touching contributes to improve reading performance.

First, we will discuss the generality of this study and present some remaining challenges. Next, we will discuss design implications that may be drawn at this stage to improve digital reading devices used in active reading.

7.1 Generality of the Study

We need to discuss the generality and the scope of this study. First, we discuss the specialty of the task. In this research, we addressed proofreading to detect semantic errors within a limited time. We selected this task because this type of reading seems to frequently include the interaction of text touching. The experiments demonstrated that in such reading, the reading performance was degraded when text touching was restricted. We need to consider how much text touching is performed in other kinds of reading and to verify the effect of text touching in these.

In our previous study, we conducted microscopic analysis of handling paper documents while reading [30]. We categorized the ways that people interact with paper documents in detail, which is hierarchically organized and consists of more than sixty actions at a bottom level, and analyzed reading behavior for various types of work-related reading based on these categories. Among them, we focus on two actions: placing a finger or an object on paper (i.e. pointing) and moving a finger in parallel to the sheet (i.e. sliding a finger along text). Table 1 presents the frequency of these two actions per minute for various types of reading. In the Paper condition of Experiment 1, participants performed pointing to text 0.92 times per minute and they performed sliding a finger or a pen 1.04 times per minute. Therefore, in this table, items of pointing whose frequency is more than 0.92 are colored in red and items of sliding whose frequency is more than 1.04 are colored in orange.

Table 1. Frequency of text touching per minute while reading. Items of pointing whose frequency is more than 0.92 are colored in red and items of sliding whose frequency is more than 1.04 are colored in orange.

Type of reading			Text touching	
Reading	Number of pages	Number of docs	Placing a finger or an object on paper (Pointing)	Moving a finger in parallel to sheet (Sliding a finger)
Proofreading	1	1	2.72	2.70
Skiming	N	1	0.12	0.00
Reading for revising	1	1	1.89	1.16
Cross-reference reading for multi-docs	N	N	2.28	0.16
Cross-reference reading between pages	N	1	2.15	0.73
Reading to answer questions	N	1	2.89	0.91
Reading to support discussion	N	1	3.08	0.06
Preparatory reading for discussion	N	1	0.91	0.22
Reading to learn	1	1	2.35	0.20
Document triage	N	1	1.13	1.38

According to this table, much work-related reading, except for skimming and preparatory reading for discussion, text touching was frequently performed. There is a possibility that reading performance might be degraded if text touching is prohibited in these reading types. We think that the task we selected in the experiments was not so special at least from the perspective of the frequency of text touching. However, we need to verify whether reading performance is actually degraded if text touching is restricted in these reading.

There are two major actions in text touching: pointing to text and sliding a finger along text. In this study, we examined the integrated effect of these two actions without separating them. However, the two different actions might cause different effects for reading. According to Table 1, the frequency of the two actions varies depending on the type of reading. If we could know how each action affects reading, we can infer how text touching affects the performance of different type of reading. Evaluating the effect of each action for reading individually is also an important future challenge.

Next, we discuss the issue of participants. Different people have different reading style. Therefore, it is apparent that the frequency of text touching varies depending on individuals. For this point, we have following two important questions. What kind of person performs text touching frequently? Even for a person who does not usually touch text during reading, is the reading performance improved if the person begins to perform text touching frequently?

For the former question, we conducted post hoc analysis for the results of Experiment 1. We compared the frequency of text touching in terms of gender (men and women), age (20's and 30's), and owning touch-based devices (owning and non-owning). A t-test revealed a significant difference only for the age [$t(22) = 2.25$, $p < .05$]. The average value for 20's and 30's were 3.59 and 9.77 respectively. Older people performed more text touching than younger people. No significant difference was found for gender [$p > .1$] and owning touch-based devices [$p > .1$]. As other factors that might affect the frequency of text touching, we should investigate the effect of their experiences for reading and writing. We need to compare the frequency of text touching between novice readers and expert readers. If we could understand the type of readers and their reading behavior, then we can provide a better support for reading depending on users.

For the latter question, we infer that reading performance would be improved if people perform text touching intentionally. That is because there was a positive correlation between the frequency of text touching and the error-detection rate in the first experiment. However, we need to verify this in future work.

Finally, we need to investigate other configurations of a tablet PC or other slate-type reading devices. In this study, we evaluated a touch-based tablet PC that allowed operating documents by touch gestures. However, users can disable this feature when using it. Disabling this feature, users can avoid a problem that unexpected behavior is caused by text touching. However, there is a possibility that the weight and glossy surface of devices might restrain text touching and we need to investigate this effect. Reading devices with e-paper such as Kindle (Amazon Inc.) are relatively light and does not provide glossy surface. They might promote text touching in comparison with touch-based tablet PCs. We need to confirm this as future work.

7.2   Suggestions

The study of text touching is not yet completed. As we described in the previous section, there are some remaining challenges to make clear the effect of text touching for various types of reading. In this paper, as a first step, we found that text touching affects reading performance in a certain type of reading. To determine the applicable scope of this phenomenon, we need more investigation for various types of reading and devices. However, in the following, we describe design implications that can be considered at this stage to improve touch-based reading devices used in active reading.

The experiments in this paper revealed three important findings. First, people will read with touching text in a certain type of reading. Second, during such reading, the reading performance may be degraded when text touching is restricted. Third, touch-based tablet devices may work on restricting users' interaction of text touching.

It is desirable that a touch-based reading device should be designed with these findings in mind, if it aims to support active reading. In most current tablet devices, touch gestures are assigned to functions to operate documents such as expanding or shrinking documents, changing the display area of documents, and turning pages. Therefore, unexpected behavior of documents might be caused by text touching, which may be troublesome for readers. In addition, if readers avoid touching text, they cannot make use of the effects of text touching such as devoting attention to some parts, comparing different parts easily, controlling the reading speed, and preventing skipping words or sentences.

Therefore, it is desirable that a tablet device used in active reading should not interfere with text touching performed during reading. To achieve this, designers of the reading device need to assign gestures that are not performed in usual reading to functions of operating documents, if the device uses touch gestures. Microscopic analysis of gestures during reading [30] would help to determine what kind of gesture we should use for handling documents.

Finally, a digital reading device might be able to promote text touching as well as prevent interfering with text touching by using visual feedback for users' behavior or by directly prompting text touching. In these cases, we can expect that reading performance might be improved.

8   Conclusions

On the assumption that text touching such as pointing to text and sliding a finger or a pen along text plays an important role for understanding documents, we conducted two experiments. The first experiment compared reading from paper and reading from a touch-based tablet device in proofreading. Results showed that the error-detection rate was higher when reading from paper than when reading from the tablet device. We inferred that this was because a touch-based tablet device did not promote the interaction of text touching during reading and this degraded the reading performance. To verify this hypothesis, we conducted the second experiment, which restricted text touching during proofreading. Results show that error-detection rates decreased when text touching was restricted. Considering these results, we suggest that a touch-based tablet device should be designed not to constrain text touching if the device is intended to support reading with frequent text touching, where active reading typically accompanies frequent text touching.

We are currently investigating the behavior during reading in detail. In this framework, we intend to conduct a detailed investigation of the effects of interaction with text. Moreover, we are currently designing a digital reading device based on the design implication described in this paper.

Acknowledgement. We thank Maribeth Back of FX Palo Alto Laboratory for her careful check for the final version of this paper.

Trademarks. iPad is a trademark or registered trademark of Apple Computer Inc. Kindle is a trademark or registered trademark of Amazon Inc. All other brand names and product names are trademarks or registered trademarks of their respective companies.

References

1. Adler, A., Gujar, A., Harrison, B., O'Hara, K., Sellen, A.J.: A diary study of work-related reading: design implications for digital reading devices. In: Proceedings of the CHI 1998, pp. 241–248. ACM Press (1998)
2. Buchanan, G., Loizides, F.: Investigating document triage on paper and electronic media. In: Kovács, L., Fuhr, N., Meghini, C. (eds.) ECDL 2007. LNCS, vol. 4675, pp. 416–427. Springer, Heidelberg (2007)
3. Chen, N., Guimbretiere, F., Sellen, A.: Designing a multi-slate reading environment to support active reading activities. ACM Trans. Comput.-Hum. Interact. **19**(3), 1–35 (2012). ACM Press
4. Dillon, A.: Reading from paper versus screens: a critical review of the empirical literature. Ergonomics **35**(10), 1297–1326 (1992). Taylor & Francis
5. Dyson, M.C.: How physical text layout affects reading from screen. Behav. Inf. Technol. **23** (6), 377–393 (2004). Taylor & Francis
6. Golovchinsky, G., Carter, S., Dunnigan, A.: ARA: the active reading application. In: Proceedings of the Multimedia 2011. ACM Press (2011)
7. Gould, J.D., Alfaro, L., Barnes, V., Finn, R., Haupt, B., Minuto, A.: Reading from CRT displays can be as fast as reading from paper. Hum. Factors **29**(5), 497–517 (1987)
8. Hess, S., Jessica, J.: Does the iPad add value to business environments? In: Proceedings of the CHI 2012 Extended Abstracts, pp. 335–350. ACM Press (2012)
9. Hinckley, K., Zhao, S., Sarin, R., Baudisch, P., Cutrell, E., Shilman, M., Tan, D.: InkSeine: In Situ search for active note taking. In: Proceedings of the CHI 2007, pp. 251–260. ACM Press (2007)
10. Hinckley, K., Bi, X., Pahud, M., Buxton, B.: Informal information gathering techniques for active reading. In: Proceedings of the CHI 2012, pp. 1893–1896. ACM Press (2012)
11. Hong, M.K., Piper, A.M., Weibel, N., Olberding, S., Hollan J.D.: Microanalysis of active reading behavior to inform design of interactive desktop workspaces. In: Proceedings of the ITS 2012, pp. 215–224. ACM Press (2012)
12. Johnson, M., Nadasa, R.: Marginalised behaviour: digital annotations, spatial encoding and the implications for reading comprehension. Learn. Media Technol. **34**(4), 323–336 (2009). Taylor & Francis
13. Kirsh, D.: Complementary strategies: why we use our hands when we think. In: Proceedings of the Seventh Annual Conference of the Cognitive Science Society, pp. 212–217 (1995)
14. Liu, Z.: Reading behavior in the digital environment: changes in reading behavior over the past ten years. J. Documentation **61**(6), 700–712 (2005). Emerald
15. Mangen, A., Walgermo, B.R., Bronnick, K.: Reading linear texts on paper versus computer screen: effects on reading comprehension. Int. J. Educ. Res. **58**, 61–68 (2013). Elsevier
16. Marshall, C.: Annotation: from paper books to the digital library. In: Proceedings of the JCDL 1997, pp. 131–140. ACM Press (1997)

17. Marshall, C., Brush, A.J.: Exploring the relationship between personal and public annotations. In: Proceedings of the JCDL 2004, pp. 349–357. ACM Press (2004)
18. Marshall, C., Bly, S.: Turning the page on navigation. In: Proceedings of the JCDL 2005, pp. 225–234. ACM Press (2005)
19. Matulic, F., Norrie, M.C.: Supporting active reading on pen and touch-operated tabletops. In: Proceedings of the AVI 2012, pp. 612–619. ACM Press (2012)
20. Minogue, J., Jones, M.G.: Haptics in education: exploring an untapped sensory modality. Rev. Educ. Res. **76**(3), 317–348 (2006)
21. Morris, M.R., Brush, A.J., Meyers, B.: Reading revisited: evaluating the usability of digital display surfaces for active reading tasks. In: Proceedings of the TABLETOP 2007, pp. 79–86. ACM Press (2007)
22. Muller, H., Gove, J., Webb, J.: Understanding tablet use: A multi-method exploration. In: Proceedings of the Mobile HCI 2012, pp. 1–10. ACM Press (2012)
23. O'Hara, K., Sellen, A.J.: A comparison of reading paper and on-line documents. In: Proceedings of the CHI 1997, pp. 335–342. ACM Press (1997)
24. O'Hara, K.P., Taylor, A., Newman, W., Sellen, A.J.: Understanding the materiality of writing from multiple sources. Int. J. Hum.-Comput. Stud. **56**(4), 269–305 (2002). Elsevier
25. Schilit, B.N., Golovchinsky, G., Price, M.N.: Beyond paper: Supporting active reading with free form digital ink annotations. In: Proceedings of the CHI 1998, pp. 249–256. ACM Press (1998)
26. Sellen, A.J., Harper, R.H.: The Myth of the Paperless Office. The MIT Press, Cambridge (2001)
27. Shibata, H., Takano, K., Omura K.: Why is paper superior to computer displays in cross-reference reading for multiple documents? In: Proceedings of the International Display Workshops (IDW 2013). SID (2013)
28. Shibata, H., Takano, K., Omura, K.: Comparison of paper and computer displays in reading including frequent movement between pages. In: Proceedings of the OZCHI 2014. ACM Press (2014)
29. Takano, K., Shibata, H., Omura, K., Ichino, J., Hashiyama, T., Tano, S.: Do tablets really support discussion? comparison between paper, a tablet, and a laptop PC used as discussion tools. In: Proceedings of the OZCHI 2012, pp. 562–571. ACM Press (2012)
30. Takano, K., Shibata, H., Ichino, J., Hashiyama, T., Tano, S.: Microscopic analysis of document handling while reading paper documents to improve digital reading device. In: Proceedings of the OZCHI 2014. ACM Press (2014)
31. Tashman, C., Edwards, W.K.: Active reading and its discontents: the situations, problems and ideas of readers. In: Proceedings of the CHI 2011, pp. 2927–2936. ACM Press (2011)

Author Index

Printed in the United States
By Bookmasters